Architectural Magazine, and Journal of Improvement in Architecture, Building, and Furnishing, and in the Various Arts and Trades Therewith

HARVARD UNIVERSITY
The   f the
Graduate School of Design

THE
ARCHITECTURAL MAGAZINE,
AND
JOURNAL
OF IMPROVEMENT IN
ARCHITECTURE, BUILDING, AND FURNISHING,
AND IN THE VARIOUS ARTS AND TRADES CONNECTED THEREWITH.

CONDUCTED BY J. C. LOUDON, F.L.S. G.S. &c.

AUTHOR OF THE ENCYCLOPÆDIA OF COTTAGE, FARM, AND VILLA ARCHITECTURE AND FURNITURE.

VOL. I.

LONDON:
LONGMAN, REES, ORME, BROWN, GREEN, & LONGMAN,
PATERNOSTER-ROW;
AND
WEALE, ARCHITECTURAL LIBRARY, HIGH HOLBORN.

1834.

May 2, 1930.

HARVARD UNIVERSITY
The Library of the Schools
of Landscape Architecture and City Planning

Gift of B. Pray from coll. of
J. S. Pray.
5813

NA
2
Ar2
v.1

LONDON:
Printed by A. SPOTTISWOODE,
New-Street-Square.

PREFACE.

We have been induced to commence an *Architectural Magazine*, from the beneficial influence which, we are informed, has attended the publication of our *Encyclopædia of Cottage, Farm, and Villa Architecture*. One of the highest gratifications we have received, since we commenced author, is to know that that work is gradually effecting a reformation in the construction of cottage dwellings and farm buildings, not only throughout Britain and Ireland, but in America and Australia. The object of the *Architectural Magazine* is to second the effect produced by the *Encyclopædia*, by improving the public taste in architecture generally, by rendering it a more intellectual profession, by recommending it as a fit study for ladies, and by inducing young architects to read, write, and think, as well as to see and draw.

In this Volume will be found a series of papers by the Conductor, the object of which is to popularise the subject of architecture as a matter of taste; and there are also several able papers, written with the same view, by Mr. Trotman, and other professed architects. This we consider to be the first step towards rendering architecture a fit study for general readers, and especially for female ones. Our reasons for introducing such papers are grounded on the principle laid down by Alison in his *Essays on Taste*, viz. that " the most effectual method to check the empiricism either of art or science, is to multiply, as far as possible, the number of those who can observe and judge."

A second set of papers has for its object the familiarising of the general reader with what are technically called the Elements of Architectural Design. The first of these, on Classical Architecture, is by Mr. Trotman, a practical architect, well known for his eminent literary talents; and the subject has been completed by our architectural draughtsman, Mr. Robertson. Gothic Architecture, to which there has hitherto been no complete Introduction, either scientific or popular, has been kindly undertaken by Mr. Picton, at once an excellent practical architect and an able writer; and this subject will be completed in the Second Volume.

The remaining papers are all of a practical nature, and either describe and criticise public or private buildings already executed, or furnish suggestions and designs for constructions in every department of the art, including finishing and furnishing; rural and garden architecture; and engineering, as far as is necessary to connect architecture with that science. The reader will find the various subjects treated on, both in the Original Communications and in the Reviews, systematically arranged in the Table of Contents.

In the Review Department we have given some account of the more important English, French, and German Works which have been published in the course of the year; and our Catalogue includes the titles, as far as we have been able to obtain them, of all the Architectural Works which have been published in Europe and America during the same period.

In the Miscellaneous Department will be found various opinions by different writers, and a variety of news, accompanied by criticisms, respecting architectural improvements going on in every part of the world, but more particularly in Britain.

For our forthcoming Numbers we have some valuable papers in hand; and we are kindly promised, by Mr. Lamb, a Series of Designs for Villas, in all the different varieties of the Gothic, Classical, and Italian styles.

In conclusion, we have to thank, most sincerely, those architects, both personal friends and strangers, who have kindly come forward to assist and patronise this infant periodical, the first of its kind that has been commenced in Britain: and we earnestly entreat all architects, and others connected with the building arts, who are desirous of advancing their profession; and our readers generally, who wish to promote the progress of architectural taste, and the universal diffusion of architectural comforts; to aid us by their contributions and their advice; and, in short, by every assistance in their power.

Bayswater, Nov. 20. 1834.
L.

BOOKS REVIEWED AND NOTICED.

General Subject.
A Plain Statement of Facts connected with the Coalition between the Society for the Promotion of Architecture, &c., and the Society of British Architects, page 275.
A Theoretical and Practical Treatise on the Five Orders of Architecture, 129.
Bakewell's Observations on Building and Brickmaking, 312.
Bennett's Artificer's Complete Lexicon for Terms and Prices, 83.
Billington's Architectural Director, Part i., 84; Parts ii. and iii., 180; Parts iv. and v., 274; Parts vi. and vii., 213.
Britton's Memoir of Sir John Soane, 310.
Crelle's Journal für die Baukunst, 237.
Dallaway's Discourses upon Architecture in England, from the Norman Era to the Close of the Reign of Queen Elizabeth, 202.
Gregory's Mathematics for Practical Men, 86.
Hope's History of Architecture, announced, 45.
Hullmandel's Art of Drawing on Stone, 86
Inwood's Studies of the Architect from Nature, 44.
Lafevre's Modern Builder's Guide, 44.
Laxton's Improved Builder's Price Book, 86.
Morisot's Journal d'Architecture Civile et Rurale, &c., 43.
Nicholson's General Treatise on Projection, announced, 372.
Rám Ráz's Essay on the Architecture of the Hindús, 267.
Rickman's Attempt to discriminate the Styles of Architecture in England, announced, 86.
Robinson's New Vitruvius Britannicus, 85, 86.
Simm's Mathematical Instruments, 371.
Skyring's Builder's Price Book, 86.
Smirke's Suggestions for the Architectural Improvement of the Western Parts of the Metropolis, announced, 137; reviewed, 177.
Sopwith's Isometrical Drawing, 369.
Warren's Hints upon Tints, 86.
Wilkins's Vitruvius, noticed, 372.

Classical Architecture.
Cockerell's Temple of Jupiter Panhellenius, and Antiquities at Egina, announced, 86.
Dodwell's Cyclopian Remains, 44, 48.
Rochette's Monumens inédits d'Antiquité, 44.

Architectural Antiquities in the Pointed Style.
Brayley's Illustrations of Christ Church, Hampshire, 45.
Coney's Interior Views of Milan Cathedral, 85.
Davis's Abbey Church, Bath (see Davis's Gothic Ornaments).
Davis's Gothic Ornaments, illustrative of Prior Birde's Oratory in the Abbey Church, Bath, 131. 238. 370.
Ferrey's Antiquities of Christ Church, Hampshire, 239. 371.
Langes Eglises Gothiques, 45.
Lockwood and Gates's Ancient Gates and Fortifications of the City of York, announced, 86.
Lockwood and Cates's Antiquities of York. See Lockwood and Cates's Ancient Gates, &c.
Raine's Catterick Church, in the County of York, 137. 273. 371.
Robinson's Details of Ancient Gates, &c., in York, announced, 180.
Salvin's Catterick Church. See Raine's Catterick Church.
Sopwith's Eight Views of Fountains Abbey, 314.

Elizabethan Architecture.
Blackburn's Architectural and Historical Account of Crosby Place, London, 44. 130.
Britton's Illustrations and Account of Cassiobury Park, Hertfordshire, announced, 180.
Clarke's Architectural Illustrations of Eastbury House, Essex, announced, 86. 240.
Clarke's Domestic Architecture of the Reign of Queen Elizabeth and James I., 204.
Robinson's Hardwick Hall, announced, 86. 372.

Modern Domestic Architecture.
Designs of Doors and Windows, in the Italian and Palladian Styles, announced, 137.
Goodwin's Domestic Architecture, 44. 132.
Shaw's Specimens of the Details of Elizabethan Architecture, 85.
Smith's Construction of Cottages for Labourers, 371.
Whitling's Designs for Shop Fronts, 180. 239.
Wild's Elementary and Practical Instructions on the Art of Building Cottages and Houses for the humbler Classes, 314. 372.

Views of Buildings recently completed.
Billington's South-west View of the Parish Church of All Saints, Wakefield, 240.
Cottingham's Prints of his Restoration of Armagh Cathedral, 239.
Newman's View of the Indigent Blind School, St. George's Fields, 180.
Wilkinson's Elevation of the National Gallery, noticed, 372.

Ornaments, chiefly for Fittings-up, Furniture, and Finishing.
A Compilation of Splendid Ornamental Designs, from Foreign Works of recent Production, 137. 371.
Carlo Antonini's Antique Roses for the Use of Architects, &c., 180.
Chippendale's Designs for Sconces, and Chimney and Looking-glass Frames, in the Old French Style, announced, 137.
Chippendale's Designs of Interior Decorations in the Old French Style, for Carvers, &c., announced, 137.
Designs for Chimney Glasses, of the Time of Inigo Jones and Sir John Vanbrugh, announced, 137.
Designs for Vases, announced, 137.
Designs of the Ornaments and Decorations of Chimneypieces, announced, 137.
Johnson's Book of Ornaments in the French and Antique Styles, announced, 37.
King's Working Ornaments, 370.
Knight's Ornaments for Jewellers, &c., 180.
Knight's Unique Fancy Ornaments, 274. 371.
Lane's Ornaments of different Eras, 44.
Lock's Book of Ornaments for Carvers, &c., announced, 137.
Lock, Johnson, and Copland's Ornamental Designs, 313.
Maguire's Ornaments in various Styles, 371.
Pether's Book of Ornaments, suitable for Beginners, announced, 139.
Shaw's Ornamental Works in Louis XIV.'s Style, 85.
Shaw's Specimens of Ancient English Furniture, 44. 371.
Trendal's Desings for Interior Finishings, 44. 136.
Uagzin on the Cast-Iron Foundery of Berlin, 44.
Working Ornaments and Forms for the Cabinetmaker, Upholsterer, &c., 180.

Local Architectural Improvement.
Trotter's Observations and Illustrations of his modified Plan of a Communication between the New and Old Towns of Edinburgh, 205.

Engineering.
Alderston's Essay on the Nature and Application of Steam, announced, 181.
Blunt and Stephenson's Civil Engineer and Mechanist, 85. 237. 240. 371.
Hallingworth's Plan and Section of the Waterford and Kilkenny Railway, announced, 181.
Jones's Evans on Millwork, 372.
Philip's Analysis of the Defective State of Turnpike Roads, announced, 86.
Sopwith's Geological Sections of various Lead Mines in Northumberland, 372.
Sopwith's Mining Districts of Alston Moor, 372.

CONTENTS.

INTRODUCTION - - Page 1.

ORIGINAL COMMUNICATIONS.

The Philosophy of Architecture popularised.

On the Means of forming a just and correct Taste in Architecture, and on the Sources from which the Principles of Design and Construction in that Art are derived - - Page 49
On the Causes of the different Kinds and Degrees of Taste which different Persons possess in Architecture - - - - 97
Architecture considered as an Art of Imagination - - - - - 145
On the Difference between Common, or Imitative, Genius, and Inventive, or Original, Genius, in Architecture - - - 185
On those Principles of Composition, in Architecture, which are acknowledged to be common to all the Fine Arts - - - 217
On those Principles of Composition, in Architecture, which are common to all the Fine Arts:—
  Sect. 1. Forms, Lines, Lights, Shades, and Colours, considered with reference to the Production of an Architectural Whole, 249
  Sect. 2. Forms, Lines, Lights, Shades, and Colours, considered with reference to the Principle of the Recognition of Art - 281
  Sect. 3. Forms, Lines, Lights, Shades, and Colours, considered with reference to the Principles of Regularity, Uniformity and Symmetry - - - - 321
  Sect. 4. Forms, Lines, Lights, Shades, and Colours, considered with reference to the Principles of Variety, Intricacy, and Harmony - - - - - 353
On the alleged Degeneracy of Modern Architecture - - - - - 148
On the comparative Value of Simplicity in Architecture - - - - 103
Remarks on the Harmony of Enrichment in Architecture - - - - 255
Architecture considered with reference to its Claims as a Fine Art - - - 223
On Character in Architecture - - 324
On Uniformity in Architecture - - 285
On Heraldic Ornaments in Architecture - 188
Architectural Maxims 80. 128. 201. 236. 266. 309. 357

Elements of Classic Architecture.

On the Extent to which the Elementary Forms of Classic Architecture are, from their Nature and Origin, fixed or arbitrary - 16
The Elements of Grecian and Roman Architecture practically explained to the General Reader - - - 108. 153. 259
Notice of a remarkable Corinthian Capital in the Vatican - - - - - 357

Elements of Gothic Architecture.

An Attempt to explain the Elements and Principles of Gothic Architecture to the General Reader - - - - - 328

Professional Practice.

On the present State of the Professions of Architect and Surveyor, and of the Building Trade in England - - - - 12
On certain deceptive Practices adopted by some Authors of Architectural Designs for Villas 117

Practical Architecture and Building.

A few Observations on the Anglo-Norman Style of Architecture, and its Applicability to Modern Ecclesiastical Edifices - - 288
On the Gin Temples of the Metropolis - 164
On London Street Houses and Shop Fronts - 113
A Method of securing Outside Shutters for Shop Fronts - - - - - 357
Remarks on Closets, &c., in Sitting-Rooms - 348
Specimens of Studies of Plan - - 226
Instructions for choosing a Dwelling-House, more particularly in a Town - - 166
On the Domestic Offices of a House - 302
Notice of some of the Ornamental Chimney Pots and Shafts manufactured of Artificial Stone by Mr. Austin of London - - 159
A descriptive Account of the Duke of York's Monument, accompanied by Plans, Elevations, and Sections, copied from the Designs of Benjamin Wyatt, Esq., Architect - 192
A descriptive Account, accompanied by Plans, Elevations, and Sections, of Hungerford New Market, recently built from the Designs of Charles Fowler, Esq., Architect - - 53
Notice of some Designs for Architectural Fountains, manufactured in Artificial Stone by Mr. Austin of London - - - 295
Design for a Villa in the Norman Style - 333
A Series of Designs, with Descriptive and Historical Particulars, of Characteristic and Ornamental Buildings, and Objects for Gardens and Pleasure-Grounds - - - 190
Notice of a very common Error in designing and building Ornamental Chimney Shafts - 63
On a Method of preventing the Damp from rising in the Walls of Buildings on Clayey and other Moist Soils - - - - 233
On an effectual Method of cutting off the Communication between the damp Foundation of a Wall built upon a moist Subsoil, and the Part of the Wall above the Ground; and on a Mode of securing the Inside of a Wall from damp forced though the Brickwork by driving Rains, Hail, Snow, &c. - - - 123
On the Use of Cast-Iron and Caithness Flagstone in the Construction of Fireproof Floors and Partition Walls in Dwelling-Houses - 71
On Cast-Iron Angles for Outside Doors - 234
The Art of Brickmaking among the Chinese 125
On Brickmaking in Egypt - - 372
On Brickmaking in England - - 312

Warming and Ventilating.

Origin and Progress of heating Hot-houses and other Buildings by the Application and Circulation of Hot Water - - 172. 368
On Ventilation, particularly as applied to Hospitals and Sick Wards - - 229
On the Ventilation of Living-Rooms, &c. - 64

Fittings-up and Furniture.

A simple and effective Preventive for the Slamming of a Passage Door - - 196
On a Method of curing Smoky Chimneys, and of ventilating Rooms - - - 233
On rendering Lath and Plaster Partitions Fireproof - - - - - 40

vi CONTENTS.

The Bruges Stove, as improved by Messrs Cottam and Hallen - - - 77
Descriptive Notice of the Russel Stove; communicated by Messrs. J. Sibbald and Sons of Edinburgh: with Remarks on this Stove, by a Correspondent resident in that City - 74
Description of an improved Roasting-Oven - 72
Notice of a Marble Table, with a Cast-Iron Pillar, constructed on an economical Principle, under the Direction of John Robison, Esq. - 308
On the Use of Slate and Cast-Iron in Household Furniture - - - - - 41
On Painted Transparent Blinds, and Tape and Line Preservers - - - - 127

Engineering.
Description of an improved Milepost invented by John Robison, Esq., and used on some of the great Roads in Scotland - - - 78
Notice of a Wooden Fence, which may be put together without the Use of Nails, Screws, or other Iron Work, invented by G. H. Cottam, Esq. - - - - - 79
Dovetailed Caps for Wooden Fences - - 235

REVIEWS.

General Subject.
A Series of Discourses upon Architecture in England, from the Norman Era to the Close of the Reign of Queen Elizabeth; with an Appendix of Notes and Illustrations, and an Historical Account of Master and Free Masons. By the Rev. James Dallaway - - 202
Journal für die Baukunst. By Dr. A. L. Crelle, Royal Prussian Architect, and Member of various Societies - - - - 237
La Propriété; Journal d'Architecture Civile et Rurale, des Beaux Arts, et d'Economie Sociale. Par T. Morisot, Architecte - - 43
The Architectural Director; being an approved Guide to Builders, Draughtsmen, Students, and Workmen in the Study, Design, and Execution of Architecture, &c. By John Billington, Architect - - 84. 274. 313
The Artificer's complete Lexicon for Terms and Prices; adapted for Gentlemen, Engineers, Builders, Mechanics, Millwrights, Manufacturers, Tradesmen, &c. &c. By John Bennett, Engineer - - - - 83
A Treatise on Isometrical Drawing as applied to Geological and Mining Plans, Picturesque Delineations of Ornamental Grounds, Perspective Views and Working Plans of Buildings and Machinery, and to General Purposes of Civil Engineering, with Details of Improved Methods of preserving Plans and Records of Subterranean Operations in Mining Districts. By T. Sopwith, Land and Mine Surveyor, Member of the Institution of Civil Engineers - 369

Historical and Descriptive.
Views and Descriptions of Cyclopian or Pelasgic Remains, in Greece and Italy; with Constructions of a later Period; from Drawings by the late Edward Dodwell, Esq. F.S.A. and Member of several Foreign Academies - - 81
An Architectural and Historical Account of Crosby Place, London. By Edward L. Blackburn, Architect - - - - 130
Catterick Church, in the County of York; a correct Copy of the Contract for its Building, dated in 1412; illustrated with Remarks and Notes, by the Rev. James Raine, M.A., Librarian of Durham Cathedral, &c.; and with 13 Plates of Views, Elevations, and Details, by Anthony Salvin, Esq. F.S.A., Architect - 273
Gothic Ornaments, illustrative of Prior Birde's Oratory, in the Abbey Church, Bath. By Edward Davis, Architect, Bath - 131. 238. 370
The Domestic Architecture of the Reigns of Queen Elizabeth and James I., illustrated by a Series of Views of English Mansions, with brief Historical and Descriptive Accounts of each Subject. By T. H. Clarke, Architect - 204

Local Architectural Improvement.
Observations, by Alexander Trotter, Esq., of Dreghorn, in Illustration of his modified Plan of a Communication between the New and the Old Town of Edinburgh - - - 205
Suggestions for the Architectural Improvement of the Western Part of London. By Sydney Smirke, F.S.A. F.G.S. - - - 177

Elementary Architecture.
Essay on the Architecture of the Hindús. By Rám Ráz, Native Judge and Magistrate at Bangalore, Corresponding Member of the Royal Asiatic Society of Great Britain and Ireland 267
A Theoretical and Practical Treatise on the Five Orders of Architecture: containing the most plain and simple rules for drawing and executing them in the present style; including an historical description of Gothic Architecture, showing its origin, and also a comparison of the Gothic Architecture of England, Germany, France, Spain, and Italy, together with details of the first, second, and third-periods of the pointed Arch or Gothic style - - 129

Architectural Designs.
Domestic Architecture; being a Second Series of Designs for Cottages, Lodges, Villas, and other Residences, in the Grecian, Italian, and Old English Styles of Architecture. By Francis Goodwin, Architect - - - 132
A Series of original Designs for Shop Fronts, forming a Collection suitable to Persons connected with the Practical Part of Building. By Henry John Whitling, Architect - 239

Designs for Ornaments.
A Compilation of splendid Ornamental Designs, from Foreign Works of recent Production 137
Knight's unique Fancy Ornaments - - 274
Locke, Johnson, and Copland's Ornamental Designs - - - - - 313

Building.
Observations on Building and Brickmaking; to which are subjoined Extracts from Testimonials in behalf of S. R. Bakewell's Brickmaking Machines. By S. R. Bakewell - - 312

Fittings-up and Furniture.
Examples for Interior Finishings. By C. W. Trendall, Architect - - - 136
Working Ornaments and forms, full Size, and in various Styles, for the Use of the Cabinet Manufacturer, Chair and Sofa Maker, Carver, and Turner; consisting of entirely new Designs, in which great Study has been bestowed in causing a Display without much Expense in Material or Labour. By T. King, Author of "The Modern Style of Cabinet Work;" &c. Parts I., II., and III. Folio - - 370

Engineering.
The Civil Engineer and Machinist. By Charles John Blunt and R. Macdonald Stephenson, Civil Engineers, Architects, &c. - - 237

Biography.
Brief Memoir of Sir John Soane, R.A. F.R. and A.S., Professor of Architecture in the Royal Academy, &c. By John Britton, F.S.A. - 310

Catalogue.
Catalogue of Works on Architecture, Building, and Furnishing, and on the Arts more immediately connected therewith, published in Europe and America during the Year 1834:—
Britain - 44. 85. 137. 180. 238. 274. 313. 371
France - - - - 44. 239. 371
Germany - - - - 44. 275. 371
North America - - - - 44
Literary Notices - 45. 86. 137. 180. 239. 314

LIST OF ENGRAVINGS.

MISCELLANEOUS INTELLIGENCE.

General Notices	45. 86. 138. 240. 275. 314. 372
Foreign Notices:	
Italy	207
France	45. 88. 242. 374
Germany	88. 243. 276
Greece	243. 375
Turkey	208
Denmark	243
North America	88
Australia	89. 276. 375
India	315
China	315
Domestic Notices:	
England	46. 89. 138. 181. 208. 244. 277. 316. 352. 377
Wales	93
Scotland	93. 142. 212. 278. 316. 380
Ireland	94. 278. 317
Retrospective Criticism	48. 95. 143. 212. 246. 279. 317. 381
Queries and Answers	48. 95. 144. 184. 216. 247. 280. 320. 391
Obituary	48. 96. 184. 320
Glossarial Index	393
General Index	395

LIST OF ENGRAVINGS.

No.		Page
	Elementary Details of Classic Architecture.	
1—9.	Egyptian architecture	19—23
10.	Grecian Doric order	25
11.	Grecian Ionic order	26
12.	Classical doorway	28
13.	Classical window	29
14.	Attic order	30
41—51.	Mouldings of Classical architecture	110
66—68.	Comparative views of the different orders of Classical architecture	155—158
122.	Roman Corinthian order	261
123.	Roman Doric order	262
124.	Composite order	264
184.	Remarkable Corinthian capital in the Vatican	356
	Elementary Details of Hindú Architecture.	
125.	Mouldings of Hindú architecture	268
126—129.	Bases and pedestals	269
130, 131.	Columns	271, 272
	Elementary Details of Gothic Architecture.	
132, 133.	Elevations of Anglo-Norman churches	291, 292
151—162.	Forms and construction of the different kinds of arches in use in Gothic architecture	331—333
203.	Intersecting Norman arches in Hoylake church	331
	Public Buildings.	
18—23.	Plans, elevations, and sections of Hungerford Market	56—61
134—136.	Plan, elevations, and perspective view of Hoylake church	293, 294
	Public Monuments.	
92—107.	Duke of York's column, with the details of its construction	193—199
202.	Obelisk on Bromsgrove Lickey	379
	Private Buildings.	
54—56.	Plan and two elevations of an Italian villa	118, 119
163—182.	Plans, elevations, sections, perspective views, interior views, and furniture of an Anglo-Norman villa	334—348
201.	Plan of a villa and grounds now forming in the neighbourhood of Sydney	376
	Ornamental Structures.	
57.	Round seat with a thatched roof	152

No.		Page
	Ornamental Objects.	
58—60.	Sundials	122, 123
69—91.	Grecian and Gothic chimney pots and shafts	150—163
137—148.	Designs for fountains	296—302
	Furniture.	
15, 16.	Cast-iron flanches and braces for tables and sideboards	41
17.	Sideboard of slate	42
32, 33.	The Russel stove	75
34.	An improvement on the Russel stove	76
35—37.	Cottam's Bruges stove	77
117—120.	Improved cock for boilers and kitchen ranges	240, 241
149, 150.	Marble table with cast-iron pillar	308, 30
206.	Bracket for towels	391
	Engineering.	
38.	Improved milepost	78
39—40.	Wooden fence without nails or screws	79, 80
116.	Improved cap for a wooden fence	236
196, 197.	Improved lamp posts	368
	Miscellaneous.	
24, 25. 62—65.	Correction of errors in the formation of ornamental chimney shafts	63, 64. 144
26—28.	Explanation of the principles of ventilation	66—68
29—31.	Cast and wrought iron supports to flagstone floors and partitions	71, 72
52, 53. 204.	Correction of errors in the architecture of shop fronts	114—116. 382
61.	Preventive for the slamming of a passage door	126
108, 109.	Errors in ground plans	226, 227
110—112.	Ventilation of hospitals	232, 233
113.	Curing smoky chimneys, and ventilating rooms	234
114, 115.	Cast-iron angles for outside doors	234
121.	Forming foundations of concrete	248
183.	Plan for forming closets in cottage villas	350
185.	Outside shop-window shutters	358
186—195.	Apparatus for heating with hot water	360—365
198—200.	Brickmaking in Egypt	372, 373
205.	Explanation of the term "curbed roof"	383
207.	Apparatus for cleaning the outsides of lofty windows	391

LIST OF CONTRIBUTORS.

	Page
A Constant Reader, London	248
A Journeyman Cabinet-maker, London	87
A Self-taught Architect and Landscape-Gardener	120
A Subscriber	279
A Young Architect	142. 211
An Observer, London	117
Amicus, London	320. 390
Ap Evan, Sam., Neath, Glamorganshire	392
Austin, Felix, New Road, London	216
B., London	96
Barnes, T. B., Newcastle under Line	320
Benham, S. H., Brighton	246
Besson, F. L., Rue de Richelieu, Paris	46. 375
Brown, John, Woodstock	91. 92
Candidus, London	319
Capper, C. H., Birmingham	234
Cottam, Edward, London	77
Cottam, G. H., Engineer, London	79. 172. 358
Cynicus, London	164
D.	138
D. S., London	140
Dymond, G., Architect, Bristol	214. 383
E. B. L.	144. 248
F., Brighton	211
F. A. M., Cowan, by Dingwall	94
G. B. W.	392
G. G. S., London	216
G. P., Brixton	315
H.	378
Hawkins, John Isaac, Civil Engineer, Pancras Vale, London	123
Hindle, W. J., Barnsley	235
Investigator, Glasgow	96
Investigator, Kent	216
I. A. F.	382
J. B., The Rectory, near Lymington	320
J. I. K., Manor Place, Paddington	383
J. R., Bayswater	383
J. R., of Edinburgh	71. 93. 94. 126. 240
J. W.	245
J. W., Dumfries	278
J. W. L.	96
J. Thompson, Sydney	377
John Milne, Edinburgh	386. 390
Jorgensen, F., Copenhagen	243
Juvenis, Birmingham	280
Kent, I. J., Architect, Manor Place, Paddington	34. 166. 302. 319
L.	138. 248. 321
Lamb, E. B., Architect, 9, Little James Street, Bedford Row	63. 333
Lavator	247
Leeds, W. H., 23, Hunter Street, Brunswick Square	226. 351
Mackenzie, J. A., Cowan, by Dingwall, Ross-shire	48

	Page
Main, James, Chelsea	125
Mallet, Robert, Dublin	391
Manners, Chas., Woolwich Common	392
Mashdoud Mohandez, Norwich	373
Milne, John, Architect, Edinburgh	64. 280
Picton, J. A., Architect, Liverpool	229. 288. 328. 381
Price, John, Architect, Derby	247
R.	379
R., Bayswater	113
R. M., Capel Street, Dublin	95
R. M., Dublin	390
R. S., Edinburgh	95
Robertson, J., Architect, 39, New Church Street, Paddington	53. 106. 153. 192. 259
Robison, John, Sec. R. S. E., Edinburgh	73. 308. 367
Rose, William, Builder, Bristol	41
Rugby, Warwickshire	48
S. C., de Loire	88
S. T., Kingston	317
Saul, M., Sulyard-Street, Lancaster	223. 357
Scrutator, London	12
Selim, Wiltshire	212
Short, William, J., Surveyor, Clapham	233
Sibbald, J., and Sons, of Edinburgh	75
T. F. L., Harwich	374
T. S., Berlin	88
T. T., Dublin	94
T. W., Banks, near Barnsley, Yorkshire	95, 96. 143. 181. 247. 280
T. Y., Vale of Alford	94
Thomson, Lieut. Colonel, Engineer, Cape Town, Cape of Good Hope	72
Thorold, W., Architect and Engineer, Norwich	248
Trotman, E., Architect, 10, Furnival's Inn	16. 103. 148. 255
W.	143. 144
W., London	378
W., Newcastle Street, Strand, London	184
W. H., Dover	209
W. H., London	285. 375
W. H. B.	223
W. L., London	45. 97
W. T.	95
W. T., Norfolk	140. 184. 213. 245, 246
Watson, J. B., Duke Street, Manchester Square	248
Wightwick, G., Architect, Plymouth	357
Wilkinson, Thomas, Liverpool	40
Wilson, Thomas, Banks, near Barnsley	216
Y. Z., London	389
Y. Z., Worcester	127
Z.	143. 391
Z., Hertford	386

THE ARCHITECTURAL MAGAZINE.

MARCH, 1834.

INTRODUCTION.

THE objects which we have in view, in undertaking an Architectural Magazine, are the same that influenced us in submitting to the world our *Encyclopædia of Cottage, Farm, and Villa Architecture and Furniture;* viz., to diffuse among general readers a taste for architectural beauties and comforts, and to improve the dwellings of the great mass of society, in all countries. The Architectural Magazine, however, will embrace a more extensive range of subjects than the Encyclopædia; since, in addition to the private dwellings of every class of society residing in the country, it will include also dwellings in cities and towns, and public buildings, in a word, the whole of civil architecture, building, and furnishing.

The study of the science of Architecture recommends itself to the general reader by the utility of its productions as an art, and by the pleasure afforded by the contemplation of these productions as subjects of taste. To young men engaged in the various professions and businesses connected with the art of building, this study presents a means of professional improvement, and, consequently, of advancement in the world; in it the landowner will find one of the principal means of increasing the value of his property; it will give to the retiring citizen an opportunity of forming his taste for building or choosing a cottage or villa residence; and to every individual who either occupies a house, or intends to occupy one, it will afford the means of ascertaining what is good or bad in construction and in appearance, and of choosing, repairing, altering, fitting up, and furnishing his habitation. Though all men do not build houses, yet all men in a state of civilisation live in them; and it must, therefore, be of some importance to every individual, to have his judgment in the choice of a house heightened by a knowledge of what points in its construction and arrangement will contribute most to his security, convenience, and comfort.

The subjects of Architecture admit of two grand divisions, public and private buildings: and, in all countries, the progress of the former seems to have been incomparably greater than that of the latter. Hence, though private dwelling-houses must have existed before, or, at least, have been coeval with, public buildings, yet there can be no doubt that the architecture of the former remained stationary for ages; while that of the latter advanced with the progress of nations: and hence, in those ages when the grandest and most beautiful temples were erecting in Greece, the most sumptuous palaces in Italy, and the most magnificent cathedrals in England, there is no evidence of much improvement having been introduced into the private dwellings even of the wealthy. The reason seems to be, that, till within the last three centuries, the mode of living of all ranks of society was comparatively simple, and very much alike in all countries having similar climates. In time, however, the general introduction of manufactures and commerce led to the improvement of domestic architecture, as it did to that of other arts, by the creation of a middle class of society; by the interchange of the productions of one country for those of another; and by the improvement of the manufactures in general use in all countries. Hence improved articles of dress led to the necessity of having improved pieces of furniture to contain them; the use of sea-coal led to the improvement of fireplaces; the use of knives and forks led to improved stoves and other arrangements for cookery; and these, and an infinity of other domestic ameliorations, led gradually to the better construction of houses.

But, though the art of constructing private dwellings has made great progress in Britain within the last three centuries, yet there still remains much to be done in the application of the modern discoveries of science to domestic purposes. The most skilfully contrived villas and mansions admit of the application of still higher skill; and the cottage of the farmer and country labourer, and the street house of the tradesman and mechanic, have scarcely yet had applied to them even that which has been already attained. The want of comfort, indeed, in the dwellings of the agricultural labourers and of the mechanics of Britain, is, as compared with the quality of their clothing and food, greater than is to be found in the dwellings of the working classes of any other country in Europe. To be convinced of this, we have only to compare the coarse brown bread and rough woollen and hempen cloth of the peasantry of the North of Europe, with their warm log houses; or the slight diet and clothing of the peasantry of Italy and the South of France, with the open airy shelters, which, in those fine climates, afford sufficient protection, and a degree of comfort suitable to the state of the occupant. In both these cases, the food, the clothing, and the dwelling are in some sort of harmony; but when we compare the clothing of broadcloth, cottons, and muslins, and the wheaten bread and butcher's meat of the English mechanic or country labourer, with his dwelling, not so impervious to the weather as that of the rudely clothed and coarsely fed Russian or Swede, and often not larger or more convenient, the inconsistency is glaring. — But we have already said so much on this subject in our Encyclopædia, that we shall not enlarge upon it here.

To those whose prosperity or fortune enables them to occupy what are considered good houses, either in town or country, some knowledge of the science and practice of Architecture would be not only a source of perpetual enjoyment, but of real use; because every accession to our knowledge gives power as well as pleasure. We do not merely allude to the preeminence which a taste for Architecture must necessarily give to every possessor of it; but also to the value of Architecture as a useful art; or, in other words, to the power of applying its principles to buildings and furniture. It may be said, indeed, that individuals so circumstanced as to be able to have handsome dwellings, can always command the services of professional men to give them advice in the choice or furnishing of a house. We allow this; and we add, that, if the general knowledge of Architecture which we advocate were of no other use than to impress the intended occupant of a house with the necessity of having it previously examined by a professional man, it would justify what we have asserted as to the benefits to be derived from architectural knowledge. The great advantage, however, which we propose to the general reader, as the result of a knowledge of the useful in Architecture (viz. of the arrangement, strength, lighting, warming, ventilating, fitting up, furnishing, &c., of houses) is, that he will know better than he now does, what comforts and conveniences he is entitled to expect from the size and rent of any given house.

A taste for Architecture, like that for any of the fine arts, is at once a source of enjoyment, and a mark of refinement. As buildings are more frequently occurring to the view than either pictures or statues, this enjoyment can be proportionately more frequently obtained; and hence it would appear to be the more desirable for the possessor. It may farther be stated, that to understand and enjoy Architecture does not depend nearly so much on what is called a natural taste, as does the enjoyment of pictures, statuary, or music. Architecture is more an art of reason than of imagination; and there is hardly any great feature of beauty or deformity in a building, the propriety or absurdity of which could not be made obvious to the most ordinary understanding, even if the possessor of that understanding had paid very little attention previously to the subject. So much cannot be said of any of the other arts mentioned.

Whatever may be the advantage to the possessor of a taste for Architecture individually, the ornament, and, ultimately, the benefit, to the whole country, arising from such a taste becoming general, would be great beyond calculation. What man, who could build his own house, and possessed any taste in this art, would be content to live in houses exhibiting such external elevations as those which at present continually meet the eye, both in town and country? Let a taste for Architecture spread generally, and our towns would soon present continuous elevations of architectural beauty, and our country residences become as celebrated for their Architecture, as they now are for their gardens and landscape scenery.

Ardently desiring such a result, one of the great objects which we have in view is the improvement, or rather the creation, of a taste for Architecture in that portion of society which occupies the best houses. This, we conceive, is to be attained in two ways: by inducing this class, and especially the female portion of it, to read and think on the subject of domestic architecture; and by cultivating a better taste in builders, carpenters, and others engaged in the practice of building, so as to induce them to erect, of their own accord, houses of a superior style. Fortunately for this last purpose, taste in an art is not necessarily connected with wealth: it may be possessed by the journeyman carpenter, mason, bricklayer, or cabinet-maker, in as high a degree as by the architect, surveyor, or learned and wealthy amateur. In all it must first exist naturally, and in all it must be improved by cultivation. Now, the cultivation of architectural taste in a man whose business is that of a carpenter or mason, and who is, consequently, familiar with architectural details, will be much easier than the cultivation of the same taste in a man of wealth, who knows no more of the practical part of building than he does of the practical part of landscape-painting, sculpture, or any other art. The great drawback in the way of the artisan has hitherto been, the want of suitable books to put him in a proper course of self-instruction. He can doubtless have access to many books treating of the five orders of Grecian architecture, and to many others containing plans and elevations of buildings; but these works can no more teach Architecture as an art of taste, than a spelling-book can teach grammar and composition.

All men born with the ordinary condition of the human faculties are naturally endowed with taste; that is, they have a predominant feeling for some one particular class of objects or pursuits: one boy has a facility in acquiring languages, another is naturally musical; and so on. Now, those feelings which have a tendency to induce the love or the pursuit of what are called the fine arts are preeminently distinguised by the term taste. This term, however, might, with equal justice, be applied to feelings having a tendency to other pursuits; such as natural history, or to any particular kind of art, trade, or commerce. There can be no doubt that many persons evince, in very early life, a propensity for prrticular trades or particular pursuits; but, though this propensity is as much entitled to be called a taste as is a propensity for music, painting, or sculpture, yet, by the conventional use of language, the term is only applied with reference to these and some other arts. According to the general acceptation of terms, therefore, those arts, the exercise of which implies creations from the imagination, are alone strictly denominated the arts of taste; while those arts are termed mechanical, the exercise of which only calls into action the reasoning powers and the physical strength. Architecture is an art which, as before stated, depends more upon reason than upon imagination; and, therefore, not being purely an art of taste, but only partially so, the imaginative faculty is less required in its professors than in the professors of painting, sculpture, or music. Let no one, therefore, who can reason, or who possesses what is called good common sense, despair of acquiring a just and correct taste in Architecture.

Architecture, as a fine art, consists chiefly in the combination of forms; and, as it is difficult to conceive any human being so deficient in intellect as not to be able to put several forms together, in the general shape of a house (for house-building to man is as natural as nest-building to birds), so it is difficult to conceive a human being whose taste in Architecture might not be greatly improved.

That improvement it is one main object of this work to effect in the minds of the mechanical artisans connected with Architecture, and more especially in the minds of CARPENTERS. The carpenter has more to do with the construction of a building than any other person employed by the architect. The word signifying architect in the Greek language may, indeed, be translated carpenter. Whether a building is to be erected of brick or stone, still it is the carpenter who forms all the patterns and guides for the bricklayer or the mason to work from. Nay, even if a cottage is to be built of mud, the first step is to procure boards adapted by the carpenter for forming moulds, by which this mud is brought into the required form; or, even if the mud is heaped up with forks, as in the cob walls of Devonshire and Wiltshire, the carpenter is required to supply what are called wooden bricks, to be built into the walls, for attaching, at a future period, the internal finishings. In the interior of a house, every thing depends on the carpenter; and most things are, indeed, done by him. The floors, and the doors and windows, are almost entirely his work; and he forms mouldings for the cornices which are put up by the plasterer. If, therefore, we could improve the taste of the rising generation of carpenters, we should have no fears of operating, through them, on all the various artisans employed in the construction of houses; and, ultimately, on the general taste of the whole community. The circulation of such works as we intend this Magazine to be will, by rendering not only professional men, but general readers, better judges of Architecture than they were before, at once contribute to the diffusion of this taste, and afford the best security for its permanency.

But, though we have singled out the carpenter as the most important artisan connected with the art of building, we are aware, also, of the powerful influence of the BRICKLAYER and the MASON. In those parts of the country where the walls of buildings are formed entirely of brick, much of their strength, and also of their durability, must depend on the BRICKLAYER. Few people purchasing houses built with brick walls are aware of the difference, in strength and durability, between a wall built throughout with sound bricks which had been for some months exposed to the air after they were burnt, and with good mortar, and a wall built with one quality of bricks for the outside, and another for the inside; or built with bricks and mortar of the best quality, but with the former hot from the kiln. In the first of the two latter cases, the wall has not the strength and durability which it appears to have; because the difference in specific gravity between the exterior bricks and the interior ones has a constant tendency to rend the whole asunder; and, in the second of these cases, the heat and absorbing power of the bricks reduce the mortar to a dry powder: so that the strength which ought to be acquired from the cohesion of the materials is wholly wanting. In modern times, when bricks cast in forms communicating to them architectural mouldings are no longer in use, the bricklayer may be said to have little direct influence in the taste of a house comparatively with the carpenter; but we are most desirous that he should acquire architectural taste, for many reasons; and chiefly because an industrious bricklayer very often becomes in time a master builder, and may often have to design houses as well as to build them.

The MASON, in all countries where stone is the principal building material, ranks next in importance to the carpenter. In Scotland there are few stonemasons, and, indeed, few artisans connected with building or cabinet-making, who have not gone through a course of architectural drawing at an evening school. In that country, the mason very frequently takes the lead of the carpenter, more especially in buildings of the humbler class; because the facings to doors and windows, the projecting stones of coins, the crowsteps on gable ends, and the ashlar work of chimney tops, all which form leading features of cottages built of stone, require no moulds or guides from the carpenter. The taste of the mason, therefore, we are particularly desirous of cultivating; because we know the extensive influence which he has over the great mass of farm buildings, cottages, and street houses, in all those parts of the country where stone is principally used for building. Every steady industrious mason ultimately arrives at building a house for himself; if he is not ambitious of doing this, he is not worth much; and, if he is enabled to do it, he naturally takes advantage of the opportunity to display his taste, whatever it may be. If nothing farther, therefore, were attained by the cultivation of architectural taste in masons, than a single improved cottage dwelling, as an example to others, and a source of gratification to the traveller of taste, our object would be attained.

THE PLASTERER, in Britain at least, was, till within the last thirty years, chiefly confined to the interior of the house; but he is now a very important artisan, having the sole employment of that material which produces such magical effects on exteriors, Roman cement. In consequence of the discovery of cements of this kind, we are now enabled to erect buildings of brick, coated over with this material, which are as handsome as those of stone, and much stronger and more durable; because the walls, with the exterior appearance of stone, have all the cohesiveness and homogeneousness of brick. By the aid of cement we are also enabled to display every kind of architectural form and ornament, in many cases, at a fifth of the expense that similar ornaments would cost if formed of either moulded bricks or of stone. Great numbers of the small houses in the suburbs of all towns are built with the savings accumulated by carpenters, bricklayers, masons, plasterers, and others connected with Architecture; and the improvement of these small buildings, through the medium of their builders, is therefore well worth attempting.

In the interior of a house, the PAINTER exercises a very considerable influence. In the higher class of houses, where different colours are employed for decorating different rooms, if the master painter be not an artist of cultivated taste, he can hardly avoid falling into error, and producing discord or monotony, instead of harmony. The painter is sometimes under the direction of the architect, and sometimes under that of the upholsterer; but he is more frequently his own master. He therefore ought to cultivate his taste, not only for the arrangement of colours, but for the choice of ornamental forms. When we consider that an ornamental house-painter has to imitate different kinds of woods and marbles; to display architectural forms and mouldings; and to imitate natural objects, such as flowers, landscapes, &c., it will appear evident, that, to excel in his profession, he must be something very superior to a mere mechanical distributer of colours. As a proof of this, some of our most eminent artists have been originally ornamental house-painters, or ornamental painters of objects connected with Architecture or domestic economy.

The trades of the GLAZIER and the PLUMBER are generally combined; because, in former times, when those subdivisions of windows which contain the glass were of lead, solder was as much required in putting in glass as putty is now. The use of stained glass is very frequently intrusted to the glazier, and we not unfrequently find it applied where it is by no means appropriate. Even if there were no point whatever of the glazier's business connected with architectural effect but this single one, it alone is sufficient to render it highly desirable that his taste should be cultivated. The business of the plumber is a most important one, especially when we consider that to him belong the distribution of water over a house, and its conveyance from the roof, the sinks, water-closets, and different other parts, underground to the main drains.

The SLATER, TILER, and THATCHER may be considered as requiring more of mechanical skill than architectural taste; but though this may be true, as far as it respects the roofs of large houses, which are not at all, or but little displayed, yet the case is different with cottages, of which the roof, next to the chimney tops, is the most characteristic feature. A good deal of taste is required for the proper arrangement of different descriptions of tiles on a roof, and also for the putting on of thatch or reeds in a picturesque manner.

In the fittings-up of a house various artisans are engaged; but the principal one, that we have not yet mentioned, is the BELL-HANGER, who requires to be a skilful mechanic.

The finishing of large houses is generally committed to the ULHOLSTERER, who employs the CABINET-MAKER, the PAPER-HANGER, and a variety of subordinate artisans, mechanics, and tradesmen, all of whom ought to be more or less acquainted with Architecture. The journeyman cabinet-maker requires to have a considerable knowledge of the mouldings and other details of both Grecian and Gothic architecture; and the master cabinet-maker ought unquestionably to be a man of taste, and to have his mind stored with all the approved forms and ornaments of antique as well as of modern architecture, sculpture, and furniture. It is true, we do not find this to be frequently the case; but the principal reason is, the deficiency of taste in the majority of the employers of cabinet-makers. In taste, as in every thing else, the supply produced will always depend upon the demand created; and where men of wealth have neither had leisure to form their taste by reading, nor opportunity to improve it by travelling, and inspecting excellent models, how is it to be supposed that they can distinguish between the good and the bad in design? All the guide that such men have in the choice of furniture is fashion, and their ambition can only extend to having something newer than the fashion which is most prevalent at the time. There is nothing, as Quatremère de Quincy, and Percier and Fontaine, have observed, more injurious to art, than this incessant craving after novelty. It corrupts the taste of the purchaser, and contributes to his unhappiness, by making him dissatisfied with whatever he possesses, when anything newer has become fashionable; and it corrupts the taste of the cabinet-maker, by creating an incessant demand for novelty, which no designer, unless he possesses a highly cultivated mind, and an almost unlimited stock of ideas, can long supply without degenerating into absurdity. Never, in any age or country, was this more conspicuous than it was in London during the first ten years of the present century; and, though it was checked in a slight degree by the classical publication on furniture of the late Thomas Hope, it has not altogether disappeared even at the present day. With this view of the subject, it is almost unnecessary for us to say how much we think the improvement of public taste, in regard to furniture, depends on the study of the principles of architectural design by the young cabinet-maker. It is, however, proper, in a marked manner, to state, that, with a view to the cultivation of the taste of the CABINET-MAKER, the UPHOLSTERER, the ORNAMENTAL HOUSE-PAINTER, the CARVER and GILDER, and other similar artisans connected with furnishing, we intend to pay particular attention, in this Magazine, to the principles which serve as guides in the general composition of lines and forms, whether of nature or of art. This has not hitherto been done in any publication addressed to the general reader; and, in attempting it, we think we shall be rendering very essential service to young men in every department connected with building and furnishing.

What are called the fixtures of a house, such as the stoves, grates, kitchen-ranges, ovens, &c., are supplied by the FURNISHING IRONMONGER; who, unquestionably, ought always to be a man of taste; since his articles are not only expensive, but of considerable durability. New fashions in them, therefore, being attended with more expense than is suitable to most housekeepers, ought to be introduced with great caution. The ironmonger is also called upon to exercise his taste, skill, and judgment in warming and ventilating; and, not unfrequently, in that humble but yet very important department, the curing of smoky chimneys. Franklin and Rumford have shown how necessary it is, for this purpose, that an ironmonger should be a scientific man; and, when we consider how much the warming of rooms and the economy of cookery depend on him, he must be allowed to fill a very important department in the completion of a house. To all the different subjects to which he is obliged to turn his attention this Magazine will be directed; and more particularly to all the best modes of warming and ventilating at present in use.

The IRON-FOUNDER is chiefly to be considered as included in

the department of the ironmonger; but cast iron now enters, in many cases, so extensively into the construction of the walls and floors of houses intended to be rendered fire-proof, and, besides, the iron-founder supplies so many important parts of the furniture, both of dwelling-houses and of agricultural buildings, that many of the articles he manufactures will frequently demand our particular notice.

We have now, we believe, enumerated the principal artisans, mechanics, and tradesmen, to whose occupations we intend to direct the attention of the readers of this Magazine; and it only remains for us to give an outline of our plan of arrangement, and to state the principles to which we mean to adhere in conducting the work.

With respect to the plan of this Magazine, every Number will be arranged in three divisions: the first of these divisions will contain Original Communications; the second Reviews, including a catalogue of all the new works on civil architecture published in Europe and America; and the third, Miscellaneous Intelligence. This last division will include notices of architectural improvements (in progress or completed) in different parts of Britain and other countries; queries and answers; and retrospective criticism on whatever has appeared in this Magazine, or in our *Encyclopædia of Cottage, Farm, and Villa Architecture and Furniture*. Though we have no intention of deviating in the slightest degree from the general outline of this plan, yet we wish it to be understood that we reserve the liberty of making such changes in it as time and experience may suggest.

In the Original Communications, every subject will be treated on the supposition that the reader is in a great measure a stranger to it; and hence every techinal term will be explained where it first occurs, and afterwards transferred to a Glossarial Index, which will be given at the end of each volume, for the convenience of reference. As numerous graphic illustrations will be required, they will be limited to subjects deemed to be of real utility; and they will, as far as practicable, be given on such a scale as to be available, as prototypes of working drawings, to the practical builder, cabinet-maker, and furnisher.

In the Review Department, the object will be rather to give a distinct idea of the contents of the works reviewed, than to display the talent or knowledge of the reviewer. No new books will be omitted; and, when room permits, accounts will be given of architectural works of first-rate merit, whether new or old, British or foreign, in order to impart to the reader a general idea of all the best books on Architecture which have ever been published. In the Miscellaneous Department, we shall endeavour to insert no intelligence which we have not good reason for believing to be true. Every query shall be inserted that is not frivolous; and, under the head of Retrospective Criticism, we will allow every article which appears in the work to be critically examined, provided that no personalities are introduced, and that the criticism is never couched in offensive language.

For the execution of this plan, we rely on the cooperation of our readers generally, and more especially on that of such practical and amateur architects as take the same views of the subject as ourselves; that is to say, who are desirous of improving society generally in architectural knowledge and taste. Indeed, our object will be, in a great degree, to induce our readers to instruct one another; and for this purpose we invite all of them, and especially young architects, to become writers. There is scarely any person who has a thorough knowledge of the art or trade which he practises, who could not write about it, if he were to try; and our experience, in the course of the nine years during which we have conducted the *Gardener's Magazine*, justifies us in asserting, that by far the most valuable contributions to practical arts and trades are likely to be made by men engaged in them; and by pupils, apprentices, and journeymen, as well as by masters. The same views are also confirmed by the success of that useful and most judiciously conducted work, the *Mechanics' Magazine*, which, directly and indirectly, has effected more for the mechanics throughout Britain than any other publication. In the course of conducting the *Gardener's Magazine*, we have seen the great advantage that journeymen gardeners have procured to themselves by becoming writers; the habits of thinking and reasoning which they have attained on subjects generally, and the power of expressing themselves with facility and accuracy in conversation, and, above all, in that most important part of every man's social duty, letter-writing. There is no more certain mode by which one man can judge of the mind of another than by his letters; and no man can write a letter who could not also write an article for a Magazine if he were to make the attempt. We invite, then, not only architects, builders, surveyors, and amateurs, but artisans, journeymen, and apprentices, of all the different arts and trades above mentioned as more immediately connected with Architecture, to become our correspondents. Let them not hesitate from any doubts as to their style; facts are what we want, and, in whatever form we receive them, they are always valuable. Independently of the endless variety of subjects suited to Original Communications, there will seldom be found a Number of this Magazine which does not contain a query that some reader may be able to answer, and also facts or reasonings, by ourselves or others, which are open to discussion under the head of Retrospective Criticism. There is probably no reader who could not communicate some news for our Miscellaneous Department; for example, of buildings projected, or carried into execution in his immediate neighbourhood; new articles of furniture, or modes of furnishing, which he has seen; new modes of warming and ventilating; or improvements in public roads, bridges, gates, or architectural fences. Let every reader, therefore, in this manner cooperate with us in eliciting and diffusing architectural knowledge and taste. The principal means of effecting the improvement of any class of society is by inducing its members to think, and the most ready mode of exciting thought in ourselves is by reading the thoughts of others similarly circumstanced.

Having now explained the objects of this Magazine; enumerated the different classes to whom it is addressed, and from whom we expect cooperation; having laid down our plan; and, finally, having stated the principles by which we mean to be guided in carrying that plan into execution, we shall proceed to lay before our readers such communications as have been sent us; not doubting but that, as our work becomes more generally known, and our contributors increase, every succeeding Number will be rendered more and more interesting.

ORIGINAL COMMUNICATIONS.

ART. I. *On the present State of the Professions of Architect and Surveyor, and of the Building Trade, in England.* By SCRUTATOR.

Sir,

I REJOICE that the Architect and Surveyor are at length to have a Periodical devoted to them. It is time they had, for never was such a publication so much required by the profession as at present; and I am confident that it will lead to the reformation of many abuses now existing among Architects, Surveyors, and Builders. It will tend to eradicate many false notions, and to correct many bad practices; and will, I hope, restore the profession to the station it formerly held in society. I am sorry to say that architects and surveyors do not now obtain that confidence with the public that they ought to have, and I think this confidence can only be restored by free discussion in such a periodical as you propose. We find that those classes which have periodicals devoted to them, have very greatly improved their knowledge and their respectability, and have had instilled into them an amicable understanding among themselves: for instance, witness what that excellent periodical the *Mechanics' Magazine* has done. This magazine was the principal cause of Mechanics' Institutions being formed, not only in London, but all over England, and it opened a wide field for communicating knowledge: it has tended to make the mechanic respected by his superiors; and has mainly contributed to make him looked upon as equal in knowledge to the aristocracy, upon whom he is gaining ground daily. In like manner, that spirited and excellent periodical the *Lancet* has tended to eradicate abuses in the medical profession; and the *Legal Observer* has done wonders even among the lawyers. If, then, these periodicals have effected so much good, it is to be hoped that yours will lead to the same results; and, if it do not, I am sure it will not be the fault of its conductor, who, I feel convinced, if he meets with support, will grapple with and expose the abuses of the profession; as well as exert himself "to improve and extend architectural taste and knowledge." If my humble exertions can be of any benefit, they are at your service; and, on the supposition that they will be acceptable, I will at once make a few remarks that are deserving of the serious attention of the members of the profession.

The first thing I shall notice is that disgraceful mode of giving evidence in courts of justice, which has made the very name of a surveyor a laughing-stock for the legal profession; his evidence in a court of law is looked upon in the same light as that of a horse-jockey in a horse cause; and can we be surprised at it, when similar evidence to the following is constantly given?

Plaintiff A and defendant B are at issue upon an account for works executed. The witnesses of A state that the work is done in a very superior manner: one witness swears that the work is fairly worth 1544*l*.; and another witness, to support him, swears the fair value is 1630*l*. Then come the defendant's witnesses, who state that the work is very badly executed, and done in a very improper manner: one of them asserts that the outside value of the plaintiff's work is 980*l*., and another surveyor says he makes the value 935*l*. Now, what are the judge and jury, who know no more about a building account than a boy of seven years old, to do in such a case? They are surprised and astonished that respectable men can be so very wide in their values; and what is the result? Why, they take the several amounts as given in evidence, add them together, and divide the amount by the number of witnesses: accordingly, the result in the above case would be, that a verdict would be given for 1257*l*. Now, let architects and surveyors reflect upon this disgraceful mode of giving evidence (and they know too well that what I have stated is pretty near the truth), and ask themselves whether it is not time that something should be done to redeem the character of their profession?

Again, do we not find it frequently the case, that gentlemen have such an antipathy to the name of a surveyor, that, if the builder were to mention to his employer that he was about to engage a surveyor to measure the works executed, he would immediately give offence; consequently, the builder is obliged to introduce the surveyor into the building by stealth. Nor can any one be surprised at it, when we witness the extortionate charges made by some surveyors, whom I shall here style *custom* surveyors. This is the manner in which they proceed: two surveyors meet to make out an account of certain works done. We will suppose the account that they have to settle is a plumber's bill. The first article is 18 cwt. of milled lead: the plumber's surveyor requires 25s. per cwt.; the surveyor for the opposite party remonstrates, and points out to him that the prime cost was 15s.; the other replies that 25s. is the customary price, and that he cannot take less. To convince his opponent, he opens an old measuring-book, and shows that 25s. has been charged in an account that he settled on behalf of Mr. Getall with Mr. Easy the surveyor, some years before; and he again repeats that it is the *custom* to charge 25s.; and that he cannot deviate from it. In the same way; he charges 1s. per foot for pipe that only cost 4d., and 1s. per lb. for solder that only cost 5d.; and so he goes on in the same ratio with all other articles in the bill. After charging so extortionately for the time and materials for making a joint to a pipe, he has the conscience to ask, in addition, 2s. 6d. for that joint, though he cannot tell why he does so, except that it is the *custom*, &c. The consequence of all this is, that the surveyor for the opposite party, if he have any conscience, cannot settle the account, and it is referred to the lawyers; it is then carried into a court of justice, where it is decided in a similar manner to that which I have before described.

Can it be a matter of surprise that there should be so little measuring, when the charges are made out in the way I have stated? As a remedy, I would recommend every person intending to build to have the work done by contract. I would contract even for a dog-kennel, until these *custom* surveyors are brought to their senses. This, I think, they soon will be; for, in consequence of the manner of proceeding which I have described, they are employed less and less every day.

Another great error, in valuing builders' work, is, that the surveyors too frequently charge but one price, whether the work be done well or ill, and that they pay no regard to the prime cost, or to the mode of payment. The latter ought to be taken into serious consideration; for, if the work be paid for as it proceeds, it will enable the builder to purchase his materials with cash, and thus generally 10 per cent. cheaper in the market, than if he had to obtain them on credit. On the other hand, if the work be not paid for till some time after it is finished, a considerable increase ought to be allowed, for the disadvantages of being obliged to purchase on credit, and for the use of the ready money necessarily laid out in workmen's wages. Something, also, should be allowed for risk, as builders are liable to have bad debts as well as other tradesmen.

Having said thus much respecting surveyors, I will now allude to one or two abuses that have lately been introduced among architects. It is now the fashion among some of the principal architects, not to allow the builder to employ a surveyor to measure his work, but to insist upon the builder leaving it entirely to the architect's clerk, or to a surveyor named by him. Every practical surveyor must at once see the evil consequences of this mode of proceeding; because he must know, that, even with the greatest caution, and with the utmost rectitude of intention, mistakes will creep in, if only one surveyor is employed; even the simple circumstance of omitting to double or treble a dimension, may make some hundreds of pounds' difference. It is this species of error that causes so great a difference in estimates for work to be performed; and frequently have I known this to be the case. I recollect certain estimates that were made for building a church, and the difference was very great between the two lowest; the parties compared books, and it was discovered that in the lowest the amount of the gallery had not been doubled: every other part was taken by both parties as accurately as could be required. What is most disgraceful in the modern practice alluded to is, that the architect's clerk or surveyor frequently charges the builder a commission for measuring; or, what is equally bad, he gets the tradesman to repair or paint his house, or to execute some other job, which the latter is obliged to do to keep himself in favour; the architect, at the same time, not forgetting to charge his employer with his commission for measuring.

Another disgraceful practice, which is either owing to ignorance or knavery, is, that some architects deceive their employers, by making very pretty and attractive drawings, and reporting that the expense of carrying these into execution will be about half or two thirds of what it actually turns out to be. In this way they obtain the sanction of their employer to commence building; and when the accounts are sent in, the employer finds himself involved too frequently in ruinous expenses. The builder, in such cases, often gets into disgrace, and is either obliged to commence an action to obtain his rights (because the architect has the knavery, in order to screen his ignorance, to say that the builder's bill is a most exorbitant one), or to have his bill cut down so low, that he is left a loser instead of a gainer, after labouring hard for 12 or 18 months. To remedy this evil, I would advise the parties intending to build, to contract with the architect for his commission, as well as with the builder for his work. This might be done in the following manner:—If the architect reports that the building will amount to 2000*l.*, his commission should be fixed at 100*l.*; and if the work exceed five per cent. beyond his report, it should be arranged that there should be a deduction, from his commission, of five per cent on the excess of the amount beyond the original estimate. Thus, if the original estimate were 2000*l.*, and the actual cost 2500*l.*, the commission of the architect, instead of being 125*l.* as it would be by the present *custom*, would be only 75*l.*; whereas, had the amount being within 2100*l.*, his commission would have been 100*l.* By thus reducing the architect's commission, instead of increasing it, when the expense exceeds the estimate, as is now the practice, the temptation to give in false estimates would be diminished; though these estimates are likely to be often made, so long as the inducement is so strong as it is at present.

Another very paltry trick common among some architects is, their custom of exacting from the builder a commission for all works done under their direction; and, if this be refused, informing the builder that his services are no longer required.

Having said thus much, allow me to point out a mode by which, I think, these abuses might be remedied. This is simply to form a society, not for eating and drinking, or backbiting their brethren, but to make rules for the governance of the profession; to make a fair tariff of prices, according to the variation of the market; to regulate the mode of measuring; and to enquire into every abuse or infringement connected with the profession. I have no doubt that if thirty or forty respectable members of the profession would form such a society, it would very soon eradicate the numerous abuses which at present exist; and that architects and surveyors would soon regain that respect with the public which they formerly possessed.　　　SCRUTATOR.

London, Nov. 1833.

ART. II.　*On the Extent to which the elementary Forms of Classic Architecture are, from their Nature and Origin, fixed or arbitrary.* By E. TROTMAN, Esq., Architect.

THE principles and circumstances which form the basis of Classic Architecture as a decorative science, are by no means so obvious to the ordinary observer as are those which constitute the foundation of the sister arts of Painting and Sculpture. In either of the latter, the efforts of the artist are purely imitative; and he who transfers to the canvass or the marble effects the most closely resembling those of nature, supplying the deficiencies of individual models by the beauties of collective observation, becomes the most complete master of his pursuit. In the study of architecture, however, the case is otherwise; the imitation of nature is of a limited and much more systematised character; and those forms and combinations which are universally received, as applicable in general to the purposes of decoration, have their origin in circumstances that would seem to be involved in a degree of obscurity, which evidence no better than traditional must fail to dissipate. Yet, amidst all this apparent uncertainty, even upon matters of fundamental importance, it is curious to observe the zeal, approaching to acrimony, with which some architectural sectarians assert against each other an exclusive authority for the most minute characteristics of their own peculiar schools. The rigid admirer of Palladian taste cherishes an indifference approaching to contempt, for the delicacy of Grecian finish, and discerns in the simple beauty of Attic profiles little else than a poverty of ornament; while the professed imitator of the models of Pericles loses sight of the force and variety of Italian composition in the excess of his abhorrence for what he considers clumsy forms of moulding and enrichment—too often content to make the elegance of parts an apology for a spiritless whole. A more comprehensive and unprejudiced view of the subject would, however, suffice to show that the genuine principles of taste cannot be thus at variance with each other; and that we should have some higher authority for appeal than the dictates of fancy, or even of precedent, when we assume an exclusiveness that belongs only to mathematical demonstration, or to the palpable evidence of the senses. It may not be amiss, therefore, to enquire how far the primitive forms of architecture are the result of a demonstrable fitness of things, thereupon determining how much is left to the province of decorative taste. In pursuing such an enquiry, it will be necessary to reject, as altogether fabulous, accounts which are so opposed to the principles of analogy and historical truth as are those of Vitruvius with regard to the origin of architectural combinations; nor can we entertain much doubt as to the degree of credit which, in a subject of such remote reference, ought to be awarded to a writer who can gravely attribute the rise of human civilisation, and even the developement of the powers of speech, to the elementary agency of fire, accidentally produced by the attrition of the forest branches under the agitation of the wind. Indeed, the statement advanced by Vitruvius upon the point in question is unsatisfactory, for a twofold reason; both because he neglects to refer the characteristics of Grecian art to their undoubted source in the prototypes of Egypt, and because also he assumes a position unsupported by the principles of constructive analogy, in asserting that the forms of architecture, as embodied in stone, were derived from those which had previously and accidentally developed themselves in structures of wood. Now, to us it appears that the whole system of architecture has its origin in two great principles; first, the principle of fitness, which provides and regulates its larger component members and masses; and, secondly, that of beauty, which adds to each of these the embellishment suited to its situation and office. The principle of fitness has regard to the properties of the material employed, to the purposes of the structure erected, and to the peculiarities of the climate possessed. This being the case, it is obvious, so far as the nature of the material is concerned, that the forms which would suggest themselves as appropriate to erections in woodwork are not those which would be in any degree significant, or even applicable, where stone was the material of construction; since the fibrous nature of the former substance fits it for a slight species of building, in which the bearings are long, and the points of support are few; while in the latter the work becomes necessarily massive, the bearings being short, and the points of support numerous. If, therefore, we would perceive in what manner the principle of fitness has given rise to the various members of architectural composition, we have only to refer to the remains of Egyptian monuments as the most venerable for remote antiquity; remains which, while they display the exemplars of classic taste, afford a grand picture of the power of art, when even emerging in its simplicity from primitive rudeness. Looking back through these to the first invention of column and entablature, we see the builder of the pristine temple adopting, in the construction of his ponderous supporting masses, somewhat of a cylindrical form, so that his pillars shall present no angles to impede the way; arranging them in a row, and giving them such a height as his unpractised judgment may deem calculated to afford a covering of sufficient loftiness for the area to be enclosed, having first insured their stability by giving them that expansion at the lower extremity, for which he would hardly need to seek an example from nature in the spreading root of the tree, or the widening base of the rock. In thus forming his line of columns, he finds their distances from each other necessarily limited by the length in which he may have been able to procure blocks to lie upon and connect their summits. Hence his intercolumniation becomes fixed at a lofty proportion, since his columns must rise to the height of a spacious avenue or chamber, while they remain confined as to relative distance by the nature of the material which they have to sustain. These columns being raised, he places on the head of each a cubical block, the top of which, by being left square, may afford a broader bed to the superincumbent mass, while its lower side is reduced to a circular form, correspondent to that of the shaft; and hence a simple capital. (*fig.* 1. *a.*) This done, he proceeds to connect the top of each to that of its neighbour by a series of blocks laid horizontally, of a depth and thickness nearly equal to the upper substance of the columns, forming thus his

epistylium or architrave (*b*). Before, however, any space can be enclosed, the whole operation must of course be repeated (unless the equivalent of a wall be adopted) by the erection of another line of columns behind the former, with similar capitals and epistylia; and the only part of the task then remaining is, to form a covering across from one line to the other, by means of large slabs of stone, of depth suited to their surface, and which, being allowed to overhang the rest of the work, will extend the area of shelter, and preserve the rest of the masonry from the effects of the weather, thus becoming a kind of cornice (*c*). In these parts, therefore, without any attempt at decoration, we obtain, upon the first and most obvious principle of constructive fitness and constructive expression, an order of architecture, rude, indeed, but complete in all the members used in Egygtian practice, which did not exhibit any thing perfectly analogous to the remaining portion of the Greek entablature, the frieze.

The introduction thus of the primitive masses was soon succeeded by the invention of mouldings, which constitute geometrical decorations of the simplest of all kinds, and are the exclusive property of architecture. These, in Egyptian works, first appear in the form of a great hollow which cornices were made to assume (*a*, in *figs*. 2 and 3.); and in that of the large

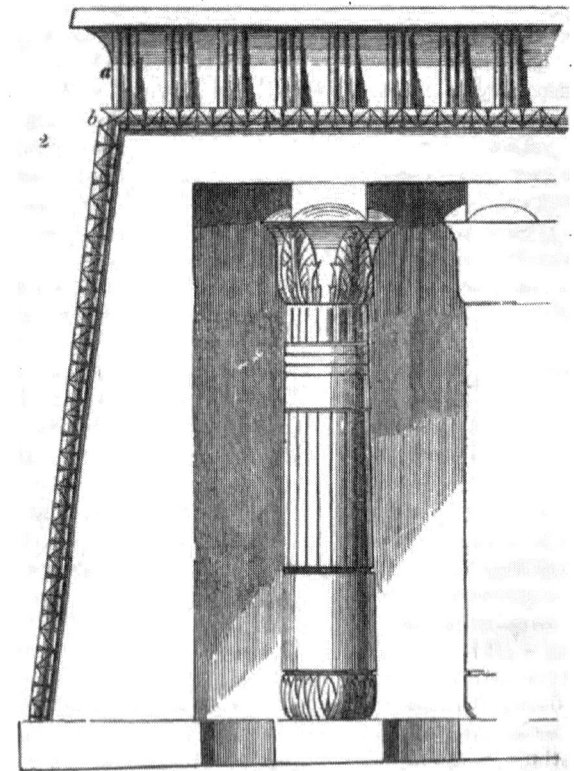

reed (*b*) which circumscribes whole compartments of columnar composition; besides others less important in the embellishments of the columns themselves; in all of which applications of moulding it is meanwhile to be observed that the absence alike of variety and of minuteness was in strict accordance with the character of the primitive members, few and bold, and with the simplicity appropriate to the earliest works of art.

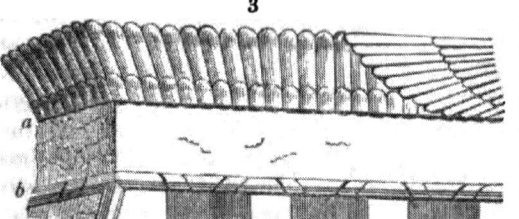

It may also be worthy of a passing remark, that the architecture of Egypt, under this form, offers a powerful, though doubtless an accidental, illustration of local as well as of constructive fitness. Placed upon far-extended plains, spotted with palm trees, but diversified by no playfulness of natural scenery, there was, in the stern simplicity of its gigantic temples, a sullen grandeur well fitted to their situation, and which seemed to bespeak them the offspring of the soil on which they rested; while the absence of all minutiæ of moulding rendered even their details conspicuous and effective at almost the greatest distance at which the eye could comprehend the mass. The adaptation to locality in these instances is the same, though developed by an opposite process, as that which makes the remains of pointed architecture, in our own country, to stand in such beautiful harmony with the variety and grouping of nature.

It will be obvious, then, how naturally an advance, even to this limited extent of architectural skill, in the adoption of simple forms, decorated by equally simple mouldings, would stand associated with that degree of mental culture which can appreciate the beautiful and the sublime in nature; and which seeks, first, by the ready vehicle of oral tradition and the language of poetry, and afterwards by the aid of the imitative arts of sculpture and painting, to perpetuate the images of those objects which excite the feelings or gratify the eye. Such an opportunity, therefore, as that which the rise of architecture afforded for the exercise of the chisel, and even for the incorporation of its performances with itself, was not to be lost; and hence it was that the subjects of nature, and particularly the products of the vegetable world, were soon laid under contribution to the purposes of decorative taste. That the summit of the column should be the first object to tempt the sculptor to the display of his powers in the execution of foliage and enrichment, was to be expected from its elevated importance, its conspicuousness, and its security from the reach of injury; and, accordingly, this

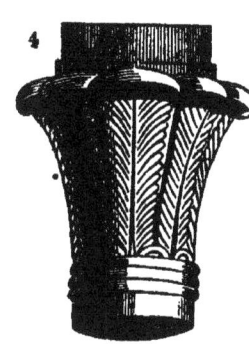

part, under the character of the capital, speedily became distinguished for gracefulness of form and elaborate elegance of design, derived chiefly from imitations of the palm leaf (*figs.* 4, 5, 6.) and lotus flower. (*fig.* 7.) The idea of analogy between the top of a column and the blossoming summit of a tree being thus suggested, the fancied resemblance was shortly carried much farther; and hence, in many instances, the column now assumed the appearance of an assemblage of reeds banded together (*figs.* 2. and 8.),

22   *Extent to which the elementary Forms of*

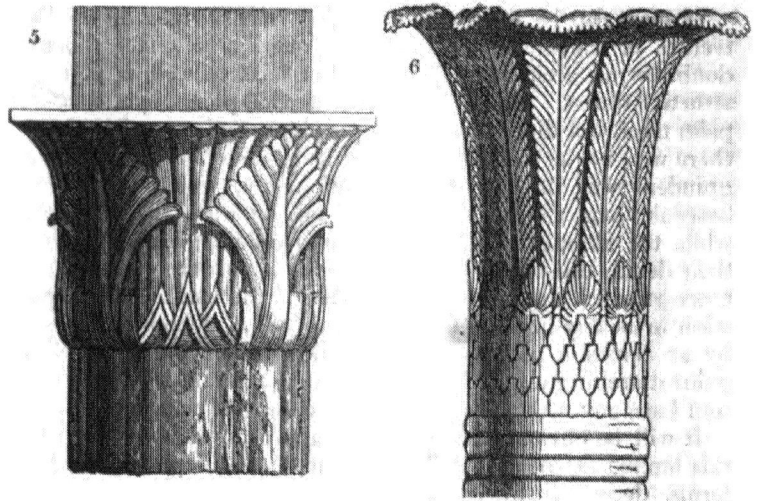

or sprang from the midst of a bed of leaves (*fig.* 2.), as an ornamental base. The reed, too, in a parallel arrangement of several

pieces, formed a frequent feature of decoration in cornices, being disposed of vertically at short intervals. (See *fig.* 2.)

Thus far, therefore, we think it must be admitted that, in these two principles of constructive fitness (we might almost say constructive necessity) and decorative relief, principally derived from the imitation of nature, we have a full developement of the origin and significancy of the essential parts of early architecture. The

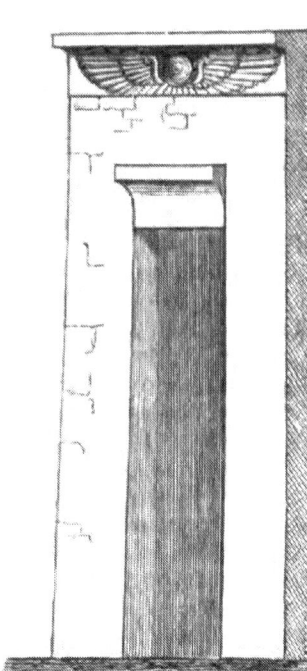

same principles will be found to extend their influence over all the minor members of composition; we shall, however, only notice, at present, that the form of apertures, as objects next in importance to the portico and the colonnade, was governed by a continued regard to fitness and utility; the upright parallelogram, or the quadrilateral opening diminishing as it ascends, being best adapted to the purposes of a doorway, from its suitableness to the admission of the human figure, and the facility with which its upper line can be formed, compared with that of more widely proportioned spaces. (*fig.* 9.) The latter reason, and the principle of unity, were sufficient to cause the same form to be retained in the windows which subsequent architecture adopted.

But passing over minor details, and viewing the advance of art as introduced from Egypt into Greece, we shall continue to discern the operation of the same laws of fitness and decorative taste as before. Utility, thus, in answer to the demands of a more variable climate, required the substitution of the inclined roof and the pediment for the flat covering and the uniformly horizontal cornice. On the other hand, the imitative or decorative principle, nourished and stimulated as it was in the mind of the Greek by the beauties which nature had lavished on the landscapes of his country, as well as by that spirit of enterprise in art proper to a rising colony, gave birth to a thousand refinements and delicacies of architectural expression. Thus, comparing with its Egyptian originals the simplest and most ancient of the Grecian orders, the Doric, we see the massive reeds, which adorn the earlier shaft transforming themselves into light flutings (*fig.* 10. *a*); the capital is neither ponderous nor overcharged with embellishment, but only so large as is requisite for utility, and with just so much of simple ornament as may make it intermediately to combine in form and character with parts above and below. The primitive epistylium now assumes a double form by its increase in height, so as to present, in its upper surface, a frieze (*b*) on which the sculptor may exercise his talent, and where his range of basso relievo may be at once conspicuously displayed and effectively sheltered; while the lower surface (*c*) fulfils its original office, and by its moulding, or fillet of separation, forms a ground line to the compositions and groups above. The cornice, too, undergoes an entire re-modification, the Egyptian reeds being converted into the triglyphs (*d*) of the Grecian frieze; while the great hollow itself is reduced to, or superseded by, the square projection of the corona (*e*), better calculated to reject the rain, in connection with slight mouldings, sufficient to satisfy the eye by affording the appearance of support from beneath, and lightness of finish above. The raising of the cornices over the pediments by the addition of a cyma (*f*), which is wanting to the horizontal cornices, not only gives importance to the portico at each extremity of the temple, but is intended to effect a purpose of utility, by confining the water from the roof to its proper current; while, again, the antefixæ (*g*), which are seen ranged along the lateral cornices, forming so elegant a mode of termination to the raised joints of the tiling, furnish one proof, among many, that the Greeks, in common with all of after-ages, held it as an architectural axiom, based upon every supposition of constructive fitness and natural analogy, that the highest place should be occupied by the lightest objects, the lower members being invested with that simplicity which is most characteristic of strength.

A continued regard to utility and expressive beauty governed the art in its farther advances. When so novel an invention as

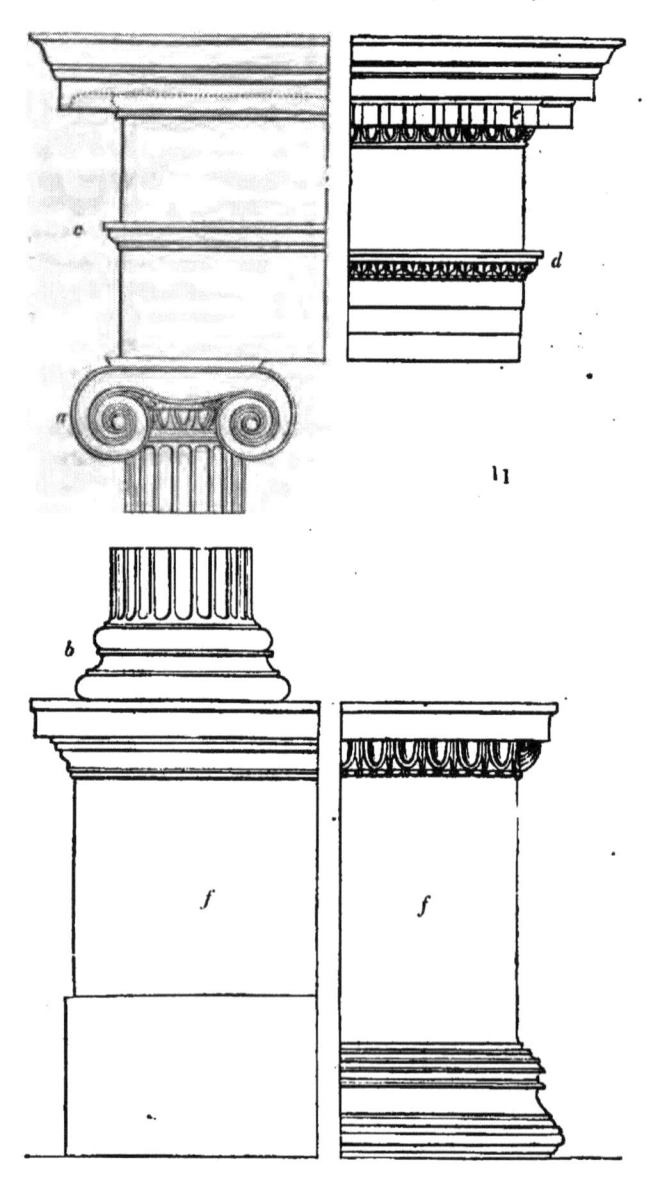

that of the Ionic capital (*fig.* 11. *a*) had been suggested by the exuberance of Grecian fancy, it became evident that a subject of such comparative richness would ill accord with the massiveness of Doric proportions. Hence the length of the column to which it was to be attached became increased; and, as the diminution of shaft could not then be so rapid as in the case of the Doric, without destroying all lightness of character by the great disproportion between the upper and lower diameters, it became necessary to supply the want of expansion at the bottom by the addition of a base (*b*), which, being composed of mouldings, should at the same time maintain a degree of elegance consistent with that of the capital. This done, the depth of the superincumbent mass must necessarily be reduced, to avoid the appearance of a tottering column; and the whole entablature was then corrected in proportion (*c*), frequently with the application of enriched mouldings (*d*), the division of the architrave into two or three faces, and the addition of dentils (*e*) to the cornice; for the origin of which last feature of detail, however, it is not easy satisfactorily to account.

To the establishment of the Doric and Ionic orders probably succeeded the use of elaborate dressings to apertures (*figs.* 12. and 13.), and the introduction of stylobates or pedestals. (*fig.* 11.*ff.*) The former, as applied to doorways, seem to have borrowed their character from the parts of the entablature; the frieze, however, being frequently compressed, and the whole reduced to a depth bearing somewhat of the same proportion to the height of the aperture as the entablature to that of the column, thus producing a due subordination to the superior mass. On the principle of fitness, the form of the architrave justly became that of the lintel, or member of support, and the cornice the member of shelter: the latter, however, viewed simply on this principle, was a matter of redundancy when it occurred beneath the protection of a portico. With respect, also, to the pedestal or stylobate, the consideration of utility displayed itself in affording, for the elevation of columns, where requisite, a platform of masonry, whose stability was insured by a firmly projecting plinth, and its shelter by the addition of a cornice moulding.

Having advanced thus far, first in an improvement on Egyptian art, and then in a great, though less decided, improvement on the variety and richness of their own, it only remained for the Greeks to proceed one step farther, but in a still diminishing ratio, to attain the perfection of the beautiful in the invention of the Corinthian order. The application of foliage in the capital of this order, according to the best existing example at Athens, is indeed such as taste may in vain attempt to surpass; but the only change, of any import, with which its introduction was associated, consisted in the elongation of the column, to accord with the increased lightness of its termination.

To this point of elevation had Grecian talent carried the detail of architecture (though without deviating from primitive simplicity in the forms of general composition to which that detail was applied), when the all-conquering hand of Rome

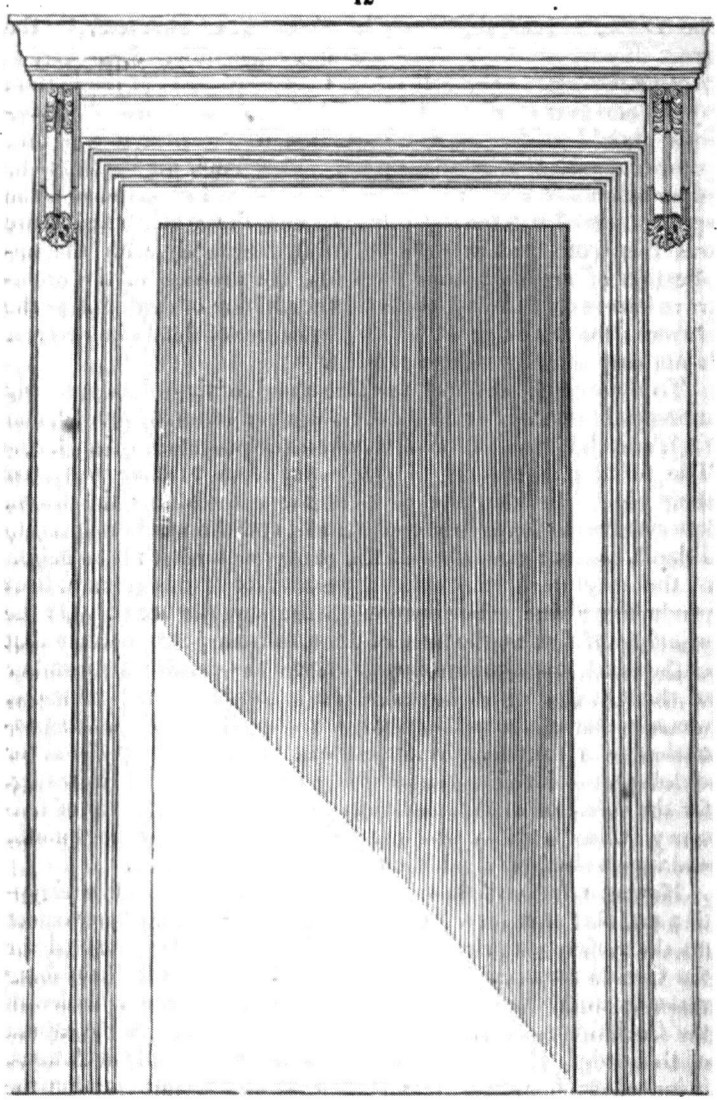

claimed the homage of the arts as well as of the arms of a world·
The variations which Roman taste introduced into the system
became most conspicuous in the combinations which succeeded
to the discovery of the principle of the arch; a discovery not
improbably suggested by the forms which masonry assumed in
walls upon a curvilinear plan. In other respects those variations

were precisely such as might have been anticipated from the character of a nation, whose martial pursuits rendered it much more susceptible of impression from the vast in composition, and the exuberant in ornament, than from the charms of simplicity and minute delicacy. Hence the preference given to the Corinthian column; hence the institution of a new order, by the blending of the Corinthian with the Ionic; hence the constant adoption of the most deeply moulded cornices for which the Greeks had left exemplars; hence the greatly increased fulness and intricacy of foliage in friezes, &c.; hence the multiplication of enriched mouldings, which supplied in dazzling show what they wanted in elegance of profile; and hence the invention of the Attic order, as, in truth, a repetition of the stylobate, for the support of statuary. (*fig.* 14. *a.*) Great as was thus the extension of the resources of composition, it was not to be expected that this insatiate pursuit after novelty of combination and richness of ornament would be uniformly favourable to true taste; and we may even be allowed to entertain a doubt whether architecture has gained much by the invention of the Composite order, which attains no increased gradation of lightness beyond the Corinthian, of which it is but an inferior modification. Certain it is, that, if the two additional Roman orders are deserving of their separate distinction beside the three of Grecian origin, nothing can be advanced more contemptibly futile and absurd than the vulgar assertion, that all the combined taste of modern times has been and must be inadequate to the production of a sixth order. To those who repeat such unfounded statements we would simply reply, that there is scarcely an old Norman doorway in any of our churches that would not furnish a capital for a new order, which should possess far more originality than can be claimed either for the Tuscan or the Composite.

Having thus arrived at that period when the architecture of the ancient world had attained its consummation of magnificence, we shall, upon a review of its progress from the earliest times, discern in all its monuments the expression of one object, that of the support of a horizontal mass of covering or entablature, by the use, first of columns, and afterwards of columns in frequent connection with arches. The support of the entablature was the end in view; the use of columns or of arches; the means by which that end was attained. Under this view of the subject, therefore, the entablature would seem to have been constituted the most important of the component masses of Architecture, and such, indeed, it is, however accustomed men may be to classify orders by a regard to the style of ornament displayed in their capitals. Thus the entablature is frequently seen to extend itself over long piles of building, which have scarcely any of columnar decoration; and it is, indeed, under a compressed form, susceptible of application altogether independently of the use of the column, though the latter can never, with propriety, stand independent of the former. Of all parts of an edifice, too, the entablature least suffers interruption, surmounting every other member of its own order, and refusing to allow even an essential mass of the structure to rise above it, without first passing across its front. It is from these circumstances, taken in connection with the effect of continuity resulting from the prevalence of quadrilateral apertures, that we shall be justified in designating all the varieties of construction which appeared in the civilised world, antecedently to the decline of the Roman empire under the general appellation of the Architecture of Horizontal Lines:

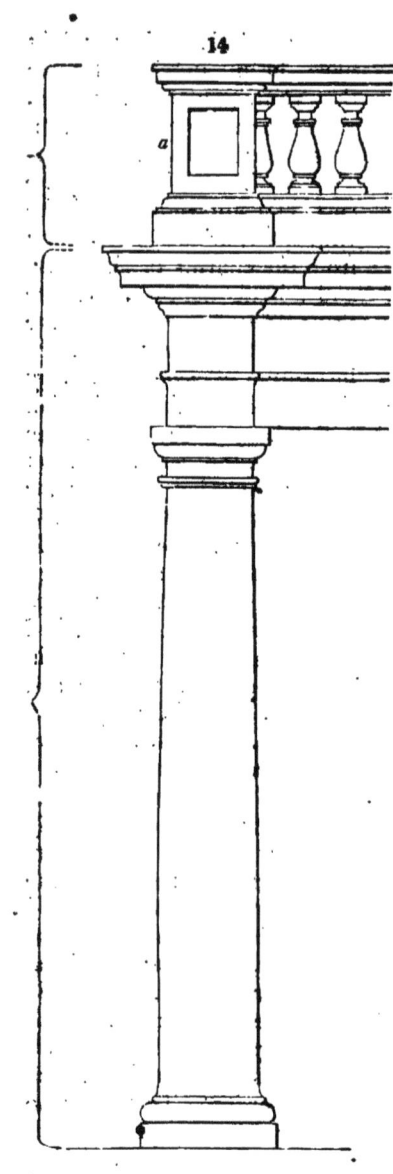

it was the work of after-ages, by the total disuse of the entablature, and the exclusive substitution for it of the arch, to introduce in the Romanesque or Norman style, and to bring to perfection in the Pointed, the other grand class of art, which connects itself with modern times, the Architecture of Perpendicular Lines.

That the architecture of horizontal lines was, by the masters of antiquity, carried to so close a promixity to perfection as to render it impossible for the taste of subsequent generations to improve upon their works, we are far from presuming to assert. True it is, however, that the Greek and Roman styles have so far excelled their early prototypes, by the appropriation and culture of all that can conduce to the harmony and completeness of their respective modes, separately considered, as to have superseded, for modern purposes, every other variety of the ancient world; insomuch that, to affect at the present time an imitation of Egyptian examples, except under very peculiar circumstances of locality and appropriation, would indicate a judgment as ill directed as his who should wish to reintroduce the rush-covered floors and wooden trenchers of our ancestors, because tired of the constant recurrence of our own carpets and dinner-services. But, idle as it would be thus to take a retrograde course in pursuit of variety, we are disposed to think that there is ample space for an opposite movement in the field of art. The Grecian school has, indeed, established for itself a style which, for the beauty appropriate to simplicity, cannot be surpassed; while the Roman works attain a picturesque splendour, more than sufficient to compensate for any want of delicacy in the detail. We may, however, well admit of a doubt, whether an earlier acquaintance with the principle of the arch would not have been productive of a wonderful addition to the variety of Greek composition; or whether the taste of the Roman might not have gained refinement, had he consulted the works of foreign talent with more of the patience of the student than of the impetuosity of the conqueror; whether, in short, the style of both might not be expected to have attained a still higher character, allowing the supposition that the patronage of Pericles had been coeval with that of Augustus, the freedom of Greece unimpaired, and national intercourse supported. The feminine grace which invests the Grecian remains, stands, indeed, in powerful contrast with the aspect of daring strength and armed glitter appropriate to the masculine form of Roman art; but characteristics as seemingly repugnant to each other have offered no obstacle to the hand of the modern master, when, with the pencil or the chisel, he would combine the dignity and beauty of opposite sexes in the figure of an angelic messenger. The remains of the Temple of Jupiter Stator at Rome, though somewhat overladen with ornament, display a beautiful illustration of the improvement of Roman details upon Grecian principles; an effect equally observable, also, in the whole composition of the elegant temple at Tivoli: and, were we required to particularise an example of the happy result of a similar combination, we could select none superior to that afforded by Mr, Wilkins in the London University,—with regret, however, that the incomplete state of the structure should leave many of its picturesque beauties to be perceived only upon reference to copies of the original design. We are much inclined to believe that the perfection of the architecture of horizontal lines is to be sought only in this union of Greek and Roman principles; an union which, while it would put to shame some of the pseudo-Athenian works of the day, would have the effect of purifying compositions of the other class from many of those frivolities and conceits which are not of classic origin, but have their rise in the practice of the modern Italian school, whose efforts for the revival of ancient architecture, though deserving of the highest praise, are to be regarded rather as exemplifying the means of pursuit than the end to be attained.

We would not, indeed, be supposed insensible to the picturesque effect of many of the peculiarities of the Palladian school; its cushioned friezes, its rusticated cinctures, its breaks, writhings, and fantastic ornaments: but we would have these at all times confined to works that are upon a small scale, considering them as at best but architectural toys, existing by mere sufferance, but becoming offensive when they interfere with the expression, breadth, and dignity, appropriate to larger structures.

It would be very possible, did the limits of our pages permit, to extend our remarks much farther into detail. We trust, however, that enough has been urged to prove that the character of the great elementary masses of horizontal architecture is founded upon the absolute fitness of things, and not upon the dictates of caprice or accident; that the contour of mouldings, as the subordinate members of decoration, is also suggested by the same law, as expressive of their office, whether in strength of support or slighter elegance of termination: and that the filling-up of composition, by an increase in the richness and lightness of its members, as they approach the summit, proceeds upon an equally fixed rule of propriety, as well as upon that of analogy to the order of nature, from whose productions the enrichments of architecture are principally copied. Beyond these limits, however, we think that the law of a demonstrable fitness ceases to be of certain application; and that the degree of delicacy and finish which shall be bestowed upon the curvature of mouldings, or the evolutions of foliage, must be left to the dictates of individual taste, that taste being most worthy of the name which can produce the most harmonious union of the beauties of the Greek and Roman modes.

One additional remark we would offer before we conclude, as worthy of attention, though its substance is in some degree implied in our suggestions at the outset, which is, that architecture, according to the principal and the customary use of the term, is the architecture of *masonry*, having for its first object the expression of the parts and method of construction, and, for its second, the application of appropriate ornament to those constructive parts. It follows, therefore, that the usually received forms of architecture will lose much, if not all, of their significancy, when applied to materials possessing different properties to those of stone, except when the appearance of stone is imitated to deception. We have indeed no vestiges of the style of decoration adopted by the Greeks in erections of woodwork; but we can entertain little doubt that the justice of their perceptions would have led them, under such circumstances, to employ an original mode, expressive of the capabilities of their material, and widely different to that plan of caricaturing columns and entablatures so frequently resorted to in the shop-front architecture of modern carpenters. We can, perhaps, scarcely refer to a better example of originality and feeling in the invention of a style of decoration in woodwork appropriate to the material and to the objects of application, than that which has been afforded by Sir Christopher Wren, in the stalls of St. Paul's cathedral; though the massiveness which is there displayed will by no means be essential, in ordinary cases, to the expression of fitness of purpose.

With these observations on the principles of constructive propriety, we shall take leave of that system of architecture founded upon the practice of the ancient world.

10. *Furnival's Inn, Dec.* 9. 1833. E. T.

THOSE of our readers who are conversant with the literature of Architecture, and who have seen Mr. Trotman's historical essay on the Tudor style of the art, in our *Encyclopædia of Cottage, Farm, and Villa Architecture and Furniture*, will, we think, agree with us in considering that essay, and the one above, as among the best which have ever been published on these two styles of architecture, and in admiring the comprehensiveness of the mind which can take such a complete and masterly view of both styles. The high literary talent of Mr. Trotman is the more remarkable, since it is very rarely found among architects who are, like him, actively engaged in the exercise of their profession.— *Cond*.

ART. III. *Instructions for choosing a Dwelling-House.* By I. J. KENT, Esq., Architect.

Sir,

THERE are few persons, whatever may be their rank in society, who have not occasion, at some period or other of their lives, to make choice of a house. Perhaps I should not be far wrong were I to say that this duty has to be performed by most men several times. How much of health, comfort, economy in living, and respectability of appearance, depends on the choice made, few people, I believe, are aware; and still fewer have an idea of the seemingly trifling, and, I may almost say, invisible circumstances, on which the comfort of a house sometimes depends. Before entering on the details of my subject, I shall just mention one of the seemingly trifling circumstances alluded to.

Suppose a new house, most substantially built, and in every apparent circumstance eligible either for purchase or occupation, and that the intended occupier or purchaser has completed his bargain without examining the subsoil, and the manner in which the foundation walls are built. On the supposition that the subsoil is dry, all will be very well, and the house will turn out what it appears to be. But supposing, on the other hand, that the subsoil should be a clay, or a stratum of moist gravel, or moist soil of any kind, and that the foundation walls should have been built with spongy bricks and bad mortar, and not with good hard bricks or Roman cement; the consequence of this will be, that the kitchen and other apartments on the ground floor will appear dry and comfortable for a year, or perhaps longer; but after this, from the bottoms of the walls acting like sponges in absorbing moisture from the soil, the damp will rise up through them more and more every year, till, at last, it will reach 6 ft. or 8 ft. above the exterior surface of the ground. I could refer to a house in all other respects most substantially and judiciously built, and surrounded by dry areas as deep as the footings of the walls, but on a clayey soil, and without cement being used in the foundations, in which the damp, in the course of eight years, has risen as high as the parlour floor; and the family occupying the house are now quite surprised at finding their furniture becoming mouldy there, after having been for years without experiencing anything of the kind. This, I think, will show the importance of using cement in the foundations of all houses placed on damp soils, and of examining the foundations under the lowest floors before taking a house, to see if this has been done. I shall now proceed to my subject.

The choice of a house will in some respects depend on the size and character of the house required, the purpose for which it is to be used, and the station in life of the party intending to occupy it. There are some things, however, common to all houses, which should be especially attended to, whether in a building intended solely for business, or in a private residence. The first points to be considered are, the nature and character of the soil on which the house is erected, and whether it is effectually drained, or is capable of being drained so as to be kept perfectly dry; for no advantages in other respects can compensate for a damp situation, both as regards health and property. A house built in a damp situation, even though the greatest care has been taken in making an artificial foundation of concrete (which has lately been done in many places), is still unwholesome; and should the materials of the foundation be of inferior quality, such as place (that is, soft half-burnt) bricks, and soft pine timber (also a common case), it will speedily decay, and be a constant and unavoidable expense. A gravelly soil is the best to build on, provided care be taken to keep out the land springs, by drains below the level of the bottom of the walls; or hard sand, if gravel cannot be found: but soft sand or clay is to be avoided if possible.

The construction of the house is a matter of serious importance to any person about to take a lease; as, by doing this, he will probably render himself liable to reinstate dilapidations, many of which may be in an incipient state when he takes possession. It is therefore quite advisable, and, indeed, is imperative on every person who is unacquainted with the nature of building, to employ a respectable architect, surveyor, or builder to examine the strength and durability of the house he is about to engage, in order to ascertain whether it is likely to remain strong and firm for a number of years. The intended tenant should also try to discover the nature of the soil, by which he will also ascertain that of the air which he will have to breathe. In low damp situations, it is well known that the air is at all times charged with a greater degree of moisture than is the case in dry open situations. A moist air suits very few constitutions, even in our humid climate, and seldom fails to bring on rheumatism, more especially in those who cannot afford to live well and take abundance of exercise.

Another important matter to be attended to, is the thorough ventilation of houses; for should the air become stagnant from want of a free ventilation, particularly in houses that have a story underground, it is highly injurious to the persons living, and particularly sleeping, in them. There should, therefore, be windows both in the back and front, and, when possible, at the sides also. From rooms in the basement story, and cellars that have neither fireplaces nor windows, there should be air-flues carried up to the open air. Care should likewise be taken that the floor in the basement story is raised above the soil, and that air is freely admitted to circulate between the soil and the floor, whether that floor is of wood or stone. Where this is properly attended to, these low rooms may be used as sleeping-rooms; but where it is not, they are by no means fit or proper for any human being to sleep in.

Stability, light, and air are three grand desiderata in every house, and should be particularly attended to in the choice of one. The roof is a part of a house which should be carefully examined; for if it be badly constructed (too common a case with the houses built on speculation, both in London and the country), with narrow gutters, and those difficult of access, you may generally expect the wet to penetrate to the upper rooms after any heavy fall of snow or rain. Many of the best houses built in London are covered with lead: this is the best covering. The next is slate, if of good quality, and with wide lead gutters with lead flushings (strips of lead covering joints) to them, and to those parts of the walls which are carried up higher than the slating. Zinc-covered roofs seldom keep out the wet many years; and tiles in London are now rarely used, except in very inferior houses.

In your choice of a house, having satisfied yourself that the site on which it is built is healthy; the drainage good; the roof properly constructed, and free of access, not merely for the purpose of keeping out the wet, but as a safeguard and means of escape in case of fire; the next portion of the building to examine is the substance of the walls, with the materials of which they are composed. The soft, half-burnt bricks, called place bricks by the builders, ought never to be employed in the walls of any building which it is desirable to keep dry. Whenever these bricks are found in the foundation of the party walls, the house should be rejected; and if they are seen in the outside of any of the external walls, you may expect every beating rain which falls to penetrate into them. Such walls suck in the water like a sponge, and give it out to all the interior fittings-up and finishings. Sound, hard, well-burnt bricks, called stocks, are the strongest, most durable, and best calculated to resist the weather, and to keep the inside of a house dry, provided the mortar used with them is composed of fresh-burnt stone lime and sharp road grit or sand, and is well mixed. The stock bricks absorb but little moisture, and that little is soon evaporated; whereas the place or soft bricks absorb a large quantity of moisture, and, allowing that to pass through them into the middle of the wall, are a long time wet; because the centre of a wall retains the moisture long after the surface is dry. It is particularly desirable, as I have before stated, for the wall of houses built on clay, or on any moist soil, to have a few courses of the brickwork above the ground laid in Roman cement.

The timber used in any building should be timber of slow growth, such as the fir of cold climates (Norway or Sweden, for example), or oak. If for work under or near the ground, the oak should be of English growth; but the American oak may be used with propriety above ground. Oak is the only timber fit for joists and sleepers (joists laid on the tops of dwarf walls) next the ground, unless the soil is particularly dry, and the floor well ventilated.

The strength of the joists and other timbers, of which the several floors are composed, is another subject of importance to every one about to take a lease of a house. If these are weak, they will necessarily shake if the tenant allows his friends to enjoy the delightful recreation of dancing on them; and though the floors may not absolutely give way, yet I have known the ceiling and cornices of many modern houses, from this cause amongst others, very unceremoniously desert their posts, and pay their respects to the floor of the room they were intended to crown. This is an accident much to be deprecated, especially as it is very likely to happen (as it did at the house of a friend of mine) at a time of all others the most annoying, viz. when you have friends with you, and are in the highest spirits, little anticipating such an event. The floors in houses of the first and second class of buildings are usually pugged (filled in, between the floor of one room and the ceiling of that below it, with mortar, &c.), to destroy sound, and as a security against fire: when this is not done, it is an unpardonable omission on the part of the builder, as the expense is small, and the benefit great. All the partitions of a house should, if possible, be brick walls. At all events, no timber partitions ought to be admitted in the basement or lower story of any house, nor in any of the upper stories, except where, from the arrangement of the rooms, the partitions on the upper floors cannot be placed perpendicularly over the lower partitions; even in this case the timber partitions ought to be trussed up so as to rest their weight upon the side walls. All timber partitions should be filled in with brick nogging. If this were universally done, and the party and other walls and partitions plastered, so as to prevent all draughts of air, it would tend more to check the progress of fire than any other mode of construction: indeed, I think, if you were to make a fire on the floor of a room so constructed, it would burn itself out, without communicating with the timber partition; or, at all events, so little would be the tendency of the fire to spread (for want of a current of air), that a very moderate application of water would put it out. But where the floors are pugged with mortar, care must be taken that the timbers are well seasoned and dried, and not taken, as is customary, even in some of our largest buildings, wet out of the Thames, sawed, and fixed, and closed up in the building in a few weeks; reeking with wet, and exuding moisture at their extremities after the weight of the superincumbent walls is put on them. The dry rot and premature decay are the frequent consequences of this careless and ignorant mode of building.

The particular character of houses in towns is, that they are many stories high, having generally one story in the basement, wholly or partially below the general surface of the ground: over this is a ground, or parlour, floor; a one-pair, or drawing-room, floor; a two-pair, or best bedroom, floor; and an attic floor. This is the general arrangement; but many houses have other attics, or garrets, above these in the roof. This arises from the high price of the ground in towns, and may be excusable in great thoroughfares, where shops let at a high rent; for even if the landlord were desirous of giving his tenant a wide frontage, to enable him to have two rooms in front, and some space behind, it would most likely be divided by the tenant, and underlet. A serious evil, however, arises from the great landed proprietors round London allowing the ground to be divided and subdivided by speculating builders or agents, so that there is now scarcely a house built with a yard large enough to dry a few clothes in; a garden is out of the question, except in some few instances, and those are far between. This is a subject worthy of the attention of the legislature; and some restraints should be imposed on landlords, particularly as to drainage and roads. If, before a landlord could dispose of his land for building purposes, he were compelled to engage to form the roads and footpaths next to his intended houses to the satisfaction of the parish, or some other authority; the sewers to the satisfaction of the commissioners of sewers; and to see that good and sufficient drains from every house were built; a penalty being incurred, if any house on his estate should be inhabited before an effectual drainage were formed, it would tend very much to the health and comfort of the middle class of society, and the poor especially.

The restraint imposed by the Building Act has, in the neighbourhood of London, tended much to produce a kind of house, called a fourth-rate house; and the smallest of these are built, principally for the occupation of the poor, in the suburbs of London, in inferior situations. These houses consist of two rooms; they have generally from 12 ft. to 14 ft. frontage, and are from 12 ft. to 14 ft. deep, having an access on the ground floor in front into the lower room, and steps outside at the back leading into the upper room. Three, four, or more have a yard and other conveniences in common. Dwellings of this description are rarely properly drained or ventilated, and therefore form nurseries for the cholera and all other diseases. They are usually let at from 3s. to 4s. per week each room.

There are some houses of this class presenting a very decent appearance, and occupied by respectable tradesmen and mechanics, having about 15 ft. wide in front by 23 ft. deep, with a basement story, cellars and wash-house, a parlour floor of two small rooms, a drawing-room floor over, and two bedrooms over that, which generally let for from 25l. to 40l. a year rent, according to the number of rooms they contain, and the conveniences they afford. The back room on the two-pair floor of a house of this description is obliged, by the Building Act, to be curbed (contracted by being carried up into the roof), which spoils the room; and the gutters are frequently so narrow at the bottom of the curb, that they convey the water into, rather than off, the house.

The next class of town house, according to the Building Act, is the third-rate house, which is from about 17 ft. to 18 ft. wide in front, and from 28 ft. to 29 ft. deep. Houses of this class generally contain the same number of rooms as the largest size fourth-rate, with an attic story over in addition: this story is sometimes partly in the roof, but more generally the walls are carried up to allow the rooms to be square. At the back of the parlour floor there is frequently built a small room, used as a dressing-room or store-room. These houses have generally two windows in the width of their front.

The next class of house, the second-rate, is of a better and larger description, and frequently possesses conveniences that cause it to be occupied by the wealthy tradesman and gentleman of good fortune. It is usually 20 ft. or 30 ft. wide in front, by 30 ft. to 40 ft. deep, with additional rooms at the back. It can, and does, in many instances, contain all the apartments required by a family keeping their carriage, footmen, housekeeper, &c.; and has attached to it, or in some mews in the immediate neighbourhood, a coach-house and stable. These houses are usually built with two windows in the width of the front, but many of them have three windows in this width. The rooms are higher and better finished than in the houses of the third and fourth classes.

The first-rate class of buildings embraces all houses containing more than 900 superficial feet on the ground-floor, and includes the residences of the nobility and gentry, and the wealthiest class of professional men and merchants. Houses of this class may be said to be unrestricted as to size, either in height or width; the other classes are, by the Building Act, restricted as to dimensions in their plan, their height, and expense; though the height and expense of a house are not now taken into consideration in deciding the rate or class to which it belongs.

A new Building Act is drawn up, and approved, which, it is expected, will pass into a law next year; and it is greatly to be hoped that in this new law the absurdities of the present act will be avoided. I. J. KENT.

Manor Place, Paddington, Nov. 16. 1833.

ART. IV. *On rendering Lath and Plaster Partitions Fireproof.* By THOMAS WILKINSON, Esq.

Sir,

IN your *Encyclopædia of Architecture*, you have suggested a very efficient mode of rendering hollow partitions solid by blowing in, if I may use the expression, powder of Roman cement and steam. It occurred to me, when I read that part of your work, that the difficulty and expense of this operation would prevent it from being generally adopted; and, having built a house of eight rooms on four stories, with a wooden staircase between, I felt not a little alarmed at the danger from fire which I was exposed to on the one hand (which I had never thought of till you pointed it out), and the trouble and expense of rendering a house fireproof on the other. After thinking on the subject for several days, and talking to my carpenter (Mr. John Brown of this place), we fortunately hit on the idea of removing the skirtings, both in the rooms and on the staircase, then filling in the space in the partition behind them with plaster, and replacing them. By this process, I have rendered my partitions what, for all practical purposes, may be considered fireproof; since, supposing the skirting-boards to take fire either on the staircase or in any of the rooms, it is evident that they could not communicate flame to the vacuity of the partition; or, supposing that, by any means whatever, the hollow part of the partitions were set fire to, it is evident the flames could not, at least for a long time, spread from one floor to another.

I assure you, Sir, that, after I perused that part of your work which treats of rendering houses fireproof, and particularly § 1790. and § 1791., I was filled with the greatest alarm, because my wooden staircase is four stories high, without an outlet to the roof, without a window communicating with a balcony, as you recommend, and with hollow lath and plaster partitions on each side; but now that I have filled in all solid behind the skirtings, I feel comparatively at ease, and though certainly not so secure as if I had solid brick partitions, yet I am confident that no fire could happen in my house that would spread so rapidly as to prevent the means of escape. Before I made this improvment, if the lower partition had caught fire, there was nothing to hinder the flames from reaching, in a few minutes, the top of the house; the smoke and flames coming out into the staircase at the interstices of the skirtings. The idea of living in a house such as that which I at present inhabit, without taking the above precautions, is to me dreadful. You have my sincere thanks for having opened my eyes upon the subject; and I trust that I shall have yours, and, if you publish this, those of your readers, for having pointed out so cheap and easy a remedy.

I am, Sir, yours, &c.

Liverpool, Sept. 1833. Thomas Wilkinson.

Certain specimens of foreign woods, received from this correspondent, will be noticed on a future occasion. — *Cond.*

Art. V. *On the Use of Slate and Cast Iron in Household Furniture.* By Mr. William Rose, Builder.

Sir,

As marble is now coming into very general use in the construction of furniture for the most wealthy classes, it appears to me that those fine plates of Penrhyn slate, which we see applied to so many uses in North Wales, might be substituted for marble in the furniture of the middling classes and the poor. The tops of all tables in general use might be made of slate with or without margins of wood, or of cast iron, or, in some cases, of copper. I know no better description of top for the tables of coffee-houses and public-houses of every description, than thick slabs of slate, their edges being bound round with copper or iron, or even zinc. The supports of these tables might be cast iron bronzed, such as those you have shown in different parts of your *Encyclopædia* (§ 1340, 1341, &c.); and when the slabs were very large, they might be strengthened by pieces of cast iron having flanches underneath, of one of which *fig.* 15. is a side elevation, and *fig.* 16. a section across the middle on a large scale, on which are seen the flanch *a*, and the two holes for screws (*b b*) in the flat plate, to screw it across the boards, or the slate slab of the table at *c*.

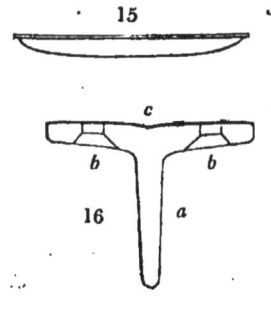

For tops of sideboards, the Penrhyn slate is particularly eligible, since it can be had in plates 10 ft. or 12 ft. long, and of equal breadth (if that breadth were desirable), and of any thickness.

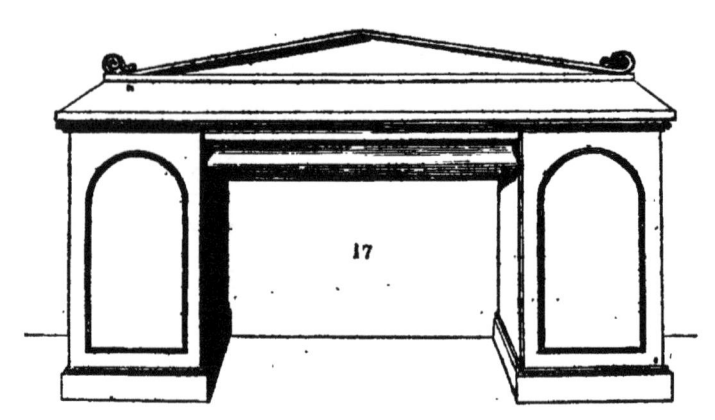

Fig. 17. is a view of a sideboard, which I had made in Bristol, of common deal, and afterwards painted so as to resemble wainscot. The top is of one slab of slate, 8 ft. long, 2½ ft. wide, and 2 in. thick. The moulding beneath it is painted of a jet black, which forms a bold contrast with the wainscot beneath, while it harmonises with the dark blue slate above. The semicircular-headed panels in each of the pedestals are also of slate, and the mouldings which surround them are painted jet black, in imitation of ebony, like the moulding under the top. The appearance of the whole is unique. The slate cost 15s., delivered at Bristol; the joiner's work, including wood, 2l.; and the painting 12s. These, I am aware, are what are called trade prices; but even if you add twenty per cent. to them, you have still a very cheap, durable, and, as I think, handsome sideboard.

I have a washhand table covered with a slab of slate, 3 ft. 4 in. long, and 20 in. wide, by three fourths of an inch thick, which slab cost only 3s. 6d. Besides the first saving of painting, there is a saving of washing every day the table is used; and as to the durability of such a top, it will probably wear out several wooden frames. In having this table constructed, I made an error in not having the raised back and sides also of slate, the framework of cast iron, and a bottom shelf for foot-pans, water-jugs, &c., of very strong slate.

I am, Sir, yours, &c.

Bristol, Oct. 1833.　　　　　　　　　　　　　　　W. Rose.

There can be no doubt that slate may be very extensively used, not merely in the commoner articles of furniture, but in the fittings-up of the offices and many of the living-rooms of houses. The panels of doors and window-shutters might be of slate; as might shelves of every description. A fixed bookcase might be formed entirely of slate; or, where economy was a main object, the styles or supports for the shelves might be of brick on edge, covered with cement, and the shelves of slate let into them. By this and other means, a library might be rendered fireproof. — *Cond.*

REVIEWS.

ART. I. *La Propriété; Journal d'Architecture Civile et Rurale, des Beaux Arts, et d'Economie Sociale, contenant: Les meilleurs modes de conserver, d'embellir, et de faire valoir la Propriété, — Les connoissances des droits et des obligations qui y sont inhérens,—Des notions d'Economie générale et domestique, — Les renseignements et instructions indispensables sur la législation et la compatibilité des bâtimens, — La description des découvertes, et des procédés utiles à la propriété et à l'habitation, — Un compte rendu de tous les monumens nouveaux, des grandes constructions, et des divers produits des arts, — Généralement, enfin, tout ce qui peut intéresser et ceux qui possèdent et ceux qui veulent posséder.* Par T. Morisot, Architecte. 4to. Paris, 1833.

WE have printed the whole of the title of this work, because we could not otherwise, in so small a space, give so complete an idea of its contents.

Architectural books in France, as in England, were, till the appearance of that of which the title is given above, almost exclusively addressed to professors, and, at all events, were very expensive. The present work is an attempt to popularise the subjects of architecture, building, and furnishing; and, to further this end, it is sold at such a low price as to place it within the reach of all classes of readers. In many respects, it may be compared to our Magazine, which has the same objects in view for English readers as *La Propriété* has for French ones. The main difference between the two publications is, that the articles in *La Propriété* seem to be chiefly compilations by the editor from other works, or translations; whereas, in our work, though we intend to have some translations and abridgments, yet the great mass of our information will be original, and furnished, not by one mind, which must necessarily soon repeat itself, but by numerous correspondents, professors, amateurs, and artisans, from all parts of the country.

In the prospectus of *La Propriété*, it is stated that " Architecture occupies less of the public attention than any other art. There are many reasons for the indifference generally displayed towards it. First, few men, however well educated they may be in other respects, know enough of the rules of this art to be able to judge correctly of its professors; and, secondly, these rules are themselves uncertain, traditional, and not united into a complete course of doctrine. The most ancient monuments of antiquity were not formed according to the rules of this art; on the contrary, it is from these monuments that those rules of art were drawn, which the masters of modern times have occupied themselves in commenting on, and which each has applied according to his own taste or genius. Thus, from the want of a fixed standard to refer to, arise the contradictory judgments which are every day passed on contemporaneous productions; and hence it is that so wide a career is open to judicious innovations, though it sometimes also admits deplorable errors."

This quotation will suffice to give our readers an idea that *La Propriété* will be conducted on liberal principles; and a very good example of the application of these principles is given in the first article of the work, which is a critique on the Palace of Deputies. The scrupulous servility with which modern architects copy, or rather reproduce, the forms of antiquity, is here criticised; and it is asked how architecture, being an inventive art, should have exhausted itself in the earliest ages of antiquity, when the wants of man were few, instead of improving and becoming more perfect as the wants of man increased and society advanced? The Romans, we are informed, imitated the Greeks chiefly in those parts of their architecture which could be suitably applied to Roman purposes; whereas we imitate every thing which is Greek indiscriminately.

It may be observed, with respect to criticisms of this kind, that in them the difference between public and private architecture ought to be kept strictly in view. We cannot be said to imitate the private architecture of the Greeks, for, in fact, we know nothing about it; but, with respect to their public architecture, the simplicity, not only of the general forms, but of the details, appears to us to render their porticoes and large public rooms suitable for all ages and countries; fitted for great public meetings, commercial or political, alike in Calcutta or in Petersburgh.

The second article in the first number of *La Propriété* is on rural architecture; in which are some very just observations on the simplicity of style, and the thorough devotedness to utility, which ought to characterise every description of farm buildings.

The next article is on legislature with reference to buildings in Paris, and on the prices of materials and labour there; both of which subjects are, of course, of considerable local interest. The article following is headed *Economie Industrielle*; in which a scheme is mentioned for establishing a magazine for imported goods at Paris, instead of leaving that city dependent on the magazines at the sea-ports. In addition to this, there are short notices of territorial property expected soon to be exposed for sale; and of certain proposed improvements in the suburbs of Paris. The next article is entitled Miscellaneous, and is followed by notices of change of residence of persons in businesses connected with architecture, the establishment of companies, &c.

This is the general arrangement of all the weekly parts of *La Propriété*; and every alternate part has commonly a 4to lithographic plate. On the whole, we are much pleased with the work; and, though it will be of no great use to English readers, we can easily conceive that the good it will do in France must be considerable.

ART. II. *Catalogue of Works on Architecture, Building, and Furnishing, and on the Arts more immediately connected therewith, recently published, commencing with the year* 1834.

BRITAIN.

1. *Godwin*'s Domestic Architecture. Part II. London, 1834. 4to. 2*l*. 12*s*. 6*d*.
2. *Trendall*'s Designs for interior Finishings. London, 1834. 4to. 15*s*.
3. *Blackburne*'s Architectural and Historical Account of Crosby Place. London, 1834. 4to. 8*s*. 6*d*.
4. *Shaw*'s Specimens of Ancient English Furniture. Part V. London, 1834. 4to. 5*s*.
5. *Dodswell*'s Cyclopean or Pelasgic Remains in Greece and Italy. London, 1834. folio. 6*l*. 16*s*. 6*d*.
6. *Inwood*'s Studies of the Architect from Nature. London, 1834. In 4to parts.

FRANCE.

Rochette: Monumens inédits d' Antiquité figurés, Grecque, Etrusque, et Romaine, recueillis pendant un Voyage en Italie et en Sicile, dans les années 1826 et 1827. Par M. Raoul Rochette. fol. 5e et 6e Liv. 2*l*. 2*s*.

Lange: Vues Pittoresques des plus belles Eglises, &c. d'Architecture Gothique. Par Lange. Liv. I. 12*s*. plates; 16*s*. Indian, sewed.

GERMANY.

Zahn, Ornamente aller klassischen Kunst-epochen. 3tes Heft. 12*s*. 6*d*. (Zahn's Ornaments of every Class used in different Eras of the Arts, &c. Part III. 4to.)

Uagzin, Von Abbildungen der Gusswaaren aus der Königlichen Eisengiesserei zu Berlin. 8tes Heft. 8*s*. 6*d*. (Uagzin on the different Articles of Taste manufactured of Cast Iron in the Royal Foundery of Berlin. Part VIII. folio.)

NORTH AMERICA.

The Modern Builder's Guide. By Manuel Lafevre. New York. fol.

Art. III. *Literary Notices.*

ILLUSTRATIONS of Christ Church, Hampshire, from Drawings by B. Ferrey, jun., is in preparation by E. W. Brayley, Esq. This work will be calculated to range, in size, correctness, and elegant finishing, with the celebrated work of Mr. Britton on British Cathedrals.

A Series of Designs for Athenian or Grecian Villas, in folio, is in preparation, and will appear early in April.

A History of Architecture, by the late Thomas Hope, illustrated by numerous Engravings from Drawings by the Author, is announced.

MISCELLANEOUS INTELLIGENCE.

Art. I. *General Notices.*

UNIONS *of Workmen* are bad, as well for themselves as their masters; for, if they fix on one ratio of prices, both for the good and the bad workmen, these are placed upon one level, and no encouragement is given to the man improving himself, if he is to receive the same as the idler. Unions, also, act injuriously against the inferior workmen; for the masters will never think of employing them, so long as there is a good workman to be had: whereas, if a bad workman could sell his labour according to its worth, the master would frequently employ him upon work that does not require a very superior hand. — *W. L. London, Dec.* 1833.

Working Over-hours. — The master and workman would be very considerably benefited if they would enter into an understanding not to allow any workman to exceed working ten hours per day; for it is impossible, if any man exceed that time, that he can perform his work properly, either for the benefit of his master, or for his own health; and it prevents him having a few leisure hours in the evening for study, or to attend institutions for the improvement of his mind. Restricting men from working over-hours will also distribute the work among a larger number of men, and will prevent many of them from roving and idling about the town, scheming and doing mischief, by forming themselves into unions; and preventing the workman who is in work, and contented, from proceeding, unless he will join their union to support them in their idleness and profligacy. If any work be required to be done expeditiously, it will be advisable to employ a larger number of hands, or, if that cannot be done, to employ a double set. — *Id.*

Art. II. *Foreign Notices.*

FRANCE.

THE reproach which has so long rested on England, that she is the only nation whose monuments require protection, is passing away, at least so far as France is concerned; for the Parisian government has found it necessary not only to surround the Exchange with an iron palisade, but also to defend the *ci-devant* Temple of Glory, the Madeleine, and the approaches to the Pantheon, by similar barricades. The works at the Madeleine, which, it is now decided, is to be a church instead of a temple, are advancing very fast; and it is said that M. Paul Delaroche is commissioned to execute eight large pictures for its interior. A new prison, which is to be finished in two years, is about to be erected in the Rue de la Roquette, to supply the place of the Bicêtre. Roland's statue of Napoleon, in white marble, 7 ft. high, is to be replaced in the public hall of the Institute, for which it was originally executed. Napoleon is represented as offering his crown and other decorations on an altar of Minerva. M. Lebas, the architect, first suggested the idea of restoring this statue. Railroads are forming in many different directions. M. Polonceau, engineer of roads and bridges, has just completed his survey for the great railroad from Paris to Bordeaux, which will have branch roads to many other places. You have, no doubt, heard of the carriages called *Les Vespasiennes*, which, in plain English, are ambulatory water-closets: they are now very popular in Paris, and a large capital is said to have been embarked in them. A mode of protecting buildings from the effects of lightning has been discovered by M. Lapostolle. He has proved, by experiment, that a jar loaded with electricity enough to kill an ox may be immediately discharged by an inch or two of straw rope. A slight pole of wood, covered with straw, and attached to a building by a strip of brass (he says) will thus serve as a conductor: and it must be allowed to be a very cheap one. Ambulatory washing machines are in great vogue among us: if you wish it, I will send you a detailed account of them in my next. The Place du Carrousel is about to be greatly enlarged by the removal of two mansions belonging to the civil list, which are now taking down. One of the halls in the Palace of Justice is being newly fitted up, in a magnificent style, with arabesques and gilding. The Parisian wits say that this is done to indulge the poor suitors with the sight of gold, their own being all swallowed up by the lawyers. Great discussion has lately taken place here respecting the obelisk of Luxor; the question being, whether it should be erected in the Place de la Concorde, according to the plan of M. Grillon, on an elegant pedestal of white marble which already adorns that Place, and which it is proposed to form into a fountain, or whether the obelisk should have a granite pedestal in the Egyptian style. Pure taste seems undoubtedly to dictate the latter; since few can conceive any harmony between an Egyptian obelisk of dark granite and a Grecian pedestal of white marble, with a rich though minute moulding, and adorned with four Tritons, each supporting a shell from which streams a sheet of water. M. Grillon has many partisans; but does not appear likely to carry his point, as the government has given notice that other plans may be sent in. It is singular that one of the objections made to the project of this eminent architect is something similar to the objection made to the plan of an eminent architect of your country; viz., it is said that, if M. Grillon erects the obelisk as he proposes, he will shut out from the Place de la Concorde the view of the Pavilion of the Tuileries and the arch of the Barrière de l'Etoile.—*F. L. Besson. Rue de Richelieu, Paris, Dec.* 10. 1833.

ART. III. *Domestic Notices.*

A NEW *Metallic Cement*, for which a patent has been taken out, consists of powdered scoria from the copper-works, mixed with stone and lime. It sets rapidly, and takes a fine metallic polish. It is now being used by Messrs. Harrison, in a large building intended for an inn, at the south-west corner of London Bridge. This cement, unlike all other kinds except Frost's, is sold mixed up ready for use. The price is 9*d.* per bushel. If the scoria, in a state of powder, were sold by itself compressed in casks, it appears to us that it would form a very desirable cement for exportation. It may be laid on in coats as thin as the fourth of an inch; but it has not been a sufficiently long time in use to determine to what extent it will crack.

A *Cock for Boilers in Kitchen Ranges* has recently been invented, which, we have no doubt, will soon take the place of all others. It is one of the most ingenious inventions which we have seen for a long time, and completely answers the purpose. It does away with the necessity for supply cisterns on a level with the boilers and for ball-cocks, and is so contrived as to keep the water in the boiler always at the same height, and to prevent a drop of hot water being drawn from the boiler, without a corresponding quantity of cold water being admitted to supply its place. As it will require several engravings to render this invention clear to our readers, we must necessarily defer a fuller account of it till our next Number.

An Oven with revolving Shelves has lately been introduced into some kitchen ranges, for the purpose of preventing the articles placed on the shelves from being burnt on the side next the fire. A spindle passes through both shelves, and through the top of the oven, where it is attached to a common bottle-jack, which is suspended from a hook in the throat of the chimney.

A new Description of Covered Gridiron, for carrying the fumes of broiling meat up the chimney, has recently been used at some of the club-houses.

Our Country Architectural Notices are at present necessarily few: but we trust to our provincial readers to supply what is most interesting, not only in rural and town architecture, but in upholsterers' and ironmongers' shops and show rooms, and in manufactories of articles used in building or furnishing. Any correspondent who may be in doubt as to the extent of the subjects which we embrace, has only to glance over the list on the cover of the portfolio in our titlepage vignette. This beautiful and appropriate ornament was designed by E. B. Lamb, Esq.

Chester. — A noble bridge of one arch over the Dee has been lately completed by Mr. Trubshaw; whose son (a most ingenious young architect and landscape-gardener, and the designer of a very beautiful conservatory and architectural flower-garden at Heath House, near Cheadle) is invited to send us a description and sketches of the bridge.

Durham. — We are warm admirers of freemasonry; and it was with much satisfaction that we observed, in an account of a meeting of the provincial grand lodge, of which the Earl of Durham is grand master, the following passage in His Lordship's address: — " I have ever felt it my duty to support and encourage the principles and practice of freemasonry; because it powerfully developes all social and benevolent affections; because it mitigates without, and diminishes within, the virulence of political and theological controversy; because it affords the only neutral ground on which all ranks and all classes can meet in perfect equality, and associate without degradation or mortification, whether for the purpose of moral instruction or of social intercourse." (*Morn. Chron.*, Jan. 28. 1834.) This is the true modern use of freemasonry. Formerly in England, and still in some countries where civilisation is not far advanced, it had other uses, such as, regulating the wages of workmen, granting protections, exercising hospitality, &c.; but now, freemasonry may be considered as a benevolent system of fellowship.

Kent. — A new pier, on the suspension principle, from the design of Mr. Lamb, is about to be erected at Greenhithe; and, close to that pretty little village, at Ingress Park, the seat of James Harmer, Esq., a beautiful Tudor villa is now building, from the designs and under the direction of Mr. Moring. The stone used in constructing this building is that of old London Bridge, and one of the alcoves, preserved entire, will be erected in the grounds as a monument of that edifice. Near this a piece of ground is laying out in the style of the Regent's Park, with detached villas and gardens; the architect and landscape-gardener employed being Mr. Lamb. The surface of the ground is beautifully varied, commanding extensive views of the Thames and the county of Essex beyond; and, from what we have seen of Mr. Lamb's plan, we anticipate a very interesting specimen of rural and picturesque beauty. Several improvements are carrying on at Canterbury, of which we expect some account from our correspondent there, Mr. Masters; and some others, at Gravesend and Dover, of which we shall be glad to receive notices.

The Rigging-house Wharf, in Woolwich yard, is under repair with a new composition called artificial stone, invented by Mr. Ranger. It is said to be so durable, that it will ultimately supersede the use of bricks and stones, thereby reducing the cost of river walls, &c., upwards of one half. A church, constructed of this new material, capable of accommodating 400 persons, has recently been erected upon the Duke of Northumberland's estate, at a cost of 800*l.* (*Kentish Chronicle*, Feb. 1834.)

We shall feel obliged to any correspondent who will give us some satisfactory particulars respecting this new composition. — *Cond.*

Art. IV. *Retrospective Criticism.*

A BOILER *for steaming Food for Cattle*, cheaper and more simple than that figured in your *Encylopædia of Architecture*, under the head of Farmery Furniture, § 1405., and yet equally efficacious, consists of a cast-iron boiler, built over a small furnace, having a vat fitted to the top of the boiler, and the bottom of the vat being pierced with holes to admit of the ascent of the steam among the food to be prepared. In this way, I boil small corn for my saddle-horses, and steam potatoes daily for my farm-horses at a very trifling expense. — *J. A. Mackenzie. Cowan, by Dingwall, Ross-shire, April* 20. 1833.

We were quite aware of this description of steaming apparatus, which, about 1804, was common in the Lothians. We have described this and other simple modes of steaming cattle-food in our *Encyclopædia of Agriculture;* and we gave the one referred to by our correspondent, in the *Encyclopædia of Architecture* as being very complete. The excellent plans sent by this correspondent, for cottages and farmeries, will be made use of in due time. — *Cond.*

Art. V. *Queries and Answers.*

A VILLA *for a sloping Site.* — " Talking of a sloping site, we are reminded of one which we would like to see Mr. Loudon or some of his friends think of for a design. Suppose a slope to the south, pretty steep too, and somewhat elevated above a public road, the whole exposure covered less or more with trees, and the background to consist of pretty high but unwooded hills, rising in the same slope: what description of villa, containing similar accommodation with *fig.* 1475., would he or they recommend for such a site?" (From a Criticism on our *Encyclop. of Architecture*, in the *Scots Times* for April, 1833.)

We feel much indebted to the editor of the *Scots Times* for the handsome manner in which he noticed the Numbers of our *Encyclopædia* as they successively made their appearance; and we are particularly desirous that some one of our correspondents should supply us with a design suitable for the situation which he describes. — *Cond.*

Camilla Cottage. — Sir, In Madame D'Arblay's *Memoirs of Dr. Burney*, lately published (vol. iii. pp. 259. and 260.), is a description of Camilla Cottage, built at West Hamble, near Norbury Park, the seat of the late amiable and much respected Mr. Lock. This description is as follows: — " The architect had so skilfully arranged its apartments, for use and for pleasure, by investing them with imperceptible closets, cupboards, and adroit recesses, and contriving to make every window offer a fresh and beautiful prospect, that, while its numerous though invisible conveniences gave it comforts which many dwellings on a much larger scale do not possess, its pleasing form and picturesque situation made it a point, though in minature, of beauty and ornament, from every spot in the neighbourhood whence it could be discovered." Several subscribers to the *Encyclopædia of Architecture* would be obliged if you would give an elevation, ground plan, and description of this (if we may so call it) *rara avis* cottage in your *Architectural Magazine*, if it be compatible with your plans. — ****. *Rugby, Warwickshire, April,* 1833.

A plan, view, and short description of the present state of the cottage referred to, if it be still in existence, will oblige us much. — *Cond.*

Art. VI. *Obituary.*

DIED, on May 20. 1833, aged 69, *M. Labarre*, a French architect of great celebrity. His principal works were the column at Boulogne sur Mer and the Exchange at Paris; he also designed the theatre at Bordeaux. M. Labarre was a member of the Legion of Honour; he was also a member of the Institute at Paris. He established a school for architecture; and many of his pupils are now eminent architects in different parts of the Continent.

THE ARCHITECTURAL MAGAZINE.

APRIL, 1834.

ORIGINAL COMMUNICATIONS.

ART. I. *On the Means of forming a just and correct Taste in Architecture, and on the Sources from which the Principles of Design and Construction in that Art are derived.* By the CONDUCTOR.

WE have before stated (p. 5.) that no one who can reason, or who possesses what is called good common sense, need despair of acquiring a just and correct taste in architecture; and we shall now endeavour to point out the mode by which this may be effected. By a just taste, we mean one founded on sound general principles; and by a correct taste, one not only founded on general principles, but on the rules and precedents which regulate details of particular styles: for example, a person of just taste may duly appreciate the general form and proportions of a Corinthian portico, but his taste may not be sufficiently correct to enable him to decide whether the mouldings which have been employed in the columns and entablatures are those which are appropriate to that order.

A very slight consideration will convince every one, that, unless he has made any art or subject his particular study, his taste or his opinions respecting that art or subject have been formed on the accidental circumstances by which he has been surrounded. A person living in a city can hardly help having some taste for architecture; that is, from continually seeing new buildings erected, he cannot avoid comparing them with those already existing, and probably judging them, in his own mind, to be either better or worse. Here, we will say, is an incipient taste for architecture, which, in a person whose mind is chiefly occupied with other subjects, may never advance a step farther. Let that person, however, be either a pupil to an architect, or a carpenter, mason, bricklayer, or any other mechanic employed in any of the trades connected with architecture, building, or furnishing, and the case will be found very different. Such a person cannot help advancing in his taste; or, in other words, forming more decided opinions as to what is good or bad, beautiful or the contrary, in the edifices or furniture which daily come before him, or in the construction of which he is mechanically employed. Here, then, we have a taste for architecture growing up with a man insensibly, as a part of his profession or trade, and, we shall suppose, without his having had recourse to books, to travelling, or to any other of the usual sources of architectural knowledge.

We shall next enquire what chance this taste has of being just and correct. Here we may observe, that the terms just and correct, like all other terms, may be taken either in a relative and limited, or in an absolute and general, sense; and, from this view of these terms, we should decide that, though the taste formed on local circumstances, such as have been already described, may be just and correct relatively to what the person possessing it may have seen and studied in his given locality, yet that it may be very deficient with reference to the architecture of the world generally.

We shall first confine our enquiries to the subject of *a just taste in architecture*. There are few persons who have not made some particular subject their study more than any other; and such persons will be at once aware, that they could never have arrived at just opinions on that subject, without having reference to the opinions formed upon it by others in different times, and under different circumstances; in short, without having reference to historical and geographical, as well as merely to local or topographical, knowledge. The first step, therefore, towards a just taste in architecture is, to know what has been done in this art in all other ages and countries, and to be able to form some idea of its present state throughout the world.

If a taste for architecture were to be formed by any individual without reference to historical data, it could only be founded on the architecture of the particular country in which he was placed, and of the times in which he lived. The architecture of that age and country might be good, or it might be otherwise; but, whichever it was, the taste which was formed on it alone could never be considered as based on such a solid foundation, as that which was formed on a due consideration of all architecture, past and present. It might be a taste for Grecian architecture, for the pointed or Gothic style; or for the Indian, or the Chinese manners; and the conventional rules of the particular style, and their application, might be familiar to the individual. Supposing that individual, however, called upon to design a building which should have a character of grandeur and beauty, and yet not indicate any style whatever: such an individual would be totally at a loss how to proceed. And why would he be at a loss? Simply, because, though he was a master of rules, yet he was ignorant of general principles; to which, in architecture as in every thing else, recourse must be had in untried circumstances.

Let us suppose, for example, a carpenter living in London, and having no other means of improving his architectural taste, than observing with attention the public buildings and street houses of the metropolis. The general idea that would be impressed on his mind, would probably be the necessity of using columns, wherever it was intended to convey the idea of architectural distinction. He would find columns of large dimensions employed in the porticoes of churches and other public buildings; of smaller dimensions, in porticoes to private houses; and of still smaller dimensions, or reduced to half or three-quarter columns, in shop fronts. Again, he would see detached square columns, supporting porticoes; and portions of square columns, under the name of pilasters, attached to the walls of all kinds of buildings; sometimes appearing to be supports to an entablature, as in the case of a returned pilaster at an angle; and at other times merely as ornaments, as in the case of double pilasters at the angles, with the corner of the wall projecting between them. From all this he would naturally conclude that there could be no good architecture without columns or pilasters. Seeing columns applied to every building, of every dimension, sometimes supporting an entablature, and at others only bearing the semblance of doing so; sometimes detached and free, the portico serving as a protection from the weather to the area of entrance underneath; and at other times attached, and affording neither shade nor protection; sometimes with their bases placed on the ground, and reaching to the entablature which crowns the building; sometimes reaching only to the height of 10 or 12 ft., and appearing to support a superincumbent wall of great height, and of a weight sufficient to crush them to the ground, if it had no other support than what was afforded by them; and at other times with their pedestals or bases over a shop front, showing nothing but glass as a foundation — he would farther conclude that the manner in which columns or pilasters were applied was a matter of no consequence, and that the great object for him to aim at, was to contrive to introduce them on every occasion, when it was considered desirable to produce a superior description of building.

Now, supposing this carpenter turned architect or builder, and required to design a grand or elegant edifice, without being allowed to use either columns or pilasters, what would he do in such a case? He would, of course, be greatly at a loss, as, thus educated, he would have no idea of a grand or elegant building without these adjuncts. Suppose, however, that he ventured to compose a design, and that, after showing it to his employer, the latter should disapprove of it in point of taste; what arguments could he offer in its justification? It is clear that he could not refer to precedent, and also, that none of his rules would apply. If, therefore, he was without a knowledge of the fundamental principles of architectural composition, he would be totally lost.

We might proceed from the column to other parts of Grecian architecture, and show that a student, in similar circumstances, would have no better data on which to form his taste, with regard to the application of pediments, cornices, and other details. We might also suppose him living in any given city, where Grecian architecture was chiefly employed, at a time when some particular fashion in that architecture, as employed by the moderns, was prevalent; or when some great leading architect gave a tone to the public taste, and was every where imitated by artists in general employment. In either case he could only acquire a local or temporary taste, founded on what he had seen.

In like manner, we may suppose a carpenter, mason, or any other architectural student, living in a town where all the architecture was in the Gothic style, and that he was ignorant of every other; in this case he would be unable to separate the idea of grandeur and beauty from pointed arches, clustered columns, buttresses, pinnacles, and battlements. Ask him to design a building without these, and he would be equally at a loss with the architect whose ideas and rules were exclusively taken from examples in the Grecian style.

No one school, therefore, is sufficient to form a just taste in architecture. This can only be acquired by the comparison of different styles, and judging between them; and by separating what is peculiar or characteristic of each style, from what is general, and to be found in all styles. Thus far as to the mode of forming a just taste in architecture.

A correct taste in architecture always implies a reference to the details of some particular style. We could not properly speak of a correct taste in architecture generally; but it would be quite proper to speak of a just taste in that sense. A correct taste, being founded on details, is far more common than a just one; because it requires little more than an exertion of memory and recollection, in treasuring up and bringing forth the details of particular styles. There are many architects who excel in correctness in the particular style to which they have devoted their attention, who, if they were questioned as to general principles, would probably be unable to define one. A knowledge of details may be most readily and accurately acquired from engravings; but, for the practical man, most usefully by the admeasurement of the best examples. In either case, recourse must be had to historical and geographical knowledge, in order to determine what the best examples are.

Having shown that a just and correct taste for architecture, as a fine art, requires a knowledge of the architecture of all ages and countries, we shall next enquire whether a knowledge of the principles of architectural design and construction might not be attained by studying architecture historically. By the principles

ART. III. *Notice of a very common Error in designing and building Ornamental Chimney Tops.* By E. B. LAMB, Esq., Architect.

Sir,

In your *Encyclopædia of Architecture*, you have very properly pointed out the difference between the bold and free style of the master, and the tame servile manner of the mere imitator. Nothing is more common in architecture than to copy without understanding the original; and this is always more evident when copyists either add to, or take something from, the object imitated. I could refer to innumerable instances of this; but I shall content myself at present with a very simple one. Builders, in common with others, seem now agreed that it is very desirable to render chimney tops ornamental; more especially in cottages, villas, and other suburban dwellings. In constructing these ornamental chimney tops, however, they generally contrive either to curtail them of their fair proportions, or to omit some member; so as, instead of pleasing, to raise up in the mind of the architect, or amateur, who knows what they ought to be, only feelings of regret and disappointment.

I shall give you an example of this from a villa in the Elizabethan style, just completed, not above a mile from town; premising, that I have not the least idea, either of the name of the architect, or of the builder. I confine my remarks entirely to the chimney tops.

Fig. 24. is a view of a stack exactly as it is, and *fig.* 25. a view of the stack as, I think, it ought to have appeared. You will observe, in *fig.* 24., that the shafts (*a*) are short and inelegant, and that the plinth and base mouldings, which I have shown in *fig.* 25., at *b*, are entirely omitted. Instead of this, in *fig.* 24. there are two panels, shown at *c*, and a sort of cornice, or row of blockings,

Indeed, the price of fish, in a short time, will probably not exceed one third, or even one fourth, of what it was in 1832. By the breaking down of this monopoly, another lesson will be added to those already lately given to dealers and tradesmen; viz. that the system of insuring, by small profits, extensive sales, is the only one adapted to the present advanced state of society in this country. — *Cond.*

under which are evidently formed for the sake of ornament; since, so far from being of any use, the panels, by diminishing the thickness of the wall, must have a tendency to render the flues more easily penetrated by the cold, and, consequently, to injure their draught. The form I have shown would not have required a greater expense of labour and material than has been incurred by building this cornice, and sinking these panels. Allow me also to point out the bad arrangement and scattered appearance of the cap in *fig.* 24.: the neck (*e*), under the cap, is much too long for the body of the shaft.

With sincere good wishes for the success of the Architectural Magazine,

I am, Sir, yours, &c.

E. B. LAMB.

9, *Little James Street, Bedford Row, Dec.* 29. 1833.

WE consider the above short communication as particularly valuable in a practical point of view; since it is only by pointing out little matters of this sort, one at a time, that the Architectural Magazine can have an influence in improving the taste of established architects and builders. The rising generation, on the contrary, require to be taught to think; and this can only be effected by scientific disquisitions. — *Cond.*

ART IV. *On the Ventilation of Living-Rooms, Domestic Offices, &c.* By JOHN MILNE, Esq., Architect.

No subject of equal importance has been so little attended to as ventilation. From the pigsty to the cottage, and from the cottage to the palace, we find the means of producing it either entirely neglected or mismanaged.

In some instances, no doubt, this essential has been attended to. The subject was scientifically considered by Tredgold, in his *Principles of Warming and Ventilating;* and, accordingly, many persons have been induced to endeavour to ventilate their dwellings; but the methods employed are exceedingly defective.

It is conceived by projectors in this way, that whatever is a good ventilator to-day will be such to-morrow; whether the wind blows in this direction or in that, in at the door or down the chimney; whether it be winter or summer; whether the apartment be warm or cold. A passage at the top, or else at the bottom, of the house, for the exit of vitiated air, is all they think of doing for it.

On the contrary, it should be borne in mind, that ventilation depends upon two exciting causes; and that, whether these are in an active state or not, ventilation is necessary.

The first of these causes is the force and direction of the wind, without reference to temperature. The second is the difference of temperature within and without the house to be ventilated.

When the wind blows hard, it forces its way into the house by every chink, and thereby forces out the air within it: but when the direction of the wind is against the door, the blast beats in whenever that passage is opened; and, according as the weather is mild or violent without, it is sufferable or otherwise within. An opening in the roof tends very much to increase the disagreeableness of this sort of ventilation, and to insure the visiter a severe cold, if not an attack of inflammation.

The second cause of ventilation is the greater temperature within than without the house; and, according as the difference is great or small, ventilation is quick or sluggish.

Almost everybody knows that warm air is lighter than cold air; and we, by experiment, find that any given volume of air decreases in weight $\frac{1}{483}$ part by every additional degree of heat. Hence, warming an apartment occasions the mass of air which it contains to become buoyant, and it would soon escape, were there an opening to allow its exit.

Now, an opening in the roof must be made, in order to permit the escape of vitiated air, and it ought to be such a one as to permit a sufficient exit of air in summer, when the difference of temperature within and without the house is small, and consequently when the ventilating current is sluggish; and it must also be just large enough to permit the escape of the same quantity of air in winter, when the difference of temperature within and without the house is great, and consequently when the ventilating current is quick: conditions which are evidently impossible, unless the ventilator can be made to open its throat in summer, and shut it in winter, just as much as is necessary.

I shall now describe a ventilator having these properties. In *fig.* 26., let $a\,b$ be a square crib, frame, or box, placed on the roof, having two doors, c and d, hung on centres at e and f.

If we can open and shut these doors according to the degree of ventilation required, our object is attained.

In order to effect this, let the end $g\,b$ of the crib project below the roof, leaving air passages, *m, n, p,* &c., between its bottom and the roof; and let the bottom of the crib be open towards the inside of the house, except in so far as it is partially closed by the damper *k*. This damper is attached to the doors *c* and *d* by pieces of cord, light wood, or iron hoops, and its weight is just sufficient to open the doors to the full extent required. Now, it is evident that a very small force of air at the under side of the damper *k* would push it upwards, and thereby shut the doors *c* and *d*; and by pushing up the damper *k*, the passage of the air by the openings *m, n, p,* &c., is prevented: but the passages *m, n, p,* &c., and the doors *c* and *d,* can never be closed completely, because, by closing the doors *c* and *d* to a certain extent, the exit of the air is prevented accordingly, and it thereby prevents the damper *k* from rising any farther; that is, the air presses upon the upper side of the damper, and upon its under side, with nearly equal force.

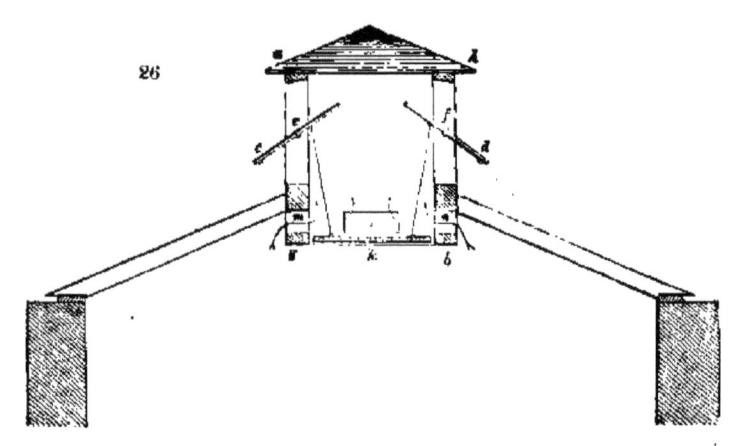

Now, the quantity of air we may want to let out will be regulated by the excess of the weight of the damper over the balancing weight at the outer ends of the doors *c* and *d*, and this weight we can add to, or take away, as we please. I have now shown that this ventilator will regulate and equalise the exit of air. It will also regulate and equalise the entrance of air into the apartment ventilated. If not, the house must be so open that it is needless to attach a ventilator to it.

Suppose that a stiff breeze blows against the door of an apartment, and that the door is opened whilst the people within are warm; the wind rushes in, compresses the air within the house, and thereby closes the damper till the ventilation goes on precisely at the same rate as before. This ventilator, therefore, is more careful and efficient than the best doorkeeper could be.

In stables and cow-houses proper ventilation is as necessary as in palaces. I shall not enter into any detail of the many bad effects upon cattle, which want of, or even uncontrolled, ventilation gives rise to; nor describe the extent of deterioration of the buildings, where there is none, or where it is ill managed; I have only to say, that, by the use of such an apparatus as that which I have now described, all the evils complained of would be prevented at a very small expense; and that in dairies it would be particularly valuable, as, by its operations, the temperature as well as the quality of the air could be easily managed.

It appears also to offer great facilities to the process of malting, and similar operations, where the temperature depends upon the draught of air.

The proper ventilation of hospitals for the sick appears to be more difficult than that of any other building. Physicians are well aware of the necessity of careful ventilation; and they frequently endeavour to enforce attention to it: but, until some self-regulating method has been adopted, I fear their humane prescriptions will be of little avail. The more irksome and painful duties which a sick-nurse has to encounter, frequently exhaust her so much, that she is reminded of this occult part of her duty only by her own sensations of heat, cold, or offensive effluvia. This is wrong; and the means of obtaining ventilation which she has in her power are no less objectionable. The windows and chimney are the only ventilators within the house, and these may be, and frequently are, opened just as much when the difference of temperature within and without the house is great, as when it is scarcely perceptible. Even although there were an appropriated opening in the roof, or in any other place, for the escape of air; if it were a mere opening only, it could neither regulate the exit nor the supply. On the contrary, as it has been already noticed, whatever shall regulate the exit, must also regulate the entrance, of the air, and *vice versâ*. Now, were there a spare flue near the apartment to be ventilated, it would not be expensive to attach an equalising ventilator to it; but, as something more must be done to increase draught at all times, I shall not describe this method farther than to point out its defects. In winter ventilation could be easily obtained, but in summer it could not; and that is the time at which it is most wanted. In the warm season it frequently happens that the heat without is as great as that within the house, and that the atmosphere is in a quiescent state: under these circumstances, little, if any, ventilation could be obtained by a spare flue. The same objection is applicable to all contrivances in which pipes or openings within the house are employed. But were the spare flue or pipe contrived in such a way as that it might be kept hot by the kitchen furnace, or other constant fire, it would be the very best promoter of ventilation that could be thought of; and, where that was unattainable, pipes upon the warmest part of the building might be employed. The longer the draught pipe is made, the stronger will be the draught.

I shall now show how the ventilating current is to be regulated in hospitals and other buildings, by the use of a ventilator such as that which I have already described. The ventilator may be placed either between the ceiling and the floor, or in the side walls; but, in either case, the ventilating or exit passages, flues, or pipes, should be carried high above the room to be ventilated, otherwise the draught will not be sufficiently strong.

In *fig.* 27., *a* is the floor of the apartment above; *b*, the ceiling of the room below; *c*, deafening; *d*, door; *e e*, air passages;

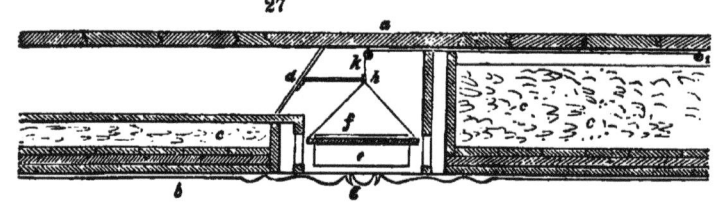

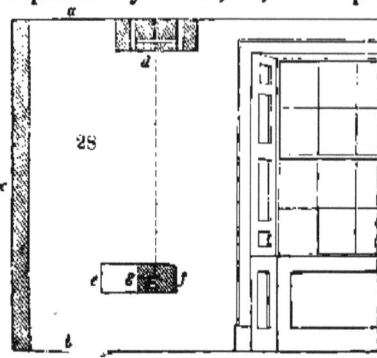

f, damper. The ventilator is understood to be in the middle of the apartment to be ventilated; and, of course, the air passage must be between two of the joists, and made to communicate with a flue or pipe appropriated to and warmed for it. No part of the apparatus is seen from below; the opening at *g* being covered by the usual ornamental patera (a flat vase; now applied to a rose-like ornament, used in floors and ceilings, to cover openings), in plaster, wood, or composition. To insure the performance of this ventilator, according to the quantity of ventilation required, the damper should be partly suspended by a cord, *h i*, which passes over one pulley at *k*, and another beyond (*i*,) at the junction of the ceiling with the side walls, and is thence carried over, and connected with a lever and weight, in the way shown in *fig.* 28. In this figure, *a* is the ceiling, and *b* the floor, of the room to be ventilated; *c* is a cross wall. The ventilator may be placed either in the side or end walls. Nothing is seen within, except the opening at *d*, and the shutter *e*, which opens into a small cavity in the wall, in which a lever and weight are made to regulate the quantity of ventilation, by placing the weight *f* nearer or farther from the fulcrum of the lever *g*, which is attached to the bottom of the damper in this instance, as it was in *fig.* 26. to its top.

The mansions of the opulent ought to be carefully ventilated; nevertheless, even in them, ventilation is often very ill attended to. In some instances the opening is made in the top of the cupola of the staircase; and certainly there is no situation better adapted for it, were it not that smoke and soot find their entrance when ventilation happens to be suspended.

Now, instead of making the exit passage in the cupola, I make ornamental openings in the plaster there, and connect these with a garret, in which the equalising ventilator is made to intercept the ventilating current; and the damper is made heavy or light at pleasure, by connecting it with its lever and weight within the parlour or vestibule of the house, and by shifting the weight, as already explained.

The area of ventilating passages will depend upon, 1st, the maximum number of persons to be admitted into the apartment to be ventilated; and, 2dly, upon the minimum difference of temperature within and without the house, at which we wish ventilation to be perfect.

According to Tredgold, " a man makes 20 respirations in a minute, and draws in and expels 40 in. of air at each respiration; consequently, the total quantity contaminated in one minute by passing through the lungs is 800 cubic inches." (*On Warming and Ventilating Buildings*, p. 69.) Mr. Tredgold, when he wrote this, had evidently not been aware of the experiments made by Pepys and Allen. In their *Essay on Respiration*, they state that an easy inspiration is about 16 cubic in.; and that the subject of their experiments made about 19 of these per minute; which gives 304 cubic in. only per minute; call it a quarter of a foot. A candle is known to deteriorate as much air as a man.

Take, as the number of cubic feet of air which you have to change in a minute, one fourth of the greatest number of persons to be admitted into the room. Suppose that this gives 500 ft. of air; and assume that the minimum difference of temperature within and without the house is about 10° Fahr.

Since the volume of air is increased $\frac{1}{483}$ by every additional degree of heat (*Dalton's Experiments*), by 10° it will be increased $\frac{10}{483}$ parts; and the heated mass will therefore be $\frac{10}{483}$ parts lighter than the air without the house.

The weight without will be affected both by its temperature and the scale of the barometer. Suppose that we assume 500 grains as being the weight of a cubic foot of air. We are now near finding the rate of ventilation; for the velocity of the current will be according to the force or buoyancy of the heated mass, and that will be the difference of weight of any equal bulk of air within and without the house.

Now, we have already asumed the fraction $\frac{10}{483}$ as the difference of volume and weight between the heated and cold air; from which we obtain $\frac{500 \times 10}{483} = 10\cdot 3$ grains, or thereabouts, of a force, per foot superficial, to put our ventilating column of air in motion.

But, from anemometrical experiments, we know that this force would give a velocity of ventilation of about 4·5 ft. only per minute, which velocity being made a divisor of the mass, 500 cubic feet of vitiated air, we have 177 ft. superficial for the area of our ventilating passages: an exceedingly large opening, certainly; but which will be much less when all circumstances are taken into account.

In order to show the utility of ventilating tubes, or flues, especially rarefying ones, I purposely omitted, in my calculation, the important fact, that they accelerate greatly the velocity of the current.

In estimating the effects to be expected from these tubes, we must not take, as I have done, the difference of weight of a cubic foot of air within and without the house, as the moving force or measure of the rate of ventilation. Instead of that, we must compare the weight of a column without, with the weight of one within the house; and the altitude of these must be equal to the height of the top of the ventilating tube above the floor of the room to be ventilated.

Now, were the top of the ventilating tube 40 ft. above the floor of the house, it is evident that, instead of the buoyant force of the warm air within being 10·3 grains only, as we had it before, it would be 40 times greater, or about 412 grains; and, accordingly, that our ventilating passages might be $\frac{1}{40}$ of what they were by the last calculation; that is, their areas might be made about 2·8 ft. superficial, instead of 777 ft.; and that such a ventilator would ventilate sufficiently 2000 persons, at a time when it is most difficult of attainment.

Tredgold has given excellent formulæ for every thing connected with this subject. I have treated it only in such a way as to make it understood by the generality of readers.

7. *Hunter Square, Edinburgh,*   JOHN MILNE.
   March 19. 1833.

WE consider this article a most important one, and wish much that some architect building a dairy, or a malt-kiln, would give a trial to the very ingenious plan indicated in *fig.* 26., and let us know the result. Mr. Milne, we have no doubt, on being written to, would engage a proper person to make a small model under his own inspection, which would remove all difficulties in regard to execution. — *Cond.*

ART. V. *On the Use of Cast Iron and Caithness Flagstone in the Construction of Fireproof Floors and Partition Walls in Dwelling-Houses.* By J. R. of Edinburgh.

THE expected reduction in the price of cast iron, from the recent improvements which have been made in the manufacture of it, will, no doubt, lead to great improvements in the construction of houses, and will render them fireproof, to a certain degree, with very little apparent change of appearance. Even at the present price of iron, much might be done by iron joisting, laid 2 ft. or 30 in. asunder, and covered with Caithness flags, the flattest, the hardest, and the most tenacious of this class of stones. They are incapable of being cut by masons' irons, but they saw easily; and, being truly flat by nature, they require no farther dressing than being sawn square. They are found of all thicknesses, from a quarter of an inch to $3\frac{1}{2}$ in., and are so strong at 2 in. thick, that no accident which can occur, in ordinary cases, could injure a square of thirty inches, or even three feet. If, therefore, joists of iron, as shown in section *fig.* 29. (in which a is the line of flagstones forming the floor;

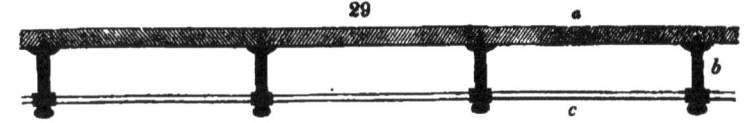

b the cast-iron joists; and c the wrought-iron rod for stiffening them), were covered with these flags, a substantial fireproof floor might be made, of any extent. In many cases, the natural surface of the stone may do; but, in conspicuous places, where neither carpet nor oilcloth is laid down, the slabs may be polished by rubbing one against another, and, when finished in this way and oiled, they look as well as Tournay marble. I have heated a portion red hot, and quenched it in water, without its cracking, or appearing to lose its peculiar tenacity. This stone might be easily got to London, as ballast, in the fishing vessels from the North, where it is prepared of such thickness and sizes as may be ordered, the joints ready sawed half way through, with the rough edge left on, to protect the sharp angle. I cannot help thinking that, if its valuable properties were known to the London builders, they would employ it largely in their works, as there are so many purposes to which it is applicable. Nothing can make better pavement; as, from its impenetrability by water, dirt never adheres to it, and, whether in rainy or in dry weather, it is always clean.

A method of making thin fireproof partitions with it, or with Arbroath stone, has occurred to me, which you may examine

Suppose a set of upright iron standards, like *a a* or *b b*, in the horizontal section (*fig.* 30. and *fig.* 31.), were erected, and stone

30

slabs, groved or plain (according to circumstances), were dropped into the spaces, a very firm partition might be built up, without re-

31

quiring any fastening, except the top course, where, of necessity, there could be no feather or ledge, as all the stones would have to be let in there. Other and better forms would probably occur on farther consideration. The corrugated iron, shown in sections 355. and 356. of your *Encyc. of Arch.* may often be used in this way, and likewise in stairs; where, if the riser were of iron and the step of Caithness or Arbroath flagstone, a light, stiff, and pleasant stair might be constructed, completely fireproof.

J. R.

ART. VI. *Description of an improved Roasting-Oven.* By Lieutenant-Colonel THOMSON, of the Royal Engineers.

Sir,

I HAVE perused your *Encyclopædia of Cottage Architecture* with great pleasure. It is a book which has long been wanted. What would I not have given for such a book when I first started in life? Even now, at the eleventh hour, I am delighted with it. I regret that I was not in England at the time your work was in progress. If I had, I should have sent you one or two designs for small cottages, which I have been in the habit of thinking nearly perfect of their kind. One of them was very similar, in its general plan, to Sir Robert Taylor's beautiful villa at Richmond, only on a smaller scale. [We shall be glad to receive these plans from Colonel Thomson, in order to publish them in this Magazine.]

This, however, is foreign to my present purpose. What I mean now to touch upon is an improvement on the roasting-oven, for which you have given some hints in your *Encyclopædia*, p. 722. By the plan which I propose, a roasting-oven of 3 ft. by 2 ft. 6 in. internal dimensions, with two or three confectioner's stoves, and one or two charcoal stoves, would be sufficient fitting for the kitchen of any small private family; and the whole expense would be covered in the saving on coals in about two or three years. I would send you a plan and section; but want of time prevents me at present. The following description of the oven, however, may suffice.

The boiler is made of plate or cast iron 2 ft. 7½ in. by 1 ft. 9 in. by 1 ft., having an opening into it on the top, near to the front, of 6 in. in diameter, for cleaning it out, or for receiving a steaming vessel for cooking vegetables, &c., in front of the oven door. There are a cock to draw off boiling water, and a pipe to supply cold water from a small cistern on the same level, with a ball cock, so as to render the supply self-acting. The upper surface of the boiler forms part of the floor of the oven. The furnace is placed nearly under the centre of the boiler. The smoke flues open from it by two slits 6 in. by 1½ in. each, gradually widening to 4½ in. by 6 in. on the level of the seventh and eighth courses of bricks. These flues proceed horizontally, branching off to the right and left, until they clear the back of the oven : there they rise to the level of the eleventh and twelfth courses, passing on each side of the oven, and separated from it by a paving tile on edge, until they reach within 4½ in. of the front, on each side of the cast-iron frame of the oven door, which is placed on the boiler, the frame having no sill. Here the smoke-flues again rise; and they ultimately join in one flue, 9 in. by 4½ in. over the centre of the door, where a damper is fixed. The opening to the furnace, 6 in. by 5 in., is formed into an inclined plane of one in three. It has no door, but is fitted with a wrought-iron spout, which also acts as a stopper, having a double back and a handle. The hot-hair flue enters from the ash-pit, immediately under the bearing-bar, and proceeds horizontally on the level of the third and fourth courses until it clears the back of the oven. Here it rises perpendicularly until it reaches the fourteenth course, where it branches to the right and left, immediately over the smoke-flues, and separated from them by a tile; the joints between the tiles being protected by a piece of slate, to prevent any smoke from rising into the air-flues. These air-flues proceed horizontally until they reach the sides of the oven near the door, where they are admitted into the oven by openings 4 in. by 2 in. each, on the level of the springing of the arch. The hot air exits at the back of the oven through an opening 4 in. by 3 in., close under the soffit of the arch at the crown. Thence it may be carried up into a drying-closet, or the hot air may be made available for any other useful purpose. Be it observed, that the arch springs from the 3-ft. sides; the back and the front being carried up perpendicularly. The entrance into the ash-pit may be closed either partially or wholly by a brick stopper, 8 in. by 6 in. by 4 in.

By this mode of construction, the internal part of the oven is kept perfectly clean; since the smoke never enters it. But when the gross particles of the coals have been carried off by the smoke-flues, and the fire burns bright and clear, the action of the furnace may be reversed, by pushing in the damper of the smoke-flue and the stopper of the ash-pit. By these means nearly the whole of the heat of the flue will be carried into the internal part of the oven, through the hot-hair flues.

The contents of the oven, which I have just described, are 165 cubit feet, which, at 1s. 2d., will give 9l. 12s. 6d. as the whole expense.

If you should deem these details likely to be useful, they are very much at your service. My object is general utility; and I know of no subject which will contribute so largely to the comfort and happiness of Englishmen all over the world, as a practical improvement in this branch of domestic economy, which may have the effect of overcoming, in some degree, that rooted prejudice in favour of long open kitchen-ranges, which roast the poor cook as well as the meat, and consume as much coals in one day as would do the work of ten in properly constructed furnaces. Wishing you every success in your useful career,

I am, Sir, yours, &c.

Cape Town, Cape of Good Hope,   ROBERT THOMSON.
   Oct. 3. 1833.

ART. VII. *Descriptive Notice of the Russel Stove;* communicated by Messrs. J. SIBBALD and SONS of Edinburgh: *with Remarks on this Stove*, by a Correspondent resident in that City.

Sir,

AT your request, we send you herewith a view and section (*figs.* 32, 33.) of what we call the Russel grate, from the idea having been suggested to us by John Russel, Esq., Lecturer on Natural Philosophy in this city. Its principal advantage consists in the fire-grate being surrounded by four cast-iron plates at an angle of 45°, which, when ground or polished, reflect more heat than most other stoves. A second advantage consists in the opening for the escape of the smoke being not larger than is necessary for the smoke alone to get away. By the smallness of this opening, there is not that waste of heated air which generally takes place in stoves where the opening is larger than necessary. Instead of having a plate of iron at the back of the fuel-chamber, a lare fire-brick is inserted there, and boxed in (filled up compactly) behind.

In cases of chimneys smoking from a want of draught, we recommend these grates, and have found them a good cure; but when the cause arises from the wind blowing down the chimney, they are not effectual, farther than making the draught a little stronger. The price of these stoves varies from 6*l.* 13*s.* to 15*l.* 15*s.*, according to the size and style of finishing.

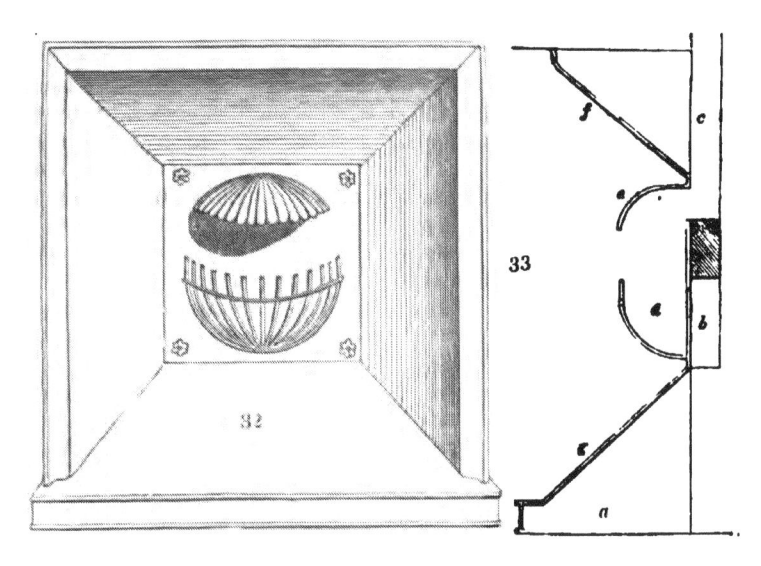

We are, Sir, yours, &c.

Edinburgh, *Oct.* 10. 1833. J. SIBBALD and SONS.

IN the section, *fig.*, 33. *a* represents the ash-pan which receives the ashes that slide down the slope *g*; *b*, the fire-brick behind the fuel-chamber; *c*, the smoke-flue; *d*, the grate for containing the fuel; *e*, the cap for conducting the smoke to the flue; and *f*, *g*, the polished sides of the grate, forming an angle of 45° with the back, for the purpose of reflecting the heat into the room.

Our attention was first directed to the Russel stove by a young architect from Edinburgh, who called on us at Bayswater, and mentioned it as being a very superior invention. From his description, we recommend him to call on Mr. Eckstein, ironmonger, Holborn, who had then recently brought into notice a projecting fire-grate like that of Messrs. Sibbald, with a wind-up cap. Our architect, having called at Mr. Eckstein's, informed us that he considered the Edinburgh invention greatly superior to his; and we accordingly wrote to Messrs. Sibbald, who sent us a letter, of which the above is the essence. We wrote at the same time to a correspondent in Edinburgh, who understands the subject of grates and heating better than any other person we know; and from him we have received the following observations. We think it right to publish them, because we are certain that there are few things relating to the fittings-up of houses respecting which people in general, and even eminent architects and builders, are more deficient in information, than parlour grates. Our correspondent says:—

The Russel grate can hardly be called a novelty; and I do not think that the slight differences which distinguish it from some others are improvements. It does very well in a chimney where the draught is always good, but will not do where it would be liable to slight occasional checks, as the smallest hesitation in the current makes the whole of the smoke come into the room. Several persons who have been induced to try these grates have been, for this reason, obliged to give them up.

Fig. 34. presents a form nearly analogous to that of the Russel

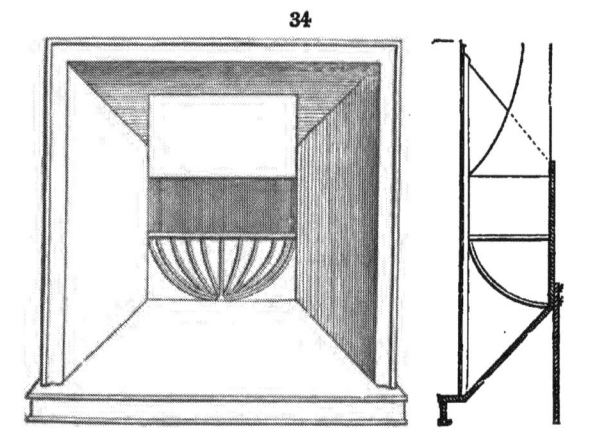

grate; but which is not liable to the same disadvantage, and which may be used in a chimney of less depth.

All forms of grates of this kind are, however, liable to an important defect; viz., that, from the great surface of the heated metal, heat is carried off to pass up the chimney. I feel satisfied, from my own experience, that the grate which I formerly described to you (see *Encyc. of Cott. Arch.*, § 1373. fig. 1243.), as being formed of three slabs of fire-brick, will heat a room with half the consumption of fuel which the best register grate would require; and, if I should ever again have to furnish a house for myself, I should have no other grate in any room of it. Any degree of elegance which may be suitable may be given to the external parts; so that its fundamental simplicity need be no objection to its introduction into highly decorated apartments. I need not add that this description of fireplace admits of being carried into execution, where ornament is no object, for a comparatively small sum.

* * *

Edinburgh, October, 1833.

ART. VIII. *The Bruges Stove, as improved by Messrs. Cottam and Hallen.* By Mr. EDWARD COTTAM.

Sir,

I SEND you sketches (*figs.* 35, 36, 37.) of the Bruges stove, as manufactured by Cottam and Hallen, who have found it to answer fully the statement given by them of it in your *Encyc. of Arch.* It will do more with a given quantity of fuel than any other stove; having the means of stewing, boiling, broiling, roasting, and baking, at one and the same time, with a small quantity of coke or cinders from any other fire.

It is simple in form, and there is not the slightest difficulty in its use. The holes in the top may be arranged as is found most convenient for the situation in which the stove is to be placed, either in a line, as in the sketch (*fig.* 35), or in the form of a triangle. One thing is indispensable for the proper action of this stove, and that is, a good draught. It must, therefore, have a separate flue.

In *figs.* 35, 36, 37. *a* is the top of the stove; *b* is the fire-pot; *g* is the hole for feeding the fire-pot; *f* is an ash-drawer; *c* is the flue; *d* is the oven door; *h* is the oven; *e* is a space for the fire to pass to the flue *c*, and for heating the whole of the top plate, any part of which will produce sufficient heat for culinary purposes; *i i i* have lids, which may be taken off, and the battery of stewpans or boilers will then be in contact with the flame. A gridiron fits on any of these openings, which has the advantage of not smoking the article broiled, the draught being downwards. I am, Sir, yours, &c.

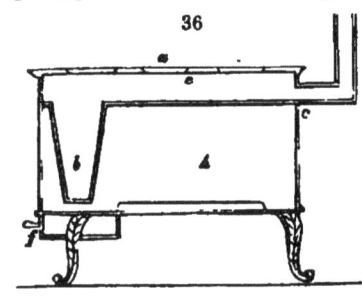

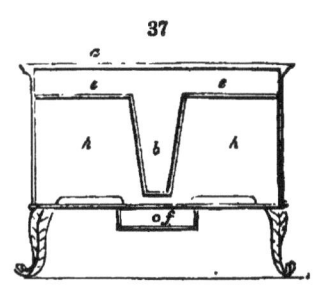

EDWARD COTTAM.

London, Feb. 12. 1834.

ART. IX. *Description of an improved Milepost invented by John Robison, Esq., and used on some of the great Roads in Scotland.* Communicated by Mr. ROBISON.

Sir,

I, SOME time ago, persuaded the trustees on the great road from Haddington to Dunbar to make an experiment with a mile-post, which I contrived so as to unite the properties of distinct notation of the distances, of indestructibility by mischievous boys, and of affording a resting-place to weary pedestrians. I have not a geometrical drawing of it at hand, from which I could take the dimensions; but the accompanying sketch (*fig.* 38.) will be quite sufficient to make you understand its construction. The portion, *a*, which is above the surface, is hollow; the top is of a shape something between those of a cheese and a flat turnip, and the stem is a hollow conical tube. The portion inserted in the ground is formed by four planes meeting in the line of the axis, and having a flat plate at bottom, as shown at *b*. The whole is fixed in the ground, by digging a small pit, setting the casting upright in the bottom of the pit, and ramming in gravel, metal, or hard rubbish round it, until the surface becomes level, or gently curved.

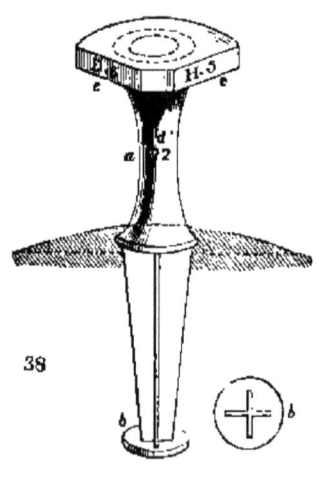

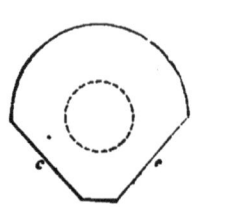

There are three distances noted on the post; first, that of the place you are approaching to; secondly, that of the place you have come from; and, thirdly, that from the capital of the country. The first two notations are on flat surfaces (*c c*), made by sections from the cheese-formed top, and the last on the stem. In the figure, Ed. signifies Edinburgh, H. Haddington, and D. Dunbar. The founders are furnished with an alphabet of letters and a set of numerals, in tin, which are struck on the pattern as required: the letters are thus cast in relief; and when the whole casting has been painted either black or white, the characters have the opposite colour impressed on them, in the way types were inked in the old mode of printing. These mile-posts are intended to be placed on the edge of the footway, next the carriage road.

I am sorry I cannot give you the items of the expense of casting and placing these mile marks; but I know it was after a comparison, in this and other respects, with other modes of construction, that the trustees adopted them, and, I understand, they have given general satisfaction to all classes.

I am, Sir, yours, &c.

Edinburgh, Feb. 1833.   JOHN ROBISON.

ART. X. *Notice of a Wooden Fence, which may be put together without the Use of Nails, Screws, or other Iron Work, invented by G. H. Cottam, Esq.* Communicated by Mr. COTTAM.

Sir,

OBSERVING that, when oak posts and rails are put together with iron nails or screw bolts, the rusting of the iron after the first shower of rain disfigures the wood, and speedily occasions its decay, I set about considering how far the use of iron might be dispensed with in such structures. The first idea that occurred to me was, that wooden pins might be substituted; but as they are liable to various objections, and do not make such a neat finish as where nails are used, I had resort to the dovetail groove, which I have thus applied: —

Fig. 39. is an elevation of a portion of railing, in which *a a*

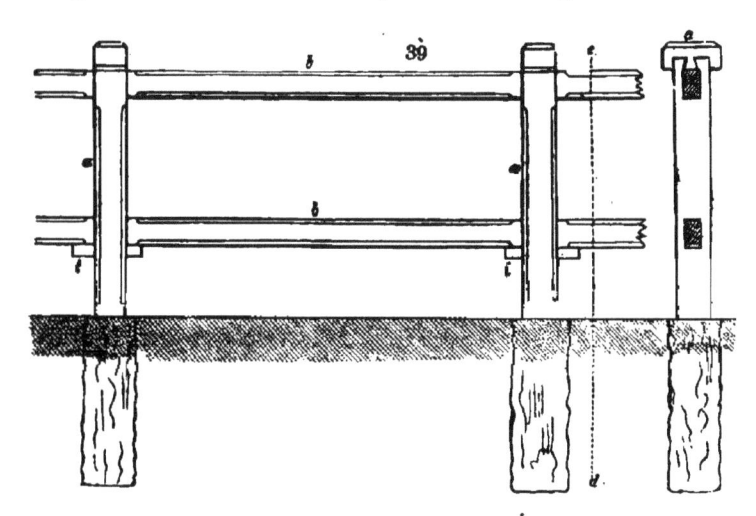

are the upright posts; *b b*, the horizontal rails; and *c*, a cross section on the lines *d e.*

On the top of each post, a dovetail groove, as shown at *fig.* 40. *f*, is worked out, into which the horizontal rails are laid, being previously joined by a dovetailed groove and tenon, as shown at *g*; the cap *h* is then pushed in horizontally over the rail, and keeps it immovably in its place. The lower rails are joined together in the same manner as the upper ones, and, being inserted in vertical mortises, are kept firmly in their places by the wedges shown at *fig.* 39. *i i*.

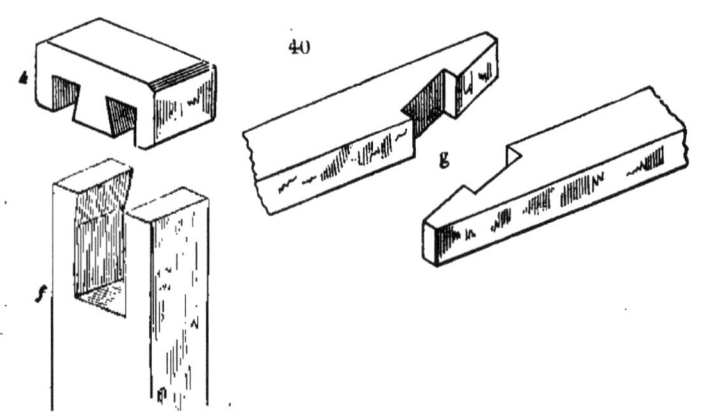

The above mode of joining rails together, which, as far as I know, is new, has all the neatness of posts and rails bolted together with iron, must be much more durable than when that metal is used with unpainted oak, and, I should think, would not be much more expensive. I am, Sir, yours, &c.

Winsley Street, Oxford Street. Nov. 1833. G. H. COTTAM.

ART. XI. *Architectural Maxims.*

PROFUSION *of Ornament* in an elevation, without any simple principle of arrangement being obvious to the eye, produces confusion. This is more or less the case with the exterior elevations of many Gothic cathedrals.

An ancient Building, known to be beautiful, is often copied and recopied in situations that have no reference to the original locality and uses of the structure. The architect is pleased with his copy, because his mind is full of the beautiful original; while the public do not understand it, but conclude that it must be beautiful, because it is placed there by the authority of a man whose taste, from his employment by government, or the nobility, they suppose to be excellent.

In Architecture, as in other Arts of Taste, the eye is frequently pleased without the mind being able to assign a reason. The effect is produced, but the cause is not immediately seen. No architect can be said to understand a building, and no critic to be competent to pass a judgment on it, who cannot refer every effect to its cause.

REVIEWS.

ART. I. *Views and Descriptions of Cyclopian or Pelasgic Remains, in Greece and Italy; with Constructions of a later Period;* from Drawings by the late Edward Dodwell, Esq. F. S. A. and Member of several Foreign Academies: intended as a Supplement to his Classical and Topographical Tour in Greece, during the Years 1801, 1805, and 1806. Imp. folio, 131 plates. London, 1834. 6l. 16s. 6d.

THOUGH the work before us is of more interest to the antiquarian than to the architect, it is not altogether without possessing some degree of utility to the latter. He may here trace the progress of masonry, from the rude Tyrinthian or Cyclopian style, in which large land-stones, or boulders, untouched by the hammer, were heaped on one another, so as to form walls of many feet in thickness, and the interstices rudely filled up with smaller stones without mortar, to the regularly coursed rustic-work of the ancient Romans. There are several intermediate styles: such as the second Tirynthian or Cyclopian style, in which the hammer is used; and the third, in which to the application of the hammer is added the use of mortar. The improved Cyclopian style comes next in order: in this, blocks of irregular size, from stone quarries, but all large, and all more or less hewn on the face, are placed on one another, so as to make close though not regular joints, without mortar. When this improved Cyclopian style is adopted with small stones, instead of very large ones, it is called the polygonal, or irregular, manner of walling; and when stones are laid in courses, and the stones themselves are not regular squares or parallelograms on the face, the walling is said to be in the acute and obtuse angled style: because, as it may be easily conceived, when, instead of vertical joists, we have sloping ones, the lower portion of one stone forms an acute angle, and the upper portion of the other, which joins it, an obtuse angle; whereas, in regular-coursed work of square stones, all the angles are right angles. It is to be regretted that the author did not live to classify and explain all the different modes of walling which he has exhibited in these interesting views; but the reader may have recourse to the author's *Tour through Greece*, to which this work, as it is stated in the titlepage, is intended to form a supplement, and to which frequent references are made.

It may amuse some of the builders of dry land-stone dikes, in Scotland, to know the classical names of their works, and what gave rise to them; and therefore we copy the following explanation of the plate which exhibits the ruins of the walls of Tiryns, said to have been built by the Cyclopians:—

"*View of the Walls of Tiryns.*— Hesiod and Homer mention the 'well-built walls of Tiryns.' Apollodorus and Strabo assert that it belonged to Prætos, for whom it was fortified by the Cyclopians. Prætos is supposed to have reigned over the kingdom of Tirynthia about 1379 years before our era. This computation would give an antiquity of nearly thirty-two centuries to the walls of Tiryns; and even this long series of revolving years does not appear too vast a period to assign to their duration, when we consider the gigantic masses of which they are composed, and the impenetrable strength which they display. Though the work of human hands, they seem formed to vie in existence with the rocks on which they are erected; and, unless they should experience the concussion of an earthquake, or be shattered by the force of artillery, they may last to the end of time. The account given by Pausanias of the walls of Tiryns accurately represents the earliest style of Cyclopian masonry. He says, that 'they were constructed by the Cyclopians, and composed of rough stones, the smallest of which was so large, that it could not be drawn by a pair of mules. The spaces formed in the walls by the irregularities of these masses were formerly filled up with smaller stones, which added more harmony to the structure.' The walls of Tiryns are, probably, at the present day, nearly in the same state in which they were seen by Pausanias in the second century; for the town does not appear to have been rebuilt or repeopled after its destruction by the Argians, about 468 years before Christ. The surprising strength and the extraordinary bulk of these walls induced Pausanias to compare them to the treasury of Minyas at Orchomenos, and to the pyramids of Egypt." (p. 3.)

"All the exterior walls of Tiryns are composed of rough blocks, that seem to have been fitted together nearly in the same state in which they were taken from the surface of the soil, or from the quarry. The vacuities left by their irregularities have been filled up with smaller stones; the largest in the walls are between 9 ft. and 10 ft. in length, and 4ft. in thickness; their usual size is from 3 ft. to 7 ft.; and the walls, when entire, were probably not less than 60 ft. in height. The interior of the Acropolis exhibits a few detached blocks, which have been hewn, and appear to have belonged to the gates." (p. 4.)

"The walls of Tiryns and Mycenæ constitute the finest Cyclopian remains that are to be seen in Greece; but these are inferior to the more stupendous structures of Norba, in Latium, which was a Pelasgic colony. Several other Pelasgic cities, whose wonderful ruins still remain in the unexplored and mountainous districts of the Volsci, the Hernici, the Marsi, and the Sabini, exhibit walls of the same style of construction, and of equal strength and solidity, with those of Argolis." (p. 4.) (See Dodwell's *Classical Tour*, vol. ii. chap. 7.)

The architect may in this work also observe what appears to have been the most ancient mode of covering the doors or other openings in walls, when lintels were not employed; and, probably, some will find, in the forms of the openings alluded to, the origin of the pointed arch. In the Acropolis of Tiryns there are the remains of a gate, 7 ft. 10 in. broad at the base, and 9 ft. high. "It is in the western wall, facing Argos, and its form probably bears the most ancient resemblance to that of the Gothic arch. It is composed of approximating blocks (in builders' language, stones corbeled over, or sailing over; from the French word *sailant*, that is, projecting), arranged in a similar manner to those in the walls of the treasury of Atreus at Mycenæ. Another gate of the same kind appears within the Acropolis of Tiryns, with a subterraneous gallery at its south-east angle. One of the gates at Mycenæ is of a similar shape; and other examples are found near Missalongi, in Ætolia, and at Thoricus in Attica: they are also seen amongst the ruins of Arpinium and Signia, in Italy." (p. 4.)

The most remarkable of these pointed gates are those to be found near Missalongi. (pl. 27. and 28.) These gates are among the remains of a ruined city, the ancient name of which is uncertain. It stands upon a rocky steep that bounds the marshes which extend along the sea coast. "In the lower part of the ruins of this city there is a chamber cut down perpendicularly in the rock. The breadth of this chamber is crossed by five parallel walls reaching to the upper surface of the rock: the six intermediate spaces, formed by the walls and the two extremities of the chamber, appear to have been covered with a flat roof. This singular edifice is composed of much smaller stones than those which were used in the walls of the city; the masonry is nearly regular; or, at least, exhibits only a few trifling irregularities, evidently more to be attributed to fortuitous circumstances than to any systematic plan. The stones are well united, but the exterior surface is rustic, or rough. Each of these walls has three apertures, or gateways, of unequal dimensions, and of a pyramidal form, terminating at top in an acute angle. Similar gates occur at Mycenæ, and at Tiryns, and they are found also in some ancient cities in Italy, which owed their origin to Pelasgic colonies. It is not easy to conceive the purpose for which these chambers were constructed, or to what use they were applied. They might have been employed either as prisons, as cisterns, or as granaries. The great door [misprinted wall] is 7½ ft. in breadth, and 16 ft. in height; the second door is not quite so broad as the other, and is 13 ft. in height; the smaller door is 10 ft. high; but the earth is considerably raised about them. The entire height of the wall is 24 ft." (p. 16.) Elevations of these doors would be simply isosceles triangles. Some of the other openings of the same kind present the same description of triangle, placed on a parallelogram; and in some, for example, in pl. 22., in the little pointed gate at Thoricus, the sides are regularly curved, so as to form a pointed arch. Indeed, were the stones of the sides of this opening not corbeled, but arched, no one would ever question its being Gothic. Thoricus, which still retains its ancient name, was one of the twelve cities of Attica; and Xenophon tells us that it was fortified by the Athenians in the 93d Olympiad (about 400 years before the Christian era), on account of its being the principal safeguard of the neighbouring mines of Mount Laurion. The remaining walls are of white marble veined with grey, procured upon the spot, and are in the third Tirynthian or Cyclopian style.

There are many curious particulars that might be quoted from this work, but we have said enough to show its interest to the architectural antiquary.

ART. II. *The Artificer's complete Lexicon for Terms and Prices; adapted for Gentlemen, Engineers, Builders, Mechanics, Millwrights, Manufacturers, Tradesmen, &c. &c.* By John Bennett, Engineer. 8vo. pp. 476. London, 1833. 12s. 6d.

FROM the title of this work we were led to suppose, before perusing it, that it contained an explanation all the technical terms employed by artificers, and a list of the present prices of all articles connected with the building trade. Instead of this, not one term in a hundred is explained; and the prices appear to have been taken from the rates which have prevailed at different periods during the last twenty years, and alphabetically arranged, without having been thoroughly examined and corrected to the time of publication. The consequence of this is, that some of the prices given are actually those at present charged; while others are those which, though they have been charged at different periods during the last twenty years, are now no longer correct.

For example: under the head of "Brick," we have, "place bricks, per thousand, 1l. 18s.; stocks, 2l. 2s.; Stourbridge fire bricks, 15l. 15s.; and Welsh ditto, 14l." Now, the price here given as being that of stocks is nearly what is now charged by the merchant for such bricks when delivered; but the place bricks are charged considerably too high, as the price of these bricks is always governed by that of stocks, and is generally from 8s. to 10s. under it. Stourbridge fire bricks are now to be had for 12l. per thousand; and Welsh fire bricks for 6l. 10s., less than one half of the price given by our author. Under the head of "Deals," the price of 12 ft. 3 in. yellow deals is stated to be 48l. per hundred; whereas the highest price at present, in the merchant's yard, is 38l. To account for this difference, the author may say his price includes profit; but if so, why did he not include profit in the prices of all the other articles; such as stock bricks, for example; which, as before mentioned, are charged nearly at prime cost? Under the head "Plate Glass," we have the prices of a plate 80 in. by 40 in., 37l. 13s.; and for 90 in. by 60 in., 68l. 18s.; whereas by the tariff for 1833, the price of the former (including profit) is 20l. 14s.; and of the latter, 45l. 8s.; so that the two glasses may be now bought for less than is stated in this lexicon as the price of one of them. Under the head of "Lead," we have white lead charged at 2l. 6s. 8d. per cwt.; though it is now to be had for 1l. 8s.; nearly 20s. difference. If it were necessary, we could point out numerous other errors and inconsistencies in the prices contained in this lexicon, but we think enough has been said on that head.

In proof that not one term in a hundred is explained, we refer to the article "Carpenter and Joiner;" which occupies about sixty pages, and contains nearly as many words which are not to be found in any English Dictionary, and of which not a single explanation is given. For many of the terms ("butt hinges," for example) we have merely a reference to some other part of the work, where, however, it is in vain to look for an explanation. Perhaps the author may say that he intended his book for artificers, who understand all these terms; but, if so, why call his book a " Lexicon, adapted for gentlemen, &c."?. It would have been better to have called the work simply a book of prices adapted for tradesmen; but, in this case, if the readers of the book are supposed to be only such as are likely to understand the technical terms, why explain to that class such words as " Cag, or Keg, a cask or barrel, which contains from four to five gallons;" " Coomb, a dry measure, containing four bushels; " " Dram, the sixteenth part of an ounce," &c. ? — *S.*

ART. III. *The Architectural Director; being an improved Guide to Builders, Draughtsmen, Students, and Workmen, in the Study, Design, and Execution of Architecture, &c.* By John Billington, Architect. Part I. 8vo, 2s. 6d. To be completed in twelve parts, to form three volumes. London, 1834.

THE first edition of this work lies before us, in one small 8vo volume. Its appearance creates suspicion, from the circumstance of there being no year mentioned at the bottom of the titlepage; no place or date to the dedication, which is to the Duke of Norfolk; no date, place, or signature to the preface; and neither engraver's name nor date to the plates. These particulars are seldom wanting to works which really are what they profess to be. On looking over the preface, in the volume alluded to, we find the following passage: — " Construction forms no part of the body of this work; but the necessary information will be found in the dictionary attached to it. Landscape-gardening, however, as connected with architecture, is not omitted, but will be found treated in its proper place." (p. x.) Now we have looked in vain, in this first edition, for the " dictionary," or the " landscape-gardening," and equally in vain for the slightest notice of an intended second or third volume, in which these articles might be contained. We have, therefore, been in the habit of looking on Billington's *Architectural Director* as, to a certain extent, an imposition on the public. If the name of Billington be not fictitious, it is, at all events, that of an architect with whom no one we have ever met with has been personally acquainted.

The second edition of this work (part i. of which has been sent us), as it is proposed to be extended to three volumes, will probably remedy the defects of the first edition; but we must confess that the address on the fourth page of the wrapper is sufficient to prejudice any thinking purchaser against it. If the publisher had wished to ruin his work, he could not, in our opinion, have taken a more effectual mode of doing so than by printing this address. We should scarcely have thought that any one could suppose that purchasers of an architectural work could be entrapped by such a passage as the following: — " The high patronage, and extensive number of subscribers, including the names of the most eminent men of the British metropolis, of which the present work can boast, are the best proofs of its undoubted superiority over many publications treating on architecture. Such persons, therefore, as may wish to secure a copy of this work, are requested to make an early application."

What is the number of subscribers; and why are not a few of the names of the "most eminent men in the British metropolis," who rank among them, given? Have these " eminent men" subscribed to the second edition without any knowledge of the first? The idea of *securing* a copy of a work like that before us is ultra — we will not say what.

The quotation of a review from the *Courier* is next given, without date; so that the reader is left to guess whether it applies to the first edition or the present one. This criticism is very properly designated a " flattering notice."

Notwithstanding the prejudice excited in our minds by the publisher's address, we will examine the part before us with care and impartiality; and we will state our opinion candidly.

This part i., then, contains a portion (32 pages) of the first edition, printed in a larger type, and on a larger page; a portion of a glossary (16 pages); and

2 quarto and 5 octavo copperplate engravings; with a printed folio table of the proportions of the Corinthian order. In the reprint from the former work, some passages are omitted, but none are added or altered. The glossary does not appear to us carefully done. For example: —" Accouplement: a framing of carpentry; also applied to signify a brace or tie." The words "framing of carpentry" give no distinct idea of what is meant. " Air trap: an aperture to admit the escape of foul air from sewers and drains." It happens to be just the contrary: an air trap is for the purpose of preventing the escape of foul air from sewers and drains. Air trunk is the term to which the author's explanation applies. — "Acanthus." We are told there are two species of this plant; the one wild, and the other cultivated: implying, we suppose, that one species is cultivated, which is not the fact; or that the cultivation of a plant makes a different species of it. This appears ridiculous to a botanist or a gardener: but perhaps it will hardly be considered fair in us to examine this glossary botanically; if it were, we should object to the scientific names not being given to the terms "Abele tree," "Acacia," and "Alder," and also to the native countries of these trees not being mentioned.

The plates are chiefly outlines. The first quarto plate contains an elevation of St. Peter's; the second is a plan of an arcade: one of the octavo plates is a very neat ground plan of a church; and the remainder are mouldings, and other details of the "five orders."

The work is cheap, and in that respect good. The British workman has hitherto been put to much needless expense by the publication of elementary architectural works in more expensive forms than were at all necessary. Till lately, indeed, architectural publishing was a sort of monopoly in the hands of only one or two persons.

The first edition of this work was almost entirely a translation from the French translation of Vignola. James Barozzio de Vignola was an eminent architect and architectural writer, who was born at Vignola, in the territory of Bologna, in the year 1507, and died in 1575. The Italian title of his work is *Regola delli Cinque Ordini d'Architettura*. It was translated into French under the title of *Traité des Cinq Ordres d'Architecture* in 1669, and has since passed through several editions in that country. A good English translation, with the plates engraved of such a size as to be really useful to the British workman, is a desideratum, but one which will not be supplied by either the first or second editions of Billington's *Architectural Director*.

ART. IV. *Catalogue of Works on Architecture, Building, and Furnishing, and on the Arts more immediately connected therewith, recently published.*

ROBINSON's new Vitruvius Britannicus. Parts I. and II. folio. London, 1833. 3*l*. 3*s*.

Coney's Interior View of Milan Cathedral. fol. London, 1834. 5*s*. — Mr. Coney's recent and premature death has left his widow in such reduced circumstances as will, it is hoped, induce the patrons of the arts, and the admirers of his talents, to encourage the sale of this fine print, which is offered at so low a price as to justify her anticipations of its success.

Shaw's Specimens of the Details of Elizabethan Architecture. Part I. 4to., London, 1834. 5*s*.

Shaw's Ornamental Works in Louis XIV.'s Style. folio. London, 1833.

Blunt, Charles John, and R. Macdonald Stephenson, Civil Engineers, Architects, &c. &c.: The Civil Engineer and Mechanist. Practical Treatises of Civil Engineering, Engineer Building, Machinery, Mill-Work, Engine-Work, Iron-Founding, &c. &c.; designed for the Use of Engineers, Iron-Masters, Manufacturers, and operative Mechanics. Division I. Imperial folio. London, 1834. 1*l*. 1*s*.

Laxton's Improved Builder's Price Book for 1834. 8vo. London. 4s.
Skyring's Builder's Price Book for 1834. 8vo. London, 1834.
Gregory's Mathematics for Practical Men; being a Commonplace Book of Principles, Theorems, Rules, and Tables, in various Departments of Pure and Mixed Mathematics, with their Applications; especially to the pursuits of Surveyors, Architects, Mechanics, and Civil Engineers. 8vo. 2d edit. London, 1834. 14s. boards.
Warren's Hints upon Tints; with Strokes upon Copper and Canvass. 12mo. London. 2s. 6d. sewed.
Hullmandel's Art of Drawing on Stone. Royal 8vo. London, 1834. 12s. half-bound.

Art. V. *Literary Notices.*

THE *New Vitruvius Britannicus*, which will contain the History of Hardwick Hall, will appear in June next.

An Attempt to discriminate the Styles of Architecture in England; with Notices of above Three Thousand Edifices. By Thomas Rickman, Architect, F.S.A. The fourth edition is in the press.

The Temple of Jupiter Panhellenius and Antiquities at Egina, being the first section of a work on the Antiquities of Greece, by C. R. Cockerell, A.R.A. and F.S.A., will be published in June next by subscription.

Architectural Illustrations of Eastbury House, Essex, by T. H. Clarke, Architect, will appear in May next.

The ancient Gates and Fortifications of the City of York, by H. F. Lockwood, and A. H. Cates, Architects, will shortly appear.

Analysis of the Defective State of Turnpike Roads and Turnpike Securities; with Suggestions for their Improvement, by F. Philips, Esq., is in the press.

MISCELLANEOUS INTELLIGENCE.

Art. I. *General Notices.*

UNIONS *of Workmen connected with Architecture and Building.* — One of the latest great strikes was that of the Lancashire builders, last year. The men persisted more than six months. The expense, to the Union, of the idle workmen was about 18,000*l.*; but the loss sustained by the working builders was four times this sum. They had refused work when there was work in abundance for all. In consequence of this refusal, many of the buildings were discontinued, and the places of some of the men were supplied by labourers brought from distant parts, and also by the introduction of machinery: so that the application for employment could not be granted. By their long cessation from work, habits of idleness, and not a little increase of immorality, had ensued. In the false hope of attaining their object, they had endured deprivations only second to absolute starvation; and now, when the day of forced repentance had come, the still farther degradation of pauperism awaited them. The failure of the strike was complete; and the disastrous consequences that resulted from it have taught a lesson to the Lancashire workmen, which, it is to be hoped, they will never forget. (*Character, Object, and Effects of Trades' Unions;* and *Morning Chronicle,* March 15.)

Cleaning Furniture. — The many accidents arising from the dangerous practice of boiling turpentine and wax for cleaning furniture induces me to send you, from my commonplace book, a receipt for the mixture of these articles, which will prove a much superior and more effectual plan than that usually adopted, and by which so many individuals have lost their lives: —

Put the quantity of turpentine required into a vessel, then scrape the bees' wax into it with a knife, which stir about till the liquid assumes the consistency of cream. When prepared in this manner, it will be good for months, if kept clean; and it will be found, that the furniture cleaned with the liquor manufactured in this way will not stain with the hand so readily as when the boiling process is adopted. But if some people must have heat in the mixture, it can easily be got, by placing the vessel containing the turpentine and wax into another containing boiling water; which will do the business as well as any fire whatever. — *A Journeyman Cabinetmaker. London, Jan.* 3. 1834.

Ventilation of Bedrooms. — There should be a constant circulation of fresh air in bedrooms. The lungs must respire during sleep as well as at any other time; and it is of great importance to have, when asleep, as pure an air as possible. It is calculated that each person neutralises the vivifying principle of a gallon of air in one minute: what havoc, therefore, must an individual make upon the pure air of his bedchamber, who sleeps in a bed closed snugly with curtains, with the doors and windows shut, and, perchance, a chimney-board into the bargain. Our health and comfort depend more upon these apparently trivial points than most people are aware of. "Confined air," says Dr. Franklin, "when saturated with perspirable matter (the quantity of which is calculated to be about five eighths of what we eat), will not receive more, and that matter must remain in our bodies, and cause disease. We may recollect, sometimes, on waking in the night, we have, if warmly covered, found it difficult to get to sleep again. We turn often, without finding repose in any position. This 'fidgetiness,' to use a vulgar expression, is occasioned wholly by an uneasiness in the skin, owing to the retention of the perspirable matter. To obviate the ill effects of this annoyance, the following rule is recommended. Preserve the same position in your bed, but throw off the clothes, and freely admit the fresh air. This will clear the skin of its perspiration, and you will experience a decided and speedy refreshment. If this be not successful, get out of bed and walk about the room; and, having shaken the bedclothes well, turn them down, and let the bed get cool. When you begin to feel the cool air unpleasant, return to bed, when you will experience the good effects of your plan. The bed itself should be so placed as to admit a free circulation of the air around it, and the curtains, if curtains there must be, ought never to be perfectly closed. It would be well if, in all the apartments, but especially in bedchambers, the upper sashes of the windows were contrived to let down; for, by this means, the admission of fresh air would be, at all times, perfectly safe; as the body, when even under such a sweat as could not, without danger, be interrupted, may receive all the refreshing, restorative, and invigorating influence of the air, without being exposed to a stream of it." Franklin himself, whatever might be the season, slept with his window open, more or less, and advised his friends to do the same; many of whom adopted the practice, and acknowledged the advantages of it. (*Glasgow Courier.*)

Mr. Bagshaw's artificial Stone for Pavements or Flooring. — We have spoken of this composition in our *Encyclopædia of Architecture*, § 2008., and have since seen testimonials in its favour from Messrs. Abraham, Newman, and Williams, architects; and from Mr. Bellman of Howland Street, London, who, having floored his shop half with it and half with Yorkshire stone, finds the artificial stone much warmer than the latter. The price of this stone is 1s. a foot, three inches thick.

Clarke's improved Blower is a tin tube, about 16 in. long, tapering about 1½ in. in diameter, at an average. At one end is a circular box, containing a wheel with four fans, which is turned by means of two multiplying wheels with a catgut rigger; these being set in motion by a winch. The velocity of the revolution of the fans draws in the air and forces it through the mouth of the tube. The price varies from 4s. 6d. to 15s. — *W. L. London, March* 15. 1834.

ART. II. Foreign Notices.

FRANCE.

It is now positively decided that a colossal statue is to be erected on the lantern which surmounts the dome of the Pantheon. A scaffold is now (Nov. 1833) erecting to place there a figure of Fame, in wood and gilt, to try the effect, before one is erected of more durable materials. (*La Propriété*, Nov. 9. 1833.)

Versailles, Oct. 1833. — There is a talk here of fitting up some of the apartments in the palace, particularly the chamber formerly occupied by Louis XIV., in the magnificent style of his age. The new furniture is to be made from models suggested by an old picture which has been found, representing this apartment in the time of Louis XIV. The bed will be remarkably splendid. The other rooms are to be converted into a historical museum; and are to be hung with battle pictures of the reigns of different French monarchs, particularly of Napoleon, so as to form a pictorial history of the wars of France, during the last century. — *S. C. de Loire.*

A new public library has been established in the city of Amiens, at the expense of a distinguished architect, M. Cheussey; who, in building it, has very cleverly contrived to make use of the materials, and especially the ornaments, of an old convent which formerly stood on the spot. (*La Propriété.*)

GERMANY.

Berlin, Dec. 10. 1833. — I am sorry that I have little to communicate in the way of architectural news. Perhaps the principal change which has taken place in our modes of construction since you were in Berlin [in 1813] is in the more general introduction of cast iron in almost every description of edifice. We have several cast-iron bridges over the Spree; and the new gates at Charlottenburg, in the style of Louis XIV., are of that metal. Some of the manufactories have their floors constructed with flanched cast-iron beams, which form abutments to brick arches. Plate iron, as a covering for roofs, has been long in use; but it is only lately that we have begun to construct rafters of cast and wrought iron, to support iron plates. The architects here consider our castings much stronger than yours; they say they have a smoother and more compact surface, which, forming a harder case, they allege must be less liable to fracture. You are, no doubt, aware that the superiority of our castings is owing to the fineness of the sand of which the moulds are made; and that the same sand which is used for casting earrings and bracelets is used also for casting joists, rafters, and cannon.

Our roads are beautifully macadamised; and a new description of ornamental milestones are in preparation, as substitutes for the old ones. Our friend Mr. —— carries with him a drawing of one of these, which he will give or lend you, if you wish to see it. I must refer you to your correspondent M. Linné for what is going on at Potsdam; and, as to the other cities of Germany, I have not, as you know, been at Dresden or Vienna for several years. You have heard, no doubt, of the improvements which Prince Metternich is carrying forward at his hereditary residence at Königswart in Bohemia; and of the chapel which he has just completed there. The country palace of the Duke of Coburg at Reinhardsbrunn, near Gotha, is, I see by the newspapers, undergoing improvements in the Gothic style, under the direction of the architect Eberhardt. — *T. S.*

We shall give an engraving and description of the milestone above mentioned, in an early Number. — *Cond.*

NORTH AMERICA.

A new Mode of warming Factories is thus described in an American paper: — "A pair of horizontal circular plates of cast iron are enclosed in a brick oven about 4 ft. in diameter. These plates weigh 1600 lbs., and operate upon each other like a pair of millstones; with this exception, that the upper one is stationary, and the lower one revolves. The upper one is set in motion by machinery; and the ordinary speed is eighty revolutions in a minute. The size of the plates, their thickness, and the velocity with which they revolve, are considerations which the size of the building to be heated must regulate. From the top of the brick enclosure, or oven, a funnel is projected; and from this the heat can be thrown off, as through ordinary furnaces, to any part of the building. In fifteen minutes from the time the machinery was put in motion (which was done by a band passed round a shaft inserted in the lower cylinder), the heat from the mouth of the funnel, in an upper story, was as great as could be borne by the naked hand.

AUSTRALIA.

The pure white Sand of Sydney, it has been discovered, is the best yet known for the manufacture of pure glass. It is without oxide of iron, or any other matter that would affect the colour of the glass: and it is free from insoluble matter, so that glass made from it is more brilliant and watery than any other, and therefore peculiarly fitted for optical and astronomical purposes. This sand is produced by the decomposition of the white sandstone which is the geological characteristic of the coast about Port Jackson, and which constitutes the great bulk of the soil about that country. This discovery, which was made by a Mr. King, is of great consequence to the colony; not only as affording a valuable article of export, which will serve at the same time as ballast; but because, from the heavy weight it makes in the hold, vessels laden with wool are enabled to take in a much larger cargo of that light yet bulky commodity, which is the only staple one of the colony. (*King's Letter to Lord Goderich*, and *Sydney Monitor*, July 20. 1833.)

Glass manufactured of the Sydney sand may be obtained of Messrs. Pellatt and Green.

ART. III. *Domestic Notices.*

ENGLAND.

ARCHITECTURAL SOCIETIES. — Endeavours seem to be making among the architects and surveyors of London and its vicinity to establish Architectural Societies. A number of young architects have met occasionally, for mutual improvement, in Exeter Hall, since 1831, and they contemplate the establishment of an Architectural College, after the manner of those of Germany. Some other architects and surveyors have had meetings, for the purpose of establishing a Society for the study of architecture and architectural topography. As soon as any thing definite has been determined on by these incipient bodies, we shall not fail to lay it before our readers. There is also a third body of architects, who meet occasionally, but chiefly, as our correspondent Scrutator informs us, for the purpose of dining together.

Architectural Exhibitions. — Some beautiful models, by Mr. Day, of ancient and modern buildings, including a model of the National Gallery now building, are exhibiting at a house near the Adelaide Rooms; and in these rooms also are some handsome architectural models. In the National Repository, in Leicester Square, a number of articles connected with architecture, building, and furnishing, deserve our particular notice, and shall have it, we trust, in our next Number, where we intend to give a more detailed account of the models by Mr. Day, &c., above alluded to.

Sir John Soane's Lectures on Architecture at the Royal Academy were completed for the season on the evening of Feb. 13. It is expected that these lectures will be published, and also that in order to commemorate the sense entertained by the profession of " the eminent services rendered by Sir John Soane to architecture, by his personal example, during a long period of honourable professional practice, and by the precepts contained in his lectures delivered before the Royal Academy; and of the generous zeal with which he has formed his splendid museum of ancient and modern fragments and models, and his fine library; and, more, particularly, of his noble gift of this collection to the nation," by striking a medal, one side of which should contain a portrait of Sir John Soane, and the other some portion of his favourite work, the Bank of England, encircled by an inscription of the following import: — " A tribute of respect from the British School of Architecture." (*Lit. Gaz.*, Feb. 15. 1834.)

Emigration of Architects. — Mr. Ross of Bristol, who furnished several designs for our *Encyclopædia of Architecture*, and who acquired very considerable public approbation by a course of lectures on architecture in Bristol, is gone to settle at New York, and has promised to become our correspondent there. Another contributor to our Encyclopædia proposes to leave London for New York, with a cargo of ornamental chimney tops, and other articles in artificial stone and papier maché, in the course of the month of May. Two other architects, our correspondents, propose going to Van Diemen's Land. Two young friends of ours, one an architect and the other a surveyor, who went from London, and settled at Sydney in 1825, are now doing remarkably well there. From one of them we have just received a long communication; but, as it requires several engravings to illustrate it, its appearance must necessarily be deferred till next Number.

The Abattoirs at Islington we consider to be among the most interesting and valuable architectural improvements which have been made in the metropolis for many years, from the humanizing influence which they will eventually have on all those connected with the trades of butcher and cattle-driver. They will also greatly diminish the amount of suffering by the poor animals themselves. A correspondent has promised us an architectural description of these structures, which we shall shortly lay before our readers.

A Public Market at Knightsbridge is projected by a company, and the designs, which we have seen, are by E. B. Lamb, Esq. The arrangements appeared to us most judicious, and we trust the plan will be carried into execution.

Fishmongers' Hall, which has been lately rebuilt close to London Bridge, is a piece of architecture of which we cannot at all approve, from the use which has been made of three-quarter columns in two of the elevations. In other respects, we believe, the building is good: but our readers will have the opinion of a professional friend on it in our next.

A handsome new Church in the Gothic Style, at Clerkenwell, has just been completed, from the designs of our highly gifted young contributor, Mr. Lamb.

A new Prison at Westminster is nearly completed, under the direction of Robert Abraham, Esq., who has kindly promised to enable us to inspect it, with a view of giving a notice of it in this Magazine.

The National Gallery, to which allusion is made by our Paris correspondent (p. 46.), has at length been commenced, from the designs of Mr. Wilkins, by the builders, Messrs. Harrison. The foundations are building of brick, and, after they have been carried to a certain height, what, in these degenerate days of masonry, is called the foundation stone, will be laid by the king.

An experimental Railway is now being laid down at Camden Town, by John Isaac Hawkins, Esq., a civil engineer, distinguished by his science and inventive powers, for the purpose of illustrating the application of Mr. Saxton's patent deferential pulley, in the propulsion of carriages. It is calculated that by the use of this pulley, with horses walking at the rate of two or three miles an hour, or using as a substitute for horses, fixed steam-engines, carriages may be propelled at the rate of thirty miles an hour, even on a surface not level or regular. This work is carrying on by subscription, and we sincerely wish it success.

The Street Architecture of London does not, in our opinion, get a tithe of the attention which it ought to have from architects; which is the more surprising, since it is likely soon to constitute a principal part of their employment. One great object of this Magazine is to give shopkeepers a taste for architecture, and thereby to induce them, when they rebuild or repair their houses, to employ such architects as can design elevations equal in dignity to that of Fearon's house in Bond Street, or in originality and elegance to that of a tailor opposite the Traveller's Club-house in Pall Mall.

A Model of the great Pyramid of Cheops was lately exhibited at the Duke of Sussex's conversazione at Kensington Palace. It is composed of 43,000 pieces of cork, and shows a vertical section of the pyramid; from which it appears that this pile was not only built upon, but round, a rock, which, it is stated, rises in the centre of the pyramid 130 ft., and on the apex of which is situated what is called the queen's chamber. The pyramid was originally covered with plaster or mortar; which made the surface even, and thus rendered the ascent so difficult as to be accounted by the ancients a great feat. This plaster having now fallen off, the ascent is easy.

The Pantheon in Oxford Street is undergoing important alterations, so as to fit it for a bazaar of a very superior description. In this bazaar there will be two new and very interesting features: a saloon, for the exposure of sculptures, paintings, engravings, and other works of the fine arts, which will be open to the public, free of expense, at all times; and a conservatory, of 88 ft. in length, and 25 ft. broad, for the exposure for sale of plants in pots. The saloon of the fine arts, from being open to the public, will tend to improve their taste in art, and the flowers in the conservatory their taste in nature. The architect, under whose direction the works are carried on, is Sydney Smirke, Esq.; who has favoured us with views of the conservatory, &c., which we intend, at a future time, to engrave.

Lancashire. — Some time ago we read an account, in a Preston newspaper, of a very interesting lecture on architecture, which had been delivered in that town. Should this meet the lecturer's eye, we invite him to become our correspondent, as we do Mr. Kenion, our valuable contributor to the *Magazine of Natural History*. We should wish to know how the Preston viaduct goes on. For architectural improvements in Lancaster and its neighbourhood, we trust to Mr. Saul; in Liverpool, we have several gardening and natural history correspondents, but none strictly architectural. For Manchester we trust to Mr. Stanway.

Middlesex. — A correspondent has pointed out to us the great want of underdraining in some parts of the metropolitan districts of roads, in consequence of which, however great may be the quantity of metal laid on, the water, rising up through it, keeps the road so moist as to render its surface a continual puddle. We could ourselves say a good deal as to the neglect of the footpaths in several places near London, and especially between Shepherd's Bush and Oxford Street, but we shall wait till after we have reviewed the excellent *Treatise on Road-making* by Sir Henry Parnell.

Northumberland. — The accommodations for the cottagers in this county are indeed too frequently very bad, often with only one, and that a very comfortless, room; but your excellent *Enc. of Arch.* is well calculated to draw the attention of proprietors to this subject, and will, I trust, have the desired effect. Mr. Green of Newcastle, your correspondent, is an architect extensively employed, and has made many ameliorations where he has had full liberty. He can render you the most valuable assistance in your highly useful undertaking. — *R. E. T. August*, 1833. We shall expect to hear from Mr. Green, and also from Mr. Falla; and we invite other correspondents, from that interesting part of the country, to send us all the information in their power. — *Cond.*

Oxford. — Sir, In August last, I passed through the show-rooms of Mr. Edwards, High Street, Oxford, and was much gratified by a number of articles there exhibited. Mr. Edwards has made great improvements on Witty's furnace, by which it is not only much more easily managed and kept in repair, but is far better adapted for heating water, either for the purposes of washing or brewing, or for circulating as a medium for conveying heat or producing steam. He has prepared, for showing to strangers, a tin model of one of his improved Witty's furnaces, which I may at some future time describe to you. The other improved articles which I saw, I shall notice under separate heads.

Kitchen Furniture. A portable roaster, formed of tin, is considered a most useful and economical apparatus for roasting meat before an open fire. The ordinary size of this roaster is about 3 ft. long, 2 ft. high, and 1 ft. deep; but some are made nearly twice as large. The front which faces the fire is open, and the back and sides are of tinned iron. The spit is let into notches in the ends, and is turned by a small wind-up jack.

Laundry. An improved ironing stove, in which the fire is enclosed in brickwork, and consequently the fuel is more completely consumed, and the heat longer retained, than in the common stoves of this kind, which are wholly of cast iron.

Bedchambers. An oval hip bath, made of tin or of copper. The depth of this bath, inside measure, is 12 in.; the base on which it stands is 3 in.; the length of the bath is 13½ in. at the top, and 19 in. at the bottom; its breadth 21 in. at the top, and 12¼ in. at the bottom; the shoulder-piece is 8 in. deep. This bath may be used as a child's bath, hip bath, foot bath, sponging bath, or even as a washing-tub.

Miscellaneous. A garden engine, with an iron frame, is an article of great utility; not only for gardens, but for washing down cobwebs, dust, &c., from outside walls. The engine lifts out of its frame, and in its place may be put the body of a common wheelbarrow, or a large basket for carrying clothes, or vegetables, or short grass. Hand-glasses of tinned iron, of different sizes, are manufactured by Mr. Edwards, and sold at remarkably low prices.

Perhaps it may be thought by some, that notices like the above are intended more as advertisements for tradesmen than as intelligence for your readers; and I admit that, at first sight, they seem liable to this objection. I think, however, that the public are as much indebted to those who bring before them notices of real improvements in domestic articles, as they are to those who treat on points of science. In all the notices of this kind which I shall send you, it will be found that my object is not less to make known the uses of the article recommended, than to give such an idea of its construction as that it can be made by other manufacturers. — *John Brown. Woodstock, Jan.* 1834.

The Architectural Improvements at Nuneham Courtenay, under the direction of Sir Robert Smirke, will tend to keep up the reputation of that noble place. But, as I know you have a correspondent on the premises, I shall leave him to describe the fine additions now making to the mansion in the Grecian style, the architectural terrace, &c. — *Id.*

Warwickshire. — A town hall, which is now nearly completed in Birmingham, will be one of the grandest structures of the kind in Britain. The general form is that of a Grecian temple; but the length and breadth are much better proportioned to each other than those of the Bourse at Paris. A description, plan, elevations, and sections are promised us by the architects, Messrs. Hanson and Welch, which we shall lay before our readers.

The Free Grammar School, in New Street, Birmingham, founded by Edward VI., will shortly be rebuilt from the designs and under the direction of Charles Barry, Esq. The principal elevation is of a highly enriched Tudor Gothic.

A new Market, in High Street, Birmingham, by Charles Edge, Esq., has been some time completed, and forms a great ornament to the town. It has done away with the disgrace, which has so long attached to Birmingham, of having no market house. We have written to Mr. Edge, and trust to him for a description and sketches.

Wiltshire. — Accounts have been received of the architectural improvements now going forward at Tottenham Park, and at Ashton Hall, in this county; but they are too long for introduction in the present Number.

Worcestershire. — In the *Worcester Herald* for November 30. 1833, is an admirable letter on the importance of the fine arts to a commercial country like Britain. It was written in consequence of an announcement of an intended exhibition of works of the fine arts in Worcester, and would be well worth reprinting in our pages, had we room. The signature to that letter is Lorenzo; and we should be most happy to reckon him among the number of our correspondents.

WALES.

Caernarvonshire. — One of the largest private residences in Britain, in the castle style, is said to be now building at Penrhyn, near Llandygai, for G. H. D. Pennant, Esq., by Mr. Hopper. This gentleman was the architect of the Gothic conservatory which was connected with Carlton House, when that building existed; and is employed on many mansions and villas now in the course of erection or improvement in Great Britain and Ireland. We should be happy if Mr. Hopper, or some of his friends, would favour us with notices of the mansion at Penrhyn and of the others alluded to. We had an opportunity of seeing several of Mr. Hopper's works, in the course of a tour, last summer, through some of the western and southern counties of England.

Glamorganshire. — Near Swansea, a new pier, roads, cottages, and various improvements, are going forward on the estate of our correspondent J. E. B., who, as a patron of the fine arts, will, we trust, send us some account of them, and of the state of architectural improvement in that part of the country.

SCOTLAND.

Edinburgh. — A new approach to this city, from the west, has been for some time in the course of execution, and is now nearly completed. It may be remarked of this road, which is carried obliquely along the south-west side of the Castle Hill, that, like the Earthen Mound, it tends to counteract the natural features of the ground: but, as the characteristic of all architectural improvements ought to be utility, this should not be objected to, unless it can be proved that the natural features and the artificial advantages are not incompatible with each other.

Cottages for the Labouring Classes. — The premium of a piece of plate, of 20 sovereigns' value, offered by the Highland Society, has been awarded to Mr. George Smith, architect, Edinburgh. (*Scotsman,* Jan. 18. 1834.)

Boring and blasting Rocks. — A newly invented apparatus for this purpose has lately been exhibited before a number of scientific gentlemen connected with this city and county. The inventor is Mr. D. Millar, road contractor and builder. The apparatus appears to be a more efficient boring instrument than any hitherto in use. It is calculated to bore or tap the depth of 100 ft. or upwards, and may be put in operation either by manual labour or steam. (*Scotsman,* Feb. 22. 1834.) An instrument for the same purpose was invented by Mr. Mallet of Dublin, 1832; of which a detailed account will be found in the *Mechanics' Magazine* for 1833. Mr. Mallet's object was to split all rocks that could be separated into laminæ by the application of male and female screws, instead of blasting, as heretofore practised, with gunpowder. The process is as follows: — Jumper holes are formed, in the direction of the proposed fracture, as at present; but, instead of filling them with gunpowder, a split female screw is inserted in each hole, and the fracture is effected by the insertion of a conical or male screw.

Cooking by Gas. — I have nearly completed a small lean-to from my kitchen, in which, by means of gas stoves, I expect to supersede altogether, or nearly so, the old processes of cooking by open fires and hot tables, and thus to get rid of various nuisances and inconveniences of heat and smells. It appears to me that this mode of cooking must lead to many beneficial changes in the culinary department, by greatly abridging the labour of the cook, enabling her to work with more comfort to herself, and to superintend more extensive preparations than any one person can, in the present way, look after. — *J. R. Edinburgh, Oct.* 13. 1833.

Further Experience of my Gas Cooking Apparatus confirms me in the opinion that it possesses many advantages. I have nine stoves in a range, varying from 4 in. in diameter to 10 in.; but I now find that even the smallest-sized ones are quite powerful enough for boiling the largest cooking pot which can be required (say for a round of beek of upwards of 20 lbs. weight); so that the expense is still less than I calculated. When all the nine stoves are burning at once, the consumption of gas is about 1 cubic ft. in 47 seconds, which at the price of gas here (9s. 6d. per mille) is considerably under a shilling per hour; and, if all the stoves were under 6 in. in diameter, the expenditure of gas would not exceed half the above quantity. It rarely happens that nine fires are required at once, as two pans boil very well when set together over one stove. In this way, you will see that the economy is as decided as the advantages in point of convenience and cleanliness. — *J. R. Edinburgh, March* 5. 1834.

Aberdeenshire Cottages. — We are far behind in cottage architecture in this part of the world; but even here your *Encyclopædia of Architecture* is beginning to work. — *T. Y. Vale of Alford, Feb.* 22. 1834.

Dumfriesshire. — The palace of Drumlanrig, which occupies one of the most striking sites in the south of Scotland, is now undergoing a thorough repair, under the direction of the celebrated Edinburgh architect, Mr. Burns. One of the handsomest gardener's houses in Scotland, in the cottage Gothic style, has lately been completed in the gardens, from designs by this gentleman. We regret to say, that, when we saw Drumlanrig, in 1831, the approach and other features in the park were altogether unworthy of such a place, and of a proprietor of so much wealth and influence as the Duke of Buccleugh.

Ross-shire. — Your *Enc. of Arch.* is invaluable in this part of the country; and various proprietors as well as myself have built specimen cottages after your models, though your improved watercloset and cesspools are what we do not here understand. — *F. A. M. Cowan, by Dingwall, April* 20. 1833.

Stirlingshire. — The observations which, you say, your correspondent, Mr. C. has made, respecting the effects which have been produced by the *Encyc. of Architecture* in Perthshire, are, I have no doubt, quite correct: I see many such symptoms here of your labours having fructified. I was lately at the Stirling cattle show, and I observed along the road, that, wherever there was a new cottage or villa in progress, something had been borrowed from your stores. — *J. R. Edinburgh, Oct.* 30. 1833.

IRELAND.

We have noticed in the *Gardener's Magazine*, vol. x. p. 62., some of the favourable reports which we have received of the influence of our *Encyclopædia of Architecture* in Ireland; which we can easily credit, considering the number of copies which, our publishers inform us, have been sent to that country. Notwithstanding disturbances which prevail in many parts of Ireland, the country is, on the whole, steadily improving. We trust to our excellent correspondent, Mr. Mallet, for notices of what is going forward, in Dublin, in those departments which concern this Magazine.

Dublin, March 10. 1834. — I have very little architectural news to send you from this place. Your friend Mr. Mallet is, I believe, very busily engaged in making experiments on bricks, stones, &c., relative to their cohesive power before and after calcination. He has also erected three of the largest water wheels in the British dominions. They are all above 50 ft. in diameter, and are connected with an immense train of mining machinery. He is now, I believe, about to erect an enormous windmill, with a tower 120 ft. high, and sails 100 ft. in diameter, for the purpose of crushing and preparing copper ore. — *T. T.*

Art. IV. *Retrospective Criticism.*

THE *Architectural Magazine* has disappointed me in not containing any thing respecting bridges, locks, docks, or those branches of architecture pertaining to canals, bridges, railways, &c., which have, for a number of years, gone under the name of engineering. If you do introduce articles on these subjects, I entreat of you never, in them, or in any other, give any calculations exclusively algebraic. If you do introduce formulæ of this description, let me recommend you, in all cases, to translate them into decimal arithmetic; for this has always to be done by the architect, or engineer, before the subject can be understood by practical men. — *An Architect. Sheffield, March* 4. 1834. Our correspondent has anticipated our views on this subject: we intend to translate all passages that we may introduce in foreign languages, as in the *Gard. Mag.,* and *Mag. Nat. Hist.,* and to explain all terms, technical or algebraic, as in the *Encyc. of Arch.* — *Cond.*

Biography of Architects. — There is one subject, which is not noticed in your prospectus, which, I think, would occasionally form a most appropriate and valuable portion of the Magazine; namely, the biography of eminent architects, &c., in all ages: nothing, I should think, would be more likely to excite that emulation, in ardent breasts, which is the sure forerunner of excellence. If I wanted to excite architectural enthusiasm in a man utterly alien to it, I conceive it could not be done more powerfully than by bringing him into St. Paul's, and pointing out to him, on the screen of the chancel — " Subtus conditur hujus ecclesiæ et urbis conditor, *Ch. Wren*, qui vixit annos ultra nonaginta non sibi sed bono publico. Lector, si monumentum quæris, circumspice."* I know not whether I have quoted right or not, for I quote from memory alone. — *R. M. Capel Street, Dublin, March* 5. 1834.

Position of the Dining-room. — Sir, I have observed that in several of the plans for farm-houses, and small villas, in your *Encyc. of Cott. Arch.,* the dining-room is farther from the kitchen than the drawing-room. This is very badly contrived; for both comfort and convenience dictate exactly the opposite arrangement. — *T. W. Jan.* 1833.

Sideboards or Shelves of Marble or Slate, I can tell, from my own experience, are very fatal to glass ware; as, from the habit of setting down glasses with a certain degree of force on a wooden table, many are broken in doing so on a stone one, till servants get accustomed to setting down glasses in a more gentle manner, as the waiters do in the coffee-houses of France and Italy. — *R. S. Edinburgh, March* 5. 1834.

Roller Blinds, &c. — In your *Encyc. of Cott. Arch.,* when speaking of roller blinds, § 673., you do not mention that the rollers are now usually made octagonal, or at least angular, instead of round. — *T. W. Jan.* 1833.

Buchanan's Gate. (See § 828. *of Encyc. of Cott. Arch.*) — A field gate only 7 ft. 4 in. wide! I wish the inventor of it would teach Yorkshire carters how to drive. A gate 10 ft. wide is too narrow for them. It is a pity, as this gate is a very pretty one. — *T. W. Banks, near Barnsley, Yorkshire, Jan.* 10. 1833.

Art. V. *Queries and Answers.*

THE *Greek Cross.* — In § 696. of the *Encyc. of Cott. Arch.,* a Greek cross is mentioned: what is the difference between this and a common or Latin cross? — *W. T. March* 16. 1834.

A Greek cross is one in which the limbs are of equal lengths, and at right

---

* Underneath lies the architect of this church and city, *Christopher Wren;* who lived upwards of ninety years, not for himself but for the public good. Reader, if you seek his monument, look around.

angles; a Latin cross has the upright limb much longer than the transverse one; and a St. Andrew's cross resembles the letter X. — *J. W. L.*

Patent Lever Flooring Cramp. — Can you, or any of your readers, give me a description of this instrument? I saw it a few years back in the National Repository, and thought it seemed a very useful invention. — *T. W. Barnsley, Yorkshire.*

Ash-pans and Hearths. — Would it not be a good plan to have ash-pans, or the part of the hearth under the grate, slope backwards, so as to throw the ashes as far back as possible? Tredgold recommends some things of the kind in his treatise *On Warming and Ventilating, &c.* — *Id.*

Towel Stands. — Might not a towel stand be fixed on the top of the washing-stand, in the same manner as a rail is often affixed to sideboards? Where room is wanted, it would take up no additional space, and would protect the wall or paper. — *Id.*

A Gothic Arch, of great Antiquity and Curiosity, is said to have been discovered, in the crypt of the cathedral at Armagh, by that eminent Gothic architect, Mr. Cottingham. Has any account of it been published, and where? Will you oblige your readers by a notice of it? A general impression rests on my mind that the cathedral at Armagh was either rebuilt or repaired by the father of the learned Mr. Ensor, now a resident in the neighbourhood of that city; but perhaps I am mistaken. I should be glad if some of your correspondents would set me right. — *Investigator. Glasgow, March*, 1834.

We have applied to Mr. Cottingham respecting the arch at Armagh, and hope to be able to give some account of it in our next Number. — *Cond.*

Street Architecture. — Which is in best taste, the mode of treating street houses singly, as in Oxford Street, or collectively, in elevations embracing several fronts, as in Regent Street? I recommend this subject, as a most important one, for discussion in your Magazine. — *B. London, March*, 1834.

Art. VI. *Obituary.*

DIED, lately, at Milan, the *Marquis of Cagnola*, a celebrated architect in that city. To this distinguished artist we owe, unquestionably, the most remarkable architectural monument of the present age. We allude to the triumphal arch which, at the end of the road over the Simplon, forms the entrance to the town of Milan. This arch, admirably adapted from the antique, is, from the elegance of its proportions, the purity of its form, the merit of its execution, and the richness of its materials, far superior to any thing else which we possess of the same kind. Destined by Napoleon to serve as a memorial of his triumphs in Italy, it has, of course, changed its object since Milan has been under the Austrian government. Its execution was, indeed, long delayed; but its author had the pleasure of living long enough to see it finished, and to know that he left behind an admirable work to bear witness of his architectural skill.

The following anecdote will show the enthusiasm which the Marquis of Cagnola felt for his art. Some years ago he came by inheritance into the possession of a very considerable fortune; and, satisfied with the competence which he had obtained by his profession, he devoted the whole of the fortune to which he had then succeeded to the construction of a villa, of which he had conceived the project many years before. In this villa he has endeavoured to realise all that luxury and good taste could imagine of perfection for such a species of residence. This work, which offered a wide scope to his imagination, occupied him so completely, that there is reason to fear it shortened his life.

Independently of the fortune that the Marquis of Cagnola acquired by his professional labours, he obtained several titles and dignities. He was made chamberlain of the Emperor of Austria, and Chevalier of the Iron Crown. (*La Propriété*, vol. ii. p. 138.)

THE
ARCHITECTURAL MAGAZINE.

MAY, 1834.

ORIGINAL COMMUNICATIONS.

ART. I. *On the Causes of the different Kinds and Degrees of Taste which different Persons possess in Architecture.* By the CONDUCTOR.

HAVING pointed out (p. 49.) what we consider to be the means of forming a just and correct taste in architecture, we shall now endeavour to show the causes of the different kinds and degrees of taste which different persons have in that art.

We have stated that, architecture being chiefly an art of reason, all persons of common sense may acquire a just and a correct taste in it; but as architecture is also, to a certain extent, an art of feeling and imagination, a perfect taste in it must not only be just and correct, but delicate, intense, and refined. Delicacy and intensity depend principally upon organisation; and refinement, conjointly on organisation and intellectual cultivation. We shall first offer a few remarks on each of these qualities as far as they relate to taste; and next point out some of the causes which operate on individuals so as to prevent the taste of any one from attaining that perfection which ought to be the *beau idéal* of all our endeavours.

A delicate taste, it will be evident to every one, must depend on the delicacy of the organisation of the individual; it cannot, therefore, be communicated by instruction, except in a very limited degree. It is very difficult for a person, who is without delicacy of taste in any art, to conceive what it is, and in what manner it operates on any individual. Some idea, however, may be formed by every one for himself, by reflecting on the difference between common feeling, in any matter where the passions or affections are concerned, and what is called delicate feeling. The difference between an ordinary taste for architecture and a delicate taste, is not less great than between common and delicate feelings in ordinary life. A delicate taste in architecture will be sensibly affected by objects and details which would pass unnoticed by those who had merely a general taste, or even a taste just and accurate. To recur to the example we formerly gave of a Corinthian portico: a man of just taste would approve of it as a whole, and, if his taste were also correct, he would examine and approve or disapprove of the details; while a man who to a just and correct taste adds a delicate one, would be sensibly affected by the mass of deep shade produced by the projection of the portico from the body of the building; the soft gradations of shadow on the dark side of each particular column; the lights softening into these shades on their light sides; the contrasted forms of the mouldings in the cornices; and the harmonious blending of light and shade among the foliage and other ornaments of the capital. Delicate taste is affected in this way, merely from the impressions made upon its organisation by the forms presented to it, without reference to the historical associations, either general or individual, which are, or may be, connected with a Grecian portico; but, when these are taken into consideration, there are a thousand ideas that will arise in the mind of the spectator of delicate taste, that would not occur either to the general observer, or to the observer possessing a taste in architecture merely just and correct.

The intensity of taste, like the intensity of passion of any kind, depends also on the organisation of the individual. Passions and affections, every one knows, may be strong, without being delicate: and their strength will be found to depend chiefly on the strength of the organisation, or, in some cases, perhaps, upon the excitability of the nervous system. At all events, no one will deny that neither delicacy nor intensity of feeling can be communicated by instruction; though these feelings, like all others, may be so far taught as to be simulated by those by whom they are unfelt. Intensity of feeling, in the common matters of life, is indicated by the party being so enraptured with some one single quality in an object, as to overlook all the others; or with the general impression, so as to overlook the beauties or faults of the details. In architecture, intensity of taste is evinced by the rapturous admiration of a building, for the display of some particular quality which characterises it: say, for example, its grandeur: and this rapture is, perhaps, carried to such an extent, as to prevent the party from seeing faults that would be obvious to a taste which did not possess intensity, or which, to intensity, added a certain degree of delicacy and correctness. Intensity of feeling with respect to any art, when the party possessing it is willing to submit to intellectual cultivation, may generally be considered as the prototype of excellence; but, on the other hand, when this intensity of feeling is so great as to overpower the judgment, and when the will of the party is too weak to submit to that degree of intellectual cultivation which would bring it under due control, it becomes a positive defect in taste.

A refined taste is one which is naturally either delicate or intense: and which has been purified and corrected by the exercise of reason and reflection. There can hardly be such a thing as a naturally refined taste; because the very idea of refinement implies the exercise of cultivation; or, in other words, the power of controlling and adjusting feelings and sentiments, by a consideration of all the various circumstances to which they are related. In general, it may be stated that no first feeling is to be depended upon, until it has been tested by an appeal to the reasoning faculties. First tastes, first passions, and first feelings of every kind, whether they are delicate or intense, are always more or less indiscriminate. A young enthusiastic architect is in raptures with whatever comes before him. He gives way to the excitement of his feelings, because these are keenly alive to impressions; while his reasoning powers are, in a great measure, dormant, from his being deficient in a knowledge of those principles of architecture by which alone the reason, as it relates to that art, can be exercised. There is always, however, hope for enthusiasm; as it is seldom found unconnected with considerable powers of mind. Wherever we find a delicate taste, therefore, or even an intense one, however crude it may be at first, if the party be endowed with common sense, and willing to improve, it may be rendered a refined one.

A perfect taste, it thus appears, includes a just taste, which is one founded on reason; a correct taste, founded on rules; a delicate taste, founded on a delicate organisation; an intense taste, founded on powerful passions or affections; and a refined taste, founded on intellectual cultivation superadded to delicacy or intensity of feeling. No one person can have any taste in architecture, whose taste may not be classed under one or other of these heads; and no one can have a taste approximating to perfection, in which all these qualities are not united in a greater or less degree. The union of these qualities in the same mind may be considered as the *beau idéal* to which the artist and the critic ought to aspire; but which, from the conditions inseparable from human nature, he can never absolutely attain.

The principal circumstances which prevent individuals from attaining a perfect taste in architecture may be included under the heads of locality, education, public opinion, fashion, and received prejudices.

The influence of *locality* on a taste for architecture is much greater than might be at first sight imagined. If we suppose an individual with a taste just, correct, delicate, intense, and refined, living in a country where any particular style of architecture prevailed, we must perceive that he would hardly be able to avoid certain prejudices in favour of that architecture. For example, if he lived in a country where almost all the churches and cathedrals were in the Gothic style, as in England, he could hardly avoid entertaining an opinion that that style is particularly adapted to churches and cathedrals; and if he went to Italy, or to Russia, where he would find ecclesiastical buildings everywhere built in the Grecian or Roman manner, he would consider them gloomy and unsuitable. In like manner, a man of architectural taste, living in a country where the houses have flat roofs, or roofs of very low pitch, as in the higher class of dwelling-houses in Italy and England, could, if he were travelling through a country where all the houses were high-roofed, as in the greater part of Germany, hardly avoid disliking them, from his prejudice in favour of low roofs. The Italian artist who was the biographer of Winkelmann relates that he, though a German, after residing many years in Rome occupied solely with the study of the fine arts, became so prejudiced in favour of flat roofs, that, when passing through Switzerland, on his road to his native country, he could not be reconciled to the high roofs of the cottages, though he was told that they were necessary to prevent the snow, when melting, from penetrating the roof. Now Winkelmann appears to have been a man, notwithstanding his prejudices, whose taste was both intense and refined, though it was far from being just, as may be learned from the following passage:—

"From Verona, we proceeded to the Tyrolean Alps. When we reached the first defile of the mountains, I observed that Winkelmann suddenly changed countenance: he then said to me, in a pathetic tone, 'See, my friend, what a horrible country; what terrible heights!' A short time afterwards, when we had entered on the German territory, he cried out, 'What poor architecture! Look at those roofs, how steep they are!' This he said with so much vehemence, as strongly to express the disgust with which these objects had inspired him. At first I thought he was jesting, but when I found that he was in earnest, I replied, that the height of the mountains had a grandeur which charmed me; and that, as to the steepness of the roofs of the houses, this ought rather to shock me, who was an Italian, than him, who was a German. 'Besides,' continued I, 'we must judge of all things relatively; in a country subject to heavy falls of snow, these high steep roofs are indispensable.'" (*Vie de Winkelmann,* p. cxxviii.)

We see, by this example, that the great in art and taste, as well as the great in wealth and worldly influence, are not more exempt from prejudices than the little. We consider it of importance to be aware of this; because the prejudices of those who are looked up to with respect are apt to mislead men who cannot, like Winkelmann's Italian friend, exercise their reason.

It is easy to conceive the influence which the prevalence of any particular style in any given locality will have on architectural taste, however good it may be in other respects; and the same may be said, not only of the style of design, but of the manner of construction, and the materials of execution. A person with a just taste in architecture, living in a country where stone was chiefly used for walls, would not be at first reconciled to walls of brick, but would be obliged to control his feelings by his reason. Where thatch is the material with which cottages are generally covered, it is difficult to avoid considering slates and tiles as cold and unsuitable for cottage roofs. Many more instances might be given; but enough, we trust, has been said, to show the unavoidable influence of locality in modifying more or less the taste of individuals.

The influence which *education* may have in giving a bias to architectural taste is so obvious, as hardly to require illustration. An amateur who has had a classical education will prefer the classical architecture of the Greeks and Romans to the Gothic style of the middle ages; a young architect who has been chiefly taught the details of the Grecian style can hardly avoid preferring that style to every other; one who has been taught to consider the Doric as the most perfect of the Grecian orders will have acquired a prejudice in favour of all buildings where that order is made use of; and so of all other styles or orders, or variations of them. As travelling may be considered a part of education, the architect of just taste, who has spent hours in exploring the architecture of caves in Egypt and India, or of tents in China, will look upon Egyptian and Chinese architecture with more favour, than the man, also of just taste, who has viewed them only through the medium of books.

That *public opinion*, or the prevailing taste of a country, has a considerable influence in biassing our taste, the opposition which is made by the public to innovations of every kind is a sufficient proof. At the present time, in England, the pointed style of architecture is approved every where, and by every body; but, during the time of Charles II., when Roman architecture was universally admired, the pointed style was as universally censured and despised, both by architects and amateurs. Thus, in architecture, as in every thing else, the influence of *fashion* is continually operating; and not only has public opinion, or the fashion of a whole country, great influence, but even the opinion or fashion of eminent individuals in that country. Thus, almost all pupils of architects have their taste more or less influenced by that of their master; and all courtiers by that of their sovereign. Every one knows that these things happen in all ordinary matters; and a very little reflection must convince them that they will happen also in matters of taste.

The received prejudices of a people or a country, with respect to the application of particular forms of architecture to particular uses, have a strong influence on the taste. There seems to be no insuperable reason why a spire should not be made an ornament to a gentleman's house in the country; and in many situations, it might be of considerable utility in pointing out the house at a great distance, or in forming the leading feature of a group, containing the different buildings which compose the dwelling-house and offices of a large mansion in the midst of an extensive demesne; but this form, being generally employed in churches, is in some degree considered sacred, and consequently its employment in villas would be too great a shock to our received prejudices. A Christian church built in the Chinese style, every one must feel, would prove offensive.

In this manner we might pursue the subject of what writers on taste call accidental associations, to show how extremely difficult, or rather how impossible, it is, for any individual to have a perfect taste; and, at the same time, to show how numerous the chances are against any two persons thinking, in matters of taste, exactly alike. Independently of the difference in the organisation of individuals, there are, as we have seen, so many other causes operating upon them in different degrees, that it is hardly possible to conceive two individuals, even if they are of similar organisation and education, similarly operated upon by external circumstances. Hence, whenever we find two persons agreeing in taste, we may generally conclude, either that the taste of the one has been formed on that of the other; or, that the one gives way to the other, whenever their sentiments are different.

Every one's taste, therefore, is the natural and unavoidable result of all the different circumstances in which he has been placed; and hence he can no more alter it, on being desired to do so, than he can change any other opinion he has formed on any subject, without tracing back the steps which led to his forming it. Hence, the necessity of charity, or mutual forbearance, in all matters of taste; and the propriety, when we state our approval or disapprobation of any object of taste, of giving the reasons on which our opinion is founded.

In arriving at this conclusion, one object which we have in view is, to suggest what we think ought to be the proper language of criticism in matters of architectural taste. In the first place, the terms good and bad taste, in an absolute sense, should seldom, if ever, be employed: since they must always be either good or bad, relatively to circumstances more or less limited. We would therefore qualify the term good, when so used, by adding another term expressive of the circumstances relatively to which it was considered good: such as, a good taste in Gothic architecture or in the Elizabethan style: or a good or bad taste in street buildings or in villas. We would prefer, however, substituting, for the term good, some term expressive of the kind of goodness: such as, a just taste in architecture generally; a correct taste in the Grecian style; a refined taste in the Tudor Gothic; a cultivated taste in Italian architecture, &c. In like manner, instead of the term bad taste, we would employ such expressions as servile taste, incorrect taste, crude taste, &c.; and, when speaking of a taste without reference to its being either good or bad, we would use such epithets as, taste of a particular age, master, or style, &c. In this way, when speaking either of the taste or judgment of an architect, or of the expression or construction of a building, we may always employ terms which shall be characteristic of the excellences or defects of the artist or object criticised; and not merely, like the terms good and bad, words conveying no other idea to our readers or hearers, than that of our approbation or dislike.

Since the taste of no individual can be perfect, and since no two individuals are likely to agree in every respect in any matters of taste, what, it may be asked, are the comparative values of a just, a correct, a delicate, an intense, and a refined taste, supposing each to be equally free from accidental influences? Our answer is, that a just or reasoning taste is decidedly the best; since a greater number of persons are likely to understand arguments founded on reason and utility, than to agree in sentiment, or to possess the same degree of imagination.

ART. II. *On the comparative Value of Simplicity in Architecture.* By E. TROTMAN, Esq., Architect.

THERE are few operations of the mind more subtle and more fallacious, than is that by which we are led to regard as identical the properties and attributes of objects that are frequently presented to our notice in close association, while they remain essentially distinct from and independent of each other. We need not wander, in search of illustrations to this remark, beyond the field which our present subject opens before us. The common recurrence of such descriptive phrases as "simply beautiful," "dignified simplicity," "graceful and chaste simplicity," has unquestionably done much to create in many minds an opinion that simplicity is one with chastity and grace, with dignity and beauty. Nor is it matter of surprise, that, in an age like the present, when all are critics, and all seekers after novelty, we should find many who, from an aversion to the extravagances of a depraved taste, adopt the opposite extreme, and, affecting a false refinement, assert the supreme importance of simplicity, be it only for the paradox which the opinion offers to vulgar minds. This opinion has, indeed, received such support, that some writers have given to simplicity the very highest place among the requisites for architectural composition; making it no less essential to the mass, than is harmony to the proportions, or beauty to the details. If, then, such distinction be claimed for this quality in art, it cannot be considered unimportant to examine the validity of such claims, as far as supported by the nature, tendency, and exemplifications of the principle of its observance. This is, indeed, the more necessary, as the principle cannot be said spontaneously to commend itself to the feelings; and therefore, in order to be maintained at all, requires the stronger support of the judgment. It may, perhaps, be fairly questioned at the outset, whether that can be an absolute rule of taste, which approves itself so imperfectly to our natural perceptions: those perceptions which are not inapt in determining upon the existence of the harmony of fitness, and the beauty of ornament: but, without insisting upon this doubt, we may examine the nature of the quality in question under some of its more ordinary applications, and perceive how far it is usually productive of the results attributed to it.

Assuming that simplicity in any work of art consists in the fewness of its component parts, and assuming also that it is the object of art to gratify the imaginative faculties of the mind without offending the judgment, we may, on asking whether such limitation of component parts is calculated to satisfy the demands of the imagination, safely anticipate an answer in the negative. If, too, simplicity be all-important to works of taste in one department, what shall exclude its authority from those in another, the gratification to be attained being derived from the same sources? Is it by rendering the parts of their machinery as few as possible, that the epic poet, the dramatist, the legendary historian, produce their most gratifying illusions? And if one or two able pens of our own times have (though not uniformly) made simplicity the garb of much beauty, has not the easy assumption of the dress tempted their many imitators to conjure up only impersonations of the ridiculous? Were, indeed, the objects of taste and of the fine arts the same with those of the useful and commercial arts, simplicity would be of paramount importance; as, in the latter, the economy of labour demands the employment of the least complex apparatus for the attainment of a given result; in the former case, however, the self-imposed toil of the imagination is its own reward; its real weariness arising from that monotony which it is the ultimate tendency of simplicity to produce.

Much of that which has been urged by many in praise of this quality arises, as we hinted at the commencement, from their having confounded it with other coexistent features in nature and in art. That the simple and the grand frequently stand combined is unquestionable; yet it is equally true that our impressions, in such cases, are produced alone by the grand; and that the grand is the result of size, which becomes effective just in proportion as the form of the beholder is, by comparison with itself, reduced to insignificance. From what other cause arises the majesty of the ocean, or of the Alpine heights, which, as illustrations from nature of abstract simplicity, do not excel the pond or the hillock? It is true that what would interfere with the simplicity of these objects would interfere likewise with their grandeur: but for this reason, that, by interrupting the effect of continuity, it would destroy also the impression of size. And if simplicity is not to be confounded with dimension, neither is it to be mistaken for grace. How both may be united in the productions of the chisel is known to every one who has seen the Elgin Marbles; but that grace is no inseparable companion to simplicity, is equally obvious to all who have paid any attention to remaining examples of Egyptian sculpture. Were we to pursue the examination of this characteristic in its varied connection with the tastes and refinements of life, it would not be difficult to show to how great an extent it has been mistaken for other and higher qualities. What is more common, for instance, than for the simplicity of a musical air to be considered identical with its sentiment and expression? Yet it cannot be denied that Handel himself has left examples of the manner in which simplicity may be made ridiculous, had we not the daily testimony of our ears to the fact. Nor, in the labours of learning, are the nature, the beauty, the sublimity, of such literary remains of past days as the English Bible and Prayer Book to be confounded with the circumstance of their simplicity of style; matters quite as distinct from each other as, in the history of character, are the oft-sung joys of rustic life from mere clownish ignorance, or the innocence of childhood from the emptiness of the idiot. It may be objected, that in thus viewing simplicity as at once non-essential and liable to excess, we are not doing justice to its claims; and that any quality in art or science may be rendered ridiculous by being overstrained in application. This remark, however, is only true as it regards qualities or excellences that are comparative: it is not correct as to those which are absolute. Absolute excellences can never be carried to an extreme. No work of art was ever too grand, too graceful, too harmonious; since grandeur, grace, and harmony are designations of absolute excellence. While, again, that some works may be too complex and too ornamental is no less certain than that others may be too simple or too poor: these terms being expressive of the extremes of qualities of comparative excellence, those of variety and ornament. The very circumstance, therefore, that simplicity is a quality comparative and indefinite, manifestly invalidates its claim to the place of an essential and absolute excellence in architecture, and in art generally. If any pretension whatever could be sustained for its authority as an absolute principle, it must be by its reduction to its primary elements. Thus received, and applied to architecture, it would render the sphere the most beautiful of all figures; the pyramid of three sides the next in merit; the ordinary pyramid, of four sides, the next; after which would come the cube of six equal sides, followed, at an uncertain interval, by the cube of the parallelogram. How little this scale of classification accords with the principles of taste developed in architecture, ancient or modern, we shall be at no loss to determine: at one glance anticipating the monotonous absurdity that would usurp the place of art, were we to consult such a scheme of approximation in the pursuit of beauty.

While, however, we deny to simplicity the character of an absolute and essential excellence in architecture, let us not by any means be supposed to assert that it is the reverse of an excellence. The truth is, as before stated, that simplicity is a quality of comparative and uncertain value; to be regarded in a negative light as standing alone, but assuming a different degree of importance as associated with varieties of circumstance: a cipher, which gives and receives significancy as attached to integral terms of admitted import. Thus when simplicity, as a relative, subserves the ends of harmony as an absolute principle, its efficiency is not to be questioned. This it does by a regard to locality, association, and significancy. The round tower that frowns from the wild rock, and the long line of massive columns, occupying, like hoary earth-born giants of a forgotten age, the Egyptian plain, are objects imposing in their simplicity; but transfer the tower in imagination to the level lawn, and the Egyptian temple to some gently varied and wooded vale, and, interesting as they would continue to be for majestic antiquity, their simplicity would cease to charm for want of the harmony of situation and accompaniment. Nor, on the ground of significancy and appropriation, will the simplicity that befits the dwelling of the citizen admit of its being magnified into the characteristic of an abode for the prince, any more than the plainness of the portico where the Stoic anciently discoursed would have been appropriate to the scenes in which modern Rome displays her religious pomps. Thus, again, simplicity is valuable where it promotes a desired expression of strength, as in the architecture of quays, prisons, &c. It is obvious, however, that this reason for its adoption ceases when the character of firmness is less requisite than that of elegance.

On the whole, we are inclined to think that the praise which has been lavished by many on the principle of simplicity in architecture, has had its origin in a twofold error, both negative and positive. On the one hand, its advocates have not considered the ultimate tendency of their position when carried out to its legitimate results; inasmuch as to make the approach to beauty identical with the approximation to simplicity is a rule which terminates in a *reductio ad absurdum*, constituting that most beautiful which is most blank. On the other hand, again, the positive error consists in their having mistaken for this principle of simplicity, another, which not unfrequently, indeed, developes itself under the same aspect; the fundamental and all-important principle of UNITY. We should find no difficulty in proving that all the excellences which are supposed educible from the former belong inseparably to the latter; while the latter disposes of unnumbered difficulties which beset the former. As to the principle of unity, it is necessary to premise, that it has, architecturally, a twofold reference; regarding, on the one hand, form and distribution, and, on the other, expression of style and purpose: the first embracing the symmetrical, the second the picturesque. Whatever praise such examples of Grecian art as the Parthenon and Theseum may have received on the ground of simplicity, it is rather for the merit of unity of form that we consider them admirable; and, though in our modern cruciform churches in the pointed style, that unity of form is not so entirely acknowledged by the eye, the unity of expression and of character is generally more than enough to satisfy the demands of taste. Again: we should scarcely select King's College Chapel, at Cambridge, as a model of simplicity; while, as an example of the supreme beauty of unity, apart from the subject of detail, it stands forth among human works in glorious preeminence. What the advocates for strict simplicity and Greek imitations may think of the merits of such piles as Salisbury cathedral, and the royal residence at Windsor, to say nothing of collegiate edifices, we know not: it is enough to know that there are those (few though they be) who talk of the impressive and the beautiful, and who can yet deny that any but works after classic models deserve the title of architecture. With respect to the last-named structures, however, we think it undeniable that they exhibit little of simplicity, with much of unity of expression; and in which of these qualities, therefore, the command of emotion principally resides, we leave to the feelings of all, who have any, to determine.

It may, perhaps, be objected, that the more closely we follow the dictates of simplicity, the more likely shall we be to render the productions of art intelligible, and their images susceptible of being at once apprehended by the eye, and permanently retained by the memory. All these advantages, however, must necessarily be insured by a regard to the principles of unity. Superfluous and irregular members of design are as much opposed to unity as to the simple and the intelligible; and whether the degree of subdivision and of ornament be greater or less, a structure characterised by unity cannot fail to leave upon the attentive mind an impression at least as distinct as would attend the inspection of a work of extreme simplicity. It may, indeed, well admit of a doubt, whether the highest pleasures which architecture is calculated to produce are those attendant on an immediate comprehension of a given subject, since, as a science for the eye and the imagination, as well as the judgment, it is its province amply to provide for the researches of curiosity. Under all circumstances, however, be the character of composition simple or elaborate, unity demands its place as the crowning excellence. We the rather insist upon this, as opposed to the boasted claims of simplicity, from a conviction that, in elevating secondary or indeterminate subjects to the rank and authority of essentials, we are inflicting injury on art, impeding our own progress, and encouraging the suspicions of those who stigmatise modern practitioners with a want of inventive power.   E. T.

10. *Furnival's Inn, April* 14. 1834.

ART. III. *The Elements of Grecian and Roman Architecture, practically explained to the General Reader.* By Mr. J. ROBERTSON.

THE *Encyclopædia of Architecture*, I have reason to believe, has created a taste for the study of that science in many individuals, especially ladies, who had no previous wish to exercise their minds on the subject. To such, therefore, a short and simple explanation of the elements of Classical Architecture may be acceptable.

What is generally understood by the term Classical Architecture is, the architecture of the Greeks and Romans. By some, this architecture is considered to be founded on the stone edifices of the Egyptians; and, by others, on the simple form of a rectangular wooden hut. Whatever may be the real origin, all agree in arranging this description of architecture in different divisions, called Orders. Of these, the Greeks invented three, the Doric, the Ionic, and the Corinthian; to which the Romans added the Tuscan and the Composite. These orders are characterised by certain arbitrary forms and proportions of columns, intended to express strength, elegance, or richness, as these qualities may be required in a building.

The characteristics of an order of Classical Architecture are, however, not necessarily confined to the column and its appendages, but extend their influence more or less to every part of a superstructure; and, although the first and chief object to be attended to, in any erection, is its fitness for the use it is intended to serve; yet, when the decorative part of the art is to be conjoined with the useful, a want of a knowledge of the orders, and their characteristics and proportions, is equally reprehensible with a too servile adherence to their details as exemplified by precedents. Architecture is not merely the art of building, for this may be exercised in the most rude state of society; but it is also the art of constructing in accordance with certain principles and rules, which reason and experience have sanctioned, as being capable of producing the most pleasing forms and proportions to satisfy at once the eye and the judgment.

Of the Orders in general. — The Five Orders of Classical Architecture are composed of certain elementary forms, few in number and simple in their nature, but which are nevertheless the essential parts of every classical architectural composition. These forms have two distinct divisions, which may be termed the principal and the subservient parts. The former consists of such parts as were essential in the construction of the wooden hut, which, according to Vitruvius, was the type of Classical Architecture. Thus, the shaft of the column, and the abacus of the capital, are said to be imitations of the trunks of trees with flat stones laid on their tops, on which the tie-beams of wood rested that supported the stratum of materials composing the roof; the plinth of the base is derived from the stones on which these trunks of trees rested. In like manner, the ends of the beams which supported the roof gave rise to the triglyphs in the frieze of the Doric order; the modillions, mutules, &c., arose from the ends of the rafters of the roof, which were seen resting on the beams; and the thickness of materials which covered the roof is represented by the corona, the predominant member of the cornice. These principal forms will be noticed more fully when describing the respective orders; and in the meantime we may add, that, although they were at first very simple and rude in their construction, the ingenuity of succeeding architects improved upon them, and highly enriched them by the assistance of the subordinate forms. These subordinate forms, which are called mouldings, have been devised in order to ornament the principal parts; and also to support, strengthen, protect, and unite them, as well as to regulate their distribution.

The mouldings in general use are eight in number.

The first and simplest is the *fillet*, a square list (*fig.* 41.) which is the smallest member in proportion to the others. Its use is to separate superior members, and to prevent the unharmonious effect that two mouldings composed of portions of circles or ellipses would occasion, when joined together.

The *astragal* (*fig.* 42.) is used as a bead or fillet with a rounded edge, in various compositions, and it is frequently ornamented as at *a*. It is chiefly employed in the orders, conjoined with a fillet, in dividing the capital from the shaft of a column;

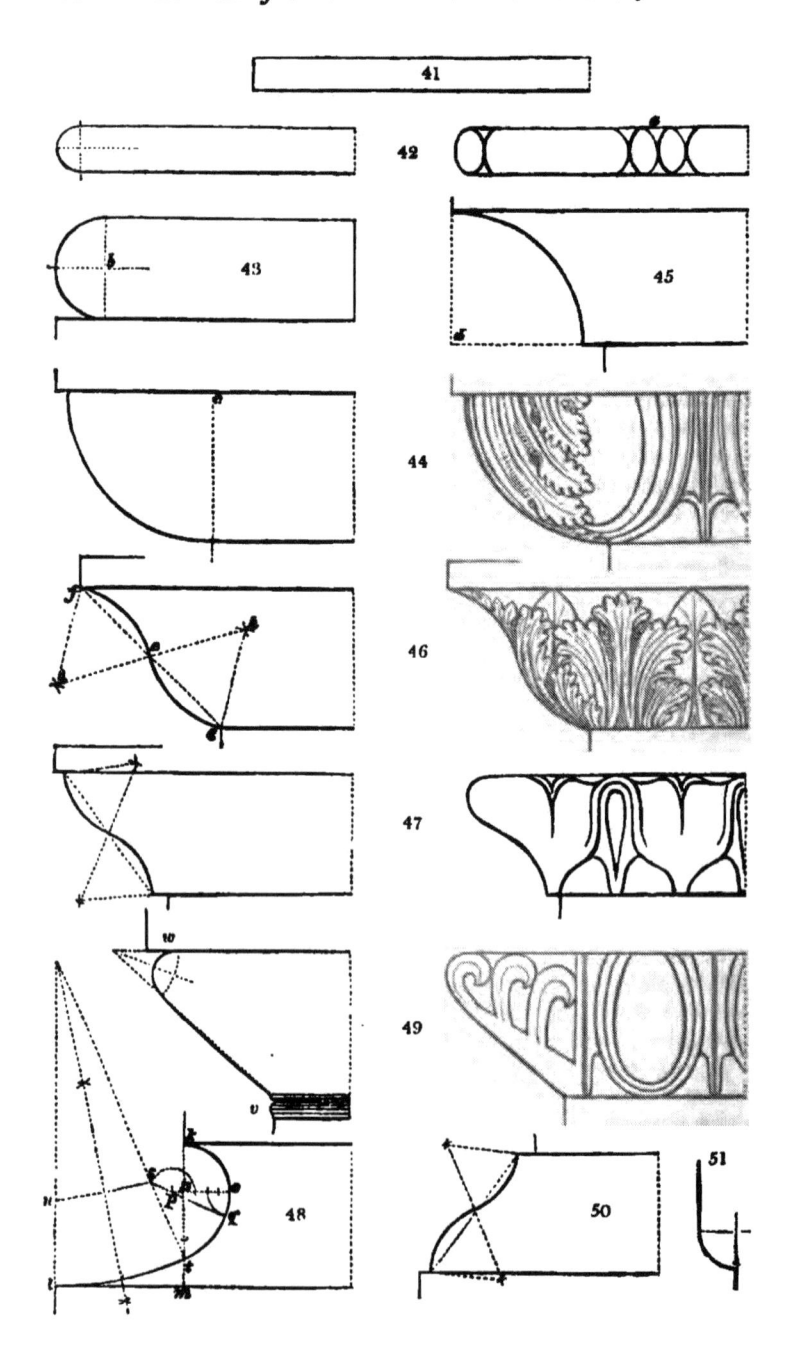

110　*Elements of Grecian and Roman Architecture,*

and it is drawn by making the profile, or rounded edge, the segment of a circle.

The *torus* (*fig.* 43.) is like the astragal, but of much larger proportion; and, from its rope-like appearance, it seems to bind and strengthen the parts where it is used. Its profile is the segment of a circle described from the centre b, which segment projects exactly to a line with the vertical face of the plinth on which the torus rests.

The *ovolo*, or quarter round (*fig.* 44.), is described from the centre c. This moulding, from being strong at the extreme parts, is chiefly employed to support other mouldings and members.

The *cavetto* (*fig.* 45.) is described from the centre d. It is generally employed in covering and sheltering other members and mouldings, as it is weak in the extreme part, which terminates in a point.

The *cyma recta*, or cymatrum (*fig.* 46.), is, from its contour, well adapted for covering other mouldings. It is described in the following manner:— When the projections are ascertained, by a scale to be hereafter described, draw the line fg, and divide it into two equal parts, as at e, which parts will form bases to two equilateral triangles; when their summits, h and i, will be centres from which to describe the two arcs that join at e, and form the cymatrum.

The *cyma talon*, or ogee (*fig.* 47.), is drawn much in the same manner as the cyma recta. It is well calculated for giving support, being strong at the extreme parts.

The *scotia* (*fig.* 48.) is employed to strengthen and contrast the effect of other mouldings, and to give a graceful winding to the profile. It is traced in the following manner:— After the points k and l are ascertained, draw the vertical line km, which line must be divided into three equal parts; then from the point n, with the radius nk, describe the arc ko; next divide the line op into five parts, which will of course make four from o to n, and one from n to p; then from p draw the arc oq, and from o describe a segment having for its radius two parts, which will determine the line that passes through the points q and p. From the point of the plinth, at l, raise the perpendicular lr; now, from p describe another arc, having for its radius two parts, this fixes the extremity of the line qs; then from s describe the arc qt, and through the points ts draw the line tr, making lu equal to ts; and from the points su raise a perpendicular line until it intersect at r, which will be the centre from which to describe the rest of the curve from t to l.

There are other mouldings, such as the *echinus* (*fig.* 49.), which is frequently ornamented with the egg and spear, but is employed plain in the capital of the Grecian Doric column, between the annulets, v, and abacus, w; the *cyma reversa* (*fig.* 50.), which is generally used below the eye in forming one of the mouldings in the bases of pedestals, &c.; and the *congee* (*fig.* 51.), on the shaft of columns.

These mouldings, with the exception of the square list, or fillet, are all portions of circles or ellipses: and, while the Greeks preferred the latter, or some other section of the cone, the Romans, in describing the contour of their mouldings, formed them from parts of the circle.

The mouldings of antiquity were frequently enriched, and in modern times this practice has been followed. In such cases, great judgment is required in giving the necessary boldness to ornamented mouldings at a great height, and but a slight indication of those near the eye. From the remains of antiquity left us, we can perceive that the ancient masters were very particular in the representation of natural objects on their mouldings; for, while the leaves which adorned the covering members were flat, like those in nature, the acorns and eggs which enriched the supporting mouldings were almost round, and nearly detached. All ornaments used to enrich mouldings must be carved out of the solid member; because, if they were added to the naked face of such members in relief, they would entirely destroy the proportion and outline of the mouldings on which they were used. The assemblage of the essential parts and mouldings which compose an order is termed a profile. The corona (fig. 10. *e*, in p. 25.) is a square flat member, which predominates in Grecian cornices, to which all the other mouldings appear subservient, and which they seem intended either to support, or to protect from injuries. The bed, or underside, mouldings are those members which occur between the corona and the frieze, and which appear to support the corona; they are common to all the orders. The fascia is the principal member of an architrave; which latter, as before observed, is the lower division of the entablature, and rests on the abacus of the capital of a column: the intention of the abacus is to serve for the better support of the superincumbent weight, by giving breadth to the top of the column.

We stated, in p. 5., that every person who possesses common sense may attain a just and correct taste in architecture; and we now state that every person who can write his name or handle a pencil may become a good architectural draughtsman. We, therefore, strongly recommend all our young readers who wish to derive pleasure from architectural productions, and more especially all young ladies, to copy the whole of the figures in the foregoing article. All that is required for doing so are, a small case of instruments, a black lead-pencil, a T-square, and a small drawing-board: nay, to all those who have, either naturally or by practice, a correct eye for forms, a pen or a pencil alone will be sufficient, without either compasses or ruler. Such a knowledge of the details of any style of architecture, as can only be acquired by drawing them, will add greatly to the enjoyment of looking at buildings where these details occur. There is no understanding any subject without first understanding its language; and there is no mode so effectual in impressing on the mind the language of architecture, as that of delineating the things to which that language applies. We therefore again recommend this practice to all our young readers; and we are certain, from our own experience (having gone through all the details of classical architecture in an architectural school in Edinburgh, in 1801, and never having forgotten them since), that it will be a source of the highest satisfaction through life, whenever classical architecture forms the subject of conversation, or whenever a classical design or building meets the eye, either in books or in reality. In order that those who copy may make the articles copied their own, we recommend them to copy on a considerably enlarged scale; but still, in doing this, there is no occasion for a formal array of colours, brushes, &c.: lines will effect everything in architecture; and the man who can represent all forms by lines, either in pencil or in common ink; who can, in fact, produce drawings in the style of the woodcuts which illustrate this work, is much more independent and possesses a much more useful talent, than he who can do nothing without hair pencils and colours.—*Cond.*

Art. IV. *Remarks on London Street Houses and Shop Fronts.* By R.

Though I have no wish to see measures generally adopted by the directors of a city, that would trench upon the liberties of individuals, yet in many cases it becomes necessary for the public good to do so. The inhabitants of the northern metropolis seem to have been aware of this, when they agreed upon the measure of confining the feuars, or builders, to a certain description of front elevation in the erection of their shops and other street houses. For the New Town of Edinburgh, an architect, under the directions of the Dean of Guild Court, furnishes the street elevations to the builders; and, in whatever way the interior of the houses may be disposed, the exterior must not be altered in any way, not even an inch either in height or width, in the foundation of pillars or windows, from that prescribed, without the special sanction of this court. Hence the uniformity of the streets of Edinburgh, and of the houses in them. These general elevations are for the most part supplied with good taste; the buildings situated at the corners of streets and turnings having an additional story, and in the centre of each line is a large house, with a pediment in front, or some other imposing feature, to harmonise with the additional stories or attics of the extreme houses.

In London, on the contrary, with the exception of some lines of buildings in the Regent's Park, and some of the new streets lately built near the Strand, this practice has been but little followed; and no one, with any pretensions to taste, can walk along the two principal streets in the English metropolis, viz., Regent Street and Oxford Street, without feeling dissatisfied with the irregularity of the buildings; and, indeed, there are not any of the other streets better in this respect. In passing along Oxford Street, we see such a variety of tastes displayed in the erection of the houses (as diversified as the faces of the individuals who inhabit them); such different heights and widths of the buildings: such unequal heights and widths of openings; and such a variety of inconsistent ornaments, of which no human being can trace the origin; and, in short, such masses of inharmonious, heterogeneous combinations, that one is led to think that each successive builder must have been blind to all around him, except his own building, during its erection, inasmuch as it forms no part of a whole with the adjoining structures. Although each building may be uniform in its parts, and form a whole in itself, its want of association with the buildings near it, which claim an equal share of notice, at once renders its combinations with such buildings inharmonious, and offers no alternation of predominant and subservient features; without which, no objects can satisfy the eye. But the most absurd architectural objects that present themselves in this city, a city famed for possessing individuals of the highest talents and purest taste, are the shop fronts.

In composing the dressings of the shop fronts in many streets, but especially in Oxford Street, it is customary to hollow out the frieze like a scotia, in order to give the cornice its proper

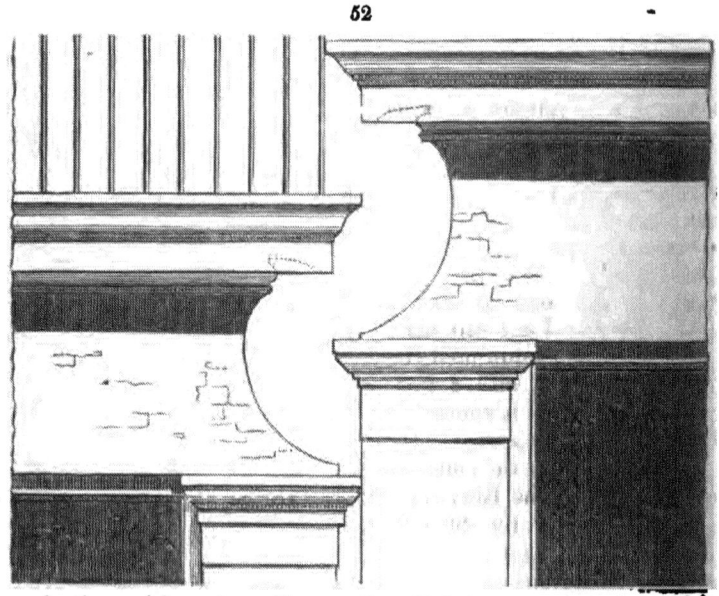

52

projection, without intruding on the adjoining property. (*fig.* 52.) This absurd practice, created in ignorance, and fostered by servile imitation, has become generally prevalent in shop fronts over the whole of London; nay, it has even intruded itself upon the untutored taste of the country carpenter; for can it be believed that, in the door-pieces of some cottages lately erected in the neighbourhood of London, this curve of the frieze has been copied to a nicety, even where the space open to the builder was unconfined on every side?

As all objects that have for their fundamental principles regularity and uniformity must influence individuals, and, consequently, affect society (for even the inmates of a dwelling in which the domestic arrangements are neat and orderly are exemplifications of this fact); and as no field of study offers easier access to individuals than architecture, being open to all, and even intruding itself upon our notice, so ought it to be the business of those who have influence, not to permit such bad taste to descend from generation to generation, but to employ every means in their power to disseminate good taste, or, at least, that sort of taste which is considered good by men of acknowledged talent. This would be a public benefit in the end, and ought to interest every individual.

To forward this object, it would be well that no house whatever should be built without an elevation being furnished by some proper person: and, even if this were supplied free of expense to the parties about to build, it would be a positive benefit to the country in the end. It may be said that, if the general elevations of streets were furnished by one individual, as in Edinburgh, it would prevent the emulative spirit of proprietors and builders, and, perhaps, produce monotony in the appearance of the streets: and further, that the various productions of different minds must be preferable to any thing that can be produced by one individual. To meet these objections, it would be necessary to have various architects employed, each to furnish the elevations of the street houses for his own particular district; and, before any building was begun, the elevations respectively should be approved of by a majority of the architects thus appointed. This would insure variety, and create competition for fame among the professional persons employed, who would each endeavour to make our streets surpass those of every other town or city, in point of beauty.

With regard to the improvement of shop fronts, or rather to the abolition of the curve in the frieze of the architrave over them, I should remark, that, in all cases where practicable, the pilasters ought to be kept far enough within the limits of the frontage of the building (even should doing so reduce the width of the windows) to admit of the proper projection being given to the cornice, without introducing the curve in the frieze. But even if the columns or pilasters are brought out to the extent of the premises on which they are used, the cornice may be finished, in a very consistent and handsome manner, against a block, supported by consols or trusses (a kind of bracket shown in *fig.* 53.). There are one or two shop fronts in London finished in this manner; and great credit is due to the architects who have designed them. Considering them as fit objects for imitation, I here annex a design for part of a shop front in a similar manner, which, from its simplicity, may be executed at a very trifling additional expense to that incurred by the shop fronts with the curved frieze. (*fig.* 53.)

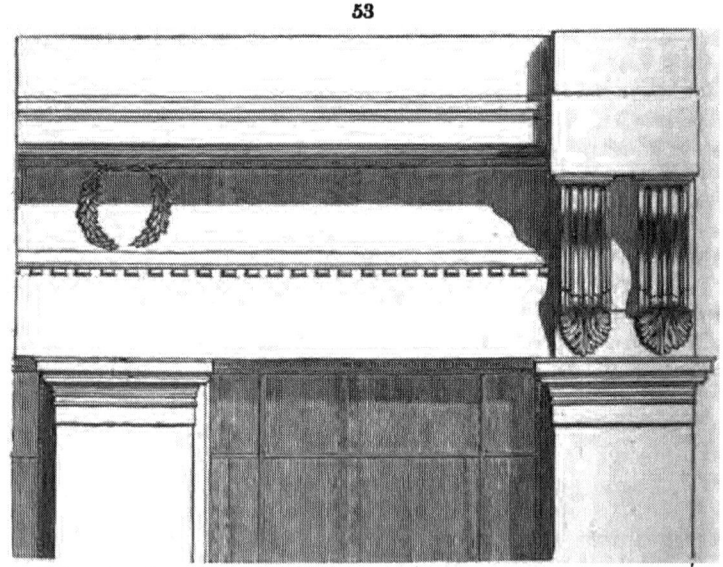

53

That the foregoing few hints may create a desire to effect an improvement in objects of such importance and such interest as the London street houses and shop fronts, is the sincere wish of the writer. R.

Bayswater, Jan. 30. 1834.

We agree generally with our correspondent, that a certain degree of superintendence is required from all municipal governments to insure public safety and convenience, and even general effect and beauty, in the cities under their control. But we do not think much would be gained by restraining the taste of individuals, when that taste does not interfere with public convenience. Employing two or three architects only, however great might be their abilities, would assuredly lead to monotony; and there can be no greater proof of this than the New Town of Edinburgh, which, though striking in a general point of view, as contrasted with the Old Town, is yet one of the tamest congregations of buildings in Europe. Were it not for the external views of the Old Town on on one side, and of the Frith of Forth on the other, the New Town of Edinburgh would be as dull as Berlin; without its redeeming points of splendid public buildings. Petersburgh is a city built from plans submitted to, and approved by, the government, with the exception of a single street called the English Line. That street is the only one in which there is a succession of varied elevations, produced by the houses having been built by different individuals for themselves; all the rest are comparatively alike, or at least were so in 1814. Under certain restrictions, therefore, we would allow every individual to exercise his own taste; and we should wish, if possible, not to see two elevations alike in any one street, but we shall return to this subject; and, in the mean time, thanking our correspondent R. for having taken it up, we invite him, and others, to continue its discussion. — *Cond.*

ART. V. *On certain deceptive Practices adopted by some Authors of Architectural Designs for Villas.* By AN OBSERVER.

IN your *Encyclopædia of Architecture*, you object, and in my opinion, with great reason, to the deceptive effect produced by accompanying architectural designs with landscapes, so as to form pictures; thereby attracting the eye to the effect of the whole, instead of the effect of the building. I am aware that there is a very plausible argument against your objection, which is, that, as the building will always be seen, in reality, in connection with surrounding scenery, it ought so to be seen in a picture: but every painter knows that by lights and shadows, by introducing forms in the trees and ground to contrast with those of the building, and, in short, by working for effect, the most indifferent building may be made, by a clever artist, to appear handsome in the eyes of those who cannot refer effects to their causes. In fact, we should no more think of ascertaining the merits of a building, either as a piece of architecture, or as a structure for a particular use, by observing it merely as a component part of a landscape, than we should think of becoming acquainted with the private character of an individual, by seeing him at a conversazione, or hearing him speak in parliament.

The deception alluded to, however, is not the only one which is practised by some architects, both in the designs which they prepare for private individuals, and in those which they publish in books. One of the practices alluded to is that of increasing or deepening the shadows of slight projections, and engaged columns (that is, columns projecting half or three quarters of their diameters) and pilasters, in such a manner as to produce an effect on paper which their projections could never, by any possibility, do in reality. To the eye of any one not practised in looking at architectural drawings, these deceptions will make the ugliest and most unscientific building look handsome. A corresponding optical delusion is that of darkening the tint of recesses, and lightening that of projections: but the most notable trick of London architects is that of casting the shadows of clouds on the plain parts of buildings; unless, indeed, the ab-

118 *Deceptive Practices*

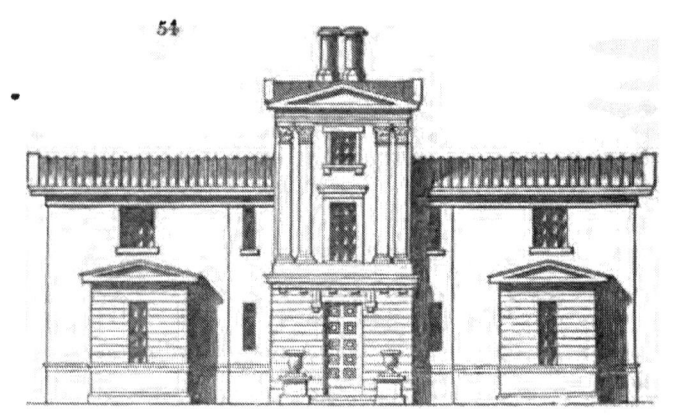

54.

surd practice of imitating mosses and weather-stains, and not only them, but even weeds and creepers, on designs for buildings not yet erected, should be considered a greater deception.

I come now to one of the greatest faults of this kind that I know of; viz., the concealment of the whole, or the greater part, of the chimney shafts. I agree with you that these ought never to be hidden in an English dwelling-house, whatever may be the style of its architecture; unless the dwelling-house is to be disguised under some other character of building. A man may choose to live in a house that has the appearance of a Grecian temple or a Turkish mosque; and if he does so, he may fairly conceal the appearance of chimneys and smoke: but, if he avows the structure in which he resides to be an English dwelling-house, let him always avow that which constitutes its chief source of comfort, its fireplaces.

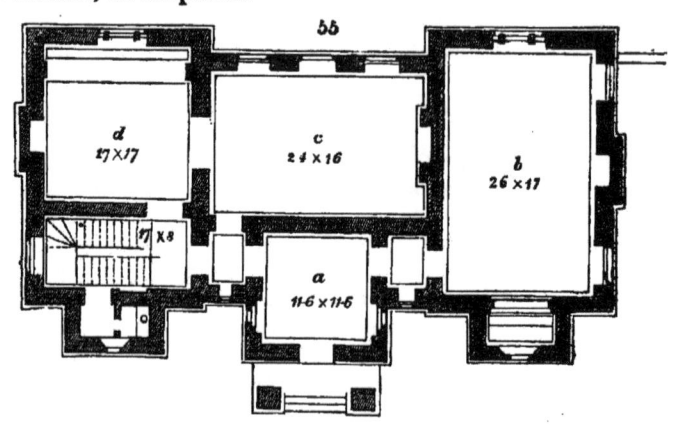

55.

Nothing can more show the vitiated taste of our architects and their employers, than their being better pleased with designs

56

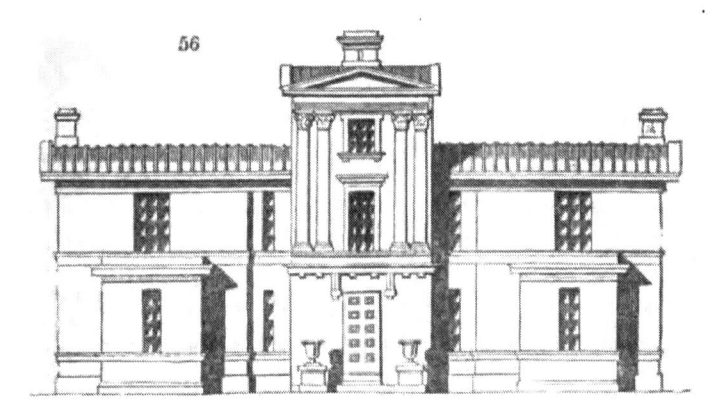

in which chimney shafts are omitted or but partially shown, than where they are boldly avowed. Let us not, however, blame the employers of architects, or the readers of architectural publications, but rather the architects themselves, for their unnational, or, I might even say, unnatural, prejudices. In former times, before the architecture of Italy became fashionable in England, there was no such thing as a house, either in town or country, without bold and conspicuous chimney shafts. Look at the houses erected by Inigo Jones, Thorpe, and all the architects of the time of Henry VIII., Elizabeth, and James I. Remove all that part of the chimney shafts of such houses which is seen above the roof, and how tame would they appear!

It will not be contended, surely, that there is anything in the nature of Roman or Italian architecture that forbids the use of conspicuous chimney shafts: those who think this, I refer to the beautiful Italian designs, by Mr. Lamb, in your *Encyclopædia of Architecture*; to the handsome Italian villa built by Mr. Barry at Brighton; or to that of Mr. Potter, at Buele Hill, in the neighbourhood of Manchester.

In order to prove what I have advanced respecting the concealment of chimney tops in published designs, I send you herewith three sketches. *Fig.* 55. is the ground plan of a villa, taken from a book of designs recently published. This plan, you will observe, is by no means objectionable; and, indeed, the two small vestibules which lead from the entrance hall (*a*) to the library (*b*), and to the drawing-room and dining-room (*c* and *d*), are to me somewhat original. In the elevation of this plan (*fig.* 54.), you will observe that the architect has shown no chimney shafts, except over the central projection: whereas it is evident, that if the elevation had been faithful to the plan, there would have been chimneys shown at each end, as I have done in *fig.* 56. I have made some other alterations in the elevation; such as removing two of the pediments; because, according to the elevation *fig.* 54., five pediments would be seen at once from the perspective view, either from the right or left angle, which would give a monotonous character, or, in other words, would be too much of a good thing. I have also removed the lines representing rustic-work in the projections; because, though they look well in the elevation, they would, in the execution, have tended to detach these smaller parts from the larger part to which they belong: besides, as rustic-work is always considered to be expressive of strength, there is an absurdity in giving the appearance of greater strength to the walls of the two low projections than is given to the walls of the main body of the house. Had the rustic-work been confined to the central projection, there would have been reason in its favour; because there extra-strength in the foundation would be required. Rustic-work should never, as in *fig.* 54., be placed over a base of plain work; because this gives the architectural expression of the stronger parts being supported by the weaker. But the alteration to which I wish chiefly to draw the attention of your readers, is that which I have made by adding chimney shafts to the ends: and I would ask all of them, 1st, Whether, considering that this edifice is to be a dwelling-house, it does not look more like what it is intended to be in *fig.* 56. than in *fig.* 54.? and 2dly, Whether *fig.* 54. is more beautiful than *fig.* 56.? If they say it is, I should be glad to know their reasons, and in what way chimney shafts, as shown in *fig.* 56., tend to disfigure it.

London, March 10. 1834.

ART. VI. *A Series of Designs, with Descriptive and Historical Particulars, of Characteristic and Ornamental Buildings, and Objects for Gardens and Pleasure-Grounds.* By A SELF-TAUGHT ARCHITECT AND LANDSCAPE-GARDENER.

As I observe the words " Garden Architecture" on the vignette of your cover, if you will permit me, I will supply you with a series of designs for what may be called decorative garden buildings.

I am aware that such buildings are much more sparingly introduced in garden scenery now, than they were a century ago, and I think very properly. I entirely agree with Uvedale Price, and the late Richard Payne Knight (and I believe that the late Mr. Repton was of the same opinion as these gentlemen), that it is in much better taste to dignify common useful edifices, such as cottages, lodges, barns, sheds, bridges, seats, &c., by better materials, better contrivance within, and better architectural design without, than to throw away money on temples, grottoes, and root-houses. But, though I allow that these useful objects ought to be first attended to, I cannot consent that the others should be excluded; and, indeed, I think most of your readers will agree with me that all exclusive plans are bad, for the simple reason that they are exclusive. Let a gentleman first attend to his own dwelling-house, the residence of himself, and of those servants and domestic animals on which so much of his own enjoyments and comforts depends; for, till his own family is at ease, he cannot be expected to think much of the enjoyments of others. Let him next see that every human being that lives on his estates, and labours for him, or pays him rent, is commodiously, conveniently, and comfortably lodged. After that, let him examine into the improvements which may be made in the lodgings of the useful quadrupeds and other animals on his demesne, or on his tenanted lands; and, having satisfied his own conscience and the opinion of good men, in all these particulars, let him then turn to the pleasing task of adding ornament to utility; of superadding to works of art what the wise and beneficent Author of nature (if we, dim-sighted and short-lived mortals, may presume thus to speak) always adds to his works, something calculated to entice and invite.

The communications which I propose to make to you, I wish to be considered in the light of hints and ideas for these inviting superadditions: some of them may not be approved of, as being too rustic; others, as being too finical or refined; some, as being paltry, and of temporary durability; and others, as being too grave and substantial for objects of ornament. I will venture to say, however, that no one design that I shall send you will be found without something to recommend it; and, if you insert one or more of them occasionally in your work, it will, in the course of a few volumes, contain a rich assemblage of ideas on this department of rural architecture.

As many of these designs will be original, some copied from published works, and others drawn from objects which have been erected, there will be no limit to either their number or variety; but still I would beg to solicit assistance from every reader of your Magazine who can help me, as well as from yourself, who have, no doubt, seen many garden decorations on the Continent, where the taste for such buildings is more in fashion than it is in Britain. For all such assistance as I may receive, I shall, with your permission, make due acknowledgment, and I hope some of those talented ladies and gentlemen, who furnish so many beautiful designs for execution on their own grounds (such as Lady Grenville at Dropmore, and the Earl of Essex at Cashiobury), for example, will not disdain to lend their aid to my humble labours in their service.

As I am more an artist than an author, my descriptions shall be short; and, as I do not think the order in which the sketches are given can be of much consequence, I shall adopt that which best suits my own convenience.

The round seat, with a thatched roof (*fig.* 57.), was erected by the Duke of Marlborough, at White Knights, about the year 1812, and is described by Hofland as " formed entirely of straight branches of the maple and the larch, beneath a circular thatched dome: the rustic pillars support an architrave of taste and beauty, displayed in the most simple materials. Thin slices from the heart of the yew tree, form medallions, which are grafted into small sprays of larchwood, with so much symmetry as to produce a surprising effect; and the pebbled floor is disposed in leaves and circles, with equal simplicity and grace. On the back of this bower is a seat which fronts the park."

Sundials are useful and interesting ornaments to gardens, and especially to parterres, whether geometrical or picturesque. Mr. Austin, the manufacturer of artificial stone, has paid great attention to the construction of sundials, and has several of very beautiful forms. I may observe of Mr. Austin's artificial stone, that he has now brought it to such perfection, that it is harder and more durable than Portland stone.

Figs. 58. and 59. are forms of sundials, with dial-plates and gnomons, of the common kind, which may be purchased for very moderate prices.

Fig. 60. is a globe sundial, representing the earth, upon which, when the sun shines, the time may be seen on either side on the equinoctial line, where the light and shade divide. The time is also denoted in summer by the shadow of the pin at the north pole on the arctic circle, and in winter at the south pole on the antarctic circle.

A much larger dial is in preparation by Mr. Austin, marked with the outlines of the several countries, the signs of the zodiac, &c.; the enlightened hemisphere of which will show that part of the earth upon which the sun then shines, the centre of which will be the meridian or noon at all places thereon; and the division of light and shade will show the rising and setting of the sun. At the intersection of the longitude and latitude (the meridian of the place on which the dial stands) is intended to be introduced a flag, to turn with the wind, the staff of which will represent the pole of the horizon. The pedestal is to be octangular, upon which will be engraven the names of the several winds, as Boreas, Zephyrus, &c., also the rhombs, or thirty-two points of the compass. The whole will form a noble and interesting object for the lawn, and an endless source of instruction and amusement for the school, as most of the problems upon the terrestrial globe may be solved by it in a manner much superior to that usually adopted; and, in fine weather, lectures may be delivered on it in the open air.

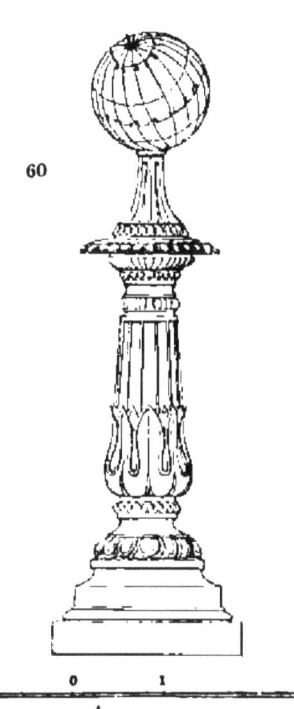

Art. VII. *On an effectual Method of cutting off the Communication between the damp Foundation of a Wall built upon a moist Subsoil, and the Part of the Wall above the Ground; and on a Mode of securing the Inside of a Wall from Damp forced through the Brickwork by driving Rains.* By John Isaac Hawkins, Esq., Civil Engineer.

In consequence of reading the excellent paper of Mr. Kent (p. 34.), I am induced to send you an account of the method I took to cure one or two of the evils against which he warns his readers.

Soon after I had taken a lease (ten years since) of the cottage I now occupy, I discovered that the damp ascended the walls to the height of a yard above the ground, and that my furniture began to be injured by mildew. Finding that the foundation was laid upon a subsoil of clay, and knowing that a cure would be effected by interposing a waterproof medium throughout the thickness of the wall, just above the level of the ground, I proceeded in the following manner: — First, I made a hole through the wall, over the ground course, taking out two courses in height and two bricks in length; consequently, the hole was 6 in. high and 18 in. wide. I filled up half this hole, at one end, with two courses of sound bricks, laid in Roman cement. It is clear that the operation could not injure the wall, the width of 18 in. not allowing of any settlement. Two courses more, of 9 in. in width, were next removed, making the hole again 18 in. wide; the half of which was then filled up with bricks and cement as before. The operation was repeated until the whole of the walls of the house were underpinned by two courses of hard bricks and three joints of Roman cement; constituting a waterproof septum, through which the damp cannot rise.

Local circumstances prevented easy access to two or three spots; and, my bricklayer not taking care that there should be three perfect joints of Roman cement in every part, the moisture still rises, in a few neglected places, in a small degree. But, with these few exceptions, the cottage, generally speaking, has been as free from damp, for nearly ten years, as if built upon a dry subsoil. The cost of 120 ft. run of wall, for the most part 14 in. thick, was about 15*l*.

In recommending this plan, I would strongly enforce the necessity of performing the operation under every part of the house, partition walls, and chimneys. I yielded to the fears of my bricklayer, and suffered the stacks of chimneys to remain untouched; the hearths on the ground floors are, therefore, damp, except when a constant fire is kept up. There was, in reality, no danger of any sinking of the stack, as Roman cement, when of good quality, expands in setting, and affords as perfect a support as the bricks and mortar which were taken away; or, rather, a more perfect support than they had afforded.

In building a house on a moist subsoil, where the expense of a waterproof foundation might be an object, a couple of courses of brick, laid in Roman cement, immediately above the level of the ground, would prevent the damp rising above those courses. I have seen a single course of slate used for this purpose with good effect; and that is, perhaps, as impervious to water as three joints of Roman cement.

Mr. Kent's just observations on the absorbing qualities of place bricks are applicable, also, in a considerable degree, to the inferior stocks of which my cottage is built. The outer walls above the first floor are only 9 in. thick; and the driving rains used to force the wet quite through them, and through the ªtering, throwing off the papering of the rooms. I cured this evil by scraping off all the plastering inside the rooms, and replacing it by a coat of Roman cement; since which time, no symptoms of damp have appeared on the inside of these walls.

JOHN ISAAC HAWKINS.
Pancras Vale, near Hampstead, London, March 15. 1834.

ART. VIII. *On the Art of Brickmaking among the Chinese.*
By JAMES MAIN, Esq.

As the Chinese are excellent potters, it is not to be wondered at that they are also excellent brickmakers. This is sufficiently apparent not only in respect to the perfect forms and durability of their common building-bricks and tiles, but in the great variety of forms and different sizes of their bricks. For common wall-work in courses, their bricks in dimensions resemble those of Europe; but, in so warm a climate as that of the south of China, many ornamental lozenged openings are required in the walls of houses, to promote ventilation; and many ornamental projections, either vertical, horizontal, or curvilinear, are required by the national taste. To execute these features, the builder never need cut a brick; the proper forms are furnished by the brickmaker according to orders issued from the architect. Hence there are moulded headers for plinths, beveled stretchers for sills, the same for lintels, &c. For mullions they have bricks of various sizes and designs, which fit as parts of the general structure with great exactness, whether as referable to ornamental effect, or security of the building.

Economy in all things is the ruling passion of the Chinese; and to this may be attributed the pains they bestow in preserving every particle of their brick-earth; and saving the time of the builder, which would be lost in reducing his bricks to the required form; and which, it seems, they consider more than compensates for the expense of the moulds.

In this country, coping bricks and tiles are sometimes furnished by the brickmaker; but few of this fraternity appear willing to leave their old beaten track. Of late years, the spirit of the celebrated and successful Wedgwood seems to be diffusing itself among the lower grades of the workers in clay; and I look forward with hope that, by means of the Architectural Magazine, many such hints as the above may be promulgated, and adopted in practice; more especially if recommended by yourself to those owners of brick-fields who may have inclination and means to carry into execution what may be proposed to them.

Chelsea, March 8. 1834. J. MAIN.

CONSIDERABLE variety in the forms of bricks existed in this country before the government duty was laid on them, as it appears evident from the houses of a superior kind, still existing, which were built in the time of William III., George II., &c. Even in houses which date so far back as the time of Henry VIII. (for example, Sutton Place, near Ripley, Surrey), a great variety of bricks appear to have been used in the cornices, window dressings, and chimney shafts. In short, an advanced state of society is by no means necessary for making ornamental bricks. At the conversazione of the London Institution, on April 16., we saw some very handsome specimens of ornamental bricks, from Nipal, quite architectural in their forms. That we still have clay fitted for making such bricks, and workmen possessing the ability to make them, is evident by the brickwork of the elaborate and unique chimney shafts of that extraordinary and splendid modern specimen of old English architecture, lately erected at Cossey Hall, near Norwich, by Mr. Backler, jun. All that is wanting to produce a return to architectural brickmaking, and to effect every improvement which our friend Mr. Main could desire, is the entire removal of the duty on bricks and tiles; and this would probably have been done some years ago when the duty was taken off slates, if the proprietors of brick-fields had had as much influence in the legislature as those of slate quarries.—*Cond.*

Art. IX. *A simple and effective Preventive for the Slamming of a Passage Door.* By J. R. of Edinburgh.

If ever you have suffered from the misery of hearing the slamming of a passage door, which is liable to be blown to by currents of air when it has been left ajar, you will not be sorry to get a simple and effectual remedy against the shock. The sketch (*fig.* 61.) is intended to represent one side of the doorcase. Instead of fixing the piece of wood, which, I believe, joiners call the checkplate, on this, a similar piece is taken, and prepared by being cut hollow on the edge *a*, which the door strikes on, and then cut down by saw draughts (slits made by the saw), as represented by the lines *b b* in the figure, leaving a portion in the middle equal to one fourth or one fifth of the length uncut; it is then securely fixed by screws to the door-post, as shown in the sketch at *c*. The door, of course, first strikes against the top and bottom extremities of this check, and must press them back before it can reach the solid part of the plate in the middle. If, therefore, the plate of wood be made of such breadth and thickness as that the united resistance of its ten or twelve springs be a little greater than the force the door strikes with, it will never reach the solid part at all, and its slamming will be nearly inaudible, however strong the current of air may be. I have found this to succeed perfectly, after all sorts of iron springs and checks have failed to remove the nuisance. J. R.

Edinburgh, Feb. 8. 1833.

Art. X. *On Painted Transparent Blinds, and Tape and Line Preservers.* By Y. Z.

As your very valuable work is devoted to a consideration of "improvements in architecture, building, and furnishing, and *in the various arts, &c. connected therewith*," I make no doubt that you will accept my apology for obtruding upon your pages a brief notice of the superior beauty of the window blinds painted by Mr. Joseph Stubbs, of the Quadrant, Regent Street. When in London, last autumn, I was particularly struck by the representation of the Thames Tunnel, then on view at the painter's residence, and my attention was the more especially directed to this kind of production from the fact of the late Mr. James Northcote, the Royal Academician, having, in my presence, adverted in terms of unqualified admiration to an interior view of Canterbury Cathedral, painted by this artist, on a window blind, some years since. I will not trouble you with my observations on the Thames Tunnel, which is probably familiar to the majority of your readers; but, as the other works of the painter may not be so generally known, a wish to assist the enquiries of those about to furnish their apartments with those truly elegant utilities, painted blinds, induces me to point their attention to a quarter in which they are not likely to meet with the disappointments to which a person of taste is too frequently subjected by the difficulty of meeting with the required excellence.

Adopting the sentiments of your correspondent, Mr. Brown (p. 92.), I venture to presume that no farther apology is necessary for an attempt to promote the satisfaction of individuals studious of displaying taste and elegance in the decoration of their dwellings. My object refers exclusively to the splendid variety of landscape scenery, both British and Continental, lately introduced in the department of painted transparencies. Among others that I saw when in town were two or three exquisite compositions from Claude Lorraine, in which the classic beauty of the design was sustained by the freshness and harmony of the tints. To enumerate all the views I saw would be impossible: the temple, the cathedral, the abbey, and the baronial pile; the monuments of antiquity, as well as the creations of modern times, aided by all the charming accessories of wood and water, attract the attention of the spectator: nature is pourtrayed in every enchanting diversity of aspect; the forest and the vale, the wood-crowned precipice and the winding path, the torrent dashing from the mountain's height, and the silent stream welling away its waters beneath a rustic bridge, by turns salute the eye.

Although the immediate object of these graceful decorations goes no further than, as a window blind, to shut out an unpleasing prospect, or the intensity of the sun, the taste, judgment, and ability of their painter, united to a commendable desire of excellence in his peculiar province, have infused into them so much of the higher requisites of art, that they are raised, immeasurably, above the common level of such productions. Elegance of design, accuracy of *local* representation, freedom of penciling, and chastened brilliancy of colour, form their main characteristics. The libraries and boudoirs of the wealthy would owe no trifling share of their embellishment to these lovely creations of the pencil. Utility comes doubly recommended, when united with ornament, and in this instance, while protecting our carpets and furniture from the destructive effects of a midsummer sun, we have the pleasure of adorning our apartments, and gratifying our eyes. I found, nevertheless, that these blinds are not more expensive than the very inferior articles which are usually to be met with.

Mr. Stubbs, I understand, has invented a very ingenious mode of preserving the tapes of Venetian blinds from the injurious influence of the sun: this object is attained by two slips of wood the length of the blind, connected as a parallel ruler, and screwed within the frame of the blind upon both sides. When the blind is about to be let down, the preserver is drawn out, and the slip of wood covers the whole of the tape which would be otherwise exposed to the action of the sun. By this simplest of all contrivances, the durability of the blind is insured for a considerable period. Probably Mr. Stubbs would oblige your readers with an accurate description of his invention, illustrated by a sketch. It could not fail to be useful, and, I am persuaded, acceptable.

Worcester, April 10. 1834. Y. Z.

Art. XI. *Architectural Maxim.*

In *judging of Buildings*, the uneducated man speaks from his feelings; and the partially educated man refers to rules. The master, on the other hand, also judges by his feelings; but his feelings are cultivated by study and long-continued observation: the feelings are thus brought to act in unison with the judgment. " A person who criticises every fine building which he sees, without vanity or presumption, with a sincere desire to find out whatever is excellent, and to understand and fully enter into the reasons for any admiration which has been generally bestowed upon it by others, yet at the same time not blindly following authority, but bringing everything to the test of his own feelings and judgment, will form to himself a habit, profitable not only when applied to architecture and the other fine arts, but in every subject on which the human understanding is exercised." (Wood's *Letters of an Architect,* vol. i. p. 5.)

REVIEWS.

ART. I. *A Theoretical and Practical Treatise on the Five Orders of Architecture: containing the most plain and simple rules for drawing and executing them in the present style; including an historical description of Gothic Architecture, showing its origin, and also a comparison of the Gothic Architecture of England, Germany, France, Spain, and Italy, together with details of the first, second, and third periods of the Pointed Arch or Gothic style: illustrated by upwards of* 100 *Steel Engravings, executed by artists of first-rate talent, including numerous diagrams, &c.* London, 1834. 4to, in 7 parts at 5s. each, or 35 numbers at 1s. each.

THIS work has been sent us by a friend, an amateur architect, accompanied by the following remarks, which we shall lay before the reader before we give our own.

" Relying upon the prospectus being literally fulfilled, which was so worded as to lead me to expect that drawings would be given of buildings executed by several of the leading architects of the day, I was induced to take in this work, in numbers, as it appeared: but, now that it is completed, I find that I have been taken in myself; for, with the exception of Chelsea church, and the new Hall of Christ's Hospital, there is no example of any thing executed by those whose names are mentioned in the prospectus. In order that you may judge whether it was a mere blunder on my part, I quote at length the paragraph in which I so cautiously put faith. ' The illustrations and examples have been carefully selected from the most approved specimens, both ancient and modern, and will include plans, elevations, and sections of various well-known and admired structures, consisting of cathedrals, churches, halls, *mansions, villas,* asylums, mausoleums, prisons, &c., most of which have been executed by architects of great skill and eminence in their profession, among whom are *Wyatteville, Smirke, Soane, Rennie, Telford, Perronet,* Clarke, Shaw, *Inwood,* Elsom, Johnstone, Nicholson, &c. &c.' Now, of the works of those whose names are in Italic, there is not a single example; and, although there are some designs for mansions and villas, they certainly are not of any that are either well-known or admired, or ever likely to be so; even supposing them, which is exceedingly doubtful, to have been ever executed. On the contrary, they are in the most contemptible taste imaginable. Let any one look at the design for a mansion in the castellated style, and judge whether it be not grossly absurd, both in plan and elevation. In regard to the first, it is as inconvenient as it was possible for human ingenuity to contrive it: in regard to the latter, it is a hideous mass of the most barbarous deformity. This is the more provoking, because far more practicable examples might have been easily obtained; carrying also with them, besides what other merits they might have to recommend them, that of possessing some authority, from their having been actually executed."

[As it is our intention, in conformity with what we have stated in p. 104., to be specific in our criticisms, whether laudatory or condemnatory, we shall here give our reasons for agreeing with our correspondent, in disapproving of this villa in the castellated style. Externally, it wants unity of character; the lower part being in Church Gothic, with a high roof, and the upper part, or central mass, which rises out of it, being castellated, with a concealed roof. These two parts are so nearly of equal bulk and importance, that they do not form a whole. A small castellated tower, rising out of an ecclesiastical structure, will not interfere with the character of a whole; but where two parts of any building are equal in bulk, or claim equal attention, and are at the same time in different styles, a whole cannot possibly be produced. In the interior, the principal apartments are scattered, instead of being connected.]

" On comparing the preface with the original address, I think I have detected the ingenious, although certainly not ingenuous, subterfuge by which the word of promise is kept to the ear, if no farther. There the paragraph I have above quoted, is reprinted, with this alteration : ' among whom we make honourable mention of Wyatteville, Smirke, &c. &c.' So that it appears, after all, their names were merely dragged in as being those of persons distinguished in the profession, not as those of architects whose designs would be copied. By what epithet can such conduct in a publisher be designated?"

The work before us ranks with Billington's *Director*, Bennett's *Lexicon*, *The New Practical Builder* (of which book the treatise before us contains many plates), and some others which we could name. These works are never seen on the tables of architects; or even in the shops of architectural booksellers; but they are hawked about in numbers among the journeymen carpenters and bricklayers, in builders' workshops, all over the country; and it is lamentable to think that these hard-working men are often induced to part with their money for such crude productions. The evil arises from the high price of standard architectural books. We shall endeavour to open the eyes of journeyman carpenters, &c., on this subject, and to create a taste among them for genuine works on architecture, which architectural publishers will then find it their interest to supply at a cheap rate.

ART. II. *An Architectural and Historical Account of Crosby Place, London; compiled from original and unpublished Sources; with an Appendix of Illustrative Documents, and fac-simile Autographs of several of its ancient Possessors.* By Edward L. Blackburn, Architect. 8vo, 94 pages. London, 1834. 8s. 6d.

THE object of the author, as stated in his preface, is " to supply the public with several facts, connected with the history of Crosby Place, which previous writers, less fortunate than himself, have not had the means of ascertaining, or of making known." (p. i.) Accordingly, the work is of much more interest to the antiquarian than to the architect. To such of the latter, however, as possess the engravings of Crosby Hall, published by Mr. Pugin, in his *Specimens of Gothic Architecture*, vol. i., the historical account of Mr. Blackburn will be a valuable addition.

John Crosby was an eminent citizen of London, in the time of Edward IV.; and he took a lease of the site of Crosby Place, in 1466, for ninety-nine years, from the prioress of the convent of St. Helen. Whether he built the house, or merely added to it, appears uncertain; but Stowe, in his *Survey of the City of London*, published in 1598, says that Crosby Place " was built of stone and timber, and was the highest house at that time in London." This, Mr. Blackburn observes, " would appear to be the earliest descriptive notice of Crosby Place;" and, as it leaves the date of its erection uncertain, he endeavours to affix its early character from " such evidence as the existing remains afford; the brief descriptions contained in the old deeds and grants of the premises; and inferences drawn from the general practice of the period in which it was [supposed to be] built."

In pursuing his enquiries, Mr. Blackburn displays an intimate historical knowledge of ancient English domestic architecture, and of the various books which have been written on it: and the work he has produced will repay the antiquarian architect for its perusal.

Crosby Place, after having been possessed or occupied successively by twenty-three different families, including the Duke of Gloucester, afterwards Richard III., several earls, Sir Thomas More, and other knights, passed, in 1678, into the hands of a family of the name of Freeman, in the possession of whose descendants it still remains. As to the building itself, the only part existing, worthy of the attention of the architect, is what is called the hall, and which was engraved by Pugin. This hall, with its lofty enriched roof, was occupied, till lately, as a packing-warehouse; but a number of architects, and other zealous amateurs of art, have raised a subscription for taking a lease of it, and restoring it to its original state. In conclusion, we agree with Mr. Blackburn in ardently desiring that the committee appointed for its restoration "may meet with that success which the nature of their object deserves; and that Crosby Hall, one of the last remaining relics of the ancient domestic architecture of London, may long remain a feature of the metropolis." (p. 66.)

ART. III. *Gothic Ornaments, illustrative of Prior Birde's Oratory, in the Abbey Church, Bath.* By Edward Davis, Architect, Bath. Imp. fol. No. 1. London, 1834.

MR. DAVIS deserves great credit for publishing this work, since it must have cost him much labour, and considerable expense; both of which he can only have incurred from the love of his profession. Almost the only letter-press the work contains is the two following paragraphs, which we quote, to give the reader an idea of what he is to expect.

"The oratory, which this publication is designed to illustrate, is almost coeval with the abbey in which it stands. The first stone was laid about 1515, by Birde, prior of the abbey, under whom the design was, for some time, diligently prosecuted. When, however, nearly completed, its progress was interrupted (probably in consequence of the ecclesiastical reforms of the period); and the structure still affords unquestionable evidence of the abruptness with which the work was abandoned.

"The subsequent history of the oratory is soon told. Though remarkable alike for purity and richness of decoration, and raised at a cost which is said to have impaired the fortunes of its founder, it was fated to experience the same neglect to which all architecture of a Gothic character was so long exposed. For three centuries it was abandoned to the mercy of parish officers; its fronts were defaced by monuments; the lower compartments of the windows were built up, and those parts permitted to remain exposed were washed and rewashed with coats of different hues, until all the sharpness of the carved work was lost, and much of the delicate tracery altogether obliterated. Thus it remained till the latter part of the year 1833. At this period, the attention of the public was again directed towards it; and, the desire for its renovation becoming general, a subscription for the purpose was entered into, by aid of which the work was commenced, and is now proceeding."

Pl. I. contains an elevation of Prior Birde's oratory, as restored in 1833. It displays two windows with heads pointed, but yet so low as to appear almost semicircular. The spandrils are filled in with very rich foliage; that over one window being different from that of the other; and the piers or buttresses are very rich, one of them having niches with canopies. II. Contains one of the principal spandrils, with a part of the full size. The ornament in this spandril consists of a branch, springing from the rib of the arch, and most gracefully wound about so as to fill the spandril with leaves of a nondescript kind, having pomegranate-like flowers, and birds appearing among the leaves; the latter, according to the taste of the time, being a pun on the founder's name. III. A spandril of another kind, with one of the leaves of the full size. The foliage here is accompanied by fruit, and the object imitated is clearly the ivy. Birds are introduced among the foliage. IV. Capital of one of the buttresses, half full size. V. A fragment, found built into the lower compartment of the windows. This appears to consist of a portion of the structure which had been superincumbent to a window; the two ribs, which serve as architraves, joining at an acute angle at some distance above the more obtuse arch of the window, and thence continued up in a straight line, and embraced on each side with foliage interrupted by crotchet-like expansions at regular distances. The price of this work is not mentioned. To the collector of Gothic details, we have no doubt it will be highly acceptable.

ART. IV. *Domestic Architecture; being a Second Series of Designs for Cottages, Lodges, Villas, and other Residences, in the Grecian, Italian, and Old English Styles of Architecture: with an Introduction, containing Observations on the English Domestic Style, by W. H. Leeds, Esq. With 42 plates, and a Plan of the Public Rooms in the Town Hall at Manchester: also with Specifications, &c., as well as Estimates, to each Design.* By Francis Goodwin, Architect. 4to. London, 1834. 2*l*. 12*s*. 6*d*.

This is one of three parts, or volumes, the first of which appeared in 1833, and the third is to follow. Speaking of the work as a whole, and with reference to others of the same kind, by Robinson, Hunt, Parker, &c., we should say, that, like them, its object is not to instruct the builder or amateur how to design or build, but to afford the man of wealth an opportunity of choosing the sort of design which he would like an architect to prepare and execute for him. As a work attractive to the eye, the present volume is inferior to those of some of the authors mentioned, partly from the very badly designed landscape scenery with which the perspective views of the buildings are accompanied, and partly from the defective manner in which they have been engraved. While we say this, we must, at the same time, state that we admire a number of the designs, and that we especially like the idea of describing them at length, and of pointing out their characteristic beauties or advantages, showing the alterations of which they are susceptible, &c. All this, in the volume before us, is the work of Mr. Leeds; and it is one in which he excels. We must confess, however, that we were rather disappointed in the introduction by this gentleman; knowing, as we do, what he is capable of producing as an architectural critic. The first two or three pages of this are occupied in cavilling at the remarks on English architecture made by the Baron d'Haussez, which, surely, were not worth serious notice. The last three pages contain a description of the public room of the new Town Hall at Manchester, of the plan of which a woodcut and an interior view are given; this structure being "one of the numerous public edifices erected by Mr. Goodwin." The description includes an extract from the highly laudatory "letter of an intelligent critic," who has borne his testimony to the merits of this public room; but which letter, we think, should, in every point of view, have been omitted, unless, indeed, the name of the writer had been given. The three intermediate pages of the introduction are more to the purpose than the six which we have mentioned; and, if we had room, we might copy some useful remarks from them. We shall hereafter give some of these remarks under our standing article, headed "Architectural Maxims," which we intend to draw from the best architectural writers, the personal remarks of our friends, and our own experience and observation.

The designs, eighteen in number, are comprised in perspective views accompanied by landscape, in geometrical elevations, and in ground plans, with one interior view, but no sections, or other details. The landscapes are, for the most part, in very inferior taste; and, in our opinion, the work would have been much better without them. In some published designs for villas, Parker's, for example, the fascination of the landscape prevents a critical examination of the building; and the general character and keeping are such as would render any structure pleasing. There is no danger of this kind, however, to be apprehended from the landscapes in Mr. Goodwin's book: these, in almost every case, detract from the effect of the buildings, rather than add to it. What are more especially offensive in our eyes are the trees, many of which are like nothing in the vegetable kingdom; some are of forms which one would imagine the most ignorant artist must have known could not possibly be found in nature; for example, those in the right-hand corner of Pl. 12. 15. and 18., where the trunks bear no sort of proportion to the heads: in Pl. 24., the trunk of a tree, on the right-hand side, tapers like the root of a carrot; and, in Pl. 35., there is a tree, the form of which sets at defiance even the uncouth shapes of the trees of Australia.

We shall now glance at the designs individually; but more for the sake of letting our readers know the contents of the work, than for that of examining them critically. For the latter purpose it would be necessary either to suppose that the reader had Mr. Goodwin's work before him, or to describe each design at such length as to give a clear idea of it, before offering our remarks. We shall confine ourselves, therefore, to such criticisms as the reader may be made to know the grounds of in a few words.

Design I. *An Entrance Lodge, or Cottage.* Some of the windows have facings, and others splayed sides, and the chimney shafts are enriched, which is all very architectural, and in good taste: but a porch is supported by two trunks of trees, with the bark on, which is rustic, and is altogether incongruous with the cultivated art displayed in the other parts of the building. II. *A Park Gate Lodge, in the Grecian Style.* This is handsome; but it has ten real and five false windows, for two rooms and three closets! This would make the house much too cold in winter, and much too hot in summer. The pantry and dairy form one room, 13ft. by 5ft., lighted by one window at each end, and three along one side! The portico is supported by square columns; "the expression aimed at by the building," Mr. Leeds observes, "being that of the least pretending form of the Greek, or columnar, style; in order to obtain which, square pillars have been preferred to round ones, both as being less expensive in execution, and as conveying the idea of greater strength than round columns of the same diameter would do." It would be absurd, Mr. Leeds very properly adds, in a case of this kind, " to argue that square columns are less beautiful than round ones; for, granting such, in the abstract, to be the case, it is for that very reason that they recommend themselves where the intent is obviously to keep down features which would only make the rest appear too homely, or require greater finish to be bestowed throughout." The chimney shafts, we are informed, " are omitted in the plate, as they would hardly be apparent in the building." We decidedly object to concealing the chimneys in cottages or small villas, whatever may be their style of architecture; for this reason, if for no other, that short chimneys never draw well. There are only two apartments in this cottage (besides the dairy, and a small closet with two windows): and the living-room has four doors and two windows! But comfort, in lodges or labourers' cottages, is seldom thought of, either by architects or their critics. III. *Lodge, or small Villa, in the Gothic Style.* Very good; and the landscape the best in the volume. IV. *Lodge, designed for G. Dodwell, Esq., Sligo.* A handsome elevation; but the interior still more uncomfortable than that of Design II. There is one living-room, 16ft. by 9ft., lighted by six windows, so large, that the apartment must be more fitted for a conservatory for plants than a living-room for human beings. There is a very small bedroom in the shape of the letter L; and, as the largest limb of the L is only 5ft. by 7ft., with a large window at one end, and a fire-place at the other, we cannot conceive where the bed is to be placed. There is one small closet, with a large window; and a small porch, with two windows. We consider such a house utterly unfit to be the dwelling of any fellow-creature. The wooden gates to this design, as shown in the perspective view, have their diagonal braces and strutting-pieces of natural curves; that is to say, such curves as can be found among crooked trees or branches; and this rude style of art we consider to be altogether incongruous with the finished and very handsome architecture of the lodge. V. *A Swiss Cottage.* Two contending towers in this design injure its effect as a whole. VI. *Gate Lodge.* The plan of this lodge contains more comfort than some of the others; but its elevation is the worst in the book. The windows and doors are architectural, and yet the roof, which projects over them, is supported by twenty-six rustic pillars, apparently trunks of trees, with their bark on. Such an incongruity can never be considered in good taste in any age, or in any country. The ground plan is in the form of a Greek cross, and the stack of chimneys is very properly in the centre; but the four edges of the thatched roof, which meet against the chimney stack, are made to embrace its sides in such a manner as to display immense concave slopes, so large, and so unsuitable for a cottage, that we know not how to designate such a deformity. VII. *A Farm House.* The chimney shafts want height, according to our taste; but, nevertheless, the design is good. VIII. *A Villa in the Cottage Style.* Original, architectural, and good. IX. Another *Villa in the Cottage Style.* Original and handsome; but we object to the rustic columns, and to Gothic labels displayed under a far-projecting thatched roof. X. *Villa in the Elizabethan Style.* Here, also, we consider the chimney shafts as too low: but in other respects the design is beautiful, and very much to our taste. XI. *Hunting-Lodge, in the Gothic Style.* Handsome; but still we think the chimneys not high enough. In subordinate matters of this kind, however, let taste be free. XII. *A Grecian Villa.* Much too plain a building either for Grecian or what Mr. Leeds terms semi-Grecian. The windows have no facings; and, after the highly enriched designs preceding it, they appear as bald and common-place as those of the brick houses of any street in London. We object also to the use of three-quarter columns in this design. XIII. *A Hunting-Lodge, or Villa, in the Italian Style.* Very handsome. There is a tower, or belvidere, with a balcony, to enable the ladies of the family "to accompany the sportsmen, during the chase, with their eyes." XIV. *Principal Park Entrance to Lissadell Court.* Handsome; but, as there is no ground plan of the lodge, we have doubts, from the elevation, as to the quantity of its accommodation. XV. *Lissadell, the Seat of Sir Robert Gore Booth, Bart., now erecting by Mr. Goodwin.* A large house, in a very plain modern style; but the arrangement, both of the principal rooms and offices, appears, on a slight view, to be good. A great fault in the perspective view is, that the building is not united to the scenery by a platform, terraces, an architectural flower-garden, or some other architectural appendage. XVI. *Small Villa, in the Old English Cottage Style.* Very good; the chimney shafts bold and free; and the whole picturesque: but here, again, we have rustic columns combined with highly enriched architecture. XVII. *An Italian Villa.* A square mass, rising abruptly from the ground, without any architectural preparation; and, consequently, not united to the scenery around. Mr. Leeds designates the style of this villa Anglo-Italian; a style which, he says, "forms a striking antithesis to the Palladian Italian, and to those dull, formal, frigid imitations of it which were tolerably abundant in England some hundred years ago." Placed on a balustraded terrace, and joined, on one side, to an architectural flower-garden, the effect would be good. XVIII. *Labourers' Cottages.* The plans of these, we are happy to say, display much more attention to the comfort of the occupants than the plans of the lodges; which, as we have already observed, are miserably deficient in this respect. We have not entered into the merits or demerits of the plans of the larger houses, or noticed Mr. Leeds's very judicious remarks on them, because architects pay much more attention to the plans of mansions than they do to those of cottages. We shall, however, quote one passage from the description of the house at Lissadell. These remarks are on the propriety of placing the offices of a large house in the country under the principal rooms, rather than in a separate wing, or in the main body of the building, on a level with the principal rooms.

" Many, we are aware, object to offices being at all sunk below the house in a country residence, where there is generally ample space for building them above ground, either as wings to the house itself, or otherwise. Undoubtedly such is the case; but there are many other things to be considered besides the facility of providing sites for them. If erected as wings, unless consistent in their architecture with the rest of the design, they will rather impair than improve the general effect, giving to the ensemble the appearance of being parsimoniously stinted, and more formal than uniform. In the next place, when thus situated, the offices in one wing are at an inconvenient distance from those in the other. Besides which, they must more or less intercept the view from the apartments in the main building. If, again, the offices be all placed together; attached to the house, yet still so situated as to be easily screened from sight, and consequently so as to be erected without any pretension to architecture; still, if the establishment be large, they must occupy nearly as much ground as the house itself: this mode, therefore, is too much like building two separate houses, in order to have the accommodations of one; to say nothing of another, and no small inconvenience in itself, namely, the distance to which the servants are removed, if not from all, at least from the greater part of the rooms in the house, and their removal in some degree from observation. On the contrary, by forming the offices in the basement, whether entirely or partly under ground, direct communication may be obtained between them and the several parts of the house, should it be so large as to require more than one access from the offices to the rooms above. Another great recommendation to placing the offices below the principal apartments is, that an unobstructed view may be obtained from every front of the house, and also that the pleasure-grounds may be continued quite round it, without interruption from out-buildings, courts, &c. In order to secure these advantages to the fullest extent, a convenient subway may be formed to the offices, for the conveyance of whatever the establishment requires; and the offices, and their out of door appurtenances, may be farther screened by a series of terraces, by means of which the lawn and pleasure-grounds may be rendered quite private." (Design xv.)

In the titlepage we are promised " Specifications, &c., as well as Estimates, to each Design." Not a single specification is given in the course of the work; but, in the appendix, there is a specification to the cottage, Design I. There are estimates to each design; but they are merely the totals of what each will cost, without stating how the calculations have been made, or what part of the country they refer to. If the cubic contents of each design had been given, the reader might have formed an estimate for himself.

The author states it to be his intention to give, in the third volume, not only specifications for the designs contained in it, but also for some of those in the first and second volumes. We are also informed that a "novel and perfectly satisfactory mode of ascertaining the cost of any building will be given" in this third volume.

The specification to the cottage, Design I., which is contained in the appendix, is so far good; but a great drawback to the utility of the book consists in its being totally without sections, or other details, which might enable a country builder to carry any of the designs into execution, or to compose any designs in a similar style. The work concludes with the author's terms as a professional man, which we give verbatim:—

" The author's terms for general plans and elevations, specifications and working drawings, either according to any of the designs furnished, or embracing any alterations proposed, are as follows: for general plans, elevations, sections, working drawings, and specifications containing full particulars and form of contract. For one or more cottages, not exceeding 200*l.*, 16*l.* For one or more, costing 500*l.*, 25*l.* For one or more, costing 750*l.*, 30*l.* For an ornamental cottage or villa, not exceeding 1000*l.*, 40*l.* For ditto, not exceeding 1500*l.*, 45*l.* For ditto, not exceeding 2000*l.*, 50*l.* For all exceeding 2000*l.*, at 3 per cent. If engaged as an architect to superintend any building amounting to 2000*l.* and upwards, provided the drawings of every kind, specifications, and forms of contract are to be furnished, the charge will be 5 per cent. on the amount of the building. The expense of the journeys to superintend, to be paid by the employer, and also the clerk of the works."

These terms are moderate; and it must be satisfactory to the employer of an architect to have some idea, beforehand, of what he will have to pay him. We would, however, in every case, adopt the suggestion of our correspondent Scrutator (p. 15.); and we would stipulate, also, that a certain sum, say 5*l.* or 10*l.*, should be deducted from his commission for every chimney that smoked within one year from the completion of the building, to such an extent as to require a cowl, or other earthenware or metallic deformity, such as disfigure so many dwelling-houses in England; the architect, of course, having the direction of the setting and arranging of the stoves, grates, &c.

The reader will observe that the architect's charge, for the plans of a cottage which would cost 200*l.* in erecting, is 16*l.* Now, this being a very serious addition to the cost of small buildings of that kind, when erected by a person of limited means, but whose taste might render him as susceptible of enjoying architectural beauties and comforts as the most wealthy, it shows the great necessity of teaching carpenters, masons, and bricklayers, not to say country builders, to be their own architects; and this it was our great object to accomplish, in our *Encyclopædia of Architecture*.

The most remarkable thing connected with Mr. Goodwin's book is, the circumstance of his employing another person to describe his designs. We know that architects often apply to artists to put in the landscapes which decorate their elevations; but we were not aware before that they also employed literary men to describe them. We think the architect ought to be capable of doing both himself. The public, however, have gained, as far as the work before us is concerned; for no person that we know is more competent to describe architectural designs than Mr. Leeds.

In conclusion, notwithstanding the faults which we have found with some of the designs, we do not think this book contains more than fall to the share of most others of the same kind. What the author appears to us to want is, a reasoning taste, which can react on his own productions. The possession of a reasoning taste would have enabled him to avoid such incongruities as putting rustic columns, which always convey the idea of temporary duration, to enriched masonic architecture, which always conveys the idea of durability. So many of the designs, however, in Mr. Goodwin's second volume, are beautiful, that we can most cordially recommend it to the public; and we look forward to the third volume, and its "novel mode" of forming estimates, with great interest.

ART. V. *Examples for Interior Finishings: consisting of single, sash, and folding doors, French windows, with shutters, chimney-pieces, &c., with their cornices and other mouldings, drawn the real size. Also various examples, full size, of cornices for rooms and staircases, base and surbase mouldings, architraves, &c., and adapted to all persons connected with the practical parts of building.* By C. W. Trendall, Architect. Large 4to, 24 lithograph plates. London, 1833. 14*s.*

THIS is a useful description of book for carpenters and builders; and, though there is nothing new or remarkable in it, there is evidence of care and attention on the part of the author. In order to give gentlemen who are their own architects an idea of the nature of this work, we shall submit a brief notice of its contents. Plate I. is a single door, with a plan, elevation, and section, showing the linings, &c. II. Parts full size for the single door, displaying the various mouldings, &c. III. Swing-door. IV. Details of the swing-door, full size. [A swing-door is one which is so hinged as to open either way.] V. Sashdoor. VI. Parts full size for the sash door. VII. Sash and dwarf door, with plan, elevation, and a variety of details. VIII. Folding-doors. IX. Parts full size for the folding-doors. X. French casement window. XI. Parts full size for the French casement window. XII. Another French casement window. XIII. Parts full size for the same. XIV. and XV. Another French casement window, with the parts of the full size, showing the meeting styles, hanging styles, window frame, meeting bar, metal bar to insert in the window sill, perforated with holes for the escape of rain water, &c. XVI. XVII. and XVIII. are chimney-pieces, with the details in full size. XIX. Cornices for staircases, full size. XX. XXI. and XXII. are cornices for rooms, full size. XXIII. Architrave mouldings, ful lsize; and XXIV. Base and surbase mouldings. All these articles and details are in the classical or modern style; and this suggests the idea, that a similar work for the Gothic, and another for the Elizabethan, manner would be useful books.

This book is published for the author, which to us is always a recommendation; since no author would undergo the trouble and risk the expense of publishing a work on his own account, that he did not feel confident deserved the patronage of the public; and no professional man, more especially, would publish a work on the subject of his profession, unless he thought it would add to his business, or to his reputation. For Mr. Trendall we hope this work may do both.

ART. VI. *A Compilation of splendid Ornamental Designs, from Foreign Works of recent Production. Adapted for the study of drawing, to assist the artist and decorator, and to aid in the various manufactures where superior ornament is required.* In 4to parts, every fortnight; to be completed in 8 parts, containing 3 plates each. London. 1s. each part.

THERE is no letterpress to the first and second parts, now before us, of this work; but the engravings in outline are most beautifully executed, and the designs, which will be equally useful to the architect, the upholsterer, the decorative painter, and even the manufacturer of cloths and papers, are eminently beautiful. The first plate is a design for the ceiling of a room; the second contains four designs for square panels, which would also serve for patterns for the seats of chairs, or for covers for tables; the third plate contains three ornaments for parallelogram panels; the fourth, a pattern for a border, and another for fringed drapery; the fifth plate, a beautiful design for a square ceiling: and the sixth, four designs for panels. These plates, which are engraved in the style of those given in the work of Percier and La Fontaine, deserve the patronage of all architects and artists; and we hail the work as the commencement of an era of good and cheap architectural publications, which workmen may afford to purchase, as well as architects.

ART. VII. *Literary Notices.*

CATTERICK *Church, in the County of York.* A correct copy of the Contract for its building, dated in 1412, illustrated with Remarks and Notes by the Rev. J. Raine, M.A.; and with 13 plates of views, elevations, and details, by Anthony Salvin, Esq., F.S.A., Architect; 4to; will appear on May 1.

Suggestions for the Architectural Improvement of the Western Part of the Metropolis, by Sidney Smirke, Esq.; 8vo. with plates; will also appear on May 1.

The following works are preparing for publication:—

Chippendale's Designs of Interior Decorations in the old French Style, for Carvers, Cabinetmakers, Ornamental Painters, Brass-workers, Modellers, Chasers, Silversmiths, General Designers, and Architects. 50 plates, 4to.

Chippendale's Designs for Sconces, and Chimney and Looking Glass Frames, in the Old French Style. 11 plates, 4to.

Designs for Chimney-Pieces and Chimney-Glasses, of the Times of Inigo Jones and Sir John Vanbrugh. 10 plates, 8vo.

A Book of Ornaments in the French and Antique Styles, by T. Johnson, Carver. 8 plates, 12mo.

Designs for Vases. 17 plates, 12mo.

Designs of the Ornaments and Decorations of Chimney Pieces of the Middle of the last Century. 20 plates, 4to.

Designs of Doors and Windows, in the Italian and Palladian Styles. 10 plates, 8vo.

A Book of Ornaments, drawn and engraved by M. Lock; principally adapted for Carvers. 6 plates, 8vo.

A Book of Ornaments suitable for Beginners, by Thos. Pether. 5 plates, 8vo.

For all the above notices we are indebted to Mr. Weale.

MISCELLANEOUS INTELLIGENCE.

ART. I. *General Notices.*

ARCHITECTURAL Students.—A correspondent recommends, "as a very useful practice for students, that they should have the general plan, dimensions, and some few particulars of a building given to them, and be required to fill it up to the best of their ability. It would also tend greatly to exercise their ingenuity, and to teach them to think for themselves, were they called upon to correct a design, whether of plan or elevation, containing something faulty, yet sufficiently remediable; without being apprised in what the imperfection consists. The utility of such practice can hardly be disputed, yet we suspect that students must generally be left to adopt it for themselves; for it is not every professor of the art who could aid his pupils in studies and exercises of this kind."—*L.* *April* 5. 1834.

Wheatstone's Figures of vibrating Surfaces.— These are published in the volume of the *Royal Society's Transactions* for the year 1833; and, as they contain a great many various combinations of lines, all regular and symmetrical, a correspondent suggests, that, like the kaleidoscope, they may assist the architect or upholsterer in forming designs for tiles, parquetted floors, carpets, oilcloths, pebble-work, mosaic floors, &c. The landscape-gardener or garden architect might also derive valuable hints from them for architectual or geometrical flower-gardens.—*D. April* 9.

ART. II. *Domestic Notices.*
ENGLAND.

MODEL of the National Gallery.—We paid a visit to Mr. Day's exhibition of architectural models, 13. King William Street, April 10th, and were much gratified. The model to which the greatest interest attaches, at the present moment, is that of Trafalgar Square, including the National Gallery now erecting, with St. Martin's Church, and other surrounding buildings. In the centre of the square is shown a large rectangular pond of water, on one side of which, opposite the centre of the National Gallery, is placed an architectural fountain. We have no objection to the fountain, but see no occasion for so much water: a circular basin, of 50 ft. in diameter, would have created the allusion supposed to be required for the name, the hero, and the fountain, and would have left an ample surface for grass, shrubs, and ventilation. With respect to the design for the National Gallery, we entirely disapprove of it, for the following reasons. As a public building, it ought to have been larger, bolder, and more conspicuous than any other range of buildings in the square; but, being of nearly the same height as these buildings, and, like them, broken into a number of parts, it will not be a sufficiently distinguishing feature. Next, as a piece of architectural composition, considered by itself, the elevation wants unity of style; and its effect is more especially injured by the two smaller porticoes of four columns each, intervening between the central portico and the projections at the extremities. These intervening porticoes are in our eyes altogether intolerable; and, even if no other change were made than removing them, the building would be greatly improved. Whenever this can be said of any part of a building or a design, the architect may rest assured that that part is an excrescence: and, therefore, is superfluous, instead of being necessary. The columns in these smaller porticoes are much wider apart than those in the main portico; which is in itself a great deformity, and which is aggravated by the circumstance of the central space, or intercolumniation, in each of the smaller porticoes, being wider than the two on each side of it, in order to admit carriages to the gateway beneath. These two circumstances give the smaller porticoes the appearance of not belonging to the main portico; and, consequently, they are felt as deformities, we should think, by the most superficial observer. We were told that they were placed there to gratify an individual (whose taste we should never think of consulting on any matter where that of the public was also concerned), and we believe it; for we cannot think it possible that Mr. Wilkins would ever voluntarily adopt such excrescences. To us, it appears that there ought to be not only a free competition for the designs of public buildings, but also a free discussion of their merits, by a committee of the general or municipal government, in public, so that that discussion might be made known through the press. There are a number of other interesting models in Mr. Day's exhibition, including one of a new cemetery, proposed to be formed at Notting Hill. This model, and that of the cemetery on the Harrow Road, show that those who have country houses to build, and grounds to lay out round them, and do not understand fully the effect which will be produced from plans and views, might employ Mr. Day greatly to their advantage. We recommend every reader, who can spare time and a shilling, to examine these models.

A Sketch of the Façade of a Design for a National Gallery, by W. H. Leeds, Esq., is now exhibiting in the Suffolk Street rooms. It is described in the catalogue as " showing a combination of two different orders on the same level, and of the same order on different levels; the columns of the same diameter throughout. The two principal galleries on the lower floor are lighted from above, the others partially so. On the upper floor are four galleries of 109 ft. in length, four of 92, and two of 93, two of 70, two of 68, &c., making twenty in all; besides a rotunda 45 feet in diameter, and four lesser ones 25 ft. in diameter, four statues in each of the wings." The author of this design appears to have spared no pains in overcoming difficulties, and in displaying original features; but we think that, in doing so, he has lost sight of simplicity and grandeur. In all buildings, a certain degree of magnitude and simplicity of general form is requisite to produce grandeur; and, where the building is farther intended to convey the idea of elegance or magnificence, there ought to be great beauty or great richness in the details. We should have preferred, either to the design of Mr. Wilkins, or to that of Mr. Leeds, a simple parallelogram in the plan, a bold portico in the centre, and a continued range of pilasters, as in Mr. Wilkins's design, from the centre to the extremities, with a highly enriched entablature, enriched niches with statues in them, and a boldly marked masonry in the basement to the pilasters. We do not say that this is the design that we should prefer above all others; but simply that we should decidedly prefer it to either of the two mentioned.

To show, however, how very different people's opinions are on the same subject, we shall here introduce that of a young friend, well versed in architecture, on Mr. Leeds's design; previously premising that we have asked several friends to send us criticisms on public buildings, in order that our readers may never rely entirely on our opinions, or on that of any one individual, and thus become the followers of another, instead of thinking for themselves. We may here observe, that, whenever we insert the opinion of another, we shall at the same time give our own; and that all opinions given in this work, which are not our own, will be given in the singular number, and with a specific signature.

" Among the architectural drawings at the Suffolk Street exhibition is a design for a National Gallery, by Mr. Leeds; which, if examined, will, I think, be found to display considerable talent, especially when considered as the production of a non-professional artist. Allowing that my opinion may not be perfectly free from partiality, I may, without any great risk of compromising my judgment, pronounce it to be a rich and varied composition, preserving the character and elegancies of the Grecian style, while it gives, in addition, greater diversity of outline and masses. The general distribution of the façade is good and effective; and the whole is so far remote from having any thing common-place about it, that not a single idea in it seems borrowed from the works of others. The uninterrupted extent of the line of columns, differing in respect to their order, but similar throughout in their diameters and intercolumniations, which constitute the leading mass; the screen walls carried up about two thirds of the height of the square pillars at the back of the Ionic colonnades, and thus admitting a view of the mass of building beyond them; and the union of those colonnades with the principal portico, forming altogether a continued covered terrace nearly 300 ft. in length; would, I apprehend, constitute a very rich, picturesque, and imposing piece of architectural scenery, especially as it would be aided in no small degree by the ranges of columns within the Corinthian octostyle. The ornaments introduced as enrichments to the Ionic frieze are novel in application, and, I think, sufficiently appropriate in character to be unexceptionable. There are many other particulars, both of general composition and detail, which it would occupy too much room to particularise here, but which will doubtless not escape the notice of those who will take the trouble to look into the drawing as well as look at it. And as any comparison would seem invidious, or worse, on my part, I must leave others to decide how far this design either excels or falls short of that of the building actually commenced. Fairness, however, requires me to observe, that the one is a mere project, while the other has undoubtedly been greatly fettered by many untoward circumstances. — *D. S. London, April* 5. 1834."

An extensive *Quay at Blackwall* has been formed for the accommodation of steam vessels of the largest class. The whole of the walling next the water has been faced up with cast-iron plates, instead of brick or stone. (*Newspaper*.)

We shall be much obliged by some account of this mode of facing up quays with cast iron.—*Cond.*

Bedfordshire.—The Duke of Bedford has called in the assistance of Mr. Barry, with a view to the improvement of the general assemblage of buildings forming Woburn Abbey, its offices, and garden buildings. Speaking of these as an architectural group, they are at present in a very scattered and unsatisfactory state; and require some grand leading feature, which, at a distance should connect them into a whole. No man is more capable of supplying such a feature than Mr. Barry; because no man, with so much imagination, combines more fully the eye of the painter with the science of the architect. Much has been done in adding to the comforts of Woburn Abbey, by Holland, Wyatt, and others, during the last forty years; but we may safely say, that, except in the distant plantations by Mr. Repton, very little taste has been displayed either in the house or in the park. What can be tamer than the pleasure-ground at Woburn Abbey? or more clumsy than the banks of American shrubs, and the petty cairn of flints and brickbats there? There is one improvement wanting, without which the place can never be looked at by us with pleasure; and that is, the approaching the entrance portico of the house on a level open road, instead of descending to it on an inclined plane between high walls, as at present. There is nothing worse of the kind in England; and yet the evil might easily be remedied by lowering the approach for some hundreds of yards before it arrived at the court-gate of the house. We are quite sure that, if this were properly pointed out to so reasonable and excellent a man as the Duke of Bedford, he would soon have it carried into execution.

Cheshire.—The design of Chester bridge is generally ascribed to the late Mr. Harrison, of Chester. In an engineering point of view, the form is objectionable, being that of the segment of a circle, instead of the curve of equilibration; consequently it derives its support from an unnecessary quantity of solid materials, built into the haunches of the arch. To an engineer who knows what a bridge in such a situation ought to have been, it appears horridly ugly; but few architects think so.—*W. T. Norfolk, March* 15. 1834.

Northumberland.—We observe, by some printed papers sent us, that Mr. Peter Nicholson, the architectural author, is now resident in Newcastle, and that a public meeting was held there, on the 31st of January last, for the purpose of setting on foot a subscription to purchase an annuity for that eminent man. The first resolution adopted by this meeting was as follows: — " That very eminent services have been rendered by Mr. Peter Nicholson (now resident in Newcastle) to scientific men in general, and to the operative mechanics of this country in particular, by his drawings connected with the construction of buildings, and by his valuable inventions and publications of various kinds, which have been the result of a long life spent in the pursuit of useful improvements in the various branches of mechanical science; and, while his conduct through life has been marked by uniform respectability of character, his devotion to science has precluded him from acquiring that competency for declining life which his talents might otherwise have enabled him to secure. This meeting, therefore, feels it due to his merits to attempt to make some provision for him, and to render comfortable the old age of a man to whom the public owes so much." It is most gratifying to observe that upwards of a hundred persons, in Newcastle alone, have put down their names for various sums from 5s. to 10l. We trust that Mr. Nicholson's admirers (and they are many) in London, and other parts of the country, will not be behind his Newcastle friends. Subscriptions will be received in London by Mr Weale, at his architectural library, High Street, Bloomsbury; and in every part of the country by any of the banks, to be transmitted to the bank of Sir M. W. Ridley and Co., Newcastle. We have known Mr. Nicholson since 1810, and have a very great respect for him. If he had been able to publish his architectural dictionary, and his other works, on his own account, he would have now been in the possession of a handsome income; but this not being the case, what is to become of an author, at sixty-eight years of age, who has nothing to depend on but his pen? He has an undoubted claim on a generous public. We have been very highly gratified by the perusal of the speeches delivered at the Newcastle meeting; and the more so, as most of them were made by architects, surveyors, and builders.

Staffordshire.— Trentham Hall, the residence of the Duke of Sutherland, is about to undergo extensive improvements. When we first heard of this, and that Mr. Barry was employed, we could not help doubting whether even he could make anything of this great, dull, flat place, with its immense mansion, as tame and spiritless as the ground on which it stands. We have seen the plans, however, for the additions to and alterations of the house, and for the formation of a large architectural garden, and we must confess that we weredelighted and astonished by them beyond measure. Let no one henceforth ever despair of a dead flat. We shall not attempt to describe the additions made to the house at present; but we may observe that the modifications of the ground, and of the large lake of water and its islands, which are proposed by Mr. Barry, prove him to have as just a taste in landscape-gardening as he has a refined and correct one in architecture. The architectural flower-garden, which will contain several acres, will be the largest and best thing of the kind in England. On one of the islands, a villa, with terraces in the manner of the Isola Bella, will be erected, as a feature to be seen from the house over the architectural garden; and a column, now erecting on a distant hill, will form another feature. The fountains of the garden, which will throw their waters as high as those at Chatsworth, Versailles, or Nymphenburg, will be supplied by a steam-engine, or by a water wheel on a distant stream; and no garden beauty will have a more striking effect in Staffordshire than this feature.

Yorkshire.— *Leeds, April* 9. 1834. I am happy to congratulate you on the publication of your Architectural Magazine; a work which has, in my opinion, long been wanted, especially in this part of the country, where bad taste is displayed daily by men who profess to be builders, but who have not the least knowledge of architecture, and who are filling our streets with such barbarous structures as would "make the angels weep." Your excellent *Encyclopædia of Architecture* has already done much; it has opened the eyes of many who build: and I sincerely hope your Magazine will do more, and attain the important ends which its conductor has in view. Having observed that you have published several notices of buildings projected, in progress, and completed, I beg to forward for your perusal the following hints of what is going on in this neighbourhood, for insertion in your pages, in case you should think them worthy of that distinction.

A *Schoolhouse* is erecting at Wakefield, from the designs and under the superintendence of Richard Lane, Esq., of Manchester. The building is already covered in, and the whole is expected to be completed about next midsummer. It was projected by a number of gentlemen in the West Riding of Yorkshire, and is called the West Riding Proprietary School. The building is in the Tudor Gothic style of architecture, and is a neat structure. The principal front extends 153 ft. in length. In the centre are two turrets, which rise to a height of 56 ft., between which is the principal entrance doorway, and a large window divided by vertical mullions. On each side of the turrets are four windows of lofty proportions, and at each end there are wings with gables, and large windows; the wings project in conformity with the centre, and about 5 ft. from the line of the building. The structure extends in width 58 ft. 6 in., rising, exclusive of the basement story, to the height of 35 ft. The chief feature in the interior consists of an entrance hall, 60 ft. by 30 ft., which is lighted by a window at each end, of large proportions. On each side are two class-rooms, severally 40 ft. by 18 ft.—There are also in the basement story several small apartments for the accommodation of the domestics connected with the institution; and a large play-room, which is entered on the back part of the building by several arched doorways. The foundation stone was laid with much ceremony by the Earl of Mexborough, on the 6th of February last. The building is wholly constructed of gritstone from the quarries at Heath, near Wakefield; except the plinth and mouldings, the stone for which is procured from Warwick Delph, near Huddersfield.

A *New Savings Bank*, of the Ionic order, from designs by Mr. Charles Mountain, of Hull, is also erecting at Wakefield. There are other works going on in the neighbourhood, which I should have noticed in this letter, had I not already extended it to so great a length: however, if you approve of these few hasty remarks, I will most willingly furnish you with every information in my power.—*A Young Architect.*

We shall be much obliged to our correspondent for accounts of the buildings alluded to, and for whatever other information he can send us, suited to the objects of the Magazine.—*Cond.*

SCOTLAND.

Communication of Sound in Public Buildings.— A number of experiments have been made this winter, in Dr. Reid's New Class-Room, Edinburgh, in reference to the communication of sound. The principal peculiarities in the class-room, in this respect, are, 1st, the great distinctness with which every sound is heard in every part, though numerous forms and pillars must intercept, to a considerable extent, its progress in different directions; 2d, the total absence of any echo, or even prolonged reverberation, which, though it may at times add to the sound, necessarily renders each succeeding sound less distinct and articulate; and, 3d, the uncommon facility with which the voice is sustained in every part of the room. The first observation made by almost every individual who visited the premises, when the class-room was building, was, that no individual could ever be heard distinctly in a room so constructed; but when they came to try it, after the room was finished, they all admitted that they never had been in any large room where so trifling an effort was required to maintain the voice at a proper pitch, either in speaking or singing. The last experimental trial was made on Friday evening, and was numerously attended. The Lord Provost and several other members of the Town Council, Sir Thomas Dick Lauder, a number of the Members of the Royal Society and of the Society of Arts, the President of the College of Surgeons, and other eminent scientific gentlemen, were present on this occasion. Dr. Reid explained the construction of the class-room, and attributed its power of communicating sound principally to the following circumstances:—

1st, To the walls being made as low as possible, though the roof is elevated in the middle of the class-room. When the walls of any building are carried to a great height perpendicularly, much of the sound that falls upon them, being reflected above the heads of the audience, is entirely lost to them.

2dly, To the inclination of the roof, which has been constructed in such a manner, that all the pulses of sound which fall upon it are reflected across as great a portion of the audience as possible.

3dly, To no part of the walls or roof being concave. Concave surfaces frequently collect the sound into foci, and ought to be avoided, except where it may be necessary to throw forward the sound in a particular direction.

4thly, To the construction of the floor, which, instead of being boarded or paved in the usual manner, presents a dull or unreflecting surface, so that, when any pulses of sound shall have once fallen upon it, they are never returned to the roof. There is, therefore, no continued reverberation ; hence, each succeeding sound is clear and distinct, never being mixed up with the secondary vibrations from any preceding sound.

5thly, To the introduction of thin boards of wood as frequently as possible, so as to produce, as it were, a large sounding-board. [Where, and how ?]

6thly, To the intersection of the roof and walls with numerous cross spars, so as to prevent the sound passing along them at any part, as in whispering-galleries, &c.

Dr. Reid, in describing the class-room, spoke in different places, and was heard in the most distinct manner, even when totally out of sight of the audience, and at the distance of upwards of 90 ft. from some of them, in situations, too, where there were numerous intervening pillars, &c. In concluding his observations, Dr. Reid mentioned his obligations to many of the members of St. Cecilia's Society, for the assistance they had given him in trying the power of the room with vocal and instrumental music. (*Caledonian Mercury*, March 24. 1834.)

We shall be much obliged to Mr. Milne, or to any other of our Edinburgh correspondents, for a plan, and sections, with such descriptive and architectural details as may be necessary to give our readers a complete idea of this class-room. —*Cond.*

ART. III.— *Retrospective Criticism.*

DAIRY *and Poultry-House.*— Sir, In your *Encyc. of Cott. Arch.*, § 1947., figs. 1721, 1722, and 1723., you give plans and elevations of a dairy and poultry house, but you do not mention how they are situated relatively to each other. I think this important, as nothing can be more offensive than the smell of a poultry-house ; and I should think, if it were too near the dairy, it would be apt to give an unpleasant taste to the milk. — *W. Jan.* 1833.

Table. — Sir, In your *Encyc. of Cott. Arch.*, § 1749., you speak of a table, which you promise to describe afterwards. This you have omitted to do. It is, indeed, mentioned a second time, § 2085., but no intelligible description of it is given. I wish you would remedy this omission in your Architectural Magazine. — *T. W. March*, 1834.

Stands for the Extra-Leaves of Dining-Tables. — In your architectural *Encyclopædia* you give two or three designs for stands for the leaves of dining-tables. They are very handsome ; but I prefer one which serves as a sideboard, or side-table : the leaves slide horizontally into grooves immediately underneath the slab, and are protected from dust by a door opening like the door of an escrutoire. I have also seen a pedestal with two arms, one near the foot, and one near the top, with grooves for the leaves to slide in perpendicularly. — *T. W. Yorkshire.*

Slate has been, for some years past, used in this part of the country for dairy shelves, skirting, and wall linings, window-sills, and the like ; but I have never yet seen it applied in articles of furniture, as your correspondent recommends. (p. 41.) The slate is procured here in large slabs, and is more expeditiously cut dry with a common hand-saw, and afterwards wrought with rasps and files, than in the manner of cutting stone and marble with the aid of water and sand. — *Z. Hertford, March* 21. 1834.

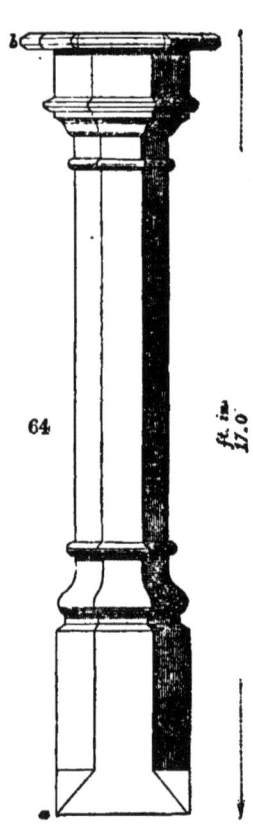

Chimney Shafts. — In fig. 25., p. 64., in my "Notice of a common error in building ornamental Chimney Shafts," the engraver has mistaken my drawing of the cap. I shall therefore feel obliged if you will correct this mistake, by inserting the accompanying sketches. *Fig.* 63. shows the way in which the cap ought to have been drawn; and *fig.* 62. is a section of the moulding: the base is similar to that of *fig.* 64. Fig. 25. (p. 64.) is one of the simplest forms of chimney shafts; but I shall now give you one of a superior description.

Fig. 64. is taken from a chimney shaft at Eastbury House, Barking, Essex: it is entirely built with brick, and rises 17 ft. above the cornice of the base on which it is placed; *a*, in *fig.* 65., is the plan or horizontal section of one half of the shaft at *a*, in *fig.* 64.; and *b*, in *fig.* 65., is the plan of the shaft at *b*, in *fig.* 64. There is a stack of five of these shafts in the centre of Eastbury House; and, by their beautiful proportions, and commanding height above the roof, they produce a strikingly grand and picturesque effect. There are many examples of brick chimney shafts still remaining in the ancient mansions of England, well deserving the attention of the architect; and, as chimney shafts form a principal feature in modern domestic architecture, their forms and situations cannot be too much studied. — *E. B. Lamb. Little James Street, Bedford Row, April* 7. 1834.

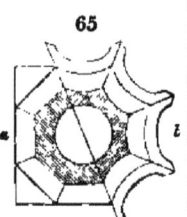

Art. IV. *Queries and Answers.*

A new Grecian Tile, &c. — In 1831, Mr. Davis presented some improvements on the ancient Greek method of tiling to the Bath and West of England Society, which are described in their *Transactions* as most ingenious and beautiful. Mr. Davis, when speaking of them, in his letter to the secretary, says, — "I believe I am enabled to produce that style of roof which is supposed to have given the first idea of the Doric order of Architecture." (*Brit. Farm. Mag.*, vol. vi. p. 111.) Should this meet Mr. Davis's eye, we shall feel much obliged by his sending us sketches, accompanied by some descriptive particulars, of the tile above referred to. — *Cond.*

Portable Smithy. — Might not a portable smithy, or blacksmith's forge, be useful in a neighbourhood of small farms, none of which were large enough to support a smithy separately? I have seen such a thing manufactured by, I think, Holtzapffel. — *W. Jan.* 1833.

THE
ARCHITECTURAL MAGAZINE.

JUNE, 1834.

ORIGINAL COMMUNICATIONS.

Art. I. *Architecture considered as an Art of Imagination.* By the Conductor.

We have already stated (p. 97.) that architecture is an art of imagination as well as one of reason and taste. When we speak of imagination, we allude to that power of the mind which consists in recalling ideas previously treasured up there by the memory, and presenting them in new combinations. Now, it is evident that a person may feel pleasure in beholding an object, without having many ideas treasured up in his memory respecting it; and this is what we have called having a feeling, or a natural taste, for an art. When that feeling is cultivated, the memory and the recollection are, no doubt, called into exercise by it; but not necessarily to that extent which would justify us in stating that the possessor of such a feeling had a taste for architecture as an art of imagination.

An art of imagination is an art which depends directly on the imagination of the artist for its creations. This, we think, is precisely what is meant when architecture is said to be an imaginative art; and hence it follows that the expression is more used with reference to the exercise of their profession by architects, than to the taste or criticism of lovers of architecture. All arts or occupations where invention, or the power of forming new combinations, in the artist or artisan is eminently required, may be called arts of imagination: for example, a machinist, who invents new machines, may be said to practise an art of imagination in doing so. The term, however, is not generally applied to the combinations of the machinist, as his inventions are addressed exclusively to the reason, and can be judged of by mathematical calculation; whereas, by the common consent of mankind, the expression "arts of imagination" is confined to those arts, the inventions of which address themselves to the feelings, and, through them, to the imagination; in short, to those arts which produce emotion, or vivid mental feeling, as distinguished from merely physical feeling. A machine on a new construction, a new composition in landscape, or an entirely new architectural design, are alike produced by the artist from the stores of his memory, passed through the alembic of his imagination: but the machine, before its beauties can be understood, requires the aid of geometrical comparisons and arithmetical calculations; whereas the landscape or the architectural design affects the feelings or the imagination at once through the eye. While we make this statement, it is, at the same time, proper to add that it only holds good with mankind in general: for it is certain that a person enthusiastically devoted to machinery, whether with or without a taste for landscape or architecture, would feel emotion; that is, a vivid train of pleasurable ideas, raised up in, or passing through, his mind at the sight of an original and ingenious machine, and, perhaps, little or none at the same degree of originality and ingenuity in a landscape or an architectural design. Every one has heard of the anecdote of the celebrated mathematician who read the *Paradise Lost* without being able to discover in it any thing that was sublime; but who said that he could never read the queries at the end of Newton's *Optics* without feeling his hair stand on end, and his blood run cold. It would seem, therefore, that every art and pursuit may become an art of imagination to him who follows it with a sufficient degree of ardour and enthusiasm: but, still, this will not justify us in departing from the general use of language, which limits the term "arts of imagination" to those arts, the main object of which is to create emotion in mankind generally.

Architecture, as an imaginative art, may be considered in two points of view; viz., as affecting the mind of the uninitiated spectator, and as exercising the genius of the architect.

The spectator who has little historical, geographical, or technical knowledge of architecture may feel a building to be grand, beautiful, picturesque, rich, ornamented, elegant, or the contrary; and yet his imagination may be but little affected by it. The reason of this is, that the imagination sees only in other things what it has first made its own by observation and memory. In the same manner, a person may be affected by music, that is, by harmonious combinations of sounds, without having the idea of a single air or tune treasured up in his mind. The enjoyment, in this case, is unquestionably far inferior to that which would be obtained by a person who had treasured up many tunes in his memory, when one of them was repeated to him at a considerable distance of time. In like manner, a person who had scarcely ever been out of London, and who had seen few pictures of landscapes, would feel pleasure in looking at a painted or engraved landscape; but this pleasure would be little, compared with that enjoyed by a spectator who had seen many paintings, and had viewed the real landscapes of the most beautiful or romantic parts of this country, or perhaps of foreign countries. The pleasure, even in the last case, would be still greatly inferior to that experienced by the landscape-painter, who would see in a picture not only an accurate imitation of nature, but a beautiful display of the science of his art. The cause of the pleasure, in the first case, is, simply a feeling for rural nature; in the second, it is a cultivated feeling; and, in the third, it is the joint exercise of feeling for this beauty, suggested, as before, by the eye, and a mental feeling for a display of the skill of the artist, suggested by the artist's imagination. Thus the exercise of the imagination adds greatly to the pleasures of taste; and, consequently, whoever wishes to enhance to the utmost his enjoyment of architectural design should be assiduous in storing his mind with ideas on the subject, by reading, by the observation of buildings of every kind, whether as designs or drawings in the portfolios of artists; or of edifices, whether in town or country, newly erected, or in ruins; and whatever may be their uses, their beauties, or their deformities; and, in short, by every means in his power.

The architect to whom architecture is not an art of imagination, as well as an art of reason, can never, by any possibility, rise above the rank of an imitative builder. He may rear edifices of great strength, solidity, and durability, very fitly arranged for the purposes for which they are built, and very correct in their architectural details; but he will never be able to produce a structure in which novelty and originality are combined with the ordinary requisites of excellence; or, when placed in a situation where rules no longer apply, to rise superior to obstacles which would be reckoned insurmountable by ordinary minds; and thus, out of difficulties, to "start" beauties. This can alone be done by the architect of imagination; and it is only such an architect that is entitled to be considered an artist possessing the powers of invention or genius.

It thus appears, that, the more an amateur or architectural critic stores his mind with ideas on architecture, the greater will be his enjoyment when examining architectural designs. It is also evident, from the foregoing considerations, that the preparatory studies of an architect must be chiefly directed to the same object; viz., that of accumulating ideas on his art; since his efforts as a designer will consist chiefly in forming new combinations from these ideas. These combinations must, in every case, be directed to the attainment of a certain end; or, in other words, to the production of an edifice which shall be adapted for certain uses, and shall, at the same time, produce a certain kind of expression of beauty or of character. Hence it follows, that an architect must not only possess genius, or the power of inventing, but also taste to compose his designs according to the principles of beauty, and judgment, or the power of reacting on the creations of his fancy, so as to enable him to bring every design, after it has been suggested by taste, under the control of reason.

Art. II. *On the alleged Degeneracy of Modern Architecture.*
By E. Trotman, Esq.

Among the hastily formed and popularly supported notions upon matters of taste, none seems to be more current than the supposition that all that is excellent in art has been transmitted to us from past ages, and that all the productions of modern skill are mere imitations of the ancient, far inferior to them in grandeur and beauty. We sometimes smile at the fictitious interest with which a pretension to remoteness of origin invests, in the sight of the zealous antiquary, the most ordinary objects; and we can indeed sympathise with the gratification with which even the shadow of a probability may be seized by some Oldbuck, whether to exemplify the principles of castrametation, or any other equally obscure. Let but the figured pottery brought to light in the course of an extensive excavation afford the least evidence of a long interment, and all its outlines are at once discovered to be replete with character and with beauty, however commonplace they might have been at the time of their formation; the grotesque and the ill-proportioned become curious, at least; and, so far from having decreased in value amid all the emulation of modern skill, the old treasure is proved to have been only lying out at compound interest. We are far from despising this feeling of deferential regard for the remains of antiquity; though it be sometimes liable to excess, and open to caricature. The architect, indeed, who has a soul for his profession, will be of all men the most susceptible of impression from matters of antiquarian interest; inasmuch as the most important remains of past ages are those of an architectural character, and in the history of such remains is involved that of nations, arts, and usages, whose every memorial becomes thus tributary to a comprehensive knowledge of his primary subject. Out of this very susceptibility, however, existing, to a certain extent, in almost all minds, as well as his own, arises the necessity for caution, lest the dictates of the judgment upon matters of taste be made subordinate to the suggestions of the feelings. In the absence of this, nothing is more common than for the observers of some mouldering relic to accompany their tribute of praise with a sigh for the inability of modern artists to produce any thing comparable with the works of their predecessors, though with the same justice as that with which the ancient poets sorrowed at the flight of the golden age, or lamented the pygmy powers of their contemporaries, as contrasted with the might of the preceding race. We have no intention, however, to follow out the developement of this principle of dissatisfaction with things present, which has always characterised the human mind; our object being rather to offer a few remarks on the complaint, as popular as it is idle, which charges modern architecture with having degenerated from the excellence of the ancient. Popular as this complaint is, indeed, it is so only among those who have bestowed but a superficial degree of attention upon the subject; yet it cannot be unimportant that the credit of the art should be vindicated before the public mind, affecting, as it does at all times, the honour of an age and nation, as well as the character of its individual professors.

At the outset, therefore, we should wish to be informed, by the objectors to the claims of modern science, what period is to be considered as constituting the boundary between ancient and modern times; and whether, upon reference to the duration of the different architectural systems of successive ages and climes, we shall not find that the inventive powers of the world, in later times, have produced revolutions as entire, as distinctive, as beautiful, and as rapid, as those which marked the earlier progress of constructive skill. Indeed, upon a chronological notice of the periods of Egyptian and Hindoo, of Grecian, Roman, Saracenic, Norman, and Pointed Architecture, we are much mistaken if the art does not exhibit, as it were, an increased impetus in its progress downwards, not without impediments and deflections in its course, but still accumulating its most resistless force for its last stage. However, without taking advantage of this division of time, as the ancient and modern, we will suppose the objection before us to contrast, under the title of modern works, those of somewhere about the last two centuries only, with the remains of preceding ages. And even here, we think, the complainants will have a difficulty in substantiating their charge, while we hold preserved among us the productions of Jones and Wren, of Kent and Burlington; to say nothing, at present, of the creations of our own contemporaries. It is true that these works may be, to some extent, impaired by an implicit deference to the practice of the modern Italian school, uncorrected by a due regard to the purer models of ancient Rome, and the chaste remains of Greece; yet this defect may well be considered as counterbalanced by the great variety of composition, and the exuberance of fancy, displayed in the productions of this period; qualities the more worthy of admiration when we consider how many of those productions were the creation of one mind. If we compare the degree of invention exhibited in the temples of Greece with that which characterises the ecclesiastical architecture of the last two centuries, to go no farther than our own country, we are far from having any occasion to fear the result. In truth, one Greek temple would represent a hundred; and it was for the sculptor, rather than the architect, to create the means of distinction between so many of the same general composition. And as to that appendage which does not admit of any comparison, since it is absent from ancient works altogether, the steeple, we are prepared, in spite of all hypercritical cavils, to think that modern architecture has lost nothing by its introduction. Unquestionably it is to the pointed style, from which this feature was originally derived, that we must look for its most successful treatment; still, however, we think that the prospect which the Londoner may obtain from Blackfriars or Southwark Bridge will be quite sufficient to vindicate the credit of our church architects of the past age, as having, in many instances, met the difficulties of this species of composition with a masterly skill. And though it be true that we have no classical precedents for steeple architecture, the most critical must confess that we have numerous examples of the application of orders upon orders, that application upon which steeple composition essentially depends; and of those examples some even claim the boasted sanction of Greek taste, as may be seen in the remains at Pæstum. We think, also, that it cannot be complained that we have failed to turn this privilege of placing orders upon orders to at least as good account as did the architects of classic times. Indeed, we should rather say, we had turned it to a better; since, if there be any circumstances which justify the use of columns upon columns, they are those which require the elevation of a lofty mass upon a very contracted base, and not, as in the Greek and Roman instances, those which allow an ample extent in connection with a limited height. After all, we should be sorry to forego the elegance of many of our specimens of steeple architecture, to satisfy the demands of a servile deference to classic precedents, which would be at once to divest our cities of all that is commanding in the distant prospect, and leave us only the sullen aspect of the dingy warehouse top and blackened gas chimney. However, our business is not with these features alone, as it is not to them that popular complaint particularly applies. To meet that complaint, then, on whatever other ground it assumes, we may anticipate the enquiry, " How is it that we see so little of grandeur and of elaborate ornament in the sacred and other edifices of the present time, compared with those of some centuries back?" This question, indeed, generally stands associated with two opinions equally untenable; the one consisting in the unqualified assumption of the position on which the enquiry rests, and the other in the conclusion that architectural science must have degenerated if that position be true. We may answer the question by noticing these two opinions separately: and as to the first, we reply, that it is not *universally* the case that the ecclesiastical architecture, for instance, of recent date, is deficient in dignity and beauty as compared with that of olden time. It is not, in truth, the work of every year, or of every century, to be raising a cathedral, provided, as we have been, by the munificence of our forefathers, with structures of that class, which seem calculated to endure as long as the earth on which they stand. We think, however, that, in the event of such a demand, we have, in the labours of Sir Christopher Wren, a sufficient proof that modern skill is quite able to meet the exigency of the case, and, as the greater includes the less, to provide for the successful treatment of all minor examples of ecclesiastical architecture. It is true, indeed, that the proportionate number of richly embellished churches is not now so great as it formerly was; but the reason for this is to be found in considerations which have no reference to any existing state of architectural science. Of these considerations, the most weighty arises from the change which has taken place in public opinion, upon matters ecclesiastical and religious, since the era of the Reformation. The influence which the priesthood of the Roman church formerly exercised over the persons, property, and services of the laity of all classes, and which induced alike the wealthy and the skilful to vie with each other in the splendour of those productions which were to purchase the peace of the departed spirit, and insure the favour of the saints, now no longer incites the liberality of a superstitious people. On the other hand, while the purer principles of the English church lead her to disclaim the system of artifice and spiritual domination, on which papal splendour has ever thriven, the reaction which, in these times of tolerance and speculation, has too generally taken place, from a state of blind subserviency to the opposite extreme of moral indifference, is necessarily far from favourable to the display of magnificence in ecclesiastical structures. While, therefore, this feeling causes the extension of so grudging a hand to the support of the outward dignity of the church, and while the increase of population demands the economical use of funds appropriated to the erection of sacred edifices, in order to increase their number and consequent efficiency, it is obviously idle to assert that architecture of this class has degenerated from its ancient splendour, when, in so many instances, its only object is that of providing the most ample and sufficient accommodation at the most economical rate; an object, certainly, never more effectually attained than in the churches of later years.

Not to insist on the opportunity afforded for architectural display, by the cheap rate of labour in former days, — an advantage which seems to us somewhat overrated, when we consider the difficulty of accumulating wealth for the purposes of building, as necessarily increased in proportion to the lowness of remuneration for work in general, — there are other circumstances which tend to explain the frequency of the magnificent structures of our forefathers. Of these, the chief are to be found in the spirit of the times, which, being incessantly occupied in the contentions consequent on the existence of the feudal system at home, and the state of our political relations abroad, rendered military pursuits the all-absorbing object of attention to the nobles, and made, at the same time, castellated structures the most frequent and the most important means and monuments of those pursuits. Besides this, the *indirect* influence of such a state of things upon architecture was doubtless far from inconsiderable, since the withdrawment of the attention of the great from objects of literature, of domestic refinement, and of social cultivation, left them to concentrate the power of their wealth upon works which tended so much to gratify their love of display as did those of architecture and its subordinate arts; works, too, for the undertaking of which, the construction of their own castles would create a taste, and the splendour and claims of the ecclesiastical establishment would at once offer ample opportunity and powerful inducement.

We conclude, therefore, that the state of society under the extremes of nobility and vassalage, dazzled as it so often was by the pursuits and splendours of military life, and subservient as it was to the ambition and power of the Roman church, from the castle-building age of Stephen down to the era of the perfection of Pointed Architecture in this country, will afford a perfectly satisfactory answer to the enquiry, how it is that our later works of eminence are few compared with those of the age of the Edwards and the Henrys. To allow that this is the case, however, and that edifices of such surpassing beauty are now less frequently raised among us than formerly, is a very different thing from our conceding that, in those instances in which architecture does now put forth its powers, it displays less ability than it once did. To form a correct opinion upon this latter aspect of the general question, we ought rather to observe what the advance of modern architecture has accomplished, under circumstances less favourable to its progress than heretofore. It cannot for a moment be the subject of doubt, that our common order of domestic and every-day buildings exhibits much more of convenience, in union with what may be called an equalised neatness of character and finish, than formerly, at a much less relative expense; nor can it be supposed that we are less acquainted with the capabilities of materials and the principles of scientific construction than were our predecessors. All this is, indeed, the natural result of that more general diffusion of property and of knowledge, which, while it forbids the display that would once have been made by monopoly, demands a style characteristic of that middle rank of life which can scarcely be said to have existed in those ages which were most prolific of splendour. It is, moreover, to be observed, that the changes which have taken place in our *ecclesiastical* architecture have been such as to provide the most commodious structures for a greatly increasing population, with regard at the same time to very different purposes of application than formerly, in the abolition of all that apparatus of processional and ritual parade by which an appeal was made to the senses of the multitude, and which required for its exhibition great space and complex arrangement. What later architects have achieved, under the restrictions of simplicity of form and economy of cost, is quite sufficient to justify the expectation, that, under more extended circumstances, their productions might rival those of antiquity. At least we entertain this hope with regard to many, and more particularly to those whose successful works in the pointed style have latterly adorned the metropolis, and various parts of the kingdom; for we must confess, indeed, that we have very little reason to anticipate much benefit from the constant repetition of the forms of Grecian temples for the purposes of Christian churches. It would be a somewhat invidious task, to enter at any length upon a comparison of the works of contemporary and past architects in detailed and specific instances, or to expatiate on the faults of some recent buildings of high pretension. We notice the most popular departments of architecture in this very cursory manner, merely for the sake of showing that the changes which they have experienced in modern times are attributable to correspondent alterations in the state of society, and of our institutions, religious and political; and that the study and profession of architecture ought not, therefore, to suffer in public estimation, for the inability to create the opportunity, or command the pecuniary resources, necessary to magnificent display.

10. *Furnival's Inn, May* 17. 1834. E. T.

ART. III. *The Elements of Grecian and Roman Architecture, practically explained to the General Reader.* By Mr. J. ROBERTSON.

(*Continued from* p. 113.)

THE object of the present article is to enable the reader to generalise on the different proportions of what are called the orders of classical architecture.

The three orders which were invented by the Greeks are considered by architects as expressive of strength, grace, and richness. The Romans subsequently invented two others, with a view to extend the bounds of strength on the one side, and of richness on the other. The proportions of these five orders are founded on the lower diameter of the columns of each; all their different members and details being drawn to a scale formed from such diameter. This scale is frequently formed by dividing the diameter into two equal parts, which are called modules, and one of these modules into twelve divisions, which are termed parts. The word module is used to signify an element in a system of measurement; which element is taken from a portion of the body to be measured. Thus, among painters, the head is a module for the measurement of the human body. Different architects have adopted different modes of forming this scale. Perrault divided the semidiameter of the Corinthian order into thirty small parts, generally called minutes. Vignola divided the module into twelve parts in the Tuscan or Doric, and eighteen in the other orders. But the more general way is to divide the lower diameter into six equal parts; and each of these parts into ten minutes: then every member of an ordonnance, or order, may be described as being, either in height or projection, so many minutes of this scale. Every order is divided into three parts; namely, the pedestal, the column, and the entablature: and these are subdivided, so that the pedestal is composed of a base, die, and cornice; the column of a base, shaft, and capital; and the entablature of an architrave, frieze, and cornice. These parts are of unequal height; and an assemblage and arrangement of the mouldings and principal details which compose them are called the profile of the order. Those profiles produce the most striking effect, in which the parts are few, and so applied as that some member may predominate in each division. This predominance of one member gives what is called expression. The following are general rules for determining the relative proportions of those parts which compose an order.

When a height is given which is common to all the five orders; that is, when they are all reduced to the same height, in order to exhibit their comparative proportions and the different diameters of their respective columns; this height is divided into nineteen equal parts. (*fig.* 66.) A conventional rule, agreed on by architects, is, that the height of the pedestal must always be one third of the column, and the height of the entablature one fourth; consequently, the pedestal requires four of these parts, the column twelve, and the entablature three. The twelve parts allotted to the column are then, for the Tuscan order, divided into seven; for the Roman Doric, into eight; for the Ionic, into nine; and for the Corinthian and Composite, into ten; and one of these parts forms the lower diameter of each respective column. The diameter is then a guide for the proportions of all the other members of the order.

When the given diameter of the column of each order is the same, their relative heights are obtained in the following manner (*fig.* 67.):— Upon a given straight line raise five perpendiculars equidistant from each other, which perpendiculars will form the axis of the columns of each order. On the first of

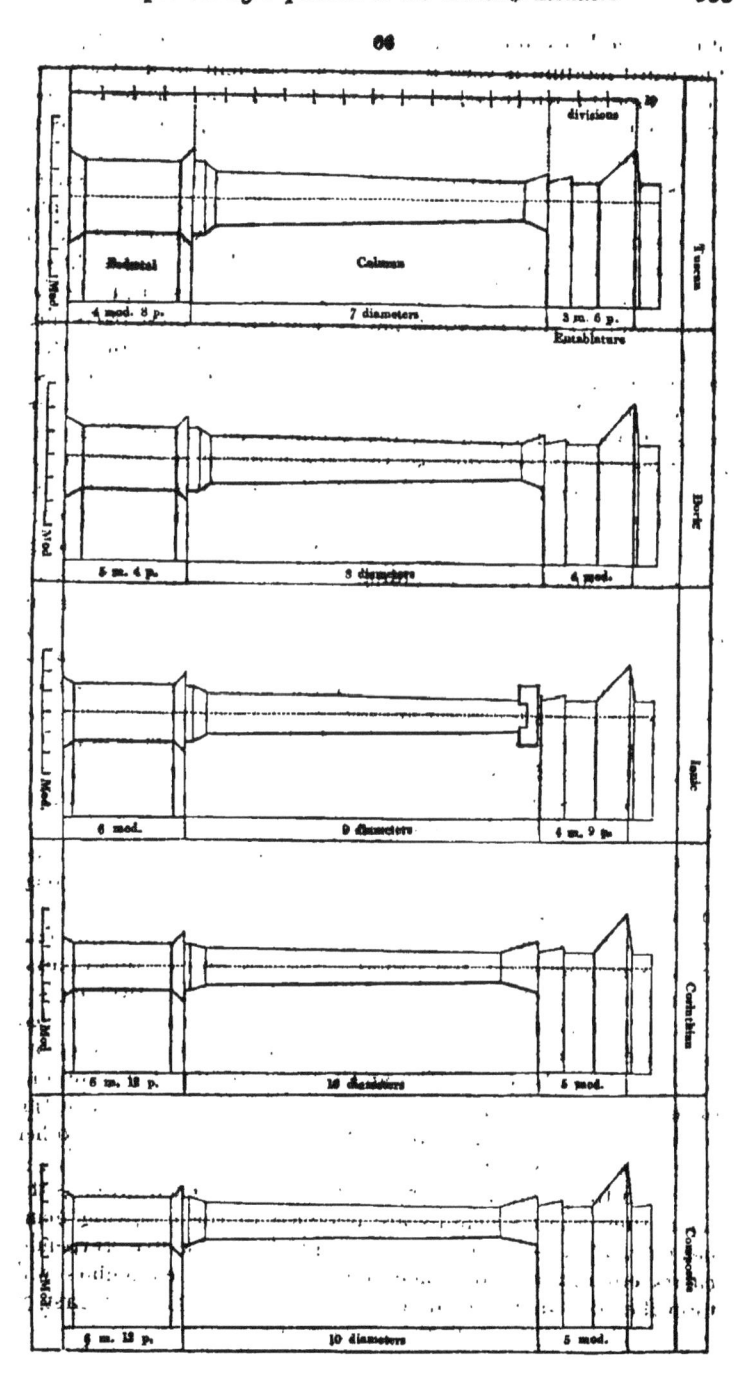

practically explained to the General Reader. 155

	Pedestal	Column	Entablature	
	4 mod. 8 p.	7 diameters	3 m. 6 p.	Tuscan
	5 m. 4 p.	8 diameters	4 mod.	Doric
	6 mod.	9 diameters	4 m. 9 p.	Ionic
	6 m. 12 p.	10 diameters	5 mod.	Corinthian
	6 m. 12 p.	10 diameters	5 mod.	Composite

these vertical lines the Tuscan order is set up by the scale of minutes; and on the fourth line the Corinthian is erected; the Composite, which is set up on the fifth line, has the same proportions as the Corinthian: then a line is drawn from the top of the Tuscan cornice to the top of the Corinthian cornice; and where this line intersects the second perpendicular is the proportionate height of the Doric cornice; where it intersects the third line, is the height of the Ionic cornice. The same is done by a line from the top of the capital, and from the top of the pedestal, of the Tuscan, to the top of the capital, and to the top of the pedestal of the Corinthian order; when the points of intersection with the intermediate perpendiculars determine the respective heights of the divisions of the Doric and Ionic orders. This, of course, must be the result, because each ordonnance, or order, when the diameters of their columns are exactly the same, increase in height in arithmetical progression.

These are the relative heights of the orders when the diameters of their columns are the same: but such a contrast would not be proper, if they were employed in the same building in stories above one another, or in any other way connected; therefore, to obtain a proportional gradation of their parts, so that they may appear consistent when thus employed, ten modules are taken from the scale of the Tuscan order, and divided into twelve parts, to form a scale of modules for the Corinthian order. (*fig.* 68.) The heights of the Tuscan and Corinthian orders are then set up from their respective scales; and the remaining part of the process is the same as that described for *fig.* 67., the diameters of the Doric and Ionic columns being found from their heights. In this case it will be observed that the diameters are not exactly the same, but decrease from the Tuscan to the Corinthian, and, consequently, all the members of the three last orders will be decreased in proportion.

Pedestals and Entablatures. — The whole height of the pedestal, which is shown with relation to the other parts of the order in *figs.* 66, 67, and 68., should be divided into nine parts, one of which is given to the cornice, two to the base, and the remainder to the dado, die, or body of the pedestal: the latter ought never to be less in height than the width of the plinth belonging to the column which it supports; and, consequently, not less in height than its own width. The following may be given as a general rule for the subdivision of the entablature: viz., the whole height, obtained in the manner shown in *figs.* 66, 67, and 68., is, in all the orders except the Doric, divided into ten parts, three of which are given to the architrave, three to the frieze, and four to the cornice. In the Doric order, the whole height should be divided into eight parts, and two given to the architrave, three to the frieze, and three to the cornice.

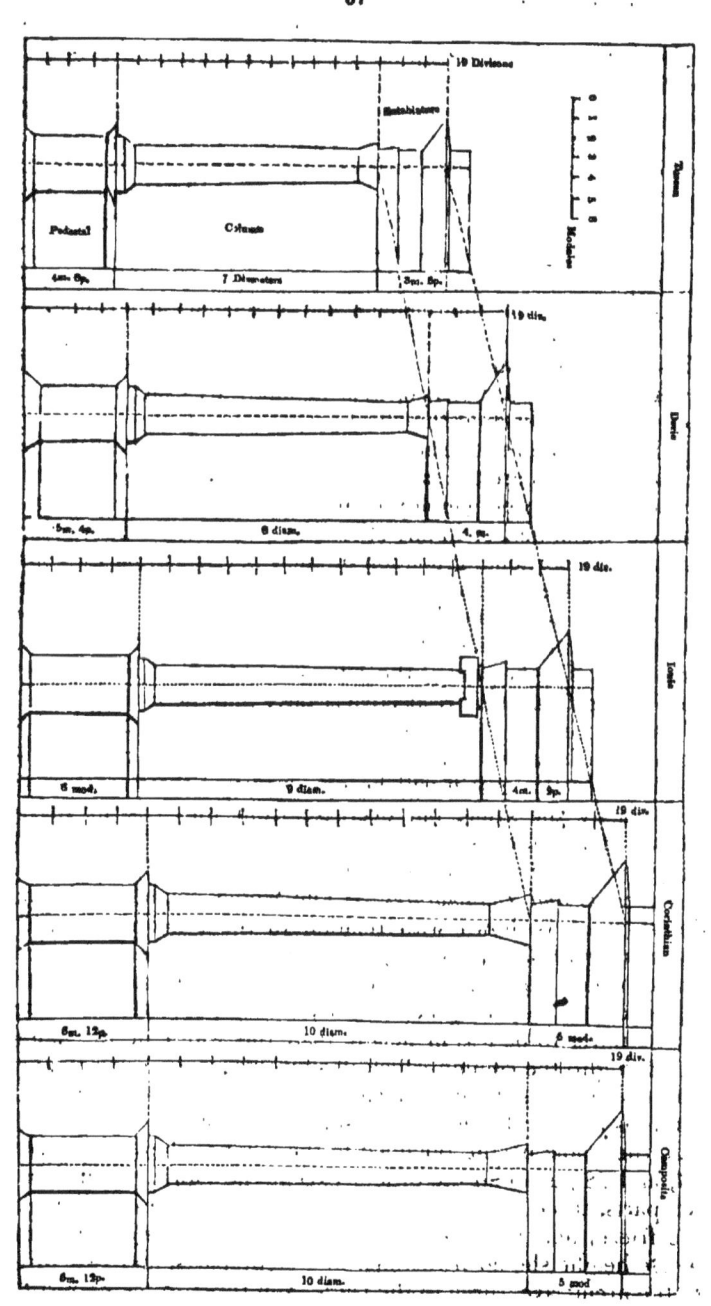

practically explained to the General Reader. 157

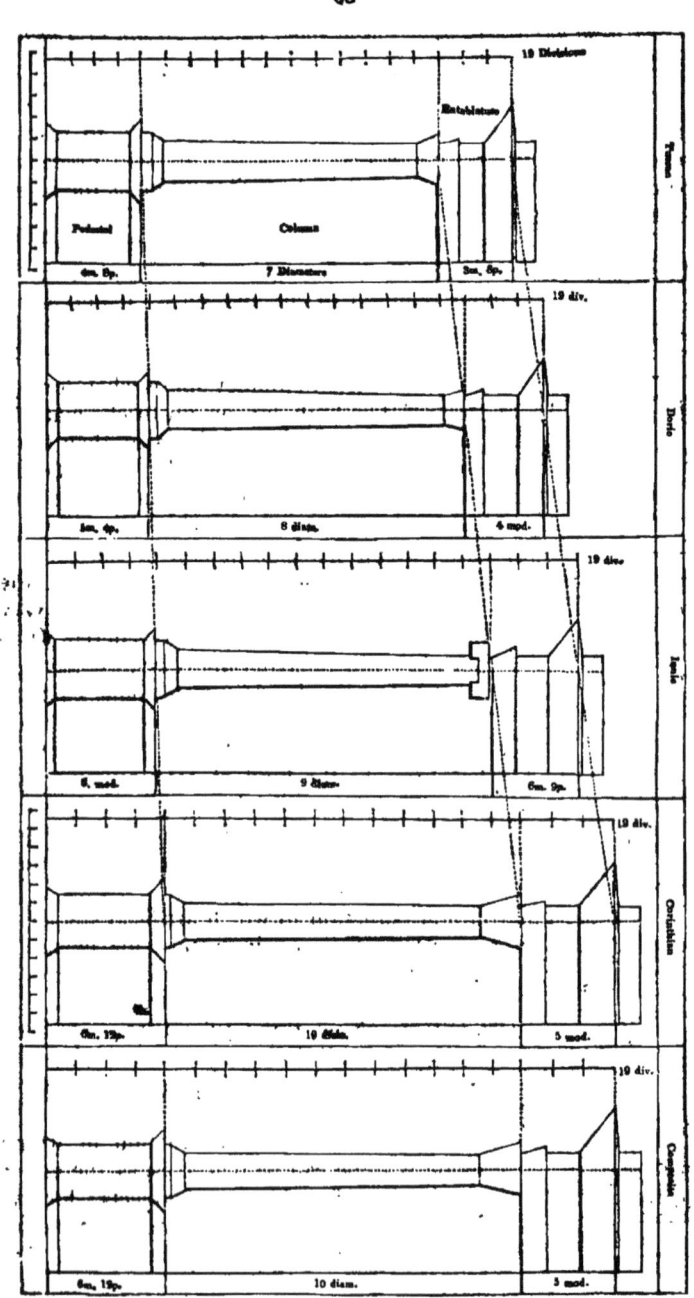

158 *Elements of Grecian and Roman Architecture.*

Art. IV. *Notice of some of the Ornamental Chimney Pots and Shafts manufactured of Artificial Stone by Mr. Austin of London.* By the Conductor.

To draw the attention of general readers to architecture as an art of taste, we consider it advisable not only to discuss general principles, as in the first paper of this and preceding Numbers, but to enter into practical details. This is the object of the following article.

The great expense of stone, in consequence, not only of the distance from which it has to be brought to London, but of the labour required to cut and chisel it into ornamental forms, has hitherto put it beyond the power of the great majority of builders to bestow much ornament on chimney shafts when formed of stone. The high tax on all bricks made in any other form, or of any other size, than those of the common building brick, prevents the modern builder from constructing those enriched brick chimney shafts which are so much admired in the mansion-houses of the time of Henry VIII. and Elizabeth. These two causes have led to the invention of artificial stone, which is now improved to so very high a degree, that it may be considered, when not placed in unfavourable circumstances, as almost equally durable with some kinds of natural stone; such, for example, as Portland or Bath stone. Mr. Austin states that he has brought the kind of composition which he employs as artificial stone, to such a degree of perfection, that his imitation of Portland stone is very nearly, if not quite, as durable as the natural material itself.

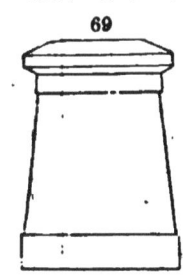

The most unfavourable situation in which artificial stone can be placed is on a moist surface, or in water: for example, when it is employed as the base or plinth of a sundial or a vase in a garden; or, as a fountain. Now, this artificial stone has been employed in all these ways for several years, without showing any conspicuous symptoms of decomposition.

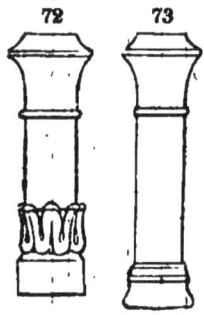

The most favourable situation in which artificial stone can be placed is, as the upper termination of architectural objects; for example, as chimney shafts or pots, acroteria, pinnacles, terminations to buttresses, &c.

160   Ornamental Chimney Pots and Shafts

74. The cause of its durability in such situations is, that, when it is wet with rain, every part being equally exposed to the weather, it very soon becomes dry. The cause of its liability to decay in moist situations is, that, in such situations, it is long in drying; and that, when frost occurs while the stone is yet moist on the surface, the well known expansion of water in freezing, ruptures it, and ultimately causes it to scale off.

When to the durable properties of this kind of artificial stone it is added, that it is as easily moulded into shape as stucco, Roman cement, or cement made of lime, sand, and smithy ashes, and that it is nearly as cheap, the public may conceive what a valuable material it is, and how well it is calculated to aid in the advancement of the decorative part of architecture. As a proof that architects coincide in opinion with what is above stated, we may observe that some of the most eminent of them who have built houses, not only near London, but in stone districts in the north of England, in Scotland, and also in Ireland, where the walls have been entirely of stone, have had their chimney shafts from Mr. Austin, in order to save the enormous expense that would be required to carve them, even where the stone is got for the labour of quarrying.

75.

Having said thus much respecting the quality of Mr. Austin's artificial stone, and its fitness for chimney pots and shafts, it only remains to give a few examples of the forms which he has manufactured; premising that we are not responsible for the taste displayed in them, and that they include but a very small part of the specimens which may be seen by the public at his extensive and most interesting establishment in the New Road, near Fitzroy Square. This establishment

76   77   78

has occupied the whole of Mr. Austin's time, and, we believe we might add, his money, for many years, and it richly deserves to be visited by all architects and architectural amateurs.

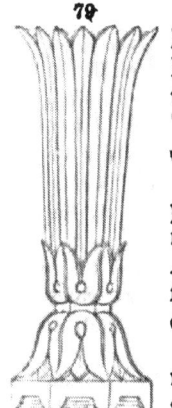

Fig. 69. is a square chimney pot of the simplest kind. Pots of this form, made of Roman cement, have been in use for the last dozen of years on the better description of houses about London. They formerly cost, by retail, about a guinea each, but they are now less than half that price.

Figs. 70. and 71. are two octagonal chimney pots, generally made of Roman cement, but far more durable in Mr. Austin's composition. *Fig.* 71., when there are five or six together, forms a very handsome termination to a stack of cottage or small villa chimneys.

Figs. 72. and 73. are elegant forms, which look remarkably well on small Italian villas, or neat blue-slated ornamental cottages. Of course, *fig.* 73. is placed on a square plinth of suitable dimensions.

Fig. 74. is a chimney pot in the shape of a baluster. The same form may be used as the shaft of a sun-dial, or as the pedestal to an ornamental vase.

Fig. 75. is composed of several pieces; and though it is a compound of forms, some of them of the Grecian class, and others belonging to Gothic architecture, yet it has been a good deal used. It is not introduced here on account of its beauty, but as aiding to form a variety.

Figs. 76, 77, and 78. are vases calculated for being used as chimney pots. *Fig.* 77. is a very elegant form, either by itself, or on a pedestal, as shown in *fig.* 88. p. 162. *Fig.* 78. is a very handsome form, and has been much used in Italian entrance lodges.

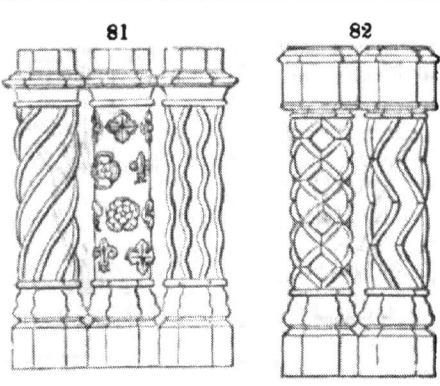

Fig. 79. is an exceedingly beautiful form, and its indented outline is better calculated for breaking the force of high winds than if that outline were smooth, as in the preceding figures, 76, 77, and 78., or even 69.

Fig. 80. represents two chimney shafts in the old English style, adapted for cottages. Shafts of this kind were generally of different patterns in the same stack, so that, formerly, when they were prevalent, they must have formed rather an expensive part of the building.

Vol. I. — No. 4.   M

162   *Ornamental Chimney Pots and Shafts*

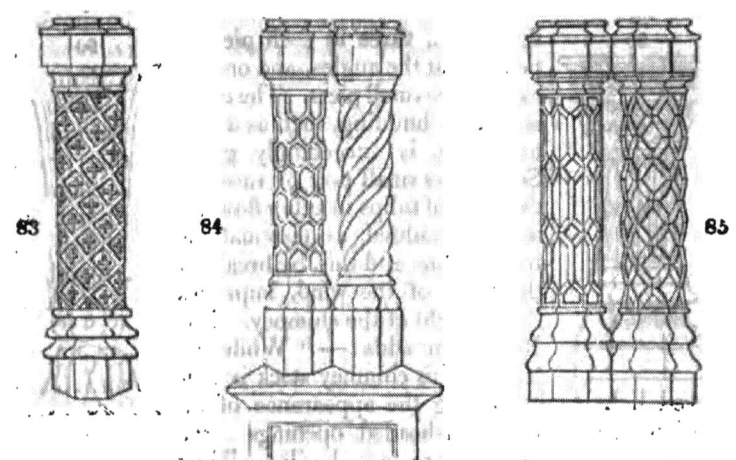

It must be recollected, however, that labour in those days was comparatively cheap.

Figs. 81, 82, 83, 84, and 85. are chimney shafts in the old English style for villas. These are made by Mr. Austin of various heights, from 5 ft. to 10 ft. and upwards; and they constitute one of the greatest ornaments to dwellings of every kind in the old English style.

Fig. 86. is a plain Gothic chimney shaft, well adapted for being placed as a termination to a flue in a subordinate description of offices, where the shafts on the house and on the principal offices are in the enriched style of *figs.* 83, 84, and 85.

Fig. 87. is a chimney shaft for a building in the modern or Italian style, which may either be used as it is, or with some termination, such as *figs.* 77. or 79.; as shown in *figs.* 88. and 90. This pedestal, or shaft (*fig.* 87.), may also be used as a support for a sundial, for a vase, for a stone basin to contain gold-fish or a curious aquatic plant, or for a baptismal font in a church.

Fig. 89. is a richly ornamented Gothic chimney shaft which may be employed for any of the purposes for which *fig.* 87. is adapted.

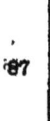

Fig. 91. represents a mode of terminating a stack of chimneys in which there are thirteen flues; viz., three in each pier or pedestal at the angles, and one on each of the small piers. The effect in a plain building, such as a manufactory, is exceedingly good. Sometimes small pots or vases, in the form of tulips or other flowers, are superadded as terminations to each flue; and this, by breaking the force of the wind, improves the draught of the chimney. Mr. Robertson adds:—" While the form of this chimney stack is rendered light by its having the appearance of an Italian screen, the arch-headed openings serve the double purpose of ornament and utility. They are useful, because the openings must create a draught, which will assist the upward transit of the smoke; while, if the stack were solid, the wind, when interrupted in its course, would pass up to the top, and thence horizontally over the flues [unless they were broken by terminating pots], and consequently prevent the free egress of the smoke. However inconsistent it may seem to see smoke emerging from a cluster of flues, in the form of a railing or screen, the advantages connected with this manner of forming a stack of chimneys, fully justify its adoption."

It is almost needless to observe, that, in all cases wherein the indigenous architecture of the country is imitated, the elements of that architecture should be employed in forming the chimney shafts and pots; and that, when classical or exotic styles are employed, recourse must be had to the elementary forms of those styles for compositions of the same kind.

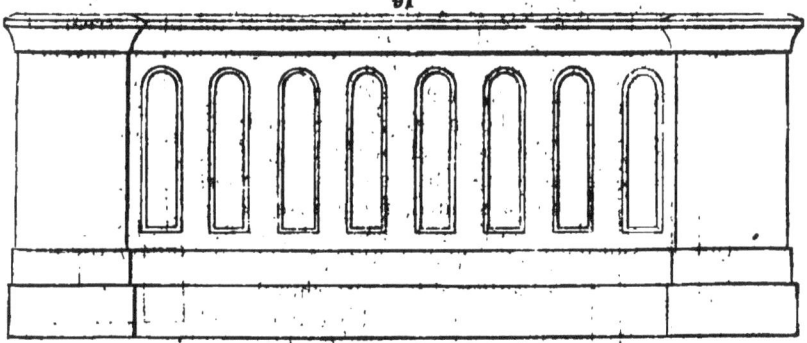

ART. V. *On the Gin Temples of the Metropolis.* By CYNICUS.

AMONG the magnificent specimens of architectural skill in this metropolis, the gin temples, if not the most ancient or classical, must be allowed, at least numerically considered, to carry away the palm in splendour. As peculiar specimens of the building art, some small portion of your readers' time may not perhaps be altogether misapplied in directing their attention to them.

It is, I believe, universally admitted, that superstition, although characterised as the 'vice of weak minds,' has nevertheless been the productive parent of all the most durable and most beautiful specimens of architecture in this as well as in other countries: indeed, I may safely affirm, without fear of contradiction, that the more absurd the superstition of the country, so in proportion has been the splendour of its architecture, and the general progress of the fine arts. We have all heard of, or seen, the gigantic pyramids and catacombs of Egypt, the massive and highly enriched cavern temples of India, the magnificent temples erected to the heathen deities in ancient Greece and Rome, the splendid mosques of Turkey, and the richly ornamented and graceful cathedrals of modern Europe; and, whatever opinions we may entertain as to the (in one point) mental weakness of their authors, we cannot but hail with reverence those feelings, which were sufficiently powerful to hand down to posterity such stately specimens of national taste and individual genius.

Admitting superstition as a vice, how can we sufficiently express our gratitude to our worthy ancestors, for extracting so much good out of evil; or to our equally worthy contemporaries, for making the most extensive vice in this city the prolific source of so much architectural display? Such costly specimens of truly classic taste were never before seen in the busy streets of London, as now meet the gratified eye of the intellectual traveller at nearly every corner of each dingy by-lane and street of this gin-drinking metropolis. I would advise any architect that has the love of his profession sincerely at heart, uncontaminated by any weak notions as to moral impropriety, to walk leisurely through Shoreditch, Old Street, Holborn, Whitechapel, the purlieus of St. Giles's, and other places, and examine and admire (for he can hardly do the one without doing the other) the numerous costly efforts of his art, which, thanks to the *spiritual* feelings of the populace, have been erected for his gratification.

Most of our justly celebrated modern architects have distinguished themselves as much by their adherence to rule and order, as by the general combination of convenience and good taste, which prevails in all [?] their works: but, the present race of gin-temple builders, with a noble independence of spirit, have indignantly shaken off all rules and trammels; and, subject only to the purse or whims of their employers, have erected order upon order in most admired disorder. He who most lavishly bestows plate glass and gilding, together with a happy corruption or combination of all the three Grecian orders into one, is the most deservedly celebrated, and the most likely to insure success to himself in these gin-drinking times.

It was my original intention to go into something like a critical dissertation on the peculiar beauties of the leading temples erected to the honour of this modern divinity; but, the more I ponder on the subject, the more unequal I find myself to the task; for, alas! who can criticise that which is subject to no rules, or describe that which is in itself indescribable?

There are, however, two or three points, which, notwithstanding the difficulty of the task, it would be unbecoming in me, as a professional man, to pass by altogether without observation. The first, which indeed must be sufficiently obvious to the most common observer, is the prevailing taste of decorating the attic story with every description of meretricious ornament; while all between the attics and the shop entablature is, in many instances, allowed to remain in primeval nakedness; a circumstance intended, no doubt, by the original inventor, to illustrate the effects produced by the numerous libations poured out to the goddess, which, at the same time that they produce crude vapours and frothy conceits in the upper story of her votaries, leave the lower parts in a state of all but perfect nudity.

The next observation I have to make is on the very late and liberal custom of hanging out a huge lamp at the entrance door; this I take to proceed from an excess of liberality in the proprietors or priests of these establishments; inasmuch as, though willing enough to profit by the vices of their poorer brethren, they are still unwilling that the poor wretches should rush into the snare uninformed as to its consequences, and therefore take this symbolical method of pointing out its injurious effects. A happy idea! and one which serves all the purpose of a signpost to a blind man: for who of their numerous tribe of worshippers would understand the lamp as a beacon light, warning them of their danger; or that it was intended, like Bardolph's nose, as a *memento mori*, reminding them of fire internal in this world, and fire eternal in the world to come!

There is one gentleman even more liberal-minded than his brethren, who has lately, in addition to the lamp before stated, surmounted his establishment with a magnificently illuminated clock, than which nothing surely can more plainly intimate the value of time to a reflecting mind. But, alas! I am afraid the worshippers are not burthened with much reflection; and well the officiating priests know it, or they would not run the risk of

hanging out such plain-speaking symbols. Much more might be added; but I am afraid I have already trespassed too much on your pages and your readers' patience, and must now bid you farewell. CYNICUS.
London, March 12. 1834.

NOTWITHSTANDING the amusing observations of our correspondent Cynicus, we are friendly to the gin temples, as they are called; because we look upon them as the first dawning of a more enriched and varied taste in street architecture than we have hitherto had in London. As to the incorrectness of the architectural taste of these elevations, we think the injury it is likely to do much less, in the infancy of this kind of improvement, than the good which the buildings themselves will effect by setting the example of increased architectural embellishment. Let other tradesmen begin to decorate the fronts of their houses; and, when this fashion becomes general, there will be a demand for a more refined taste, which will not fail to be supplied and displayed. We question much whether the ultimate arrival at good taste in this way may not establish it on a surer foundation, than if the architects of streets had begun at once by correct and elegant designs. It is not by being led blindfold into that which is excellent, that excellence is established; but by passing through error, and undergoing correction; and finally learning from experience what excellence really is, and, of course, appreciating it accordingly. — *Cond.*

ART. VI. *Further Observations on the Choice of a House.* By L. J. KENT, Esq. Architect.

HAVING carefully examined the nature of the soil, the drainage of the premises, the strength and durability of the walls and timbers, and the ability of the roof to keep out wind and water; the next subject to which I will direct your attention is the manner in which the house is lighted; as the cheerfulness and healthiness of a house depend much on abundance of light, and that the light be equally distributed. A room is always more cheerful when light is admitted at both ends: when this cannot be obtained, choose a room where the windows are placed in its longest side, and, if possible, at one end also; but on no account choose a room to pass the day in, that is lighted by a borrowed light, or a skylight. Our happiness depends much more than is generally supposed on the cheerfulness or dulness of the room which we occupy during the day, and on its fittings-up and furnishing: it is next to impossible to have buoyant spirits and agreeable thoughts in a dark half-lighted room.

The windows, to light a room cheerfully, should be brought down as low as the nature of the occupation of the room will allow, and be carried up as high nearly as the cornice. None of the sashes should be fixed, and particularly all the upper sashes should be made to open; as the confined air is more speedily and effectually expelled by opening the upper than the lower sashes, and therefore, in sleeping-rooms, the upper sashes should be opened every fine day. Unfortunately, in houses occupied by the poor, the upper sashes are seldom hung; and the close unwholesome air is therefore never effectually dispersed, even when the windows are opened.

All windows should be provided with shutters inside, where comfort is an object. They afford the only effectual means of excluding the light, which is sometimes so desirable in cases of illness; and they keep the rooms warmer in winter, and cooler in summer, to say nothing of affording security from thieves. In the best rooms they should be made to fall back into boxings, contrived to receive them during the day; but, where the rooms are small, the shutters may be made to slide up and down, in order that they may occupy less space, and not prevent you from having curtains to the windows.

Smoky chimneys are an insufferable nuisance; they are in some situations very difficult to cure, and they arise from a great variety of causes. One, amongst others, is building the openings too shallow, in some instances only 9 in. deep: they should never be less than 14 in., and are better if 18 in. You may then have an old-fashioned, it is true, but convenient and satisfactory, safeguard against fire, where, as it frequently happens, a fire is left in a room without any one to attend to it; I mean, the circular wire fireguard, which turns round in front of the fire, when you require its use, and passes out of the way behind the grate when not required; and which is, like a sincere friend, always ready to be used when most wanted.

While examining the fireplaces, see if the hearth slabs are very narrow: if they are, you may expect the chimney-pieces to be of an inferior description. Marble chimney-pieces should be carefully looked to, as it frequently happens that they are contracted for at some incredibly small sum, compared with their appearance, and put together with old marble, the stains in which often become visible again, when they are exposed to the heat of the fire. The sides, or profiles, the slips, and the soffits, or undersides, of the shelves, are often not more than one fourth of an inch thick, and sometimes they are even less than that. All these things it is of importance for the tenant to examine; as, should the chimney-pieces fail, and become dilapidated, he will be called upon by his landlord to restore them to a sound state and condition, at an expense most likely greater than their first cost.

The floors of the inferior kinds of houses are mostly laid with white deals 9 in. wide, and often not more than ¾ in. thick. They should be generally of yellow deal, and never less than 1 in. thick, at least they should be invariably so in the basement story; and they should never be of soft spruce deals. These deals may easily be detected by your finding small round holes in the boards of the floor, where the hard knots have fallen through; for, from the soft spongy nature of this timber, it shrinks so much, when thoroughly dry, that the knot falls out. From the shrinking of this wood, the joists of floors laid with it often open a quarter of an inch wide, so as to require the floor to be taken up and relaid, or slips or fillets of wood fitted into each joint; and if you do not remedy the evil, the water, every time the floor is scoured, finds its way through these open spaces on to the ceiling of the room below, and not only discolours, and even destroys it, but in time decays the laths, as well as the plastering. In good houses, batten floors, that is, floors laid with narrow boards 1¼ in. thick, are used in all the best rooms: inch deal floors are put in the upper servants' rooms; and 1¼ in. yellow deal floors in the rooms that have boarded floors in the basement story. Floors of the best kind are doweled with pins of hard wood, or of iron, driven into the edges of the boards, and connecting them closely together, without nailing them to the joists. As a substitute for doweling, floors are nailed only on the outer edge of the boards, through which edge the nails are made to pass obliquely into the joists, so that, when the floors are finished, no nails appear.

Whenever you find the soffit of a window or doorway sunk, so as to impede the door or shutter from closing easily, it should be examined: it will generally be found to arise from the weakness of the lintel, and that the arch in brickwork, which should be turned over every opening where it is possible, has been omitted. This must be remedied without delay, or it will get worse.

The internal appearance and comfort of a house depend much on the staircase; and there are two classes of persons, the very young and the very old, who are materially inconvenienced by an ill-constructed staircase. The best staircases are those without winders [those steps where the stair makes a turn, without a landing, and which steps, of course, are broader at one end than at the other]; where the height is divided into two or three flights of steps, by half paces or spaces, or quarter paces. [A pace, or space, in a stair is a level or platform, occurring between flights of steps, and not forming a landing-place, or platform, to a floor.] In a good staircase the height of each step should not exceed from 6 in. to 7 in., and the width of the tread should be from 11 in. to 12 in. Of the two evils, viz., a high rise and narrow tread without winders, or an easy rise and broad tread with winders, choose the staircase with the winders, as the easiest and safest: but never choose a staircase, the steps of which are continued straight up a whole story without landing-places or winders. Stone staircases are very desirable: they are, when properly constructed and executed, much superior to wood, as they are noiseless, and a security in case of fire. Knowing that the public always fully estimate their value, some builders have erected stone staircases in the houses they have built; but, to avoid expense, or from ignorance, they have executed them so improperly, that the lives of those who pass up them are in great danger. This remark refers to stone staircases let into 4 in. timber partitions, which are brick-nogged [wooden framework filled in with bricks], and have pieces of wood nailed above and below the steps, to keep them from falling. The half-pace landings are sometimes composed of two stones carried across the opening of a window, the window being part below and part above the landing. A stone staircase should never be pinned into a wall of less than 9 in. thick; but when the steps are of a considerable length, that is, above 3 ft. 6 in. out of the wall, the wall should be 14 in. thick. Another piece of negligence is not uncommon; the party-walls, in such houses as have stone staircases (which are first, second, and sometimes even third rate houses), being lofty, and containing a great number of flues, and being only two bricks thick, it follows that a great part of the wall, instead of being two bricks thick, is only two half bricks thick, between which the flues pass: so that, when the mason cuts into the wall to fix the end of the step, the flue is broken into, and part of the step passes into the flue, and is there left for the soot to lodge on; and, if carelessly pinned in, the smoke, should the skirting be of wood, is thereby allowed to escape into the house. This evil is often occasioned by the carpenter cutting into a flue, when making a hole to fix the bearers for his landings, which having wedged, he, without directing the bricklayer to fill up the spaces he has left round the timber with brick and mortar, fixes the skirting, and the evil is often not found out until the chimney takes fire. Where there is any doubt or suspicion of this being the case, it would be advisable to make fires in the flues, and put some damp hay or straw on these-fires, so as to cause a large quantity of smoke to ascend, and then to open the windows; by this means the evil, if it exists, may possibly be detected.

The next subject (and it is one of great importance to the comfort of a house) is water. The facility of obtaining water in the upper part of houses in London and its vicinity, and the moderate charge made by the water companies for high-service, may, I think, induce you to require a capacious cistern in the roof, if possible; or, at all events, on the attic or two-pair floor of all houses of 60*l.* or 70*l.* a year and upwards. The expense of a cistern and pipes to convey the water to the upper part of a house (supposing the house unfinished, or undergoing a thorough repair) is so small, at the present low prices of plumber's work, and the advantages of having an abundant supply of water in the upper part of your house so great, that, where the difficulties to be overcome are not of a very serious nature, every one who assists in his comforts, the saving of his servants' time, and the means it affords, in cases of fire, of saturating the floors with water, and thereby preventing the fire from spreading downwards, will seriously consider this subject before he decides on allowing the opportunity of obtaining these advantages to pass by him. Besides saving the time of carrying water from the basement story up three or four flights of stairs, a cistern in the upper floor affords the means of having a bath at but little expense; of providing your servants a sink on the attic or two-pair floor; of having a water-closet in the upper part of the house (a great convenience, particularly where there are children, or two families, in a house); and of supplying any or all of your best bedrooms or dressing-rooms with water, by means of a fixed basin, with a supply-pipe and cock; and which may also have a plug and waste-pipe, carried either into the trap of the water-closet, or into the rain-water pipe. This is a comfort that can scarcely be estimated by any one by whom the luxury of it has not been enjoyed.

In the choice of a house, therefore, the capaciousness, construction, and situation of the cisterns for the supply of water are matters to be carefully looked to; or you may, perhaps, find it necessary to incur a considerable expense in providing the quantity of water you need, should the house you are about to take not require to be repaired, and should you thus not have a convenient opportunity of fixing a cistern in the upper story. In the present day, every privy should be a water-closet: let the construction of it be ever so common, still water should be supplied, and that liberally. Where the expense of a proper closet is inconvenient, or the occupancy of the house of an humble kind, an iron hopper set in brickwork, and supplied with water by a pipe and cock, will answer the purpose. Connected with the water-closet is the drain, by which the water is carried off from it, and, generally, the sinks and other parts of the house. From want of proper care in the construction of the drains, many houses, otherwise very comfortable and healthy, are rendered the reverse, by offensive and noisome smells. This arises either from there not being proper traps, or from the covering or sides of the drains being insecure, and permitting the impure air to escape. Enquiry should be made as to the construction of the drains before a soil-pipe is permitted to enter one. Where soil is permitted to enter a drain, the drain should be rendered with cement half round (the) bottom inside, and all over the top outside, and covered with earth, of which clay is the best kind.

Attention should be directed to the fastenings, which are often of a cheap and inferior description, and thus are a source of continual annoyance, from the locks getting out of order, and the bars, bolts, &c., not acting properly.

Closets, when properly fitted up, and of a sufficient depth to be useful (that is, when the shelves are at least 12 in. wide), are a very great convenience; but, when the shelves are only 8 in. or 9 in. wide, the closets generally become sluts' holes, and the receptacle of all the rubbish of the house. When they are put up independently of the plastering, that is, unconnected with the plaster, or with the walls not plastered at all, they should be lined all round with deal, and made air and dust tight. If it can be avoided, they should never be placed against an external wall, unless the wall is battened. [To batten is to fasten narrow strips of wood against a wall, on which plaster laths are nailed, or canvass stretched, so as to preserve a vacuity between the plaster or the paper and the wall.] External walls, indeed, should always be battened in good rooms, as there is but little dependence on freedom from damp when the external walls are plastered on the brickwork, and the precaution of battening is neglected.

It frequently happens, even where the principal walls, roof, and floors of a house are sound and strong, that the middle partitions are infirm and weak; these, therefore, you should examine; for it is too common to find, either from the bad materials used in the walls in the basement story, or from neglecting the foundation, or, more frequently, from the bad construction of the timber partitions, that they sink. The consequences are, that the floors become out of a level, the doors do not fit their openings, the gutter-plates that rest on these partitions sink, and cause the water to lie in a pool in the hollow part, and the plastering and cornices crack. This, although a serious evil, is not always insurmountable, as it frequently occurs from the hasty manner in which buildings, particularly those built on speculation, are erected, the partitions being plastered before the building has settled to its proper bearing; and, when arising from this cause only, it may be remedied. One of the first questions asked by many gentlemen who are about to have a house built, or to have alterations made, is, "How soon is it in your power to get the works completed?" and, generally speaking, the shortest possible time is allowed. This is a great error: a sufficient time to dry and season the materials (particularly in the bricklayer's and carpenter's work) should be allowed, before the joiner's work or plasterer's work is begun, in order that the defects arising from the shrinking of the timbers, and any unequal settling of the brickwork, may be remedied before the finishings are fixed. Should any settlement take place afterwards, the finishings, being attached to the brickwork and rough timbers, must necessarily partake of any unequal settlement or change of position that may occur in them.

L. J. KENT.

Manor Place, Paddington, March, 1834.

ART. VII. *An Account of the Origin and Progress of heating Hot-houses and other Buildings by the Application and Circulation of Hot Water, instead of by Fuel or Steam.* By GEORGE COTTAM, Esq. F.H.S. Z.S., Associate Member of the Institution of Civil Engineers.

As the practice of warming buildings by steam preceded that of heating them by means of the circulation of hot water, it may not be uninteresting to notice the commencement and rapid progress of that invention; more particularly as the mode of heating buildings by steam is very similar in its operation to that of heating them by hot water.

The first notice recorded of heating chambers by steam is to be found in the *Philosophical Transactions* for the year 1745, wherein it is stated that a Colonel William Cook had suggested the idea of warming apartments by the application of steam: it does not, however, appear that he carried his intention into effect.

In the third number of the *Journals of the Royal Institution*, Count Rumford mentions heating by the application of steam, and proceeds as follows:—" This scheme has frequently been put in practice, with success, in this country, as well as on the Continent." From this passage we might infer that heating by steam was well known in this country at the period alluded to; but I have never been able to ascertain where, or by whom, it was adopted. Buchanan, however, in his *Essays on the Economy of Fuel and the Management of Heat*, remarks:—" I have not been able to learn that any thing of importance was done previously to the use of steam in warming cotton mills, although we find a patent for heating by steam was granted to John Hoyle, dated 7th of July, 1791, and to John Green, dated the 9th December, 1793."

About the same period, Mr. Watt, being engaged in making various experiments on steam for other purposes, was naturally led to consider the subject of applying it to the warming of buildings. Buchanan informs us that, about the year 1784 or 1785, probably during the intervening winter of those two years, Mr. Watt had recourse to steam for the purpose of heating the apartment wherein he usually wrote. This room was 18 ft. long, by 14 ft. wide, and 8½ ft. high; and the apparatus consisted of a box or heater formed with two side plates of bright tinned iron, about 3¼ ft. in length, by 2½ ft. wide, kept an inch distant from each other, by means of stays, and joined round the edges by other tin plates. This box was placed upon its edge near the floor of the chamber, being furnished with a cock to let out the steam, and a pipe, proceeding from its lower edge, communicated with a boiler in an under-apartment; the said pipe serving to convey the steam, and return the water. The effect produced by this apparatus was less than had been calculated by Mr. Watt, which may now be explained, by the experiments of Professor Leslie on the heat transmitted from a polished surface.

Mr. Bolton, at the close of the year 1794, assisted the Marquess of Lansdowne in the improvement of an apparatus, erected by a Mr. Green, for warming his library by means of air heated by steam: the use of this apparatus was, however, abandoned, in consequence of some defects in the pipes or joints. Twelve months afterwards, Mr. Bolton superintended the erection of a similar apparatus for his friend Dr. Withering's library. This apparatus, as regarded heating, proved altogether satisfactory; but it was soon obliged to be disused, in consequence of the pipes, which had been constructed of copper and softly soldered, emitting, in some parts, a most disagreeable effluvium, which rendered it unpleasant to Dr. Withering, who was then in an infirm state of health, and suffering from a disease on his lungs. The apparatus was in consequence removed to Soho, near Birmingham, where Mr. Bolton proposed its being erected at his own residence, in which he was then making considerable improvements; having, among other things, resolved to heat every apartment in the house by means of steam. A boiler was, in consequence, fixed in one of the cellars; but circumstances subsequently intervened to prevent the plan from being carried into execution.

About the year 1798, we find that Mr. Watt heated his bath by steam; and, in the course of the ensuing year, that Messrs. Bolton and Watt proceeded to fix cast-iron steam-pipes in various mills and manufactories throughout England and Scotland. These pipes soon came into general use; and, in 1807, Buchanan published his pamphlet containing an *Essay on the Warming of Mills and other Edifices through the Medium of Steam.*

In 1810, Buchanan published his *Practical and Descriptive Essays on the Œconomy of Fuel and Management of Heat,* which were duly noticed in the various scientific periodicals of the day. The use of steam having thus become general for warming public edifices, cotton and other mills, it was forthwith applied to horticultural purposes, such as forcing-houses for grapes, pineries, &c.; and was most efficiently resorted to by those spirited cultivators, Messrs. Loddiges of Hackney, on a grand scale, for heating their forcing-houses and stoves, where it was attended with so much success, as to supersede the use of brick flues. This favourable trial caused it to be adopted in various similar but minor establishments, where, however, it was not attended by equal success, from causes I shall more particularly demonstrate when engaged in comparing the value of warmth derived from hot water, with that produced by steam. This brings me down to the period when heating by hot water first came into notice, in consequence of the experiments of a most ingenious and spirited gentleman, Anthony Bacon, Esq., of Aberaman in Glamorganshire, and, subsequently, of Elcot in Berkshire. The gentleman in question having made some experiments at his first residence in Wales, proceeded to put his plans into practice, more in detail, at his last-mentioned estate, where he immediately perceived the great advantage of heating forcing-houses by means of hot water. In consequence of these primary steps, a letter was addressed to the Horticultural Society of London, by Mr. Whale, gardener to Mr. Bacon, subsequently published in the *Gardener's Magazine* (vol. iii. p. 196.), which brought this system into notice; and, on its being generally adopted, several persons started up as claimants of the invention, when the *Gardener's Magazine* for 1828 became the grand arena for discussing the disputed point. Among the foremost claimants were Mr. Atkinson, Mr. Bacon, and Messrs. Bolton and Watt. During the progress of the discussion, numerous statements were adduced, by which it was most satisfactorily proved by Mr. Bacon, that he had preceded Mr. Atkinson in the idea, as well as in the trial; and that the latter gentleman derived his knowledge of the plan from inspecting Mr. Bacon's machinery. It became no less evident, from the facts elicited, that the idea or principle did not originate even with Mr. Bacon, as the Marquis de Chabannes had taken out a patent for precisely the same invention in the year 1814; and had also published a pamphlet, in 1815, containing plans, amply developing the nature of his patent, and proposing to diffuse heat through the medium of hot water, as applicable to vineries, hot-beds, pineries, dwelling-houses, &c. As a farther proof of the efficiency of his plans, he proceeded to put them in practice at the shops, Nos. 36. and 37. Burlington Arcade, as well as at No. 1. Russel Place. An extensive conservatory and vinery at Sundridge Park, near Bromley in Kent, the seat of Sir Samuel Scott, Bart., was also heated by the Marquis de Chabannes, in 1816, by means of hot water. The dwellings previously mentioned were publicly exhibited, and might, consequently, have undergone the inspection of those persons who laid claim to the discovery in the years 1821, 1822, and 1823. Notwithstanding this, and although the Marquis de Chabannes appears to have been the first individual who made the plan public in England, Messrs. Bolton and Watt stood forward as claimants to priority as to the adoption of the system in question; for, in a letter addressed to the editor of the *Gardener's Magazine*, under date March 18. 1829, and published in that work, vol. iv. p. 304, we find as follows:—

" We may briefly observe, that the attention of this firm has been directed to the employment of steam and hot water as ——... for the transmission of heat upwards of *fifty years*, and they have been used by us, with that view, under almost every modification, in the warming of rooms for all the various operations of manufactories, for habitations, for the heating of baths, vats, and various other purposes. Preference was given to the one or other according to the circumstances under which the application of heat was required, steam being naturally preferred for the more rapid diffusion of a high temperature, and water substituted when the heating of that liquid to a low temperature, or the steady maintenance of such a temperature in a room, was the object to be attained. The application of these principles to the warming of hot-houses has not attracted much of our attention, not possessing ourselves any house of that description; but the adoption in them of modes of heating practised in other buildings, where analogous desiderata were attained, must, we conceive, be a natural consequence of the diffusion of the practice.

"Whenever the horticulturist determined it to be a primary consideration, in the heating of the hot-house, to preserve with the least fluctuation any given degree of atmospheric temperature, the advantage of employing water, in preference to steam, for the attainment of that end, was obvious, and could not fail to present itself to any mind conversant with its use for that purpose. The practicable attainment of it could not be attended with difficulty, as it had long been effected under analogous circumstances."

From the above observations it would appear that the system of heating by hot water was in use in England in 1778; but the assertions contained in this letter do not seem to agree, in point of time, with the origin adduced of the discovery, by Messrs. Bolton and Watt, of heating by means of steam. After every enquiry that has been set on foot, it appears that the earliest date, at which the appropriation of steam by Mr. Watt for the purposes of warming buildings was resorted to, took place in his own apartment during the year 1784 or 1785, which experiment proved extremely defective; while the steam apparatus adopted by Doctor Withering (previously adverted to) was not set up until the year 1795 or 1796. The first perfect machinery used for this purpose was erected in the cotton mills of Mr. Lee of Manchester in 1799; and we find Buchanan, as previously observed, publishing his *Essays on warming Mills and other Structures* in 1807, and his *Essay on the Œconomy of Fuel and Management of Heat in warming Mills and other Buildings* in 1810; wherein very frequent mention occurs of Messrs. Bolton and Watt, yet no notice whatever is taken respecting the circulation of heat by means of hot water passing through pipes having been adopted by those gentlemen. This omission appears very singular; since it might have been naturally supposed that so simple, efficient, and beautiful a system of diffusing heat could not possibly have escaped the penetration and industry of such a genius as Buchanan, had it been then known to have attained public use. What tends more to create astonishment at this silence upon his part, is, that we find a very extensive list inserted in his works, of all buildings wherein steam had been applied for the purposes of warming, drying, and heating. Another work was also published by Tredgold, in 1824, *On the Principles of warming Public Buildings and Hot-houses by Steam*, wherein no mention whatsoever is made of hot water being circulated through pipes, for the purpose of heating buildings; although he alludes to the idea of cooling apartments by means of the circulation of cold water through pipes. In addition to the above observations, it may be necessary to remark, that, in the progress of a discussion that continued for six years, no previous claim was made to that adduced by the Marquis de Chabannes; neither has a single hot-house, stove, building, or any apparatus whatsoever, been pointed out, as having existed anterior to those erected by the marquis. Under the above considerations, I am rather tempted to suppose that Messrs. Bolton and Watt must have misunderstood the application made to them by the editor of the *Gardener's Magazine*. I cannot terminate these remarks without observing, that it would not only have been interesting, but satisfactory, had Messrs. Bolton and Watt, when communicating their information to the Magazine above quoted, pointed out two or three of the buildings wherein they had put their earliest applications of the hot-water system into effect. However, notwithstanding the observations previously adduced, I find the plan of warming rooms by hot water preceded that of heating by steam, as it appears that a physician of the name of Bonnemain, in or before the year 1777, possessed a large building, several stories high, heated by the circulation of hot water through metal pipes; and that, by means of the same process, he produced artificial incubation, having hatched chickens for the court of Louis XVI., and regularly supplied the markets of the French metropolis, as will be more fully detailed hereafter. It is by no means improbable that Mr. Watt, or Dr. Black, or some of the other eminent men in communication with him, might have perused Bonnemain's description of the apparatus he had adopted. However, there can be little doubt but the Marquis de Chabannes was perfectly conversant with the plans which had been resorted to by Bonnemain.

In my next article, in continuation of the present, I shall describe the apparatus employed by M. Bonnemain, which he called a *calorifère*, and employed on a large scale for the hatching of chickens; and I shall next describe, in succession, the methods of Chabannes, of Bacon, of Atkinson, of Fowler, of Kewley, of Weeks, of Perkins, and, in short, of all our British engineers to the present time.

REVIEWS.

ART. I. *Suggestions for the Architectural Improvement of the Western Part of London.* By Sydney Smirke, F.S.A. F.G.S. Large 8vo; pp. 117, with a folding map, and two lithographic views. London, 1834.

THIS work is characterised by great moderation and good sense; and is, therefore, the more likely to attain the end which its author has in view. This end we shall lay before our readers in the following brief abstract: —

The author commences by what some will, perhaps, consider rather an unnecessary task; viz., that of combating the usual arguments against improvement; and by showing, that, owing to the immeasurable increase of our traffic, it is necessary to have our streets straighter and wider. He next goes on to show the great obstacle thrown in the way of alterations, by the dread of interfering with the property of individuals; and regrets that more of the land on which London is built did not belong to the crown, or to corporations. The most striking improvements in the metropolis, he says, have been made either by the crown officers, or the corporation of London and its dependent companies. The same has been the case in most of the provincial towns. It is under a sense of the great difficulties that lie in the way of all improvements, in such a metropolis as London, that the author has studiously endeavoured to exclude from his pages all chimerical projects; and he therefore expects "something more than the usual amount of attention which similar lucubrations have hitherto received." He has given few suggestions, indeed, which do not recommend themselves as improvements; and many of them demand only a comparatively moderate outlay of capital. " It should be remembered," he says, " that the increased value of ground and houses, in the immediate vicinity of the parts improved, would, in many cases, be a source of considerable profit. As soon as a communication between different parts of a city is established, by opening a wide, commodious, and direct avenue, the public are not slow to accept the advantages which it offers: houses of a higher consideration and value are immediately required in it; and it is not difficult to conceive, that, in many instances, the owner of the property may be more than repaid for any loss of space to which he may have submitted." (p. 11.) This is perfectly true; while, at the same time, it confirms the author's preceding remark, that the great obstacle to improvement is, where the property is divided into fractions of not more than one, two, or a few houses each; instead of being in masses, built on half an acre, an acre, or upwards.

In the case of London, Mr. Smirke observes: — "It should not be overlooked that a great part of the west end of the town is covered with houses built long before the existence of the present Building Act; and that they are consequently precarious property, requiring a higher insurance, a greater annual expenditure in repairs, and, therefore, obtaining a lower rent, than houses of a more recent date and better construction." (p. 12.)

In this part of his work, the author remarks, " that no mechanical art has, within late years, experienced improvements more numerous and important than that of building. An old house in London is rarely pulled down without revealing a construction faulty in principle, and careless in execution. Common sense is shocked by finding a thick wall of brickwork, carrying, probably, three or four floors besides the roof, built over a void space, upon a piece of timber, the ends of which are, of course, liable to become rotten in a few years; and the whole of which may be, and often is, reduced to ashes in a few minutes: yet this mode of construction was universal, until lately, in our shops, and, in truth, is still allowed to be practised by some builders, who have not yet opened their eyes nor used their understandings. The substitution of iron for timber is an improvement in the art of building that can hardly be overrated: it has banished at once the unwieldy girders which our ancestors were wont to truss, until they could hardly support their own weight; it has given us pillars that neither fire nor water can affect; and may almost be said to have afforded us the means of erecting an indestructible house. The very expensive, and often unsuccessful, process of piling for foundations has but of late years yielded to the use of the artificial concrete substratum; the surprising strength and imperishable nature of which give it a value that cannot be too highly estimated by the architectural practitioner. The mode of baking bricks in clamps, instead of kilns, is a practice unknown until recent times, by which their hardness and durability are greatly increased; whilst, with regard to timber (the other most important material of a building), it is hardly extravagant to say, that the late introduction of the tanking process [by which timber is saturated with corrosive sublimate] bids fair, at no distant period, to render the destructive ravages of the dry rot a matter of tradition. Such are some of the improvements (and there are many others not necessary to be enumerated here) of which the proprietor of land in the streets of London may avail himself at the present day, to increase the value and permanence of his property." (p. 14.)

We pass over what the author says on the importance of the improvement of a city to the health of its inhabitants; not altogether because this, to the readers of such works as that of Mr. Smirke, is self-evident; but, because we think we can occupy the space which we can devote to the review of this work more usefully to our own readers.

Mr. Smirke has abstained from saying much on the opportunities which improvements, in the widening and straightening of streets, would offer of increasing the architectural beauty of street buildings; because he very wisely considers this as an object but of secondary importance. The inferiority of London, in point of architectural merit, to many of the Continental capitals, our author observes, " must have forced itself on the conviction of every traveller who has quitted the shores of his native country; and our neighbours are ready enough to draw thence very plausible inferences in disparagement of our taste and genius. That the standard of public taste is lower in England than on some parts of the Continent, must probably be conceded. In those branches of our manufactures which more especially seek aid from the arts of design, our general deficiency in this respect is evinced by an almost total want of originality. French books of patterns are the text books of our operative artists, who seem ambitious of nothing beyond a successful imitation. In carpets, cottons, silks, paper-hangings, and furniture, there is alike the same poverty in decorative design. Even the natives of China and India are in some respects our masters; for the delicacy, variety, and richness of their designs are not unfrequently even beyond our imitation. In consequence of the incompetency of English manufacturers on this point, our French neighbours have usually been successful competitors with us in all those branches of trade that depend on the arts of design; and thus our want of feeling for the fine arts, and the defective cultivation of the public taste, become important in the view of the political economist himself.

" A man of ordinary observation, who has had an opportunity of becoming acquainted with the principal cities of Europe, has only to walk through the streets of London, to convince himself that we are at present a people deplorably devoid of a taste for the picturesque. Where, except in this country, shall we find streets of interminable length, composed of houses without cornice, architrave, or any of the most simple features of architectural decoration? We look in vain for a Corso, a Strada Nuova, a Canal Grande, or a Herren Gasse; and the noblest and wealthiest of the most opulent country in the world are, for the most part, content to shelter themselves, during the season of their residence here, in houses utterly destitute of all the dignity or grace of architecture.

" The slow progress of our national museums and galleries, and the inadequate funds destined for their completion and support, are proofs, it is to be feared, of the same tasteless habits; of the same Bœotian insensibility to the attractions of a refined and rational pleasure. It is indeed humiliating to contrast our parsimonious tardiness, in this respect, with the bold munificence of other countries. Whilst we have been deliberating and doubting, Berlin has raised a beautiful gallery, worthy alike of its accomplished author, Schinkel, and of the country that has earned celebrity by so many enlightened reforms. Even the state of Bavaria, a country of very limited territorial extent, can point with just pride to the noble work of Klenze; a production, in point of magnitude and magnificence, far removed beyond the range of our economical conceptions. In addition to this latter gallery, Munich has lately raised another monument to its taste, in the Glyptothec, consisting of a range of sculpture galleries sumptuously finished, and covering a prodigious extent of ground; a magnificent public library is in progress; whilst a theatre, larger than the largest in London, a royal palace, an observatory, and many other buildings of great beauty and importance, are striking evidences of that enlightened taste for the peaceful and elegant arts which distinguishes the present sovereign of Bavaria."*

Mr. Smirke next proceeds to enquire what aid might be reasonably expected from the legislature, towards the adoption of some systematic general plan of municipal improvement; and he suggests the examination and collation of the different acts which have been passed on the subject of London improvements, in order to select what was good; and also the formation of a permanent Board, or Municipal Commission. Nothing better, perhaps, could be suggested under the present circumstances of the metropolis; but, in our opinion, the whole space included under London and its suburbs, say within a circle of five miles from St. Paul's, with power of extension, ought to be formed into a representative municipal government; and, this having been done, every thing connected with general improvement would come under the cognizance of a proper department, and be discussed in public, and consequently open to the criticisms of the press. No system that we can think of is calculated to be more perfect than this; and the legislature is now making approximations towards it, in the present corporation reforms.

Before the author proceeds to describe his plans in detail, he takes a brief retrospective view of the west of London, from the time of the Norman princes to the present day; and, proceeding from the western gate of the fortifications nearest to the Thames, named Lud-gate, he surveys the whole country as far as the village of Charinge, and the Marsh of Westminster, on the one hand; and to Clerk's Well, Old Bourne Bridge (now Holborn), and the village of Tybourne, now Mary on the Bourne, or Marylebone, on the other. But we pass over this entertaining part of the work, having barely left ourselves room to enumerate the most obvious improvements proposed.

Among the general principles to be kept in view in laying out the streets of a town, one of the first is, to admit of its being penetrated in all directions in straight lines. A second is, that, towards the centre or most public part of the town, the streets ought to be broader than at the remote and less frequented parts. By streets penetrating in all directions, it is not meant to be implied that there should be diagonal streets through square compartments of buildings; but merely that there should be a facility in passing from any one part of the town to any other part. This, it is obvious, may be effected in a town composed wholly of squares of buildings, provided these squares are not too large. When they are very large, this can only be accomplished by streets in oblique lines. The most perfect form of the ground

---

* We saw the work of Klenze alluded to, the Pinakothec, and also the Glyptothec, at Munich, in 1828, and we have given an elevation of the Pinakothec in the new edition of our *Encyclopædia of Gardening*, p. 145., and of the Glyptothec and a plan of its surrounding garden in the *Gardener's Magazine*, vol. ix. p. 401. The Tuscan palace at Munich we consider a much grander piece of architecture than either; an engraving of it will be found in our *Encyc. of Architecture*, p. 953. — Cond.

plan of a large town would be that of a circle, with all the public buildings in the centre, and all the streets either radiating from that centre, or forming concentric circles or segments to it. Such a plan, combined with what we have called breathing zones, or public gardens, promenades, and places for markets, &c., we have given in the *Gardener's Magazine*, vol. v. p. 687.; and we have there shown how it might be applied to London, and to towns generally. Mr. Smirke's improvements are all projected on the same fundamental principles as those which we have laid down; but the most scrupulous regard has been had to apply them in such a way as to require the least possible number of houses to be taken down. A straight line is very properly, in our opinion, never made a desideratum by Mr. Smirke; unless where a number of small houses and narrow lanes come in the way; as, for example, in St. Giles's, and in some parts of Westminster.

It only remains for us slightly to mention a few of the lines proposed by Mr. Smirke; because, though the principle is of general interest, yet its application to London renders the details local. Oxford Street is to be continued in a straight line to Holborn; Piccadilly through Leicester Square to Covent Garden Market, and thence to Temple Bar; the Strand through the Mall in St. James's Park to Chelsea; St. James's Street, across St. James's Park to Rochester Row and Lambeth Road; the Haymarket is to be continued to Oxford Street; and St. Martin's Lane and Wellington Street, from Charing Cross and Waterloo Bridge, into Oxford Street and Holborn, &c. A number of other subordinate improvements, and particularly one for building villages for the working classes, we must defer noticing till a future opportunity.

ART. II. *Catalogue of Works on Architecture, Building, and Furnishing, and on the Arts more immediately connected therewith, recently published.*

BILLINGTON's *Architectural Director*, Parts II. and III., 8vo, price 2s. 6d. each. The plates in these two numbers are very accurate, and very well executed.

Whitling's Designs for Shop Fronts, 4to, 12s. 6d., is announced.

A View of the Indigent Blind School, St. George's Fields, erected from the designs of John Newman, Esq. F.S.A., Architect, forms an interesting architectural engraving, well worth purchasing by the architect who collects materials of this kind. This fine print is published for the benefit of the Charity; and the price is only 4s.

Working Ornaments and Forms for the Cabinetmaker, Upholsterer, &c., 2 Parts, large folio, price 10s. each, are published.

Knight's Ornaments for Jewellers, Chasers, Die-Sinkers, &c., 4 Parts, 4to, 5s. each.

Antique Roses; being a Series of One Hundred Examples from the most celebrated Remains of ancient Rome, for the Use of Architects, Sculptors, Modellers, &c. &c. Selected by Carlo Antonini; and drawn on Stone by Wm. Doyle. No. I. 4to. To be completed in 25 Parts, at 3s. each. London, 1832.

The part before us contains four plates: the first three are antique roses, taken from the cloisters of the church of Santa Maria del Popolo in Rome; and the fourth is a large antique rose from the Pantheon. They are beautifully lithographed, and must be valuable as patterns to carvers, modellers, plasterers, &c. The present number is dated 1832; and it is not stated whether any others have been published. Mr. Doyle, we understand, has had great experience in painting on glass, and is a teacher of architectural drawing.

ART. III. *Literary Notices.*

ILLUSTRATIONS, *with a Topographical and Descriptive Account, of Cassiobury Park, Hertfordshire*, the seat of the Earl of Essex, by John Britton, F.S.A. &c., is about to be published by subscription. Cassiobury is interesting in an antiquarian point of view; and also on account of its noble Gothic mansion, its beautiful garden scenery, and its very picturesque lodges and cottages; erected, for the most part, from the designs of the present earl. Mr. Britton's work will consist of about 40 pages of letterpress in folio; and, at least, 30 embellishments by Turner, Alexander, Hearne, Elridge, and Pugin. The publication will be limited to 150 copies: 20 of which will have the plates coloured, price 6 guineas each; and the others will be 3 guineas each.

Plans, Elevations, Sections, and Details of the ancient Gates, Fortifications, and other interesting Buildings in York, by P. F. Robinson, Architect, will shortly appear.

A Plan and Section of the Waterford and Kilkenny Railway, with Reports, &c., by R. M. Hallingworth, price 20s., will be published by subscription. A list is already printed of subscribers' names; among which we are glad to see those of a number of architects.

An Essay on the Nature and Application of Steam, by M. A. Alderson, Civil Engineer, will be published as soon as 200 copies are subscribed for at 10s. each. This essay was honoured by the award of the highest premium ever yet given by the London Mechanics' Institution. A large portion of the work is devoted to the application of steam to the purposes of warming, ventilating, drying, cooking, &c.

For the above notices we are indebted to Mr. Williams, of the Architectural Library, Charles Street, Soho.

MISCELLANEOUS INTELLIGENCE.

ART. I. *Domestic Notices.*

ENGLAND.

ARCHITECTURAL *Drawings and Lectures.* — At the last soirée at Kensington Palace, given by His Royal Highness the Duke of Sussex, Mr. Britton exhibited about sixty of his interesting drawings, which have been made to illustrate his lectures on architectural antiquities. These drawings were arranged on the two sides of the gallery library, and were disposed to show the various styles and eras of architecture, as existing in the excavations of India, the temples of Egypt, those of the Grecian Acropolis, also in Rome; then the decline of the Roman architecture, and the introduction and progressive changes and varieties in the Christian architecture of the middle ages; next the castellated class, and lastly the old domestic, from the Norman advent to the revival of the Italian orders in the time of Henry VIII. His royal highness, the lord chancellor, and many noble and distinguished visiters, appeared to take a great interest in this mode of displaying the nationalities and peculiarities of design and execution of so many edifices of such remote times. Any thing that can thus be done to give a fashion or publicity to architecture, either ancient or modern, is entitled to general approval. Mr. Britton has lately given one of his lectures (that on ancient castles) to very large audiences, to the literary and scientific societies of Windsor, Hampstead, and Southwark; and he is to repeat the same before the Marylebone Literary Institution, in the course of the summer. The third number of his *Dictionary of Architecture and Archæology* has been long delayed, as well as the third and concluding part of the *History, &c., of Worcester Cathedral*, in consequence of urgent demands on his time, from the distracted state of parties in his parish (St. Pancras), by public societies and private engagements. He has, however, written memoirs of two of his old friends, viz., Sir John Soane and Sir Jeffrey Wyatville, for Fisher's very beautiful work, *The National Portrait Gallery.*—T. W. *April*, 1834.

Exhibition, Somerset House. — We took a cursory glance at the architectural drawings on the 12th inst. There is nothing very striking; but a number of designs at, and a few above, mediocrity. We shall notice only those few of which we retain most recollection. Among the public buildings, the first which we shall mention is *A Design* (886.) *submitted to the Fishmongers' Company, in December,* 1831, which we prefer to that executed, from its noble detached portico, and the general style of grandeur and originality which pervades it. There are several other designs for this Fishmongers' Hall, almost every one of which (particularly 892.) appears to us better than that which has been adopted; chiefly because the latter has no detached portico, while it has a number of attached columns: thus incurring expense, without producing an adequate effect. *The Perspective View of a Design for a Royal Exchange* (893.), which obtained the gold medal in the Royal Academy in 1833, surprised us not a little. As a piece of architectural composition, it belongs to the school of attached columns. Specimens of this school may be seen in a portion of the elevation of the Treasury, where the columns are of no use, but to support an entablature, and darken the windows under it; or in Trinity Church, New Road, where the columns support little vase-like ornaments. In the design (893.) there appeared to us, to be above a hundred of these attached columns; and only one portico with the columns free. With respect to the drawing, we were still more surprised than we were at the design: it is of a very inferior description, as any one may be convinced of, by comparing it with 938., drawn in the same simple style, but with great accuracy, distinctness, and beauty. *The Design for a National Pantheon* (898.), *proposed to be erected in Trafalgar Square,* looks more like a monumental column or obelisk joined to a fountain, than a place for containing busts or statues. *The intended Suspension Bridge across the River Thames* (925.) is too light and fragile in appearance. The first point to be attended to, in a bridge, is the expression of strength. Here the piers in the Gothic style are pierced with windows and arches in all directions, so as to convey the idea of lightness and weakness. Again, the fundamental principle by which effect is produced is contrast; and, in a suspension bridge, there is a fine opportunity of contrasting simple massive piers with the light open work which suspends the roadway of the bridge from the chains carried by these piers. We are quite sure that any architect of a reasoning taste will feel the force of these objections. *The View in the lower Quadrangle of Hungerford Market* (942.) forms a beautiful architectural picture; as do the views of the same market, 879. and 943. *The Design for a new Temple Bar* (947.) we trust will never be executed: to do so at the present day, would argue as much wisdom as placing a partial dam across the Thames, by restoring the obstruction at old London Bridge. *Perspective View of the proposed Free Grammar Schools, Birmingham, selected by the Committee as One of the Three best Designs for the Premiums.* (952.) The general effect of this design is good; but, on looking into the detail, we find far too much care bestowed on the towers and angular buttresses for a school, and far too little on the chimney tops, to be in harmony with the angular buttresses. A parapet of pediments raised against the side of the roof is too obviously merely ornamental; and, besides, gives intricacy in a part of the design where repose would have had a better effect. *The Design for the Termination of an Aqueduct* (1013.) has too many parts for producing effect; and it has nothing characteristic of its being the termination of an aqueduct. Grandeur ought to have been aimed at, instead of variety. *The Design for an Architectural Institution* (1020.) is architectural, and apparently suitable; and we should be glad to receive the plans and sections, with a description of what is intended by the author, for publication in this Magazine. We should also be glad to receive the ground plan of 1021., for the sake of showing the internal arrangement. The elevation of this design we think far too extravagant for execution in the present day. Architects seem to forget that this is no longer the age of gorgeous public buildings.

Among the designs for dwellings, we do not recollect any of preeminent excellence. We were most pleased with the *Interiors intended for Coombe Abbey, near Coventry. The Entrance Gallery* (932.) is in the Elizabethan style, and very fine, as is *the Entrance to the great Dining-Hall.* (1012.) . *The Draw-*

ing-room (927.) is in the style of Louis XIV., large in extent, and very gorgeous and characteristic in design. *The Sketch of the North Front of Emo Park, Queen's County, Ireland* (913.), shows a fine architectural basement or terrace, which most of the designs for villas in the present exhibition want. *The Cottage in Hayling Island* (914.), and that *at Dichley, on the Derby Road* (915.), are suitable and picturesque. *The Design for a Castellated Mansion* (919.) is not sufficiently high for the castellated style, in proportion to its breadth; and it ought to have been placed on a broad architectural basement. *The Villa in Surrey* (920.) seems classical and varied. *A Mansion in Scotland* (926.), surrounded by its terrace walls, has a characteristic effect. *Claydagh House* (929.) rises from a platform bounded by a balustrade, agreeably to our taste. *The Interior of the Library at Leigh Park, Hants* (956.), (which we saw last summer), is exceedingly good, both in reality and in the design. *The East View of Cossey Hall, Norfolk* (958.), is beautifully drawn; but the subject does not form such a good whole as it might have done, had the drawing been smaller, or the picture larger. It fills, in fact, too much of the paper, and has neither enough of background nor of foreground. As to the design itself, its details, in an architectural point of view, are of surpassing beauty. (See a notice of Mr. Dighton's model of this building below.

Among the models, that for a *Chapel to the General Cemetery Company* (873.) executed in Maltese stone, is by far the most beautiful, both as an architectural design and as a model. That for completing the *Buildings at Whitehall*, is covered with attached columns, or with columns detached, but only a foot or two from the wall to which they belong, and consequently merely ornamental. There is not a mode of disposing of columns more repugnant to our feelings than this. Half columns may actually be of some use, as adding to the strength of the wall; but columns detached, and yet affording no useful shade or protection, while they occasion nearly as great an expense as porticoes, are wholly without either grandeur or utility. *The Model of the County Courts at Kerry, in Ireland* (874.), is one of which we should much wish to lay the ground plan before our readers.

Such are our opinions respecting a few of the architectural drawings and models exhibited; but we must beg our readers to recollect that these opinions were formed at one visit; and that, as they are put down from recollection, we may sometimes have referred to the wrong number. If we have leisure, we shall take another view, and give a second notice. In the meantime, if any artist thinks we have formed an erroneous judgment of his works, let him recollect that these criticisms are not anonymous, and are therefore likely to be sincere. We shall be happy to insert any reply to them; only premising, that the party replying shall assign his reasons, and give us, either publicly or privately, his name. This we require, on the principle that all replies to criticisms having the responsibility of a name, should have a similar responsibility. We shall also be glad to have the criticisms of correspondents on any of the architectural designs in the present exhibition, whether they have been noticed by us or not.

The Model of Cossey Hall, Norfolk, the Seat of the Right Hon. Lord Stafford, was inspected by us at the house of the modeller, Mr. Dighton, in Mount Street, Grosvenor Square, May 12. The late Lady Stafford was noted among the nobility as a woman of great taste generally, and more particularly for her taste in, and knowledge of, architecture. The improvements at Cossey Hall were begun some years ago, under her direction; the architect employed being J. C. Buckler, Esq., son of the architectural antiquary of that name, and well known for his profound knowledge of the Gothic style in all its details, and for his great taste. The model before us consists of a series of quadrangles, forming one general parallelogram in the plan. The building is placed on ground which slopes gently to a river, and the principal living-rooms are in the upper quadrangle, and along one entire side of the parallelogram, terminating near the river in a large conservatory. The opposite side of the parallelogram contains chiefly the offices, stables, &c. The architecture is chiefly remarkable for the very great beauty of its details; most of which are executed either in red or white brick, made and burned on the spot. The only decided principal mass is the upper one, containing the entrance hall; the remainder consists of a series of masses in succession, forming a continuous elevation from the offices near the river, to the entrance hall and chapel at the other extremity. The model, not being quite completed, does not yet display either the grand entrance or the chapel, but the situations for both are pointed out. Along the drawing-room front there is a very broad paved terrace, supported by a forest of piers, surrounded by Gothic arches; and from this terrace there is a magnificent double flight of steps to the lawn. There is one gateway to the kitchen court, another to the stable court, and an entrance gate from the river, all of very great beauty. The model, however, is chiefly remarkable, and will be chiefly useful, for the very great accuracy, beauty, and character of the details — of the buttresses, towers, turrets, chimney tops, gable ends, cornices, string-courses, terminations to dormer windows, finials, finishings to gateways, &c. &c. The fidelity and beauty with which these details have been executed by Mr. Dighton are almost beyond praise. We could wish that he would make casts of all of them, and indeed of the whole building, so as to put it in the power of architects all over the country to possess themselves of a model, which could not fail to be of great use in aiding their invention, and correcting and purifying their taste in the Gothic style. We could wish to see Mr. Dighton employed in modelling some of the other fine buildings in the country; such as Alton Towers and the buildings in the Enchanted Valley, Eaton Hall, the proposed improvements at Trentham Hall, &c.

The Pantheon Bazaar, Oxford Street (noticed p. 91.), is nearly completed; and we were favoured with a private view of it on the 12th of May. We expect soon to be able to lay before our readers such plans, elevations, and sections of this large and magnificent building (to which there is nothing of the kind that can be compared in the metropolis), as will give them a complete idea of it; and will show them how much beauty of effect may be combined with a speculation having profit for its object. We shall also point out what we think superfluous in its elevation. The bazaar will be opened to the public on the 28th of May.

Art. II. *Queries and Answers.*

Pargetting. — In your *Architectural Encyclopædia* you mention a new kind of pargetting, composed of lime and powdered brick; but you do not say in what proportions they should be used. I shall feel much obliged by your giving the exact proportions, as well as the manner of use, if it differs from that employed in the old method. — *W. T.* March, 1834. The powdered brick is used instead of sand, and in the same proportion. There is no difference in the mode of laying it on. — *Cond.*

Brickmaking Machines. — What are the respective merits, or otherwise, of Mr. Cundy's patent brickmaking machine; and that of Messrs. Fortnum and Fencke's (or some such name), of a more recent date, and lately employed at Peckham Rye; and of the Russian patent one of M. de Chomas; or of any other that may have been invented? — *W. Newcastle Street, Strand, London, April* 24. 1834.

Art. III. *Obituary.*

DIED, at his house at Camberwell, April 29., *William Froome Smallwood*, Esq., Architect, at the early age of 34 years. Mr. Smallwood was eminent as an architectural draughtsman, particularly in the Gothic style; and, as a man, he was much esteemed and beloved by all who knew him.

THE

ARCHITECTURAL MAGAZINE.

JULY, 1834.

ORIGINAL COMMUNICATIONS.

Art. I. *On the Difference between Common, or Imitative, Genius, and Inventive, or Original, Genius, in Architecture.* By the Conductor.

In our preceding article (p. 145.), we have shown that every architect must necessarily have the power of invention; or, in other words, be a man of genius. The amateur architect may understand the art, have a love for it, and possess a good taste in its productions; but he is not supposed to possess the power of designing new buildings — that is, of displaying architectural genius.

In the infancy of all arts, the artist must have drawn his materials from nature, and created an art by the exercise of his inventive powers; but, in an advanced state of society, such as that to which we have now arrived, the artist derives his materials from the works of artists who have preceded him, and thus, as it were, works at second hand. In the former case, he must necessarily display inventive genius; and in the latter, imitative genius only.

The difference, then, between imitative genius and inventive genius consists in this; that, in the former case, the artist composes with elements already prepared to his hand by his predecessors, and that, in the latter, he forms elements of his own, and composes with them.

The architecture of all ages and countries may be reduced to two primitive elements; viz., the roof, and the prop by which that roof is supported. The kind of roof, and the kind and manner of applying the props, must have varied in different countries, according to the climate, the building materials furnished by the soil, and other circumstances; and from this difference have arisen the different manners of building, or styles of architecture, which are characteristic of different countries. Each of these styles consists of a number of parts and details; such, for example, as columns, pedestals, architraves, cornices, pediments, &c., in the Grecian style; and arches, buttresses, gables, mullions, labels, tracery, &c., in the Gothic manner. Now, an architect of the present day, in composing either a Grecian or a Gothic building, has the forms, the proportions, and all the different details of the parts mentioned, ready fixed to his hand, and from these he proceeds to design, or compose, whatever description of structure may be required of him. It is evident that, in this case, the mental powers required of the architect are incomparably less than if he had first to invent all these details, and next to invent a mode of combining them together, so as to produce the structure required. In the latter case only would he be entitled to be considered as possessing an inventive, or original, genius.

The first grand step, in the progress of architecture, was, the fixing of the details of what are called the different orders of Grecian architecture. This done, there could afterwards be little demand for original genius in that style,. till either a building was to be applied to a purpose to which it never 'had been applied before; or a material used in construction, which had never been so used previously. The introduction of the arch to the Grecian style, producing what may be called Roman architecture, must have been an exertion of original genius. So, afterwards must have been the invention of the pointed arch, which may be considered as the second grand step made by architecture, and which has led to all the different varieties of the Gothic style. The union of sculpture with architecture, when it first took place, must have been an exertion of original genius; and so also must have been the application of heraldry to that art, which took place during the age of chivalry. The use of painting, whether exteriorly or interiorly, must also have been at first an effort of original genius. Since architecture, whether regarded as to its different styles, or as to the different arts which have been united with it, seems thus to have exhausted all the sources of invention, it may be asked whether there is now any room for the exercise of original genius in the art. The answer is easily found from its past progress. Original genius in architecture may be called forth now, and in all future times, as it was in all past times, by the application of architecture to a purpose to which it was never before applied; by the use of a material in construction which was never before so used; and by the union of an art with architecture which never was before united with it.

In Britain, within the last century, three descriptions of structures have been introduced, which might, to a considerable extent, have called forth original genius. The first of these, in the order of time, was plant-houses, or structures for the growth of tropical plants, or the production of a summer climate during winter. Here was a purpose to which architecture had never been before applied, together with the more extensive use of a material (glass) than had ever before been made. No original genius, however, was displayed in consequence of this invention; for, as every one knows, all plant-houses merely display the forms, either of Grecian, or of Gothic architecture.

A second occasion for the display of original genius in architecture took place when cast iron was first employed as a material of construction. The most remarkable structures formed of this material have been bridges, some of which exhibit a certain extent of original genius, and others little beyond the ordinary powers of imitative composition.

The third description of structure, to which we have alluded, is suspension bridges. Here we have the application of architecture to a purpose to which it never was before applied, viz., to the pillars or towers which support the chains; and the use of a new material in bridge-building, viz., wrought iron in the forms of chains and rods, for supporting the road-ways. The suspension of the road may fairly be considered an exercise of original genius; but the supporting towers, as far as we know, have never displayed any thing more than such an adaptation of Grecian, or of Gothic architecture, as can only be considered an ordinary exertion of common or imitative genius. In some cases, indeed, even this ordinary exertion of the power of imitative composition has not been made. For example, the pillars of the Hammersmith Bridge are in the Grecian or Roman style, and consist of square columns, supporting architraves; the suspension chains passing through these pillars, under the architraves, instead of over them. Now, considering the construction of these pillars, as an imitation of the original type of wooden props supporting the beams of a roof, the intervals between these props being filled in with clay, the chains appear to have no other support than that of a mud wall. This mud wall, or filling in between the wooden props, was never intended in the slightest degree to support even the architrave; and, for an artist to employ it to support the chains, which carry the whole weight of the bridge, argues either an utter disregard, or an utter ignorance, of the spirit of Grecian or Roman architecture.

It is no defence of this violation of the imitative principle to say that the filling in is of stone, and, therefore, as strong as any other part of the pillar; for, if the imitative principle is given up, then the pilasters, and the architrave over them, are wholly without expression or meaning. In this, and every similar case, where classical architecture is employed, the chains, the support of which is the main object of the pillar, ought to have passed over the upper part of the architrave, and been carried by an appropriate description of acroter, in the composition of which the artist might have exercised his inventive powers. The whole pillar would then have been employed in supporting the chains, instead of only the most inferior and weakest part of it.

As subjects on which architects might display a degree of genius, perhaps as original as can be expected in the present improved state of all the arts, we may suggest the idea of taking the forms of the oldest styles of Gothic and Hindoo architecture, and applying them to the composition of dwelling-houses, and furniture adapted for modern use. For example, the Norman, or circular-arched Gothic, of which there are but few specimens remaining, might be taken; and, from the forms and details already existing in that style, other analogous forms and details might be invented, suitable for all the purposes of domestic building and furnishing. From these details, partly furnished by precedent, and partly by the inventive powers of the artist, designs for houses and for furniture might be composed, totally different from any thing that has hitherto appeared. This would, perhaps, be as great an exertion of original genius as could be expected in the present age.

Before, however, any architect attempts to design even within the ordinary sphere of invention, he ought to have made himself acquainted, as far as practicable, from books and other sources, with all that has been done by his predecessors, in all ages and countries. The more richly he stores his mind with the ideas of others, the more likely will he be to bring forth new ideas of his own; for a new idea can be nothing more than a new combination of ideas which had previously existed. By making himself thoroughly master of all the ideas of others, the architect becomes, not only capable of inventing with facility for all ordinary purposes, but of inventing in what may be called a cultivated style of art, as compared with that crude style of invention sometimes seen in the productions of untutored genius.

"The inventions of cultivated genius, Dr. Browne remarks (Lect. xxxvii.), " consist in the suggestions of analogy, as opposed to the suggestions of grosser contiguity." The latter are those of the ignorant inventor, who disdains storing his mind with the ideas of others; the former, those of the highly educated artist, who has made himself master of all that has been done in his art.

This, and the three preceding articles on architecture as an art of taste and of imagination, we consider as preliminary to a series of articles, which are to follow, on the art of composition in architecture.

Art. II. *On Heraldic Ornaments in Architecture.* By W. H.

It is the aim of the professors of every art, to please those who, from their acquirements, are likely to be the best judges of their productions; and, in this attempt, the architect, if he succeeds, is generally happy enough to obtain also the praise of the public. The opinions of the great mass of society are formed by the impressions that present themselves to the senses, and it is the chief end of science to make these impressions favourable. When the attention is attracted by the appearance of an edifice, the eye is naturally struck by the decorations of its exterior;

and, from the scrutiny that is bestowed on the ornamental parts, they are riveted in the recollection; while the remaining portions of the structure are often regarded with comparative indifference. It need scarcely, then, be urged, that the importance of a proper choice and appropriation of external ornament, in architecture, is increased by the universal notice that is taken of it. This consideration has suggested the following remarks upon the application of heraldry, as displayed in sculpture on the public buildings and mansions of distinction in this country.

In the first place, it should be observed, that the intention of these displays is to perpetuate claims to the honours of ancient lineage and rights; and any view as to their symbolical details producing an ornamental effect is a secondary consideration. In complaining of this disregard to appearances, it is not, however, meant to throw any contempt on heraldry as a study, or on the uses of it with reference to history and biography.

Armorial bearings are usually very indefinite and speculative types of their real meanings; and, except by those who use them, or who have made them the subject of particular investigation, they are little understood. The illustrative emblems expressed on them are, to a great extent, composed of the representations of signs and figures that never had existence but in the imagination; and which, consequently, have no natural objects to which they can be compared. Even where animals and other objects from nature are delineated, they are in most cases in distorted attitudes and positions; and are often metamorphosed by the junction of two or more species in one. A device or composition of this sort can rarely be gratifying to the sight, unless it is clearly intelligible. The simplest imitations of familiar objects make stronger impressions on the feelings than the most original efforts of fancy. The curiosity that is excited by heraldic exhibitions cannot be gratified by confusion in details; and the admiration due to the beauties of an edifice is often deteriorated by the imperfect effect produced by that part of it which is intended to be ornamental, and which, as before remarked, is always most conspicuously offered to the view.

One of the most remarkable instances of the employment of an heraldic figure in London is that of the lion on Northumberland House in the Strand; and it is perhaps the least objectionable of all, so far as the statue is concerned, because, from its correct execution, it conveys a true conception of what it is meant for: but, on account of its striking and very conspicuous situation on the summit of the building, and from its being the first object seen, there are few beholders who retain any clear idea of the house itself, more than a general impression of the space it occupies, and that there is a lion above it. This circumstance renders it questionable, whether the lion does indeed constitute an ornament to the architecture of Northumberland House, although it may in itself be admired. The dragons on the Guildhall of the city of London, also, not only overpower every thing else by their prominent position, but, as specimens of imaginary and hideous deformity, they do not recall any pleasing associations whatever. With only referring in a general way to the various sphinxes, satyrs, and other monsters, that are exalted in so many instances and situations, almost to the horror of the passers by, there are two cases of present date that have drawn a great share of the public gaze; viz., the hall of the Goldsmiths' Company, and that of the Fishmongers' Company. The defective locality of the former, and the bold station of the latter, together with the similarity of their uses and coinciding dates of erection, have very naturally led to many comparisons between the two. In both of these buildings, the armorial bearings of the companies are placed as conspicuously as the nature of their respective architecture will admit. In the Goldsmiths' Hall, the supporters (the figures on each side of the arms) consist of two animals, if they may be so called, having the bodies of horses and the extremities of bulls, with one horn each, from which they take their name of unicorns. In that of the Fishmongers, the supporters are two objects, having their upper halves the images, in the one of male, and in the other of female, human beings, with their lower halves representing those of fishes. There are also on both buildings sea monsters, half horses and half fishes. With respect to the workmanship or sculpture of these monsters, it is not intended here to criticise it; for, indeed, it would not be fair, even if it were faulty, to blame an artist who was required to represent things that have no prototype in nature, and in the designing and execution of which no stricter rules than those enjoined by custom were to be adhered to. Neither of the designs spoken of can give any satisfaction to those who do not know their meaning; nor is it to be supposed that those who do, can receive any sensation of delight from the inspection of monstrous forms, that must either draw forth contempt and ridicule, as where the beauty of the human proportions is partly changed to those of beasts, or produce impressions bordering on disgust.*

There are, probably, many persons who will not agree with these opinions; but they are stated with a view of making known

* In *Jameson's Journal* for April, 1834, it is argued that the ancients were most minutely accurate in their imitation of natural objects when they composed the fantastic creatures of their fancy; inasmuch as each of the parts employed to form the whole is, when taken separately, an accurate imitation of some thing which exists. To be convinced of this, Marcel de Serres says, we have only to glance over the remains of the purer periods of Greece and Rome, and, to a certain point, also of Egypt. Antique monuments preserve the traces of species which appear to be no longer found on the globe. — *Cond.*

the notions of all those whom the writer has ever heard converse upon the subject. That the public do sufficiently appreciate the production of really beautiful and classical sculpture on buildings, is attested by the almost unqualified approbation that several such instances, at the western part of the metropolis, and, indeed, in all the other places where they have appeared, have met with; and it is to be regretted that the taste of the public, in this particular, should be neglected, and almost abused, by the exposure of compositions to their view with so little that is classical, beautiful, or intellectual; and so much that is unsightly and unmeaning, as appears in heraldic ornaments on architecture generally.

As a defence of these animadversions on the use of monsters, the employment of the centaurs in the Athenian remains might be adduced as a precedent; and, as such, it is a very good one. But it has been pronounced, by those whose judgment in such matters is esteemed, that these should be regarded as instances of the most astonishing triumphs of art, in representing objects favourably, which would otherwise be disagreeable; and therefore this precedent must form an exception to the rule, especially when the difference of the times may in the one case give a qualification, and in the other a negative, to their propriety. There is also another circumstance that rather authorises the use of heraldry; and that is, the legislature requiring the royal arms to be seen in the churches of the established religion; and the importance of these edifices gives considerable weight to the authority. It should, however, be remembered, that these arms, though subject to similar censure, are familiar even to children; and that the intention of placing them there is altogether so national, that any want of attraction in their actual appearance is overbalanced by a friendly prejudice in the minds, and it is to be hoped in the hearts also, of those who behold them. As a concurrent fact, it might not be amiss to mention, that the national fervour or enthusiasm of a neighbouring country has led them, in many instances, to shew forth the letter N worked in bricks or stone on the fronts of houses, to their utter disfigurement, as the significant, and to them almost charm-working, initial of Napoleon.

As the tenour of the preceding observations is against the use now made of heraldry, it may perhaps be inferred that the writer wishes to exclude it entirely from architecture. This is by no means the case: these observations are only thrown out as a hint that, where buildings are publicly situated, the public have a right to comprehend what is exposed to them; and that, where heraldic ornament is attempted, it should not overpower the architectural expression of the building. Objects that are confused, or unsuitable, may as well be kept back altogether.

London, April, 1834.

ART. III. *A descriptive Account of the Duke of York's Monument, accompanied by Plans, Elevations, and Sections, copied from the Designs of Benjamin Wyatt, Esq., Architect.* By Mr. ROBERTSON.

THIS monument, which is now complete, and crowned with the statue of his late Royal Highness the Duke of York, forms a very striking ornament to the neighbourhood in which it stands; and, as it occupies the exact centre of the great opening from Carlton Gardens into St. James's Park, it is in a most imposing situation, whether viewed from the latter place, or from Regent Street.

The sum collected by private subscription for the erection of this monument amounted, in the year 1829, to 21,000*l.*; and this sum was shortly afterwards (by the interest thereon, and by further contributions) augmented to 25,000*l*. In the same year the committee of noblemen and gentlemen for managing the application of the fund thus raised, invited a few of the most eminent architects to submit designs for a monument to commemorate the public services of the late Duke of York, as Commander-in-Chief of the British Army. The competitors accordingly delivered in their designs, accompanied by estimates, in the month of August, 1829; but the committee did not come to a decision on their merits until the month of December, 1830, when the preference was given to the designs of Mr. Wyatt; which designs were then finally adopted. The monument was erected by Mr. Nowell of Grosvenor Wharf, Pimlico, who was under an engagement to complete it in every respect, with the exception of the statue, within a period which should not exceed two years, and for the sum of 15,760*l.* 9*s.* 6*d.* He completed his task in about one year and eight months; and he has certainly done it in a most substantial and workmanlike manner.

The architect and builder were put in possession of the ground on the 25th of April, 1831; the excavations commenced on the 27th of the same month, and they were finished in twenty-eight days. These excavations were dug to about 22 ft. below the general surface, in order to obtain a solid stratum of natural earth; and an artificial foundation was then formed by a large body of concrete, of sufficient magnitude to fill up the excavation, and of sufficient solidity to sustain the superincumbent weight of the monument. This artificial foundation was in form the frustum of a pyramid, covering a space of 2809 superficial ft. at its base, and having a surface of 900 superficial ft. at the top.* A course of Yorkshire stone slabs, 7 in. in thickness, was laid all over the surface of the concrete when brought up the half of its height, that is, at 11 ft. 6. in. above the level of its base

* The concrete was brought to its proper line of inclination by means of boards fixed at each of the four angles, and lines occasionally strained from one angle to another; and the concrete, when once brought to its proper position, firmly retained that position.

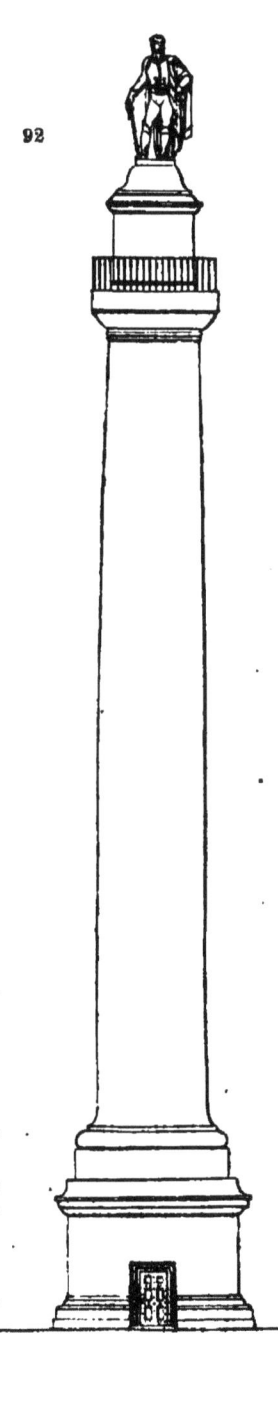

line, in order to equalise the pressure from above; and a second course of stones was, for the same purpose, laid upon the top of the body of concrete. This foundation, which was laid on the 25th of May, 1831, was finished on the 25th of June; and in three weeks afterwards the masonry was commenced; for by this time the concrete had become as compact and solid as if it had been a natural rock of granite.

The masonry was begun by a course of rough granite being laid on the top of the Yorkshire stone slabs; and the pedestal, which is 16 ft. 8 in. in height, and consists of ten courses, is built of the famous Aberdeenshire grey granite. The capital and base of the column are also of grey granite, but of a darker tone of colour than that of the pedestal; the shaft of the column, and the acroter or upper pedestal, are built of Peterhead red granite. The shaft, from the top of the base to the bottom of the capital, consists of twenty-six courses: on the west side there are seven apertures, and on the east side six, for the admission of light to the staircase. The column, which is of the Tuscan order, is 94 ft. 4 in. in height, including the base and capital: the inferior diameter is 10 ft. 1¾ in., and the lower diameter is 11 ft. 7½ in.; so that the proportion of the column is fully eight diameters. The acroter, which is 12 ft. 6 in. in height, and consists of seven courses, forms at once a covering to the staircase, and a pedestal for the statue to stand on.

The upper bed of the abacus (on the outer edge of which there is fixed a plain substantial iron railing) forms a gallery, to which we ascend by winding stairs through the interior of the column; and from which there is a delightful and extensive view of the surrounding scenery: the outlet to this gallery is by a door in the east side of the acroter. The stairs consist of 168 steps of 2 ft. 4 in. wide: each course in the shaft is exactly the height of five steps; and these five steps in one course are placed alternately at right angles to those of the preceding course; so that four stones, each containing five steps, form one complete round of the staircase.

From the manner in which the bond stones are employed in the shaft of this column, the structure would be of sufficient strength even for a lighthouse surrounded by the ocean; and this peculiarity of construction is, that the five steps of each course, as well as the newel or central pillar, together with the stone which forms the outer wall, *are cut out of the solid block!* This circumstance (in addition to the manner of joining the courses by dovetailed keys, and the way in which the ends of the steps that form the newel are spiked or plugged to each other) shows that the courses of the column are bound together in the most substantial manner.

Fig. 92. is a geometrical representation of the monument. The entrance, which is at the top of the stairs leading from the Park, fronts the south.

Fig. 97. is a plan of the pedestal. In this plan, *a* is the entrance; *b*, the outer casing of grey granite; *c*, the inner casing of red granite; *d*, the projection of the mouldings of the base; and *e*, the situation of the first riser of the spiral stairs. The newel of the staircase in the pedestal part is 2 ft. in diameter; and there is a landing over the doorway, which is the only one there is in the whole height.

Fig. 98. is a plan of the lower diameter of the shaft, in which are seen the aperture (*f*) for admitting light to the staircase; and the dovetailed keys (*g*) at each joint. The outside wall in this plan is 2 ft. 7 in. in thickness; and the newel is 1 ft. 6 in. in diameter, from the top of the pedestal to the level of the gallery.

Fig. 95. is a vertical section of the shaft, showing the openings for admitting light (*f*); and a section of the keys (*g*) which pass down through the whole course, and are inserted 2 in. in the middle of the stones of the courses immediately below.

Fig. 93. is a plan of the smaller diameter of the shaft. In this plan the thickness of the outer wall is, from the diminution of the column, only 1 ft. 10½ in. The keys and joints are shown at *g*.

Fig. 94. is a plan of the acroter and upper bed of the abacus. In this plan *h* is the situation of the last riser of the stairs;

with Plans, Elevations, and Sections. 195

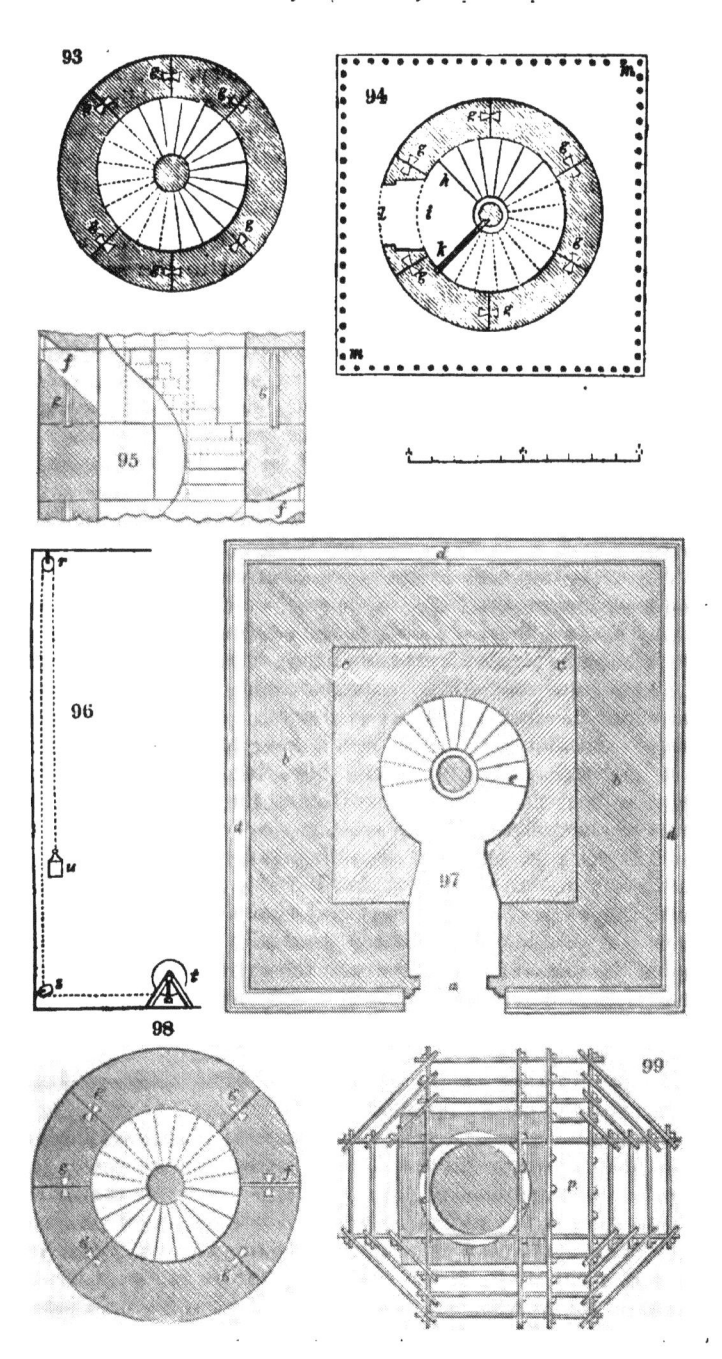

i, the landing; *k*, a large stone slab 4 in. thick to finish the landing; and *l*, the door leading to the gallery, *m*.

Fig. 104. is a section of the base and base mouldings of the pedestal.

Fig. 101. is a section of the cornice of the pedestal.

Fig. 100. is a section of the capital of the column.

Fig. 105. is a section of the base of the acroter.

Fig. 103. is a section of the cornice of the acroter.

These five figures of details are all drawn to the same scale, to show their relative proportions.

Fig. 102. is a horizontal section of one of the dovetailed keys, on a large scale. The length, as represented in the section, is 7¼ in., the width 4 in. at the two ends, and 3 in. in the centre. In a vertical direction they pass down through each course of the shaft at every joint, and 2 in. into the solid stone of the course below, as before observed, and as shown at *g* in *fig.* 95. They are of Yorkshire stone, and grouted in with Parker's best cement. In *fig.* 102., *n* is the joint in the stones of the outer wall, through which those keys pass, and *o* the cavity for the grout.

When the masonry of the monument was completed, in the month of December, 1833, the statue, which is by Mr. Westmacott, was not finished; and, as the artist at this time required several months longer for its completion, it was thought advisable to remove the scaffolding, notwithstanding the great expense that would be incurred by its re-erection; as, had it remained through the winter, the ropes would have become rotten by the frost, and the scaffolding would have been thereby rendered unsafe to bear the weight of hoisting up the figure. When the statue was completed, Mr. Nowell, in a very short time, erected a simple yet ingenious and scientific scaffolding of mere poles and ropes; and on the 8th of April, 1834, the statue of his late Royal Highness (having slings and chains round the arms, to which the tackle was attached) gradually ascended at about double the rate of the movement at the extremity of the minute hand of an ordinary-sized church clock, in presence of a vast number of spectators. The hoisting up of the figure was completed at half past seven o'clock the same evening.

Fig. 99. is a plan of the scaffolding. The statue was drawn up through the parallelogramic space at *p*.

Fig. 106. is a geometrical representation of the scaffolding, looking to the west. In this elevation are shown the space (*p p*) between the perpendicular poles, through which the statue was raised, and (*q*) the beams to which the blocks were attached.

The responsible task of raising the statue was performed with much ease and safety. It was elevated by means of four machines placed on the ground, which were worked upon the principle of the windlass. Four large blocks were attached to the beam at

with Plans, Elevations, and Sections. 197

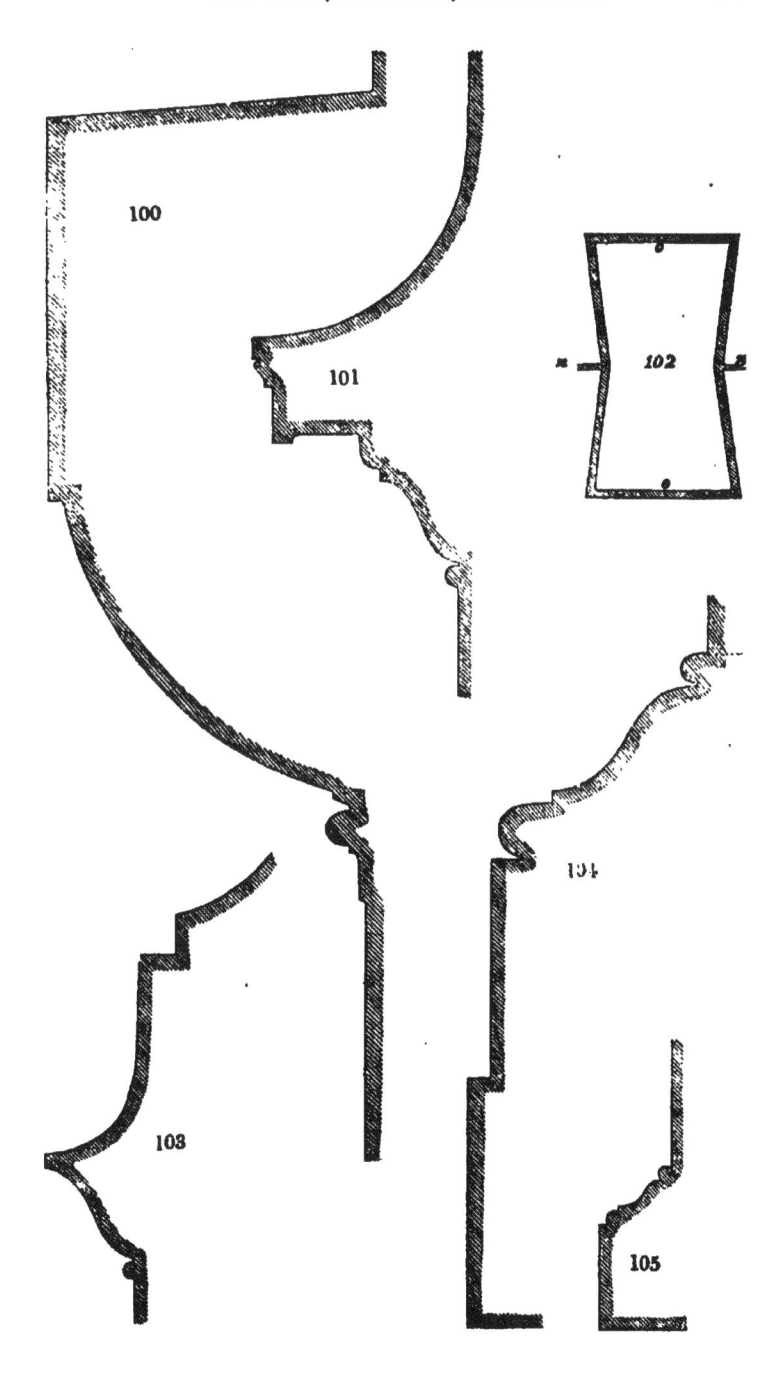

198   *Description of the Duke of York's Monument,*

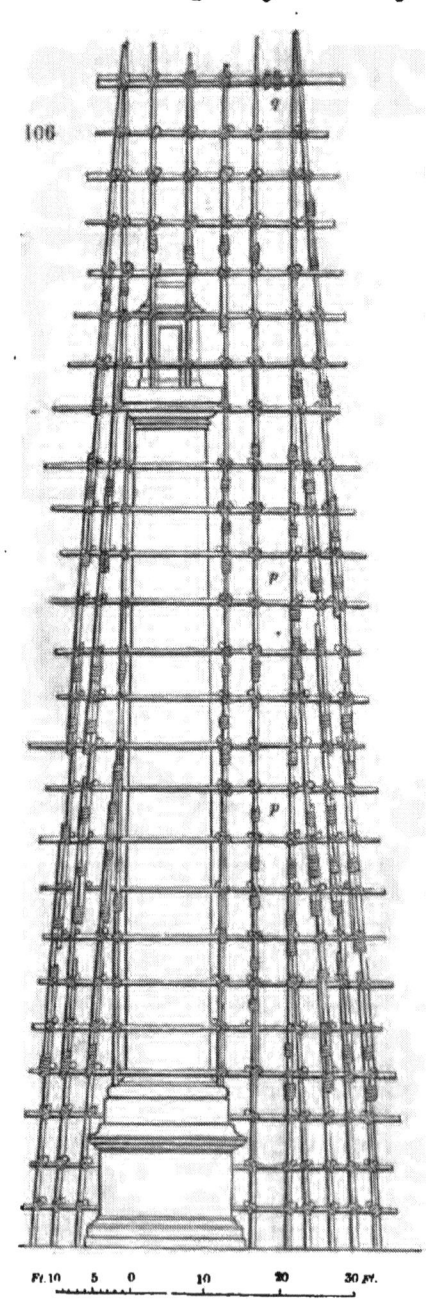

q in *fig.* 106.; and four smaller ones, called snatch blocks, were fixed near the ground. From the crabs, or machines, the ropes passed through the snatch blocks up to the larger blocks or pulleys at the top, and then came down to the statue, to which they were attached. By referring to *fig.* 96. the process will be readily understood. In this figure let us suppose *r* to represent the four large blocks fixed to the beams at the top; *s*, the snatch blocks, or four smaller ones, at the bottom; *t*, the crabs; and *u*, the weight to be raised. The figure was fixed on its pedestal by means of bars of wrought iron, 4 in. square, which passed down through the body and legs from the waist, and protruded through the heels of the boots. These two bars were inserted 2 ft. into the solid stone, and firmly fixed with solder.

Fig. 107. is a view from St. James's Park, showing the relative situation of the monument with the buildings that surround it. In the foreground are seen the elegant structures of Carlton Terrace, and, in the distance, the Athenæum, and the Travellers' Club-house.

The whole height of this monument is 123 ft. 6 in., and it is therefore

107

about the same dimensions as the column of which it is a copy, namely, the celebrated Trajan's column at Rome. The height of the statue is 13 ft. 9 in., which makes the whole height, from the ground line to the top of the figure, 137 ft. 3 in.; but when viewed from the bottom of the steps, at the level of St. James's Park, the altitude is 155 ft. 3 in.

It may not be uninteresting to compare the dimensions of this monument with that of Fish Street Hill, London, erected by Parliament from the designs of Sir Christopher Wren, to commemorate the burning of the city in the year 1666; and with the monument erected to the memory of Lord Melville in St. Andrew's Square, Edinburgh. This latter monument is of much the same form as that of the Duke of York; but the column is fluted, and the pedestal ornamented with festoons. It is built of Killala stone, from the designs of William Burn, Esq., architect, Edinburgh; the building was executed by Mr. Alexander Armstrong of that place, and completed in August 1832.

	City Monument.	Duke of York's Monument.	Melville's Monument.
	Ft. In.	Ft. In.	Ft. In.
Height from the ground to the top	202 0	137 9*	1:2 7*
Diameter of the column	15 0	11 7¼	12 2
Circumference of the pedestal	128 0	75 0	72 0
Height of the pedestal	40 0	16 8	18 4
Height of the gallery from the ground	170 0	111 0	120 10
Height above the gallery	32 0†	23 6‡	31 9‡
Number of steps in the stair	365	168	196
Time taken in building	6 years.	1 year 8 months.	

Although the Duke of York's monument is much inferior in magnitude to that of Fish Street Hill, and to Melville's monument (the statue on the latter is 18 ft. high), it must nevertheless be looked upon as an undertaking of no ordinary merit: for, whether we consider the peculiarity of the artificial foundation; the successful method of forming the casing, or wall of the staircase, the steps, and the newel, all out of one piece; the difficulty of procuring blocks large enough for this purpose from Scotland, and that of finding vessels with hatchways sufficiently large to admit these blocks into their holds; the hardness of granite to work with the chisel; and the many other contingent circumstances; we must look upon this monument as a great and magnificent work.

It may be worthy of a passing remark, that the stairs of this monument, as well as that of Melville's monument, wind round to the left; while the stairs of the City monument wind round to the right; and the stairs to the "whispering gallery" of St. Paul's wind round a well-hole on the left. There is an important advantage in having spiral stairs winding to the left; because, in that case, the handrail, which ought always to be on the right in ascending, is attached to the outer wall, and therefore a person holding it in going up, walks upon the broadest part of the steps.

* Including statue.   † Including blazoned urn.   ‡ Including statue.

The contemporary press seems to consider, with reference to the statue, that the figure is too clumsy, and that Mr. Westmacott has fallen into an error by associating the order of the Garter with boots and cuirass belonging exclusively to cavalry uniform. I shall leave this part of the subject to be decided by competent judges, and content myself by remarking, in conclusion, that I think the gentlemen of the committee have fully discharged their duty, and that they have been singularly fortunate in selecting an architect so eminently qualified to furnish the designs for this noble structure, and a builder who thoroughly understood those designs, and worked up to them in a tradesman-like manner.

The monument was opened to the public on Wednesday the 23d inst., at 1s. per head; and I understand that the funds which will be thus raised are to be applied to the relief of the widows and orphans of soldiers.

Bayswater, April 26. 1834. J. ROBERTSON.

ART. IV. *Architectural Maxims.*

In Bookcases, Wardrobes, and all similar articles, the space between 3 ft. and 7 ft. from the ground is all that ought to be appropriated to shelves; as it is only between these points that a person can conveniently reach any thing. All above and below these points, if it is used at all, should be cupboards for bulky articles seldom wanted. — *T. W.*

Doors should be hung on the side nearest the fire, whether they are in the same wall, or at right angles with it; otherwise they will draw out the smoke every time they are used.— *T. W.*

Unity of Forms and Lines. — In every building, in order to preserve unity of expression, there ought not only to be prevalent the same forms, but the same character of lines. In correctly Grecian architecture, the forms extend in length, the prevailing lines are horizontal; in the Pointed style, the forms exceed in height, and the prevailing lines are perpendicular to the horizon; in Roman architecture when the arch is introduced, in the Anglo-Norman style, and in the Elizabethan manner, there is, or ought to be, a harmonious combination of horizontal, perpendicular, oblique, and curvilinear lines.

Congruity of Forms. — When two forms totally different, as a circle and a square, are unavoidably placed together, unless the one is a great deal smaller than the other, they will never form a whole.

Effect of Habit on the Taste and Judgment. — A vicious combination may become tolerable, and even satisfactory, by long habit; for example, the barn-like form of the body of a church, and its tower or spire.

REVIEWS.

ART. I. *A Series of Discourses upon Architecture in England, from the Norman Era to the Close of the Reign of Queen Elizabeth; with an Appendix of Notes and Illustrations, and an Historical Account of Master and Free Masons.* By the Rev. JAMES DALLAWAY. 8vo, 447 pages. London, 1833. 14s.

MR. DALLAWAY is advantageously known to the public by several works on architecture and sculpture, which evince, on his part, an ardent love of those arts, and great knowledge as an architectural antiquary. The work before us consists of six discourses; the first four of which relate to the Gothic architecture of churches and cathedrals; the fifth, to military architecture; and the sixth, to Tudor and Elizabethan architecture. The appendix contains collections for an historical account of master and free masons.

From the above outline of the contents of this volume, our readers will conclude that it is replete with interesting information on the subjects on which it treats, and we only regret that our necessarily limited space prevents us from either giving an analysis of the work, or such extracts from it as will confirm them in such a conclusion. The work is characterised by an accumulation of facts, rather than by arguments or speculations; and on that account it is the more valuable for the purpose of enabling the young architect to form correct historical ideas on the subject of the Gothic style. No young architect ought to stop short in the acquirement of architectural and antiquarian knowledge, till he can refer every church, cathedral, or old mansion, which comes in his way, to its precise era. For want of this knowledge, we frequently find architects, even of reputation and extensive practice, committing anachronisms in the Gothic style, by placing in the upper story of a building details which belong to a period antecedent to those employed in the lower story. This departure from the order of time, though it may escape detection by general observers, and even men of a good general taste, is yet exceedingly offensive to those who are so far enlightened as to see in it a deviation from truth and propriety.

In the discourse on military architecture, there is more curious information than might be expected respecting a style which, as far as its original uses are concerned, may be considered as long since extinct. This style is classed as — 1. Saxon or Roman; 2. Anglo-Norman, from 1070 to 1170; 3. Norman, from 1170 to 1270; 4. Style of the Crusaders, introduced by Edward I. in 1272; 5. Style of Windsor Castle, by Edward III., 1350 to 1400; 6. Style of the fifteenth century, 1400 to 1480; and, 7. Castles in the reigns of the Tudors. Lists are given of the castles belonging to each of these classes; and, as most of them are delineated in published works, the student who has access to the British Museum may, with far less trouble than might at first sight be imagined, make himself master of the peculiarities of each particular class. Here, then, is a fine opportunity for an architect to display inventive genius on the principle before laid down in our Essay on the subject. (p. 185.) We invite young artists, therefore, to compose seven different designs for small villas in the seven styles of castle architecture above enumerated; including, for each particular design, all the interiors, fittings-up, and furniture which ought to belong to it. Had we seven cottages to build in seven different situations, in a mountainous country, and were not limited as to expense, we would build fragments of castles, of seven different styles, above enumerated; and to each fragment we would add the rooms requisite to form the cottage. These rooms, with their roof, should, of course, be in some of the various modern styles, so as to form a contrast with the style of the castle: at the same time the cottage should be so subordinate as to unite with the ruins of the castle in forming a whole; and ivy, and creepers, and trees, might be employed to harmonise the composition.

Discourse VI. is on the Tudor style, and the architecture by which it was succeeded, until the close of the reign of Queen Elizabeth. The Tudor style commenced with the fifteenth century, and exhibits vast mansions, in which the characteristic style of the castles of the preceding age "was not entirely abandoned, but superseded and mixed up with a new and peculiar manner." This style was neither ecclesiastic nor military, but something between both. A great number of small rooms were formed, for lodging a multitudinous household; and some of an enormous size, for a display of hospitality; but there were very few arrangements either for comfort or convenience. This style began to undergo variations under Henry VIII., by Holbein, at once an architect and a painter, by the introduction of the Roman style, and the modifications of it adopted in France. It was further changed, during the reign of Elizabeth, by the introduction of the Italian ornaments and designs of John of Padua. John Thorp was the most celebrated architect of this reign; but Mr. Dallaway gives the names of nine others, all eminent. This discourse is full of data on which to study the characteristics of this, now the most fashionable and prevalent style of old English domestic architecture.

The historical account of master and free masons abounds in curious matter. The author investigates, " I. The various designations of master masons, and their associates and operatives, which may be authenticated either from their epitaphs, in the magnificent structures where they had sepulture, or from the contracts with patrons and supervisors. II. An enquiry into the true claims of ecclesiastics, with respect to their having been the sole designers, or architects, of cathedrals and their parts, exclusively of the master masons whom they employed, and who were required only to execute plans already allowed them. III. Of architects who practised in England, during the middle ages, concerning whom documentary evidence is adduced in a series." (p. 411.)

But we must conclude our remarks; having, we trust, said enough to show that Mr. Dallaway's *Discourses* deserve a place in the library of every reading architect.

ART. II. *The Domestic Architecture of the Reigns of Queen Elizabeth and James I., illustrated by a Series of Views of English Mansions, with brief Historical and Descriptive Accounts of each Subject.* By T. H. Clarke, Architect. Royal 8vo, 24 pages; 20 lithographic plates, and 2 woodcuts. London, 1833. 1*l*. 1*s*.

THE Elizabethan style of building, Mr. Clarke informs us, in his preface, " is much better adapted for country residences than any other; being much less expensive in the arrangement and decoration. What," he asks, " can be more suitable characteristics of an English mansion, than a noble picture or banquet gallery, spacious staircases and halls, and windows admitting an abundance of light and air?" In these sentiments most architects, we believe, will concur, as we do most heartily; and, it necessarily follows, that we highly approve of the design of the work before us. We regret, however, that we cannot say much in favour of its execution. The lithographic plates convey a tolerable idea of the effect of the different buildings exhibited, but they are not sufficiently distinct to enable us to make out any of the details. With respect to the descriptions, though the author states, in the titlepage, that they shall be " brief," yet we did expect something more than merely three or four lines, as in some instances; or even a fourth of a page, which exceeds the extent to which most of the notices are carried. In some instances we are merely told the name of the county in which the building was erected, and left to discover what part of the county it may be situated in, and even whether it does still exist, or has been destroyed, as is the case with some of the mansions, views of which are here given. The author might very well have filled up two pages with descriptive and historical particulars of each design, accompanied by outline engravings on wood of the various details of each. The work would then have been of very great value to the architect in a scientific and practical point of view, and would have lost none of its attractions to the general reader, as a book of picturesque architectural scenery. We strongly recommend the author to take these remarks into consideration, when his work comes to a second edition.

The subjects illustrated are: — Wimbledon House, destroyed early in the 18th century; Eaton Lodge, Aston Hall, Grafton Hall, Stanfield Hall, Beckford Hall, Bromshill House, Fenn Place, Queen's Head, Chastleton, Bereton Hall, Holland House, Houghley House, Streete Place, Montacute House, Westwood House, Wakehurst Place, Carter's Corner, Eastbury House, and East Mascall, all lithographs; and the south front of Eastbury, and an old house near Worcester, woodcuts.

We have been most gratified with a view of Montacute House, and with the descriptive notice of it, which is decidedly the best in the work. We shall quote it entire; premising that many of the houses built during the reign of Henry VIII., had the form of the letter H for a ground plan, in compliment, as it is supposed, to that king; and the plan of Montacute House shows that the same compliment was paid to Elizabeth. This mansion was erected in Somersetshire, " between the years 1580 and 1601, by Sir Edward Philips, sergeant at arms to Queen Elizabeth. The cost of its erection is said to have amounted to nearly 20,000*l*. The form of the plan is that of the letter E, intended, perhaps, by Sir Edward as a mark of respect to his royal mistress. The house is built of stone found on the estate, of a rich brown colour, ornamented with gables, a balustrade, pinnacles, and enriched cornices. Between each window of the second story are niches, occupied by figures in ancient costume; the chimney shafts present columns of the Doric order. On the central compartment are the arms of the family, and over the entrance is the following inscription, dictated by the true spirit of old English hospitality: — ' Through this wide-opening gate, none come too early, none return too late.' The building, which is 92 ft. high, is divided into many and spacious apartments, among which is a magnificent banquet gallery, 189 ft. long, and 21 ft. wide." (p. 19.)

ART. III. *Observations, by Alexander Trotter, Esq., of Dreghorn, in Illustration of his modified Plan of a Communication between the New and the Old Town of Edinburgh.* 4to, several plates. Edinburgh, 1834.

MR. TROTTER is well known in Scotland as a gentleman much attached to architecture, and as one who has paid great attention both to territorial and municipal improvements. For several years past, he has bestowed particular attention on the means of improving the city of Edinburgh, and especially of forming a more convenient and elegant line of connection between the old town and the new. Mr. Trotter has spared neither labour nor expense in making his ideas on this subject known to the citizens of Edinburgh, by engraved plans, views, &c. In 1828, he printed *A Plan of Communication between the New and the Old Town of Edinburgh*, accompanied with six large folding plates, besides detailed engravings in folio. A second edition of this work was published in 1829; and, after a great deal of discussion, some of Mr. Trotter's plans being thought too expensive, he prepared and published those which form the subject of the work, the title of which stands at the head of this article.

It is highly gratifying to us to observe how very general the spirit of improving towns is in almost every part of the island; and certainly, with reference to Edinburgh, the changes which have taken place there during the last fifteen years appear to be greater, in proportion to the size of the city, than those which have taken place within the same period in London. With respect to Mr. Trotter's plan, we have not a sufficiently distinct recollection of the streets and public buildings of Edinburgh to speak of it in detail; but, from the bare inspection of the delineations, we can state, that, in the alterations proposed, great and obvious leading principles are kept in view. For instance, easy communication between the city and the country; easy intercommunication within the city; broad streets; and open spaces round all public buildings. These are principles, the application of which was nowhere more wanting than in the old town of Edinburgh; and though (if they were applied to the extent proposed by Mr. Trotter) the character of that crested ridge of old dusky buildings, which forms the principal feature of "Auld Reekie," would be in a great measure destroyed, yet this is as nothing when compared with the convenience and magnificence which it would produce. It is ridiculous to suppose that the distinctive character of the old town can be kept up, and the modern improvements of which such a town is susceptible introduced. Crowdedness, darkness, and filth are the characteristics of old towns; open airiness, light, and cleanliness, of new ones.

There is one circumstance in Mr. Trotter's plan, respecting which we have some doubts; and these doubts could only be removed by local inspection. It appears to be an object with Mr. Trotter to reduce the surface of the Earthen Mound to a level, or nearly so, from one end to the other; probably in order that it may serve as a base line to the views of the Castle from Prince's Street. But to reduce the Mound to a level requires two distinct degrees of acclivity (from B to L in the plan), in the street which is to connect Prince's Street in the new town with the High Street in the old town. The acclivity in a part of this line will be 1 in 15; while, on the Mound, it will be 1 in 20. Now, instead of lowering the Mound at one end, we should prefer either retaining it at its present height (by which means the ascent of the second rise would be reduced to nearly 1 in 19), or raising it sufficiently to render the whole slope, from the Institution on the Mound to St. Giles's church, one plane of the same acclivity in every part. No effect or beauty, in our opinion, should ever be attempted at the expense of permanent convenience. This is the only doubtful point that we have, with respect to Mr. Trotter's modified plan.

The next point on which we have to offer a few remarks is, the mode in which the two valleys between the new town and the old are proposed to be planted. According to Mr. Trotter's engraved views, these hollows, which are, " in most parts, between 30 ft. and 40 ft. below the level of Prince's Street," are shown as planted with timber trees, or trees of a timber-like size. Now, we contend that, whether with respect to the salubrity of the two valleys, or to the beauty of the scenery to be produced in them, the articles planted should be chiefly low shrubs. These valleys have no natural outlet; the upper one being dammed up by the Mound, and the lower one by a market and other buildings close to the North Bridge. Unless, therefore, the sun and the wind are freely admitted, to dispel the exhalations which will unavoidably accumulate in these basins, they cannot fail to prove reservoirs of malaria. That the beauty of the scene would be incomparably greater if it were planted in such a manner as to be looked down on, both from the old town and the new, as two grand panels of vegetation, is perfectly clear to us; though we have not room to enter into such details as may convince those who are of a different opinion. By clogging up these two hollows with high trees, they will be rendered useless to the inhabitants as places of air and exercise; and the distinctive character of the localities of the old town and the new will be destroyed.

MISCELLANEOUS INTELLIGENCE.

Art. I. *Foreign Notices.*

ITALY.

A Suspension Bridge has been thrown across the river Garigliano, on the high road from Naples to Rome, where, for a long time, a miserable ferry was the only means of conveyance. It is 230 ft. in length, and cost 75,000 ducats. (*For. Quar. Rev.*, May, 1834, p. 471.)

The Roads in the Kingdom of Naples have become an object of increased attention on the part of the government. They are divided into three classes: the royal roads, which are maintained at the expense of the treasury; the provincial roads, for which 1,000,000 ducats are paid by the communes. Meantime manufactures are spreading very fast over the kingdom. From all this, it appears that that beautiful country is not so stationary and indolent as many people are apt to suppose, because they seldom hear any tidings from that quarter. (*Ibid.*)

TURKEY.

The sultan has ordered the erection of a building on a larger scale at Constantinople for the manufacture of great guns, on the principle practised at His Majesty's arsenal at Woolwich, from the designs and under the superintendence of Mr. William Barlow, a talented young English architect and engineer, who has been at Constantinople for some time past, making all the necessary arrangements for commencing the same. — *W. J. S. Clapham, May*, 1834. A school of architecture has also been established by command of the sultan. (*Galignani's Messenger.*)

ART. II. *Domestic Notices.*

ENGLAND.

At a Lecture on the Pyramids of Egypt, at the Royal Institution, some weeks ago, which we had the pleasure of attending, not only models of the pyramids, but specimens of the stone of which they are composed, were produced. This stone is a soft calcareous agglutination of shells; and not granite, as many erroneously suppose, from the circumstance of the Egyptian columns, obelisks, and statues being chiefly of that material. At the same meeting, models of several obelisks were exhibited, in one of which might be remarked the great beauty and unity of effect produced by the pedestal of the obelisk having sides sloping in the same plane as the sides of the upper part; or, in other words, of the pedestal being a frustum of a pyramid, of which the upper part was also a frustum, the continuation being broken by the narrowing of the upper part of the pedestal.

A Course of Lectures on Civil Engineering is now delivering at the London University, by Dr. Ritchie, which, it appears to us, well deserves to be attended by young architects. Besides the subjects of strength and stability, the pressure of water, its force in motion, its velocity in pipes and rivers, &c., the motion of air in tubes and in chimneys, and warming and ventilating, form part of the course.

The personal Friends of the late eminent Civil Engineer, Mr. Thos. Tredgold, have set on foot a subscription for his orphan children; who, since their father's death, have lost their mother; and, in addition to this, their eldest sister, who acted as a mother to the younger children, has lately died. Thos. Telford, Esq., the president of the Institution of Civil Engineers, is at the head of this subscription; which, we are sure, will command the attention of all who know any thing of Mr. Tredgold's character.

Tothill Fields Prison, May 23. — We were shown over this building by its architect, Robert Abraham, Esq., attended by his clerk of the works, Mr. Buller. Every part of the prison, its uses, and the mode of its construction, was minutely pointed out, and described to us; and the impression left on our minds by the whole is, that it is one of the most perfect prisons that has ever been erected. The outline of the ground is irregular; but that of the court-yard, which is surrounded by the prisons, is an octagon. The entrance is from the south side, directly opposite to which is the governor's house; to the right of the court-yard are the prisons for females, and to the left those for males. The back part of the governor's house is semicircular; exterior to which there is a semicircular platform, and, beyond that, parallelogram prisons radiating outwards, with yards between. The governor, from his back rooms, can see into all these yards and prisons; and, on the ground floor, there is an admirable contrivance for the turnkeys to see into all the prisons and yards without being seen by the prisoners, which reminded us of the plan for a Panopticon workhouse or prison, by Jeremy Bentham, which was carried into execution by his brother, the late General Bentham, by desire of Catherine II., in Petersburg, and which we saw there in 1813. The various arrangements for classification, separation, security, warming, ventilation, cleanliness, and inspection, are as admirable as are the details of execution. The whole is fire-proof. The work was performed by contract; the different parts being contracted for separately by different contractors. For example, the entrance iron gate is by one contractor, and the inner gate by another. The work could not be better executed than it is; and, what is remarkable, and proves the profound study of the subject, and practical skill of Mr. Abraham, is, that the cost, so far from exceeding the estimate, as is almost always the case, falls short of it some thousand pounds. This prison does the greatest honour to Mr. Abraham; and we hope that, for the good of the public, he will publish the plans of it at large, with all their various details, descriptions, and specifications. Many of the details are original, and most ingenious. There is a fine panoramic view from the roof of the chapel, which is over the governor's house; and we could not help remarking, when looking from it to the towers of Westminster Abbey, how many architects there are who could erect an equally sumptuous cathedral, and how few there are who could contrive and execute such a prison; the effort in the one case is chiefly imitation, but in the other it is invention.

Cheshire.—The spire of a church which had deviated from the perpendicular 5 ft. 11 in., and was split several inches apart a long way up the centre, has lately been set straight and reunited by Mr. Trubshaw. The spire was built on a naturally sloping situation; and its weight is estimated at about 1500 tons of stone. In all sloping situations, the lower side (whether of churches, towers, houses, or even walls or roads, unless the foundation be rock), has a tendency to give way first; but more especially when the foundation, as in this case, was of two different kinds of subsoil. On the upper or fast side of the spire, the ground underneath was of slaty marl; while that on the lower side of it was of a sandy marl. Mr. Trubshaw, after examining well the outside of the foundations, commenced digging down the inside. After having got below the level of the footings (lowest stones of the foundation), he " proceeded to bore a row of auger-holes clear through under the foundation of the high side, the holes nearly touching each other. These holes he filled with water; and, corking them up with a piece of marl, let them rest for the night. In the morning, the water had softened the marl to a puddle; and the building gradually beginning to sink, another row of holes were bored, but not exactly so far through as the first row. They were filled with water as before; and the high side not only kept sinking, but the fracture in the centre kept gradually closing up. This process was continued till the steeple became perfectly straight, and the fracture imperceptible. (*Weekly Dispatch*, April 7.)

Kent.— The town of Dover, which is so romantically situated at the extremity of a valley between two important fortifications which rise majestically above it, has become this summer one of the most attractive places on the coast. The consequence which it has attained, not only as a port, but as a place of fashionable retirement, is likely to be much increased from the extensive improvements which are going on in all parts of the town. Amongst the first of these is the harbour, which for years past has been subject to an accumulation of beach at its entrance. This is to be removed by means of the back water, which is to be brought in immediate contact with it by means of a noble tunnel of brickwork, 30 ft. wide and 16 ft. high, and at its extremity diverging into several branches of iron pipes 7 ft. in diameter, which can be discharged in any direction as the situation of the bar may require. A quay wall of masonry, 300 ft. in length and 25 ft. high, is also in progress; which, together with the excavation, and other works connected therewith in progress, renders it peculiarly interesting to the scientific observer. A new church, called the Holy Trinity, in Stroud Street, near the Bank, is becoming an object of attraction: it is a Gothic edifice, and its principal elevation next the street is to be of stone, with pinnacles terminating the body and aisles. This building will be completed in the course of a year. A new crescent fronting the sea, forming three groups of buildings, from a design of

P. Hardwick, Esq., of London, is about to be erected by some spirited individuals in the town: when completed, a carriage drive and a fine walk will be formed, encircling the bay, and affording to the visiters and townspeople one of the most delightful promenades in the kingdom. The want of a good approach to the town coastwise has long been felt, but this is now about to be remedied: a wide and handsome street has been built, leading from the bottom of the castle hill towards the market-place, and is soon to be thrown open to the public. That old relic of antiquity, the *Maison Dieu*, has lately been disposed of by the crown; and it is much to the honour of the corporation that they have made arrangements for securing the preservation of this ancient structure, which forms a striking object on entering the town. This building, like many others, was probably erected at different periods, from the style observed in its several parts; but the alterations which it has undergone, since it has been in the possession of the crown, have so mutilated it, that it is now almost impossible to ascertain its original form. The project of the railway from London to Greenwich being continued to Dover, is much talked of. Plans and a prospectus are now before the puplic; and it is to be hoped that ere long this grand undertaking will be in progress; thus giving to this town another important advantage, which its natural situation so justly entitles it to. — *W. H. Dover, June* 5. 1834.

Norfolk. — *Boring for Water at Diss.* Some well-borers, under the direction of Mr. David Greenley of Northampton Square, London, have been for some months engaged in boring a well at Messrs. Taylor and Dyson's brewery, at Diss, in Norfolk; and have succeeded in obtaining an abundant supply of pure water, at a depth of upwards of 600 ft. from the surface. The well was sunk, a few years ago, for the purpose of supplying the brewery with water; but, in consequence of the immense quantity of sand continually rising whenever the pumps were worked, it has been almost useless. Many efforts had been made by different well-sinkers to deepen the well and get rid of the sand, without success, the sand rising as quickly as dug out: but Mr. Greenley has conquered all difficulties, and obtained an abundant supply of pure water. We have conversed with Mr. Greenley on boring for water, and he has promised us a paper on the subject. We are persuaded that, if the facility with which water may be procured by boring, in many situations, were better known to builders, Artesian wells would be much more generally in use.

Somersetshire. Bristol. — *The Elements of Beauty and Deformity* were discussed in a lecture delivered at the Mechanics' Institution, Bristol, April 22., by John Withers, Esq. The object of this lecture was to point out the radical forms of those objects which we are accustomed to consider beautiful, or the contrary; and to assign reasons why certain forms should produce certain emotions. The various previous theories of beauty were briefly adverted to; and Mr. Withers endeavoured to prove that beauty was in all cases the result of "harmony and subordination in variety." (*Bristol Mercury*, April 26. 1834.) We are much gratified at hearing of lectures of this kind being delivered to mechanics; because we feel confident that, by infusing good taste into this class, whether those of the workshop or of the garden, the general taste of the country will be most effectively improved. We intend to have, in every Number of this Magazine, at least for a considerable time, an article on some department of taste as a science, so as ultimately to render every thing respecting taste and beauty familiar to every reader. In the mean time, we have applied to Mr. Withers, through a friend, for an abstract of his lecture.

Surrey. — We referred to the bricks at Sutton Place in p. 126.; and we find the following mention of them in the *Gentleman's Magazine*, vol. i. new ser. p. 488., which we consider valuable, as confirming our opinion both of their beauty and their durability: — " Sutton Place presents the finest specimens, perhaps, extant of the stamped and baked clay of the fifteenth century, formed into huge bricks 14 in. long by 9 in. wide, and 3½ in. thick; and also into coins, mullions, weatherings, &c., all of which are impressed with their proper mouldings; and the cavettos enriched with a tracery of running foliage, and other appropriate ornaments. The bricks are marked alternately with R W; and with a tun and bunches of grapes, within borders of Gothic ornament. A rebus for Richard Weston is evidently intended. The colour of this brick or artificial stone is excellent, a light warm ochre, resembling Caen stone. The material is of a close texture, and rendered extremely hard by the fire of the kiln. Time has made little or no impression on it. The effect of the minarets on either side the hall-door, composed of this brick, and of the coins and parapet of the building, is exquisitely rich; and, in any edifice of the period that has yet come under my notice, unrivalled."

Sussex. Brighton. — There are a variety of things in this hotbed of trickery and favouritism that would startle you were I to name a tithe of them in one epistle; nay, which would rouse the ire and indignation of every true lover and professor of architecture and the building arts. You shall be furnished hereafter with the particulars of a job that was concocted here, between three and four years ago, which was a complete architectural robbery. An invitation was given to architects to furnish designs for a public building (offering a premium, &c.), that was restricted not to cost more than from 12,000*l.* to 13,000*l.*; and the design (out of from sixty to seventy that were submitted) of a favourite was selected, that ultimately cost the town between 30,000*l.* and 40,000*l.* The building consequently erected is now one of the most villanous monuments, of good materials and workmanship thrown together pell-mell, that ever disgraced this or any other age.* — *F. Brighton, April,* 1834.

The Church at Hove. — A letter on this subject appeared in the *Brighton Herald* in March last, a copy of which has been sent us; and from it we make the following abridgment: — " Mr. Basevi, architect of London, and son of Mr. Basevi, a resident in Hove parish, Brighton, offered, at a parish meeting, on Sept. 20. 1833, to furnish plans gratuitously for rebuilding the church of Hove on its own foundation. Of course, this offer was accepted; and he was consequently appointed architect to the church. Notwithstanding this, at a subsequent meeting, in Feb. 1834, Mr. Basevi, sen., endeavoured to get some compensation voted to his son for these plans; and this the writer of the letter alluded to considers not in accordance with fair dealing on the part of Messrs. Basevi towards the parish; and, on the part both of the parish and of Messrs. Basevi, towards professional men in general: the gratuitous offer of the plans having, no doubt, influenced the parish in choosing their architect. The letter in the *Brighton Herald* is signed Fair Play; but the writer of it has authorised us to give his real name and address: viz., *S. H. Benham. Brighton, April* 14. 1834.

Yorkshire. — *Leeds Court House* is undergoing considerable alterations and improvements, from the designs and under the immediate superintendence of our talented townsman, R. D. Chantrell, Esq. — *A Young Architect. Leeds, May* 5. 1834.

Hull. — *A Memorial in honour of the late Mr. Wilberforce* is about to be erected in this place; for which a design has been submitted, by Mr. Clarke of Leeds, that has been approved of. It is a column, at the top of which will be a statue of the philanthropist: the height of the whole is to be 100 ft. —*Id.*

Huddersfield Parish Church. — This ancient edifice is about to be rebuilt in the perpendicular Gothic style, with crypt and buttresses, from designs by Mr. J. P. Pritchett, architect, of York. The cost of rebuilding will amount to nearly 3000*l.* — *Id.*

---

* We admit this sentence, for the sake of protesting against the use of expressions similar to those contained in it, without assigning reasons. All such modes of condemning any object go for nothing with us, because they afford no proof that the party using them is any judge. Let our correspondent give us the name of the building, and state his reasons in detail for disapproving of it. —*Cond.*

SCOTLAND.

Edinburgh Society of Arts.—By *Jameson's Journal* for April, 1834, we find that a number of interesting communications, on architectural subjects, were laid before this very useful Society during the months of January and February, 1833. Among these are, an Improved Ventilating Warm Air Stove, by Mr. Symington, of Kettle, Fife; on constructing Public Buildings in relation to the Theory of Sound, &c., by Mr. Wm. Reid, architect, 27. Charlotte Street, Glasgow; Model and description of a Window calculated to insure the safety of Glaziers and Painters, by Mr. Rutherford, sievemaker, Haddington; description of an accurate and cheap Air Pump, by Mr. Dunn, 50. Hanover Street, Edinburgh. If this instrument could be rendered available for exhausting air in an apparatus for cooling wines, water for drinking, butter, &c., so as to supersede the use of ice, it would be most valuable; we have no doubt that such an instrument will shortly be invented, and made so cheap as to be within the reach of every family. It would add much to our domestic comforts, especially in the south. An Essay on the Causes of Obstructions in Water Pipes, by J. S. Hepburn, Esq., promises to be valuable, as does another by Mr. Davidson, 123. High Street, Edinburgh, on the Use of the Siphon for draining marshes, mines, lakes, &c. Lastly, a model and description of a Chimney Pot for preventing the return of smoke, occasioned by downward currents, by Mr. Shillinglaw, 5. Cheyne Street, Stockbridge. We do not know whether it is the intention of the Society to publish these papers and others; but if it is not, and if it were consistent with the rules of the Society, we should be very glad to receive notices of them for publication. These notices would be best made out by the authors of the papers; but we have no wish that they should do so, if it at all interferes with the views of the Society.

Mr. Perkins's Mode of heating by Hot Water seems to be making rapid progress in Edinburgh. Besides churches, manufactories, warehouses, &c., which he has already heated, it is reported that the Register Office will soon be added to the number. We also hear that Lord Corehouse, a man of great taste, who employed Mr. Blair as an architect to design a mansion in a romantic situation on the borders of the Clyde, and our correspondent, Mr. Main, to lay out his grounds, has sent for Mr. Perkins.

ART. III. *Retrospective Criticism.*

ADVANTAGES of a Taste for Architecture.— I daily feel the truth of an opinion you express in your Introduction (p. 3.), that a taste for architecture is most desirable for the possessor, because it is so easily indulged in. A person possessing this taste can scarcely go any where without having it gratified, and at no expense; whereas a taste for paintings, sculpture, &c. can seldom be satisfied without a large expenditure. I think the Magazine will have the same effect, with respect to architecture, that the *Gardener's Magazine* has had with respect to gardening; viz., it will diffuse a general knowledge of the subject, and draw attention to it: if it have this effect, it will do a world of good in various ways; for it is surprising how few have any knowledge of architecture, except those who follow it as a profession. Mr. Bennet, M. P. for Wilts, is the only gentleman I have heard of, in this part of the country, who has a good practical knowledge of building. He designed the stables at Stockton House, which are in the old English style, and do great credit to his taste. — *Selim. Wiltshire, April* 28. 1834.

The Architectural Magazine, No. II. — The stoves mentioned, p. 74., remind me of a tale I heard many years ago, about the stoves of an amateur named Ledsam, who lived, I believe, in a midland county, some sixty years since. These stoves were contrived so as to serve two rooms; for, by being placed in the partition wall, and turning upon a pivot, they could instantly be applied to either room. Sometimes one side of the stove had a fire in the grate, and the other (as is usual in the summer season) was filled with a bouquet of flowers. For the sake of amusement, Mr. Ledsam would divert his friend's attention from the fire for a moment, and, when they turned their eyes again, they beheld the flowers, instead of the fire, and *vice versâ*. He had also a trap on the table, in the vestibule, to detect dishonest visiters: a half crown lay on the table, and appeared very easy to filch, but the moment it was touched, an iron hand started up, and grasped the thief round the wrist, like a handcuff. — I fancy I could contrive a simpler wood railing than Mr. Cottam's, and yet fulfil all the requisite stipulations. — The practical graziers and cattle drovers here are opposing the *abattoirs* (p. 90.), or rather the removal of the Smithfield market, tooth and nail. The consumer could decide the matter, by giving the sixteenth part of a farthing per lb. more for country-killed meat. Depend upon it, as soon as railroads are common, nothing else will appear in London. [We hope that, if this should not be the case soon, *abattoirs* will be erected all round the town, to prevent the necessity of driving cattle through it either to the Islington abattoir, or to Smithfield.] — I hope to see in one of your early Numbers a sketch of the tackle used in hoisting the Duke of York's statue to the summit of the pillar in Carlton Gardens. [See p. 195.] A very curious exploit of this sort is described in the *United Service Journal* for February last. It recounts the very simple means used by Captain Lloyd, and his companions, to ascend the peak of a mountain in the West Indies, which never had been ascended before.— You would serve architecture very much by getting up petitions to take off the *double* duty now charged for ornamental bricks. Mr. Pease is trying to get the whole off, but it cannot be afforded at present. I fear the duty on bricks is a sad tax on rural labour. The double duty does not produce much revenue, but acts like a prohibition against the use of ornamental bricks.

Your Sheffield correspondent (p. 98.) may say what he pleases about what has "gone under the name of engineering." It recalls to mind a case which came under my own experience. A schoolfellow of mine, after being articled five years with the great Sir Jeffery Wyatt, came to spend a week with me, about the time the London Bridge plans were in agitation. "Why don't you try for the Bridge?" says I. "So I will," says he, "if you'll build the foundation." This affords the true clew to the reason why engineers are called in to build bridges, docks, &c. As the world goes now, the best way is to acknowledge engineering and architecture as two distinct professions, and to employ professors of both where first-rate works are required. — *W. T. Norwich, April* 21. 1834.

Ventilation of Living-Rooms. — I consider that the ventilation of living-rooms is of great importance, and have long desired to be acquainted with an efficient and economical mode of accomplishing it. I do not, however, think that Mr. Milne, in his article (p. 64.), has disclosed the desideratum. Suppose that four persons are spending an evening together in a room ventilated by his method, and five more at once join them; the air of the room becomes more heated and rarified, the damper of the ventilator is raised, and its doors partially closed; and, consequently, the change of the air of the room goes on less rapidly, when circumstances require that it should go on more so. For bedrooms no better method of ventilation, I believe, can generally be adopted than that of keeping open the sashes a little at top and bottom; a practice I have been in the habit of following for more than twelve years, and which, when judiciously managed, I never found injurious to either delicate females or infants, when they are in tolerable health. On the contrary, I have no doubt that it is beneficial to every one, as compared with the too general practice of sleeping in close rooms; especially if the bed curtains are drawn close also. We much want some complete mode of ventilation, which in winter should be combined with warmth, so that the air from without, which takes the place of that which escapes, should not enter the apartment at too low a temperature; and in summer it ought perhaps to be united with some drying process, because the night air at this season is frequently charged with an unhealthful degree of moisture. — *G. Dymond, Architect. Bristol, April,* 1834.

The alleged Deceptions practised by Architects. — In p. 117. there is an article " On certain deceptive Practices adopted by some Authors of Architectural Designs for Villas. By an Observer;" in which, though there is a good deal of truth in some of the remarks, there still appears to me to be much overstatement, and not a little absurdity.

Your correspondent commences with reprehending the custom of " accompanying architectural designs with landscapes, so as to form pictures." Now, would he think it an unfair thing of the proprietor of the house, if, after its completion, he was, for the purpose of giving a distant friend an idea of his new abode, to send him " a picture" of it as it really existed, with the accompanying landscape correctly shown, so as to display the fitness of the building to its situation? Would he have him represent his villa, which he had surrounded with every thing that the taste of the architect and landscape-gardener could devise to render its situation picturesque and delightful, as an isolated mass, midway betwixt heaven and earth, without ground for it to stand upon, without clouds to overshadow it, and without trees or shrubs to surround it? and this merely to avoid *making a picture* of what he was labouring to render picturesque; or attracting his friend's " eye to the effect of the whole, instead of the effect of the building;" when he had been spending his time and his money in making the whole beautiful, when the architect had been employing his talents in rendering the building suitable to the ground, and the landscape-gardener (if not identical with the architect) had bent all his endeavours on rendering the ground still more suitable to the building? Your correspondent would surely not wish him to act so absurdly. Yet in what essential point does this imaginary case differ from the case in point? In the one case, the gentleman gives his friend a representation of the villa *as it is;* and, in the other, the architect gives the gentleman a representation of it *as it is to be.* The only difference is, that the one is a present, and the other an anticipated, representation: and, if the latter is an unlawful thing, the architect must close his office, and lay by his square and his compass; he may form his design in his head, and give verbal descriptions of it to the employer and the workman, but for the future he must scrupulously avoid putting pencil to paper, for fear of returning to the deceptive practice of drawing what does not exist.

What your correspondent seems, on this head, most to fear, is, that the architect may be " a clever artist;" and therefore able, " by lights and shadows, and by introducing forms in the trees and ground, to contrast with those of the building," to make " the most indifferent building appear handsome! But if the architect be so clever an artist, and if he have so accurate a knowledge of the effect of light and shade (the very essentials of architecture), he can surely exercise his talents as well on the structure itself, as on the mere representation of it, and may be able to render it something more than a " most indifferent building;" and, if he be so admirable a landscape-gardener, he can certainly produce the effects in execution which he has so successfully imitated in painting.

Your correspondent next remarks, that he " he should no more think of ascertaining the merits of a building, either as a piece of architecture, or as a structure for a particular use, by observing it merely as a component part of a landscape, than he should think of becoming acquainted with the private character of an individual, by seeing him at a conversazione, or hearing him speak in parliament." Now, if he had said that he should not think of judging of its internal arrangement, by its effect as part of a landscape, there might have been some aptness in the similitude; but does he really mean to say that the situation of a building should not affect the design? That villas and town houses may change places without injuring the effect of either? The passage certainly implies this. Till, however, I find that villas are in the habit of visiting their city friends, that men of science take their houses with them to conversaziones, and statesmen bring their country seats with them to parliament, I, for one, shall endeavour to suit my buildings to the situations I intend them for; trusting that they will remain stationary where I place them.

The next deception alluded to is that of giving a false idea of the projections and sinkings, by incorrect shadowing. This is certainly a very improper practice wherever it exists, though I should not have thought it likely to be very prevalent, from the little temptation which it seems to offer; as it certainly would have appeared to me that an architect who could not produce a good design, would not possess science enough to render this deception effective: but here I am set right by your correspondent, who informs us that " these deceptions will make the ugliest and most unscientific building look handsome!" I should presume that he grounds this charge upon some one case which has come under his notice, and that this is the case of the same misguided person alluded to under the foregoing head. If this be correct, the present instance exhibits, in a far more striking manner than the former, both the preeminent talents and the singular infelicity of that highly gifted, but most wayward and unfortunate, individual. In the former instance, by means of lights, shades, and surrounding scenery, he made an indifferent building look handsome; but, in this, he produces the same effect, on the ugliest and most unscientific building, by only a slight variation of the shadows. Surely no parallel case is on record! An architect who, by merely varying lights, shadows, and surrounding forms, can produce such magical effects; and yet, when he comes to attempt a design, produces nothing but what is of the "ugliest, the most unscientific," or at best, of the "most indifferent," character! — if such a man should, at any time, be brought to bend his talents on the actual building, which he has hitherto so strangely neglected, instead of prostituting them to the deceptive practices, in which he has met with such unprecedented, though mischievous, success, we may then expect from him nothing short of a masterpiece of art.

The practice of "darkening the tint of recesses" is not a deception at all, when done in an artistlike manner; and, when done badly, the architect is the sufferer by the deception. It is absolutely necessary, in a geometrical elevation, where the front and back parts are shown of equal height, to vary the tint in such a manner as in some degree to indicate the comparative distances of the parts; the greatest deception that could be practised would be to tint them all alike, so as to make them all appear as if on one face. Casting accidental shadows on plain parts, is a blamable practice, where it is calculated to convey a false idea of the building; but there are cases where, in execution, particular circumstances will prevent a part from being a prominent feature, which will not at all affect it in a geometrical drawing. In these cases, the practice alluded to may be very serviceable, and not unfair. The practice of imitating mosses, weather-stains, &c., is to be condemned, not on the ground of their being shown on "buildings not yet erected," for this reason would have equal force against making drawings of the buildings at all, but because it is representing blemishes and defects which, in execution, the architect would wish to avoid. If, however, the architect chooses to show creeping shrubs on a building where it is intended that such should be planted, he is by no means to be blamed.

In most of your correspondent's remarks on chimney shafts I quite agree with him. In the Gothic, Italian, or even Grecian styles, they may be rendered far from unpleasing; but still, if the architect finds that they will interfere with his design, he is no more to be blamed for concealing them, than for hiding the roof by a parapet, brickwork with stucco, or deal with wainscot or mahogany graining. The practice of not showing them in the drawing, when they will appear in execution, is certainly reprehensible; but there are many cases where, their introduction being injurious to the composition, the architect has, with much pains and management, contrived to gather over the flues into a back part of the building, where they will not at all form part of the principal design, but where, in a geometrical drawing, they would show as high as if they were in front: in these cases they are very fairly omitted in the drawing of an elevation to which they do not belong. This *may* be the case with the design adduced.

I will trespass no farther than to apologise for having made my remarks so lengthy; but I think, when your correspondent is at such pains in raking together charges against the profession, it is but fair to allow architects to defend themselves.— *G. G. S. London, May* 10. 1834.

Mr. Austin's Chimney Pots and Shafts. (p. 159.) — In this article, you have introduced some ornaments among the chimney shafts, that were not intended for such; and, fearing that they may meet the eye of those by whom they were designed, I think it should be remarked they were not intended to be used as chimney pots by me. Fig. 74, p. 160, is a sundial pillar; figs. 77. and 79. are oriental vases, modeled expressly for the new grand Pantheon Bazaar, under the immediate direction of Sidney Smirke, Esq., architect; fig. 87. is a pedestal designed for one of the principal rooms in Ironmongers' Hall; and fig. 89. is an enriched Gothic font or pedestal, restored from an example in Henry VII.'s Chapel. It should also be observed, that the chimney shafts are drawn to a scale of a quarter of an inch to a foot, and the other ornaments to a scale of half an inch to a foot, except fig. 69., which is to a larger scale, being the smallest-sized chimney pot made. — *Felix Austin. Artificial Stone Works, New Road, Regent's Park, June* 7. 1834.

Durability of Austin's Artificial Stone.—With regard to the durability of my artificial stone, you say (p. 159.) that I "consider it very nearly, if not quite, as durable as Portland stone." Now, I beg most confidently to assert, that I consider it *more durable, and considerably superior* to Portland stone; having for several years made fountains and reservoirs of large dimensions that have withstood the severest winters, and having had basins in my own yard, where the water contained in them has been frozen into solid bodies of ice, which have not sustained the least injury. The only precaution necessary, is that of breaking a hole in the surface of the ice, and the reason for this is evident; for as the water, when transformed into ice, occupies more space, and the surface, when frozen, does not allow the water below it to expand, if a vent in this or some other way were not afforded to it, it must necessarily break the vessel. The hole in the surface of the ice, by affording the water an opportunity of escaping through the aperture (which must be occasionally reopened), prevents the vessel from bursting. That water does escape through the hole in the surface will appear from the little hillock of ice that forms itself round the aperture.— *Id.*

ART. IV. *Queries and Answers.*

PLATE-WARMER. — Have you seen the following very great improvement on the common plate-warmer? If you have, as you study comfort, I think you will approve it. It appears to be a pedestal for a bust to stand upon; but, when opened, is found to be lined with tin, with shelves for plates, and a place at the bottom for a heater. The effect is much superior to the usual ingenious mode of hiding a fire from everybody at dinner. There is one objection; and that was, when I saw it, that there was a smell of burning wood: but this I attributed to the newness of the timber of which it was constructed. At any rate, your correspondent, Mr. Mallet, might produce a very elegant piece of furniture for the purpose in cast or wrought iron. — *Thos. Wilson. Banks, near Barnsley, Jan.* 18. 1833.

Concrete for Foundations. — Amongst the numerous plans which have been adopted for securing the foundations of buildings, this appears now to occupy a prominent place. I should feel obliged if any of your correspondents would inform me of the proportions of materials, and what is considered as the best to use. — *Investigator. Kent, June* 6. 1834.

THE ARCHITECTURAL MAGAZINE.

AUGUST, 1834.

ORIGINAL COMMUNICATIONS.

ART. I. *On those Principles of Composition, in Architecture, which are common to all the Fine Arts.* By the CONDUCTOR.

THE principles of composition in any art must necessarily depend upon the end which that art is intended to effect. The objects of architecture may be reduced to three; utility, durability, and beauty. The principle of utility determines the situation, dimensions, arrangement, and local relations of buildings; that of durability, the mode of their construction, and the nature of their materials; and that of beauty, their appearance as objects of taste. The first two of these objects we shall pass over for the present, as being, from their practical and mechanical nature, much more generally understood than the latter; and we shall, therefore, limit our observations, in this and some succeeding articles, to the principles of composition in architecture, with reference to the production of beauty.

Beauty in architecture, as in other arts, and as in nature, is of many kinds; but in architecture all these kinds may be included in two classes: first, those kinds of beauty which result from a combination of what may be called the elementary materials of architecture as a fine art, without reference to the works of preceding artists; and, secondly, those which result from architectural combinations which have reference to the works of preceding artists.

The elementary materials of architecture, considered as an art of taste, are forms, lines, lights, shades, and colours. The principal element, however, is form, which may be said to give rise to lines, lights and shades, and, to a certain extent also, even to colours.

The elements of architecture, considered as an art established by preceding artists, are to be found in the elementary forms of the different styles of building; such as the Grecian, the Gothic, &c., with all their numerous varieties and subvarieties. We shall confine ourselves, in this article, to those fundamental principles of composition which apply to architecture, in common with all the fine arts.

The first principle in all combinations, whether of lines, forms, colours, or sounds, is that of producing *a whole.* The reason why this is a fundamental principle is, that the mind can only attend to one sensation at one time; and hence, that where more objects than one are presented to it, they must be so presented as to produce only a single sensation. A single sensation, produced by a number of objects, may be called a composite sensation, as opposed to a simple sensation, or one produced by a single object. For example, a hundred bricks, if strewed promiscuously over a piece of ground, could only be looked at separately one after another, and would therefore produce a hundred separate sensations: but, if these bricks were thrown together in a heap, they might be observed by one glance of the eye; and in that case would produce only one single sensation or impression on the mind. If the heap were large, and the spectator placed so near it as that he could not see the whole at one glance, he would then experience a confusion of sensations; because he would see those bricks which were near the eye individually, and others, farther from it, in parts; without, however, being able to see the heap as a whole. This example illustrates two subordinate principles in the formation of a whole; that of *contiguity*, or the necessity of bringing those parts which compose the whole in contact; and that of *distance*, or the necessity of adjusting the dimensions of the object, or its distance from the spectator, to the powers of vision in the human eye.

If we suppose the heap of bricks to be at such a distance from the eye as to be taken in at a glance, and consequently easily comprehended as a single object; and if we further suppose it to be in the form of a cone, or a pyramid; this will give an additional idea or sensation: but even this additional sensation may be still easily included in the one composite sensation produced by the whole. We may next suppose the pyramid arranged like steps; this will not interfere with the idea of a whole, though it will add still farther to the composite nature of the sensation produced by it. If we suppose these steps alternately of white and black marble, the object may still be viewed as a whole; but if the lower half of the pyramid were to be of steps of one colour, and the upper half of steps of another colour; or if the lower half were arranged in steps, and the upper half without steps, then the mind would receive two distinct sensations, that produced by the lower half, and that by the upper half; and these two sensations would no longer unite in forming a composite sensation of easy comprehension; that is, in forming a whole. From these particulars, two conclusions relative to the composition of a whole may be deduced: first, that a great number of simple sensations may enter into the idea of it; and, secondly, that all these simple sensations must unite in forming one composite sensation. Thus we arrive at two familiar principles, viz., that of *the necessity of the unity of the whole,* and that of *the necessity of the connection of the parts which compose it.*

That the human mind is adapted for viewing, as a whole, an indefinite number of parts, may be rendered evident to every reader, by his considering the number of particulars that enter into the composite idea of the meaning of a written or printed sentence; say of one thousand letters, in a hundred words. In casting the eye rapidly over such a sentence, the meaning is caught at once; but it can only be caught in consequence of each of the thousand letters in that sentence having produced its separate simple sensation; each of the separate words having also produced its separate composite sensation; and each of the members of the proposition, or subject of the sentence, having also produced its composite sensation.

We may here mention, incidentally, that in this way what is called the association of ideas may be formed: the sight of a letter leads to the idea of words and sentences; and the sound of a word leads to the idea of its separate letters. The view of a single brick raises up in the mind the idea of a wall or a house; and a house calls up in the mind the idea of the bricks, and of all the other component parts of which it is constructed. It is, in many cases, by the exercise of the mind in tracing these associations, that the emotion of beauty is experienced; and this emotion of beauty is to be considered as the result of a composite sensation, in the same way as what may be called a sensation of beauty is produced by a single sensation, from viewing any agreeable form or colour.

On looking at any pleasing object, whether in nature or in art, it will always be found, on analysing it, that, whether it be merely agreeable, or supremely beautiful, it still forms a whole: this quality of forming a whole being independent of every other description of beauty, and yet being common to all the different kinds of it. On the other hand, no composition whatever, though its parts, when taken separately, may each be of the greatest beauty, will please when these parts are put together, unless in that state they form a whole. Parts, also, which, if viewed separately, have little or no beauty, may, when combined in due subordination to the principle of unity, form a beautiful whole. A multitude of objects enter into the composition of those landscapes which include a considerable portion of distant scenery. Many of these objects, taken separately, may not only be of little beauty, but may be disagreeable, or even deformed; yet some one principle, by operating alike on this immense number of seemingly discordant particulars or sensations, reduces them all to one agreeable composite sensation. This principle, in the background of a natural landscape, is distance; and, in the foreground of a natural landscape, is continuous light, or continuous shade. In like manner, all discordant compositions may be rendered accordant, if not positively beautiful, by some uniting principle which may be applied in common to all their parts. The whole of a discordant landscape may be reduced to unity of expression, by increasing the distance of the picture from the eye, by excess of either light or shade being thrown over every part of it, or by sameness of colouring; and a house, or other building, which, in respect to its forms, its lines, or its style, is discordant, may be rendered tolerable, by being whitewashed in every part, or by being stained in every part with dark tints, so as to give the whole an appearance of age and antiquity. We are far from saying that by processes of this kind beauty can be produced; we only assert that discordant parts may be reduced to a whole, and that deformity may be neutralised, and thus rendered accordant, or at least tolerable. Our object in stating these things so much in detail, is, if possible, to convey to every reader an idea of the paramount necessity of the principle of a whole pervading every composition whatever. We shall next proceed to develope other principles.

Every work of art, to give pleasure to the human mind as such, must be recognised as a work of art. This is self-evident. If it were possible for an artist to form imitations of trees, stones, rocks, ground, or animals, all so perfect as to be undistinguishable from similar productions of nature, they would be considered as natural objects: and, consequently, whatever gratification they might otherwise afford, they could give no pleasure as works of art; since, as before observed, to enable them to do so, it must be known that they were formed by the hand of man. The heap of bricks, before referred to, was recognisable as a work of art, from the artificial forms of the bricks: had the forms of which this heap was composed been natural, such as small stones, gravel, or lumps of earth, unless the shape of the heap had approached to some regular geometrical or artificial form, it would not have been recognisable as a work of art, and could have given no pleasure as such. The recognition of art, therefore, is a primary principle in architecture, as, indeed, it is in all the fine arts, even in those which are considered the most purely imitative. Hence it is that the irregular style of landscape-gardening, as described or treated by some who seem to consider it a mere imitation of natural scenery, is, in so far as it perfectly attains such an end, no fine art at all. How, indeed, can there be any art in that work which, when in its perfect state, must necessarily be mistaken for nature? Landscape-gardening is, doubtless, like architecture, to a certain extent, a fine art; but not by virtue of its creating fac-similes of natural scenery. No work of man can rank as a fine art, in the composition of which the recognition of art is not a fundamental principle. How this is to be effected, in the imitation of natural scenery by landscape-gardening, is suggested in *Gard. Mag.*, viii. 701. and ix. 682.; and will be developed, in all its details, in our *Encyclopædia of Landscape-Gardening*.

The next principle which we shall notice, as generally applicable to the fine arts, is *regularity*, or the recognition of regular art. A hut may be recognised as a work of art, however rude or anomalous its form; because, according to human experience, its sides, its roof, and its door could never have been arranged, so as to form a hut, by chance. Such a hut is satisfactory as a work of art, but nothing more: but a hut in a square form gives additional satisfaction by the regularity of its figure; which gives an idea not only of art, but of cultivated or improved art. There can be no doubt, therefore, that the love of regularity is strongly implanted in the human mind; since regularity is the first principle which displays itself in the works of man composed with a view to beauty. A regular form is a solid which is composed by a repetition of similar surfaces; thus, a cube is included between six similar surfaces or planes, and a polygon is composed of many similar planes or surfaces: both these figures are uniform. The essential principle of regularity is repetition, and, in uniformity, repetition of the same form. In a cube, this regularity is of the simplest kind; in two cubes placed together, it is somewhat more composite; still more so when three are joined, and when these are of different degrees of magnitude, or when different forms are employed. In this way *repetition* becomes the essential principle, or parent, not only of regularity and *uniformity*, but of *symmetry*, or the correspondence of parts; and thus, by causing one half of an elevation to reflect the other half, several different forms may be employed in the same design, without detracting from its regularity.

The restless activity, the love of change, or, in other words, the thirst for novelty, in the human mind is such, that we are no sooner gratified with the appearance of art, than we require regular art; and no sooner with regular art, than we require symmetrical art. From symmetrical art, the next step is to irregular art, the object of which is to produce variety.

Variety gives pleasure by exercising the mind, and by exciting its attention to one thing after another in a continuous train of sensations; the things being different, but yet allied and connected. Variety is produced, not so much by a great number of different things, as by changes in the combination of a few things. To recur to our bricks: though each brick be nothing more than a solid parallelogram, or what geometricians call a parallelopipedon, yet a thousand or ten thousand bricks may be distributed on a flat surface; either in scattered, but yet connected groups, or in a line, so as to produce an assemblage exhibiting continuous variation of position. If we suppose them placed in a line; then, in commencing at one end of this line, and tracing all the projections and recesses in it, from one end to the other, it will be found that they are produced by a very few elements of composition: by presenting the flat side of the brick, its narrow side, or its end; by presenting these at different distances from an imaginary straight line, along the front of the varied line; by placing the bricks at greater or less distances from one another; and so on. Now, the cause of the variety thus produced is obviously contrast in the position of the bricks; for there is no difference in their form or colour, or in their light or shade, or even in their lines, further than what is produced by their position. *Contrast*, therefore, is the essential fundamental principle of variety.

The variation which we have described may be called simple variety, or variety of the lowest kind; in the same manner as a square or parallelogram house, or a round or conical hut, may be said to possess simple regularity, or regularity of the lowest kind. It is easy for the reader to conceive, that, by introducing other forms along with the square into the composition of the regular house, a composite kind of regularity may be produced; and also, that by employing different other forms of objects besides that of the parallelogram, a composite variety will be effected along the supposed line formed by the bricks. When a great number of different forms are employed in composing variety, the result may he denominated *harmony;* and when a great number of parts, similar in form, but different in size, are employed, the result is *intricacy.* In harmony, in intricacy, and in every modification of variety in architectural productions, or in all productions the beauty of which depends chiefly upon form, the essential principle will be found to be contrast either of form, or of position — or of both.

The greatest exertions of any art, in its highest state of refinement, may be all reduced to the combination of regularity with variety: including, under the former term, uniformity and symmetry; and, under the latter, intricacy and harmony.

We have now endeavoured to illustrate the four grand principles of composition, applicable to architecture in common with all the fine arts: viz., 1. The principle of a whole, founded on the necessity of unity of sensation; 2. The principle of the recognition of art, founded on the immutability of truth, or the necessity of a thing appearing to be what it is; 3. The principle of regularity, including uniformity and symmetry, founded on the inherent love of order existing in the human mind; and, 4. The principle of variety, including intricacy and harmony, founded on the desire for novelty, occasioned by the activity of the human mind.

ART. II. *Architecture considered with reference to its Claims as a Fine Art.* By W. H. B.

THE influence of a taste for the fine arts in softening and civilising man has been universally confessed. Nor is this taste advantageous only in its effects upon society: the individual himself who possesses it derives from it some of his sweetest and purest pleasures. The fine arts, then, are worth some study; since the enjoyment arising from the contemplation of their beautiful productions must increase with the spectator's knowledge of their principles. He will receive gratification from them in proportion to his knowledge of them, and in proportion as he is competent to investigate and analyse their perfections. The uncultivated man, who sees a painting for the first time, is, no doubt, delighted; but his feeling, though it may break forth in a cry of admiration, can scarcely be compared with the pleasure experienced by a man of cultivated mind and elegant taste, who, without being so much of the artist as to have his attention engrossed by technical details, can judge of the truth of expression, the skilful arrangement of the groups, the grace and fidelity of the drawing, the judicious management of the light and shadow, and, in short, of such other essentials to excellence as may characterise the performance. Were the supposed uninitiated person to behold a piece of sculpture equal or even superior, as a work of art, to the painting, he would probably look upon it with a less delighted eye, because he would not understand it so well. The cold and colourless marble, however exquisitely chiseled, would, we think, be less easily appreciated by a stranger to the arts, than the bright and gay tints of the painting, which would remind him of the hues as well as of the forms of nature. If a work of architecture, however magnificent it might be, met the eye of our novice, it is likely that his pleasure, did any exist, would be more vague and unintelligible than in either of the former cases; for painting and sculpture find their models in the natural objects around, whereas architecture has no such resources, but presents forms and combinations peculiarly its own. As painting and sculpture imitate what all have seen, the rudest, though entirely ignorant of their principles, may receive from them that sort of pleasure which a successful imitation ever causes; especially an imitation of the works of nature, which all, in a greater or less degree, instinctively admire. But with architecture it is otherwise. Here the observer, if delighted at all, is delighted, not with any resemblance to well-known objects, but with abstract beauty of form and harmony of proportion, which, compared with imitative merit, are less manifest sources of gratification; and which, to be valued, must, in some sort, be understood.

The highest beauties of architecture consist in unity, harmony, and expression; and, as these beauties are quite independent of resemblance to nature, they cannot be perceived and felt as they should be, unless some knowledge of that wherein they consist be possessed.

The great mass of individuals actively engaged in other pursuits do not possess this knowledge; and, though many would like to add to their other attainments some acquaintance with architecture, few care to seek it in those learned and elaborate treatises where alone it is to be satisfactorily found. There may be few who cannot distinguish between the style called Gothic and that borrowed from the relics of Grecian and Roman antiquity. Probably most know the prominent features of the "five orders," which, though exclusively applicable to the style of the modern Italian school, were, for a long time after the revival of letters, duly credited by the public, as including all the varieties of the architecture of the ancients. But let us conceive a classic structure deprived of its columns; and perhaps not one of the class above referred to would be able to pronounce whether the building was in Grecian or Roman taste, or to which (if to any) of the "five orders" its proportions and enrichments belonged. Of course, such a spectator would be incompetent to tell whether the building was in the pure Grecian style of the age of Pericles, or in the inferior taste which prevailed under Roman domination; or, again, whether it was in the ancient Roman or in the modern Italian manner. Yet between these there is so great a difference, that the observer would perceive a total alteration in the character of the design, if it were to be changed from one manner to another. It is evident that such a spectator cannot tell wherein the beauties of architecture consist, as he cannot discriminate between the styles, and form a definite opinion upon their respective claims to admiration, and the reasons for their excellence or demerit. If it be said that to do this would require a sort of professional lore, important, perhaps, to architects, but uninteresting and unnecessary to others, it may be replied, that others criticise without scruple the works of architects, and thereby justify architects in demanding from them a knowledge of the principles of architectural composition. This demand is more especially reasonable in cases where the judgment of non-professional individuals is decisive with regard to the adoption or rejection of designs; as in the case of competitions for the erection of public buildings, &c. Independently of this consideration, there is much to be said in behalf of this study, as adding a new and prolific source of pleasure to those already possessed by persons of taste: for though architecture, from its artificialness, requires some study to be appreciated, and though its beauties are so abstract that it has been called "the metaphysics of the arts," yet these beauties are displayed in the eyes of all, and whichever way we turn they meet our view. Galleries and exhibition rooms must be resorted to for paintings and sculptures; but architecture is conspicuous in every street, within doors and without. The increased dissemination of knowledge, and consequently of taste, by which these times are characterised, has had, among its many other effects, that of calling into requisition the art of ornamental design, in every dwelling the proprietor of which has the means of combining with domestic convenience that which pleases the eye. To the truth of this remark the recent alterations in the metropolis bear abundant testimony. Unless, therefore, too much has been assumed with regard to the general vagueness of information in this matter, we have works of art constantly before our eyes, from which the mass of observers can only derive a sort of undefined pleasure; and even that is modified, in many instances, by the consciousness that much of the gratification which the harmonious proportions or other merits of buildings are capable of yielding is lost to them. If they could decide upon the claims of the different styles, and determine why one edifice is more beautiful than another, they would look upon the architectural works rising up around them with intelligence and satisfaction.

The history of architecture affords many proofs that the sound judgment of a few skilful and well-informed artists can make no head against the prevailing opinions, crude and erroneous though they be, of the million who look upon their works. Fashion, as in all else, is in the present instance omnipotent. The inventive genius of Jones, the elegant taste of Wren, and the bold originality of Vanbrugh, could not prevent those eminent men from joining in the blind and unaccountable contempt with which our fine old Gothic cathedrals (notwithstanding their venerable grandeur of aspect, and marvellous skill of construction) were regarded for two hundred years previous to the latter end of the last century. The public, then, being the judge to whose decisions all must bow, will pronounce sentence well or ill, as that public is well or ill informed. Mere natural taste will not enable the uninformed to give a clear and well founded decision upon works of architecture; and, till the public become possessed of sufficient architectural knowledge to enable them to do this, perfection in architectural works never can be attained.

If, then, a nation's progress in the fine arts depends upon public taste, which again depends upon knowledge; and if such progress, till eminence be attained, is an object worthy of ambition, it is surely desirable that the public taste should be cultivated peculiarly with regard to architecture; as that, more than any other art, bears evident and palpable witness to the refinement and civilisation of a people. The intelligent stranger, passing through a city, can judge of its architecture; though he may not have time to examine its productions in any of the other arts.

It is quite impossible to compress within the limits of a paper like the present, all that might be said on a subject involving, as this does, numerous considerations, and admitting of copious illustration: but I shall have gained my end, if I have at all succeeded in showing that architecture, being more artificial, and at the same time displaying its works more conspicuously, than the other fine arts, demands and deserves more study, before it can be appreciated by the public; and that attention to the subject would not be ill bestowed, but would augment the enjoyment of individuals, and influence beneficially the taste of nations.

Art. III. *Specimen of Studies of Plan.* By W. H. Leeds, Esq.

Too frequently do we meet, even in houses of a superior class, with instances of strange, nay almost wilful, inattention to architectural regularity, and also to convenience; a defect which, though pardonable enough in the first draft of a plan, is inexcusable when suffered to pass into execution without correction. I have observed some houses that would almost convince any one that the chief object, on the part of the architect, was to get through his task with the least possible trouble and expense of thought; the defects in them being such as a very little study would have prevented.

As even a single illustration (and I could bring forward fifty) will prove more satisfactory than mere allegation, and likewise enable the reader to determine whether I am too presumptuous in making the above remark, I shall now, for the purpose of exemplifying some of the careless oversights alluded to, and at the same time pointing out how, in that particular case, obvious faults might have been avoided, exhibit part of the plan of a villa, which forms one of the subjects in Britton's and Pugin's *Edifices of London*.

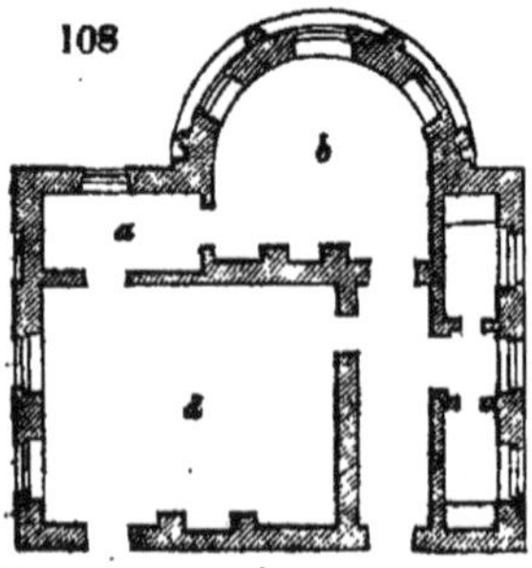

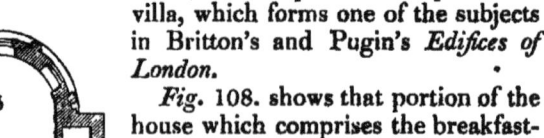

Fig. 108. shows that portion of the house which comprises the breakfast-room (*b*), and smaller drawing-room (*d*), which latter is *en suite* with a larger apartment of the same denomination measuring 51 ft. by 22½ ft., and decorated with columns. In a residence containing such an apartment as the one last mentioned, it is but reasonable to expect that all the other sitting-rooms, however unpretending they may be in themselves, should exhibit careful study in their respective plans. Instead of which, we here perceive that, in the breakfast-room (*b*), no regard whatever has been paid to symmetry, the chimney-piece being thrown out of the centre, in order to admit a door from the corridor, on the same side of the room; which door, again, comes so close to the fire-place, that it cannot but occasion much positive inconvenience. Had the room been of the usual form, and had there been no windows on the side facing the fire-place, the irregularity just pointed out would have been neither so observable nor so objectionable; but here, the centre window and the chimney-piece being placed obliquely to each other, it becomes so marked as to be positively offensive. The architect, no doubt, adopted the readiest mode; but that this mode was the best, or that he had no alternative but either to put up with this blemish or to make such alterations as would too much disturb the rest of his plan, I must be permitted to doubt. At all events, the next figure (*fig.* 109.) points out how I would have disposed the plan, so as, at all events, to avoid the imperfection which now disfigures the room *b*. According to the alteration here introduced, not only does the breakfast-room (*b*) become perfectly symmetrical, but it acquires greater extent and variety, while the door communicating with the corridor is so placed as not to interfere at all with what is, strictly speaking, that side of the room itself. So far, perhaps, the alteration will be allowed to be an improvement; it may, nevertheless, be objected, that it is attended with no small sacrifice, namely, the loss of the little anteroom, or rather *inter*-room, *a* (*fig.* 108.), besides what is taken in on the opposite side. According to my view of the matter, however, the room *a*, which is only 6 ft. wide, is so utterly insignificant in itself, and so evidently a mere passage, that much would be positively gained in effect by reducing it, and rather considering it a kind of alcove belonging to the adjoining drawing-room, but separated from it by a glazed door; placing a sham door with a mirror in the corresponding angle, and between these two doors the fire-place, the chimney of which would connect itself with that of the breakfast-room. The reason for making this change in the situation of the chimney-piece is obvious; because it would then present itself at once to those who entered from the other drawing-room.

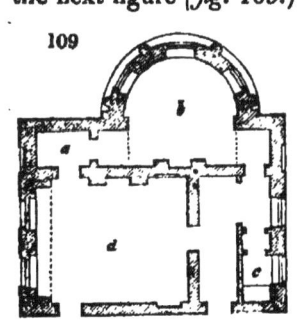

It will also be seen that, in order to have the distance between the window and the side wall exactly the same in both angles, the plan (*fig.* 109.) encroaches a little upon this room; and also that, for the purpose both of bringing the doors nearer to an angle, and of improving the proportions of the room, the windows being in one of the narrower sides, the windows themselves are placed in a kind of break or bay. Another advantage attending this latter change is, that, instead of being, as before, out of the centre of the wall, this chimney-piece is placed equidistant from each angle. In our opinion, what is thus lost in size, in this apartment, is so inconsiderable in itself, as to be a mere trifle in comparison to what would be gained in point of general appearance. The breakfast-room, on the other hand, would be proportionally enlarged, and moreover so greatly improved, and so closely connected with this drawing-room, yet still kept sufficiently detached from it, that it might occasionally be made use of as an additional evening-room.

The other variations from the original plan hardly call for any remark, except it be that transferring the door from the corridor either to the middle (as in *fig.* 109.), or to the other angle of that wall, is, upon the whole, attended with one recommendation, namely, that it is more remote from the water-closet (*c*); while, as the window in the corridor could not be seen from the room, the depth, or rather want of greater depth, in this part of the plan would not be so obvious.

Taken together, the variations appear to improve the rooms *b* and *d* very materially as to appearance; and to enlarge the former, much more than the latter is diminished. Besides, as the alcove, or cabinet, if it deserve that name, would be separated from the latter room only by a glazed door; as far as regards effect, and a very considerable degree of effect too, that would more than make amends for what is actually taken away from the room itself. Instead of a window facing the door, I should greatly prefer lighting this alcove through an ornamental aperture in the ceiling; which is perfectly practicable, because there happens to be no upper rooms over this part of the plan. A large mirror might then occupy the place of the present window, by which means a very striking vista would be formed when the doors of the whole suite were thrown open. Beneath this mirror might be a slab, supporting vases and other ornaments; which, together with a few casts and busts arranged against the walls with the light falling upon them from above, would form a very pleasing little architectural scene, obtained at a trifling expense.

It may, indeed, be objected, that, after all, this would be *only* a closet. Very true; yet those who have seen the closets of this description in Sir J. Soane's house, will admit that this is not only well worth having, but far better worth some cost of study than many things on which it is generally bestowed. The display arising from furniture and movable ornaments may be obtained at any time; not so, that which it is the province of the architect to create, and which, if omitted by him at first, is rarely thought of afterwards, and is not always, indeed, attainable, except by undoing his work, for the purpose of supplying his deficiencies.

As a still farther improvement, even upon the plan (*fig.* 109.), a very slight modification of it would suffice to convert the room *b* into a complete circle of about 16 ft. diameter, by continuing the cornice of the bay or semicircle quite round, and having draperies to enclose that part of the plan: in which case, the spaces cut off from the room might be lighted from the ceiling, like the adjoining alcove. This may probably seem to be abandoning one advantage just now held out in defence of the proposed alterations, and rather to contract than to enlarge the available space of the apartment. These draperies, however, might in general be left undrawn; since they, together with the form given to the ceiling, and carpet also, would sufficiently indicate circularity of plan, and show how it might be produced at pleasure.

What has been just stated will be sufficiently intelligible without another woodcut; at least to those who think it worth their pains to satisfy themselves as to its practicability. Those, on the contrary, who take no interest in the subject, will rather approve of the omission, and thank me for here terminating my remarks.

ART. IV. *On Ventilation, particularly as applied to Hospitals and Sick-Wards.* By J. A. PICTON, Esq., Architect.

THE processes of warming and ventilating public buildings are so closely connected in principle, that they ought never to be attempted separately; yet we frequently see large sums of money thrown away in vain struggles to perform what a little attention to the principles of pneumatics would have shown to be impracticable. In churches, chapels, theatres, and other buildings where great numbers are assembled in a small space, the rarefaction of the air proceeds with such rapidity, that little difficulty is experienced in obtaining a circulation sufficient to keep the atmosphere tolerably pure. The greatest art required is in proportioning the apertures for the admission and exit of air to each other, and to the quantity of pure air requisite for the supply of the greatest number the building is capable of containing; and also in so arranging them, that the change of atmosphere may take place without any perceptible draft or current. There is rather an important defect observable in most of the apparatus employed for warming public buildings by heated air; viz., that, when the apartment is sufficiently heated, and it is desirable to prevent the temperature rising, there is no mode of immediately effecting this, but by stopping the supply of air entirely, or by opening the windows, so as to admit an unpleasant draft. This might easily be accomplished by connecting a cold-air flue with the flue for heated air; having a register for closing it either wholly or partially, so that the temperature of the air admitted might be regulated with the utmost nicety.

The ventilation of hospitals and sick-wards, so as to secure a constant and regular change of atmosphere (whatever may be the difference of temperature within and without the building), is by no means an easy task. The self-regulating principle, at first sight, appears extremely desirable, as it relieves the attendants of all trouble and responsibility. The mode pointed out by your correspondent Mr. Milne (p. 64.) is extremely ingenious and elegant; but, in its adaptation to the purposes now under consideration, I am afraid it would fail, from the operation of several causes. In the first place, as it depends for its efficacy entirely on the *excess* of temperature of the air in the room over that without, should the difference be very slight, or the excess be the other way, it would become wholly inoperative. Suppose, for instance, the temperature in the open air be 80°, and inside the apartment 65° or 70° (no very uncommon case), and the rerafaction produced by respiration equal 10°; it must be evident that the circulation will be extremely languid, if, indeed, it exist at all, and at a time of the year, too, when most needed. In a room of the description I am now speaking of, the rarefaction of the air, by respiration, proceeds comparatively slowly; and it is quite possible for the air in a room to become unfit for respiration with little or no increase of temperature. As the specific gravity of the carbonic acid gas and the nitrogen emitted from the lungs does not differ materially from that of pure atmospheric air, it is only by its affecting the general temperature of the air in the apartment that the circulation is produced. Another disadvantage attending the plan is, that the delicate balance which is necessary to be preserved would be extremely liable to be deranged in the damp atmosphere of this country, whether the pivots on which the louvre-boards work are of metal or of wood. In high winds, too, the effect of the air externally on the broad surfaces of the louvre-boards would tend greatly to derange their operation. The principal disadvantage of the plan, however, consists in this: its obvious tendency is to preserve a certain relative proportion between the external and internal temperatures; or, in other words, to quicken the circulation when the difference is great, and to diminish it when the difference is small, without reference to the absolute height at which the thermometer may stand; hence it necessarily follows, that, if the apertures are calculated to change the air with sufficient rapidity in the heat of summer, when the difference is very slight, they will occasion an enormous waste of heat in the winter, when the difference is very great, by carrying off the air too quickly; or, on the other hand, if calculated for ventilation as required in the winter, they will fail to answer the purpose in the summer. If it be replied, that the equilibrium of the dampers can be occasionally altered, so as to require a greater or less pressure on the lower surface to produce the same effects, it is obvious that the great advantage of the self-regulating principle will be entirely lost. I am quite prepared, however, to admit that the principle is an excellent one, and, could the practical defects I have pointed out be avoided, it would be well worthy of a trial.

Perhaps the very best method of ventilating any building, where it is requisite to produce an artificial current, is by having a fire in a close chamber in the roof or upper part of the building, the only supply of air to which is procured by means of flues communicating with the different wards or rooms to be ventilated. These flues, which might be furnished with registers or slides to adjust the ventilation, would cause a constant and regular change of atmosphere under all possible circumstances, and at all seasons of the year. This plan, however, would in all cases be expensive, and in many instances impracticable. Probably the next best mode is to let the air admitted be, as nearly as possible, of the temperature which it is desirable to preserve in the apartment; with a sufficient number of apertures, furnished with slides, in such situations in the upper part of the room as may be most convenient, for the exit of the air. When the air in the apartment is warmer than that outside, of course it will have a constant tendency to rise and escape. In the heat of summer, if it is possible to procure a supply of cool air from below ground, and at the same time to heat the air above the room, so as to cause it to rise, it is evident the cooler air will be forced by the atmospheric pressure to supply its place, and a temperature below the average of that outside will be maintained. In the Lock Hospital lately erected by the trustees of the Liverpool Infirmary, designed by myself, and executed under my superintendence, an attempt has been made to combine these advantages, and hitherto with complete success. The wards for patients are rooms about 50 ft. by 20 ft., and 13 ft. 6 in. high, containing about fifteen or sixteen beds in each. There is no basement story, and the vacant space under each floor communicates with the external air by a number of small gratings. Two air-flues in the jambs of each fireplace are open below, and communicate with the back of the grate just above the floor. The grates, of which there are two in each apartment, are registers, with air-chambers running completely round the back and sides, but separated in the middle. *Fig.* 110. shows the plan of the grate and jambs, and *fig.* 111. the front view : *aa* are the flues on each side the fireplace; *bb*, the air-chambers; and, by a lining of brick inside, the air is made to pass within 3 in. of the heated back and sides of the grate; *cc* are the slides for the admission of warm air into the apartment. These grates were executed by Messrs. Pooley and Son, of Liverpool. It will be seen by the plan, that none of the heat at the back and sides of the fire is lost; but, being communicated to the air admitted from below, a fine stream of air, warmed, but not heated unpleasantly, is constantly pouring through the orifices into the room. For the escape of the air, there are six flues provided in each ward, about 14 in. by 9 in. each, built in the walls, and opening at the top into the space between the ceiling and the roof, with two apertures to each flue from the room, one at the top near the ceiling, and the other a little above the floor, each furnished with a slide. For the escape of the air from the space under the roof, pagoda caps, formed of concentric rings of cast iron, about 2 ft. in diameter, are fixed, one on the roof of each ward. If it is required to preserve as much heat as possible in the apartment, by closing the whole of the upper slides, the air being able to escape from the bottom apertures only, the whole mass of air in the room must be heated to one temperature before any can be permitted to escape. In like manner, by opening or closing any portion of the slides for the admission or exit of the air, the temperature and ventilation may be regulated at pleasure. In the summer, the air in the space under the slates, being highly rarefied by the direct action of the sun's rays on the upper surface, is continually passing off through the caps; while the air admitted through the apertures *c c*, coming from the subterranean space below the floor, is considerably below the temperature outside. In addition to this, the windows can, of course, be opened when requisite; and, being all on one side of the rooms, and a considerable height from the floor, any unpleasant draft is avoided. Of the efficiency of the above plan, I can speak with the utmost confidence;

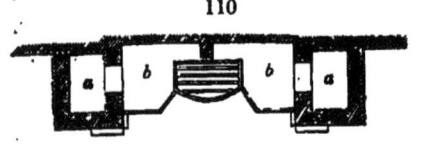

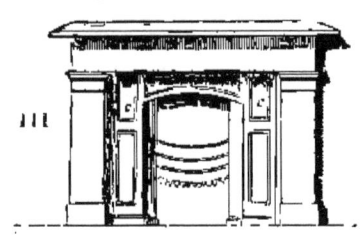

and its simplicity and cheapness will, I think, be evident on inspection. The warmth diffused by the grates is such, that, though two are fixed in each ward, of the size mentioned above, it has never been found necessary to use more than one at a time.

Liverpool, April 18. 1834.

ART. V. *On a Method of preventing the Damp from rising in the Walls of Buildings on Clay and other moist Soils.* By WILLIAM J. SHORT, Esq., Surveyor.

ON reading Mr. Hawkins's article (p. 123.) on the means of preventing injury to walls, &c., from damp, it has occurred to me that the following method might be employed to prevent the damp from rising in walls, at the same time that it provided ventilation sufficient to keep dry and preserve the timbers of the ground floors. When building the house, I would leave, as the works proceed, a vacancy or channel in the centre of all the walls, as shown at *a* in *fig.* 112., laying over the same, slabs of hard

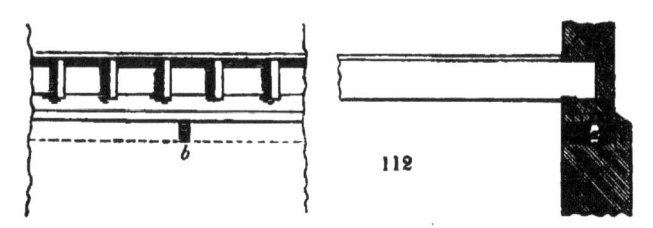

cheap stone or slate, which may be chamfered off so as to form a neat finish to the plinth round the outside of the building. At various intervals, I should propose that small openings communicating between this channel and the interior of the building (as shown at *b*) should be made; so that a current of air from the exterior may be driven through the channel and openings under the floors, in order to sufficiently ventilate the same.

The only increased expense will be the difference between a course of stone or slate and a course of bricks; as leaving the vacancy or channel will be, if any thing, a saving.

Clapham, May, 1834.

ART. VI. *On a method of curing Smoky Chimneys, and of ventilating Rooms.* By Mr. SAUL.

I HEREWITH send you a sketch of a plan for curing smoky chimneys. It is the invention of Mr. R. Hall, of this town, a professed chimney doctor. I have seen several rooms where it has been adopted, which have been completely cured of smoking. As the plan is very simple, it may be executed at a trifling expense.

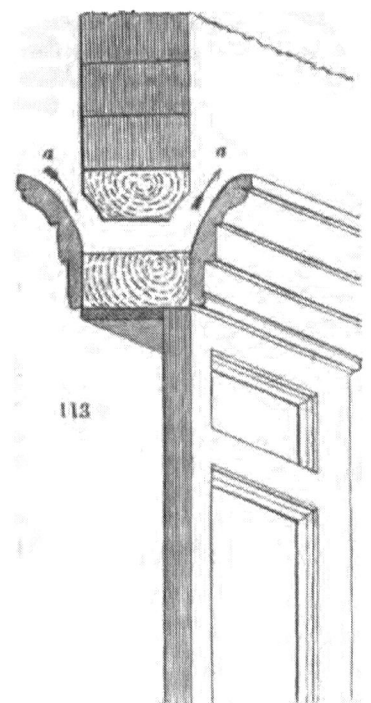

A current of air passes over the door behind the architrave or moulding (aa in *fig.* 113); the arrows show the way by which the air enters; and, as it rises direct to the ceiling, a person sitting in the room feels no draft whatever.

This plan may be adopted without disfiguring the room in the least, as the architrave is taken off and rounded on the back part, and is then replaced in such a manner that the aperture by which the air enters is not seen.

Sulyard Street, Lancaster,
May 3. 1834.

Art. VII. *On Cast-Iron Angles for Outside Doors.* By C. H. Capper, Esq., Civil Engineer.

I have often thought that outside doors might be greatly improved by having cast-iron angles at the bottom, in the following manner:—In *fig.* 114., a is the upright style; b, the bottom rail;

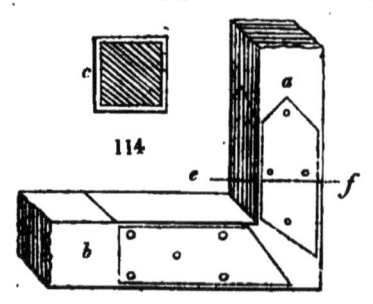

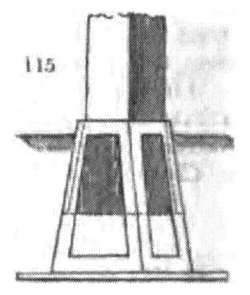

c the horizontal section at ef, showing the top of the iron angle foot, and the section of the style. The expense of these angular pieces of cast iron would be about 7*s.* or 8*s.* a pair. There would be much saving of labour in making door frames in this manner; and, as the angles of doors constructed wholly of wood are liable to rot, those with cast-iron angles would have a great advantage over them.

The same plan may be applied to posts for parks, &c., by having iron sockets (*fig.* 115.) made very light, and to fit on to the part to be inserted in the ground. These sockets may, I think, be made at from 3s. 6d. to 4s. each; and, of course, there will be a saving of timber when they are used.

Birmingham, June 16. 1834.

ART. VIII. *Dovetailed Caps for Wooden Fences.*
By W. Y. HINDLE, Esq.

A DESCRIPTION of a wooden fence which may be put together without the use of nails, screws, or other iron-work, is given in p. 79., in which the inventor states that wooden pins, "are liable to various objections, and do not make so neat a finish as where nails are used." Now, I shall feel obliged if you or any of your correspondents will point out in what respects wooden pins are either unfit or inelegant for works of this description.

I think Mr. Cottam's dovetail cap is liable to several objections; namely, the expense, and the increased number of grooves and tenons, which, by receiving, and for a long time retaining, moisture, are known to decay in a very few years. A great portion of the rain which would fall on the cap would, by means of the dovetail, be conducted to the ends of the rails, which, together with the dovetail, would shortly be rotten. I am of opinion that the end of the dovetail is more unsightly than a wooden pin, though certainly neater than the wedges under the bottom rail, shown in Mr. Cottam's sketch. This method of fastening would not prevent the top of the post from being moved sidewise, as there is nothing to tie the rail firmly to the post. The cap, by swelling and shrinking, as the weather was moist or dry, would soon become loose; and, when cattle (as is frequently the case) rubbed themselves against it, it would fall off, and the rails probably be lifted from their bed and broken.

I should suggest the fastening of the upper rail in the manner shown in the accompanying section (*fig.* 116.), where *a* is the cap, having one end of a strong wooden pin (*c*) driven tight into it.

The corners of the cap, formed so as to drip the water at four points clear of the rails, are shown at *e e*; and the rails (*d d*) are overlaid and fastened in the post (*b*) by the pin (*c*). The bottom rail need not have any fastening farther than being overlaid, as the bottom end of the post (being fast in the ground) could not be moved aside.

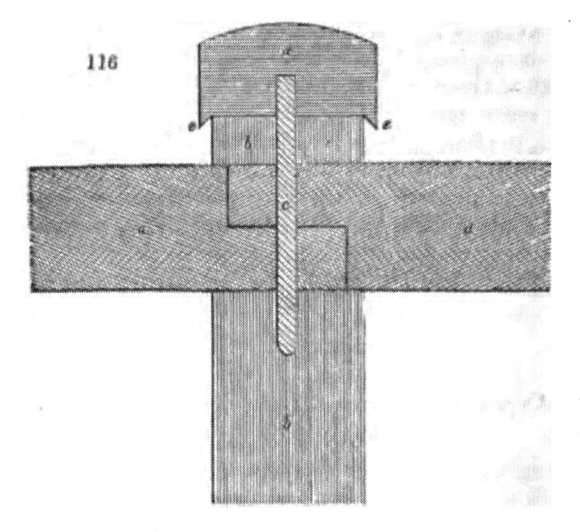

Barnsley, April 13. 1834.

Art. IX. *Architectural Maxims.*

If *Blank Windows* are ever allowable in original compositions, it can only be where they form a part of a system of windows. To introduce them where they form no part of such a system; that is, where there are no real windows at all in the elevation, as in the exterior elevation of the Bank of England, and in the front of the National Gallery at Charing Cross; is contrary to every sound principle of architectural composition.

Pediments. — There are few things more objectionable in Grecian or Roman architecture than that of placing a pediment where it could not, by any possibility, be on a large scale the end of a roof, or on a small scale the protection to a door or a window.

Imitation and Invention. — Architecture, as an art of mere imitation, may be judged of by rules and precedents; but as an art of invention, it must be judged of by general principles. In imitating an old castle, priory, or abbey in a modern villa, all the peculiarities, and even faults, of the originals may be copied, in order to keep up the illusion; but, in composing an original design in the castle or abbey styles, the general forms, details, and manner of composition, require only to be attended to.

REVIEWS.

ART. I. *The Civil Engineer and Machinist: Practical Treatise of Civil Engineering, Engineer Building, Machinery, Mill-Work, Engine-Work, Iron-Founding, &c. Designed for the Use of Engineers, Iron-Masters, Manufacturers, and Operative Mechanics.* By Charles John Blunt and R. Macdonald Stephenson, Civil Engineers, Architects, &c. Division I., containing Boulton and Watt's Portable Twenty-Horse Steam-Engine complete.

ACCIDENT prevented our obtaining a sight of the first division of this magnificent work, in time to give it such a perusal as would enable us, in the present Number, to place it in a clear light before our readers, and to aid them in forming a correct notion of its peculiar merits. A cursory glance at its contents, however, is abundantly sufficient to warrant our high commendation; and to elicit a strong desire that the public may, by liberal support, encourage the authors to proceed with profit, as well as pleasure; for sure we are, that nothing short of the pleasure of producing excellence could have induced them to incur so much labour and risk as are evident on the face of this publication. From our hasty inspection, it appears that Boulton and Watt's 20-horse steam-engine is accurately delineated; that the details are correctly given, and with a minuteness that must delight every person seeking sound information on the subject. We confess that we have repeatedly seen the prospectus of this work stitched up in the numbers of some of our scientific journals, and we felt it as obtruded upon our notice by some determined book-maker; but we passed it over as another of those traps with which we have before been caught, and induced to part with our money, and waste our time, in the endeavour to pick out a few grains of corn from among a large quantity of chaff. Our satisfaction is indeed great at finding ourselves so agreeably disappointed, in observing that the performance exceeds every thing that could be expected from the promise. We purpose, in our next Number, to enter more minutely into the particular merits of this highly useful work, a division of which, it is announced, will be published every six weeks, price one guinea; a sum very moderate indeed, for twelve folio engravings, besides letter-press descriptions. Nothing short of an immense sale can remunerate the proprietors.— *C. C.*

ART. II. *Journal für die Baukunst.* In zwanglosen Heften. *Journal of Architecture.* In Parts, published occasionally. By Dr. A. L. Crelle, Royal Prussian Architect, and Member of various Societies. Vol. VII. Part I., with 6 Plates. 4to. Berlin, 1833.

DR. CRELLE is considered one of the most scientific architects in Germany, and he is at the same time a man of letters.

He can hardly be said to be in much practice as an architect, though he enjoys the situation of president of the architectural council, or, as we should say, board of architecture, of his Prussian majesty. We intend to give an account of all the principal articles in the six preceding volumes of Dr. Crelle's work; not only for the gratification and instruction of our readers, but to show them that the literature of the architecture of Germany is much more copious than that of England.

Art. 1. in Part I. of the seventh volume, now before us, is entitled, "Some remarks on fire-proof stairs," by M. Engel, a Russian architect. The author proposes to include the stairs in a square tower, with a small well-hole, or square in the centre. This would give, to form the central well, four piers, which are to be connected by arches in the direction of the stairs. These arches are to support, in common with the side walls, the steps composing the stairs. Such staircases are to be met with the Old Town of Edinburgh, and in Paris; and in various stone-built towns on the Continent. In this country, the surrounding piers, walls, and arches might all be built of brick; and the steps over the brick arches formed of artificial stone. Art. 2. is the description of a floating sluice in North Holland, translated from a French work. Art. 3. is the description of a Dutch causeway, made with clinker bricks; a kind of road very common in Holland. This paper, and the preceding one, are rendered very plain by excellent engravings. The fourth article is on paper roofs; of which it appears that there are a number, both in Russia and Sweden; and, according to a note by the editor, also in Germany. Art. 5. is entitled "The Church of Kraschen, with some remarks on the style of the middle ages in church building," by M. Rimann, architectural surveyor at Wohlau, in Silesia. This article is illustrated by some engravings; which we intend to have copied; and we shall give them, along with the translation of the article (to us the most interesting one in the part), in a future Number.

ART. III. *Catalogue of Works of Architecture, Building, and Furnishing, and on the Arts more immediately connected therewith, recently published.*

BRITAIN.

GOTHIC Ornaments, *illustrative of Prior Birde's Oratory, in the Abbey Church, Bath.* By Edward Davis, Architect, Bath. No. 2. Imp. folio. London, 1834. 5s. 6d.

The engravings in this second number are still better executed than those in the first. They are as follows: — 1. A panel or compartment, filled with a flower. 2. A finial, or upper canopy, forming a corbel. 3. Part of a cornice, with the frieze beautifully covered with foliage. 4. Part of a transom, with one of the heads, from the lower compartment of a window. 5 Bosses (small projecting ornaments, like rosettes), from the exterior.

A Series of Original Designs for Shop Fronts, forming a Collection suitable to Persons connected with the Practical Part of Building. By Henry John Whitling, Architect. 4to. London, 1834. 12*s.* 6*d.*

In the preface, the author states that his object, in submitting this work to the public, is, "to demonstrate the practicability of producing, in shop fronts, an effect of a pleasing and appropriate character, without resorting to that ultra system of decoration, which at present so extensively prevails in the metropolis." As a work of art, his book, he says, has no pretensions whatever; his objects being cheapness and utility. There are twenty-two plates of elevations, most of which are plain and neat, and three of sections of the pilasters, cornices, and entablatures. There is one trifling objection, which we have to most of the designs, which is, that at the ends the cornices are generally returned. Now, as any one may observe, when walking along the streets of London, and as our correspondent R. has pointed out (p. 113.), these returns can seldom be carried into execution, without disfiguring the elevation. A much better plan, we think, would be, to finish the entablature against a block, in the manner shown in fig. 53. p. 116.; or in any analogous manner, so that each design might be completely independent of that adjoining it, with respect to execution. With this correction, the work will be useful to builders and carpenters. We do not like the half and three-quarter columns stuck on as mere ornaments, and we think young architects ought to have courage enough to reject all such prostitutions of one of the noblest features of architecture, and genius adequate to finding an unobjectionable substitute.

FRANCE.

Le Père la Chaise, ou receuil de plus de 150 desseins au trait des principaux monumens de ce célèbre cimetière, avec leurs échelles de proportion. Par Quaglia, ancien peintre attaché à l'Impératrice Joséphine. Paris, 1834. 12 francs.

Tarif des Prix des Ouvrages de Bâtiment. Par un vérificateur expert. Paris, 1834. 1 tom. 12mo. 3 francs.

Constructions de Charpentes. Par Krafft. Renfermant des planches relatives aux travaux maritimes et navigation; écluses de toutes grandeurs, vannes, caissons pour la construction des vaisseaux, docks, claire-voies jetées, digues et murs de quai, machines pour couper les herbes et nettoyer les canales, &c. 28 plates, with explanations, forming one vol. folio. Paris, 1834. 36 francs.

This is evidently a very important work; the machine for cutting the weeds of and cleaning canals, is probable that of Bétancourt.

Traité de l'Art de la Charpente. Par Krafft. Carpentry and Joinery, as applied to the interiors of houses. 31 plates, and detailed descriptions. Folio. Paris, 1834. 24 francs.

Construction des Bâtimens et d'Habitations en Charpente. Par Krafft. 82 plates, with explanations. Folio. Paris, 1834. 54 francs.

Art de la Charpente. Par Krafft. Contenant plus de 500 modèles de ponts tournans, ponts de bateaux, ponts levis à coulises et à bascule, machines à épuisement, batardeaux, pilotis caissons, grues, &c. One vol. imp. folio; 63 plates, with explanations. Paris 1834. 48 francs.

Krafft, as will be seen by our Paris letter, died lately. His works, the most valuable of which are enumerated above, are in general estimation throughout the Continent.

ART. IV. *Literary Notices.*

MR. COTTINGHAM is about to publish some prints of his restoration of Armagh Cathedral.

Ferrey's Christ Church, Hampshire, will be out about August 10.

Mr. W. Billinton, architect and civil engineer, Wakefield, is publishing by subscription, a south-west view, 21 in. by 16 in., of the parish church of All Saints, of that town.

The following Works have just appeared: — Clark's Plans, Elevations, Sections, and Details of Eastbury House, Essex, in large 4to; 2*l*. 2*s*. Blunt and Stephenson's Civil Engineer: Division I., The Steam Engine, 12 plates, 1*l*. 1*s*. Lockwood and Cater's Ancient Gates and Fortifications of the City of York; royal 4to, plates; 18*s*. Dodd's Mechanics for Practical Men; 8vo; 7*s*. 6*d*. Pugin's Fourth Part of the Second Series of Gothic Examples; 1*l*. 1*s*. — J. Weale. *Architectural Library*, 59. *High Holborn, July* 12. 1834.

Ram Raz on Hindu Architecture; 4to, with numerous plates; 1*l*. 11*s*. 6*d*. This work, which is very curious and interesting, we shall review at length, in our next Number.

MISCELLANEOUS INTELLIGENCE.

ART. I. *General Notices.*

DYEING *Maple or Satin Wood with Cochineal.*—I observe, in a London newspaper, a notice of the invention of a mode of embellishing maple or satin wood by dyeing it with cochineal. This is an old Swedish practice. In that country they use knotty pieces and roots of the birch, which they appear to plane with a plane which is not very sharp, so as to throw up the fibre more in some places than in others: they then dip these thin boards into dyes of various kinds; and, as the raised fibre imbibes colour faster than the smooth cut parts, a delicate variety of tint is easily produced. The boards, when dry, are smoothed and varnished, and make very beautiful furniture.—*J. R. Edinburgh, Feb.* 8. 1833.

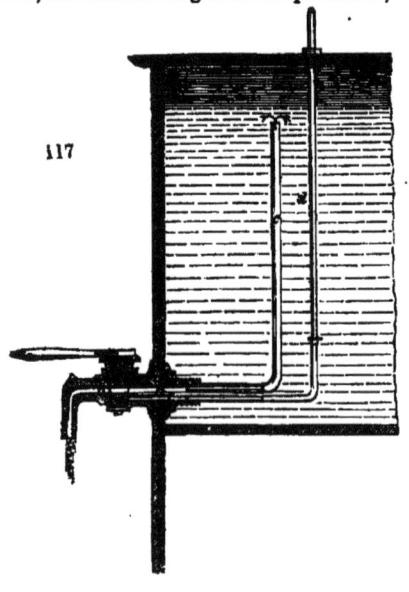

A Cock for Boilers, in Kitchen-Ranges of a superior description, is mentioned p. 46., and the following is a description of it, taken from the *Repertory of Arts,* vol. i. n. ser., p. 154. *Fig.* 117. represents a section of the cock, and the other parts connected therewith: *a* is the plug; *b*, the hot-water passage; *c*, a pipe connected with the hot-water passage; *d*, cold-water supply pipe, leading from a tank or reservoir, whence the supply of water to the boiler is obtained: the pipe *d* leads to the cold-water passage *e*, and thence to the water passage *f*, when the plug is turned for the purpose of withdrawing hot water. *Fig.* 120. is an end view of the cock, which shows the hot-water passage, and also two cold-water supply passages. *Fig.* 118 shows the plug separately, with the hot-water passage *a*, and cold-water passages *e* and *f*. *Fig.* 119. is a section of the cock for the purpose showing the cold-water passages *c*. and *f*. These three last figures are drawn to double the scale of *fig.* 117. The advantage of such cocks is, that the turning of the handle, to draw hot water, acts upon the cold-water passages by means of a double plug and barrel in the cock, so that an equal quantity of cold water is admitted in the boiler to that which is withdrawn from it; and, as these two water passages are adjusted to each other, the boiler will always contain an equal quantity of water, and thereby do away with the danger of its bursting from the circumstance of the water becoming low; therefore, by the application of cocks of this description, the boiler will at all times be properly supplied, and the height of the water in it cannot vary in the slightest degree.

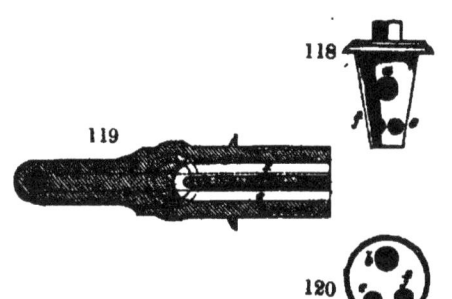

It will be seen that, when the cock is opened for the passage of the water, which will flow down the pipe c, into the water passage b, at the same time the water will descend from the supply tank, by the pipe d, into the cold-water passage e, and thence through the plug into the water passage f, which communicates with the boiler. The hottest part of the water will at all times be withdrawn, in consequence of the pipe c ascending to just below the surface of the water in the boiler; and the water, of course, can never be drawn through the cock unless the water line be above the pipe c.

The pipe through which the hot water is withdrawn, and the supply pipes, are regulated to such a nicety, that even the downward pressure of the column of water, and the expansion of water in a heated state, are considered in their construction. It is also evident that this arrangement of the supply may be varied, and applied to all sorts of boilers, where a change in the supply of water is desired.

Slabs of Slate fixed in a Bed of Concrete, as a Substitute for Granite Sleepers for Iron Rails.—This plan is in contemplation for the London and Birmingham railroad; and, with a view to prove the strength of slate so bedded, some experiments were made, July 2., on the premises of Messrs. Cottam and Hallen, in the presence of Mr. Solly the chairman of the company, Mr. Stephenson the company's surveyor, Mr. Palmer the engineer, and other gentlemen; from which it resulted, that slate, of a certain thickness, will answer all the purposes of granite, as a sleeper for the rail, at less than half the expense of that material. It was found, by the hydraulic press, that a cubic inch of slate will sustain a pressure of three tons and a half; and that, consequently, slate of an inch and a half thick is more than equal to any pressure which it can be required to support on the railroad. Slabs of slate, of sufficient size and thickness, may be had for the purpose in abundance, from the quarries in Wales, Cornwall, and Ireland. It will require some ingenuity to fix them in the concrete, so as to prevent them from being shifted from their places by the vibrating motion of the wheels of the engines and waggons. In order to ascertain the best mode of effecting this object, it has been arranged that 300 of 400 yards of the Birmingham and London railroad should be laid with slate sleepers in the first instance. (*Morn. Chron.*, July 7. 1834.)

Slate has lately been used as flooring for shops in London, and it has also been laid down in the Strand as foot pavement; in order to prove, by experiment, its durability relatively to that of Yorkshire flagstone. Its strength is such, that it might be used in all warehouses instead of boards for the floors; and thus, by means of cast-iron joists, such buildings might be most effectually rendered fireproof. In common dwelling-houses, fireproof partitions, and fireproof chests and closets, might be formed of the same material joined by iron or copper.

ART. II. *Foreign Notices.*
FRANCE.

THE *new Protestant Church* has been opened in the Rue d'Aguesseau. It is in the Gothic style, and is remarkably chaste and light. The windows are of stained glass. The drapery of the altar-piece is not quite equal to the rest of the decorations; but we understand it is only temporary. This church is capable of containing about 800 persons. — *L. May*, 1834.

Abattoirs are erecting at Boulogne, Caen, and many other towns in the French provinces; and it is expected that, in a very few years, not a single head of cattle will be slaughtered throughout France at any private establishment. Suspension bridges are also in progress over most of the secondary rivers. The section of architecture in l'École des Beaux Arts distributed prizes, at their meeting on the 10th of January last, to M. Boulanger and M. Gounod, for designs for a school for the children of chevaliers of the Legion of Honour; and to M. Guenepin and to M. Boulanger, for designs for aviaries in pleasure-grounds. Trottoirs (or, in other words, paths for foot-passengers) are about to be added to all the streets of Paris; so that persons may, in future, walk through that bustling capital without fear of either mud or cabs. M. de Mauneville has invented a machine for making parquetted floors, or rather for preparing the boards of which such floors are made; which promises to bring parquetted floors again into fashion. M. de Mauneville's establishment is at Troussebourg, near Honfleur. In the architectural department of the salon for 1834, M. Clerget has a picture, representing the supposed original appearance of the Temple of Augustus and Livia; the ruins of which are still in existence, at Vienne in Dauphiné. These ruins are sufficiently preserved to make it easy to form a general idea of what the temple once was; but M. Clerget differs from M. Rey (who gave a view of it formerly) as to the details. Under the name of religious historical architectural studies in the middle ages, M. Albert Lenoir has exhibited the ancient façade of St. Laurent, at Rome, as exemplifying the style of the fourth to the ninth century; St. Maria Toscanella, for the Byzantine school of the eleventh century; and the cathedral of Parma as an example of the style of the twelfth century. Besides these views of ancient edifices, there are some designs for modern buildings. Among the latter are, a plan for uniting the palaces of the Louvre and the Tuileries, and one for restoring the Théâtre Français. Two designs were exhibited for a pedestal for the statue of General Hoche, to be erected at Versailles; but neither of them have been accepted. In fact, after all, it is found so difficult to make a pedestal for this statue (which, by the way, was originally designed for the Temple de la Gloire, now La Madelaine), that M. Marochetti, sculptor of the department, has agreed to form a new statue and pedestal complete, for the same sum as it would cost to adjust a pedestal only to the present statue! M. Douchain, architect, of Versailles, is to do the building part, and the government is to supply marble. It is estimated that the expense will be about 22,000 francs. Among the articles in the "Exposition des Produits de l'Industrie" are the decorations of a room all in steel: doors, chimney-piece, clock, candelabra, and, in short, all the usual ornaments of a drawing-room, are in steel. The effect is singular, but somewhat gloomy.

With regard to architectural news, the celebrated Château de Pompadour, to which so many historical recollections were attached, has been nearly destroyed by fire; and plans are already on foot for rebuilding it. An architectural society has been established in Paris, under the title of Société Libérale des Constructeurs d'Edifices publics et particuliers; and persons wishing to become members are directed to apply (postpaid) to M. Douchin, Rue Aumaire, Nos. 3. and 5. The Church de la Madelaine is at last completed; but I shall speak more in detail of this edifice in my next. Krafft, whose works on carpentry are considered the best in France, died lately, at the age of 65.

GERMANY.

Women Mortar Carriers. — At Vienna, women are always employed to carry mortar. In 1827, when Mr. Hawkins, the engineer, was building a sugar-house there, nine stories high, he employed a hundred bricklayers at one time, and fifty female mortar carriers. These women carried the mortar up four-story ladders outside the building; and thence up seven other ladders inside, from story to story. Each woman serves two bricklayers; and, when these bricklayers leave work, the woman who attends on them cleans their trowels and other tools, and wraps them up in the men's aprons, and puts them in a secure place till the morning, when she must have them ready for the men at their time of beginning to work. It is singular that a custom which, we are apt to think, belongs only to a very rude age, should prevail in such a highly civilised and humane society as that of Vienna, where all classes, from the lowest to the highest, are educated, and where all, without exception, are polite. But in this very country, where women are thus daily employed in the labours of men, it would be thought shocking if a female were to be seen on the outside of a coach. Such are the anomalies of society.

DENMARK.

In the Annual Exhibition of the Danish Academy of Arts, which opened on April 1., out of 305 subjects, there were 44 of architecture and machinery. (*For. Quart. Rev.*, May, 1834, p. 466.)

Copenhagen, June 10. 1854. — The king has given orders to repair the palace of Rosenburg, and it is said that he intends renewing the furniture, partly from the cabinet-makers and upholsterers in Paris and London. You are no doubt aware that the rooms in this country, as in Sweden, are generally finished in water colours; and that paper, and also wainscoting, are very uncommon. The king intends to have the principal rooms papered with some of the newest French papers; and the grand hall of entrance, which is at present painted in imitation of freestone, will assume the character of marble. All the windows on the principal floor will be renewed, and narrow astragals and plate glass used, as in the best houses of London and Paris. Your horticultural correspondent, Petersen, is making various improvements in horticultural buildings, respecting which he will no doubt write to you very soon. — *F. Jorgensen.*

GREECE.

Since peace has been established, the rich Greek merchants have purchased immense estates from the Turks, in the Island of Negropont; and a plan is now in agitation for rebuilding Athens on the opposite coast. The engineer Cleanthes has been employed to form a plan for this purpose; but his plan has not given general satisfaction, as it is thought he has consulted private interest rather than public convenience in the arrangement of the streets. The city is intended to contain 80,000 inhabitants; and the engineer proposes to combine in it imitations of the Palais Royal and the Tuileries of Paris, the Place of St. Mark at Venice, and all the other most celebrated architectural ornaments of the different cities of Europe. The city is to be about three miles from the port, with which it is to be connected by a kind of faubourg. All the streets and public places are to bear the celebrated names of antiquity. (*La Propriété*, June, 1834, p. 375.) There seems something very absurd in setting about building a town for a given number of inhabitants; and still more so in the idea of transferring to Greece imitations of modern squares and buildings, and giving them classical names. There is, however, little danger of the scheme being carried into execution.

An engineer has been sent to Syra, to superintend the construction of various edifices, rendered necessary by the increase of commerce. Among them are a lighthouse, an entrepôt for merchandise, and a new lazaretto. The latter is much wanted. (*Athenæum*, vol. for 1834, p. 324.)

ART. III. *Domestic Notices.*

ENGLAND.

Fires in London. — One cause of the frequency of fires in London is the imprudence of persons wishing to put up stoves, &c., in cutting into party walls, without having any regard to what may be on the other side. In this manner the flues of stoves, &c., are often brought dangerously near woodwork; and if, from any incidental cause, a fire is made of rather more than ordinary potency, the wood in the next house, on the other side of the wall, becomes ignited, and a fire ensues, for which, at first, there appears no assignable cause. There is a law which obliges all persons intending to make alterations in the party walls of houses in London, or to make exterior additions to, or alterations in, them, of any kind, to give notice to the district surveyor; but though it is generally attended to with respect to exterior alterations (for these, being seen by everybody, are soon noticed by the surveyor), it is as generally neglected in the case of interior ones. In a case which came before the Lord Mayor, June 19. 1833, the party wall of a house in Snowhill had been cut into to such a degree, for the purpose of setting a kitchen stove, that a hole was actually made into the next house; and the party wall became so hot, when the kitchen fire was lighted, as not to be endured by the hand. The person who inhabited the house into which the hole was cut, stated that the paint had become all blistered with the excessive heat. The Lord Mayor said, that often, in setting up a kitchen range, workmen cut into the backs of the cupboards of the kitchen in the next house, and in a short time afterwards a fire broke out, for which no one could account.

Mr. Nixon's Show Rooms and Warehouses, in John Street, Oxford Street, contain at present a number of specimens of inlaid French furniture, and of tables, looking-glass frames, and other articles, in the style of Louis XIV., all imported from France. Among these are included a number of the mouldings, architraves, and other members used in the fitting-up of rooms, belonging to that period, and a number of marble chimney-pieces. The work on these marble chimney-pieces is nothing like so good as the best English workmanship, but the charm of their being really French is all-powerful. Such is the effect of this charm, that many articles of Louis XIV.'s time are purchased, admired, and imitated, for no other reason than their antiquity. — A mode of printing coloured flowers on velvet, newly invented, and practised by the French, is so perfect and beautiful, that we do not see how it can be discovered (unless by its durability) from painting by hand. Mr. Nixon has imported several covers for chair bottoms of this material; and nothing can exceed the brilliancy of their colours, and the accuracy and delicacy of their execution. The flowers, inlaid in tables, cabinets, and in different ornamental pieces of furniture, are of a richness and beauty that is hardly to be conceived by one who has never seen them; and they are so well represented, that they may be known in a moment by any florist. We had great pleasure in looking over Mr. Nixon's collection, on May 23.

Separating Sea Water from its Salt. — This was effected by Mr. Fraser of Long Acre, upwards of twelve years ago. His plan was, to employ a particular description of cooking-range adapted for ships, which boiled and distilled at the same time. An improved plan of effecting the same object has lately been brought into notice by Messrs. Wells and Westrup, who have taken out a patent for a machine for converting sea water into excellent fresh water. The process was exhibited in a vessel in the river near Westminster Bridge, 14th June, 1834, before a number of scientific gentlemen. The conversion is effected by distillation, the condensation being produced by passing the pipe, by which the steam is carried off, through the side of the vessel, into the river or the sea, and returning it into the vessel again at a sufficient distance for condensing the steam; which then flows out in a stream of pure fresh water. The top of the cistern in which the sea water is boiled is formed to allow cooking-kettles to be placed in it, and, of course, any thing contained in them may be boiled by the heat of the steam, so that the cooking for a ship's company may be performed by the same process that shall supply them with a sufficiency of fresh water. The process converts nine tenths of the sea water contained in the cistern into pure fresh water, in about twelve hours. The cistern by which the process was performed on Saturday, contained about 133 gallons, and in twelve hours about 120 gallons of fresh water was produced. The gentlemen present all tasted the converted fresh water, and pronounced it excellent. (*Morning Advertiser*, June 16. 1834.)

Subscription for Mr. Peter Nicholson. — Sir Jeffery Wyatville, with his usual munificence, has written to Mr. Weale to request that he will put his name down to the subscription for Mr. Peter Nicholson for 10*l.* — *J. W.*

The Collection of Books of the late Mr. Taylor, of the Architectural Library, High Holborn, is to be sold by auction on July 21., which will afford a fine opportunity for architects to enrich their libraries. Mr. Taylor's premises have been taken by Mr. Weale, who has already removed to them his stock of architectural books from Broad Street.

The Obelisk of Luxor, mentioned p. 46.— In the *Mechanics' Magazine*, Nos. 570. and 571., for July 12. and 19. 1834, there is "An Account of the transportation of the obelisk of Luxor to Paris," illustrated by six engravings. It is extremely interesting; and we would recommend every young architect, who does not take in the *Mechanics' Magazine* (though we should think there are few who do not), to purchase these Numbers, and to bind them up as a supplement with the first volume of the Architectural Magazine.

Norfolk.— Perkins's system of heating by hot water is making great progress here, under the superintendence of Messrs. Parlour and Sons. Mr. Coke of Holkham, is building a wall 9 ft. high round his park, which is 14 miles in circumference. It will cost 5000*l.* per mile, and it is to go on at the rate of two miles per annum. It is to be game proof. Building is in a very dull state here; so much so, that many of the best joiners are unemployed. In p. 205., Stanfield Hall is mentioned. There is a modern staircase in a Gothic hall in this mansion, and a frightful one it is. I am aware of the want of precedent for Gothic staircases; but Mr. Salvin has surmounted that obstacle nobly, in our Norwich cathedral, in the ascent to the pulpit. I have just received Blunt and Stephenson's new work; and it is certainly a very splendid one. I have been fully employed of late, principally in my manufactory. I shall shortly get up a very elaborate machine for drying paper as it comes from the making-machine (Fourdrinier's). I am glad to see Mallet's name again in your Magazines. I have read Junius Redivivus's article on your *Encyc. of Architecture*, in *Fox's Repository*. The great engineer, ——, has made a grand blunder at Denver Sluice in this county. It will probably be the last job he will have in the Fens.— *W. T. Norwich. July* 6. 1834.

Sussex. — *The Worthing Clock Tower.*—In pursuance of a public invitation to architects, of the 26th November, 1832, for designs for the erection of a building for the reception of a clock with four dials, to be placed in the most conspicuous spot in South Street, Worthing, several designs were submitted, and one in the Gothic style, by Mr. S. H. Benham, architect and surveyor, of Brighton, was adopted. Some doubt having been raised as to the stability of Mr. Benham's design, if carried into effect, he explained the principles of its construction, in a letter addressed to the *Brighton Guardian*, from which the following is an extract: — " The figure of my plan is octangular (a figure which I preferred, as being best suited to the site), and 18 ft. in diameter. The outer wall is 12 in. thick, with pointed arch openings in each side, and supported at the angles by buttresses 1 ft. 3 in. thick, 2 ft. 6 in. in projection, and 30 ft. in height, diminished and weathered (beveled so as to prevent the rain from lodging) upwards, to receive the clock room, and the open belfry surmounting it, the walls of which are also 12 in. thick, and are connected with the outer walls by an arched corridor 3 ft. wide; thereby giving additional and considerable strength to the height, for the purpose of securing greater stability to the diminished superstructure, springing upwards from the base line altogether from 50 to 60 ft.; the centre of the dial from the ground line being 40 f.t The angles of the diminished clock room are also supported by buttresses of ample dimensions, springing directly from a deep weathered coping of the sub-structure of 30 ft., before named, finished by crocketed finials, from 4 to 5 ft. in height, above the clock room, and terminated by pinnacles. The belfry (which is 5 ft. in the clear, and 7 ft. externally) stands down upon the top of the weathered cornice, encompassing the upper part of the clock room; and, within the pinnacles, crowned by a cyma-recta roof crocketed at the angles, and terminated by a finial of suitable proportions. The depth of the foundations of the structure would, of course, be determined by the nature of the soil; their thickness would be 18 in., with inverted arches under every opening; and, under the arched corridor, formed by the outer and inner walls: thus giving a good and substantial base-work to erect the superstructure upon. It is well known to mathematicians that, the nearer the figure of a plan approaches to a circle, the stronger it is in its constructive principles. Hence engineers, in the construction of batteries or walls of defence, invariably adopt for their plans many-sided figures, viz., pentagons, hexagons, heptagons, and octagons, and very frequently plans resembling (in outline) stars, in consequence of their great strength at the angles over every other kind of figure, and carry such works into effect with less materials; these figures possessing greater strength than any other kind of plan which has its walls at right angles. The strength of a building is not dependent upon a mass of materials being throw (pell-mell) together, without regard to sound principles. The acme of science is to acomplish great ends with small means, and this can only be done upon sound principles. Now, with regard to the material, I propose using, for the sake of economy, "Ranger's patent stone," a material that can be used for one third less than the brickwork, and Parker's cement; this stone is most assuredly the best and strongest for the purpose, in consequence of its being cast in blocks, varying in height, length, and thickness, as circumstances may require for the work."—*S. H. Benham. Brighton, May 5. 1834.*

ART. IV. *Retrospective Criticism.*

THE *Architectural Magazine*, No. I.—I agree with Scrutator to the very letter, and have no fear of common sense prevailing ultimately. Mr. Trotman's remarks on Egyptian Architecture (p. 20.) reminded me of an idea I have long entertained, viz., that Egyptian architecture is peculiarly applicable to engineering work, particularly for the piers, &c., of suspension bridges. [It has been applied to smelting furnaces by Dr. Macullonch.] Mr. Kent condemns zinc roofing. I think you ought to inquire whether he includes Mosselman's zinc, so highly spoken of in the *Mechanics' Magazine*, vol. xx. Mr. Trubshaw (p. 47.) and myself were engaged, simultaneously and without concert, in righting leaning towers, about two years ago. Mr. Ranger's stone (p. 47.) reminds me of your inquiries respecting Brunel's marvellous arch in the Tunnel yard: perhaps you can get at it now. My mother used to steam dumplins, near thirty years since, with an apparatus like that of Mackenzie. (p. 48.)— *W. T. Norwich, March* 15. 1834.

The Architectural Magazine, and Architecture as a Study for Ladies.—I rejoice in the anticipation of the happy results which must inevitably follow the circulation of your Magazine. The *Encyclopædia of Architecture* has done much towards improving the taste for architecture, and creating a desire for a more extensive acquaintance with its principles and practice; but the information conveyed by the pages of the Architectural Magazine is presented in such an inviting form, as to render it more generally useful, and better calculated to accomplish the design of its conductor: it being a book not intended for the study merely, but for the table of every one who has the least pretension to taste, or who has any feeling for the higher enjoyments of domestic life. The Magazine will consequently become an able auxiliary in the cause of education; and hence it is I anticipate so much; for now (and not till now have they been able) will our females make architecture their study. It is my decided opinion, and I have frequently expressed it, that neither architecture, nor the fine arts generally, will flourish in this country, till they become branches of female education; and I would suggest that you should write an article, expressly dedicated to females, for the purpose of calling their attention to this very important subject, and that you should lose no opportunity of impressing on them, as they value their own happiness and that of their children, the necessity of the study of architecture. Then would follow, as a necessary consequence, the fine arts, landscape-gardening, floriculture, horticulture, &c., and our ladies would become active, healthy, intelligent, and happy; and would diffuse those blessings to all around them. — *John Price, Architect. Derby, June* 21. 1834.

ART. V. *Queries and Answers.*

INCONVENIENCE *of lofty Windows.* — My upper windows here are 8 ft. high, and the upper sashes are fixed; the stonework projects a good deal; so that I tremble every time they are cleaned: and how a glazier would contrive to put one of the topmost panes in I cannot tell. No ladder can be brought near enough; and a man standing on the sill of the window cannot reach 8 ft. high. An ordinary glazier's bench or stool is of no use in such a case as this. What is wanted is a raised platform, which may be easily fastened to the window, and shall, at the same time, have an upright shaft, by which a man may support himself. *Experto crede.* Make your windows less than 8 ft. high, or let the upper sashes be made to slide. A plank, supported on a trestle in the room, and tied to a ladder outside, which may also be taken hold of by the workmen, is all I can think of. Can any of your readers suggest a better plan? — *T. W. The Banks, Yorkshire,* 1833.

Sideboards for small Rooms. — I saw, some years since, a kind of dumb waiter, which would be very suitable for a small dining-room sideboard. It consists of three leaves, which, when not wanted, lie close together, and form a neat side-table: when wanted, the centre pillar is contrived so as to allow of their rising up, and forming three tiers of leaves. I have not a sufficiently accurate recollection of it to be able to send you a drawing; but I doubt not that Mr. Dalziel will recognise the description, and explain it to you: and I think you will agree with me in considering it a very clever and useful piece of furniture, where space is valuable. One of the most elegant, because most simple sideboards, for a similar purpose, that I ever saw, was only a slab, partly screwed to the wall, and partly supported by two brackets, that were placed so as to include about one third of its length between them, which was fitted up with book-shelves, I think; but would have been more appropriately accompanied by a cupboard. If Mr. Dalziel, or any other of your correspondents, could give me a working-plan, &c., of a dumb-waiter sideboard, I should be much obliged. — *T. W.*

Washing and Wringing Machine. — Seeing a wringing machine figured in your *Encyclopædia of Cottage, Farm, and Villa Architecture and Furniture,* I send you an account of a washing and wringing machine which I have had in use for some years. It was made by Bullman of Leeds, who took out a patent for it, some years since. In mine, the operator, if only one, stands at the end opposite the wringing apparatus, and works the washer by means of a lever that plays from right to left: but, unfortunately, the maker never thought it necessary to consider that it would probably be worked by a woman; nay, it requires a span that is not very convenient to a tall man. An improvement has been made in these machines, by which the washer is worked by a person or persons at the sides, and moves along, not across, the machine. Bullman has also a mangle on the principle of the wringing machine. Perhaps some of your correspondents could favour us with a description of both machines. — *Lavator.*

Colouring of Plaster Casts. — Can any of your correspondents inform me what the colouring is composed of, and how it is used, on the plaster casts from the frieze of the Temple of Lysicrates, now in the new room at the British Museum? — *E. B. L. London, July* 9. 1834.

Composition of Concrete, for Foundations. (p. 216.) — In answer to Investigator, I have used concrete in the proportion of five of loamy gravel to one of stone lime. Dry brick rubbish may be used with the gravel; or, in fact, any other material, if carefully spread, and used sparingly. These proportions will be found to answer well. This kind of foundation is not very new; for Carter informs us that the foundations of Westminster Abbey, erected 1245, consists of flints, irregular stones, rubble, and mortar, forming together one almost impenetrable body. In many of the ancient remains of castles, particularly in Kent, the foundations are made in this manner.— *L. London, July* 5. 1834.

Concrete, &c. (p. 216.) — Take Thames-washed shingle, and Dorking lime fresh from the kiln and finely powdered, in the proportion of six bushels of shingle to one bushel of lime, with a due quantity of water. These are to be intimately and properly mixed in small quantities (say a small barrowful), and then thrown from a stage at least 5 ft. high, while hot, in equal layers; every layer to be well rammed. — *A Constant Reader. London, July* 4. 1834.

Concrete Foundations (p. 216.) are usually made with Dorking lime; but I apprehend any water lime will do as well. We use, for waterworks, lime burnt at Heyden in this county. There is also a capital lime made at Reach and at Burwell, in Cambridgeshire, which is used in waterworks all over the Fen country: both these limes are sold at the kilns for about 6d. per imperial bushel. This is very important; for, with Dorking lime, concrete foundations cost nearly as much as brickwork, all things considered. With regard to the proportions of material, I should advise experiments to be made with local materials, to determine them. Pieces might be formed of not less than a foot cube; or, what is better, an old tea chest might be filled with them. The lime should be fresh from the kiln. I believe concrete was first suggested by Semple, in his *Treatise on Building in Water;* 4to, 63 plates; Dublin, 1777. — *W. Thorold. Norwich, July* 6. 1834.

Concrete. (p. 216.) — Whenever I have used concrete in the foundation of buildings, I have had a wide square trench dug out, about 8 in. wider than the lowest course of brickwork, and to such a depth as to insure a tolerably firm foundation. *Fig.* 121. will show this more distinctly. In this figure, *a* is the floor line; *b*, the ground line; and *c*, the concrete. When the trench is made, I have coarse and fine gravel thrown into it together (just as they come from the pit), to a thickness of about 4 in.; I then have it grouted with thin hot lime, only just enough to bind the gravel together. The mixture must now be rammed down hard. Course after course must then be laid, and so treated; till the mass reaches to within about 18 in. of the ground line. The proportion of hot lime to the gravel is about one eighth part only, which I think is enough. It was Walter's Sutton flare-burnt lime which I used. I think this plan better than first mixing the gravel and lime, but this may be a mere matter of opinion. The mixture hardens in a few days, in the most complete manner. After the brickwork is built on it, immediately fill the sides of the trench with earth, ramming it in well, to prevent the rain from affecting the concrete — *J. B. Watson.* 30. *Duke Street, Manchester Square, July* 9. 1834.

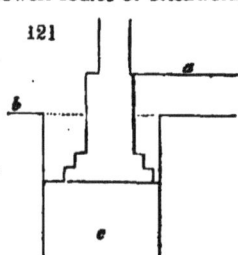

THE ARCHITECTURAL MAGAZINE.

SEPTEMBER, 1834.

ORIGINAL COMMUNICATIONS.

ART. I. *On those Principles of Composition, in Architecture, which are common to all the Fine Arts.* By the CONDUCTOR. Sect. I. *Forms, Lines, Lights, Shades, and Colours, considered with reference to the Production of an Architectural Whole.*

HAVING laid down what we consider to be the fundamental principles of composition in the fine arts generally, we shall now show the manner in which they are applied in architectural composition; but always, it must be remembered, with reference to that art considered in an abstract point of view, as the art of combining artificial forms, lines, lights, shades, and colours; without reference to the uses of buildings, or to particular styles of architecture. By separating these elements of composition from the ideas of use, of expense, of propriety, of fitness, and, above all, from architectural style, we shall be the better able to analyse our ideas respecting them, and to show to the young and inexperienced student their independent influence. The principles of composition applicable to the different styles of architecture, and having reference to the use and duration of buildings, will be subsequently considered.

The first principle which we laid down (p. 217.) is that of the necessity of producing a whole, in order that the composition may be easily comprehended by the eye. The reason given for this is, the unity of the human mind, which can only properly attend to one thing at a time. Hence, as we before stated, the necessity of the unity of the whole; and of the connection between the parts, either really by absolute contiguity, or apparently by seeming contiguity. To these elements of a whole, we added that of what artists call distance, or the adjustment of a whole to the eye.

It is scarcely necessary to observe, that the parts composing every whole must either be, or seem to be, in contact with each other. This is self-evident; for, as the object, in producing a whole, is to combine several different things so as to produce the effect of one; if these different things were apart from each other, they would form several objects, instead of a single one. The adjustment of an object, or of a collection of objects, to the human eye, is equally necessary to our comprehension of such objects as a whole. If they are too near, the limited angle of vision cannot embrace them, and they can only be seen partially, or in succession; and thus, a series of impressions will be produced, instead of a simultaneous one. If, on the other hand, they are too far from the eye, the angle of vision will not be sufficiently filled; intervening objects will enter into the picture on the retina, and the eye and the mind will be distracted. In order to facilitate the comprehension of a combination of objects as a whole, it is found advantageous, in artificial composition, to arrange them within the limits of some well-known and easily comprehended figure. Thus, a whole, however intricate and numerous may be its parts, will be much more readily comprehended if its outline assimilates easily to the form of a square, a parallelogram, a semicircle, a triangle, or any such familiar geometrical figure, than if it were really in the form of any two of these figures combined; or in a form so irregular, as not to be easily reducible in the mind, at the first glance, to any common figure. If we examine what passes in our minds when we are attending to any new object, with a view of impressing it on the memory, we shall find that, if forms be an important element in the object or scene, we compare them in the mind with other forms with which we are already familiar; and, as mankind generally are more equally acquainted with geometrical or abstract forms, than they are with the forms of particular things, hence new forms are more frequently compared to circles, squares, triangles, &c., than they are to the sun, to trees, or to the human figure. Such a lake is said to be round or oval, and not sun-shaped or egg-shaped; and such a mountain flat or conical, and so on. We state this, lest it should be thought that there is any magic in the form of a triangle, a cone, or a square, &c., as applied to groups; and to show that, in reality, these forms are merely made use of in idea, as helps to the memory. Having made these remarks on the paramount importance of the principle of a whole, we shall now proceed to show how a whole may be produced by forms, by lines, by lights and shades, and by colours respectively.

In combining *Forms* into a whole, these forms must be more or less of the same kind. If the whole consists of few parts, then little variety of form can be produced; if it consists of a great number of parts, then a variety of forms may enter into the composition. Suppose a whole to consist only of two parts. In that case, if one of the parts were a cube, and the other a globe, or a semi-globe, it is evident that a whole could not be produced; because there is no congruity between these two forms. In order to display a cube and a semi-globe in the same composition, either a number of intervening forms become requisite; or the one form must be incomparably smaller than the other. In general, there should be one prevailing form in every composition, or at least one prevailing character of form. Suppose what may be called the initiatory or fundamental form to be the square, or the cube; then, the parallelogram, as being of the same character, may be combined with it, so as to produce every requisite variation. The square, or cube, can only produce variation by being made larger or smaller, or by being repeated; but the parallelogram admits of being made narrower or broader at pleasure, and it farther admits of being placed either on its side, or on its end. Both squares and parallelograms admit of being placed either at right angles or obliquely to each other; and this is a farther source of variation, though still perfectly consistent with the production of a whole.

Suppose the circle or globe to be taken as the initiatory element of composition: in that case we have the globe and the cylinder, both capable of being increased or diminished at pleasure; but both, when applied to architecture, incapable of producing that degree of unity combined with variety to which the square and the parallelogram may give rise; because the cylinder, though it may, like the parallelogram, be varied in length or diameter, cannot, like the parallelogram, be placed on its broad side. A building, therefore, in which round towers are the prevailing forms, can never have so much variety as one in which the towers are rectangular, other circumstances being the same. If, however, rectangular forms are combined with round towers in such a manner as to preserve unity of effect, the variety produced will be so much the greater.

We have now to consider how a whole is to be produced by means of *Lines*. Here it may be necessary to begin by observing that there are, properly, no such things as lines in nature; but that the word is used by artists solely with reference to art; that is, to the appearance of lines which is produced by forms, and to the necessity of beginning with lines in all graphic delineations of objects. If the forms of a composition are as they ought to be, so also will be the lines. The consideration of lines, therefore, may be viewed as the treatment of forms in the abstract; or as an assistance to us in the composition not only of forms, but even, as will be hereafter seen, of lights, shadows, and colours; since every thing which has length and breadth is necessarily bounded by lines.

As, in every building that constitutes a whole, there are certain prevailing forms, so there will also be found in the same building a prevailing character of lines. Where the parallelogram is chiefly laid on its broad side, there the horizontal lines will prevail: where it is chiefly placed on its end, or where the cylinder or round tower is the principal form employed, there the prevailing lines will be perpendicular. Oblique and curvilineal lines are seldom found in buildings, except as indicative of roofs; and these roof lines, in all harmonious structures, will be found to have one prevailing tendency. If they are straight lines, then their degree of obliquity, or the angle which they form with the horizon, will generally be found to be the same, or nearly so, throughout. If they are curvilineal, they will, for the most part, be either segments of circles, or, if not of circles, of ovals or of ellipses, having the same transverse and conjugate diameters. A very extensive composition, however, may, in its roof lines, combine straight, oblique, and curvilineal lines; though this cannot be done without producing discordance or incongruity in small buildings.

The *Lights* in an elevation are produced by the breadth and the prominence of the forms; and the *Shades*, by the recesses, and by horizontal and perpendicular projections. Considering the lights produced in a composition in an abstract point of view, they ought to form a whole, independently of the shades, of the forms, or of the lines. Thus, there must be one prevailing form of light in every structure; and this will naturally result from one form prevailing more generally than any other, and from one general tendency of the lines. In an abstract point of view there must be one prevailing form of shade; and this, in its turn, will depend on the prevailing form of light. In buildings where the perpendicular forms and lines prevail, there perpendicular lights and shades should be prevalent; and in those where horizontal or oblique lines are most conspicuous, the lights and shades will follow the same direction. In analysing the elevation of a building, we shall find it possible that the forms and the lines may be in harmony, without that harmony extending to the lights and shades: thus, suppose the parallelogram form to be prevalent, and the building to consist of a number of long narrow parallelograms set on end, joined by broad parallelograms set on one side; the effect may be good, considered merely with reference to forms and lines; but if all the projections are at an equal distance from the main body of the building, then all the lights on these projections will be equally clear, and all the shadows produced by them equal in width and depth of shade. But to produce a whole, it is requisite not only that some of the projections should be broader than others, in order to give main features of light, but that some of them should exceed in projection, as well as in width, in order to give shadows exceeding in depth. Inexperienced persons, who cannot separate the effect of lines from the effect of lights and shades, are thus very apt to form an erroneous conception from outlines of buildings seen on paper; and, on the other hand, draftsmen, aware of the effect of lights and shades, in order to render a drawing on paper pleasing to the eye, increase them beyond what the projections would actually produce, and thus deceive the spectator.

Colour, it may be thought, has very little to do with buildings, or, at least, with their exteriors; but this is a mistake. In every building, even of the most monotonous-coloured stone, there must of necessity be two colours; that of the walls, and that of the glass of the windows. If the roof is seen, there will probably be three colours; and, if the doors and other woodwork are not painted to imitate the walls, there will be four colours. If there are facings to the doors and windows; or if there are columns, or pilasters, or angle stones, of a different colour from that of the common material of the walls, there will be five colours; and if the roof have lead on the hips and in the valleys, or flashings round the dormer windows, there will be six colours. Finally, if veined stone or marble be used, either for the common material of the walls, or the columns, pilasters, or facings, there is no limit to the number of colours which may occur in a single elevation. The consideration of the subject of colours, therefore, is of importance in architecture; merely with reference to a building, considered independently of every other object: but when we view a structure, as situated in the country, and surrounded by verdant scenery, the colour becomes of increased importance.

What, then, constitutes a whole in the disposition of colours? The prevalence of one colour throughout an elevation; and this one colour assuming throughout the same general character of form and tint. Thus, if the walls of one front of a house are built of yellow brick, the principle of a whole will be violated by building the other front, or the sides, of a brown or a red brick; or if the principal front of a house is of Portland stone, and the other sides of Yorkshire or Bath stone, or of brick, the principle of a whole, with regard to colours, will be totally destroyed. The same may be said of the colours of the roof; for if one side were of red tiles, and the other of blue slate, the principle of a whole would be as completely destroyed, in that part of the building, as in the other case it was in the walls. It may now be asked, how the principle of a whole, with regard to colours, is to be maintained in a building, the walls of which are of one colour, and the roof of another; for example, white or red walls supporting blue or black roofs? Undoubtedly, where the roofs are very conspicuous, and the colours both of the walls and roof very bright, the principle of a whole is totally destroyed. A barn-like, blue, slate roof, fresh from the slater, and red walls newly erected, or walls newly whitewashed, present a most discordant picture, and one which can only be reconciled to an eye conversant with harmonious colouring by the effects of time and the weather in neutralising both colours. Where the colours of the roof and of the walls are in unison, as in common brick buildings with tiled roofs, a whole, in respect to colours, is produced; and this whole would give much more satisfaction than blue slate roofs on white walls, were it not for certain prejudices against tiles on account of their commonness or meanness. The only way in which a building, having the colour of its roof totally different from that of its walls, can be rendered tolerable when quite new, is by concealing the roof, or flattening it to such an extent as to allow only a small portion of it to be seen. This is one reason why edifices with concealed roofs are generally more satisfactory to the eye, than those where the roofs are conspicuous. In old buildings, such as cathedrals, where the roofs and the walls are alike grey with age; in cottages, where earthen walls, or walls of stone of a grey or dingy colour, are covered with thatched roofs; or in cottages with brick walls, having tiled roofs, the whole produced, is, with respect to colours, an unobjectionable composition.

In the cases of buildings in the country which are surrounded by vegetation; or in others on eminences without trees, and backed by the sky, the colour of the building, including both the walls and roof, ought to be such as not only to form a whole of itself, but also to form a whole, when combined with the surrounding scenery, or the sky. Large conspicuous roofs, of a blue or of a green colour, are alike unsuitable for both situations; because blue does not harmonise with green, nor with the sky; and because green is monotonous in one case, and discordant in the other. The colour of a building, to be opposed to the sky, ought to be of some whitish, yellowish, reddish, or brownish tint; avoiding, as extremes, blue and green. The same observation will apply to buildings intended to be placed in the midst of verdant scenery, and more especially to such as are of small size, and which must of necessity, form component parts of a composition, and not a whole by themselves. At the same time, it must be observed, that small artificial objects, placed in the midst of natural ones, such as a white cottage with a blue slate roof in a wood, though considered in the abstract as inharmonious, yet in the reality, by the reflection of the lights and shadows of the surrounding objects, may be rendered harmonious, and consistent with the idea of a whole.

We shall enter on the subject of colours more in detail, when we come to develope the principle of variety, as applied to architectural composition. In the meantime, we are most anxious to impress on the minds of our young readers the great advantages to be derived from founding their knowledge of architecture on principles, rather than on rules. Hitherto, in this country, at least as far as we know, there has not been the slightest attempt to teach architecture on any other basis than that of precedent; and the consequence is, that the minds of most architects are incapable of tracing effects to first principles; that is, to those causes which operate altogether independently of what has been done by their predecessors. The metaphysics of architecture, however, as of all the arts of taste, and indeed of all arts whatever, form by far the most important part, with reference to their improvement; for how can the human mind be satisfied by those by whom its nature is not understood?

Art. II. *On the Harmony of Enrichment in Architecture.*
By E. Trotman, Esq.

We suspect that there is no error more common among the superficial observers of architectural composition, than the misapprehension of the character and application of enrichment. The eye of the vulgar is delighted with the greatest possible superabundance of carved work; and even the uninitiated man of taste, who has withal obtained some general ideas on the subject from buildings and from plates, may perhaps entertain the notion that the use of enrichment is scarcely governed by any considerations than those of pecuniary expenditure. And even where the observer was able to discriminate between the enrichments appropriate to different styles of architecture, there is little reason to expect that he would be able to discern upon what principles that appropriateness was founded; whether, indeed, it had any other basis than the conventional sanction of association, or were, on the other hand, supported on the fixed laws of fitness and harmony. To the architectural student, this subject, indeed, affords occasion for enquiries of peculiar interest, the result of which will be somewhat different to the impressions which he may have experienced upon the first investigation of architectural ornament, when a warm imagination suggested that little was to be done but to give free license to the rovings of the pencil. It too often happens, however, that this license is found to be least attainable when most needed; but were it otherwise, and could we at all times seize and embody the visions of richness and of beauty which may flit before the eye of the imagination, our success would be at best but very imperfect, vigorous as our compositions might chance to be, unless they were subjected to the test of fitness to the purposes of association, harmony, and expression. In what manner this principle of fitness is developed and sustained by examples of confessed authority, we will devote a few lines to investigate. It is indeed to be admitted at the outset, that the origin of most of the varieties of architectural enrichment is attributable to accident, the accidental varieties of climate and locality; but the same may be observed, in a great measure, as to the different styles themselves to which such matters of detail belong. It is for us, therefore, to notice how those circumstances, which, in the latter case, governed the suggestions of casualty, and, in the formation of style, imparted to them a specific complexion, exercised in the former also an assimilating influence, so as to invest details of common origin with a character inalienably appropriate to that of the style in general to which they stand applied. Thus while the productions of the vegetable world afforded the same patterns to the Greek and to the Roman artist, the uses made of them by the two were essentially different. In the taste which led the Greek to select the honeysuckle as the constant favourite, we recognise that love for beauty in its simpler form which governed the composition of their temples at large. In the graceful neatness which characterised the play of curves in that enrichment, and the delicate relief and finish which gave brilliancy to the contrast of its lights and shades, the same feeling prevails that imparted to the profile of every moulding its elegant contour. The lotus, the egg, the rose, the wreath, exhibited all, in form and in arrangement, additional instances of the simplicity that is at once understood, united with the beauty that is instinctively admired; and, where the richer foliage of the acanthus obtained admission, its treatment was conducted upon the same principles, without any complex masses or convolutions. It will be seen, therefore, how that spirit which educed from earlier prototypes, and from the exigencies of the case, the Grecian system, pervaded the composition of all the ornamental details applied to that system, and gave unity to the whole. With how little effect would the same embellishments have appeared in connection with the lavish grandeur of Roman composition! Here, then, the mind that dictated the display of large and picturesque masses and redundancy of moulding, seeking to impress by profusion rather than to captivate with grace, bestowed upon its details of foliage characteristics of correspondent boldness and exuberance. The enrichments for individual mouldings were now multiplied beyond enumeration: the honeysuckle, to be received at all, must be mingled with and supported by the acanthus; while the latter, again, was treated with a freedom unknown to Grecian foliage; its richly undulating masses being employed in frieze and panel with an unsparing hand. Festoons and garlands, coffers and flowers, frets and guilloches, were now used in unprecedented profusion and richness. In all such varieties of Roman ornament, we observe that the delicacy and smoothness of Greek enrichment were as much neglected, as its thinness was carefully avoided. The Grecian detail bespoke the cultivated genius of the geometrician; the Roman, that of the painter. To the former, indeed, belonged the charm of beauty in simple outline; to the latter pertained the fulness and the force which result from grouping of masses, and breadth of light and shade. While, then, a little practice will enable the student to detect those peculiarities which constitute the difference between the Grecian and the Roman treatment of ornamental foliage, it will be well for him to follow out the examination of the causes of this difference, which will lead to the conviction that the characteristics of distinction are not arbitrary, but are the consequence of that peculiarity of mind which, pervading all the systems of architectural practice, gave to the whole unity and decision; a peculiarity of mind, in the case of Roman art, strikingly national, which, after the reception of the first fundamental principles from the taste of the Greeks, forbade submission to the dictates of any foreign school as to the cultivation of those principles, knowing no other law than the suggestions of splendid schemes and inexhaustible resources.

A still more powerful illustration of the manner in which the genius of an individual system thus governs the character of its enriched details, with a view to the preservation of unity, will be displayed upon an examination of the composition of foliage in the great style of northern climes, and of what we are accustomed to call the dark ages. The period, indeed, that gave birth to and fostered the style of pointed architecture, was confessedly one of moral and of literary darkness; but we think it is undeniable that the flights of the imagination in search of the wild and the awful are, for the most part, in the inverse proportion to the depth of scientific knowledge and the extent of matter-of-fact calculation. Thus it was with the style of our Henries and Edwards; the authors of which, in attaining for their works that inimitable sublimity which affects every heart, looked not abroad for the helping hand of classic accomplishment, but regulated their designs by the analogies of nature and by the dictates of experience. The genius of their great style was that of mysterious grandeur. It was in the exhibition of this characteristic that its resources were most fully and advantageously developed, however successfully they were applied to the attainment of all minor purposes of the picturesque and the beautiful. As compared with the mathematically proportioned architecture of preceding ages and of classic lands, this system presents itself to the imagination rather as the creation of the mighty spirits of the air, than of the earth-born race of man. The ponderous materials that remain suspended aloft, as if thrown forth in the playfulness of some invisible hand, whose power arrested them ere they fell, and fixed them in their course, bespeak an agency like that which is fabled to sustain the coffin of the Arabian prophet, rather than the calculating skill of the labouring artisan. How do the spreading vaults of pointed architecture, its flying buttresses, its massive pendants, its slender shafts, its widely ramified windows, its overhanging tabernacles, proclaim the daring of that power which could give order to the masonry, the wondrousness of that hand which could bestow the durability of ages on fabrications to all appearance so perilously slight! It were itself the work of a lengthened essay, to notice the means by which all the details of this style are made tributary to the production of this effect of the magically sublime. Our business is at present more especially with the character of its ornaments of foliage, which are equal in beauty, and superior in variety and in nature, to those of other styles, while they display an adaptation to harmony of effect altogether admirable. This adaptation is not only the result of that freedom of composition for which these accessories are remarkable, but is more particularly the consequence of that peculiar management of light and shade by which Gothic foliage is distinguished from every other kind. In other styles, when the outline of a piece of foliage is fully drawn out, the shadows follow of course in the direction of the stems and their indentations; here, however, the shadows usually cross the lines of the stems and veins of the leaves, generally assuming a circular form, and sometimes describing a succession of concentric curves, like the rippling of the disturbed water where a stone has fallen. Hence an elaborate piece of foliage, in the best period of the art, is strongly marked with the shadows of knobs and protuberances, its edges at the same time being less finished and defined than those of classic composition. All this, indeed, every architect knows, and every student may know who has access to our cathedral or collegiate antiquities, or who, in the absence of this advantage, can refer to the works of Halfpenny, Pugin, Atkinson, Shaw, and others, upon this subject. Our object is especially to remark that this peculiarity of light and shade is strikingly in accordance with the genius of the pointed style. It is not, indeed, favourable to our immediate comprehension of the subject of design; no details in this style are so, otherwise the effect of the mysterious, as one great attribute of the system, would be at an end. Its excellence is, that, while it offers to the eye an aspect of great richness, from the playful sprinkling of shadows, it retains the interest of the beholder by developing the figure of the ornament gradually upon a more careful examination, presenting to him a double instead of a simple picture; one in the distribution of chiaro-scuro, and the other in the composition of outline. Hence, after the inspection of this as well as all other ornamental detail which contributes to the charms of pointed architecture, the casual observer will confess that an effect of peculiar power has been produced upon his mind; but, on his endeavouring to recall the means by which it has been gained, he will find his efforts altogether eluded. This is not to be done by confusion of decorative forms: it is, on the other hand, a remarkable exemplification of the adaptation of methods to the attainment of the great ends of harmony; an instance of that architectural might of our forefathers, the effects of which are as irresistible, as its principles are deep and recondite. An accurate observation of these points of distinction between the enrichments of foliage peculiar to different styles is, of course, fundamentally necessary to correct composition; and that, as we have endeavoured to show, not on the ground merely of that habit of association which makes us identify certain forms of ornament as appropriate to certain systems, but more especially, also, on account of that innate fitness of parts to the production of unity in the whole, which distinguished ancient art; a characteristic resulting from the unity of feelings, wants, and circumstances, which affected the minds of those who created the several styles; a characteristic, also, which cannot safely be disregarded, until it shall have been proved that the successful cultivation of any particular mode of architecture depends upon some other principle than that of the use of correct component parts under a correct arrangement.

We had intended to notice some farther matters as affecting the *application* of ornament; our limits, however, forbid us at present to proceed; and we leave the reader, therefore, to examine and dilate upon the principle of generic fitness which we have here laid down, as he may find opportunity.

Furnival's Inn, July 15. 1834.

Art. III. *The Elements of Grecian and Roman Architecture, practically explained to the General Reader.* By Mr. Robertson.

(*Continued from* p. 158.)

Of *the Grecian Orders respectively.* — The *Grecian Doric* was the first order which was invented; and in the simplicity of its forms there are many traces of the essential parts necessary in the construction of the primitive hut; having the triglyphs in the frieze as representatives of the joists; and, as representatives of the rafters, what are called mutules in the under side of the cornice, with inclined soffits to show their inclination in the roof, and generally chiseled to give a sort of roughness, in imitation of the ends of the rafters. (See the under side of the cornice, directly over *d*, in fig. 10. p. 25.) In the first age of this order, the columns were extremely short in proportion to their width, and they were placed on the floor, without either pedestal or base: indeed, the shortness of the shaft, and the tapering form, being the frustrum of a cone, are still characteristics of this order. The column was originally without flutings, and the capital exceedingly simple, having no annulets to separate it from the shaft: a very rough, ill-shaped, quarter-round moulding, bearing the abacus, was employed instead of the echinus; and its projection did not exceed the lower diameter of the column. In the best examples of this order, the column is from five to six diameters in height; the shaft is without a base, but is occasionally set on a plinth, and it has twenty elliptical flutings, that meet in a sharp edge without any fillets to divide them. The capital is one half of a diameter in height, and very simple; having only a plain square abacus supported by a very flat ovolo of great projection, and five or six annulets to separate it from the shaft. The distinguishing features of the entablature are, the triglyphs in the frieze and the mutules in the cornice. The architrave and frieze occupy each more than one third of the whole height of the entablature; the remainder being given to the cornice. The peculiar grandeur which belongs exclusively to this order renders it well adapted for situations where grave solidity and solemnity are desired. (See fig. 10. in p. 25.)

The *Grecian Ionic* (see fig. 11. in p. 26.), which is said to have been invented by the inhabitants of Asiatic Greece, is the second of the Grecian orders. The height of the column is generally less than that of the Roman Ionic; but the entablature is much bolder, and more simple, being composed of fewer parts. The characteristic features are the volutes of the capital, which are placed flat on the column, and the enriched ovolo which connects them. The Grecian Ionic is generally fluted; and it has an air of grandeur, which is, perhaps, not so fully possessed by the Roman Ionic. The best examples are those which are copied exactly from the temple of Ilissus. This order, from its graceful appearance, is very suitably employed in the interior of dwellings; and externally in porticoes, colonnades, &c. The details of the Ionic orders will be more fully explained under the head of Roman Ionic. (p. 263.)

The *Grecian Corinthian* (*fig.* 122.), which is a perfect masterpiece of art, and which is said to have been invented by an Athenian sculptor (though this has latterly been much disputed), is the third and last of the Grecian orders. The most striking feature is the capital, which is of great height, and is enriched with leaves. Both the Greeks and Romans executed this order, in their temples and public buildings, in the most highly decorated manner. The entablature was richly ornamented; having its architrave with three fascias of unequal height, and the frieze decorated with foliage; the bed mouldings of the cornice, and the mouldings of the architrave, were highly enriched; and the column was fluted. Although the general property of this order is, that it admits of the greatest degree of ornament, it is frequently executed with much propriety in the most plain and ⁊le manner. Its slender delicacy advances it to the highest

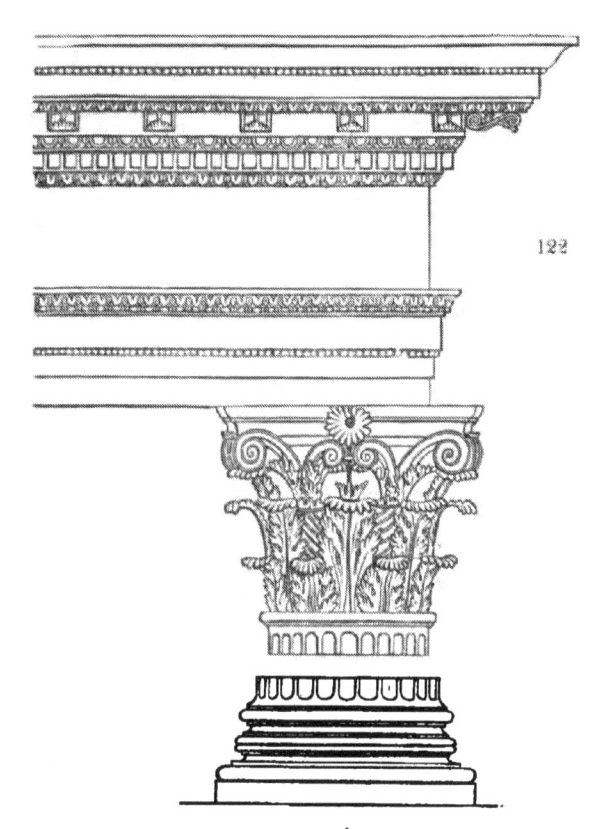

practically explained to the General Reader. 261

degree of lightness consistent with solidity; for it is generally admitted that a column of wood, or stone, of more than ten diameters in height, has the appearance of being incapable of supporting an entablature. This order appears to have been better understood, and more happily executed, by the Romans, than any of the other Grecian orders; and, as the proportions of the Grecian Corinthian are exactly the same as those of the Roman Corinthian, I shall describe its other characteristics under that head. (p. 268.)

Of the Roman Orders respectively. — The *Tuscan* (see fig. 14. in p. 30.) is the most massive and solid of all the Roman orders; and, as it is composed of but few parts, and these without ornament, its characteristic features are massive proportions and great simplicity. It is said to have been invented in Tuscany; but modern writers have contended that the Etruscans have, in its composition, only slightly deviated from the Doric order; because, when the latter is divested of its triglyphs, mutules, &c., it is nearly the same in appearance as the Tuscan. The chief objects of the Tuscan order seem to be utility and economy; as, while it is stronger, it is at the same time more easily executed than any of the other orders. The Tuscan order is most fitly employed in any edifice expressive of strength; such as prisons, markets, barracks, &c. The column, including the base and capital, is seven diameters in height; and, indeed, no order of more massive dimensions can be employed with advantage in any elegant edifice, except the Grecian Doric, which is rendered light by its great diminution.

The *Roman Doric* (*fig.* 123.) is characterised by its bold and massive appearance; and its distinguishing features are the

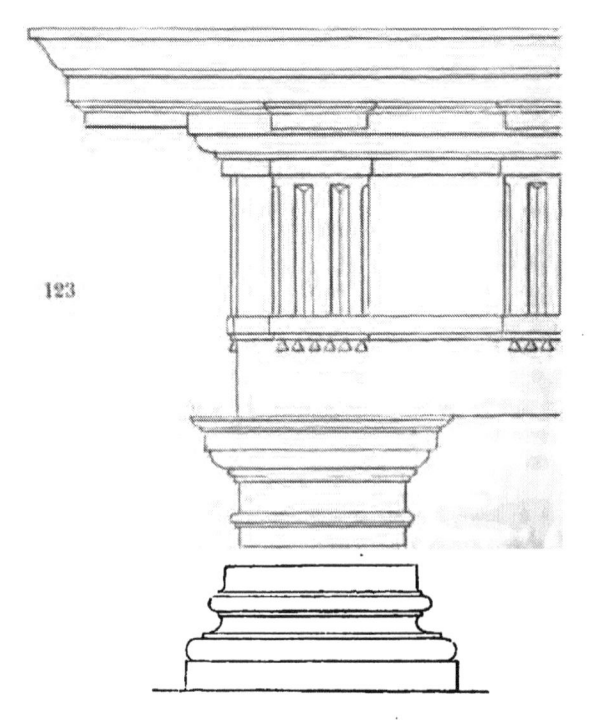

123

channeled projecting intervals in the frieze, called triglyphs. These are placed over the centre of the columns: they serve to regulate the intercolumniations, and are at such distances that the metopes, which are the spaces between the triglyphs, are left exactly square. This order is next in strength to the Tuscan; but it is less simple in expression, and possesses more symmetry in its members. The column is frequently fluted, like that of the Grecian Doric, and is sometimes placed on a base only, but generally on a base and plinth: the height of the column, including the base and capital, is eight diameters. This order may be well employed in churches, cemeteries, and in commercial structures, where strength and security, combined with gracefulness, are the desired objects.

The *Roman Ionic* is distinguished by the volutes or scrolls of the capital; and in this particular differs essentially from the Grecian Ionic. In the latter, the volutes are placed flat on the shaft, as before observed, and are seen in the front and in the rear, each side having the appearance of a baluster; but the Roman Ionic capital has the volutes placed diagonally, or on the angles, with the abacus hollowed out on the four sides, and consequently presenting the same appearance at the sides as in the front and rear. The pedestal in this order is higher in proportion, and less simple in the combination of its parts, than in the Doric. The column is frequently fluted; and, when this is the case, there are twenty-four flutings, of a semicircular form, having small intermediate fillets to separate them. The column, including the base and capital, is generally nine diameters in height. The light and graceful appearance of this order is a medium between the grave massive character of the Doric and the elegant richness and delicacy of the Corinthian, and it is well employed, like the Grecian Ionic, in the interior of dwellings; or externally, where it is placed over the Doric order.

The *Roman Corinthian*, like its Grecian prototype, is characterised by the height of its capital being in general more than one diameter of its column, and by the delicacy of its ornaments, which are leaves supporting small volutes. The capital assumes the form of a vase, the lower part of which has two rows of leaves, one row above the other, and eight in each row; the upper part has a third row of leaves, which support eight small volutes, and these in their turn support a decorated concave abacus. The other characteristics of this order are, the divisions of the cornice, which has both modillions and dentils; the decorated frieze; and the unequal divisions of the architrave. The column, including the base and capital, is ten diameters in height. This order (as before observed) admits of the highest degree of enrichment; and, in all cases, it has an air of dignity combined with beauty. It may be well employed in magnificent edifices, both externally and internally.

The *Composite* (*fig.* 124.) is, as its title imports, a composition, and it is formed from the Corinthian and Ionic orders. The capital, like that of the Corinthian, is in the form of a vase, having two ranges of acanthus leaves: it is distinguished from the Corinthian capital by having the scrolls or volutes as well as the enriched ovolo of the Ionic; but in other respects the column is similar to the Corinthian, both in its general proportions and in the details of its mouldings. The entablature is frequently made more simple than that of the Corinthian, and is composed

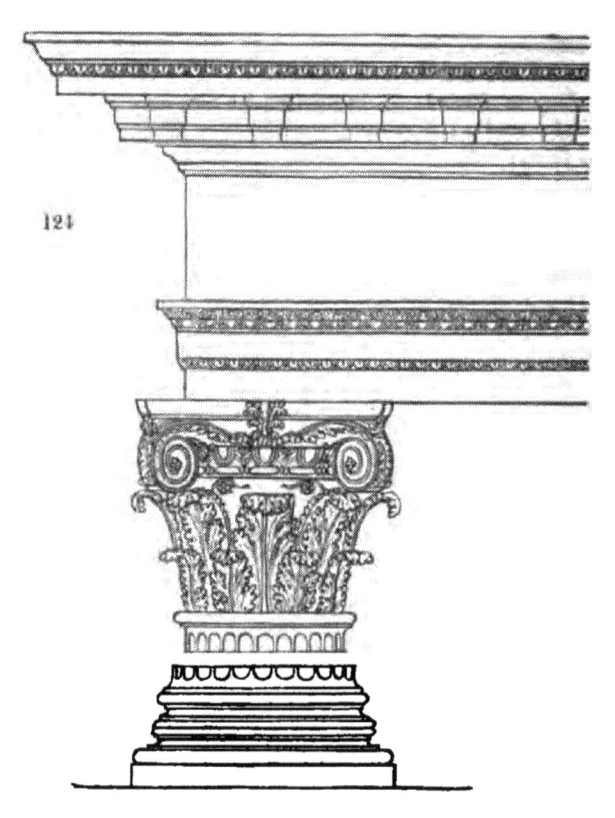

of fewer parts; the cornice has the blocks and dentils of the Ionic, and the architrave has a single fascia. While the members of the Corinthian predominate in the column, those of the Ionic are most conspicuous in the entablature. It has been justly disputed whether the Composite deserves the name of a distinct order; and it has been considered even less entitled to this epithet than the Tuscan, which, as before observed, is only a simplification of the Doric. The three Grecian orders possess all that is included in the five Roman orders; for, while the Doric at one extreme is expressive of strength and solidity, and the Corinthian at the other extreme is expressive of delicacy and richness, the Ionic, as an intermediate order, is expressive of grace and elegance. A variety of orders, of the Composite kind, have been invented by the Romans, having the proportions of the Corinthian, but each differing in the ornaments adorning the capital. The order generally termed the Composite has been selected, by architectural writers, from the others, and is of the general appearance described and figured above. This order is never seen to advantage in connection with the Corinthian; and the inventors of it seem to have been aware of this, for they generally employed it in the erection of triumphal arches, theatres, and other structures, where it was quite unconnected with the other orders.

The Diminution of Columns. — The shafts of all the columns of the five orders are diminished in diameter as they rise. The columns of the ancients were tapered from the base to the capital in a straight line, in imitation of trees; but in the best examples there is a swelling in the middle of the shaft: indeed, this convexity is necessary to prevent an optical delusion which would make the sides of the frustum of a cone, when of a considerable height and tapering in straight lines, to appear concave. The general way of diminishing columns is to commence the diminution at one third of the height of the shaft, and to make it, at the top, not less than one eighth nor more than one sixth of the upper diameter.

Pilasters must not be regarded as imitations of columns, as they owe their origin to the necessity of giving more solidity to the walls of the cella (the part enclosed by walls, and sometimes called naos) of Grecian temples, in which they were originally used merely as supports, without either base or capital. Subsequently, in order to give pilasters more elegance, as well as to ornament the walls of the cella, a base and capital were added to them; differing, however, from those of the columns with which they were connected. The Romans were the first who gave the same base and capital to pilasters as those of the columns behind which they were placed; and modern architects have not only followed this practice, but have given them the same proportions, ornaments, names, &c., as are given to the columns with which they are associated. The Romans frequently entirely detached the pilasters from the wall against which they were placed, and as frequently employed them without any columns being placed before them; they have also used them in a variety of ways in connection with insulated columns.

In the best examples of the present day, pilasters have their bases, capitals, and entablatures the same height as those of columns; but, while the proportion is the same, as it regards the height of capitals, the breadths are different, and the developement of the form of a pilaster gives a greater space to each of its faces, because it is quadrangular.

Pilasters are distinguished, in the same manner as columns, by the names of Tuscan, Doric, Ionic, and Corinthian; and, when employed in connection with columns, they are frequently diminished in the same proportion as the columns themselves. When they are placed very near the columns in front of them, they ought to project from the wall about one eighth of their diameter; but, in large porticoes or peristyles, where they are placed at the distance of 8 ft. or 10 ft. behind the columns, their projection must not be less than one sixth of their diameter; and their projection, when on a line with columns, should be regulated by that of the latter. In the last-mentioned case, when the entablature is continued without breaks over both pilasters and columns, the former are diminished on the front face only, leaving the sides perpendicular. When pilasters are employed alone in an architectural composition, their projection ought not to be less than one fourth of their diameter, as this gives great regularity to the returned parts of capitals, especially when these are of the Corinthian order. Half pilasters are frequently used, two of which meet in internal angles; but the irregularity of the cornice, when thus employed, shows the necessity of avoiding the practice whenever it is possible to do so. Pilasters, like columns, are occasionally fluted; but the exact number of the flutes is not determined by antique examples: they are, however, always employed in uneven numbers; and when the pilaster projects less than half a diameter, the flutings are never made in the returned part.

Bayswater, August, 1834.

ART. IV. *Architectural Maxims.*

ARCHITECTURAL *Criticism*, when it explains to what circumstances buildings owe their power of pleasing, and what tends to increase and what to diminish that power, is of great value to the practical architect, and a great source of instruction and enjoyment to the amateur. It teaches the architect what he has to avoid, and what he has to imitate; by what different modes of composition he can produce the same effects; or how to produce different effects by similar modes of composition. (*Woods.*)

Imitation in Architecture. — There are two modes of imitating the architecture of other countries; one true and legitimate, the other false and heterodox. The true mode is less an imitation than an adoption; being the reception, in the manner of an alphabet, of the system, rules, and taste of a foreign style, and adapting them to native habits and customs. Thus it was that the Romans adopted the architecture of Greece, converting the orders of Attica to the uses, habits, and climate of Italy. (*Elmes.*)

Criterion of Excellence in Architecture. — We may judge of details by rule; but the only true method of estimating the excellence of an architectural composition is by the sentiment it produces upon a well-regulated and cultivated mind and heart in a healthy body. To render this criterion the more certain, repeat the inspection under different circumstances. (*Woods.*)

REVIEWS.

ART. I. *Essay on the Architecture of the Hindús.* By Rám Ráz, Native Judge and Magistrate at Bangalore, Corresponding Member of the Royal Asiatic Society of Great Britain and Ireland. 4to, pp. 64, 48 plates. London, 1834. 1*l.* 11*s.* 6*d.*

THIS work, if we are not mistaken, will go far towards altering the generally received hypothesis respecting Hindú architecture. Most writers, among whom is included Quatremère de Quincy as the most eminent, consider Indian architecture as of Egyptian origin; but it is clear, from the work before us, that it has a much closer affinity to Grecian architecture than to that of Egypt, or of any other country. It is proper to state, however, that there are three tolerably distinct kinds of architecture existing in India. First, the architecture of the caves, which may very fairly be considered as having some analogy to that of Egypt, and which Quatremère de Quincy appears to confound with the architecture of the pagodas; secondly, the Gothic or Saracenic architecture of India, supposed to have been introduced by the Mahometans; and, thirdly, the Hindú architecture described by Rám Ráz.

Rám Ráz, who died in India before his work was published, was induced to undertake it as a topic " worthy of his abilities and talents," by Richard Clarke, Esq., a member of the Royal Asiatic Society. Rám Ráz, though descended from kings, was born of poor parents; and owed the little education which he received, when a boy, to mere chance: a portion of that education, however, consisted in learning to read and write the English language. He began life as a clerk to the adjutant of a native regiment; and rose in the civil service till he attracted the attention of a public functionary, who procured for him the responsible and highly honourable post of judge and magistrate. He knew the Sanscrit, and several of the native dialects; and also algebra, geometry, geography, and astronomy. We mention these particulars, to enable the reader to form his own opinion of the competency of Rám Ráz to produce a work on architecture. Speaking of his undertaking in the preface, he observes: —

" The subject of Hindú architecture is curious, and highly deserving the attention of the antiquarian and the philosopher. A correct account and accurate elucidation of the art of building practised by the Hindús must throw considerable light on the early progress of architecture in general. Some of the western authors have traced a certain resemblance in the leading features of the buildings in Egypt and India, and have thence concluded that there has very early been a communication of architectural knowledge between the two countries. But it is not altogether improbable that this resemblance may be merely owing to accident; inasmuch as, in architecture as well as in every other art indispensably necessary to the comfort of mankind, two or more nations may possess something in common, without having any intercourse with each other; for, the wants felt by man being the same, it is not surprising that the remedies resorted to for supplying them should be also similar or nearly so. If, on the other hand, however, both these countries had actually any communication in early ages, it is hard to determine which of them may have been indebted to the other. The western writers on antiquities have not placed this matter beyond a doubt; and, for my own part, I will not venture to affirm any thing with certainty, until I have collected sufficient information to form an opinion as to this alleged affinity in the architecture of Egypt and India. I humbly presume, therefore, that, until the *Silpa Sástra* (architecture) of the Hindús is correctly illustrated and laid before the public, the question as to whether the art owes its origin to the one or the other of the two countries, must remain problematical." (p. xiii.)

In the essay, we are informed, as we are in Columella and Vitruvius, respecting the agricultural and architectural writers of the Greeks and Romans, that the Hindús had been in possession of numerous treatises on architecture and sculpture, but that very few traces of them remain. The names are given of nine out of forty or fifty treatises, of which some shattered fragments may still be found in Southern India. One of these, entitled *Mánasára*, is the most perfect that now exists. It treats at most length on building sacred edifices, but includes private dwellings, villages, and cities; embracing a variety of relative topics, distributed through fifty-eight chapters. The date of this work is unknown; but the antiquity given to it by tradition is altogether extravagant, some placing it three or four centuries before Christ, and others ten! Of the Mánasára, and other fragments of treatises, Rám Ráz observes, that " the architectural portions of them, if divested of all the extraneous matter with which they abound, contain little more than a dry detail of the technical names, and of the proportions of the several members of a sacred edifice. Considerable portions of these works are replete with minute descriptions of religious rites to be performed on various occasions, from the commencement till the completion of a building; as well as rules and aphorisms for predicting the future destiny of the builder." (p. 12.)

The first chapter of the Mánasára treats of the several measurements used in architecture, sculpture, &c.; and the second, of the qualities of an architect (*sthapati*), who, as Vitruvius recommends, is required to be " conversant in all sciences;" and, farther, to be " ever attentive to his avocations; of an unblemished character; generous, sincere, and devoid of enmity or jealousy." (p. 14.) Nearly similar qualifications are required for the surveyor or measurer (*sútragrahi*), and most of them for the joiner and the carpenter:—" It is impossible to build houses without the aid of these four descriptions of artisans: therefore, let the enlightened twice-born (the Brahmins, or men of the first class, &c.) gratify them in every respect. Woe to those who dwell in a house not built according to the proportions of symmetry." (p. 15.) The third chapter treats of the nature and quality of ground on which buildings are to be erected; it is very copious and very curious. Minute directions are given for constructing a plough, and for ploughing the ground on which the house is to be built. This being done, " let sesamum seeds, pulse, and kidneybeans be sown, with incantations pronounced over them; and let due reverence be paid to the spiritual teacher; and let the oxen, and the plough to which they are attached, be presented to him. When the crops are matured, let them be grazed on by cattle, and let cows remain on them for one or two nights. The ground will become purified by the froth flowing from the mouths of the cows, and by their ordure; after which, you may commence building in the centre thereof." (p. 19.) A long chapter gives directions for ascertaining the cardinal points by means of a gnomon, in order to place the building in a particular position relatively to the east. Passing over a number of chapters, Rám Ráz next notices the Hindú orders, which, he says, consist of four principal parts; namely, the pedestal, the base, the pillar or column, and the entablature. The Hindú architects, like those of Europe, include the base and capital when they take the height of the pillar or column. They also compare the various parts of an order to the several parts of the human body, much in the same manner as is done by Vitruvius.

There are twelve different descriptions of *mouldings* used in the composition of pedestals and bases, as shown in *fig.* 125. Of these, the name of the circular kinds (marked 10 in the figure), *cumuda*, signifies literally *Nymphæ'a esculénta*, and corresponds with the astragal, bead, and torus mouldings of the Grecian orders. The *padma* moulding (11), literally *Lòtus*, is supposed to resemble a petal of that flower. The mouldings (1 to 9) are all quadrangular, and answer to the Grecian fillets and plinths. A *capotum* (12) is the section of a moulding made in the form of a pigeon's head, from which it takes its name. It is a crowning member of cornices, pedestals, and entablatures; the beak of the bird serving the purpose of a spout to throw off the water falling on the cornice, and in this respect performing the office of the Grecian corona.

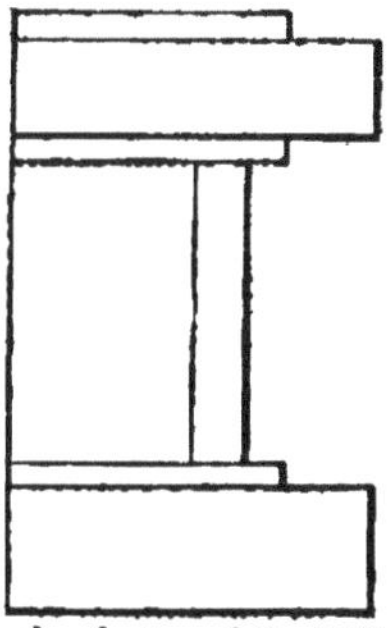

For the composition of *pedestals*, the Hindú architects, we are informed, have " a multiplicity of contradictory rules," as the reader may easily conceive by glancing at *fig.* 126., which is one of the simplest, and *fig.* 127., which is one of the more elaborate of twelve examples given by our author in his first plate. The rules for proportioning the different parts of these pedestals are given at great length, and we recommend them to the perusal of those who are learned in such matters.

Of *bases*, twenty-eight different specimens are given, of which *fig.* 128. is the most simple, and *fig.* 129. the most elaborate.

The chapter on *pillars* treats of their various forms, dimensions, and ornaments. " Let the height of a pillar," says Mánasára, " be divided into twelve, eleven, ten, nine, or eight parts, and one be taken for the breadth of the foot of the shaft; and, the same being divided again by a number of parts, of which the height of the pillar may consist, let the upper extremity of it be diminished by one of those parts respectively." Cásyapa, another Hindú architect, says, " the height of the pillars may be three times that of the base, or six or eight times that of the pedestal. The breadth of the pillar may be a sixth, seventh, eighth, ninth, or tenth part of its height; if it be made of wood or stone, one third or one fourth; or one sixth of the height, if it be a pilaster joined to a wall." (p. 29.) Pillars may be square, or octangular, or with sixteen, with five, or with six sides; or cylindrical. The whole shaft may be of the same form; or, in pillars of other forms than square, the bottom, middle, and top may be quadrangular, and the intermediate spaces of other forms. Directions are given for ornamenting columns. Columns are divided into seven sorts or orders, according to the number of diameters which they are in height; the first sort is six diameters in height, with a high base and pedestal, and an entablature of more than half the altitude of the column. The capital to this order is equal in height to the upper diameter of the shaft, and its projection is equal to its height; and so on.

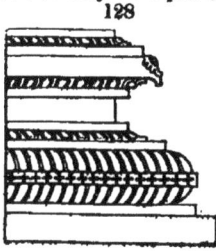

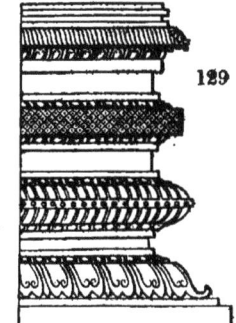

In comparing the Hindú orders with those of Egypt, Greece, and Rome, Rám Ráz observes: —

" The second sort of column in the Hindú architecture may be compared with the Tuscan, the third with the Doric, the fourth with the Ionic, and the fifth with the Corinthian or Composite pillar. This affinity between the columns of India and of Rome and Greece is so striking, that one would be apt to ascribe it to something more than mere chance: but there are other columns in the Indian architecture not only one diameter lower than the Tuscan, but from one to two diameters higher than the Composite.

" The Egyptian columns appear to have no fixed proportion in regard to thickness and height. In some of the specimens of the ruins of Upper Egypt, the height of the columns consists of from four to six times the lower diameter; which last proportion coincides with that of the first sort of the Indian pillar. The orders of India and of Greece and Rome are remarkable for the beautiful effect of their proportions; a circumstance to which little regard has been paid by the Egyptians. Both the Indian and Grecian columns are diminished gradually in their diameter, from the base to the summit of the shaft; a practice which has never been observed in the Egyptian: on the contrary, a diametrically opposite rule has been observed in their shafts, which are made narrower at the bottom than at the top, and placed upon a square or round plinth. The proportion in which the diminution at the top of the columns of the two former is made, seems to have been regulated by the same principle, though not by the same rule. The general rule adopted by the Hindú architects in this respect is, that the thickness at the bottom, being divided into as many parts as there are diameters in the whole height of the column, one of these parts is invariably diminished at the top; but in the Grecian and Roman architecture, the diameter of the upper part of the shaft, in a column of 15 ft. in height, is made one sixth less than its thickness at the base; and in a column of 50 ft. the diminution is one eighth. The higher the columns are, the less they diminish, because the apparent diminution of the diameter in columns of the same proportion is always greater according to their height; and this principle is supposed to have been discovered with great scientific skill, and is adduced as one of the proofs of the highly refined taste of the Greeks: but we observe that precepts derived from the same principle have been taught and practised in India from time immemorial.

" The plan of the Grecian and Roman columns is always round; but the plan of the Hindú columns admits of every shape, and is frequently found in the quadrangular and octangular form, and richly adorned with sculptured ornaments. The form of the Egyptian pillars, too, is circular, and their shafts are often fluted like the Corinthian; but the fluting of the Indian column resembles neither the one nor the other. The decorations of the Egyptian columns often consist in representations of ' a bundle of reeds,' tied up with a cord on the top, having a square stone placed over it; in some specimens are also found bindings or fillets in various parts of the shaft, and in the intervals between them reeds and hieroglyphics are represented. But there is nothing like these ornaments in the Indian orders, except in the columns found in the excavated temple of Elephanta and some other places, and which differ materially from those employed in other situations in Hindústan. There are no fixed intercolumniations in the Hindú architecture, as are found in the Grecian; but the spaces allowed between pillar and pillar in different Hindú buildings are found nearly to coincide with the Grecian mode of intercolumniations, though in too many instances they differ widely from it, and the same may, perhaps, be said of the Egyptian colonnades.

" The Indian pedestals and bases are made more systematically, and afford by far a greater variety of proportions and ornaments, than the Grecian and Roman. In the European architecture, the forms and dimensions of the pedestals and bases are fixed by invariable rules, with respect to the orders in which they are employed; but in the Indian, the choice is left to the option of the artists. The capitals of the Grecian columns invariably mark the distinction of the several orders: those of the Indian are varied at pleasure, though not without regard to the diameter and length of the shaft; and the forms of the plainest of them, though they have in reality no-

130

thing in common with the Grecian orders, are found at a distant view to bear some resemblance to the Doric and Ionic capitals; but those of a more elaborate kind are sometimes so overloaded with a sort of filigree ornaments, as to destroy the effect of the beautiful proportions of the whole. The Egyptian capitals, on the other hand, are formed into elegant vase shapes, decorated with the stalks, leaves, and blossoms of the lotus, and occasionally with palm leaves, which latter ornaments are supposed to have given the first idea of the Corinthian capitals. And in some specimens, the Egyptian capital is composed of the representation of the head of the goddess Isis. The entablature of the Indian order admits of little variety, as well in its composition as in its relative proportions; whereas the same member, in the Grecian and Roman architecture, is varied for each order both in form and magnitude. The massiveness of the Indian entablature offers a striking contrast to the lightness of the Grecian; but the richness of the former may be said to be unrivalled.

"In the existing treatises on Hindú architecture, no mention is made of anything like a substitution of human figures for columns to support the entablature, but the shaft is directed to be adorned with the figures of demons and animals; yet various examples are to be met with in which human figures, as well as representations of animals, are employed in bold relief in the sides of pillars in temples and porticoes, but by no means like those found in Egyptian architecture. The antiquity of this invention in India is not determined, but the Grecian architects refer the origin of their caryatides to the commemoration of their captivity of the Caryan women, while others assert that it was derived from an Egyptian source." (p. 40.)

For the forms and details of the different orders of Hindú columns, we must refer to the work itself. We cannot, however, resist the temptation of giving two specimens of columns, one with a pedestal, and the other without. (*figs.* 130. and 131.)

The ninth chapter of Mánasára treats of villages and towns, of which there are said to be eight sorts; and plans of several of these are given. All of them are surrounded by walls and ditches for protection: some of the villages are exclusively for brahmins; others for hermits; one for holy mendicants; and so on. Speaking of private houses or mansions for these villages, it is said that they may consist of from one to nine stories, according to the rank of the persons for whom they are built. "The lower class of persons must on no account construct their houses of more than a single story, or ground floor." Outcasts are to live in huts, not nearer any village than 4000 yards. Every house is to have a raised seat or pedestal on each side of the door. A whole page of this chapter, it is stated, is taking up in enumerating the various sorts of gifts and donations [*] to be made to the artists on the completion of an edifice; and, finally, in denouncing dire misfortunes to those who withhold such presents from them. (p. 47.)

The next chapter treats of cities, to which succeed twelve successive chapters on vimanas, or pyramidal temples, gopuras, or pyramidal gateways, and on the great pagoda, or monastery, as it would be called in Europe, of Tiruvalúr. The extracts from these chapters are illustrated by numerous beautifully lithographed plates, for which we must refer the architect to the work itself. The vimanas and gopuras vary in height from one to sixteen stories, and they are made round, quadrangular, or with six or eight sides. "The form of the edifice may be uniformly the same from the basement to the summit, whether it be square, oblong, circular, oval, or the like; or it may be of a mixed nature, composed partly of the one, and partly of another form." (p. 28.) These temples are divided into five sorts with respect to their magnitude: namely, the moderate, the bulky, the victorious, the admirable, and the universally beloved. The dimensions and proportions of a number of examples are given, commencing with a vimana of a single story, and terminating with one of fifteen stories; there are also gopuras of from one to twelve stories, and a ground plan and isometrical elevation of the large pagoda before mentioned, and of which there is a beautiful model in the Museum of the Royal Asiatic Society. The work concludes with directions for preparing *chunam*, or cement, as practised by the Hindû artisans of the present day.

Chunam is made from gravelly limestone, or from shells washed out of saltwater marshes, burnt with charcoal, and then powdered. The powder is mixed with clean, sharp, river sand, in various proportions, according to the use for which it is intended. For finer works, the powder

---

[*] The practice of giving a present to the builder, in addition to the sum contracted for, was formerly common in Europe. In the contract for the building of Catterick church, Yorkshire, dated 1412 (see p. 273.), there is a clause stating that, if the work is completed by a certain time, the money is to be paid to the builder, and a cast-off gown of his employer's given to him into the bargain. (For farther instances, see the work alluded to, p. 11.)

is very finely ground, and the water used in preparing it for mortar is generally mixed with molasses or coarse sugar. It seems this article is considered by modern practitioners, " who have had the most extensive practice in building, as an indispensable ingredient in a durable and hard cement."

It is remarkable, that, throughout the whole work, not a single word occurs on the subject of arches, though many of the vimanas and gopuras terminate in domes; there are, however, no arched openings, as doors or windows, and this circumstance seems another indication of the affinity between the Hindú style and that of Greece.

In conclusion, we have to observe that this work is curious in a historical point of view, as a record of a style of architecture which has no more chance of being revived, than the religion of the people to whom it belonged has of being perpetuated. The latter is overcharged with superstitious observances, only calculated for an age of general ignorance; and the former consists chiefly of gorgeous structures, overlaid with ornament, which could only be erected under a despotic hierarchy or monarchy. Such structures, indeed, could only excite the admiration and wonder of an abject people: for, in ages of darkness, though refined beauty makes no impression on the people composing the mass of society, they are easily awed by obvious indications of great wealth and power; they require something to fear and serve, rather than something to love and enjoy. In a historical point of view, the work of Rám Ráz is likely to be eminently useful to the painter, the scene decorator, &c., and it may afford some hints for the composition of ornaments to the architect, the cabinet-maker, and the designers of ornaments for different descriptions of manufactures. There is hardly any design in the work that we should consider deserving of being copied exactly, but the manner of some of the designs might be imitated and purified. The Royal Asiatic Society has rendered the British public a valuable service, in publishing so original and expensive a work at so low a price; and there can be no doubt the volume will find its way into every good architectural library.

ART. II. *Catterick Church, in the County of York; a correct Copy of the Contract for its Building, dated in* 1412; *illustrated with Remarks and Notes,* by the Rev. James Raine, M.A., Librarian of Durham Cathedral, &c.: *and with* 13 *Plates of Views, Elevations, and Details,* by Anthony Salvin, Esq. F.S.A., Architect. 4to, pp. 22. London, 1834.

WE cannot give a better idea of this work than by quoting a part of the introduction; and we request the reader to contrast the enthusiasm therein displayed for the Gothic style, with that shown for the Grecian, by the German architect Klenze, in a passage from one of his works, given p. 275., from the *Foreign Quarterly Review* for July, 1834: —

" The object of the present publication is to make known the original contract for the building of Catterick church, in Yorkshire, dated in 1412; of which we undertake to give an accurate transcript, with notes and explanations, and engravings illustrative of it and of the fabric to which it gave rise. Our ancient church architecture is again in the ascendant, proudly triumphing over all the various abominations of that dark age of English design and execution which commenced at the dissolution of religious houses, and extended, with a few exceptions, to the beginning of the present century. During this long period, men not only did not build after our good old English models, but they manifested, in far too many instances, an anxiety to destroy. Too ignorant to appreciate, they affected to despise; and too proud to feel ashamed, they gloried in their deeds of destruction. There may be still in the land those who care for no design but what they, in the folly of self-importance, determine, in spite of wiser heads, to be the best; and there may be men, pretenders to the name and qualifications of architects, ready to carry such degenerate plans into vile execution; but their number, we rejoice to say, is rapidly decreasing. Such has been the reaction, that public opinion has, with one or two late melancholy exceptions (we are now speaking of the north of England), compelled men to act, if not to think, aright; and public opinion is not yet at rest. So rapidly is the study of our national architecture reviving, that he who has it in his power to bring to light such documents as that which forms the substance of the following pages, illustrating the cost of workmanship in times of old, and giving the various technical names of parts and things as they were used at their respective periods, many of which have been long forgotten because they were no longer required, will be thanked for his pains by all those genuine architects whose slightest meed is praise. The contract for the church of Catterick has much to recommend it to the architect; and still more, perhaps, to those who take a pleasure in tracing the English language during its early history. In both points of view, it is of peculiar interest." (p. 6.)

This contract is, indeed, of very peculiar interest; and Mr. Rickman says that "a copy of it ought to be in the hand of every rational antiquary, that it may explain genuine architectural terms, and guide his search for similar documents." In the contract, the word "lavatory" is used to designate one of those water niches always to be found immediately within the entrance of a Catholic church, and, by modern architects, called the "piscina;" and the annotator proposes to substitute the former word for the latter in future. The improvement is so obvious, that we have no doubt it will be generally adopted. No reference is made in the contract to working drawings; and it is suspected that models in wood, or drawings on wooden tablets, were in use in these times; and were generally made by the ecclesiastics, who were, for the most part, the church architects of this and preceding periods. The average wages of a mason, when Catterick church was built, was 7d.; a carpenter, 5d.; and a quarryman, 3¼d. per day. The amount of the contract was 114l., worth at least 684l. of present money; and, it is thought, the builder was amply paid for his workmanship, notwithstanding the smallness of the sum. The plates are beautifully etched; and, as an architectural curiosity, the work is well worth procuring by every man of taste.

ART. III. *Catalogue of Works on Architecture, Building, and Furnishing, and on the Arts more immediately connected therewith, recently published.*

BRITAIN.

KNIGHT's Unique Fancy Ornaments. In five parts, containing six plates in each. Published monthly. 4to, part 1. London, 1834. 4s.

The plates are most beautifully engraved. The frontispiece is a framework of scrolls, foliage, flowers, quadrupeds, birds, and insects, in the style of Louis XIV., and exhibits a good deal of fancy, and expertness in composition. Plate 2. contains fanciful borders and panel ornaments, in the style of Louis XIV.; plate 3., ornaments for panels and compartments, in a less grotesque manner; plate 4., ornaments in the style of Louis XIV.; plate 5., ornaments for vessels in the same style; and plate 6., ornaments in the same style, of various kinds. There is no letterpress. The work will be particularly useful to ornamental house painters, modellers, weavers, and, in general, to all ornamental manufacturers.

Billington's Architectural Director, &c. Parts 4. and 5. 2s. 6d. each.

We noticed, p. 180., the second and third parts of this work, and commended the accuracy of the plates. The same remarks may be applied to those given with the present number. One of these contains a transverse section of St Peter's Church at Rome; another, the elevation of the Buon Campagna Palace, in the same city; the third is a ground plan of the Giustiniani Palace; and the three remaining ones are details of the Tuscan and Doric orders.

Part 5. contains a plan and elevation of a private house in Rome; ornaments of mouldings; capital of a Corinthian pilaster; proportion of entablature; plans of arcades; and crowning entablature. Both Parts contain portions of the letterpress description of the plates, and of the dictionary. The latter as far as the article Carpentry.

A Plain Statement of Facts, connected with the Coalition between the Society for the Promotion of Architecture and Architectural Topography, and the Society of British Architects. Pamphlet, 8vo, pp. 28. London.

The object of the author is to give " a complete *exposé* of the irregular proceedings of the Society of British Architects;" but, as we do not wish to enter into the merits of the case, we merely recommend his pamphlet to those who do.

GERMANY.

Stern: Theorie der Kettenbrücke, und ihre Anwendung. Theory of Chain Bridges, and its application. 4to. Berlin, 1834. 10*s.*

Klenze, Leo von, Court Architect at Munich: Sammlung Architectonischer Entwurfe, &c. Collection of Architectural Designs, &c. Fol. Munich, 1832.

Menzel, Carl A.: Versuch einer Darstellung des jetzigen Zustandes der Baukunst. Essay on the present State of Architecture. 8vo. Berlin, 1832.

MISCELLANEOUS INTELLIGENCE.

ART. I. *General Notices.*

'ANTICIPATED *Universality of Grecian Architecture.* — Never has there been, and never will there be, says Leo von Klenze, more than one *art* of building (*eine Baukunst*), namely, that which was brought to perfection at the epoch of the prosperity and civilisation of Greece. Before this perfection was attained, it was necessarily preceded by many attempts; so, too, after the art itself was overthrown and trampled upon, both by time and by barbarians, some reverberations of it were yet sensible. Thus there were many modes of architecture (*Bauarten*) after as well as prior to its existence as an *art*. Grecian architecture alone is marked by universal propriety, character, and beauty; although any mode of architecture is capable of affecting us, and has a certain value of its own, when it is a really national style, and has grown up out of the religious and civil habits of a people. This Grecian architecture, taking it in the most extensive sense of the term, comprehends two leading epochs of its formation; namely, that in which all the apertures and intervals are covered by horizontal lines, and that when the arch was discovered and applied to similar purposes.

If we examine into and attend to this twofold developement of Grecian architecture in its elementary principles; and, in forming a style for ourselves, keep in view those precious remains of art which are yet preserved to us both in Greece and in Italy; Grecian architecture can and must be the architecture of the world, and that of all periods: nor can any climate, any material, any difference of manners, prove an obstacle to its universal adoption.

The history of art, he afterwards continues, like that of the world, proceeds step by step: just emerging, therefore, from out of the magnificent wretchedness (*das grandiose Elende*) of the middle ages, partly surrounded only by the remains of the most debased period of Roman art, partly attracted only by what was most homogeneous in it, viz. its bad taste, the artists of that period (the fifteenth and sixteenth centuries) could not possibly restore architecture to its native dignity, however meritorious their endeavours to do so may have been.

The gross architectural solecisms of a Buonarotti, the still more flagrant absurdities of a Giulio Romano, Maderno, and Borromini, which naturally resulted from them; the tasteless puerilities which reached their climax under Louis XV.; and, lastly, all the unmeaning and spiritless imitations of detached Grecian forms of a still later period, were any thing but calculated to arrest the defects observable in the works of the fifteenth century; so that an important task was still reserved for architecture in these our own times, when Grecian antiquity has been opened to us by so many literary and statistical works.

For some time past intelligent men of all countries have been labouring for the accomplishment of this object; and we also have added our endeavours to theirs; nor have we feared to set our face manfully against the mechanical workman system, derived from Vitruvius and Vignola, or against the empty groundless theories of praters about art, and the low miserable notions of those who see in architecture no other purpose or value than that of protecting ourselves as economically as possible against rain, heat, and cold. (*Introduction to Klenze's Collection of Architectural Designs*, as quoted in the *For. Quart. Rev.* for July, 1834, p. 108.)

A new Method of diffusing Light through a Theatre has been discovered by a mechanic at Venice. By the aid of parabolic mirrors, the light of many lamps is concentrated over an opening made in the ceiling of the theatre, and reflected down on a system of plano-concave lenses, of a foot in diameter, which occupy the aperture, and convey into the theatre the rays of light which arrive at them parallel, and depart from them divergent. From the pit the lenses are alone perceived, which resemble a glowing furnace; and, although the luminous focus is sufficient to light the whole theatre, it does not dazzle, and it may be viewed without fatiguing the eyes. The apparatus being entirely concealed, it accommodates itself readily to all the changes which the representation may require. It likewise occasions neither smoke nor bad odours, and has none of the inconveniences of the ancient system. (*Times*, July 12. 1834.)

Art. II. *Foreign Notices.*

GERMANY.

THE *two greatest Architects in Germany* are Karl Friedrich Schinkel of Berlin, born in 1781, and Leo von Klenze of Munich, born in 1784. A very interesting account of some of the principal works of these artists, and of the present school of architecture in Germany, is given in the *Foreign Quarterly* for July, by a valuable correspondent of this Magazine. We have made several quotations and abridgments from it, which will appear in this, and in the succeeding Number; but every architect ought to peruse the entire article.

The Walhalla, or hall of the gods, which is erected on the hill Donaustauff, near Regensburg, is a magnificent temple-formed structure, in the most classical Doric style, with a noble portico, consisting of eight columns in front, and an inner range of six others; and on each of its sides are seventeen columns, the whole formed of marble, and raised on a substructure, in which is formed an ascent between massive walls of Cyclopean architecture. As its name imports, this edifice is intended to become a kind of universal German Pantheon, in which will be deposited monumental busts of the most illustrious citizens and heroes of Teutonia. In the interior is a magnificent frieze, executed by Wagner the sculptor; and the pediment of the portico will also be enriched by a suitable subject in relief. (*For. Quart. Rev.*, July, 1834, p. 112.)

NEW SOUTH WALES.

A Model for a Government House has recently been finished by Mr. Chadley, the surveyor. A project for erecting a magnificent town-hall in Sydney has been brought forward by Mr. Poole the architect, and it is warmly approved of by several influential persons. It is also in contemplation to erect a floating bath in Sydney Cove. (*Sydney Gazette*, Oct. 5. 1833.)

Art. III. *Domestic Notices.*
ENGLAND.

LANCASHIRE.—*Mr. Huskisson's Monument in St. James's Cemetery, Liverpool.* A statue of this celebrated statesman has been completed by Gibson, a Liverpool artist, now in Rome, which is said to have given very general satisfaction; but the very reverse seems to be the case with respect to the building now erecting to receive the statue; and the following is an abstract of a criticism, which a correspondent has sent us, and which has appeared in the *Liverpool Chronicle* and the *Liverpool Mercury*. We entirely agree with the writer, and sincerely wish, with him, that it may not yet be too late to have the upper part of the temple thrown open.

"Mr. Huskisson's monument is a circular temple from the ground to the top. One third of the height is in plain rustic work, with a small entrance door to the south. On this rise ten half columns, fluted, of the Corinthian order, and solid masonwork between them almost to the capitals; on this a dome roof, with ten circular lights, terminating with a cross on the top. I am at a loss to know what sort of ideas the architect must have possessed, to erect a building which so much resembles the round-house at Everton, to place a marble statue in, the execution of which cost 1200*l.*: only think for a moment of the effect of a figure 7½ feet high, standing on a pedestal 3¼ feet high, shut up in a small circle, and even part of that cut up by a stair. It will be impossible for a spectator to have any other than a distorted view. It is a general rule, in viewing works of art, to go no nearer than what the extreme height or breadth may be. The famous Benvenuto Cellini said, that a whole-length figure should at least have seven points of view to know and appreciate it properly. It may be said you can have seven points of view here; but if you had seventy, it would be of little use, so long as the space to view it in is so confined that it will be like a horse in a mill, round and round, you cannot get a yard or an inch out of the track. The architects of the present day seem only to study how neat they can make a small model to be looked at on a mahogany table, regardless of the site, or how it may appear when erected. The mistakes that have lately taken place in the metropolis confirm this remark. At Buckingham Palace, for instance, after the building was up, it was found that the centre was too large for the wings; they were taken down and rebuilt, and now the centre is found to be too small for the wings. The dome, also, has been removed; and, when the architect was questioned about it before a committee of the House of Commons, he said *he was not aware* that it would have been seen from the Park. I would propose, as this statue was intended for a public monument, and one to be seen by all and at any time, that a meeting of the subscribers be called without delay, so that the building may be altered.

"This building is said to be a copy of Demosthenes's Lantern; but this it is not exactly. The tomb of Lysicrates, in the Capuchin Convent garden at Athens (commonly called Demosthenes's Lantern, built 333 years before the Christian era), was complete with open pillars to the base. It was not closed up between for some hundred years. This tomb is an open circular temple on a square base, and the grand effect produced by placing a circular temple on a square base is well known, not only from this at Athens, but from Adrian's Tomb at Rome, the temple at Tivoli, &c. It is bad taste to have the circle to the ground, because it gives the building too much the effect of a limekiln or pottery work. There is no small door reserved in the Athenian tomb, and that in the side of Mr. Huskisson's monument has a disagreeable effect; it ought to have been concealed. If the pillars had been complete and open, there would have been no occasion for a door, as the size of the building would have permitted visiters to the Cemetery to view the statue near enough without entering the building, and the effect would have been grand. On the one side the rich foliage of the trees as a background to relieve the white marble, on another the rocky banks of the Cemetery; the beautiful effect of the rising or setting sun, or the pale moonlight glimmering through the pillars; would have added to the grandeur and solemnity of the place. On inquiring the reason for shutting up the figure, I was told it was to preserve it from the weather. It has been proved that the marble the figure is made of will stand the weather for ages entirely exposed; but this would have had sufficient shelter with the dome top, standing as it does in a hollow, and surrounded by the rocks of the Cemetery.

" There is yet time, before the figure arrives, to rectify this, and it behoves the subscribers to bestir themselves, and to prevent so beautiful a statue being consigned to this *dark lantern.* When it was proposed, it was intended for a public monument, but it is likely now to be a private one, and not to be seen without the attendance of the *custode* with an iron key and the visiter with a silver one."

It is probable that the architect of the Huskisson monument was not aware that the filling up of the spaces between the columns was a modern addition; for we find the same tomb of Lysicrates with the fillings-in between the columns, copied as a tower, or *campanile*, to one of the chapels in Regent Street, which was erected a few years ago, either from the designs of Mr. Nash, or from those of some one in his office. Nothing can show a greater poverty of taste, or more innate slavery of mind, than the practice of indiscriminately copying whatever was done, or supposed to be done, by the ancients. It will be disgraceful to Liverpool if this hybrid temple is allowed to remain as it is. — *Cond.*

SCOTLAND.

Renfrewshire. — A *beautiful Granite Sarcophagus*, from Egypt, has lately been placed in Hamilton Palace. It was found in one of the pyramids, and is said to have contained the mummy of one of the ancient kings, which has been recently sent to the Edinburgh museum. The sarcophagus measures 7 ft. in length by 3 ft. in breadth, and, in the middle, about 3 ft. in depth on the outside; and weighs about 4½ tons. Over the whole surface are engraved pictures and hieroglyphics, very much defaced. (*Elgin Courier,* May 16.)

Selkirkshire. — *A Bridge of a novel Description* has been erected over the river Ettrick, at Fauldshope, in the Forest of Selkirkshire. It consists of a single arch upwards of 76 ft. of span, an exact semi-ellipse; the rise from the chord line being only 20 ft. The whole is constructed entirely of rubble whinstone; and it is believed to be the largest arch of this description in Great Britain. The curve line of the arch, notwithstanding the extent of the span, and the humble description of the materials of which it is composed, remains mathematically correct. This spirited attempt on the part of the agents of the Duke of Buccleugh, in producing, at a moderate expense, so useful a structure, of such simple materials, it is hoped will not be overlooked by road trustees and architects. Messrs. Smith of Darnick are the builders by whom the bridge was planned and executed. — *J. W. Dumfries, July* 3. 1834.

All masonry is essentially either cementitious, that is, depending for its strength on the use of mortar; or mechanical, that is, depending for its strength on the proper cutting of the stones, and bedding them one upon another. The masonry of the bridge above mentioned is of the cementitious kind, and good mortar must have been used. Were Roman cement employed with rubblestone instead of common martar, we have no doubt that arches of much larger span than 76 ft. might be built of rubblestone. Indeed, as it has been proved that concrete will bear an immense weight, we seen no reason why an arch should not be composed of that material in all situations where it might be found cheaper than any other. We should be glad to hear of something of the kind being tried; a dome roof, for example. — *Cond.*

IRELAND.

Cathedral of Armagh. — The Lord Primate of Ireland (Lord John Beresford, Archbishop of Armagh) has subscribed 8000*l*. to the restoration of the ancient cathedral of Armagh; the foundation stone of which was laid by the

Very Rev. the Dean, on the 21st of June last. The vast superstructure of the venerable tower, weighing 4000 tons, is to be supported, during the relaying of the foundation of the piers, without removing a single stone from the upper part of this immense tower, by means of some very ingenious mechanism invented by Mr. Cottingham, the architect. (*Newspaper*.) We should be much obliged to Mr. Cottingham for some account of the mechanism alluded to. — *Cond.*

ART. IV. *Restrospective Criticism.*

MR. EDWARD BLORE, architect to the late additions at Lambeth Palace and Buckingham Palace, designed the mansion for Lord Corehouse, not Mr. Blair, as you have stated in p. 212. The house in question is beautifully situated on the Corehouse falls of the Clyde, and is a happy adaptation of the early English style of architecture to the requirements of the present day. The grounds, which are highly picturesque and romantic, commanding from their heights most extensive views over the beautiful vales of Clyde, combine with the house to render this one of the most tasteful retreats in this part of Scotland. — *A Subscriber. July*, 1834.

Mr. Main informs us that he only laid out a flower-garden and designed a green-house at this seat, and not the grounds generally, as we had supposed when we wrote the paragraph in p. 212.

Regarding the Performance of my equalising Ventilator, I beg to remind Mr. Dymon that the increase of heat, which he notices in p. 213., also increases the velocity of ventilation; and that the force of the current closes the door of the ventilator only so far as to admit the same quantity of air to escape in any given time, whether there are "four" or nine persons in the room; and that, therefore, his position, that the "change of the air in the room goes on less rapidly," is not correct; and that, in order to ventilate sufficiently his additional "five" visitors, he has only to shift the weight upon its lever, at hand in the room or in the vestibule, as directed in my description.

But it may be said that this attention to the lever and weight would be troublesome, and likely to be forgotten; and so it would, were it necessary to make an adjustment of the opening of the ventilator, as often as "four" or "five" persons joined or left a company. That, however, is a case which is not likely ever to occur. We are not to suppose that "four" persons are so cooped up in a room, where ventilation is so nearly adjusted to what they require, that the introduction of a few more visitors would bring the whole company to the expiring point. On the contrary, we must always ventilate freely, in such a way as that a little more heat may not be offensive. But, even supposing that such a degree of nicety of the rate of ventilation were contended for, it could be obtained neither by a mere opening in the roof, nor by opening and shutting a window; which, although it were practicable, and attended with no injurious consequences, could not be so easily done as to adjust the weight upon the lever of my ventilator. Indeed, independently of the impossibility of effecting even an equality of the rate of change of the air, by opening a window, it is admitted by Mr. Dymond that, in summer, "the night air is frequently charged with an unhealthful degree of moisture:" and for this reason I object to his plan of ventilating sleeping-rooms, by keeping the windows open all night.

On the supposition that the bedrooms are the higher parts of the house, I would advise air to be taken in, in summer at least, at the base of the house. In winter, I would keep the bedrooms comfortably warm by heated water, or by fire, and the windows shut: I would make the ventilator at the highest part of the room; carry its passage to the highest point possible, either in a chimney or in a tube; intercept the passage with an equalising ventilator; and keep the door of the bedroom a little open. By such an arrangement, the room would be purified at least from the light azotic gas expired by the sleepers, by its ascending through the ventilator; and complete control might also be exercised over its exit; and, of course, over the entrance of a fresh supply of air; while, at the same time, the other pernicious part of the expired air, the carbonic acid gas, which is 22 per cent. of the air breathed, being much heavier than common air, will rush out at the door of the room like water, whenever its temperature shall become at any time so low as to prevent its escape by the ventilator. Moreover, the fresh supply of air, entering at the base of the house, will gradually lose its "moisture" by the absorbing quality of the walls, &c. That such is the fact, Mr. Dymond may satisfy himself by using a hygrometer at the place where the moist air enters, and another in his bedrooms.

I am not, however, to be understood as signifying that the constitution and habits of some persons may not admit of ventilation effected in the way recommended by Mr. Dymond. We know that the aboriginal inhabitants of the warmest parts of America sleep in hammocks, suspended from a tree, and in open sheds, where they are nightly covered with dew, which to them is harmless, but to a European destructive. The celebrated Franklin also slept continually with his windows open; but his constitution was naturally robust, and he observed such a regimen of diet, drink, and exercise, as few persons would willingly confine themselves to. Indeed, such examples are far from warranting the practice, under a climate so variable as ours.

In conclusion, I beg to state that the weight which I propose (p. 68.) for regulating the opening of the suspended damper may be made sufficiently heavy to counterpoise it; and that thereby the proposed counterpoising weight attached, in fig. 28., to the lower margin of the external door, would be unnecessary, and that equality of ventilation could still be nearly obtained by changing the position of the weight upon its lever. I would observe, also, that the internal air passages, marked *m*, *n*, *p*, fig. 26., which permit the air to get above the suspended damper, should be made large; and in such a way as that they may not be closed by it, even when it is pushed up by hand, so far as to close the external door altogether.

From this arrangement, Mr. Dymond will see that, according as the external door becomes shut, the air between it and the suspended damper becomes compressed, and, reacting upon the upper side of the damper, prevents its ascent, and thus keeps the external door from being ever shut, farther than to allow an escape of air equal at all times, whatever pressure may be applied. In p. 69., for "scale," read "state" of the barometer; and in p. 70. for "777" read "177." — *John Milne, Edinburgh. 8. James's Square, July,* 1834.

Art. V. *Queries and Answers.*

WINDOWS. — Should not the lower edge of windows be rather farther from the floor than the height of the chair backs, to prevent the shutters from constantly knocking against them? I know many persons prefer windows reaching to the ground; but I doubt whether they can be defended on optical principles, I mean with reference to the internal effect: but let the oculist and artist settle that. Let the former say whether a strong light, reflected up to the eye, is good; and the latter decide whether it does not confound the direct and reflected lights and their shadows. It is a point worth consideration, if we are to act from reason, and not from custom, or mere fashion. I should be glad to hear the opinions of some of your readers on this subject.— *T. W. Yorkshire, Jan.* 1833.

Cements. — Which is the best of all the different cements sold in London? I think there are at least half a dozen kinds. — *Juvenis. Birmingham, July,* 1834.

THE

ARCHITECTURAL MAGAZINE.

OCTOBER, 1834.

ORIGINAL COMMUNICATIONS.

ART. I. *On those Principles of Composition, in Architecture, which are common to all the Fine Arts.* By the CONDUCTOR. Sect. 2. *Forms, Lines, Lights, Shades, and Colours, considered with reference to the Principle of the Recognition of Art.*

WE have shown (p. 220.) in what way the Recognition of Art becomes a fundamental principle in the fine arts. We hear much of the imitation of nature, as a guide in art; but it must never be imagined that, by the phrase "imitation of nature" is to be understood the making of a fac-simile of nature; that is, such a copy as might be mistaken for the original. There could be no art, or creative power, displayed in this; and, consequently, such an imitation could afford no more pleasure to the copier than that which he could derive from the hope of deceiving the spectator; while the spectator, even supposing him to be completely deceived, would experience no satisfaction different from that afforded by the original. Suppose that a person undertook to construct an artificial tree to fix in a hedgerow, or on a lawn, and that it was so exactly like the natural trees near it, that no person could distinguish it from them; what credit would we give to the mechanist who put the work together? Clever he might certainly be; because he had produced such a perfect fac-simile as to deceive us; but we could never allow that he had a talent equal in rank to that of the man who could draw a tree on paper, or paint one on canvass. Every one feels, in a moment, that the power of doing the latter requires a superior degree of mind; and that, while the tree, in the one case, is a mere mechanical production, in the other it assumes the rank and dignity of an emanation from the mind of man; in short, of a work of art. This, we think, is quite sufficient to show, that it is no part of the business of an artist to deceive; that every work of art, to sustain that character, must be avowed as such; and that the essential distinctive principle of works of art is, that they are evidently the creation of man.

All the great principles or instincts which belong to human nature display themselves more or less in the savage state of nations, and in the infancy of individuals. Now, after the savage has acquired a small stock of food and clothing, in what way does he decorate his dwelling, or ornament his person? Does he cover the former with turf or creeping plants, or grow shrubs over it, in such a manner as to make it pass for a grassy hillock, or a thicket of bushes; and does he wrap the skins in which he is clothed round him in such a way as to imitate nature in the deceptive sense, and make himself pass for a wild beast? No: he builds and dresses in such a way, rude though it may be, as to mark both his dwelling and his clothes as his own work; and, indeed, strives to make them as different from the simple works of nature as his means will possibly allow. What are the first indications given by infants of their taking an interest in the objects around them? A desire to touch them; next to possess them; and, lastly, to show their skill in imitating them. We repeat, that it is this skill, or creative power, which constitutes the essential principle of art.

We allow, at the same time, that there is a kind of art, or rather of manufacture, which passes with many for art, which gives some persons a certain degree of satisfaction. To this kind of art may be referred those fac-similes of ruins, fruit, flowers, and even animals, which may be, and often are, mistaken for originals. But this is mere mechanical repetition, and not creative imitation; which, to belong to art, must always be avowed to be such, by the imitation being evidently of a different material from the original.

The principle of the Recognition of Art, then, we shall consider as firmly established; and equally so, that which flows from it, viz., that every work of art must bear external evidence that it is the work of man, and not the work of God. A very few words will show the application of this principle to forms, lines, lights, shades, and colours.

In those arts which imitate the forms of nature, such as painting and sculpture: in the first, art is recognised in the materials, and in the manner in which objects are imitated by colours on a flat surface; and, in the latter, in consequence of the employment of stone or plastic materials, to imitate forms without colour. But the principle of the recognition of art is still farther displayed, both in painting and sculpture, by the artist imitating the forms of the species, rather than that of the individual before him. Even in taking portraits of a particular landscape, tree, man, or animal, this is or ought to be done; and always is done when the work produced assumes the character of a work of art, and is not intended to be a mere graphic memorandum of a particular scene or object, with all its individual peculiarities. It seems almost needless to add, that what will apply to form, applies equally to lines; by which, indeed, form must be indicated. When the central form, or the form of the species, is imitated, the central lines, or lines expressive of the species, must necessarily be included in the imitation. The one, in short, cannot exist without the other. The same observations will apply to lights, shades, and colours, with reference to the imitation of natural objects: but we have, we trust, said enough to show that the principle of the recognition of art applies even to those arts which imitate the forms of nature, and in which, at first sight, it might be thought impossible so far to deviate from the form of the object imitated as to render the recognition of art obvious in that particular.

In architecture, and in the sculpture of artificial forms, such as vases, &c., art is at once recognised in all forms which are bounded by straight lines, and included in perfectly flat surfaces; or by circular or regularly curved lines, and perfectly globular or curvilineal surfaces. There is no such thing in external nature as an absolutely straight line, or one curved with perfect regularity; and hence there is no such thing as a perfect square, a perfect parallelogram, or a perfect circle or oval, in general scenery. Nature affords many approaches to these and other regular and symmetrical forms, but she leaves it to man to perfect and complete them. All forms, therefore, which may be defined as geometrical, that is, all which are perfectly regular or symmetrical; in short, all which are formed by the repetition, more or less frequent, of the same parts or lines, must be at once recognised as belonging to art.

The art of architecture is, more than all others which are classed with the fine arts, an art of artificial forms; and the reason for this is to be found in the principles of architectural construction, with which, as they are not common to all the fine arts, we have, at present, nothing to do. Whatever may be said of the ornaments of architecture, no one will assert that the great masses of a building, or even its doors, windows, roof, and chimney tops, are imitations of nature. Neither will any one assert that these masses, doors, windows, roofs, and chimney tops may not be combined in such a manner as either to be beautiful and satisfactory, or otherwise. We need hardly remind our readers that it is the object of the chapter, of which the present article is a section, to show in what manner the forms of architecture, and the lines, lights, shades, and colours produced by these forms, may be combined so as to produce architectural beauty.

In the general forms or masses of architecture, it will be found that, the more the forms of nature are deviated from, the higher will be the style of the building. A cottage with the walls of mud, or of turf, or of round land stones or boulders, is low in the scale of art, compared with one the walls of which are of brick, or of squared stone; and a house where the stones are not only squared, but smoothly hewn, and rubbed to perfectly flat surfaces, ranks still higher in the scale. If an architect were to imitate the perpendicular face of a rock in the walls of a house, and if he were to make his doors and windows in the form of cracks, chasms, or other holes of a natural or accidental character, he would cease to be an artist.

If it is easy to comprehend how art is to be recognised by forms and lines, it is not less so to display a character of art in lights, shades, and colours. There is hardly such a thing in nature as an even distribution of light over a flat surface; for this reason, that there are few or no truly flat surfaces in nature. The exception is the surface of a still lake; but even that is varied by the reflection of the surrounding scenery, or of the clouds of the sky. The same may be said as to shades and colours: there is no continuous flat shade, or flat tint, in nature; because, as before mentioned, there are no continuous surfaces. Hence, whenever artificial forms are introduced, there, not only lines, but lights, shades, and colours, should be evidently artificial also. Hence, in colouring rooms, the groundwork on which the ornaments are placed should be always one even tint of colour; and the ornaments bordering or distributed over such a tint should never resemble fac-simile copies of nature, but always display the average or specific form of whatever object they may be intended to represent, and be disposed in such a manner as to be recognised as artificial. Flowers, for example, should not be painted as if they had been thrown against a wall or a ceiling at random; but they should be disposed in regular borders, wreaths, or groups. It must be recollected, at the same time, that to this, as to all other principles and rules, there are exceptions. For example, if it is desired to surprise, puzzle, or confound, then a disorderly distribution of the parts of a composition, or its ornaments, will attain that end, which would be altogether defeated by an orderly distribution of them.

In the details of architecture, and more especially in its sculptured ornaments, natural forms, such as foliage and flowers, are commonly imitated. Here art is recognised not only by the material employed, but by the more regular symmetrical, or otherwise artificial, character of the imitation, and by its approaching the average form of the species, rather than that of the individual. Hence close imitations of nature, even though in stone, are never so pleasing as those which, though scientifically correct with reference to nature, have, at the same time, a decidedly artificial character. There are many ornaments belonging to the early period of Gothic architecture liable to the objection of being too close imitations of nature; and those rustic columns, applied to cottages, which not only have their bark left on, but even retain parts of their branches, are particularly obnoxious to, and altogether inconsistent with, a character of art. If we examine the objectionable ornaments alluded to, we shall find that the principal cause of our displeasure is the want of a character of art in the imitation. The general form of the flower, of the leaves, and of the stalk connecting them, will be found to be such as might have been produced by a cast from the originals; in other words, we shall find the piece of sculpture a fac-simile of an individual flower, instead of an imitation, according to art, of that flower as a species.

Art. II. *On Uniformity in Architecture.* By W. H.

The developement of the organ of order in the human system, by the application of it, in every description of physical arrangement, is at once the most conclusive proof of its existence, and of its imperative nature. As an acquired rule of life, it is an habitual possession, but it is more primitively of an instinctive origin; because those who are most distant from its acquirement are equally ready to own its supreme value, and to envy it in others. In commercial affairs, the want of it is a disgrace; in domestic life, it is the matron's ambition; in dress, it is perfection. It is admirable in business, for its convenience; at home, for its comfort; and personally, for its example. The influence it has upon architecture produces, as one of its results, uniformity.

In defining the expression uniformity, it is considered as alluding to the correspondence or similarity of the parts of an object, or of objects collectively, with each other, in the formation of a whole. Architecture, which is often mentioned in the same breath with painting and sculpture, must on this topic be separated. The copyist of nature, in the various forms of creation, finds nothing either so far similar in itself, or with other objects, to justify the term uniformity in its representation. Were the human figure to be delineated in a geometrical manner, with each limb corresponding in altitude to its opposite, it certainly might then be uniform, but it would not properly depict life; and, in fact, any attempt to extract such a principle of exactitude from the appearances of natural productions must fail, when their infinite multiplicity of variations seems quite to banish such a thought. Although architecture, in this particular, cannot claim to be an imitative art; it is the more so one of invention, in suiting itself, by constructive uniformity, to the reasonable habits and tastes of mankind. How far this view is effected, and of what real consequence it is, are intended to be the subject of the following remarks.

In erections of more than ordinary altitude, as, for instance, towers, steeples, domes, and the like, where they are seen from many points of view, and at considerable distances, rising above inferior objects, they usually present the same appearance in each prospect. In the case of such a building being on a circular plan, a more complete uniformity can be achieved than in any other form; and hence such a form becomes the most simple and compulsory occasion for its adoption. When the purposes of a structure will admit of, and be best answered by, uniformity in its interior arrangement, it follows, as a matter of course, that the same may be kept up throughout its exterior; provided it is insularly situated; and no architect would neglect such an opportunity, by not adopting so desirable a method. This kind of uniformity may be generally attained in designing sepulchres, baths, fountains, and minor architectural erections; but its most frequent and important application is in churches, and other buildings, either for congregational or limited assemblies. In many of such instances, it happens, as in St. Paul's Cathedral, that the whole building, both plan and elevation, may be bisected by an imaginary line, with the nicest impartiality; leaving to each half the exact reflection of itself in the other: though each, being so separated, is no longer uniform, but derives its merit in this respect from being exactly similar to the other; thus producing, as it were, a united effect, by a twofold accordance. This manner of disposal in architecture, while it leaves every room for uniformity of details and general similitude of character, works its ultimate advantage, by restricting its great likeness to the smallest possible number of portions; and which, to judge by the above example, powerfully conduces to grandeur. There is a singular specimen of uniformity, somewhat of this class, in the Banqueting-house at Whitehall, where the front and its reverse are precisely similar, though, of couse, completely hidden from each other.

The next species of uniformity is, where utility requires a varied internal plan, and defies any connection with regularity. Having now touched upon it in situations where it must be the architect's pleasure, we arrive at the other side of the question, and pursue him in his perplexity. If a plan cannot be uniform, an elevation is, notwithstanding, to be so; but then it is not only one elevation, but often four. In this regard, circumstances seldom desire more than the style to be maintained in each, although each is expected to be distinctly uniform in itself. An evidence of this appears in the New Post-Office, having four elevations, each complete, and all greatly differing, except in general character. These peremptory demands in the adaptation of outside forms in buildings have led to many of the most ingenious contrivances and schemes; but, at the same time, have, doubtless, often been the means of contracting and perverting many of the noblest designs. Uniformity is often thus purchased at the expense of convenience, and by the use of deceptions, in the shape of blank representations of entrances and windows with their appurtenances, in places where they never could really appear; and this kind of subterfuge extends itself to many other items. Invention is racked in the struggle for uniformity under difficulties, in proportion to the importance in which it is held. In this attempt, unless the end is perfectly and manifestly attained, it is an abortive effort, and the struggle stands confessed; but, being so attained, the evidence of the difficulty vanishes. The near approach to it fails by its only blemish, and its total absence would be preferable. As an example, the four turrets of the Tower of London are something similar, though no two of them accord in dimensions, or in details; the effect of which is almost ludicrous. To turn from so feeble a specimen of architecture, to one of the most gigantic in talent of modern times (it is alluded to with the utmost respect); the Bank of England discovers a case in point, which is lamentable, from the very excess of its own merits in other respects; and, evincing, as it does, every proof of originality and excellence, it makes the regret the greater that such a composition should suffer, even in a slight degree, from the irregular form of the plot having caused a partial want of uniformity in that erection.

There has been a question mooted respecting the fronts of street houses, as to the comparative advantages of their being collectively uniform, as in Regent Street; or separately so, as in other streets; and this class of buildings now presents itself, in reference to our subject. There requires no greater argument of the collective method being favourable to the appearance of a town, than that most of the great alterations in London (which have been designed by the most eminent architects) have been made with this view; but it becomes a doubt whether it is reasonably conducive to a mercantile effect, that our streets of business should resemble a succession of mansions; or whether the individual purposes and wishes of the occupants are answered or defeated by it. Ask, on this point, a few of the tradesmen of Regent Street their opinion of the new houses in the West Strand (also built collectively), and we presume that they will admire them: but, in their own cases, not one of them is content: the linendraper's elevation is not gay enough; the tavern is too modest; the bookseller's is not sufficiently classical; and so on. Each is dissatisfied, because he is not distinguished from his neighbours; and he endeavours to distinguish himself by every means in his power, by his mode of showing his goods, and also by colouring the plastering of his house differently from others: and certainly, in Regent Street, where there are almost as many stone colours as houses, this completely succeeds in breaking the illusion intended by the design. In private streets, where the same objection to uniformity is not so likely to exist, the idea can be better carried into effect; and therefore it is only in such situations that, in the opinion of the writer, the collective plan can be satisfactorily applied.

It appears that the ultimate end of uniformity in architecture consists in its chief attribute, which is, the assumption of importance; and that the gradations of its consequence keep pace with the respective purposes of buildings. The reverence and awe excited by a church or a palace are not looked for in a cottage. A rigid uniformity, indeed, is almost inconsistent with an unpretending pastoral erection; which, though not so imposing, is often much more touching to equally laudable sympathies. The humble pretensions of a common building may be accredited as fit and unassuming, so long as they are evidently the result of convenience, or even accident; but, when uniformity places them in array as something to enforce attention without being worthy of admiration, it defeats itself, and humility is rendered meanness. In conclusion, while, as a matter of taste, uniformity is only arbitrary, so far as it is desirable in conformity thereto; yet, when desirable, as a matter of practice, it is perhaps the most absolute principle for adherence that occurs in architectural design.

London, July, 1834.

ART. III. *A few Observations on the Anglo-Norman Style of Architecture, and its Applicability to Modern Ecclesiastical Edifices.* By J. A. PICTON, Esq., Architect.

THE ecclesiastical architecture of England, from the time of the Conquest to the Reformation, yields to that of no other country in variety, elegance, and originality. The gorgeous magnificence of our cathedrals, the simple beauty of the village church, with its " tapering spire that points to heaven," the gloomy grandeur of the timeworn remains of our monastic edifices, open up, to all lovers of the grand, the beautiful, and the picturesque, never-failing sources of gratification and delight. The pointed style of architecture, after remaining in abeyance upwards of two centuries, has, within the last fifty years, again attracted a considerable degree of the public attention; and the adaptation of this style to sacred edifices, as well as the beauties of its distinguishing features, are now very generally acknowledged and appreciated. Since its revival in modern times, it has obtained a copiousness of illustration which leaves little to be desired; and, from the increasing partiality of the public generally, it bids fair to remain lord of the ascendant, in ecclesiastical structures at least, for some time to come. It cannot but appear singular, with all this feeling in favour of Old English architecture, at a period, too, when a search for novelty is one of the distinguishing characteristics of the modern school of the art, that the Norman style, confessedly the parent of all the subsequent varieties of the pointed style, and the source from which many of its beauties have been derived, should have met with so little attention. One reason for this indifference may be, that it is generally considered as simply a debasement of the late Roman style of art; a spurious descendant from the Italian school; too servile a copy to assert any pretensions to originality; and far too rude in its details to be ranked along with its prototype. I am quite willing to admit that, to a certain extent, this opinion has some degree of plausibility; but it will not, I think, be difficult to prove that this style maintains a character sufficiently marked to render it worthy of some consideration; and, though not possessed of all the majesty of the Roman remains, or of the lightness and grace of many specimens of the pointed style which succeeded it, that it still has sufficient merit to render it worthy of being rescued from the neglect in which it has hitherto remained. It is true, there has been no lack of writing on the subject; for, perhaps, those *cruces antiquariorum*, Saxon architecture and the origin of the pointed arch, have elicited more learned discussion and elaborate argument than any other subjects connected with architectural antiquities. What I complain of is, that no practical use has been made of the patient research and laborious investigation thus called into action, and that, notwithstanding all that has been written, so very few buildings should have been erected in this style: and yet, perhaps, there is no style of architecture with which, under certain circumstances, so picturesque an effect may be produced at so comparatively small an expense. To call the public attention to the peculiar features and capabilities of this style is the object of the present article.

The general characteristics of Norman architecture are massiveness and strength, with a considerable degree of rudeness and weight in the minor parts of the earlier specimens; but growing gradually lighter in its proportions, until it finally merged into the early pointed style. Its elements of composition are few and simple: the column and arch constitute its principal features. These, however, are capable of a vast variety of combinations; and, indeed, I should be disposed to consider its merit to consist chiefly in simplicity of outline, combined with picturesque effect in the detail. It requires no intricate tracery, no crocketed pinnacles or canopied niches; and no rich paneling or heraldic devices: and these circumstances peculiarly adapt it to the purposes of the village church, or parochial chapel. Every person who has a correct taste for propriety in architectural embellishment, must have remarked with pain the bald nakedness of many of our modern (so called) Gothic churches, where ambition of design seems to have waged ineffectual war with poverty of means. Frequently, everything is sacrificed to the appearance of the exterior; and, but for the shape of the windows, it would be difficult to discover what style or order the interior is intended to display: and, where interior decoration is attempted, straight coved ceilings without groins, piers supporting arches cut into a flat wall, and other such abominations, are but poor substitutes for the carved oak or stone groins of our ancestors.

A principal, I might almost say, an essential, feature of our old churches is their division into three aisles, with the centre rising above the side aisles, forming what is called a clere-story: and this arrangement is not at all adapted to modern convenience, which generally requires galleries for a congregation of moderate number. If the roofs of the side aisles are elevated, to admit of height for galleries, the centre part must be raised so high as greatly to increase the expense, besides injuring the hearing; or the clere-story must be omitted, and the centre kept down to the level of the sides, which greatly injures the effect both of the exterior and interior, however correct the details may be. Many of the smaller Anglo-Norman churches have no side aisles; so that no feeling of correctness is invaded by building modern churches on the same principle, which, for the reason just stated, would effect a considerable saving of expense.

In this I would not wish to be misunderstood. I am no advocate for slavish imitation, and consider it much better to endeavour to imbibe the spirit of our old architects, than servilely to copy their works; but the revival of pointed architecture in this country being, as far as it extends, an attempt to imitate, as far as possible, our ecclesiastical remains, consistency and good taste require that, in buildings erected for the same purpose, respect should be had to the general principles as well as minor details.

The enriched mouldings and other ornaments in the Norman style, although extremely diversified, are, with few exceptions, such as any country mason might easily execute, as rudeness of execution is of little consequence; a bold relief and decided character being of more importance than a high degree of finish. In erecting a church in the pointed style, the cost of a tower or spire forms a very serious item in the estimate, in consequence of which it is not unfrequently omitted altogether, to the disappointment of the public, and the regret of all who comprehend the principles on which the effect of the style depends. The main lines being in a verticle direction, some prominent feature is required in which they can be developed to ome extent, or the effect of the whole is lost. In the Norman style, the verticle lines are subservient to the horizontal ones, so that no prominent part of the kind is required; a simple belfry being all that is requisite. A tower is objectionable, in buildings of this style, on another account: the Norman architects lavished all their skill, and a greater portion of their expenditure, in ornamenting their west fronts, which, even where there are towers at the west end, as at Lincoln, are generally thrown into one broad *façade* without any projection, as is almost universally the case in buildings of a later date.

There are a few village churches scattered throughout the country, which have almost miraculously escaped the ruthless hand of time and the barbarous improvements of modern churchwardens, which may serve as exemplifications of the above remarks.

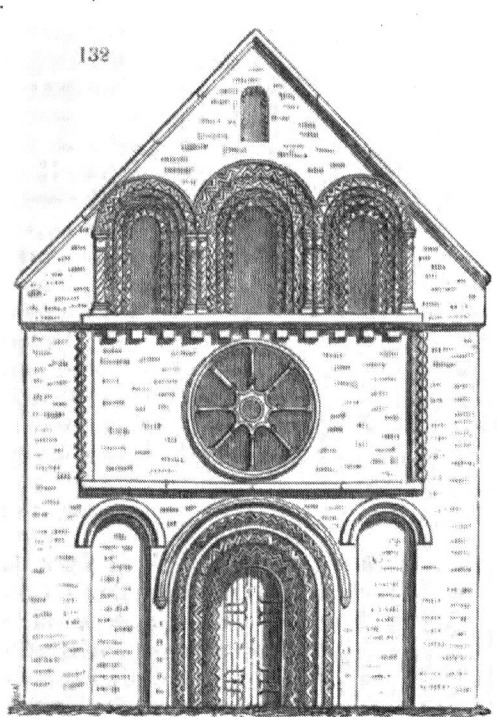

Fig. 132. is the elevation of the west front of Iffley church, Oxfordshire, restored.

Fig. 133. shows the west end of the chapel of St. Leonard's Hospital, Stamford, Lincolnshire.

These may suffice to give a general idea of the effect of the Norman fronts, though there are many others well worth attention, among which may be mentioned Stewkley, Buckinghamshire; Castle Rising, Norfolk; Adel, Yorkshire; Tickencote, Rutlandshire, and the transept of Winchester cathedral. If a tower is considered an essential requisite, perhaps one of the simplest is the short one in the centre of Iffley church, which may be seen in Britton's *Architectural Antiquities*, vol. v.; Castor Tower, the tower of Bury St. Edmunds, and the lower portion of the western towers of Lincoln cathedral, which may be found in the same volume, may also be consulted with advantage. For a country church, however, I am disposed to consider a belfry far more appropriate, particularly where the funds are circumscribed.

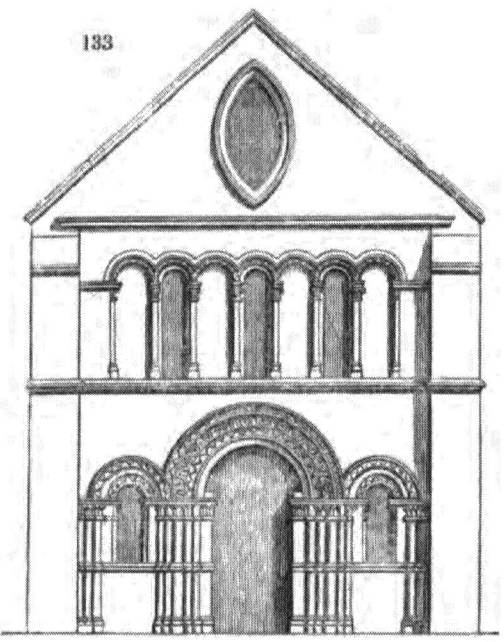

In illustration of the above remarks, I will proceed to describe a small church lately erected under my superintendence, at the village of Hoylake, in the county of Chester, at the mouth of the river Dee, about nine miles from Liverpool. In designing buildings of any description, but more particularly churches, if architects presume to deviate from the styles generally adopted and understood, they have frequently a host of ignorance and prejudice to contend with. This, however, I am happy to say, was not the case in the present instance; the Rev. C. L. Swainson, of St. Mary's Edge Hill, Liverpool, by whom and by whose benevolent family the principle part of the expense was defrayed, having himself originated the idea of introducing the Norman style.

Fig. 134. shows the north-west view. The west front is adopted, with a few modifications, from the west end of Castle Rising, Norfolk, which is one of the most picturesque little objects in the kingdom. The general effect will be sufficiently obvious without any detailed description. The side windows are finished with detached columns, and a deeply recessed archivolt, above, with bold chevron or zigzag mouldings. A plain parapet crowns the side walls, supported by corbels, consisting of human and wolves' heads. The buttresses are flat, and of one width to the top, where they are finished by plain set-offs. One of the principal differences between the plans of our modern churches and those erected before the Reformation is the want of a chancel. In churches erected at the present day, a small recess for the altar, generally flanked by a vestry at each side,

to Modern Ecclesiastical Edifices. 293

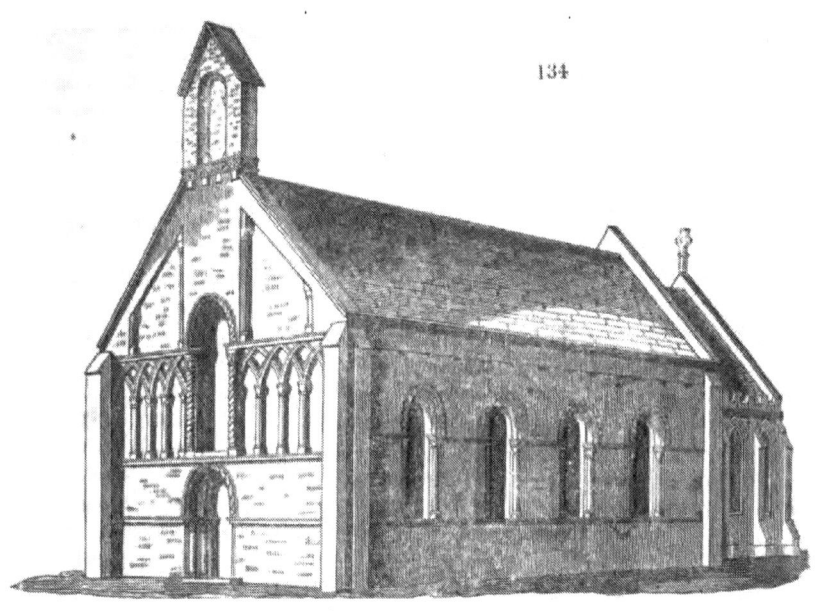

134

is the substitute. The chancel, in old churches, constituted a main feature of the building, even when there were no transepts; and it is frequently a source of great beauty and variety, from its having been erected at a different period from the nave or body of the church. This arrangement has been attempted in the present instance, as will be perceived from the ground plan (*fig.* 135.). The chancel is erected in the early pointed style of

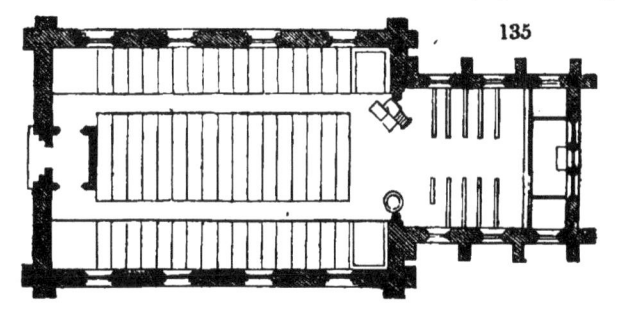

135

the thirteenth century, with narrow lancet windows, and bold projecting buttresses; the walls being finished with water table and embattled parapet. The east end is shown in *fig.* 136. The east window is similar to several in Salisbury Cathedral and Beverley Minster. Internally, the building is open to the frame timbers of the roof, which are moulded, and painted in imitation of dark oak; the trusses are bracketed down the walls, and rest on stone corbels, carved into grotesque heads. The chancel is divided from the church by a very deeply moulded Norman arch, ornamented with chevron mouldings, and springing from the capitals of two Norman columns. At the east end and flanking the altar on each side, are two wooden screens, with cast-iron tracery, in the perpendicular style, forming two small vestries. The front is an exact copy of a very beautiful Norman one at Lullington, Somersetshire; and the cover is constructed of antique carved oak. In the pulpits and desk, the porch, and details generally, the consistency of style is scrupulously maintained. There are no enclosed pews, the whole of the seats being open benches, with the elbows at the ends raised and carved into *fleurs-de-lis.* The exterior, and most of the ornamental work in the interior, is executed in red sandstone. The whole expense, after deducting the drawback of duty on the timber and glass, was about 1900*l.* The church affords accommodation for 466 sitters.

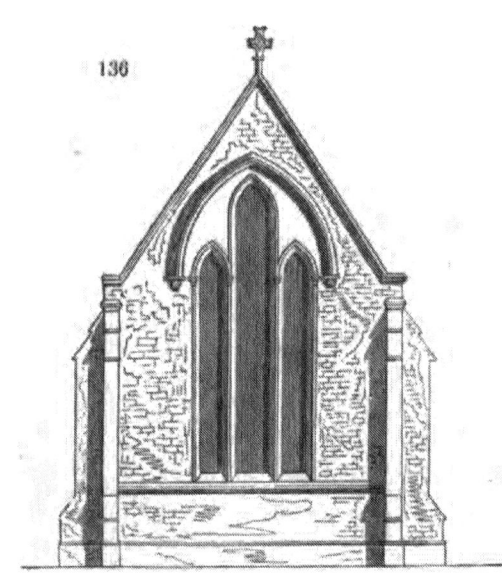

I have been induced to send you this detailed description from an earnest desire that a correct taste in architecture should be more generally diffused; and that the principles and capabilities of each style of the art should be more studied and better understood by the public at large. Then, and not till then, may we expect to see something like consistency in the adaptation of edifices to the scenery and locality in which they are to be placed. The Grecian temple or Roman Pantheon, adopted as a Christian place of worship, in a city, is tolerably consistent and harmonious; but, when transferred to the sylvan glades and rural valleys of England, can never call forth those emotions and associations excited by the " ivy-mantled tower ". or rude buttress of our own indigenous architecture. The columns on " Sunium's marbled steep " may suit the sunny skies and balmy air of the classic shores of Greece; but in the situation of the church described above, on the bleak strand of the

Irish Sea, exposed to all the fury of the north-western blasts, which, in a few hours, sometimes convert the country for miles round into a sandy desert, I think it must be acknowledged that the stern massiveness and grotesque combinations of the Norman style are much more appropriate.

The observations at the commencement of this paper do not, of course, apply in cases where the funds will admit of the varieties of the pointed style being correctly carried out in their principles and details. This, however, particularly in small edifices, is seldom the case. English architecture has revived under very different auspices, and in a very different state of society, from that in which it was carried to such a pitch of perfection. The almost inexhaustible resources and command of labour and skill which were formerly lavished in the erection of splendid edifices, for the purpose of a mistaken, though, perhaps, well-meant, superstition, are now expended in diffusing the comforts and conveniences of life among all classes of society. The standard of the necessaries of subsistence is elevated; and, in consequence, the wages of labour are raised. But whilst this result is greatly to be rejoiced at, we can see no reason why taste in design and correctness of detail should be at all inconsistent with economy in expenditure. This can only be accomplished by the more general diffusion of architectural knowledge among the public who employ and judge, as well as the architects who design. To this end, such publications as the *Encyclopædia of Architecture* and the *Architectural Magazine* are eminently conducive: and that they may effect a reformation in the architectual taste of the present and future generations is indeed "a consummation devoutly to be wished."

Liverpool, June 9. 1834.

ART. IV. *Notice of some Designs for Architectural Fountains, manufactured in Artificial Stone by Mr. Austin of London.* By the CONDUCTOR.

WE have more than once remarked on the obligations which architecture is under to the manufacturers of Roman and other cements, and of artificial stone. We have also noticed (p. 159. and p. 216.) the great degree of perfection, with reference to hardness and durability, to which Mr. Austin has brought his composition... All that appears farther wanting is, to make known generally to architects, and to amateurs of architecture and garden scenery, what can be effected in this material, at a price (as may easily be conceived) extremely moderate when compared with that of real stone. We have already (p. 159.) shown some of Mr. Austin's designs for chimney pots and shafts, and shall, at present, give figures of a few of his fountains.

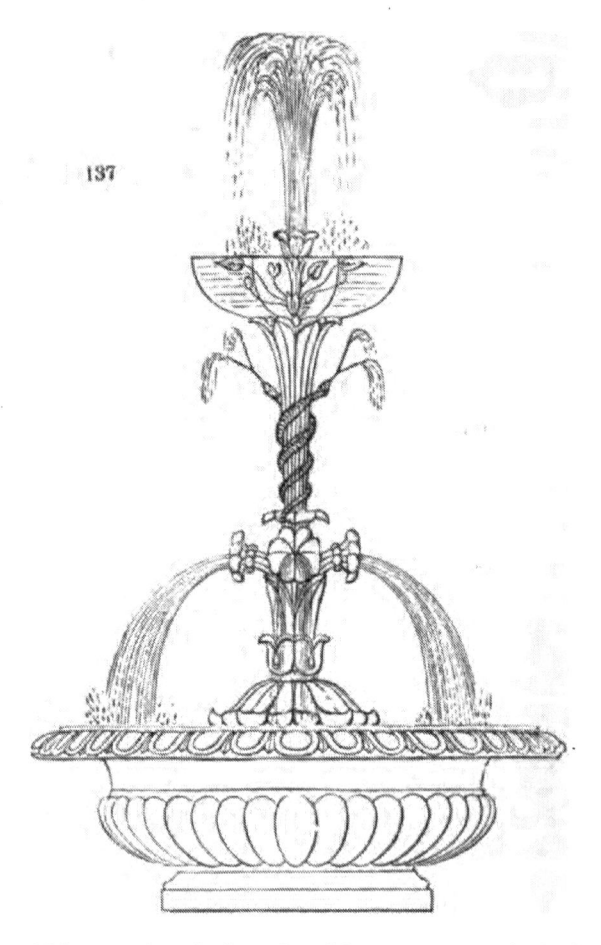

Fountains, it may be observed, are ornaments particularly suitable for architectural gardens; and, as these gardens are every day becoming more common in the country, because every day the art of harmonising architecture with landscape scenery is becoming better understood, we anticipate a corresponding increase in the employment of architectural fountains. All town gardens, by which we mean chiefly those in front of street houses, may be considered as architectural; and for them such fountains are particularly suitable. The same water, which is now supplied by the water companies direct to the kitchen cisterns, might first pass through the fountain; and, from its basin, be conducted to the cistern. In the winter season, during

138

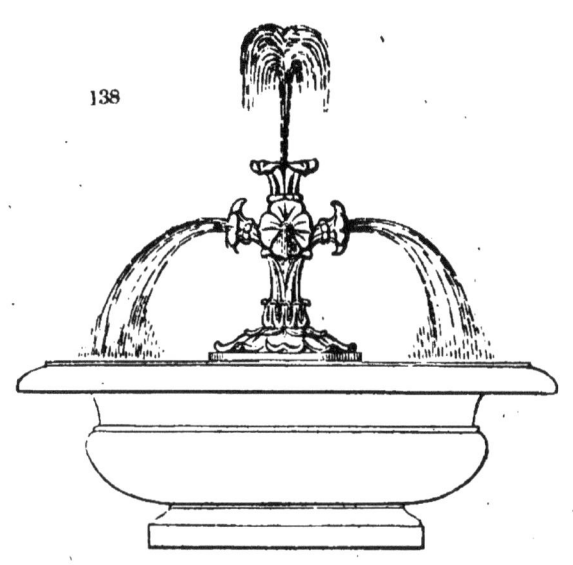

severe frost, this would be impracticable, but there could be no insurmountable objection to it, at least as far as we are aware, in the summer season. During winter, the fountains, though without water, would still be handsome as architectural ornaments; in the same manner as trees are still handsome at that season, though without leaves. All the water which enters kitchen cisterns should, in our opinion, be made to pass through a stratum of filtering materials; and this would free it from any impurities which it might receive while in the basin of the fountain.

139

The improvement of street houses, in various ways, seems to be making considerable progress. Public attention has lately been roused, on this subject, by those numerous erections called gin temples: every shop front that is renewed displays a somewhat more cultivated taste than it had before: square stone chimney pots are not unfrequently introduced; and balustrades in cement or artificial stone are, in many cases, substituted for plain brick parapets. Facings or dressings to windows are also more frequent than they used to be; but on this point, as Leigh Hunt has well observed, in his *London Journal*, we are still lamentably deficient; the windows and doors of whole streets being nothing more than what Mr. Woods, in his excellent *Letters*, &c., calls "mere holes in brick walls." A substitute for these facings is, in some houses, made up by flowers, trained up a sort of exterior architrave, formed of wire; and flowers, whether in open balconies, covered with verandas, on common window sills, or on the upper part of the entablature of shop fronts, form delightful ornaments to the most crowded parts of the metropolis; and, happily, are every year increasing. There are scarcely three houses together, in the whole length of Oxford Street, that do not display flowers at the windows, on the house top, or in the shop. The china shop, No. 209. in Oxford Street, has a beautiful crop of grapes both outside and inside. Ivy and Virginian creepers run up considerable portions of several fronts, and the day will perhaps come when every lamp-post will have an ornamental plant of some sort climbing round it. The house the most elegantly ornamented with flowers, between Bayswater and St. Paul's, is decidedly No. 5. St. George's Terrace, Oxford Road; where the wire architraves before mentioned are introduced, and covered with luxuriant creepers; and the balconies of the windows of five stories are richly stocked with geraniums and other beautiful flowering plants. We conclude this digression by referring to what Leigh Hunt has recently said on this subject, in Nos. 21, 22, and 23. of his *London Journal*.

We do not expect by this article all at once to render fountains a popular ornament in town gardens; but if it should be the means of introducing only one or two of them in the gardens of those long rows of houses lining the New Road, the Kent Road, and other suburban roads, we shall be satisfied with the beginning. That this article, and others which have appeared, and which shall appear, in the *Gardener's Magazine*, on foun-

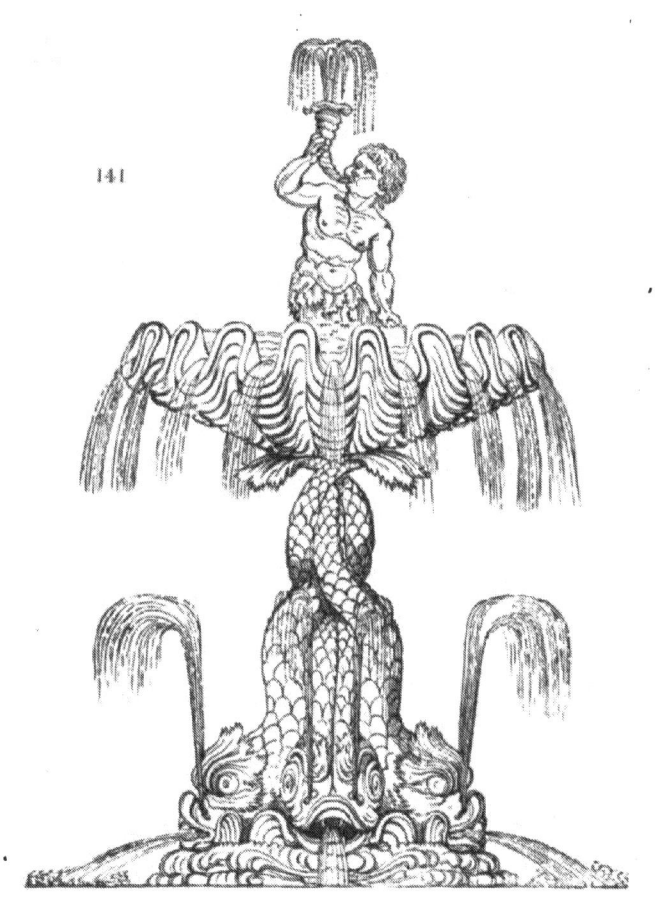

tains, vases, statues, and other architectural garden ornaments, will render them more general in villa gardens round the metropolis, and in architectural and flower-gardens in the country generally, we have not a doubt. We know, indeed, that this has already been the result, Mr. Austin having given us the names of many places to which he has supplied the stonework of fountains; and Mr. Rowley, the addresses of above a hundred noblemen and gentlemen, in different parts both of Great Britain and Ireland, to whom he has supplied the engineering apparatus for such foun-

tains. See *Gard. Mag.*, vol. vii. fig. 129.; vol. viii. fig. 42.; and vol. ix. fig. 62. to 69.: see, also, *Encyclopædia of Cottage, Farm, and Villa Architecture*, p. 987.; and the *Encyclopædia of Gardening*, new edit. In the historical part of the latter work there are many beautiful designs for fountains executed in different parts of Europe; and, among others, that of a pagoda fountain, 100 ft. high (p. 333.), which was intended to be erected by the late Earl of Shrewsbury, in the Enchanted Valley at Alton Towers, Staffordshire.

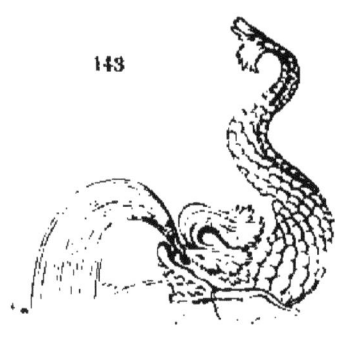

All the designs figured in this article have been executed, and most of them may be seen, at Mr. Austin's very interesting museum. *Fig.* 137. is an elegant design, which may be seen in operation, in the Conservatory at the Pantheon Bazaar. The basin from which the upper jet springs is of crystal; it contains a painted copper water lily, from the flower of which the jet issues, and also gold fish. It appears to us that there is a baldness about this crystal vase, when compared with the richness of the other parts of the composition; the rim ought surely to have projected, or to have shown some lines. We do not altogether approve of spreading the leaves of the water lily about in a natural-looking manner; more especially as they are painted green. They approach too near to a facsimile imitation, and ought, we think, to have been more sculpturesque; or, in the language of our article on the principles of art, &c. (p. 281.), that the recognition of art should have been more perceptible. Fountains of this kind, terminating in elegant glass vases containing gold fish, are particularly suitable for green-houses and conservatories.

Fig. 138. is also a conservatory fountain, composed of a portion of *fig.* 137., fixed over a basin or tazza vase, of a simple, but elegant shape. We introduce it not only to show a reason why Mr. Austin can compose a great many different kinds of fountains out of a given number of what may be called elementary parts, but to demonstrate that, several of his fountains being composed in this way, they must necessarily be less expensive than if all the separate parts of each design were modelled expressly for it.

Figs. 139, 140, and 141. are dolphin fountains, and *figs.* 142. and 143. are dolphins that can be put as supports to tazza vases, so as to form a fountain somewhat in the style of *figs.* 140. and 141. It will be observed that the same triton serves both for *fig.* 139. and *fig.* 141.; which contributes, as we have said above, both to variety and cheapness.

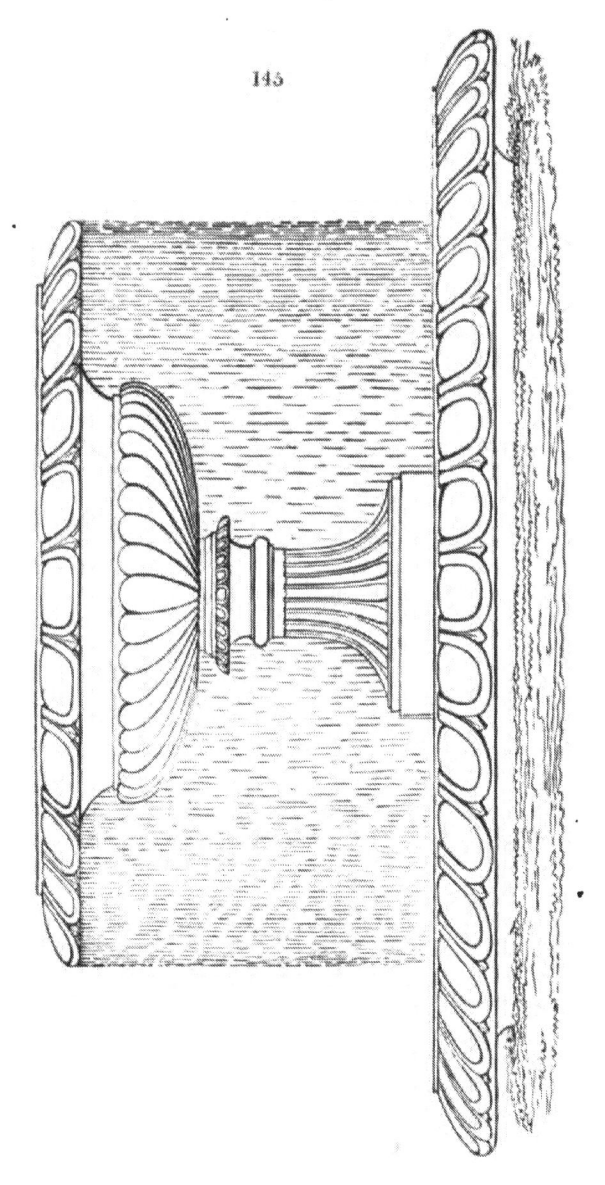

Fig. 144. forms one of three supports to a beautiful tazza fountain erected by Mr. Austin, for Lady Amherst, at Montreal House in Kent.

Fig. 145. consists of two separate parts; the tazza or basin, and the vase from which the water overflows. In this basin may be placed a pyramid of tazza vases, diminishing gradually in size, one above another, commencing with the one in *fig.* 145., and terminating with *fig.* 146. or *fig.* 147., according to the height of the source from which the water is supplied; or a nozzle, forming the water convolvulus, *fig.* 148., may furnish a termination to the whole.

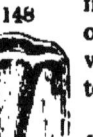

The tazza or lower part of *fig.* 145. may form a basin for *figs.* 139, 140, 141, &c.; as the tazzas of *figs.* 137. and 138. may be used as basins for other figures or small jets.

Art. V. *On the Domestic Offices of a House.* By I. J. Kent, Esq., Architect.

The *Kitchen*, a most useful and necessary apartment in every house, being chiefly used for the preparation of food, should be furnished with every thing necessary to enable the cook to perform her duties. It should be as lofty as circumstances will allow: this is a most important point, and should be attended to in all houses. In small houses, it is especially necessary, as low kitchens are generally dark, and light is essential both to cleanliness and comfort. In many third and fourth rate houses in London, the kitchens are so low and dark, that the servants employed to wash up the tea things, glasses, and other articles, generally, in such houses, washed in the kitchen, cannot see when they are clean. When cooking is going on, the whole kitchen is filled with steam; the tin covers and other utensils, which ought to look bright, become dim, and everything has an air of dirt and untidiness. In houses of these classes, therefore, the kitchen ought always to be made more lofty than it is at present; and, instead of the lowest, it ought to be the loftiest apartment in the house. In most parts of England, the kitchen is in the basement story, or on the ground floor; but in Genoa, and many other towns in Italy, it is in the upper story of the house. This is convenient for the escape of smells, but very inconvenient in almost every other respect. Sometimes the kitchen is on the same floor with the dining-room, but detached from the house, and under a flat roof, covered with lead, or, what is termed in London a lead flat. When this is the case, the flat should be pugged (stuffed between the roof and the ceiling with some non-conducting substance), and ventilated, so as to keep out the intense heat, which would otherwise penetrate the lead. In houses of a superior description, the kitchen should be not only lofty and light, but also well ventilated, or supplied with air flues for carrying off the steam, and the effluvia from the food. When this precaution is neglected, even in lofty kitchens, the steam hangs like a cloud below the ceiling, and the smell of the food, when cooking, is often found very unpleasant. Sometimes the escape of these effluvia to the living-rooms of the house is prevented by pugging; but this only confines them to the kitchen, while the air flues carry them away into the open air.

Where practicable, the kitchen should look to the north, or the north-east, as should all those domestic offices which require to be kept cool. When the kitchen is under ground, as is frequently the case in England, particularly in large towns, this is not of so much consequence; but it should always be as near as possible to the dining-room. In large houses it is desirable to have a private communication between the kitchen and the dining-room, by a passage (and staircase, if the kitchen, &c., are under ground) leading into an anteroom, or waiting-room for the servants, adjoining the dining-room. This passage should be thoroughly ventilated, so that any escape of effluvia from the kitchen, &c., may be dispersed before it reaches the anteroom. The anteroom should be furnished with broad shelves, fixed to the wall, with drawers beneath, to hold such articles as may be wanted by the servants waiting in the dining-room. In some houses there is a hot table, warmed by pipes of hot water, or flues, to set the dishes on, when brought from the kitchen, before they are carried into the dining-room.

A kitchen should be dry: the walls must therefore be preserved from damp, if the kitchen be under ground, by building them in cement, at least as high as the level of the floor; and, where ground is against any of the walls, it may be necessary to build an inner wall one brick thick, and hollow, against the outer wall; or to build a dry area, carried down below the level of the floor of the kitchen, which area should be ventilated and drained. The floor should be of rubbed Yorkshire stone, laid on brick walls at least two courses of bricks high above the ground. If the foundation is damp, concrete 1 ft. or 2 ft. thick, composed of clean gravel and fresh-burnt stone lime, should be thrown in first, on which the walls should be built; and air should be introduced and made to circulate freely under the stone floor, for which purpose air gratings should be fixed in all the outward walls, and openings for the air to pass through left in all the walls on which the paving is laid.

In very large kitchens, a portion of the floor opposite the fireplace, about the centre of the kitchen, and from 6 ft. to 10 ft. square, according to circumstances, should be of wood; that is, of oak joists and sleepers laid on brick walls, with a deal or oak floor. On this wooden floor the table should be placed, and by this means the cook may generally be able to avoid standing on the stone floor. The skirtings should be made with cement (not wood), wherever there are stone floors.

The ceiling of a kitchen should be always plastered; for, if this is not done, the effluvia arising from the cooking collect, and remain between the joists, in spite of all the ventilation you can provide; the spaces between the joists also afford shelter for flies, spiders, &c. As the ceilings of kitchens should be scraped, whitewashed, cleaned, and whitened (or coloured), every year, the expense of plastering is soon repaid by the diminution of the surface; the sides of the joists making a surface of one and a half times more than the whole of the ceiling.

The doors should be all made to open towards the fireplace, otherwise the opening and shutting of them will be likely to cause the chimney to smoke.

The fireplace should be capacious in proportion to the quantity of cooking required; from 4 ft. to 8 ft. or 9 ft. wide, and never less than two bricks and a half, or 1 ft. $10\frac{1}{2}$ in. deep. Large fireplaces should be 2 ft. 3 in. to 2 ft. $7\frac{1}{2}$ in deep; the range can then have a proper boiler at the back, supplied with water by a pipe from the main cistern, and regulated by a small feeding cistern, so that the boiler will always be full of water: where this plan is adopted, you will have a supply of hot, if not boiling, water at night as well as by day. A screen extending the width of the opening of the fireplaces is quite necessary, when much cooking is required, to render the kitchen complete and comfortable; this may be used as a hot closet, as well as a warmer for the plates and dishes, and it likewise saves fuel, by accelerating the roasting of the meat. In large kitchens there should be a hot plate and preserving stoves on one side of the fireplace, and a boiler on the other; these should be covered over, at the height of 6 ft. or 7 ft., by a projection or canopy from the wall, open in front, and communicating with a flue for carrying off the steam and effluvia from the meat. There should be one or two large closets, from 3 ft. to 4 ft. wide, and at least 18 in. deep, for holding spices and other things that may be wanted by the cook.

The principal furniture required in a kitchen are, a table as large as the size of the apartment will allow, and made very strong; and a dresser or dressers. The tops of these dressers should be 2 in. thick, and the drawers about 2 ft. wide, and 7 in. deep. The space under the drawers is sometimes enclosed with doors, and sometimes open, having a pot board the whole width and length of the dresser, and raised 3 in. or 4 in. from the floor. There should be good locks on one or two of the drawers, and two iron or japanned handles fixed on each. A mill for coffee, one for pepper, and another for the finer spices, may be fixed to the ends of the dressers. Ranges of rails, furnished with hooks, should be fixed to the wall for the dish covers, and round towel rollers behind the doors. There should be an ash grate and pit under the fireplace, and in large establishments a smoke jack, as it is not only the best for roasting meat, but is always ready. Where there is no smoke jack, a bottle jack is generally employed as a substitute; and this, when not in use, should be hung on a hook purposely fixed in the wall, with a small hook near it, for the key. A bottle jack should always be used with a tin stand or case, called a hastener, moveable, and standing on feet, with a dripping-pan fixed in the bottom. This case is open to the fire in front, but closed at the back and sides. It should be of block tin, and should be kept very bright inside, that the rays of heat may be reflected back on the meat. Sometimes the hastener is made to serve also as a plate-warmer. When the bottle jack is not used with a hastener, or, at any rate, not fixed to it, there should be a small notched brass crow fixed to the mantelpiece for it to hang upon.

The Coal-cellar should be placed as near to the kitchen as possible, and should be sufficiently large to hold coals for nine months' consumption. There should be a ready access to it from without, for the men to shoot the coals into it.

The Scullery should be as close to the kitchen fireplace as possible. It should be paved with Yorkshire stone or brickwork, and need not be more than 9 ft. or 10 ft. high.

In every scullery there should be a stone sink as large as the space will allow, 7 in. to 8 in. thick, leaving room for a plate rack at one end. Under the plate rack, or by the side of it, should be a slanting drip-board, to convey the water that runs from the plates and dishes into the sink. A waste pipe should be fixed in the bottom of the sink, and taken into the drain, with a bell stink-trap and grating over it; or the waste pipe may be taken into a trap in the drain, and the grating soldered into the sink. Under the sink, or in some other convenient part of the floor, should be fixed a large airtight stink-trap, to carry off the water when the floor is cleansed. There should be no sink stone (a stone pierced with holes to allow the water to run off, but without any cover), as that is the most frequent means by which noisome smells escape from the drains. Hot water should be supplied to the sink by pipes taken from the cistern into the boiler at the back of the kitchen fireplace, and there coiled round several times; then conveyed to the sink, and afterwards to the washing-troughs in the wash-house, when they are situated below the level of the cistern: cold water should be also conveyed to the sink, which may be done in pipes direct from the cistern.

The Larder, or safe, for keeping the meat and other provisions in, both before and after they are cooked, should be large, and, indeed, sufficiently capacious to contain all the provisions. It should be effectually protected from the sun's rays, and yet have a complete circulation of air all round it, if possible: it should be so placed as not to be near the dust bin or beer casks, or any other place from which dust or putrid or other bad smells can arise: it should be enclosed all round with fly-wire panels in wood framing, and should be raised above the paving, in order to admit air at bottom, and to keep it dry. The ventilation should be free at top, and be protected from rain by a double roof: it should be lofty, and should have strong iron bearers, with hooks to slide on them, so that the meat may hang above the head; and shelves, from 18 in. to 2 ft. wide round, to put dishes on. A separate safe should be provided for vegetables and fruits, and for game, if there is any quantity of it. For large safes, where it can be contrived, there should be an inner door, with a space between the doors, to enable the cook to shut the one before she opens the other. The outer or first portion of the safe may be used for those provisions that will be wanted first. For small families, one or two iron safes, hanging from some beam in the ceiling, contrived so as to be drawn up out of the way by lines and pulleys, when not in use, with one or more shelves in each, and having fly-wire all round, are far better than the safes placed against brick walls, as is most usual.

The Cistern. — Over the scullery may be the cistern intended to supply the whole of the basement story with water. This, whether inside or outside of the building, should always be covered over, and have a flap in the cover to give access to the pipes. The best kind of cistern is formed of quartering framed together, with the bottom and sides boarded and lined with lead. The lead at the bottom should, in ordinary cases, be 7 lb. to 8 lb. weight to the foot, and that at the sides 5 lb. to 6 lb. to the foot; but, where the water has a tendency to corrode the lead (for instance, if at all impregnated with any kind of salt), the lead should be proportionably thicker. The pipes to supply the cistern, as well as the pipes from the cistern to serve the different sinks, &c., should be of the kind called by the lead merchant extra-strong pipe; particularly those pipes that are laid under the ground, and those that are outside the building, and are exposed to the frost in winter. All pipes outside the building should be covered over, to protect them from injury by blows or frost. The cocks should always be of the very best manufacture, or they will be constant sources of annoyance and expense.

The Beer Cellar and the Wine Cellar. — These cellars should not have any communication with each other. Both should be arched and dry, and neither should ever be placed, if it can possibly be avoided, under the yard: if, however, such a situation be inevitable, the cellars should have solid spandrils, and be covered with two or three courses of plain tiles laid in cement. The wine cellar should be fitted up with bins, and, where large enough, divided so as to form an inner and an outer cellar; perhaps the best method of dividing the bins is by walls half a brick thick, and carried up to the top with horizontal York stone shelves every 3 ft., to divide the bins in their height. As some wines require a warmer temperature than others, the pipes that are to supply the several sinks with hot water may be carried through some of the bins, or through that portion of the cellar which is separated by a brick wall, and thus a warm cellar may be obtained at very small expense.

In large or first-rate houses, a butler's pantry, or footman's room, a housekeeper's room, and a servants' hall are indispensable. These rooms should all have wood floors in the centre, with a course of stone paving, 2 ft. wide, all round against the walls. The floors should be laid hollow on brickwork, as described for the kitchen, and the skirting should be of cement. An air flue carried up from the hollow space under the floor, close to the chimney, would be very desirable, to keep up a constant current of air under the floors. The sinks in these rooms (of which there should be two in each, fitted up in a window recess) should be lined with lead. They should be each about 18 in. or 2 ft. long, and 12 in. or 15 in. wide, side by side, and about 12 in. deep; each should be covered with a flap, and have the space beneath it enclosed with doors, to form closets, with a shelf in each. One of the sinks should have a brass grating, about $3\frac{1}{2}$ in. diameter, soldered into the bottom, with a wood drainer for decanters, &c.; and the other a washer and plug with a chain. A waste pipe should be soldered into each sink; but none of these pipes must be taken into the drain without the intervention of some trap, otherwise the foul smells from the drains will be a source of annoyance. Waste pipes of this kind are sometimes allowed to empty themselves into the open area over a sink-stone trapped.

The Housekeeper's Room should have a series of closets, 2 ft. deep; some with shelves for linen; others for pickles and preserves; and, again, others with drawers for stores of various kinds.

The Footman's Room, or Butler's Pantry, should have, in addition to the sinks, a large dresser fitted up with drawers and closets underneath; with a wide shelf continued all along the room, above the level of the top of the door. Adjoining this room should be a fire-proof plate closet, ventilated and kept sufficiently warm to prevent it from being in the least damp. The pipes that convey the hot water to the several sinks may be made to pass round this plate closet, as well as through the wine cellar, as, when damp gains admittance, it causes double trouble to the footman, by tarnishing the plate. The plate closet should be fitted up with shelves lined with thick drugget.

The Passages should be well lighted and ventilated; otherwise the smells arising from the drains, the kitchen, &c., will be carried up into the body of the house, the air above being more rarefied than that below. The passages should be paved all over with stone or brickwork, with the skirtings of cement, and the walls plastered with stone, lime, and sand, lined out into blocks, in imitation of stones, and coloured. Plastering of this kind is much more durable than plastering composed of chalk, lime, and dirt, such as is now generally used, and is very little more expense. The bell board should be fixed in the passage between the kitchen and the servants' hall; each bell should have a pendulum attached to the spring, and the names of the rooms written on the bell board below the bells.

Manor Place, Paddington, July 25. 1834.

Art. VI. *Notice of a Marble Table, with a Cast-Iron Pillar, constructed on an economical Principle, under the Direction of John Robison, Esq.* Communicated by Mr. Robison.

I send you herewith a rude sketch (*fig.* 149.) of a marble table with a cast-iron pillar, the latter cast in a portion of the mould of our street-lamp pillars. I had it cast of the proper length, with a flat plate at the top, as shown in *fig.* 150., and by putting it in the lathe, and dressing the top plate and edge of the bottom moulding parallel to each other, I have insured the verticality of the pillar and the parallelism of the table with the floor of the rooms, which is scarcely ever seen in pillar tables with heavy tops.

The screw-bolts, for screwing the base of the pillar to the plinth on which it stands, are shown at *a.* It makes a very handsome piece of furniture, yet is very moderate in its cost. The Pyrenean marbles are very cheap at Toulon and Bordeaux; and, as there is a constant communication between the latter place and London, by the wine ships, nothing is easier than to get slabs or tables of any dimensions from that quarter. Marble steps, slabs, flower-tables, garden seats, &c., might be cut at Bordeaux for British use, from drawings sent from England.

Marble tops of 42 in. in diameter, and with a raised border, cost at Bordeaux, in 1832, from 75 to 85 francs; and the same size, when without a raised border, from 40 to 45 francs. The freight from Bordeaux to Edinburgh is 50*s.* per ton, and the duty 3*s.* 6*d.* per cwt.

WE have lately heard of a new and most valuable caster invented for tables by the author of the above communication, who has promised us an account of it. It is very strong, will not require oiling for many years, and is not liable to go out of order.

ART. VII. *Architectural Maxims.*

ARCHITECTURE *is the oldest and most sublime of all the Arts;* and though it must excite the feelings through the medium of thought, yet, perhaps, the feelings which it does excite are, on that account, only so much the more powerful. (*A. G. Schlegel.*)

Qualifications of a Critic. — No man can be a true critic or connoisseur, who has not a universality of mind, and who does not possess that flexibility, which, throwing aside all personal predilections and blind habits, enables him to transport himself into the peculiarities of other ages and nations, to feel them, as it were, from their proper central point; and which enables human nature to recognise and respect whatever is beautiful and grand under those external modifications which are necessary to their existence, but which sometimes even seem to disguise them. (*A. G. Schlegel, on Dramatic Literature,* vol. i. p. 3.)

To check Empiricism. — The most effectual method to check the empiricism, either of art or science, is to multiply, as far as possible, the number of those who can observe and judge. (*Alison.*)

Genius, at least what is generally so called, is the child of imitation. It is in vain to endeavour to invent without materials on which the mind may work, and in which invention must originate. Nothing can come of nothing. (*Reynolds.*)

REVIEWS.

ART. I. *Brief Memoir of Sir John Soane, R.A. F.R. and A.S., Professor of Architecture in the Royal Academy, &c.* By JOHN BRITTON, F.S.A. 4to. London, 1834. (Not for sale.)

THIS memoir was prepared, by Mr. Britton, for Fisher's *National Portrait Gallery*. It is accompanied by a beautifully engraved portrait of Sir John Soane, by Thompson, after a painting by Sir Thomas Lawrence; on which Mr. Britton remarks, that "it not merely delineates the features of the countenance, but marks the air, the expression, and the apparent thinking of the living model." On the titlepage there is a beautiful group of vases from the Soanean Museum, engraved on wood by Thompson, after a drawing by Harvey; and in the last page there is an antique bas-relief, drawn on wood by the same artist, and engraved by Williams.

In Mr. Britton's introductory remarks, he states, that no architect, since the days of Vitruvius, has had his name and works known by a larger portion of the public than Sir John Soane. Sir Christopher Wren, who, like him, designed many large edifices, also lived to an old age, and was almost a martyr to litigation and splenetic criticism; but, in those days, the press was but of limited range. Now, however, the press is all-powerful, and Sir John Soane has been assailed by it because he has been fortunate and popular; and has attained wealth and honours. Every part of London can show buildings designed by Sir John Soane; and, in his work entitled *Designs for Public and Private Buildings*, folio, 1828, will be also found the plans of numerous villas and mansions, executed by him in different parts of the country. "These, however, are not the only objects that have tended to keep the name of Sir John Soane before the public for more than half a century; but, as Professor of Architecture in the Royal Academy, and as Author of various pamphlets and volumes on his professional studies, and from having been an extensive and liberal benefactor to many institutions connected with the fine arts, sciences, and literature of the country, he has acquired no small portion of publicity and distinction."

"The public character of an artist," Mr. Britton observes, "is generally indicated by his professional works, which form the chief legitimate objects of commentary for the biographer. Raphael, Wren, &c., have left decided proofs of their talents;" and, of Sir John Soane, Mr. Britton adds, "it may suffice to point to the Bank of England, and say, 'That is his work;' and we will venture to assert, that, on careful examination, it will be found to manifest a fertile fancy, great abilities, and varied attributes of architectural skill. It is stamped with the broad mark of the artist's own genius, and is contradistinguished from the designs of all his predecessors and contemporaries."*

Sir John Soane was born at Reading, in Berkshire, in 1756; and, when a boy, he was placed in the office of George Dance, an architect of eminence. There young Soane "soon displayed those attributes of genius, zeal, acuteness, and perseverance, which generally lead to fame." When a student in the Royal Academy, he obtained a prize medal; and was made one of its travelling students, with a small annual stipend. He left England in 1777; and, after having been some time in Italy, returned to England, with his portfolio well stocked with sketches. He was tempted to visit Greece; but resisted the

---

* To the interior of the Bank of England, we understand, our author's remarks will apply; but as to the exterior, with the single exception of the north-west angle, we do not know a public building so little to our taste in the metropolis. There is a want of unity of design throughout; and what can argue a greater deficiency in one of the qualities assigned by Mr. Britton to the architect, viz. fertility of fancy, than the introduction of blank windows in the boundary wall of an aggregation of buildings? — *Cond.*

temptation, because his associates were to be young Englishmen of fortune. While at Rome, he made a design for a senate-house, and one for a royal palace: views of which are in the work before alluded to. The palace was to be erected in Hyde Park, with a series of magnificent mansions extending from Knightsbridge to Bayswater. This design was much approved of by Lord Camelford; who became a warm friend and patron of the young architect when he settled in London, in about 1780. From this time to 1788, Sir John Soane was chiefly engaged in making designs for country mansions. In that year, he succeeded Sir Robert Taylor as architect to the Bank of England; and, soon after, commenced his professional operations as bank architect, by making an elaborate ground plan of the whole range of offices in their present state, with another as he proposed to arrange them. " Several houses, with a church, were to be purchased and pulled down; and the whole was to be an insulated stone edifice, constructed in the most suitable and substantial manner, without external windows; calculated for extended durability, and to resist fire." An essay on the merits of the bank, as a piece of architecture, will be found in *Illustrations of the Public Buildings of London*; 2 vols. 8vo.

Mr. Britton next notices some designs for public buildings, made by Sir John Soane, which were never executed; and others which have been only partially carried into execution. Among the latter are designs for the Board of Trade and Privy Council Offices (a model of which will be found in Mr. Day's collection, p. 138.). The new law courts at Westminster are referred to, as a test of Sir John Soane's abilities and science.

Within a limited space, Mr. Britton says:—"The architect has arranged and erected seven public courts, adapted for the accommodation of judges, counsel, lawyers, juries, witnesses, spectators, &c.; with appropriate corridors, retiring and waiting rooms, apartments for officers, &c. . . . The works were prosecuted with rapidity; and were very far advanced, when some architectural amateurs of the House of Commons found fault with the design, and obtained an order of the House to pull down a large mass of the building. Still farther, they recommended and secured the same sanction for an architectural design of their own, in what they called the Gothic style, to be built, and added to the architect's interiors, in which there is nothing Gothic." In consequence of frequent and severe remarks on these law courts in the House of Commons, and by the public press, Sir John Soane published a folio volume, in 1828, entitled *A Brief Statement of the Proceedings respecting the new Law Courts at Westminster.* "This work contains all the plans, elevations, views, &c.; and," Mr. Britton says, "may be referred to as a literary, graphic, professional, and political curiosity; eminently calculated to afford useful suggestions to young architects, and even to barristers and statesmen."

"Without the aid of illustrations," Mr. Britton observes, "it would be useless to make farther comments on Sir John's designs;" and, in conclusion, he adds, " It is but justice to say, that, in making estimates, in a comprehensive knowledge of the value and quality of materials, in directing sound construction, and in the skilful arrangement of plans, Sir John Soane is allowed, by his professional brethren and rivals, to possess and exercise on all occasions a discriminating judgment." (p. 12.)

We shall conclude our notice with some account of Sir John Soane's house and museum in Lincoln's-Inn-Fields; which he has, with such commendable liberality, bequeathed to the public.

Sir John Soane's house, in Lincoln's-Inn-Fields, is distinguished by having a stone veranda, or screen, in front. The interior and the museum have constantly received additions up to the end of the year 1833; and, by act of parliament passed that year, Sir John Soane "has settled on trustees, for the benefit of future architects, and for the gratification of artists and amateurs, his inestimable museum and library. To preserve these, in their entireness, within the walls which were purposely raised for their reception and display, and in union with the numerous and original architectural forms and effects which belong to the house, the most prudent and strict clauses are introduced into the act; and the interest of 30,000*l*., with the rent of an adjoining house, are appropriated and granted to support and uphold the premises, and provide for a suitable domestic establishment. The whole is to be opened, for public examination, and for the study of artists, at certain times, and under due regulations; and thus a commencement is made towards supplying that desideratum, a national architectural academy. The Soanean Museum may be hailed as a novelty in this country, and probably in the world; and cannot fail of proving highly beneficial to the student in architecture, and more particularly to those persons of ardent and keenly inquisitive dispositions, who can neither afford time nor money to travel and examine the ancient edifices of distant countries. Of this truly novel and munificent donation to the public, it may be proper to give a very brief account; for it constitutes an important, a prominent feature in the biography of its proprietor and founder. A very concise catalogue of the contents of the museum and library, and a list of its pictures and drawings, would occupy a very large volume. They consist of several thousand books and MSS.; some hundreds of architectural fragments, casts, and models; numerous pieces of ancient and modern sculpture; an immense collection of architectural drawings; and several fine pictures, by Reynolds, Lawrence, Hogarth, Turner, Calcott, Howard, Jones, Canaletti; together with many objects of virtù and rarity. These are dispersed and arranged over nearly the whole of the house, from the attics to the basement floor. At the conclusion of the professor's twelfth lecture, at the Royal Academy, March 21. 1833, Sir John, speaking of his house and its contents, said:—'This collection, which is now my absolute property, I hold henceforth as a trustee for the country; and, when I can no longer give my personal care to its protection and enlargement, that duty will devolve on others; who will exercise this trust under such regulations as will insure the perpetuation of those national advantages, to the promotion of which I have dedicated a large portion of an active and anxious life.' " *

If envy be ever allowable, that man may well be envied who has been the architect of such a fortune, who has maintained through a long life such an unspotted reputation for probity and honour, and who, in the prospect of terminating his career, can leave behind him such a monument.

ART. II.' *Observations on Building and Brickmaking: to which are subjoined Extracts from Testimonials in behalf of S. R. Bakewell's Brickmaking Machines.* By S. R. Bakewell. Pamph. 8vo. Manchester, 1834.

THERE is an account of this tract given at some length in the *Mechanics' Magazine*, No. 578., for Sept. 6. 1834, to which we refer our readers; observing only, that the intelligent editor of that work considers Mr. Bakewell as having made important improvements in the art of brickmaking: which improvements, he thinks, will ere long be universally adopted. One of these consists in a more rapid and perfect manner of mixing and tempering the clay; and another, in employing a machine to press the clay, when in a half-dry state, into the mould before burning. The machine for pressing is very simple, and easily worked; though it is capable of communicating a pressure to the bricks, when in a half-dried state, of more than two tons. The bricks, when pressed, fired, and ready for the builder, have the upper and under face of each, and also the two ends, indented or countersunk, about a quarter of an inch deep, and within an inch of their edges. This enables the bricklayer to make much smaller joints than he can with bricks as they are at present formed; while the mortar which fills the cavities forms a sort of

---

* A ground plan, with views of the different apartments, and of several architectural and sculptured objects, with a descriptive account of the house, are published in a quarto volume, entitled *The Union of Architecture, Sculpture, and Painting*, by John Britton, F.S.A.

dowel to hold the walls together. In short, it is clear to us that both the beauty and durability of these bricks, and of the walls in which they are used, must far exceed anything hitherto to be met with in this country; and we can only hope that Mr. Bakewell's improvements will speedily come into use in the neighbourhood of London. Walls properly built of good sound bricks of the common manufacture, and with good stone lime and Thames sand, we consider as far stronger than any description of stone walls, except those formed of large blocks; but those formed of bricks manufactured in Mr. Bakewell's manner will be both more handsome and more durable than any brick walls heretofore erected. The great strength of brick walls is the result of their homogeneousness, supposing, of course, that they are properly built with the best mortar; and their durability depends jointly on their homogeneousness, and on the thorough vitrification of the bricks of which they are composed.

ART. III. *Catalogue of Works on Architecture, Building, and Furnishing, and on the Arts more immediately connected therewith, recently published.*

BILLINGTON's *Architectural Director, &c.* Parts 6. and 7. 2s. 6d. each.

Part 6. contains a transverse section of a church at Genoa; ornaments of mouldings; a door in Rome; plan and elevations of a house in Rome; impost and architraves of the five orders, and a Doric door. The letterpress consists of a comparative table of the general proportions of the Ionic Order. The descriptions of the orders, &c., go as far as p. 224., and there are eight pages of the lexicon.

Part 7. contains three plans of houses in Rome; two plates of ornament; a plate of the Composite Order; one of the crowning entablature, and another of details of the same order. The letterpress includes a table of the Corinthian Order of Vignola; the directions, &c., for drawing the orders, go as far as p. 264.; and there are eight pages of lexicon. In the latter, the second term which occurs is "Clear-story windows;" and we have, as an explanation, "windows which are without transomes:" whereas the words "clear-story windows," as every Gothic architect knows, mean simply over-story windows; being applied to the windows in the upper stage or story of the naves of churches, which are over, and clear and detached from, the aisles. This part of the work, as we said before, is singularly imperfect.

Locke, Johnson, and Copland's Ornamental Designs. 4to, 25 plates. London, 1834. 9s. 6d.

These designs are intended for the ornamental painter, carver and gilder, and printed paper and printed cotton manufacturer. They also include shields, compartments, masks, &c. They were originally published more than half a century ago; and this work is a reprint, with a view to supply the present demand for the grotesque fanciful ornaments commonly said to be in the style of Louis XIV. A good deal of fancy is certainly displayed in these ornaments; but it is fancy of the most inferior kind of art, a fancy which is chiefly exercised in combining into a whole lines and forms which have little or no meaning of themselves. Were lines and forms representing natural objects (such as trees, flowers, animals, insects; or artificial objects, such as buildings, statues, sculpture, furniture, &c.), so combined, there would then be a higher degree of fancy displayed; more mind, at all events; and, according to the taste and talent of the artist, some degree of sentiment of love, or admiration; or of the elegant, the romantic, the rural, or the classical, instead of the mere picturesque, or more frequently the grotesque. This last term is very properly applied to subjects like those before us; since, as far as they do imitate natural forms, they are chiefly shells, or such fragments of shells or other marine productions, as are used in grottoes. This book is abundantly cheap, which is the best thing we can say of it.

ART. IV. *Literary Notices.*

ELEMENTARY *and Practical Instructions on the Art of building Cottages and Houses for the humbler Classes.* — An easy method of constructing earthen walls, adapted to the erection of dwelling-houses, agricultural and other buildings, surpassing those built of timber in comfort and stability, and equalling those built of brick; at the same time effecting a considerable saving in the expense, as it may be performed by any person without previous experience, and in any climate: to which is added, a practical treatise on the manufacture of bricks and lime, and on the arts of digging wells, and draining, rearing and managing a vegetable garden; of the management of pigs, poultry, sheep, and other cattle; making of bacon, hams, &c., for winter stock. The whole applied for the use of emigrants, to the better lodging of the peasantry of Ireland, and to those districts to which the benevolence of landed proprietors is now directed. With six plates of plans and elevations, and several woodcuts of details. Lond. 8vo.

Eight Views of Fountain Abbey, intended to illustrate the architectural and picturesque scenery of that celebrated ruin; etched on copperplate from original drawings by J. Metcalf and J. W. Carmichael; with a historical and architectural description, by T. Sopwith, author of various works on architecture, the surveying of mines, and land-surveying. Lond.

MISCELLANEOUS INTELLIGENCE.

ART. I. *General Notices.*

VERANDAS *and Windows.* — There are some excellent remarks on the subjects of these parts of a house in *Leigh Hunt's London Journal*, No. 31. for August, 1834. This Journal, which is published weekly at three halfpence, is, in our opinion, the most delightful of all the cheap periodicals of the present day. It treats of the same subjects as the *Spectator* of old, and is, in our times, what the *Spectator* and the *Tatler* were in the reigns of William III. and Anne. If there are any of our readers who do not take it in, we recommend them, at all events, to purchase numbers 21, 22, and 23., for the sake of the architectural remarks which they contain. Verandas, Leigh Hunt observes, hide shabby windows, and form a balcony for flowers. Windows down to the floor admit light from below, instead of from above, and let in draughts of air across the floor so as to chill the feet. The outsides of windows in this country are almost universally eyesores. "Look at the windows down the streets at the west end of the town, and they are almost all mere slits in the walls, just such as they make for barracks and workhouses. The windows of an Irish cabin are as good, as far as architecture is concerned. The portholes of a man-of-war have as much merit. There is no pediment, no border; seldom even one visible variety of any sort, not a coloured brick." (p. 161.) Boxes of flowers, placed on the outsides of windows, Mr. Hunt thinks, give a liberal look to the house, and, he adds, "keeps up a good-natured kind of intercourse between the inmates of a house and those who pass it." Imagine, he says, whole streets adorned with flowers, and multitudes proceeding on their tasks through avenues of lilies and geraniums. A few seeds, and a little trouble, "would clothe our houses every summer, as high as we chose, with draperies of green and scarlet." Ivy wards off the rain, and keeps walls dry. So much for the outsides of windows. Mr. Hunt next considers windows from the inside. A window is a frame for other pictures besides its own, and it may be made, by curtains and blinds, either to harmonise with what is without, as well as with what is within; or to improve or conceal, as may be found desirable, the objects looked to. The inmates might see through roses and geraniums, or through a painted blind; or through one part of the window which looked on a pleasing object, while the other part might be shaded by a curtain or a blind, or a plant, to prevent the eye from seeing what were better concealed. " Shutters should always be divided in two, horizontally, as well as otherwise, for purposes of this kind. It is sometimes pleasant to close the lower portion, if only to preserve a greater sense of quiet and seclusion, and to read and write the more to yourself; light from above having both a softer and stronger effect, than when admitted from all quarters. We have seen shutters, by judicious management in this way, in the house of a poor man who had a taste for nature, contribute to the comfort and even elegance of a room in a surprising manner, and (by the opening of the lower portions, and the closure of the upper) at once to shut out all the sun that was not wanted, and to convert a row of stunted trees into an appearance of interminable foliage, as thick as if it had been in a forest." (p. 170.) A window "put high up in a building," and commanding a distant prospect, gives a sense of power and superiority to earth, and is in fact sublime; hence the grandeur and beauty of those clusters of round-arched windows in the upper parts of Italian villas, in campaniles, and in the bell and prospect towers of this country. High rooms are always healthier than those on the ground floor, and the healthiest quarters of towns are almost always the highest. For that reason the time may come when sitting-rooms will occupy the place of garrets. We again recommend the articles from which these remarks are extracted to every reader.

Art. II. *Foreign Notices.*

INDIA.

CEMENT, *in India* (p. 272.), is not only mixed up with a coarse sort of molasses, but finely powdered brickdust is frequently put in it. Might not those ingredients add to the hardness and durability of British cements, and even of Austin's artificial stone? The chunam of India, after two or three years, becomes so hard that it can hardly be broken, and the flat or terrace roofs made of it last for generations without cracking, or admitting a drop of water, notwithstanding the continued heavy rains to which they are exposed at certain seasons. — *G. P. Brixton, August* 21. 1834.

CHINA.

The Architecture of China, as far as we can gather from *Gutzlaff's Journal of a Voyage along the Coast of China,* in 1831, 1832, *and* 1833, appears to be a variation of that of the Hindús, as described by Rám Ráz (p. 257.), but, as there are few splendid buildings, in consequence, chiefly, of there being no established religion, or wealthy church hierarchy, the style is in very few places fully developed. The forms and proportions of the columns are the same as those in Hindú architecture, and also the curved lines of the roofs. In the smaller buildings there appear to be ornaments not to be found in the work of Rám Ráz; but there is nothing sufficiently different, in the component parts of this mode of building, to constitute a different style, which must always depend on main features, and not on ornaments. The houses of the common people in China are of mud, and consist but of one apartment; those of the better circumstanced are of brick. It appears from Gutzlaff's book, and also from a notice of it in the *Westminster Review,* No. 41., for July, 1834, that the idea generally entertained of the Chinese being averse to the introduction of strangers into their country, is a delusion propagated by the East India Company in support of their monopoly. That monopoly being now in a great measure destroyed, we may soon expect to have travels in the interior of China by European artists, architects, and cultivators, who will convey to us more correct notions of Chinese architecture, sculpture, costume, landscape scenery, gardening, and agriculture, than we have yet obtained.

In building in Canton, and other parts of China, immense quantities of pepper, and pepper dust are employed; so much so, that the greater part of the pepper raised in the Island of Penang is sent to the Canton market, where it generally bears a higher price than it does in London. The pepper dust is mixed with the plaster used for the last coat of the insides of rooms, in order to diffuse an agreeable odour, such rooms not being painted. The whole pepper is mixed with the mortar used in the walls; because it is found to stop the ravages of the white ant, one of the most destructive insects in tropical climates. — *G. P. Brixton, August.* 21. 1834.

Art. III. *Domestic Notices.*

ENGLAND.

A HANDSOME *Entrance to St. James's Park*, from the north end of Duke Street, which has been recently laid open by the removal of several old houses, is about to be formed by the Commissioners of Woods, Forests, &c. The proposed communication consists of two flights of steps with landings between, and parapets on each side, and enclosed at each end by very handsome iron gates between stone piers. It will run parallel with the east flank of the new State Paper Office, and will materially improve Duke Street. It has been designed by Messrs. Chawner and Rhodes, the crown surveyors, and is to be erected under their superintendence. — *Amicus. August* 7. 1834.

A writer in the *Times* suggests the idea of pulling down St. James's Palace, and making a grand entrance to St. James's Park on its site. We should prefer the continuation of Pall Mall in a direct line to the park, and having a proper entrance formed there, together with the execution of the other improvements in St. James's Park, the Green Park, and Hyde Park, suggested by Mr. Thompson, in the first volume of the *Gardener's Magazine* (p. 281.). One of the greatest beauties in this plan is, that it would bring Kensington Gardens to Pall Mall; where, by the gateway proposed, persons on foot might enter, and, passing through a tunnel under the road at Hyde Park Corner, proceed, unmolested by horses or carriages, to the farthest extremity of the gardens. Were the bridge across the Serpentine River yet to build, Mr. Thompson's paper might have had the effect of preventing such an absurdity from being committed; but, in 1826, when it was published, the bridge was already commenced; and, besides, at that time, government was not much in the habit of attending to the suggestions of the press. By our postscript to Mr. Thompson's paper, however, and by letters in the *Times*, we had the satisfaction to get the pieces of water brought to one level, and to prevent the absurdity of a bridge of five arches being built over a dry bank; which bank, in the plans at the office of the Commissioners of Woods and Forests, was represented as a waterfall.

Cambridgeshire. — *Fitzwilliam Museum.* The syndicate appointed by the University of Cambridge to receive plans and estimates for the rebuilding of the Fitzwilliam Museum have extended the time for receiving such plans, from the 12th of November next, to the 10th of April, 1835. (*Times,* August 1834.) If we were to refer to the parties in London where particulars are to be obtained by architects intending to compete, we should subject ourselves to the advertising duty; but, as this is expected to be taken off next year, we shall then be able to render more service to the profession by notices of this kind than we can now do. Till this takes place, we may observe, that the architectural booksellers of the metropolis are at present the most likely persons to give information to architects on such subjects.

SCOTLAND.

Leith Harbour has lately been surveyed by Mr. Cubitt, an eminent London engineer sent down by government. The object is to ascertain how far it is practicable to construct a low-water pier and wet docks, which would evidently greatly facilitate the entrance and exit of vessels. The present high-water harbour was constructed some years before the Union; and, though it has since undergone repairs at different periods, it has never been rendered properly efficient.

The Commissioners for improving the City of Edinburgh were recommended to consult Mr. Cubitt the engineer, respecting some points in their improvements on which there existed a difference of opinion; but, strange as it may seem, these commissioners could not even agree as to the propriety of asking Mr. Cubitt's advice. Judging from the Edinburgh newspapers, the commission does not appear to work well.

IRELAND.

On the Dublin and Kingston Railroad there seem to have been some terrible blunders made by the engineers. Four or five of the land arches have tumbled down, and more are expected to follow. — *S. T. Kingston, July*, 1831.

An Analysis, chemical and mechanical, of all the principal Bricks made in Britain is about to be undertaken by our correspondent, Mr. Mallet of Dublin. For this purpose, he would be glad to receive specimens (average samples) of all the different kinds of bricks made in England, Scotland, and Ireland. Each specimen should be a whole brick, taken from near the centre of the kiln. It should be carefully labelled with the name of the maker and the brickfield, the general character of the brick, and whether the clay was ground in a mill or merely mixed, and how long it was exposed. Each brick should be wrapped up in paper; and all those brickmakers who are nearer London than Dublin, may send their bricks, carriage paid, to the care of the Conductor of the Architectural Magazine, at Messrs. Longman, Rees, and Co., Paternoster Row. Mr. Mallet observes, that his object is to deduce the best possible proportions of alumina, silica, iron, and, perhaps, lime, that will produce the best bricks for general purposes. This, he says, has been attempted on a small scale, but never properly executed, to his knowledge. It is a vast labour, and a most important one. Those of our readers who take an interest in this subject will, we trust, use every means in their power to second the efforts of Mr. Mallet, by sending him specimens either to his residence, 94. Capel Street, Dublin, or to our care, agreeably to the directions given above. The result of Mr. Mallet's analysis, taken in connection with the mechanical improvements of Mr. Bakewell, noticed p. 312., promises a great change in brick buildings. At present, when society is in what may be called a transition state, this is, perhaps, of less consequence than may appear at first sight, because the fashions in house and shop building change much oftener than the decay of the structure; but when all are more equally enlightened, and, consequently, more nearly alike in wealth, it will be found desirable to have buildings of greater durability, as well as of greater beauty. Instead of one mansion and a hundred miserable mud cottages, we shall have ten villas and eighty comfortable cottage dwellings of brick.

ART. IV. *Restrospective Criticism.*

The Porticoes of the London University and the new National Gallery. — It affords me great satisfaction to find that, in his excellent paper on Grecian architecture, your very able contributor, Mr. Trotman, has borne his testimony to the merits of the portico of the London University, respecting which many newspaper writers have had the hardihood or the ignorance to assert that no one, save Mr. Wilkins himself, ever saw anything to admire in it, although its beauty was never disputed until the architect had given offence by his strictures on that of St. Martin's church. Not only had it escaped the censure since attempted to be levelled against it, but it had actually been spoken of in terms of unqualified admiration, and that, too, by some of the parties who have since laboured with might and main to bring that and Mr. Wilkins into discredit; thereby proving their praise to be as timeserving and valueless as their malevolence is base and contemptible. In the introduction to the second volume of the *Public Buildings of London*, Mr. Britton passes a brief, yet sufficiently liberal, encomium upon the University and its portico; while both Mr. Hosking and Mr. Wightwick, the latter more especially, speak of it in the language of genuine admiration. To the suffrages of the two last-mentioned gentlemen, both of whom are professional architects, and consequently not liable to the suspicion of having any private interest to serve in extolling the work of a living brother in their art, to their suffrage may now be added that of Mr. Trotman. What renders their testimony the more important is, that, while the others published their opinions of the building in question previously to the attack of the newspapers upon Mr. Wilkins, the fourth has delivered his perfectly uninfluenced by the sneers directed against the architect and his building. Hardly is it to be supposed that such writers would voluntarily commit themselves, by thus warmly commending what they did not believe to possess real merit. So far, therefore, is the assertion above alluded to from being true, that the portico of the University has, perhaps, obtained stronger and more unequivocal approbation than almost any other contemporary structure. So very far, too, is mere abuse from being calculated to set aside, that it rather tends to corroborate, what has been said in its praise; because, if those who are evidently anxious to bring that piece of architecture into discredit assign no reasons, nor enter into any criticism, it may be concluded either that they are so ignorant of the art as not to be able to make any remarks, or that they cannot discern any fault in it. It is true that one individual (Mr. Gwilt) has affirmed that the columns look like a row of Dutch skittles or nine-pins, and so, perhaps, they may in his eyes; yet that is no fault of the architect, rather of the order itself, and of both Grecian and Roman architecture altogether. The columns themselves are unobjectionable; the disposition of them far more imposing, and more classical withal, than in any other examples in this country; the result most happy, in a due admixture of richness and simplicity, of picturesque and architectural effect; consequently, if it is still far from satisfying Mr. G.'s fastidious taste, it must be this system itself which is defective. Or it is possible that he conceives the principles of ancient architecture to have been greatly amended and perfected by the Italian school; and that the latter, rather than the former, ought to be our guides. Much is it to be regretted that he did not take the trouble to explain himself, and to point out what it is which, in his opinion, causes the columns of the London University, in particular, to bear so fatal a resemblance to nine-pins. He might very properly, too, have animadverted, at the same time, on the exceedingly bad taste of those who have lavished their admiration upon so contemptible a piece of design; which, by the by, would have answered the purpose quite as well as denying that it has obtained any admiration at all.

Whether it was altogether becoming in Mr. Wilkins himself to refer to his own portico as an illustration of the superiority of Greek principles, I conceive to be a point of very minor importance, and as not at all affecting the building itself, although advantage has been taken of it to reproach Mr. Wilkins for his offensive vanity. It is amusing, however, to observe how very tenderly an equal or even greater degree of the same failing is treated by those who affected to be disgusted with it in so self-sufficient a person as Mr. Wilkins. Not many weeks ago, in reviewing Sir John Soane's *Professional Life*, the *Literary Gazette* quoted a very remarkable passage, rendered still more noticeable by its being printed in capitals, wherein Sir John speaks of his designs for the new law courts at Westminster in a tone of the highest satisfaction. Nevertheless this effusion of self-commendation called forth not even the slightest reproof. This and a variety of other circumstances tend to show that the allegations brought against Mr. Wilkins were dictated by a determination to censure; and that criticism has been grievously warped and perverted to an ungenerous purpose. Let works of art be appreciated according to their actual merits or defects, and not cried up or disparaged on totally extrinsic grounds. For my own part, I should admire the London University ite as much as I now do, had it been erected by any one else; neither do I ider that I am thereby pledged to an equal approval of the building lately commenced in Trafalgar Square. In fact, after seeing the model of it in Mr. Day's exhibition, I begin to entertain some misgivings on the subject. All the effect arising from columns is confined to the centre and the two pavilions, in which is placed the entrance leading to Castle Street, &c.; and as in these latter the centre intercolumns are necessarily very much greater than suits the other proportions, perhaps it would have been more judicious to have omitted columns here altogether, and applied them elsewhere (in the parts immediately adjoining the portico, for instance), whereby greater importance would have been given to that division, and it would have been rendered both more varied and more continuous. According to the model, the two intercolumns on each side of the portico look bare and unfinished, all the upper story being merely blank wall between the antæ, instead of there being more enrichment than in the corresponding spaces elsewhere. So far, this is anything but an improvement on the first design, where there were niches above, and a plain unbroken surface below, whereby breadth and repose, together with the appearance of solidity, were given where propriety called for them. In the altered model, again, although the centre dome is more elevated, its design by no means accords so well with the general character of Grecian architecture as the first one. Another circumstance which, although not easily avoidable, operates very disadvantageously to the whole, is, that the lower part of the structure is perforated with windows, while the upper is solid.

In making these observations, I am well aware that Mr. Wilkins must have had no ordinary difficulties to contend with, owing to limited space (limited, I mean, as to depth), and to being restricted, in the height of his order, by making use of the columns which belonged to the portico of Carlton House. It is not improbable, however, that the model may yet undergo many corrections; and I, for one, sincerely hope he will reconsider some of the things I have thus taken the liberty of pointing out. — *Candidus. London, March*, 1834.

Doweled Floors (p. 168.). — In my last paper on the choice of a house, some mistake has arisen respecting the explanation of doweled floors, which I shall feel obliged by your correcting by the insertion of the following lines. Doweled floors *are* nailed to the joists; but in such a manner as for the nails not to be seen. The first board that is laid is nailed on one edge, by the nails being driven straight through the board, the heads of the nails being afterwards concealed by the skirting; and, on the other edge, by nails driven in slanting, through about half the thickness of the board to the joist below. Dowels or pins, either of iron or wood, are previously let into the board at given distances, one end of each projecting, in order that it may be fitted into a hole made in the thickness of the next board, which is not to be nailed on the edge where it is joined to the first board. The whole floor is laid in this manner, each board being nailed only on one edge, and that through half its thickness, except the first board and the last; both of which are nailed on both edges, the nails which would otherwise be seen on the outside being hidden by the skirting. The dowels are for keeping the boards firm on the side on which they are not nailed.

The best floors are framed, parquetted, or inlaid with different kinds of wood; but doweled floors, even of deal, are far superior to either folding or straight-jointed floors, which are those in most general use. Folding floors (see *Encyc. of Cott. Arch.*, fig. 62.) are made of boards of different widths, and the joining of them in length forms an awkward mark or seam. The straight-jointed floors are made of boards of the same width, but are joined at irregular distances. The folding floors have each board nailed on both edges on the surface of the board; but the straight-jointed floors are nailed on the edge on one side like the doweled floors, and on the surface of the board only on the other side, as a substitute for the dowels or wooden pins which hold the boards together in doweled floors, as without some support the boards would not be firm. The straight-jointed floor is much superior to the common folding floor, and it is generally used for the principal rooms in third and fourth rate houses. — *I. J. Kent. Manor Place, Paddington, July* 28. 1834.

Art. V. *Queries and Answers.*

THE *best general Work on Architecture for a Beginner.* — The title, price, and publisher of such a work is wanted by — *T. W. Barnes. Newcastle under Line, July* 25. 1834.

Concrete. — Have the walls of any house been formed entirely of concrete? Would not this, in many parts of the country, be a cheaper mode of building than either brickwork or rough stone? There can be no doubt of its durability, provided the work were executed properly. A system of frames and moulds could be put up so as to admit of laying on the concrete in layers, in the same manner as in building in *pisé*. At all events, fence and garden walls might be built in this manner. Would it not, also, be a good material to substitute for macadamised stones, or common pavements in the streets of towns; provided the layers were made sufficiently thick, and had proper time allowed to dry and harden before they were travelled over. — *J. B. The Rectory, near Lymington, Aug.*, 1834.

Method of righting a Tower. — Can any of your readers give me some account of the method used in righting the tower of a large pin manufactory in the London Road, Southwark? I have heard that it was a very novel, ingenious, and successful experiment; and executed (I believe) by Mr. Smith, builder, of Woolwich. — *Amicus. London, Aug.* 7. 1834.

Art. VI. *Obituary.*

DIED, on Sept. 2., at his house in Abingdon Street, London, in his seventy-ninth year, *Thomas Telford*, Esq. F.R.S. &c., and President of the Institution of Civil Engineers. "This eminent engineer and most excellent man " was a native of Langholm, in Dumfriesshire, which he left at an early age. His gradual rise, from the stonemason and builder's yards, to the top of his profession in his own country, is to be ascribed not more to his genius, his consummate ability, and persevering industry, than to his plain, honest, straightforward dealing, and the integrity and candour which marked his character throughout life. Mr. Telford had been for some time past, by degrees, retiring from his professional business; and, of late, chiefly employed his time in writing a detailed account of the principal works he planned, and lived to see executed; which account he had only finished a few days before his death. There is hardly a county in England, Wales, or Scotland in which his works may not be pointed out. The Menai and Conway bridges, the Caledonian Canal, the St. Katharine's Docks, the Holyhead roads and bridges, the Highland roads and bridges, the Chirke and Pont-y-Cyssyllte aqueducts, and the canals in Salop, and other great works in that county, of which he was surveyor for more than half a century, will immortalise the name of Telford." (*Morning Chronicle*, Sept. 5. 1834.) "Mr. Telford was also a poet, and wrote in the *Scots Magazine* under the signature of 'Eskdale Tam;' and in Currie's *Life of Burns* will be found some beautiful verses, by Mr. Telford, to the memory of that poet." (*Mech. Mag.*, No. 578.) Mr. Telford is the author of the articles " Architecture, Bridge," &c., in Brewster's *Encyclopædia;* and he has the merit of being the first practical man to point out, in the former article, the philosophical principles of architecture, as contained in Alison's *Essays on Taste*. It was about the time this article was published (1815 or 1816) that we first became acquainted with Mr. Telford; and we can add our testimony to that of all who knew him (we may safely say, without exception), of his high moral worth and affable manners. His life and works will no doubt be published.

THE ARCHITECTURAL MAGAZINE.

NOVEMBER, 1834.

ORIGINAL COMMUNICATIONS.

Art. I. *On those Principles of Composition, in Architecture, which are common to all the Fine Arts.* By the Conductor. Sect. 3. *Forms, Lines, Lights, Shades, and Colours, considered with reference to the Principles of Regularity, Uniformity, and Symmetry.*

Regularity, we have shown (p. 221.) to be the first step in the progress of art, and (p. 283.) that it is generally by this step that art is first recognised. Regularity is resorted to, in the primitive state of every people, in the practice of all those arts, the object of which is to please. In the rude ages, the first books were written or recited in rhyme, which in language is the recognition of art. The species of motion expressive of joy, in which time was kept, was considered dancing; and songs, whether of joy or grief, were considered music, when the same sounds were repeated at regular intervals. In sculpture, and in painting, we find that the principle was recognised in the stiff attitudes of the figures, and the upright regular forms of the trees or other objects introduced. In rude architecture, it is rendered obvious by the total absence of variety.

Uniformity must necessarily have been nearly coeval with regularity, since, in architecture, it merely implies a form composed by the repetition of similar surfaces. When this form is repeated at the same intervals of space or time, uniformity is joined with regularity. Thus a cube is uniform, and when a series of cubes are joined in succession, so as to form a line, the mass of building becomes at the same time regular.

Symmetry being a conspicuous beauty in the human figure, in all animals, and, indeed, in most natural objects, would soon attract attention after uniformity and regularity. A statue would be carved with both hands and both feet in the same position, long before any attempt was made to vary the attitude or the drapery; and full-face portraits, which showed both eyes, would be painted long before profiles, or three-quarter faces.

These three primitive beauties, regularity, uniformity, and symmetry, may be referred to one common principle; viz., Repetition. In regularity, a form is repeated at regular distances without reference to the number of times, or to the production of a whole; in uniformity, a form is simply repeated or doubled, without reference to the formation of a whole; and in symmetry, a form, whether simple or composite, is repeated or doubled on each side of a centre, with reference to the formation of a whole. The elevation of a building may be perfectly regular, the windows may be of the same form, and at the same distances, and their repetition may be carried to any extent, without forming a whole. In like manner, a building may be uniform; that is, the general form either of the whole building, or of its prominent details, may be repeated or doubled without forming a whole. For example, two double cubes, each containing an even number of windows, may be joined together, so as to form a building perfectly uniform; and yet not so as to form a whole in architectural composition. A whole not only consists of distinct parts, but these parts must always be put together in such a way as to produce an obvious centre; and this centre must be essential to the composition. Now, a regular building, such as a street, whether with or without a colonnade, may be cut into any number of parts, and each part would have just as good a claim to being an architectural whole, as the whole mass of building had when joined together in the form of a street. In like manner, a uniform mass of building, such as two cubes placed side by side, might be cut into two equal parts, and each would remain uniform, without either in their separate or conjoined state having ever formed a whole. This would be more especially the case, if the windows, doors, or other parts, in each elevation, were in equal, and not in odd, numbers. If they were in odd numbers, there would be one window, door, or other part, in the centre, and this must necessarily be cut in two, when the two cubes were divided; and, if the two cubes were to be reunited, the same sides must again be placed together. On the other hand, if the windows, doors, or other parts, were even, it would be of no consequence which sides were placed together. Thus it appears, that as every whole must have a centre, which is essential to it, so a uniform building with an irregular number of windows, doors, or other parts, forms a nearer approach to a whole, than a uniform building with a regular number of parts. In general, the test to discover a whole in any building is, to imagine it cut down the centre; not always through the centre of the mass of materials, though this will be sufficient in regular and uniform buildings, but through the centre of the composition. If the two parts separated can be joined together again in any other way than that in which they were combined before, a whole was not originally produced. The great distinctive character, therefore, of a symmetrical building, or other artistical composition, is, that it forms a whole; but this is by no means the case with a building or other object which is merely uniform, or regular. We shall now endeavour to show the application of the principle of repetition, in its three modes of regularity, uniformity, and symmetry, to forms, lines, lights, shades, and colours.

Whatever may be the general *Form* of a buidling, considered as a whole, that character of form ought to be the prevailing one in all its leading parts and details. This is sufficiently obvious; for, if different forms were employed in the details, without any regulating principle, they could never be recognised as belonging to the same composition; and a consistent whole could not, therefore, be produced. Suppose a building to be in the form of a double cube, one placed over the other, with windows on every side. The principle of Uniformity requires that these windows should be parallelograms, that being the form presented by the elevation of the double cube; and the principle of Regularity requires that they should be repeated at the same distance from one another throughout. The forms being the same, and the distances between these forms being also the same, on all the four sides of the building, the result would be uniformity and regularity. There may be very little beauty in this result; because it is wholly without either symmetry or variety; and, if of small size, equally without grandeur; but the beauties of uniformity and regularity, though of the simplest and rudest kind, are here in absolute perfection. If the building were of considerable magnitude, that circumstance alone, taken in connection with uniformity and regularity, could not fail to produce the emotion of grandeur in the mind of the spectator.

Symmetry, we have stated to be the result of the repetition of forms round, or on each side of, a common centre. Thus, if an addition to a double cube were made on one side, and that addition repeated on the other side, the result would be a symmetrical whole. It does not follow that the whole thus produced would be good; because the addition might be round, in which case there would be a want of uniformity in the whole; or it might be too small, or too large, in either of which cases there would be a want of proportion; but still, provided the repetition were correctly made on the other side, the symmetry would be perfect. Symmetry, in short, is nothing more than one half of an object, consisting of a combination of different parts, reflecting the other. There are no forms, therefore, which may not be employed in a symmetrical composition; all that is essential being that there should be a centre, which cannot be dispensed with, and that the forms arranged on one side of it be reflected by those on the other side. Where symmetry is joined with variety and harmony; that is, where cultivated symmetry is aimed at, there are certain licenses which may be taken in departing from regular or mechanical symmetry; but these belong to a higher kind of beauty.

The production of regularity in *Lines, Lights, Shades,* and

Colours, will be easily understood from these details respecting regularity in forms. Where the forms are regular, the lines must of necessity be regular also; for we are not now speaking of the lines of ornament employed to decorate regular buildings. The term uniform lines may be considered a contradiction; but it must be recollected that the term is only used by artists, and with reference to art. Uniform lines, therefore, are lines bounding uniform objects; and symmetrical lines, lines bounding objects which are symmetrical. Regular lights and shades will be produced by regular projections and recesses; and a uniform object must necessarily be uniform in its lights and shades. Though the treatment of colour in elevations is of far less importance than in interiors, yet, where regularity should prevail, the neglect of colour in windows may materially interfere with the effect; and the same may be said both with regard to uniformity and symmetry. Blank windows, that is, recesses indicating windows, but without glass, in any description of building founded on the principles of regularity or uniformity, always injure the effect, by interrupting the series or system not only of colours, but of lights and shades. Blank windows may, however, be introduced in symmetrical buildings; provided that when they occur in one half of the composition, they are reflected in the other half. They are, however, always more or less defects, and should be avoided if possible.

Art. II. *On Character in Architecture.* By W. H.

It has been recommended by a distinguished and exalted professor of architecture (Sir John Soane), that architects should endeavour, above all things, to give character to their compositions, as being one of the chief and most speaking excellences in design; and upon this subject it is intended to offer a few considerations as to the effects of its influence, the causes by which it is itself influenced, and, generally, of what it consists.

Character, as a term in architecture, must be distinguished from style, for there may be many characters in the same style; and also from expression, for there may be many expressions contributing to the same character. By style is understood a particular description of order; but character alludes to the specific manner in which such style may be applied. Expression, when details only are spoken of, is synonymous with character; but, as every member conveys a distinct expression, it is left for their combination in an entire erection to decide and confirm its character. Although character is, in fact, the simple, though forcible, language of the features in architecture, it is, notwithstanding, the most abstract, and, it may be said, even the most immaterial, attribute that strikes upon the mind. It is immaterial, because it derives and realises all its essentials from the effects produced by collected objects relatively, and not so much with regard to the objects themselves. To exemplify these positions or assertions more clearly, and touching the progressive influence which they respectively have on our feelings, it will be found that, on the view of an edifice, we recognise its style, we perceive its expressions, but we are impressed with its character. Hence it becomes, as it were, the conducting medium between the intrinsic beauties and qualities of the art, and the pleasures and feelings they excite. If space or vastness improve its commanding character, the response is wonder; if delicacy or minuteness invite examination, it is met by concern and curiosity; if variety vaunt forth its merits, it is respected for richness and value; and to uniqueness, too humble almost to claim its due, taste renders its cheerful tribute to harmony. The vividness of these impressions may be more or less biased by preconceived ideas, or prescience of the purposes of an erection, with which the character should have some affinity; but as this may, and probably will, be different with each individual, the cause rests entirely with him, and does not concern any effect of the architecture.

The influences which act upon character from without, that is, by means entirely foreign to itself, are considered to be these two, locality and aspect. Locality, which includes every distinction of region and climate, it will be easy to prove, has as many distinct powers over the operations of character in building. The pyramids of Egypt, the pagodas of India, the mosques of Turkey, and the cottages of Switzerland, all partake of their several localities, and of the notions that might naturally be suggested by their respective climates and scenery. Locality, however, within our own land, is equally subservient to our subject; for instance, we will suppose ourselves placed before a prospect of a great eminence with a building on its summit, having, for its details, turrets, battlemented walls, and pointed apertures: the character suggested by such a locality would be that of a castle; and, to show that it is the scene only that so influences the character, we will imagine that in the valley beneath there is an erection having a similar combination of parts; but there, at once, they are altogether changed in our imagination; and the same expressions that in the one case formed the striking idea of a castle, in the succeeding instance assume only the characteristics of a village church. The mere circumstance of an approach to a building being altered as to its level, will sometimes make a very sudden and great difference in the effects which its character had previously produced.

There is not any very perceptible difference in the actual construction of buildings in this country which may be attributed to their being exposed to any particular severity of weather on certain aspects. The influence, then, that character in architecture receives from this cause may be reduced to the single circumstance of the power of the sun, as it varies shadow, and, to a certain extent, colour. A northern aspect, with the sun during the greater part of the day behind it, is not only enveloped in shade itself, but casts a shadow on all before it, which is a kind of type of the gloom that is generally felt to be its characteristic impression. A southern aspect, consequently, obtains the greatest duration of the sun's rays on it; and is the most influential, by the depth and perspicacity which it gives to the details; and (contrary to the northern aspect) it receives additional clearness from the reflection of the ground before it. The eastern and western aspects are, of course, neither so long nor so powerfully under this influence of the sun. As the habits of society in general have introduced rather an artificial change in what may be called daytime, they have not much opportunity of judging of the effects of the sun when in the east; and it already begins to retire from that aspect by the time they are leaving their houses: therefore, as we are speaking of effects worked upon their minds, the eastern aspect has not so great a share of their favour as the western; because, when the sun is in the west, and even setting, it is, with the fashionable world, comparatively midday. In porticoes, especially, where the force and depth of the shadows are most important and desirable, their character is much deteriorated by being subjected to so negative an influence as either the northern or eastern aspects receive. In instance, a portico, erected after a very pure Grecian Doric example, to a chapel in Stamford Street, being nearly due north; and the Ionic portico to the new Law Institution in Chancery Lane, being nearly due east, are considered (without speaking in the least reproachfully of the architecture) to be very unfortunately placed; and are, thus far, evidences of this point. A comparison between the north and south elevations of a church or other building, being constructed exactly similar, will better show the difference of character caused by aspect than any other illustration. The most successful method that has been adopted of remedying this detrimental effect of aspect, seems rather to consist in the use of internal recesses from the line of a building, in preference to extraneous projections, which often fail in procuring the desired effect. Perhaps the north front of Somerset House may have received this consideration, as to a great extent it may be applied to this principle; but a more evident case occurs in the church of St. Mary Woolnoth, in Lombard Street.

Having thus pursued the subject in the view of its influence upon the mind, and also the influence it receives; the third point of view in which it presents itself concerns its composition, or in what it consists. Perhaps the fact of its having been represented, in the first place, as an immaterial subject, may make it appear rather paradoxical to descend at once to the consideration of its reality. It is immaterial, from the expanse of its description and its indefinite nature; yet, like character in the human disposition, it is only such by its maintenance; and the construction that aids that maintenance forms the reality from which it is extracted as an essence. Character in architecture, then, is, in brief, originated and upheld by the consistency of combined expressions. In the design of an erection, the data of some previously executed model are often taken for adoption to a greater or less extent; but, to have also a claim to originality, there must be sufficient variation to avoid its being a copy, and yet sufficient similitude in such variation to preserve its character. A too close adherence implies servility; and, again, too great a freedom with any given basis, is at the risk of its injury. It is the confusion of having one datum in an original model, another in the present purpose of the building, and a third in the architect's invention, that is so likely to occasion a mingling of the whole together, and probably the destruction of all character in the architecture. This has been much complained of in the modern addition of a steeple to the primitive and ancient form of a temple, as in St. Martin's, St. Pancras, and other churches, where (independently of the alleged defect in construction, which consists in placing the steeple over the pediment, and which is irrelevant to our topic) it produces an equally important defect, by the injury which it does to the character of the architecture, by the union or rather confusion of two very opposite expressions. Simply, the appropriation of a particular order is the most usual and prevalent course; and this, while it leaves the widest scope for originality in its adaptation, limits the data to those which are available with the greatest facility as precedents. Hence increased novelty of form, produced from the same materials, becomes the main cause of distinction in character; and in the aptness of these changes, and in the suitableness of these variations, lies the great art of producing this effect. Of course, novelty, for its own sake alone, can be achieved with a much freer hand by breaking forth from all precedent whatever: but the preceding remark is made with reference to architecture of an orthodox kind (if such a term may be used), and not to any occasional eccentricity. Indeed, the architecture which is least known, and which is most remarkable for its singularity, is the farthest from what could be desired in character; the perfection of which is comprised in its producing the same unequivocal admiration from the greatest possible number of minds. Instead of which, there can scarcely be two similar opinions of any building, the only deducible proofs of the worth of which, the absence of all comparison, are wrapped up in the conceit of the inventor.

In conclusion, the writer is well aware that he has very superficially treated a subject (having only regarded architecture in its exterior, and *en masse*), which, if fully entered into, would lead to many points of improved interior arrangement and of organised compilation. He has only attempted, by the foregoing observations, to acquaint the reader with the current of thoughts (however vague) which would probably have never even occurred to himself but for the recommendation of the eminent individual first mentioned.

Sept. 1834.

ART. III. *An Attempt to Explain the Elements and Principles of Gothic Architecture to the General Reader.* By J. A. PICTON, Esq., Architect.

THE great master of architecture in modern times, Sir C. Wren, has laid it down as a maxim, that "architecture aims at eternity, and is therefore the only thing incapable of modes and fashion." This, however, like every other dogma, is liable to exceptions. Undoubtedly, grandeur in conception, unity in design, harmony in proportion, and elegance in ornament, will always command admiration, whatever may be the particular mode or style exemplified. Still it is curious and interesting to mark the change and variation which have continually been in progress in the public estimate of architectural excellence; and perhaps it would be difficult to point out two periods in history separated from each other by the interval of a century, in which the principles and practice of architecture have not differed widely and materially. Since the first dawn of light which history has thrown upon the progress of the human mind, the acknowledged principles of taste have undergone continual modification, from the various states of civilisation, from the progress of mechanical science, and from that variety of ebbs and flows to which the ever-shifting current of human affairs is continually liable. At every period, however, that great principle and source of all improvement, the aspiration after something nobler and better than what the present scene affords, has been constantly at work, when not entirely repressed by violence; and, though in all cases moulded by external circumstances, and frequently diverted into unworthy channels, in every branch of art, but more particularly in architecture, it has been the source of a variety of styles; and yet of a beauty and fitness in each, to which "a thing incapable of modes and fashions" never could have attained.

Down to the period of the revival of classical architecture, the various modes hitherto practised, whatever might be their other merits or defects, had something of originality to recommend them; but originality, at the present day, is utterly proscribed. Any absurdity, if it can but be brought forward under the sanction of precedent, is sure to meet with some patrons and admirers; but woe be to the unfortunate wight who should dare to introduce any novelty of his own! He is hunted down as fair game by the common consent of the purists, periodists, and five-order men; and his professional reputation, if he ever possessed any, is in imminent danger of being sacrificed. The task of the present generation is confined to the adapting and combining of the materials already accumulated. It is in the selection and combination of these that talent and taste are to be exhibited.

Amongst the various modes of architecture which are presented to our notice, none possess greater claims to our attention than the indigenous style of our own country, commonly called the Gothic or Pointed style. Now that the Italian mania has happily passed away, it is pretty generally acknowledged that there are other sources of beauty and grandeur besides those which have emanated from the schools of Vignola and Palladio, and a reaction has taken place in favour of the Gothic style to such an extent, that some knowledge of its principles is absolutely requisite for every person who professes any degree of taste or judgment in architecture. Independently of its intrinsic excellence, the remains of this style are scattered in such profusion about our native isle; they form such prominent features in the lovely scenery of England, and are connected with such a variety of pleasing associations, that I can imagine no study more delightful to a person of refined taste and cultivated understanding, than that of its rise and progress, principles and details. There is a very common but very erroneous impression existing, that the study of architectural antiquities is dry, technical, and uninteresting. Can this be the case of a pursuit which depends almost exclusively for its interest on the imagination, and the association of ideas? The ancient architecture of England is closely identified with the brightest periods of our history; with the triumph of liberty at Runnymede, and with the glories of Cressy, Poictiers, and Agincourt. We mark, too, in its progress, the advancement of civilisation and the arts, from the barbaric pomp of the Norman conquerors, through the chivalrous gallantry of the times of our Edwards and Henries, down to the gorgeous magnificence at the period of "the field of the cloth of gold." Can we then look on it with indifference and apathy? To apply the words of our great moralist, " Far from me and my friends be such frigid philosophy! That man is little to be envied, whose patriotism would not gain force upon the plain of Marathon, or whose piety would not grow warmer among the ruins of Iona."

For the benefit of such of your non-professional readers as

would wish to acquire a general knowledge of the subject, I propose, through the medium of the *Architectural Magazine*, to give a popular view of the leading principles of the Gothic style, to enable any person of ordinary discernment to discriminate between the different periods and varieties, and to appreciate their peculiar beauties. I shall begin with a few words as to the nomenclature and classification of this style. Most writers on this subject have taken exception to the term "Gothic," as applied to the architecture of the middle ages. Mr. Rickman, to whom every student of architecture is under the deepest obligations for his very valuable publications, gives to this mode the general epithet of "the English style:" this, however, seems too exclusive and narrow an appellation. We are scarcely justified in rejecting the claim to belong to this style, of such magnificent structures as the cathedrals of Strasburg, Mechlin, Ulm, Vienna, or even Notre Dame, and the cathedrals of Normandy, although they may differ in minor points from edifices contemporaneously erected in England; while the appellation of "Christian Architecture," bestowed upon it by that indefatigable and judicious antiquary Mr. Britton, is, on the other hand, far too comprehensive; as that term would include the eccentricities of the Byzantine school and the bizarrerie of the Italian Tedesco. After all, where lies the valid objection to the use of the term Gothic? and, although originally applied in ridicule and contempt, I think it will not be difficult to prove that it is quite as expressive, and conveys ideas quite as definite, as any other term. The words Doric, Ionic, and Corinthian, applied to styles of architecture, lead us to the conception, whether correctly or not, of the modes of building employed by the Dorians, Ionians, and Corinthians. In like manner, the Gothic style, not to quibble about the precise period or manner of its introduction, was undoubtedly originated and carried to perfection by the descendants of the cognate races of Saxons, Franks, Normans, and Germans, branches from one common Gothic stem, and by them alone. "We are sometimes too apt to forsake the vulgar, when the vulgar is right;" and in this case, whether correct or not, the term "Gothic" is likely to survive any other appellation which has yet been given to the style.

With respect to classification, that of Mr. Rickman, decidedly the clearest and most judicious which has yet been suggested, is, with some slight modifications, that now generally adopted. He subdivides Gothic architecture into four periods:—

1st, The Semicircular, or Norman; extending in its pure state from the time of the Conquest to the reign of Stephen, A. D. 1136; and, with the mixed or transition style which succeeded, to about the year 1190.

2d, The Early Pointed; from the reign of Richard I., 1189, down to the reign of Edward I., 1307.

3d, The Decorated; which prevailed during the greater part of the fourteenth century.

4th, The Perpendicular, sometimes called the Florid Gothic; which commenced about the reign of Richard II., and prevailed during the whole of the fifteenth century and the early part of the sixteenth, down to the period of the Reformation.

The arch being the most promising and distinguishing feature in this style of architecture, I shall close these introductory remarks by a short description of the different forms of arches introduced, with the periods during which they principally prevailed: these, and any other illustrations which may be necessary, will be in the simplest possible style, to enable any person who can handle a lead pencil and a pair of compasses to make himself master of their contour and method of delineation.

The semicircular arch (*fig.* 151.) is the only one employed in edifices erected prior to the reign of Stephen, A. D. 1136. From that period to the end of the twelfth century, it is found associated with pointed arches, as in the circular part of the Temple Church, London, built about 1180; and in that of St. Bartholomew the Great, West Smithfield, built some time during the reign of Henry II., in which last the great arches at the intersection of the transepts of the original church are pointed, and the arches of the chancel semicircular. The clere-story windows of the present church are of later date.

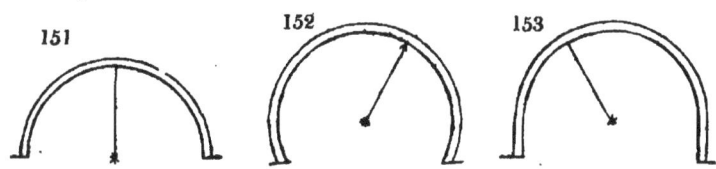

There are two forms of the horseshoe arch (*figs.* 152. and 153.), in which the centres are above the line of the springing. This arch is not common; but is sometimes introduced along with semicircular arches, apparently for the sake of variety.

Fig. 154. is the segmental arch, in which the centre is below the springing line. This form is rarely combined with semicircular arches. Its general application was to interior doors and openings, during the early and decorated periods; but even in these it is not of frequent occurrence.

Fig. 155. is the lancet arch, the height of which is greater than its width. Where this arch is used for the main outlines of doors, windows, and other openings, they

332   *Elements of Gothic Architecture.*

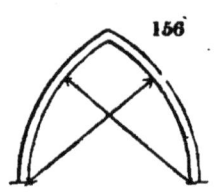

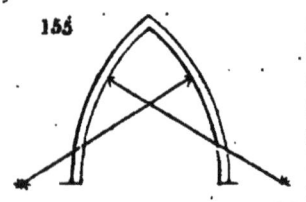

may safely be attributed to the early pointed period. The transept of Beverley Minster, and the nave of Lincoln Cathedral afford beautiful specimens of this form of arch. In the composition of tracery and wood carving, the lancet arch is continued through all the varieties.

Fig. 156. is the equilateral arch, of which height and width are equal.

Fig. 157. is the drop arch, the height of which is less than its width. *Fig.* 158. is the pointed segmental, the centres of which are below the line of springing.

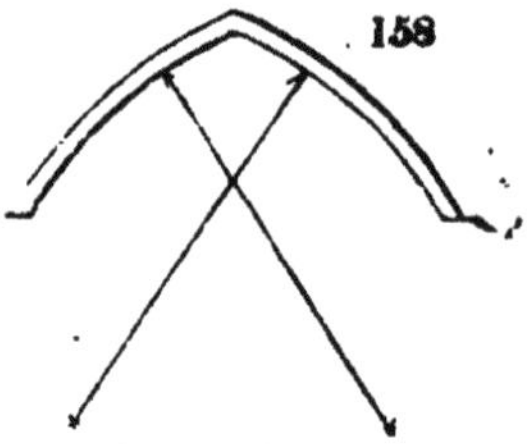

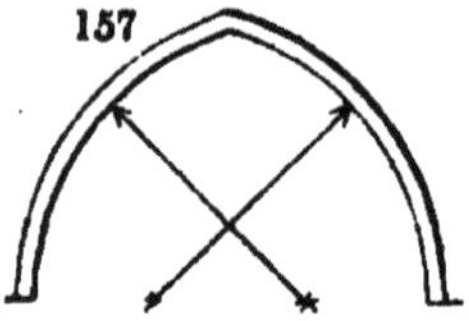

The three last-mentioned arches are used indifferently in the early, decorated, and perpendicular styles.

Fig. 159. is the pointed horseshoe. This form of arch occurs in a few buildings in the mixed or transition style, immediately succeeding the Norman. The choir of Canterbury Cathedral, erected A. D. 1184, offers the finest specimens.

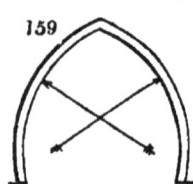

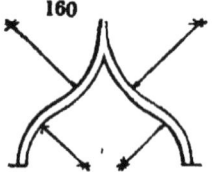

Fig. 160. is the ogee arch. This form was never used for the main arches of doors and windows of ancient buildings, as is sometimes absurdly done at the present day. Its use was confined to tracery, niches, tabernacle work, and other ornamental situations. The ogee form was also frequently applied to the canopies of doors and windows in the late decorated and early perpendicular.

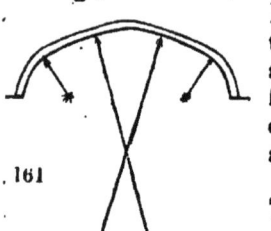

Fig. 161. is the four-centred or Tudor arch. This form belongs exclusively to the reigns of Henry VII. and VIII., after which time the Gothic style ceased to exist in any degree of purity. This peculiar form of arch has sometimes led to a separate classification of this period, under the denomination of Tudor Gothic; but the mere form of the arch hardly seems sufficient to warrant this multiplication of classes.

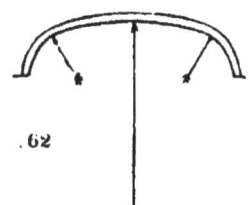

Fig. 162. is the three-centred or elliptic arch. This arch is sometimes, though very rarely, met with in England, in buildings of the late perpendicular: it frequently, however, occurs on the Continent; but marks the debasement and near approach of the extinction of the style.

It will be perceived, by the foregoing remarks, that the form of the arch is not, in most cases, sufficient of itself to determine the period or class to which an edifice belongs. Recourse must be had to the mouldings, tracery, buttresses, and other details, which will be noticed in future articles.

Liverpool, Aug. 23. 1834.

ART. IV. *Design for a Villa in the Norman Style of Architecture.* By E. B. LAMB, Esq., Architect.

THE situation of this villa is supposed to be on a gentle slope, backed by rich woody scenery, and facing a highly cultivated country.

Fig. 163. is the ground plan. In this figure, *a* is the porch; *b*, the hall; *c*, the principal staircase; *d*, the drawingroom; *e*, the library; *f*, the dining-room; *g*, the passage leading to the dining-room, and opening on the lawn; *h*, the passage leading to the domestic offices; *i*, stairs leading to the level, the kitchen, &c., which is lower than the rest of the building; *k*, domestic offices; *l*, conservatory; *m*, lobby between the drawingroom and conservatory. The entrance is by an ascent (*a*) of two flights of steps to the porch, which is on a level with the principal floor. This porch has a simple groined roof, springing from columns in the angles. On the left of the arched entrance is the hall door: *b* is the hall, also simply groined in the same manner. The hall is lighted by a rather small window glazed with stained glass. Opposite this window is the door to the domestic offices; and at the end are two arches, one communicating with the principal staircase (*c*), and the other with the passage to the dining-room, ending with a sash door to the lawn, &c. This door should have a rich stained glass border, and crimson head. The passage should have a simple ribbed ceiling, in imitation of oak: the appearance should be rather dark and intricate, to increase the effect: the colour of the walls should be dark stone, rather resembling the effects of age than otherwise. From this passage would be seen the staircase; and from the extremity near the

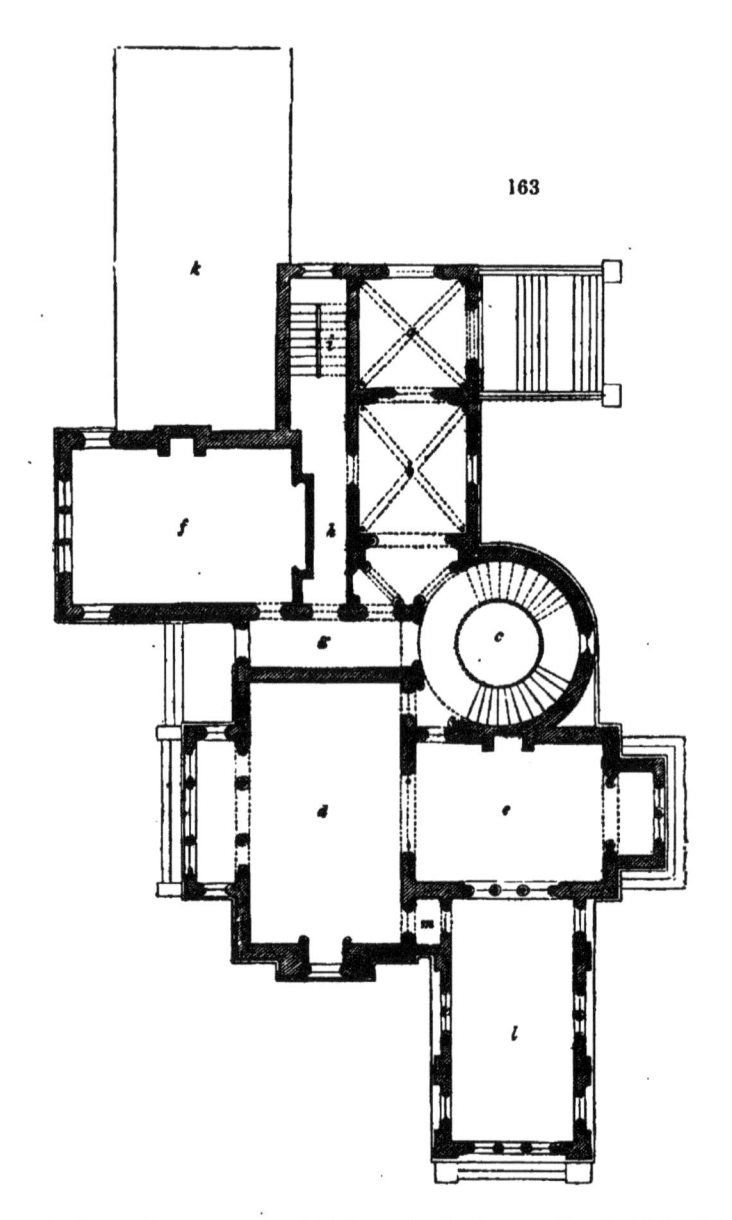

sash door the contrast of light and shade would, I think, be agreeable. Directly opposite the archway to the passage should be a rich stained glass window in the staircase. The staircase should also be lighted by the small windows round the top of

in the Norman Style.

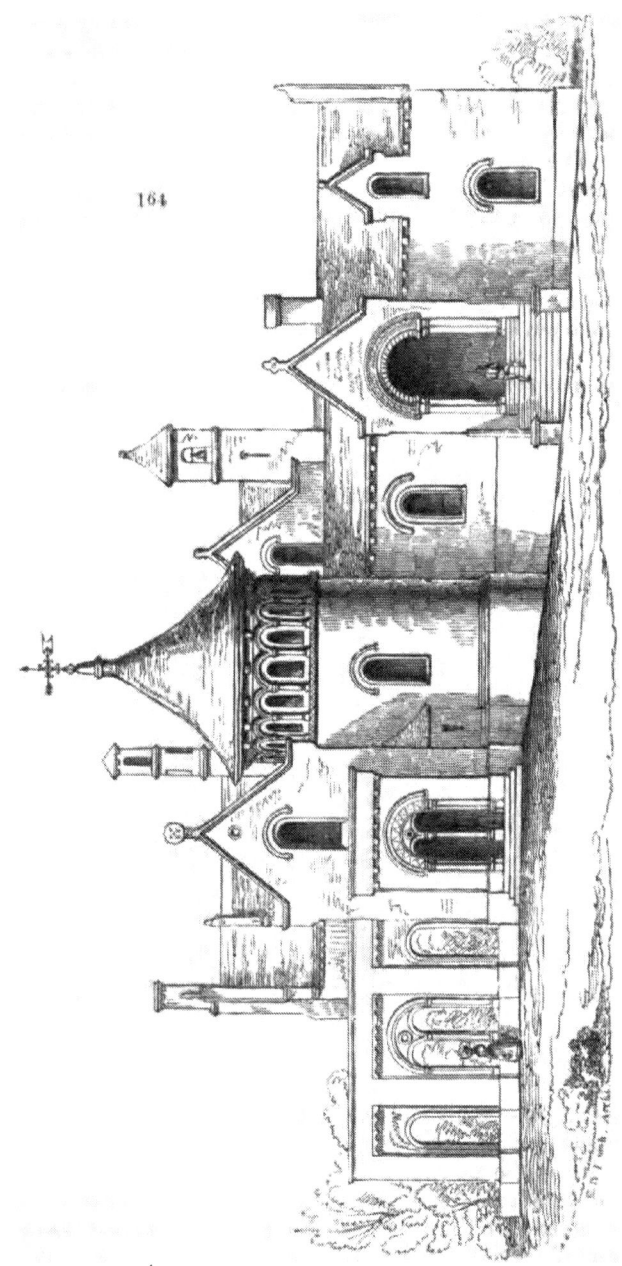

the tower, which are shown in the elevation. (*fig.* 164.) The roof of the staircase is groined, the ribs painted various colours, and the bosses gilt. From the centre boss is suspended a lamp, shedding rather a dim though still glowing light on the stairs at night. The upper windows should be glazed with rather a dark-coloured glass; and the stairs should be of stone without nosings; that is, without a moulding on the front edge of the tread or step. The staircase should not be geometrical (self-supported), but raised upon columns and arches; and should not go higher than one story. The handrail and balusters should be of bronze, with an oak capping.

From the staircase we proceed to the library, or general sitting-room. (*Fig.* 163. *e.*) This room should be fitted up in a neat manner, partaking rather of the grave than of the gay. The south window is placed in a recess, the external elevation of which is given in *fig.* 165., to a larger scale. The ceiling of

165

this room should be in nearly the same form as that of the drawingroom; but not so richly decorated. The arch of the recess should be on columns, and it should be enriched with the usual decorations. To give a little more light, and also to add to the interest of the room, there should be a small skylight in this recess, glazed with warm-coloured (red or yellow) glass. The window should have coloured glass borders; but the centre lights should be plain; quarry (*carré*, square) glazing (or casements) would be quite inadmissible in a modern building, therefore we are under the necessity of substituting plate or German sheet glass; but this evil will not materially affect the architecture of the building. The windows communicating with the conservatory (*l*, *fig*. 163.) should consist of three arches with tinted borders, corresponding with the other window. The fireplace shall be described hereafter. The large archway leading to the drawingroom is shown in the view of that room. (*fig*. 182., p. 348.) This archway might be closed either by full drapery, or doors richly carved. In either case they should be in the centre of the jamb. If the archway be closed by doors, they should be made to slide back into the wall; and if by curtains, they should draw back into a similar recess. Thus contrived, they would never be in the way. The small doors of the room should be framed and ornamented in a corresponding manner; the architrave should be moulded, or only splayed; not projecting, as that would not be consistent with this style of architecture. The doors may be either circular-headed or straight-headed; but, for this design, the circular head is most in harmony.

Now, having drawn aside the ample folds of the rich drapery, and introduced you to the drawingroom, I shall first call your attention to the ceiling, which is in the most general form of ceilings of the Norman period. It might be more arched; but, as I have a room over this, and as I must have windows in the side wall, there will not be space for a deeper-arched ceiling; and groining I do not consider perfectly consistent with a drawingroom. This ceiling is ribbed, and at the intersection of the ribs are carved bosses gilt. The hollow of the rib is also gilt. The rib is of oak; the panels are coloured blue, or any other colour that may suit the taste of the occupants; or they might be ornamented with various devices, and many colours; but not with heraldic devices, as heraldry was not known to the Normans. The great recess, with its arches, &c., has been before mentioned. Over the fireplace is a window of richly stained glass. The other windows should only have stained borders; for, if the whole were of stained glass, it would tend to darken the room too much. The window over the fireplace should slide into a groove; and a plain glass window might be substituted at pleasure, as it would be agreeable to view the country when either in the bud or at the fall of the leaf, and at the same time to feel the genial influence of a cheerful fire. Of the furnishing of this room it will be scarcely necessary to say anything, as the general view (*fig*. 182.) will give some idea of its appearance. The colours should be in perfect harmony; and a lively character should be given to the whole. Chairs, sofas, tables, stools, chiffoniers, articles of *virtù*, a few elegantly

338 *Design for a Villa.*

bound books, vases for flowers, musical instruments, with other elegant articles of refinement, taste, and ornament, should be strewed about the room in most picturesque disorder.

I have not mentioned curtains, except those used to divide the rooms; and these have been omitted purposely, as unnecessary in a room which is highly architectural: but, if they must be had, they may be hung inside the recesses, so as not to interfere with the architecture. Modern Gothic upholstery, with its unconnected burnished gold cornices, suspended by holdfasts, and thick unmeaning festoons of drapery, would be highly unsuitable. The smaller arches should be turned upon columns rising from the plinth, which should be sufficiently high to receive a cushion; thus forming a pleasant and agreeable seat. The large arch should be open, and the window opposite carried down to the ground, so that, by descending two or three steps, you would come on to the lawn. Windows constructed in this manner, when hung as doors, always have a cheerful effect.

If you are not already tired of my villa, we will next proceed to the dining-room. (*fig.* 163. *f.*) The joists of the floor above this room should be shown, or, at least, an imitation of them; but, if the real joists were left open, it would be necessary to have a double floor, to prevent any noise being heard above. Perhaps it would be better to show only the girders, which should be simply moulded, with a few gilt bosses, and corbels to support the ends. The ceiling should be of light oak, or coloured to represent that wood, and not highly varnished, as that would, by its glossy appearance, destroy the illusion. Near to the entrance of this room is an arched recess for the sideboard, at a convenient distance from the passage (*h*) which leads to the domestic offices. The prevailing colour of the dining-room should be rather of a rich tint, and the furniture more massive, and placed in a little more regular order than in the drawing-room; though, at the same time, care should be taken that the whole does not have a heavy effect. The window at the end should be in three arches, with some coloured glass; and the side windows should correspond with it.

In the composition of architectural interiors, the same principles should guide us as in the composition of a picture; and it will generally be found that the best pictures, for breadth of effect and light and shade, are those where the ceiling or upper part is a mass of shadow and repose, and the lower gradually inclining to light. Thus the light colour should rather rise from the ground than the dark; though the general practice is quite of an opposite nature. On noticing the interiors of our ancient domestic buildings, it will generally be found that this principle is the leading cause which produces so pleasing an effect of light and shade. Their richly carved ceilings are interspersed with heraldic devices and gilt bosses, and ribs and panels of an endless variety of form and colour, which produce depth of tone and intricacy of effect; and the whole combines in general harmony to create agreeable shadow and repose. The long line of vaulting in our cathedrals, with the sparkling bosses and rich tracery which so frequently adorn them, produce a mysterious effect upon the beholder, that is increased by the richly wrought tracery of the window heads, and the stained glass of various hues; the whole throwing a shadow upon the roof, which produces sensations frequently felt, but difficult to be described.

Passing from the drawingroom through the small lobby (*m*), we come to the conservatory (*l*). This is certainly one of the most awkward things to design in the Norman style; but, as I should like such a thing attached to a small villa of this kind, I must make the best I can of it. The roof should be semicircular, on iron ribs, entirely glazed; and the sides should have such openings as would be in character with the rest of the building. The door leading to the conservatory should be glazed with plain glass; and the window at the end should correspond with the library window. If this building were filled with rare plants tastefully arranged, I think it would be an agreeable addition to both the drawingroom and library.

I will not think of troubling you to go up stairs, as I need merely say that the whole of the upper rooms will be in the same character; and if any objection should be made to the windows rising in the gable, as seen in the elevation (*fig.* 164.), and thus preventing the room from having a flat ceiling (as I am aware a prejudice exists to that effect), let me observe that the ceilings will be ribbed, and supported on corbels, which will entirely take away the unsightly appearance; in fact, the general effect would be an improvement, particularly as the room would be of a very good height (about 12 ft.) in the centre.

Having described the principal rooms, let us now retrace our steps along the passage (*h*), only to show you the situation of the domestic offices: *i* shows you the position of the back stairs leading to these offices, which are under *k* and the diningroom (*f*). Under the hall, porch, and passage (*h*) are cellars, &c. The back stairs leading to the servants' bedrooms also communicate, by a passage similar to that marked *h*, with the principal part of the house.

Thus, having completed our cursory survey of the interior, we will step outside. First, let us consider the building as a whole. (*fig.* 164.) My object has been to produce a picturesque effect; though how far I have succeeded it is not for me to say. The great aim, in designing villa architecture, is to consider, first, what will be the effect upon an uneducated observer, and then, if possible, to study for the critic. I place the uneducated person first, as he has the fewest prejudices to get over; and therefore you must design for him *en masse*. I do not think contemptuously of the opinions of this class of persons, but I place more reliance upon those of another class; viz., the architects of reason. They stand as a medium between the two extremes of the uneducated and the educated; and their criticisms are often severe, but just. A building that cannot stand the test of reason is a mere jumble. The last critic I have to encounter is the

in the Norman Style. 341

antiquary; and of him, perhaps, I shall feel the scourge. How fortunate would be the architect who could satisfy all! To do that is scarcely within the scope of human ability. I will, however, try my chance to please as many as I can. First, I have endeavoured to give a picturesque outline to the building; next,

342 *Design for a Villa*

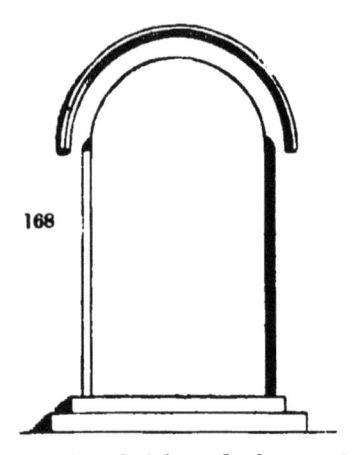

I have tried to arrange it on the principle of fitness; and, lastly, I have started with a character which I have endeavoured to keep, as well as the change of manners and customs would allow me.

The Norman style of architecture comprises the period between the reign of William I. and that of Henry II. The characteristics of this style are, generally, massiveness, round arches, various mouldings, and rudely sculptured figures; but with ornaments which are frequently of rich and elegant design. Many of the ornaments and mouldings resemble those of Roman architecture; which affords evidence of the Norman having been originally a modification of that style; though, in the latter part of the period when the Norman style prevailed, its increased complexity, rich groining, and varying outline formed a unity, style, and picturesque effect exclusively its own.

I have not confined myself entirely to the details of one villa in the following figures, thinking that perhaps a variety of forms would serve better to illustrate the Norman style, as far as it may be necessary to proceed at present.

Fig. 167. is a design for a Norman porch. This porch is square on the plan, with a groined or open timber roof, covered with tiles on the outside. Lead was frequently employed as a covering for roofs in old English buildings; but slates should

in the Norman Style. 343

170.

never be used in Gothic architecture. Slates were not only never used by our forefathers, but are a very inharmonious material for buildings in any of the old English styles; and when a proper material can be obtained, sufficiently durable, there can be no excuse for using any other. As this porch is designed for a modern building, I have put sash doors to it; as this would give a view of the rich arch and scenery from the inside of the hall. Over the door-head is a basso-relievo. This situation, in Norman buildings, was very generally appropriated to sculpture, usually religious subjects; but, for domestic buildings, there is an infinite variety of subjects applicable to this purpose: history and chivalry would be particularly adapted to it; and might form an additional source of interest if of coeval style with the architecture, or if relating to any heroic action performed by the ancestors of the proprietor of the villa. Detached figures should be sparingly introduced in the exterior; as such subjects, in the Anglo-Norman buildings, were generally saints or other ecclesiastical personages, and were but rarely introduced in domestic buildings; though I would not entirely exclude either single figures or basso-relievos, when an applicable subject occurred.

172.

At the sides of the porch are small openings, that may either be glazed with stained glass or left entirely open.

Fig. 168. is a plain doorway with a label moulding over. The angles of the jamb are splayed. This kind of splay would also suit internal doors of a plain style.

Fig. 169. is a doorway and door of a later period than the last. Here, in the door head I have shown some rich scroll ornaments, which were frequently used in similar situations. In the west

A A 4

front of Rochester Cathedral are some very good specimens of this kind of ornament, though the arch mouldings are plain zigzag heads with a plain bead. The zigzag is a very common moulding used in the decorations of the Norman style. The columns in this doorway are twisted, and have plain bases and capitals; and the door is ledged, having scroll hinges. Scroll hinges, at the period alluded to, were frequently of such elaborate design as to cover the whole door; and, by their multifarious ramifications, they produced a rich and sparkling effect. There are several specimens of plain square-headed doors still remaining in some of our ancient cathedrals.

Fig. 170. is a plain window with a label; and *fig.* 171. is a window with columns and moulded arch. The impost moulding is extended to receive the label in this window; but this was not always the case, as will be seen in *fig.* 165. These windows appear deeply sunk into the wall; but they do not, in fact, require a very thick wall, as, generally, the great depth of the architrave of a Norman window is on the inside of a building; so that any objection to this style on that score is easily obviated. Breadth of design and composition may be thus obtained without heaviness of detail in appearance or reality.

Fig. 165., p. 336., is the library window shown externally. Windows divided by mullions were not unusual among the Normans; and some very early specimens may be seen in St. Alban's Abbey.

Fig. 172. is a singular window, from Faxton church, Northamptonshire. It is only 2 ft. high in the clear, and is an early specimen of the introduction of cusps (the points formed in the upper corners of the window, by the uniting of the two curves).

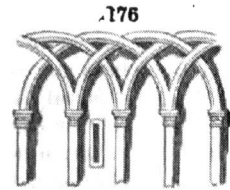

Fig. 173. is another specimen of the introduction of cusps in the head of a window. A window similar to this is to be seen in the south front of Canterbury Cathedral, which may be considered of the date of 1184.

Fig. 174. is a square-headed Norman window, drawn from a sketch by the late W. F. Smallwood, Esq. It is taken from some building in the Netherlands; but, having misplaced my memoranda relating to it, I regret I cannot name the building from which it was taken. I believe there is a specimen of this kind of window in the Jews' House at York; but the occurrence of square-headed windows in this style is very rare. However, this would be a sufficient precedent for the introduction of one in any modern composition.

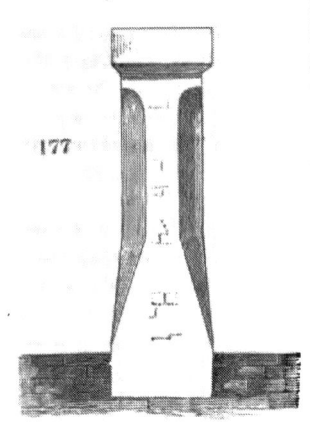

Fig. 175. is a specimen of interlacing arches. I have shown these in the upper part of a tower (which might be used for a staircase), in order to exhibit a manner of finishing the angles with small beads or columns, which produces a pleasing effect. Here is also shown an arch cornice. Cornices were of many forms; in arches, moulding-blocks, cables, chains, billets, zigzag, &c. When of blocks, they were carved in various ways; the same design being seldom twice used in the same cornice. Corbel heads, and rude imitations of animals, were among the decorations of these blocks, together with flowers, which were frequently of good and chaste design.

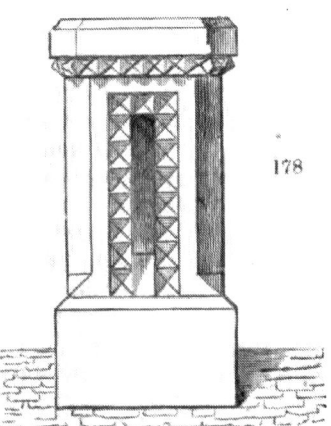

Fig. 176. is another specimen of interlacing arches. These are interesting, as I believe it is now generally admitted that the intersecting arch was the origin of the pointed style of architecture.

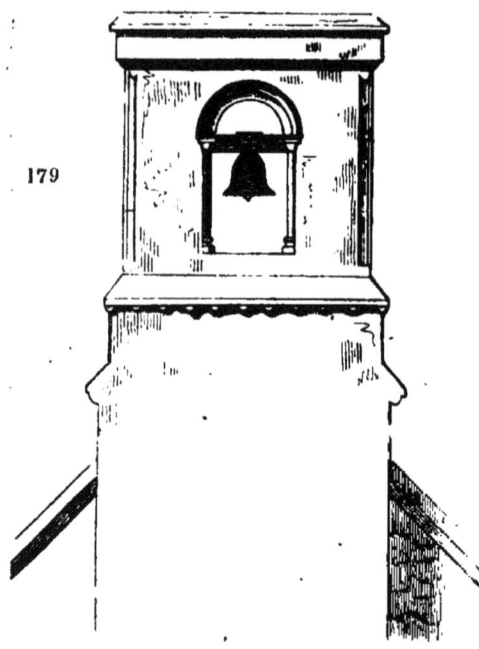

Fig. 177. is a plain chimney shaft in the character of the Norman style. Here we have a difficulty to overcome, as the Normans did not use flues: their habits and the wood fires did not require them; and, in fact, flues were very unusual till about the reign of Elizabeth. That the Normans had fireplaces is true: as there are many specimens now extant of very beautiful workmanship: but they were usually built in the external walls, and the smoke was permitted to escape through a hole a little above the mantelpiece. In the great halls the fires were made in the middle of the room, and the smoke escaped through the louvre boards at the top of the roof: but, as this would not suit a modern building, we must have chimney shafts as much in character as possible.

Fig. 178. is a design for a chimney shaft rising from the roof.

Fig. 179. is a bell tower with a flue on each side. This is for an external wall; and it is aided in its appearance by the buttress-like projection on each side. The buttresses in the Norman style were generally but slightly projected from the wall, and they were frequently ornamented with angle columns or beads, or the angles splayed.

Fig. 180. is a turret chimney shaft, for a cluster of flues. This is suited to the angle of a building, and there would be very little difficulty in turning the flues into it. In fact, this would be one way of preventing smoky chimneys. This form may be called a disguised chimney shaft, but it should not be used to the exclusion of all others; which, when they show their intention, add greatly to the appearance of comfort, and stamp the character of the building.

Fig. 181. is a fireplace agreeably to the feeling of the Norman style. Of course it is of much smaller dimensions than

in the Norman Style. 347

those of our ancestors; as the different fuel now used does not require so large an opening.

Fig. 166. shows a few articles of furniture in the Norman style. In the British Museum are preserved some ancient chessmen of Norman character: the kings, queens, and bishops are represented as seated in chairs, the backs and sides of some of which are carved with very beautiful scroll ornaments. Some have a more simple kind of decoration, and some have their backs ornamented with interlacing arches, with columns and a kind of mosaic work; the whole serving to show something of the style of furniture used in those days. I need scarcely say, that there are many specimens of diaper and mosaic work that would form good subjects for carpets and papering for walls; or, what would look better for walls, moulds might be formed to impress the plaster, so that it would have the appearance of rich ornamental sculpture. In the nave of Bayeux Cathedral, Normandy, there are some very excellent examples of this kind of decoration. In internal decoration we need not scruple, for want of precedent, to use composition ornaments, when the chief ornaments of the Temple Church were of this material before their restoration, and the beautiful and elaborate west door is still of the same material.

ART. V. *Remarks on Closets, &c., in Sitting-Rooms.*
By W. H. LEEDS, Esq.

IN p. 48. of this Magazine, an enquiry is made respecting Camilla Cottage, on account of the ingenuity with which, as appears from the description, concealed closets, cupboards, and recesses were there introduced. If a house be already built, there may be a good deal of difficulty in devising anything of this kind, without reducing the size of any one of the rooms; but in the case of one that is to be built, there can be hardly any difficulty whatever in providing as much accommodation of that kind as can possibly be required, especially in a building of the cottage class; because any external irregularity occasioned by placing closets or recesses of any kind where they would form projections from the outer walls might, instead of proving blemishes, be so treated as to conduce materially to picturesque character and effect. But perhaps the principal reason, and a very sufficient one it is, why architects have bestowed no study upon contrivances like those in question, is, that few people care to have a closet of any kind, however completely it may be concealed from observation, in a sitting-room; and, of course, in any other part of the house, where appearance is of no importance, there can be no occasion to aim at disguise, unless so far as it may conduce to actual security in case of an attempt at robbery. Besides, closets and cupboards may be, and actually are, made use of even in handsomely furnished rooms, with this difference, that, instead of being sunk within the walls, they form articles of furniture capable of being removed at pleasure. What, for instance, is a chiffonier, to all intents and purposes, but a cupboard, that may, should there be occasion, be applied to exactly the same uses as any other cupboard of the same size, although of a different description. Again, if anything larger be required, partaking more of a closet than cupboard size, a piece of furniture resembling a glazed bookcase, with silk curtains behind the glass, supplies it at once; and, where economy is a consideration, furniture of this kind may be made quite handsome enough without being expensive. Another advantage attending such conveniences is, that, besides their usefulness, chiffoniers and similar articles serve to give a more finished and comfortable appearance to a parlour or sitting-room than chairs and tables do alone.

Should it happen that the rooms are small, then, indeed, more articles of furniture than are actually required may oftentimes prove an inconvenience, and occasion a crowded huddled-up appearance. But as either the conveniences alluded to must be abandoned altogether, or space allowed for them in some way or other, it becomes entirely a question of choice, with any one who is about to build, whether he will avail himself, as far as possible, of the full extent of his plan, in order to have the rooms as large as it is possible for them to be; or whether he will give up any space, or else in any degree extend his plan, in order to obtain farther convenience. In making a plan for a small residence, there certainly is no difficulty in bringing in closets or recesses of any kind, where they would not at all interfere with the space allotted to the sitting-rooms; but then there are people who wish for closets, and yet must have every place and passage just as large as if there were nothing of the kind; people, in short, who expect an architect to be, not exactly the bottle conjurer, but able to get a pint and a half into a pint mug. "They do not understand plans, not they; but surely closets may be made without either reducing any one of the rooms, or making any addition whatever to the building." The only way of dealing with such persons, who, it is to be hoped, are now becoming scarcer than formerly, is for the architect so to arrange his plan, in the first instance, that whatever space be appropriated to closet room shall seem quite incapable of being turned to account for any other purpose.

Of course, it is impossible to pretend to lay down rules, or even offer any definite instructions, in regard to what may be accomplished by various and very different methods. Without explanatory cuts, moreover, it is exceedingly difficult to point out satisfactorily, and so as to prevent misconception, what is obvious and intelligible at first sight when expressed in a diagram. One mode, however, may here be mentioned in general terms, which is that of making a double instead of a single partition between two rooms, and forming closets and recesses out of the intermediate space thus left. Of these closets, some might belong to one room and some to the other; or else to one only, as should be deemed most advisable. Supposing, in a small house, for instance, with only two moderate-sized sitting-rooms, the dining-parlour to be divided from the other apartment after this manner: besides what is gained, in respect to the convenience of closets, there is this additional advantage, that sounds, as, for example, of persons conversing together, could not pass from one room to the other, but would be almost as completely intercepted as by a solid wall of the same thickness as the two partitions and the closets between them. Consequently a doorway, with double doors, might be formed, leading from one apartment to the other, so as to afford a direct communication, free from the objection which would attend it were there only a single door between the two rooms.

The annexed sketch (*fig.* 183.) of part of a plan for a small cottage villa shows something of the mode above recommended, but so extended as to admit a small light closet between the two sitting-rooms. This closet or small lobby (for its size does not entitle it to the name of room, it being, in fact, little more than the space of a bay window,) would conduce to external effect, and likewise to some effect and variety within, as the window recess would afford a very convenient situation for stands of plants and flowers; or a small conservatory, opening to this bay, or one side of it, might be added to the present plan. In regard to external effect, there would, as may be seen by the plan, be sufficient contrast between solid surfaces of wall and the parts occupied by windows; and that sort of indication of intricacy which arises from the plan itself being not obviously pointed out by the elevations, and therefore leaving something to imagination.

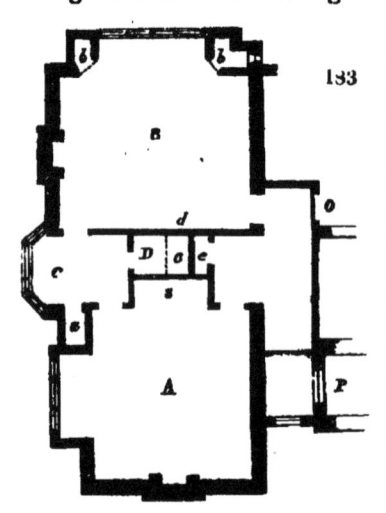

In *fig.* 183., A is a dining-parlour, 17 ft. by 18 ft., with a recess for a sideboard at *s*; B is a drawingroom, 21 ft., by 15 ft., having two closets (*b b*), with jib or masked doors in the panelling of the window recess; the whole of the bay being intended to be wainscoted. At *d* is a panel communicating with *c* behind, c is a lobby communicating with both rooms, having a large closet at D, and a smaller one at *a*. Symmetry not being of importance in such a case as occurs here, the doors are not placed in a line, in order to prevent a direct view from one room to the other: *p* indicates the situation of the porch; *e* is a closet in the vestibule for great coats, &c.; and *o* is a door leading to the staircase, and beyond to the domestic offices.

Besides the closet D, which is as accessible from either the dining or the drawing room as if its door opened immediately into either, a smaller secret closet or cupboard might be made in the lower part at *c*, having a sliding door in the dado or lower part of the wall, in the drawingroom, at *d*. Or a cupboard of a similar description, having another below it opening into *c*, might be fixed higher up, and effectually concealed, not only from observation, but even from discovery, by placing before it either a mirror or a glazed print or drawing in a double frame, so contrived that the inner moulding would slide aside, and give access to the door of the cupboard.

It is obvious that the same expedient might be easily adopted almost anywhere, if no more than a shallow cupboard or recess of a few inches in depth be required. Whether there is any instance of this particular contrivance having actually been executed, the writer knows not: possibly there may, although he is not aware of it. He cannot, however, say that the idea is perfectly his own; because he met with the first germ of it where no one would think of looking for it, and where it is likely to remain as safe from discovery by architectural readers as if it had been studiously hidden in the most secret cupboard ingenuity could devise; namely, in Tieck's tale of *Die Gemählde*, or The Pictures.

23. *Hunter Street, Brunswick Square, Sept.* 1834.

ART. VI. *Architectural Maxims.*

FIRST Conception.— In every work of art, great or little, even down to the least, all depends upon the conception. (*Goethe.*)

Influence of Beauty. — Men are so inclined to content themselves with what is commonest, the spirit and the sense so easily grow dead to the impression of the beautiful and the perfect, that every one should study to nourish in his mind the faculty of feeling these things, by every method in his power: for no man can bear to be entirely deprived of such enjoyment; it is only because they are not used to taste of what is excellent, that the generality of people take delight in silly and insipid things, provided they be new. For this reason, one ought every day to hear a little song, read a good poem, see a fine picture, and, if it were possible, to speak a few reasonable words. (*Goethe.*)

MISCELLANEOUS INTELLIGENCE.

Art. I. *Domestic Notices.*

DEVONSHIRE.— *Exeter New Market.* On August 20. the Chamber met for the purpose of receiving a report from the committee appointed to examine ninety-nine plans, sent in by numerous architects for these markets; when the premiums were awarded as follows: — For the upper site, 100*l.* to Mr. George Dymond of Bristol [our correspondent]; 50*l.* to Mr. Henry Lloyd of Bristol; and 25*l.* to Mr. Andrew Patey of Exeter. For the lower site, 100*l.* to Mr. Charles Fowler of London [the contributor of a design for a villa in our *Encyclopædia of Cottage, Farm, and Villa Architecture and Furniture*, and architect of the Covent Garden, Hungerford, Portman, and other markets, all of which we hope in time to engrave and describe]; 50*l.* to Mr. Ambrose Poynter of London; and 25*l.* to Mr. J. B. Bunning, of London. Means are about to be adopted to produce, from the said plans, one for each market, embracing the best and most useful portions contained in them. (*Exeter Flying Post*, Aug. 21.)

We are much gratified at observing the liberality of the Exeter Commercial Chamber, and the success of our talented friends Mr. Dymond and Mr. Fowler; but we were not less surprised and chagrined to observe a letter, signed An Architect of Thirty Years' Standing, in the *Times* of August 25., in which a candidate among "more than eighty, who had sent in plans, estimates, and specifications, with a letter not to be opened unless the candidate were successful, complains that his drawings were returned, on the 24th of August, rolled up in a single sheet of paper, tied round loosely with a string, unsealed, addressed to me, and without my sealed letter, which confidential letter they must have opened to have obtained my name." Our readers are aware that, in cases of this sort, the unsuccessful candidates are informed by advertisement that their plans, &c., will be sent where ordered. We are at a loss to conceive why this rule has been departed from in the present instance; and we hope the Chamber of Exeter will give some explanation on the subject.

The Exeter Athenæum, a building intended as a public library and literary institution, like the London Institution, and the Royal Institution, of the metropolis, was commenced early in September. We have not heard the name of the architect; but report assigns the design to our classical correspondent, Mr. Wightwick of Plymouth.

Northumberland. — *Bellingham Bridge* having long been in a state of decay, the foundation stone of a new one, from the design of our correspondent, Mr. Green, architect, Newcastle, was laid on August 22. The bridge will consist of four segmental arches of 50 ft. each. The contractors are Messrs. Welch [we suppose Messrs. Hanson and Welch of Liverpool and Birmingham], who purpose having the arches turned by the end of December. The cost of the bridge will be defrayed by private subscription. (*Newcastle Courant*, Sept. 6.)

Newcastle is undergoing great improvement, in the widening of streets, and in the opening up of new lines of communication from one extremity of the town to another. A corn market is also in contemplation, on a grand and commodious plan, in a central situation. (*Ibid.*, July 12.)

Mid-Lothian. — *The large wooden Piles* upon which the suspension chains of the Newhaven pier are supported have been so much injured by minute marine insects, that it has been found necessary to case them with thick sheet iron.

Inverness-shire.— *A new County Hall*, including a courthouse, sheriff-clerk's office, depository for county records, &c., was commenced in Inverness, in the first week of May last. At the same time, the foundation stone was laid of the United Charity School. The masonic rites usual on such occasions were rigidly observed, the first stone of both edifices being laid in the northeast angle, by the Grand Master of the Northern Lodge. (*Elgin Courier*, May, 1834.)

THE ARCHITECTURAL MAGAZINE.

DECEMBER, 1834.

ORIGINAL COMMUNICATIONS.

ART. I. *On those Principles of Composition, in Architecture, which are common to all the Fine Arts.* By the CONDUCTOR. Sect. 4. *Forms, Lines, Lights, Shades, and Colours, considered with reference to Variety, Intricacy, and Harmony.*

VARIETY is the next beauty that is sought for after Symmetry. To produce variety, it is commonly imagined that a great number of things of different kinds are required to be brought together, or that a great number of different kinds of qualities must exist in the same thing. This, however, is to confound variety with diversity. Diversity requires, for its production, a number of things, or of qualities, different in themselves; variety requires only the same thing, or the same quality, placed in different points of view. An almost endless variety may be produced by the position of objects of any one form; for example, by grouping cubes or globes on a flat surface: but diversity would require not only the same variation of position, that is to say, the same grouping, but a difference in the forms, or in the colours, or in both, of the articles grouped or distributed. The Contrast in the Position of objects of the same kind is the cause, or fundamental principle, of Variety; and the Contrast in the Forms or other qualities of the articles brought together is the cause, or fundamental principle, of Diversity.

Intricacy may be described as variety rendered complex, or intricate, by the number of the parts, and by the necessary concealment from the eye of many of them. A small number of cubes may be grouped on the ground, in threes, fours, and fives, in such contrasted positions as to produce considerable variety; but, to render this variety intricate, a considerable number more cubes would be necessary. Instead of groups consisting only of three, four, or five cubes each, such an additional number would be required as would be sufficient to conceal partially one or more cubes in each group. Thus, as, in variety, the cubes might all be placed side by side, so, in intricacy, one or more of the cubes must be placed above one or more of the others. The concealment thus effected must, however, never be so complete as to render a discovery hopeless; because the chief property of intricacy is to engage the eye and the mind, by exciting the curiosity in search of what is unseen, but is yet apparently discoverable. Contrast and Concealment, therefore, are the principles of Intricacy.

To produce Harmony, objects require not only to be contrasted, as in Variety, and partially concealed, as in Intricacy, but to be opposed, as in Diversity. In short, Harmony in composition, whether in Language, Music, Poetry, Painting, or Architecture, admits of the use (in the sense of art) of every property possessed by the materials of the art in which the composition is produced. By the phrase "in the sense of art," we intend to limit the properties of the materials employed to those which are suitable to the art in question: for example, in painting, the material employed is colour; but when we state that every property of colour (the material of painting) may be made use of in harmony, it is not to be understood that we refer to colour either with regard to its chemical or its mechanical properties. From the contrasted position of objects springs Variety; from contrast in position combined with partial concealment, Intricacy; from contrast in form, Diversity; and from all of these combined, Harmony.

In a style of writing which aims at nothing more than correctness and variety of expression, no violent or abrupt transitions from one mode of diction to another; from the prosaic to the poetic style, or from the grave to the gay, for example; are admissible. In a harmonious style, on the contrary, the most sudden transitions of diction and of language are not only admissible, but essential, in order to give that degree of force which renders the effect of harmony so much more intense than that of mere variety. In music, melody may be considered as analogous to variety in written composition, since it consists of simple sounds arranged so as to produce variety by their position, and by the duration of the intervals which occur between them, and does not admit of either violent contrasts or discords. Harmony, however, requires something more than a mere variation of position and intervals; it requires a combination of sounds, according to given principles, to form concords or discords; and the occasional introduction of these discords is essential to the perfection of the composition. What is it that constitutes the difference between the melodious and smoothly flowing verses of Pope, and the harmonious forcible poetic compositions of Dryden, but the violent transitions, and bold and sudden contrasts, in the compositions of the latter poet? Claude's landscapes are varied and beautiful, for the same reasons as Pope's poetry; and the landscapes of Salvator Rosa are bold, forcible, and harmonious, on the same principle as Dryden's poetry; viz., the employment of qualities violently opposed, along with others varied and united.

The highest praise that can be given to an architectural composition, without reference to its expression, is, that it presents to the eye a harmonious whole. It may possess various other qualities, having reference to the purpose for which it was erected; to its expression of that purpose, or of grandeur; to its architectural style; or to its antiquity, strength, durability, &c.: but, viewed simply as a composition of lines, forms, lights, shades, and colours, the highest praise that can be given to it is that of being a harmonious whole. A building may be a regular whole, a symmetrical whole, or a varied whole; but it must be something more than all these to be a harmonious whole.

Having endeavoured to show what constitutes Variety, Intricacy, and Harmony in composition, in the fine arts generally, our next business should be to apply these general principles to the elementary qualities of architectural composition: but no one who has understood this article and the four preceding, on the same subject, can be at any loss in forming a varied, an intricate, or a harmonious composition, by means of forms, lines, lights, shades, or colours, or by all of these combined. He may not be able at first to form such a composition as will perfectly satisfy either himself or others: but to this he will arrive by practice, and by testing his productions by the principles which we have laid down. A mere knowledge of these principles will not, alone, make an eminent artist; but where nature has supplied the necessary organisation, or where an individual has been taught to become an artist as a profession, without reference to his natural taste or faculties, a knowledge of these principles will enable him to react on himself, so as to criticise his own works and those of others, or, at least, to prevent him from committing gross absurdities. An artist, however great may be his taste or his genius, who cannot test his own works or those of others by the principles of sound criticism; who cannot turn his mind in upon itself, and analyse the feelings and emotions which give rise to the productions of his pen or his pencil; will be in continual danger of committing some error or absurdity, which persons wholly without genius, and even far inferior in abilities to himself, may detect, in consequence of their knowledge of principles, and their power of analysing what passes in their own minds. Hence it happens, in the present state of the education of artists, that a just and correct taste is safer than a brilliant genius.

Having, in this article, brought to a conclusion our outline of those principles which are common to all the Fine Arts, we shall next commence a series of papers on the principles more especially applicable to Architecture.

Remarkable Corinthian Capital.

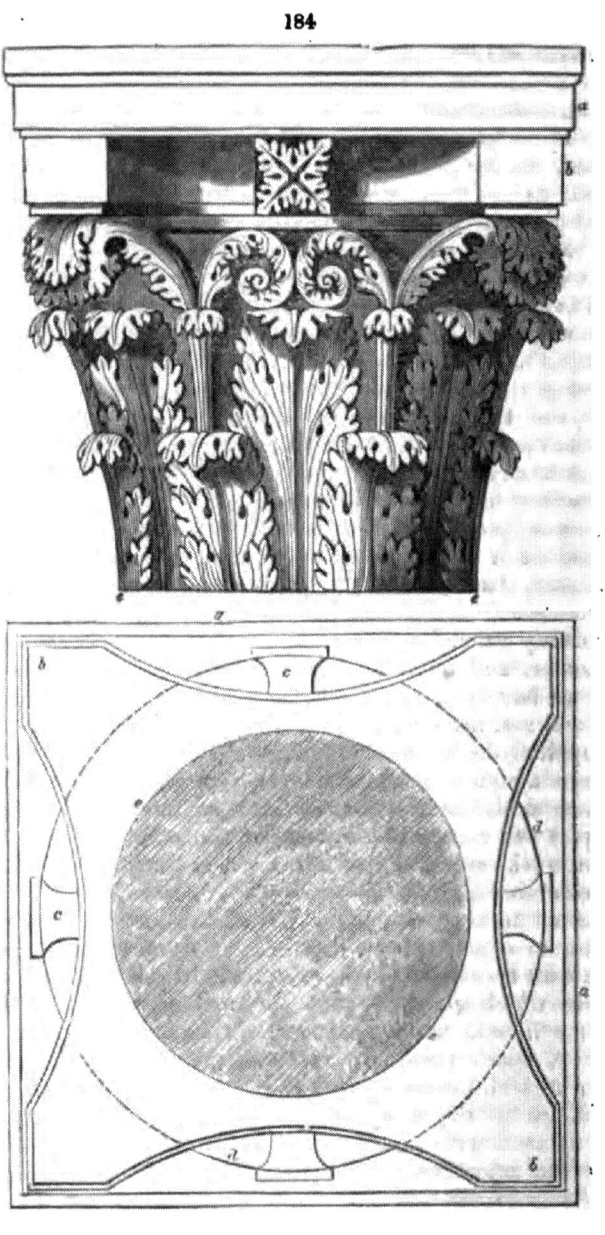

184

Scale of original, 3 in. to 1 ft.

a a, Abacus; *b b*, horns; *c c*, rosettes; *d d*, lip of vase; *e e*, upper diameter of column.

ART. II. *Notice of a remarkable Corinthian Capital in the Vatican.* By G. WIGHTWICK, Esq., Architect.

IT was my chief occupation, while a student at Rome, to glean whatever architectural rarities I could find in the gallery of the Vatican; and I have now by me many drawings, from exquisite examples of the antique, for the first time (I believe) geometrically delineated to accurate measurement. They consist of vases, altars, candelabra, two very curious marble chairs, and a remarkable Corinthian capital, the plan and elevation of which (*fig.* 184.) are herewith forwarded for your publication, should you coincide in my opinion of its worth.

You will observe that its chief peculiarity consists in the square abacus, and the omission of the volutes. The horns curve inward, as usual; but, instead of the one diagonal, they exhibit two square faces, parallel with the right angle of the abacus. The lip of the vase shows itself with considerable prominence, and the central rosette rests upon it, entirely protected above by the abacus, and beautifully relieved by shadows on each side.

It has often struck me that the curved abacus of the Corinthian was particularly unsuited to very small circular porticoes, owing to the too strongly marked opposition between the convexity of the entablature and the concavity of the abacus. This defect is obviously avoided by the square abacus of my example, which gives also a simplicity to the capital, and recommends it as peculiarly fitted to porticoes (whether circular or square) where a foliated capital is desired, without the orthodox but expensive accompaniments of a fluted shaft and modillion cornice.

I have had it accurately modelled, and cleverly executed in Portland stone, by Messrs. Andrews and Greenham, of Plymouth; and the fact of its having been much admired by all who have seen it, is the motive for this communication.

Such of your travelling readers as may chance to come near Plymouth, may see this curious example practically illustrated in the residence of H. Collins Splatt, Esq., at Brixton.

Plymouth, September, 1834.

ART. III. *A Method of securing Outside Shutters for Shop Windows.* By Mr. SAUL.

HAVING been applied to for a plan for securing outside shop front shutters, the following is the method I have given, which may be of interest to the readers of the *Architectural Magazine*, as it differs from any that I have seen published.

The window is 8 ft. wide, and 7 ft. high. There are fourteen shutters, and only one bolt is required in securing the whole;

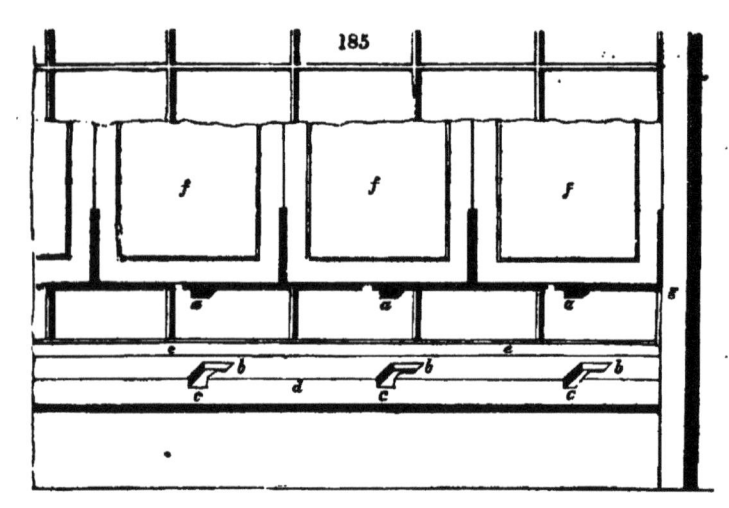

this bolt is fixed on the seventh shutter, but it might be fixed on any of the others except the first or last. Each shutter has attached to the corner plate a stud (*a a*, in *fig.* 185.), which slides back into the groove in the window sill at *b b*; so that, when the shutter to which the bolt is affixed is put up, it secures the whole, as the others are prevented from moving back to *c c*. The window sill (*d*) has got a brass plate fixed upon its upper surface, to prevent the studs from breaking out. The bottom rail of the window is represented by *e e*; and the window shutters (*ff*) are raised up, to show more clearly the studs and the grooves in which they slide. When the stud enters at *c*, and is thence moved to *b*, the shutter comes close up to the style *g*, so that it cannot be taken out until it is moved backwards the width of the stud. The upper ends of the shutters slide in a groove the whole way.

Sulyard Street, Lancaster, July 28. 1834.

Art. IV. *An Account of the Origin and Progress of heating Hothouses and other Buildings by the Application and Circulation of Hot Water, instead of by Fuel or Steam.* By George Cottam, Esq., F.H.S. Z.S., Associate Member of the Institution of Civil Engineers.

(*Continued from* p. 176.)

We shall now proceed to give a chronological detail of every discovery that has taken place in regard to heating through the medium of hot water introduced into metal pipes, commencing with the apparatus of M. Bonnemain, who appears to have been the earliest practiser of the useful and efficient method adverted to. The following quotation, referring to M. Bonnemain, is translated from the *Dictionnaire Technologique* of 1827: —

"The Egyptians were, from time immemorial, in possession of a method of hatching chickens, without the help of hens, by means of furnaces of a particular construction, known by the name of *mamals*. The inhabitants of the village of Berne, at certain seasons of the year, also employed furnaces heated by means of lamps, in hatching chickens for sale; but their process, the result of long practice, and favoured by the climate of their country, does not generally succeed in other countries; and therefore, after making numerous experiments, in order to obtain similar results, all those who were engaged in the pursuit have abandoned it, owing to the uncertainty of success resulting from their essays. M. Reaumur has also published many ingenious observations on artificial incubation; but M. Bonnemain, a French physician, is the only person who, after studying with great care all the circumstances which promote the natural incubation, has been able to hatch eggs in a constant manner, and even more certainly than is in general found to take place with the fowls in our poultry yards."

M. Bonnemain's apparatus consists, first, of a *calorifère*, intended to cause the hot water to circulate; secondly, of a regulator, adapted to maintain an equal degree of temperature; and, thirdly, of a stove, kept constantly heated to the degree proper for incubation, whereto is also attached a cage for the purpose of keeping the chickens warm for the first few days after being hatched. We shall now proceed to describe these three parts successively.

The *calorifère* is so constructed as to transmit the heat of the fire to all parts of the stove, by means of tubes, through which the hot water circulates. In *figs*. 187. to 191., it is delineated in plan, section, and elevation. It is composed of a copper cylindrical fireplace (A), containing a grate (B) which separates it from the ash-pit. The fireplace is every where surrounded by the water in the cylindrical boiler (c), which boiler has likewise fire tubes, though which the flame, smoke, and heated air from the fire are made to circulate; and, in consequence, the greater portion of heat is communicated to the water before it escapes through the chimney.

An *adjutage*, or connecting joint (*d*), affixed upon the top of the boiler, as displayed in *fig*. 186., forms a communication from the interior of the boiler with the vertical tube *d g*, which is united with the horizontal tube *e f*, whereto is soldered a long transverse tube, or adjustment; into which an equal number of tubes, as 6, 8, 10, &c., are fitted. This row of tubes is introduced through the partition wall into the stove, through which it passes in a gently inclining position, and, passing out on the opposite

186

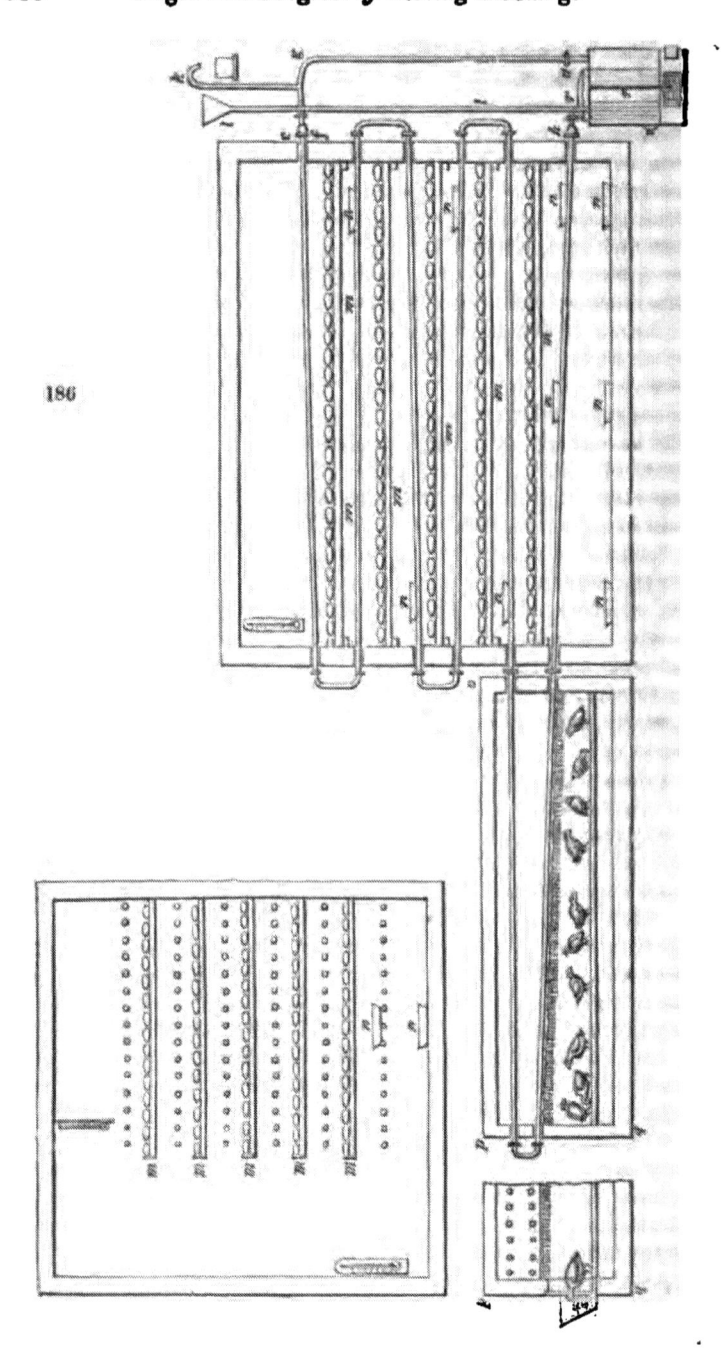

side, the same tubes are curved, and again enter the stove about 8 in. or 9 in. below; thence passing through it, they again traverse the partition wall, and are then bent and passed through the stove, and so on two or three times repeatedly: the last two times, however, M. Bonnemain caused them equally to traverse a kind of cage (*o p q*), having a sheepskin with the wool adhering to it suspended therein, under which the young birds could nestle and keep themselves warm. The row of tubes was then once more united in another transversal tube (*h*), at the bottom of the stove, to which was adapted another tube, descending to the bottom of the boiler on one side, and also above the top of the boiler, thus rendered convenient for filling and emptying the boiler with water. In such case, however, it is requisite to interpose between the mouth of the tube and the bottom of the boiler a capsule of copper, affixed by three branches, so that the heated water should not be directed towards this orifice, and thereby abate in its action of boiling. It is no less desirable to solder to this tube, along the whole of that portion passing through the water, a double envelope full of air, so as to prevent the descending water from becoming re-heated previously to passing into the boiler, whereby the force of its circulation is diminished. An open tube (*k*), raised above the highest point of the first-mentioned tube (*g*), serves to allow the air contained in the water to escape; the other tube (*l*), fitted to the basement of the boiler, as previously specified, but which is elevated above the level of the highest circulating tubes, has a funnel at the top whereby the boiler is to be filled with water. For the purpose of better comprehending the construction of the *calorifère*, we shall now proceed to give a detailed explanation of the figures representing this apparatus, the same letters of reference indicating the correspondent parts in all of them.

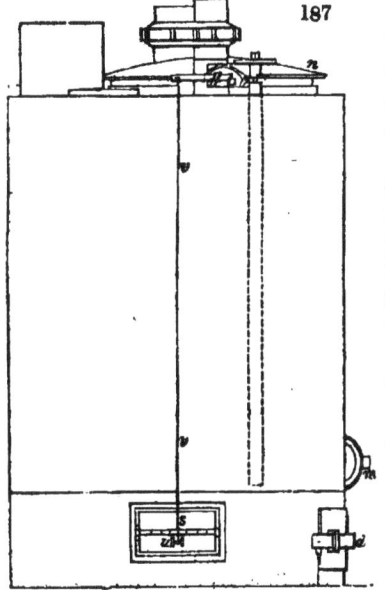

Fig. 187. Exterior elevation of the *calorifère*. *Fig.* 188. Plan of the upper part of the same having its cover removed. *Fig.* 189. Vertical section of the same, displaying the flues or tubes for the products of the combustion to circulate through. *Fig.* 190. A plan taken at the level of the grate. *Fig.* 191. A section of the furnace and its chimney. *Fig.* 192. Side elevation of the regulator and section of the tube enclosing the iron rod. *Fig.* 193. Birdseye view of the dial and levers of the regulator. *Fig.*194. Front view of the register door. *Fig.*195. A section of the same.

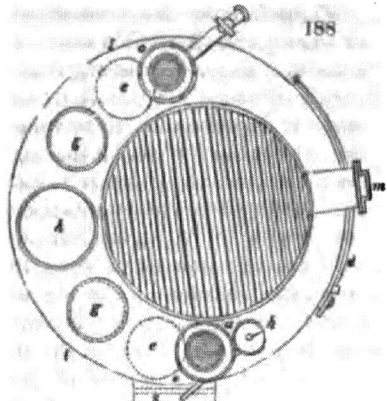

The last four figures are drawn upon a scale three times larger than the former. *a*, The fireplace; *b*, the grate; *c*, the ash pit; *d*, the door of the ash pit; *e e*, tubes whereby the smoke, &c., ascend from the fireplace through the aperture *f*; *g g*, other tubes, down which the smoke, &c., pass from the tubes *e e*; *h*, a larger tube, serving as a chimney to convey away the products of the combustion, which enter through the tubes *i i*, and escape by means of the tubes *g g*; *l*, the exterior case of the *calorifère*, the whole space comprised between the same and the exterior sides of the tubes and fireplace being filled with water; *m*, the mouth of a corresponding opening, serving to light the fire and clear the grate; *n*, the cover of the furnace; *s*, the register for the air to feed the fire, contained in the box or case (*t*) projecting beyond the exterior of the apparatus; the register turns upon the axis *u*, being moved by the rod or wire *v*: *x* is an iron rod; the lower end being screwed, and turning towards the left, in a female screw of brass (*y*) affixed to the bottom of a leaden tube, at the upper part of which is a short square tube of brass (*z*) acting upon the claw (*á*) of the curved lever (*b'*), &c.; while the square tube is guided through an aperture, also formed square, in order to prevent the leaden tube from turning round.

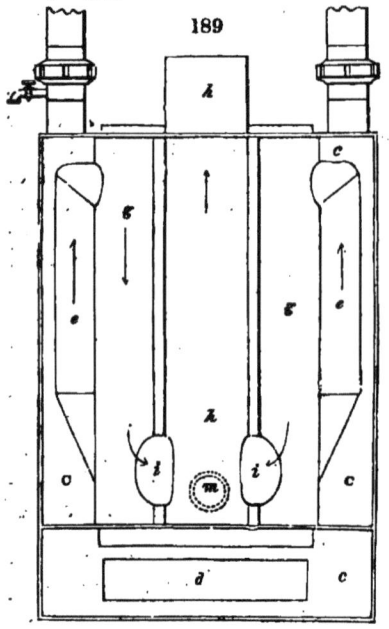

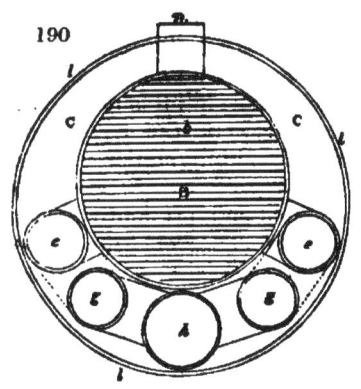

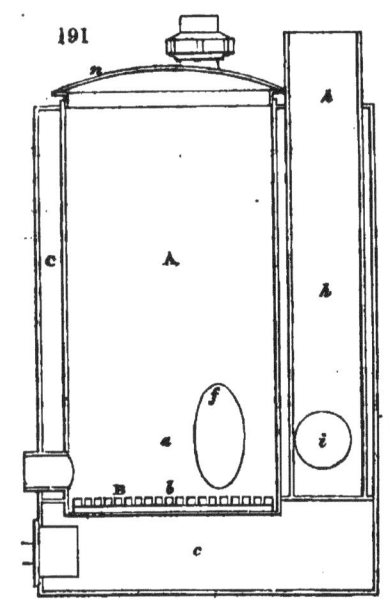

Every object being disposed as above stated, we proceed to raise the cover (*n*) of the furnace (*fig.* 187.), and throw in as much charcoal or wood as may fill half or two thirds of the dimensions of the furnace; we then replace the cover, and open the mouth of the furnace (*m*), and thereby introduce lighted charcoal. As soon as the fire begins to burn, we close the mouth, and open the door (*d*) of the ash pit, until a draught is established, when we close all the openings. The products of the combustion, which are disengaged from the fire, are then introduced, at the opening *f*, into the two ascending tubes *e e*; they then ascend the tubes *g g*, passing through the large tube *h h*, and thence to the chimney. During the passage of the gaseous products of the combustion, they communicate to the water in the boiler a great portion of their heat, and finally enter the chimney at a temperature but little elevated. It may readily be imagined that the water heated in the *calorifère*, rising by means of its specific levity through the tube *d*, *fig.* 186., from the summit of the boiler, creates a progressive movement throughout all the tubes, which again return to the boiler a corresponding quantity of water through the tube *r*, which is precipitated downwards to its lower part. This circulatory movement, once established, continues as long as the water is heated in the *calorifère*, because the temperature is never equal throughout all parts of the apparatus. We consequently infer that a perfect equality of temperature never can exist, owing to the continued loss of heat escaping from the exterior of all the tubes. In the mean time, the temperature of the air enclosed in the stove varies but little from that of the several tubes whereby it is traversed; and as the curves of the tubes on the outside of the stove afford little surface to be cooled by the surrounding air, so the force of the circulation uniformly in the ratio of the difference between the temperatures of the water issuing from the *calorifère* and re-entering the same, does not become greatly diminished, even when a large portion of its heat is expended, outside of the stove, in maintaining a gentle heat in the cage (*o p q*) adjoining. We therefore find, the more the water is cooled passing through the last circumvolutions of the tubes, the more active is the circulation in all parts; and, consequently, the more equal is the temperature of all the tubes that heat the stove, and of the air within it. Indeed, to prevent the loss of heat as much as possible, the *calorifère*, and all those parts of the tubes placed on the exterior of the stove, are enveloped in lists of woollen cloth.

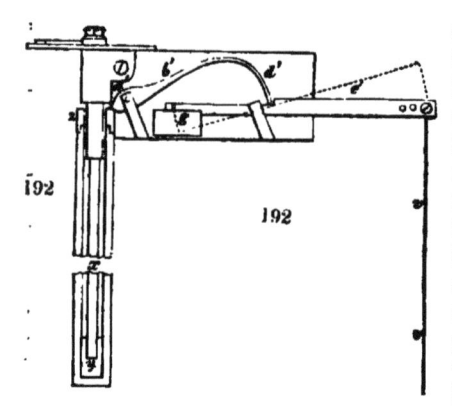

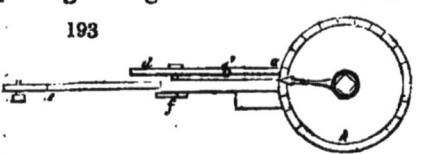

M. Bonnemain, having thus applied the principles of heating with so much skill, was always enabled to maintain in his stoves an equal temperature, scarcely varying so much as half a degree of Reaumur's thermometer; but, as it was not sufficient to have thus far solved the problem, he contrived that this degree of temperature, in all parts of the stove, should be constantly maintained at that point which was found most favourable for promoting incubation. It was by means of the following apparatus, or regulator of the fire, that he attained this desirable object.

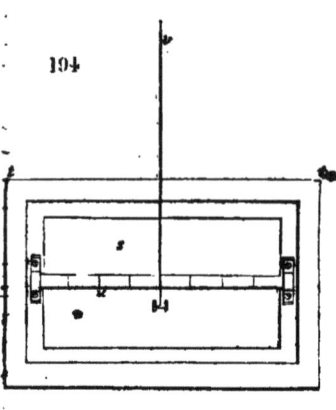

The action of this *regulator* is founded on the unequal dilatation of different metals by heat. A rod of iron (x, fig. 192.) screwed, as above mentioned, at its lower extremity, is united to a female screw of brass (y), which is enclosed within a tube of lead termi-

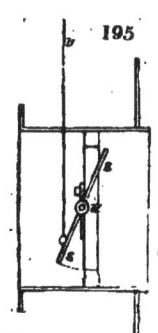

nating at its upper end in a ring of brass (z). The leaden tube is plunged into the water contained in the *calorifère*, by the side of one of the tubes (g). The dilatation of lead being greater than that of iron, at an equal degree of temperature, and the rod being also enclosed within the tube, it is heated much less than the tube; and, when the temperature is raised to the degree required, the lengthening of the tube brings the ring (z) into contact with the claw (a') at the shorter end of the bent lever (a' b' d'); but when the slightest increase of heat again lengthens the tube, the ring (z) raises the claw of the lever, but, by reason of the greater length of its opposite arm (d) that end descends much more. This movement is communicated near to the axis of a balanced lever (e), placed below the end of the former one, and thereby greatly increases the motion of the lever e', which movement is forthwith transmitted by the iron wire (v) to the register (s), which diminishes or entirely suppresses the access of air to the fire. The combustion then abates, and, the temperature falling a little in consequence, the leaden tube shortens and is disengaged from its contact with the claw of the lever (a' b' d'); and the counterweight (g) fixed in the lever (e) causes the other extremity to rise and open the air register (s), thus affording a wide passage for the admission of air, when the combustion acquires a renewal of activity. Hence it becomes obvious that, the temperature of the *calorifère* being regulated, the tubes circulating through the stove must constantly dispense the same quantum of heat for any given period. Nevertheless, this condition did not suffice for uniformly preserving an equal temperature in the stove, in consequence of the temperature of the open air so greatly varying. In order to counterbalance this influence, M. Bonnemain fitted, upon the upper end of the iron rod that supports the regulating tube, an index, contrived in such a manner as to turn the rod, and, consequently, the screw (y) at its lower end, so as to lower or raise the leaden tube. In the former case, the claw at the shorter end of the lever (a' b' d') falling from it, causes the air register to open, and raise the temperature higher than the dilatation of the leaden tube permitted; and thus a higher temperature is obtained, and regularly continued. If, on the contrary, the tube be raised by turning the index in an opposite direction, the air register affords a less opening, whereby a temperature considerably lower is produced. Hence we find that it is easy to determine, *à priori*, the degree of temperature which we would communicate to the water circulated by means of the *calorifère* through the rows of tubes in the stove. In order to facilitate the means of regulating his *calorifère*, M. Bonnemain caused divisions to be engraved upon a dial plate beneath the index, and inscribed the words "*stronger heat*" or "*less heat*" upon this plate; thus pointing out the direction in which the index should be turned, in order to produce the one or the other effect. M. Bonnemain's *calorifère* and regulator, by means of appropriate modifications, might thus be usefully applied under garden beds, so as to preserve the temperature expedient for vegetation at all seasons of the year; or, in producing an abundance of early crops of vegetables. Successful experiments of this description were resorted to at the *Jardin des Plantes* at Paris. This ingenious apparatus may equally be applied to maintain the proper temperature in greenhouses, apartments, and more particularly in stoves, when the alcoholic or acetic fermentations are to be produced, or the crystallisation of sugarcandy, tartaric acid, &c., is to be effected.

When it is requisite to hatch chickens, &c., in the stove previously described, a fire should be kindled in the *calorifère*, and by means of the regulator the degree of heat fitted to produce incubation is obtained in the stove. The eggs must then be ranged near each other upon the shelves with borders to them (*m m, fig.* 186.) fixed under each row of tubes. It is expedient not to cover, during the first day, more than the twentieth portion of the superficies of the shelves, and to add every day, during twenty days, an equal number of eggs, so that, on the twenty-first day, the quantity of eggs first deposited will be for the major part hatched, and every day nearly the same number of chickens will be obtained; which, however, may be regulated by the demand at any particular season of the year.

During the first days of incubation, whether natural or artificial, the small portion of water contained within the substance of the egg evaporates through the pores in the shell: this is replaced by a small quantity of air, which is necessary to support the respiration of the chicken. But as the atmospheric air which surrounds the eggs in the stove at that degree of temperature is either completely dry, or but little humid, so the chicken would greatly suffer, or finally perish, from this kind of desiccation. The aqueous vapour which exhales from the breathing of the old fowls while hatching, in some degree prevents this ill effect; but, nevertheless, in dry seasons, this vapour is hardly sufficient; and thus, in order that the eggs may be better hatched in the dry seasons, the hens cover them with the earth of the floor of the granary. In artificial incubation, to keep the air in the stove constantly humid, they place in it flat vessels, such as plates (*n n*), for example, filled with water. When the chickens are hatched, they are removed from the stove and carried to the cage (*o p*); where they are fed with millet. There are also partitions in the cage, to separate the chickens as they are hatched each day, in order to modify their nourishment agreeably to their age. Artificial incubation is exceedingly useful in furnishing young fowls at those seasons when the hens will not sit; and in some situations to produce, or, as we may say, to manufacture, a great number of fowls in a small space.

Prior to the Revolution, M. Bonnemain had set on foot a very lucrative establishment, whereby the court of France and the various markets of Paris were abundantly supplied with poultry at all seasons, and, consequently, at those periods of the year when the farmers had not the means of furnishing that delicate commodity. The disastrous effects of the revolution that subsequently took place occasioned the abandonment of this useful institution, and thus the French capital was deprived of the beneficial results of the discovery. M. Bonnemain, however, after a lapse of time, renewed his project; but as sufficient funds were wanting to direct his plans with that assiduous care he had previously bestowed upon them, the results were not so advantageous as to warrant their continuance; and the attempt was thus ultimately adandoned.

ART. V. *Notice of an improved Lamp Post in Use in Edinburgh.* By JOHN ROBISON, Esq., Sec. R.S.E., &c.

THE lamp pillars in use in this city are, I think, worthy of your notice: they, in the same way as the mile marks (p. 78.), combine durability, effectiveness, and economy, with a graceful outline. I had to contend with much prejudice and opposition in getting them introduced; but they have now made their way into some twenty or thirty different places, including New South Wales. Previously to their introduction here, it was held as an axiom that square lanterns were better fitted for gas lights than globes, and that their maintenance was less expensive. Experience has proved both positions to be false, as, by providing, in the construction of the top, a chimney for the discharge of the watery vapour of combustion, it is found that the globes remain undimmed in all weathers, and protect the flame from being blown out when the wind extinguishes that in the lanterns. The expense of repairing damaged lanterns is also found to exceed that of renewing broken globes in a very unexpected proportion. The lamp pillars serve the purpose of indicating the names of the streets, which are cast in relief on the bar against which the lamplighter's ladder is reared, and are painted white.

The lamp pillar consists of two pieces of cast iron, and a frame of wrought iron for the support of the glass. *Fig.* 196. is a view of this lamp pillar, with all its parts complete. *Fig.* 197. is a section of the same, showing the construction of the parts within.

In erecting the pillar, the base (*a*) is set on the stone by the assistance of a spirit level, and the butts (*b b*) are bedded into the stone, level with the pavement, and secured by lead. The shaft (cc, previously adjusted to its base at the foundery) is then slipped on it, and the key driven through as at d, which confines the shaft and the base firmly together.

The lamp iron, or frame (e), is attached to the head of the pillar; and is secured, upon the same principle, by two screwed pins at f. The cross bar (g) for the lamplighter's ladder to be placed against, is made flat on the face, and a little thicker below than above, to allow of the light striking on its surface, on which the names of the streets, &c., in which the lamps are to be placed is to be cast in relief on both sides. The pillars are to be painted of a dark colour, and the letters made white.

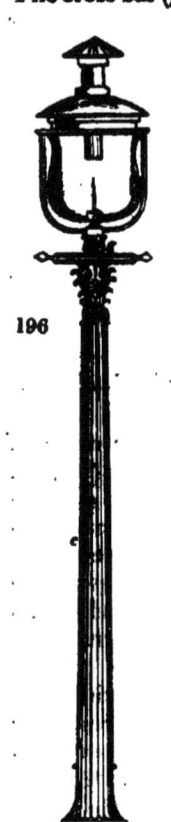

The glasses are open at bottom, with an inch and a half aperture as a vent hole; but, in order to prevent the wind from disturbing the flame, a disc of tinned iron slides on the gas pipes to a regulated distance from the opening.

The covers are constructed as shown in the figures, having a chimney in the centre, for the purpose of maintaining a current of air through the interior of the lamp; and to carry off the watery vapour generated by the combustion of the gas, which would otherwise condense on the surface of the glass, and obscure the light.

The experience of last winter has shown that this construction of lamp post possesses an important advantage over those previously used here. It throws very little shadow beyond its own base; the lights burn steadily in the most stormy weather; the casualties to the glass have been much diminished; and the difficulty of climbing the pillar (from the absence of projecting ornaments) has put a stop to the stealing of the brasswork in the burners. The dust, likewise, from finding no lodgment, is washed away by every shower.

Edinburgh, February, 1833.

REVIEWS.

ART. I. *A Treatise on Isometrical Drawing as applied to Geological and Mining Plans, Picturesque Delineations of Ornamental Grounds, Perspective Views and Working Plans of Buildings and Machinery, and to General Purposes of Civil Engineering; with Details of Improved Methods of Preserving Plans and Records of Subterranean Operations in Mining Districts.* By T. Sopwith, Land and Mine Surveyor, Member of the Institution of Civil Engineers, Author of "Geological Sections of Mines," "Account of Mining Districts," &c. With thirty-four copperplate engravings. 8vo, pp. 239. London, 1834.

IN his preface, the author informs us that his object is "to elucidate the principles of isometrical projection, and to explain its application to a variety of useful purposes." After stating its suitableness for geological maps and plans, and sections of mines of every description, he adds, that "for plans and elevations of buildings, and for working details of machinery, isometrical drawing possesses such decided advantages, that a more extended knowledge of its principles cannot fail to insure its almost universal application, in preference to every mode of perspective drawing. In representing gardens and pleasure-grounds, not only a correct plan of the mansion, and the various walks, lawns, or plantations, can be shown, but also the height and pictorial aspect of the trees, shrubs, green-houses, &c. For this and various other purposes, isometrical drawing will be found an agreeable occupation to amateur artists, and especially to ladies, who are thus enabled to combine the beauties of landscape, architectural, and flower painting, with useful and correct delineations of pleasure-grounds, houses, gardens, or other objects." (p. vii.)

Our readers who are aware of the extent to which we have used isometrical projection in our *Encyclopædia of Cottage Architecture*, in our *Illustrations of Landscape Gardening* (a new series of which will speedily appear), and in the *Gardener's Magazine*, will not be surprised at our entirely agreeing with Mr. Sopwith in recommending isometrical drawing as by far the best kind for general use in architecture, land-surveying, and landscape-gardening. In truth, this description of drawing has been employed in these three departments of delineation from the earliest period; and the only difference between the practice recommended by Professor Farish, Mr. Joplin, and Mr. Sopwith, and that formerly practised by surveyors and architects, is, that the modern practice is founded on principles and reduced to a system, which the other was not. In the British Museum is a work, by the architect and engineer Caus, entitled *Hortus Palatinus*, printed at Frankfort in the year 1620, in which a number of the plates, both of the garden and the palace, are in tolerably correct isometrical drawing; and we have seen a number of drawings by old English architects in the same style. With regard to maps of estates, the old mode of giving the elevations of the trees, fences, gates, houses, &c., is nothing more than isometrical projection, made by the eye without any knowledge of its principles. It thus appears that this description of drawing is the most ancient and natural of any, as well as the most useful.

On the subject of its utility in architecture, Mr. Peter Nicholson, one of the first practical mathematicians of the age, has the following remarks, which may be considered conclusive in its favour: — " Isometrical projection combines the uses of perspective and geometrical drawings of plans, elevations, and sections. It is of equal utility with perspective in showing how the parts of a design are connected together, and has this advantage over it, in exhibiting the measures of those parts. Much study is required, in order to carry a complex design which is represented by geometrical drawings into execution, from its being necessary to represent the object by as many separate drawings as it has faces. Hence the advantage which isometrical projection has over geometrical drawings, in uniting all the faces of an object; and, consequently, representing the object itself by one drawing."

Having, as we conceive, shown the great value of this description of drawing to the architect, surveyor, and engineer, we have only at present room strongly to recommend Mr. Sopwith's book as by far the best, and indeed the only complete, work that has yet appeared on the subject. Every part of it is rendered easily comprehensible, even by a person who knows scarcely any thing of geometry; and every mode of the application of isometrical drawing is beautifully illustrated by engravings. Mr. Sopwith shows, and indeed it is self-evident, that the term isometrical perspective is incorrect; isometrical projection is the true designation, from which the practice of isometrical drawing is deduced. This isometrical drawing consists in a certain proportional enlargement of some parts of the projection, in order that both the geometrical ground plan and the isometrical elevation may be measured by the same scale. It is an important point, therefore, for such of our readers as wish to make themselves acquainted with the difference between isometrical projection and isometrical drawing, and to bear it in mind afterwards. We shall speak of the suitableness of this mode of drawing for gardening purposes in our *Gardener's Magazine*.

ART. II. *Working Ornaments and Forms, full Size, and in various Styles, for the Use of the Cabinet Manufacturer, Chair and Sofa Maker, Carver, and Turner; consisting of entirely new Designs, in which great Study has been bestowed on causing a Display without much Expense in Material or Labour.* By T. King, author of "The Modern Style of Cabinet Work, exemplified in New Designs;" "Designs for Carving and Gilding, &c. &c. Parts I., II., and III. Folio. London, 1833. 10s. each.

THIS is a most beautiful work, and one that will be of the greatest use to the practical man, especially to him who lives in the country. The designs show considerable originality, and, as it appears to us, good taste; and they are on such a large scale that no workman can have any difficulty in carrying them into execution. Each part is complete in itself.

Part i. contains, supports of sideboard tables; a termination of a sideboard back; sideboards; rosettes and studs for turning and carving; a loo table; card and loo table feet; pilasters and columns; commodes; a flower-stand; and a support for a card table.

Part ii. contains, centre ornaments for friezes; stump feet; legs for tables; brackets; pillar supports for commode shelves; cantilever supports for commode shelves; panel corners; tops for bead panels; nulling combined with other mouldings [a nulling is a turned moulding representing strings of beads of different sizes and forms, but generally globular, oblong, ovate, or spheroidal, which was very common both in furniture and cornices about a century ago]; contours of mouldings, Grecian and Gothic.

Part iii. contains, chair legs; uprights and spindles for chair backs; chair splats; an arm-chair top; ornaments for sofa backs, and for the end of a couch or sofa; legs for sofas or couches; a drawingroom chair back; the back of a hall chair. This part also contains short explanations, on one page, of the thirty plates which compose the work. Several of these plates are of the size of a whole sheet; so that the work is as cheap as it is good.

ART. III. *Gothic Ornaments illustrative of Prior Birde's Oratory, in the Abbey Church, Bath.* By Edward Davis, Architect, Bath. No. III. Imperial folio. London.

THE first plate in this number exhibits a canopy in the angle near the entrance; the second, bosses from the compartments under the window; the third, one of the principal spandrils, with part of it full size; the fourth, another of the principal spandrils, with part full size; the fifth, a pedestal under a canopy. The whole of these are most ingenious in design, and beautifully drawn and printed.

ART. IV. *Catalogue of Works on Architecture, Building, and Furnishing, and on the Arts more immediately connected therewith, recently published.*

FRANCE.

PONCELET: Mémoires sur les Roues Hydrauliques. 4to. 7 fr.

La Propriété, Journal d'Architecture Civile et Rurale, de Beaux-Arts, et d'Economie Sociale. 8vo. In monthly numbers. Paris.

Picturesque Travels in Ancient France. The parts relating to the province of Languedoc are now in course of publication. The volumes already completed are five in number, and comprise Upper Normandy, Franche-Comté, and Auvergne.

Compte de Lasteyrie: Collection de Machines, Instrumens, &c. 4to. New edition, to be completed in twenty-two parts, of which six are published.

D'Aubuisson de Voissins: Traité d'Hydraulique à l'Usage d'Ingénieurs. Large volume, 8vo; with four plates.

GERMANY.

Meyerheim and Strack's Architect, Part IV.: Antiquities of the Old Mark of Brandenburg. 10 dollars for the four parts.

Von Rinz: Baronial Castles of the Grand Duchy of Baden. 1 vol., royal folio; with sixty plates. 130 fr.

Crelle: Journal für die Baukunst, &c. Vol. VII., Part IV.; and Vol. VIII., Part I.

Crelle and Dietlein: Principles of Bridge-Building, &c. Berlin. 5¾ dollars.

ENGLAND.

Treatise on Isometrical Drawing as applicable to Geological and Mining Plans, Picturesque Delineations of Ornamental Grounds, Perspective Views and Working-Plans of Buildings and Machinery, and to General Purposes of Civil Engineering. By T. Sopwith. 34 copperplates. Demy 8vo, 16s.; royal paper, 1l. 1s.

The History and Description of the Architecture, Construction, Materials, &c., of Eastbury, Essex. Imperial 4to. 2l. 2s.

Compilation of splendid Ornamental Designs from foreign Works of recent production. 4to, 24 plates. 10s.

Maguire's Selection of Ornaments in various Styles. 4to. 9s.

Knight's Unique Fancy Ornaments. Four parts, 4to. 16s. Five parts will complete.

Shaw's Elizabethan Details, Part III. 4to. 5s.

Shaw's Ancient Furniture, Part VIII. 4to. 5s.

Smith on the Construction of Cottages for Labourers. 8vo. Plates. 4s.

The Antiquities of Christchurch, Hampshire. By B. Ferrey, Architect. 4to. 2l. 5s.; royal paper, 3l. 7s. 6d.

Lockwood and Cates's History and Antiquities of the Gates, &c., of the City of York. 4to, five plates, 18s.; large paper, in folio, 30s.

Cattrick Church, in the County of York, illustrated; with Notes by the Rev. J. Raine; and with 13 plates of Views, Elevations, and Details, by A. Salvin, Architect.

Britton's Survey of the Borough of Marylebone; fine large coloured map, in a 4to case. 1l. 1s.

Blunt and Stephenson's Civil Engineer, Part II. Atlas folio, 1l. 1s.

Treatise on the principal Mathematical Instruments employed in Surveying, Levelling, and Astronomy, &c. &c. By F. W. Simms. 8vo. 5s.

Oliver Evans on Mill-Work; a new edition by T. P. Jones. 8vo, 25 plates. 18s.

Account of the Mining Districts of Alston Moor, Weardale, and Teesdale, in Cumberland and Durham. By T. Sopwith. 12mo, plates. 4s. 6d.

Geological Sections of Holyfield, Hudgill, and of Vein and Silver Band Lead Mines in Alston Moor and Teesdale. By T. Sopwith. 4to, plates. 10s. 6d.

Art. V. *Literary Notices.*

ELEMENTARY *and Practical Instructions on the Art of Building Cottages and Houses for the humbler Classes,* and for the better lodging of the peasantry and industrious classes in this country, as well as for the use of emigrants; 8vo, 8 plates and 27 woodcuts; 7s.; is in the press.

Mr. Robinson's *Hardwick Hall* will be published in December.

Mr. Wilkins will shortly publish two of the principal books of Vitruvius, which relate to *Civil Architecture,* with copious notes.

Mr. Weale will soon publish, from Mr. Wilkins's drawing, a *Geometrical Elevation of the National Gallery,* in a folio print.

A General Treatise on Projection, showing the various modes of delineating lines, plane figures, and solids, by Peter Nicholson, Architect, is preparing for publication.

For the above notices and the preceding catalogue we are indebted to Mr. Weale.

MISCELLANEOUS INTELLIGENCE.

Art. I. *General Notices.*

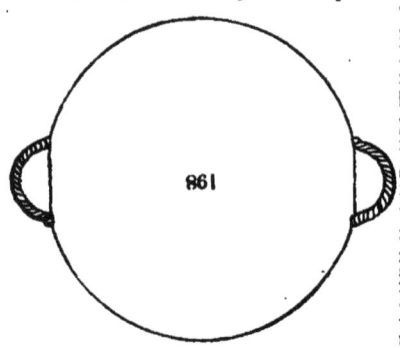

BRICKMAKING, *in Egypt,* is not confined to any particular class. Most of the common labourers, and many of the mechanics and tradesmen, as well as farmers, possess the tools for making bricks; and the following is an account of their mode of proceeding:— Near the bank of the Nile, or any other place where water and rich soil may be found, one or two men go into the water, and, with a rude instrument, like a carpenter's adze, they cut about two or more feet deep, and six or eight feet long: the breadth is according to circumstances. After they have cut about a load of soil, they mix with it one sackful of broken straw, cut about a quarter of an inch long (the quantity of this material must be proportioned to the quality of the soil), and a certain quantity of ashes. After these materials are well mixed together, they are ready for moulding. One man takes a *borrshane* (*fig.* 198.), and goes to the other who is in the pit, who fills it up with the mixture; and then the first carries it to a barren place, or common. When a sufficient quantity has been carried to this place, the labourers spread the cut straw over the ground where the bricks are to be made. The brickmakers then get each of them a vessel (see *fig.* 199.) full of water, and then sit each to his work. They fill the moulds (*fig.* 200.) with their hands, and when each mould is full, they dip their hands into the water, and pass them over the surface of the brick to smooth it; and then, taking up the mould, they leave the brick on the ground to dry, and so on. When the desired quantity of bricks are made, they are left to harden in the sun; and when they become dry on the upper surface, they are turned over, till they become thoroughly dry, and hard enough for immediate use, or for burning.

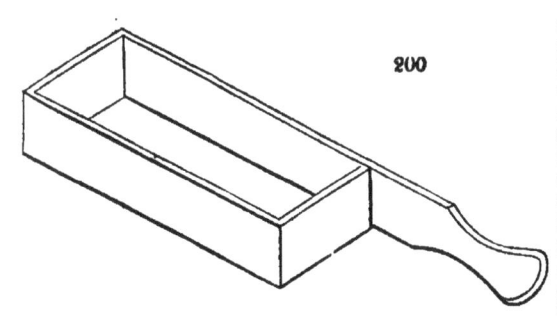

Fig. 198. represents the *borrshane*, in which the labourers carry the brick earth: it is made of the leaves of the palm tree, and is a circular mat with two handles. *Fig.* 199. represents the pot for holding the water, in which the labourers moisten their hands to smooth the bricks which they are moulding. *Fig.* 200. is a representation of the mould, made of wood. — *Mashdoud Mohandz. Norwich, Sept.* 29. 1834.

The Ancients conducted Water in Pipes. — It is stated in Professor Vince's *Principles of Hydrostatics for the Use of Students in the University of Cambridge*, p. 18., that "the ancients, not being aware that a pipe would convey a fluid to a level as high as the reservoir, carried water in pipes only down hill. To convey water to a place only a little below the water in the reservoir, having a valley between, they built aqueducts, instead of carrying a pipe down the hill, and then up again.

Now, the word "aqueduct," as applied to the works of the ancients, is so sure to raise in our minds the image of those splendid remains to be seen in every direction around Rome and some other ancient cities, that a most erroneous idea appears likely to be perpetuated, by its employment as above in a book written expressly for instruction on points of this nature. For it never can be true, that, as a practical measure, it would, under all the circumstances, have been more advisable to construct "pipes," or rather tunnels, "down hill and then up again" for the purpose of conveying the streams of the magnitude with which Rome was watered, than to follow the gradual descent of the land with open aqueducts, and, when necessary, to cross the valleys at the most advantageous places. The enormous thickness of masonry requisite to confine these streams in tunnels after their descent from the Sabine and Alban hills, and the difficulty of repairing it when out of order, sufficiently exonerates the ancients from the charge of ignorance in employing the mode of construction they adopted.

In London, we confine the use of water almost exclusively to domestic purposes; and most convenient it is to have water at command on every floor of the house, obtained by the well-known principle that, when conveyed through pipes, it rises to the level of its head. But in Rome, which has no good natural springs, where the climate is hot, and where water was, as it still is, an object of magnificence as well as use; where the daily use of the public bath was a salutary fashion adopted by all, and where the public games sometimes depended on the supply; a good many pipes, fifteen or twenty miles long, would have done little towards supplying the demand of so large a population; and nothing but the gigantic idea, which that gigantic nation could alone afford to execute, of conveying whole rivers across the plain into the city, was calculated to render it, what it still is, the best-watered metropolis in the world.

That the ancients used water-pipes is well known: those of earthenware are frequently found as perfect as when first laid down; and it is quite impossible to understand how they could use pipes in connexion with the transmission of water, and not arrive at the knowledge of what now appears to us so obvious a principle — that it will rise through them to the level of its reservoir; especially when the complicated refinements of the ancient baths, and the general skill in engineering manifested by the Romans, are considered. The want of metal might, perhaps, have limited the use of pipes in cases where it was necessary to resist great pressure; but there is at Fréjus a fountain supplied by a restored Roman aqueduct, which the writer of this article is inclined to believe may be a case in point. Fréjus stands low; and, although I had not time to examine the course of the aqueduct, I am of opinion that the water is there conveyed by a pipe "down hill and then up again."

Let the learned engineers of Cambridge turn to the first work which professes to treat of the aqueducts of the ancients, and they will find them accused not only of using water-pipes, but of conducting water by them, in siphons, over hills. — *T. F. L. Harwich, Sept.* 1834.

ART. II. *Foreign Notices.*

FRANCE.

PARIS, Sept. 1834. — Never did any monument of antiquity cause a greater sensation in Paris than the Obelisk of Luxor. No sooner had the Pacha given permission to the French government to remove this fine monument, than 500 Arabs were employed, at the expense of the French nation, for that purpose. The French engineers who superintended the work created quite a sensation in Luxor; even the dancing-girls learnt French; and when the obelisk was removed, machinery of extraordinary ingenuity was contrived for getting it on board ship, and relanding it on its arrival in France. At length it reached Paris; and then the question was, what was to be done with it? Some advised it to be placed in the Basse Cour of the Louvre, beside the Sphinx which had lain there for the last twenty or thirty years; some recommended the Place de la Bastille; some the Champ de Mars, and some even the Pont Neuf. Numerous other places have been suggested; but objections have been made to all. For a long time, as I before observed (p. 46.), the Place de la Concorde was thought the most likely to be fixed on; but now it is said that it will be placed at the rond-point de Courbevoie, beyond the Pont de Neuilly.

Many projects are in agitation for improving the pavement of the streets in Paris. The Rue Vivienne and the Rue Richelieu have already undergone repair. The kennels in these streets have been formed of long pieces of flagstone hollowed out to receive the water, and firmly bedded in a mortar formed of cement and lime. Extensive improvements are about to be made in the Champs Elysées and the Place de la Concorde. There are to be fountains in each square of the place, and in different parts of the Champs Elysées. All the paltry buildings in the latter are to be removed, and handsome houses substituted. The arch at the Barrière de l'Etoile, at last, seems likely to be finished: two statues of Fame have been placed on the Parisian side, and models for the other sculptures are said to be prepared. The Museum of Natural History, which has been long talked of, has been commenced. It is to comprise a gallery for mineralogy and geology, hot-houses, houses for animals, reservoirs and conduits of water, &c. The gallery is to consist of a centre and two wings. The centre will be 300 ft. long; and the wings, which are to contain the herbarium, library, theatre, &c., 120 ft. long, and 45 ft. wide. The hot-houses are to consist of two pavilions entirely covered with glass, each 60 ft. long, 36 ft. wide, and 36 ft. high. At the extremity of one of these pavilions are to be two ranges of curvilinear hot-houses, presenting a surface of 140 square yards of glass. The church of St. Dénis is being repaired;

but, as this is out of the city, I will return to the public works of Paris, the most important of which is a monument which is to be erected in the Place de la Bastille, in memory of the revolution of 1830. It is to consist of a bronze column in the Doric order, surmounted by a statue of the Genius of Liberty. The monument will have for its basis three plinths, or steps: the first of red Flanders marble, circular in the plan, of 30 yards in diameter, and nearly 1 yard in height above the pavement; the second will be of white marble, about 18 yards in diameter, and 3 yards high above the first, exclusive of the cornice over it; the third will form a square of 8 yards on each side, and will be elevated about 9 ft. above the cornice of the second; it will also be of white marble. Above this will be placed a pedestal of bronze, 6 yards square, and 6 yards high. The column will be $3\frac{1}{4}$ yards in diameter at the base, and 25 yards high. It will be surmounted by a lantern 4 yards high, on which will be placed a statute, which will make a total elevation of $46\frac{1}{4}$ yards from the pavement. These measurements are not very exact; but I expect soon to be able to send you an engraving representing an elevation of the entire design. The staircase will be of bronze, and will consist of 205 steps. Two sides of the bronze pedestal will bear inscriptions in gilt letters; and the two others will be ornamented with symbolic figures. All the ornaments will be gilt, and the torus of the base of the column will be ornamented with laurel leaves. On the shaft of the column will be inscribed, in gilt letters, the names of the citizens who were slain in the revolution of July, 1830. The capital of the column will be gilt; and also the statue of Liberty, which will hold a flambeau in one hand, and a chain, broken, in the other. The preparatory works were commenced in 1833, and the total expense is estimated at 900,000 francs. — *F. L. Bésson. Rue de Richelieu, Paris.*

GREECE.

Athens. — According to some of the French papers, the Greek architect Kleanthos, who has been commissioned to prepare plans for laying out the new city, has been removed from his post, in consequence of his favouring some of the present occupiers of the ground intended to be built on. Upon the same authority, we are informed that it was his idea to bring together all the most striking beauties of the principal cities of Europe; the Piazza di San Marco at Venice, the Palais Royal, the Tuileries, &c. &c. If such was literally to have been the case; if the architect really intended to desecrate the classic site of Athens by copies of the Parisian buildings, and so to Frenchify the new Grecian metropolis, his dismissal is not a circumstance for regret. At all events, it is certain that Klenze set out for Greece on the 16th of July in order to give the government his advice as to the project for the future city and the residence of its sovereign. It seems that it is intended to provide at first for a population of about 80,000 inhabitants, besides those in the Piræus, which is to constitute a seaport town. — *W. H. London, Sept.* 1834.

AUSTRALIA.

I have to thank you for Part. I. of your *Encyclopædia of Cottage Architecture*, sent to me through the medium of the editor of the *Sydney Gazette*. You will think it strange, but the admirable arrangements that it describes do not seem at all suited to our colony: not only the climate, but the habits of the people, the servants, and the mode of living peculiar to a new country, seem to militate against those refinements that even in an old country cannot be easily introduced. We require refinements of a different description; and I never take up a work on any of the countries bordering the Mediterranean, but I observe many little things, the results of experience, that might be introduced here with advantage. Could you not devote some papers in the *Architectural Magazine* to the architectural arrangements suitable to our colony, pointing out the different styles of building and interior distribution used in the domestic architecture of Spain, Italy, Barbary, and Syria? Such papers would be very useful to us, though they might perhaps be profitless to you.

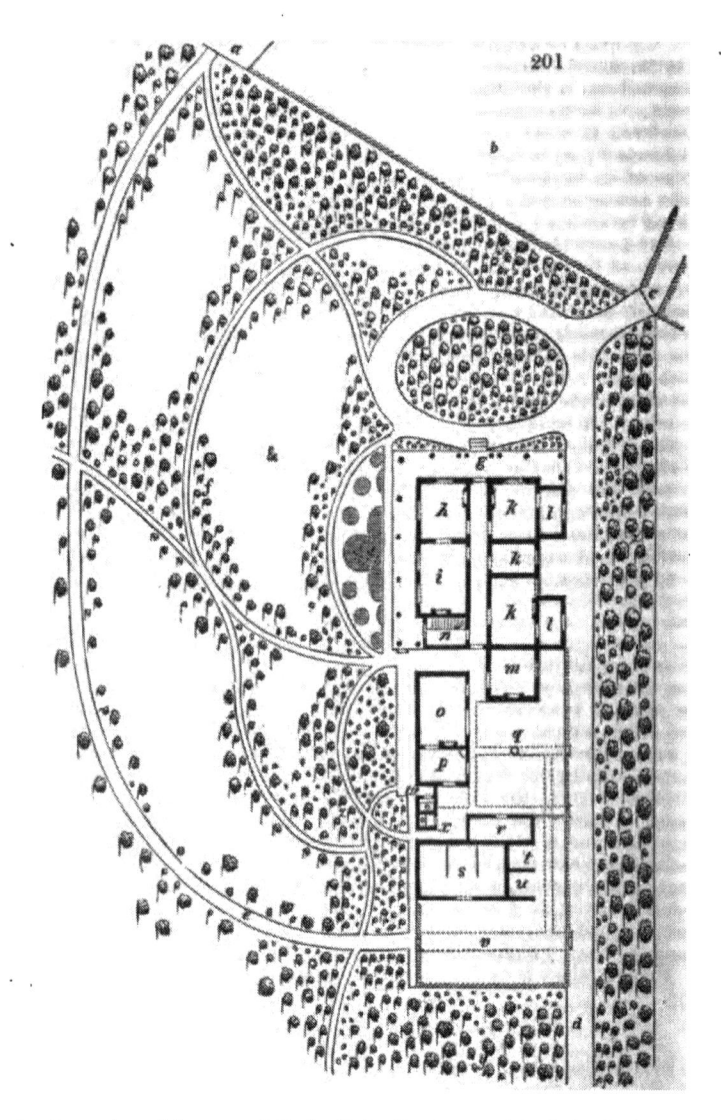

I send you a sketch of a design for a cottage (*fig.* 201.), which my father-in-law intends building near Sydney. The ground plan was given to me by Mr. Lewis, with whom, I believe, you are acquainted.

The house is to be an éxact square, and only one story high; the cellar is to be under the drawingroom, with stairs from the storeroom leading to it. Two dressing-rooms and the storeroom are taken out of the veranda. The ground falls to the north-west. The kitchen-garden (*a*) and the paddock (*b*) are already formed; *c* is the entrance road; *d*, a back road to the vineyard and the woods; *e* is a private road to the stable-yard and offices; *f*, walks on the lawn; *g*, the veranda, under which is the main entrance to the house; *h*, dining-parlour; *i*, drawingroom; *k k k*, bedrooms; *l l*, dressing-rooms; *m*, nursery; *n*, storeroom and stairs to cellar; *o*, kitchen; *p*, back-kitchen and washhouse; *q*, well; *r*, wood-house; *s*, stable; *t*, gig-house; *u*, tool-house; *v*, stable-yard; *w*, best privy; *x*, servants' privy; *y*, natural wood; *z*, shrubbery; and &, flower-garden.

The two principal aspects are north-east and south-east: these are the most agreeable here. The north is too much exposed to the sun, and so is the west; and the west is also exposed to the hot winds, or Australian simoom, in the summer; and, in the winter, to very keen cold winds. The south is altogether an objectionable aspect, on account of the prevailing winds coming from that quarter being always cold, and very boisterous. The rain and the generality of storms also come from the south. So powerful, indeed, is the rain, that all the sides of the houses that face the south are plastered; for, if this is not done, the rain penetrates the bricks or stone, and makes the walls always wet. You will observe that, in the plan of the cottage (*fig.* 201.), the kitchen is detached: this is desirable, not only on account of the heat, but also to cut off all communication with the convict servants, and to avoid the smells, and the flies, which are very troublesome in summer, yet it is necessary that the kitchen and all other out-buildings should be connected with the house by covered ways; for it rains here so tremendously, or rather spouts, that it is impossible to move in it without being thoroughly wetted.

Sufficient attention has not yet been paid here to arrange a house according to the proper aspects and prevailing winds. Besides what I have mentioned just now, the sea breeze is very potent near Sydney: in summer it sets in about ten or eleven o'clock, and then, after a time, gradually dies away until sunset, when it sets in again. This wind comes from the north-east, and is very refreshing after a hot day, or a hot morning; from seven to ten o'clock being the hottest part of a summer day in regular weather.

It appears to me that thick walls, with recesses, and houses two or three stories high, with balconies and windows commanding different aspects, would be more agreeable than the large-roofed cottages that are mostly adopted here; but the fact is, that this is the cheapest mode of building, as roofing is not expensive, shingles being universally used instead of tiles. The Indian *chunam*, or plaster, has not yet been introduced: this would make the houses in the town much more healthy and agreeable. Sydney is, I am afraid, becoming very unwholesome, the houses being too much crowded, and proper arrangements for drainage, &c., not having been made when the town was originally laid out. I have found my own health, and that of my children, sensibly improved by merely moving to a residence within the reach of the sea breeze. — *J. Thompson. Sydney, Aug.* 10. 1833.

Art. II. *Domestic Notices.*

ENGLAND.

Both *Houses of Parliament* were burnt to the ground, on the night of Oct. 16.; and it is said to be the intention of government to rebuild them on the same spot. Perhaps this may be desirable, on account of the offices in the neighbourhood; but, we must confess, we should have preferred a more open and elevated site. Were it not that we should regret to see the space intended to be left open at Charing Cross covered with buildings, we should have pointed to it as a suitable situation. A large and lofty quadrangular building there might easily be made to contain both Houses of Parliament, with all the offices and other appendages necessarily connected with them. At all events, before anything is done, either in the way of rebuilding on the ancient site, or on a new one, we hope that the whole architectural talent of the country will be invited to send in designs and suggestions; and that these will be impartially examined by a competent commission. We constantly hear of cases in which plans have been advertised for in competition, while the architect who is to be employed was appointed beforehand; and the only use of advertising for the plans was, to admit of his gaining hints from them. We should be glad to expose this practice; but, notwithstanding the frequent occurrence of the circumstance, we have not been able to prevail on any of the architects who complain of such treatment to authenticate a case by their names.

New Churches. — A correspondent has sent us the *Fourteenth Annual Report* on the subject of building new churches; from which it appears that additional churches are to be erected at ten different places, and that plans have not yet been received for them. Our correspondent complains that he has been unable to procure any farther information at the office of the commissioners, in George Street, Westminster. All we can do is to give publicity to his complaint, not having, as he enquires, "any interest with any of the commissioners;" and, like him, not choosing to make any enquiry, where a necessary preliminary, as he alleges, is to "fee the clerks for their trouble."

Cambridgeshire. — *The Fitzwilliam Museum, Cambridge.* The time allowed for sending in designs for the building about to be erected for this purpose, is now extended till the 10th of next April. There is little doubt but that the competition will be strong in point of numbers; and we hope it will prove equally strong in point of talent. The subject itself is of a class highly favourable to display, and well calculated to bring out the original talent of those who are gifted with it. We trust, therefore, that the design selected for execution will be creditable to the national taste; and prove an additional architectural gem to the university and town of Cambridge. — *W. London*, 1834.

Fitzwilliam Museum, Cambridge. — It is strange that the document furnished to architects contains no programme whatever relative to the intended building, nor any information as to what is required, beyond a plan of the site itself, which affords an extent of about 360 ft. in front, by 150 ft. in depth. It is true, farther information may be obtained by direct application to the vice-chancellor; but even this, it should seem, will be given only to those who are disposed to make drawings and estimates for the purpose, "gratuitously." In our opinion, this is a very zigzag and rather unintelligible way of proceeding on such an occasion. If it is desired to limit the competition, wherefore are architects in general invited to it by public advertisement? and if, again, the competition is to be perfectly open to all, why clog it by difficulties that must entail so much trouble upon those who will have to answer the applicants for information, separately and individually? — *H. Sept.*, 1834.

Devonshire. — A splendid new masonic hall was completed, early in September, at Tiverton; and it was dedicated on Sept. 10., eleven lodges, from different parts of the county, being present. The hall is attached to the Angel Inn, near the river Exe. At the end, opposite the entrance, stands the chair of the W. M. [worshipful master], under a rich canopy, supported by two pillars in front, of white and gold; the whole raised on three steps of chequered work. The chair of state is also white and gold; with crimson velvet seat and arms, adorned with masonic emblems embroidered with gold; altogether got up in a first-rate manner. On each side of the chair and canopy are two other canopies; and at the back of these is a crimson and blue painted drapery, which extends across the whole end of the room. The floor is painted black and white chequer-work; forming a pavement of great beauty, the design of Brother Captain Hodges. The walls are painted around with niches, in which are placed statues of the old Fathers of Masonry; of whom the initiated will discover mention made in the volume of Holy Writ. The ceiling contains, in the centre, a large circle, extending the full diameter of the room, representing the interior of an open cupola, with the sun shining through the centre; and on the sides are depicted the twelve signs of the zodiac. Midway between each end of the room and this large circle are two smaller circles, with masonic emblems. In an ornamented recess, at the lower end of the room, stands the organ; a very good instrument, having eight stops. The remaining furniture of the lodge is exceedingly handsome; being, for the most part, presents from some of the brethren. Over the seat of the J. W. [junior warden] floats a beautiful banner, belonging to the chapter; and, opposite to this, over the seat of the secretary, another white silk banner is suspended, on which is admirably painted the subject of Abraham offering Isaac; in allusion to the name of the lodge *Fidelity*. The splendid banner last mentioned, together with the niches containing the statues, the elaborately ornamented and highly finished ceiling, and also the drapery at the head of the room, were executed by that talented and much respected artist, Brother L. E. Reed of Tiverton. This superb hall was the admiration of all who saw it, whether the initiated or others. It is certainly a credit to "The Lodge of Fidelity;" and will be a lasting honour to the liberality and spirit of the craft of Tiverton, so far as the internal decorations are concerned: we cannot, however, say so much for the exterior, this being by no means answerable to the beauty within. The entrance is exceedingly bad; and we hope soon to hear that a suitable porch is made to this temple, dedicated to religion, morality, and science, and sacred to a pure system of ethics, veiled in mystic allegory. A copious account of the ceremonies which took place on the occasion of the opening of this hall will be found in the *Exeter Flying Post* of Sept. 11. 1834.

Monument erected to the Memory of the late Earl of Plymouth, on Broomsgrove Lickey. — The ceremony of laying the foundation stone of this monument was performed, on the 15th of May, by Lord Lyttelton, who acted as grand master mason. The form, as will be seen by the engraving (*fig.* 202.), is that of a simple obelisk, standing on a pedestal 17 ft. in height, and about 20 ft. square. The whole height of the monument will be, according to the drawing, 91 ft. 6 in. The pedestal (on the sides of which there are inscriptions in sunk panels) is approached by three steps, which run all round; and these, together with the structure, are formed of the elegant Anglesea marble. The situation chosen by the committee for this monument is the top of the Lickey Hill, which is a few yards to the left of the coach-road proceeding from Worcester to Birmingham; and the obelisk, when the trees around the spot are felled, will, from its lofty locality, be seen at a great distance. This monument is from a design by Mr. John Hanson, architect; and the contractor is Mr. John Welch, who has undertaken to complete the structure in five months from the time that the foundation was laid. It differs from other monuments of this description, in having the faces of the pedestal battering; that is, the die of the pedestal is narrower at the top than at the bottom where it rests on the plinth, which harmonises well with the pyramidal form of the upper part. — *R. June*, 1834.

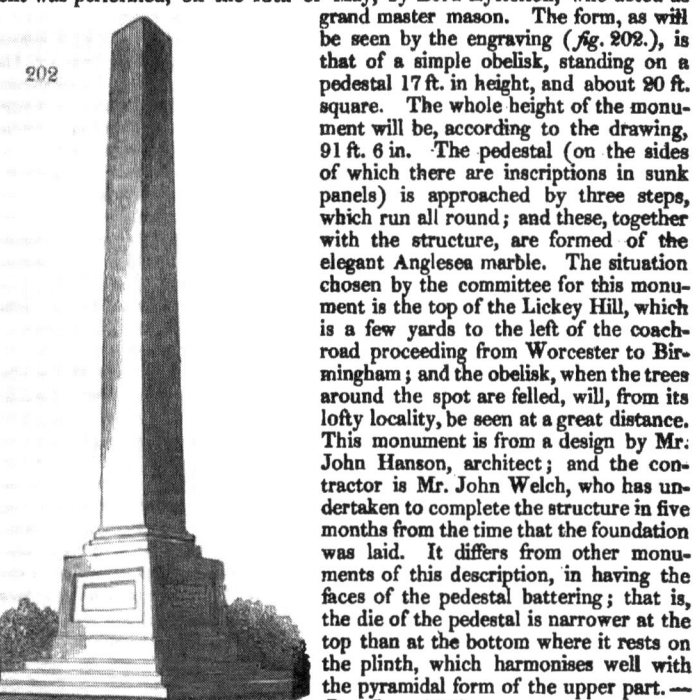

The Birmingham Town Hall. — While in England, I saw the whole of the new Birmingham Musical Hall, on the evening it was first lighted with gas;

and previously during the day. It is a noble structure; but, I think, very defective in some respects. None of the stones for the building (which are the hardest limestone I have seen) were cut by the steam-engine, as was, I think, stated in the *Mechanics' Magazine*. The organ is the most stupendous machine conceivable; and the effect of the whole, when standing in front of it, very august. But the ceiling, to my taste, is in an execrable style: divided into three great squares, containing circles; with very deep radial panels and borders á la Grec, and between the quarter panels poor meagre ornaments. The light was utterly insufficient: it came from globes, in the side windows, containing triple argand burners. I do not think they will ever light it effectually, without some great central light. The windows and galleries have an excellent effect; and that of the exterior, seen a good way down the street, from the majestic attitude (if I may so speak) of the building, is grand. The roof, I am sorry to say, appears to be sinking rapidly in many places; in some, as much as 7 or 8 inches: it is all covered with lead. I could not get into it; but I wish you would get plans of it, for the *Architectural Magazine*, from some correspondent. Externally, when I saw it, it seemed to me to indicate such derangement inside, as would soon become dangerous. — *R. M. Dublin, Sept.* 19. 1834.

SCOTLAND.

Cenotaph to the Memory of Sir Walter Scott. — A printed "*Address to the Committee and Subscribers of an intended Cenotaph to the Memory of Sir Walter Scott, Bart., at Edinburgh,*" has been sent us by Mr. Britton. Its object is to erect a cenotaph in the form of a cross; and it is stated that Mr. Britton has made some designs illustrative of his opinions and suggestions.

In recommending a cenotaph for Sir Walter Scott, at Edinburgh, in the form and general character of a Christian cross, Mr. Britton observes: " I am influenced by the conviction, that a design of this kind is more analogous to the present age, to the partialities of the deceased, to the pervading character of his writings, than any other species of architectural composition. Neither Egyptian, Grecian, nor Roman, could be made to impart that locality and nationality of sentiment which belongs to the architecture of the middle ages: this brings with it, and belongs to, the chivalric and romantic annals of Great Britain; it blends the military and monastic; it unites the civil and ecclesiastical emblems of by-gone days; it may intimate the gloomy, almost impregnable, castle of the rude and haughty baron; and also the gorgeous and sainted minister of the catholic devotee. Whilst the one furnishes dungeons and halls, galleries and cells, lofty embrasured towers and moats, drawbridges and portcullises; the other is designed and adorned with all the luxuries of architectural composition and sculptural ornament. These are objects and associations belonging to ' *The Lady of the Lake,*' ' *The Lay of the Last Minstrel,*' ' *The Antiquary,*' ' *Kenilworth,*' ' *Peveril of the Peak,*' &c. &c., and these unfold to the fancy of the antiquarian architect an exhaustless store for combination and composition. A design in the form, and with some of the peculiarities, of the stone cross, is susceptible of great variety of surface, as well as great power of expression. Whilst its architectural members may indicate something of the military and monastic character of the middle ages, its sculptured enrichments ought to display some of the prominent personages and characteristic incidents of the bard's and novelist's creative fancy. The engraved and sculptured designs of the ancient Egyptians and Greeks have lasted for many centuries, and are examined and investigated with intense interest and delight by artists and antiquaries of the present age; so may future connoisseurs and antiquaries look with curiosity and delight at the *Scott Cenotaph* (if appropriate), which an admiring public may raise to his fame. Instead of armorial insignia, which generally are as unintelligible as Egyptian hieroglyphics, and have little that is emblematical or historical in their designs, I would introduce a series of sculptured subjects, both in statues and basso-relievos, to tell tales of the author and of his writings; and these subjects should mark and characterise certain interesting scenes, personages, and events which are rendered familiar to the reader of Scott's works. I would also call into action and laudable rivalry the talents of modern artists, and put their designs on permanent record, and in immediate association with the name and memory of Scotland's boast." (p. 4.)

Aberdeenshire. — A round tour, 76 ft. high, and 17 ft. in diameter at the base, has been erected at Muthil, near Peterhead, in commemoration of reform. The tower contains a stone staircase, which leads to a circular apartment at the top, with windows commanding beautiful and extensive views in every direction. This tower has been erected by a local subscription; and we consider it as doing the highest honour to the subscribers, since they could have no motive whatever of a grossly selfish nature. We would rather see one such tower, than a thousand of such columns or obelisks as those erected to Lord Melville, Lord Plymouth, or any other noble or wealthy individual, by his dependants or friends, which are, for the most part, no proof of real merit. In the notice of this tower, given in the *Scotsman* of Sept. 3., it is stated that the apartment at the top has four windows, answering to the four cardinal points. This has a very good effect exteriorly in a square tower; but in a round one, it is very bad. Three windows would have been better: but any number above seven would have been better still. What is the reason? Four windows can never be seen in such a point of view as either to give the expression of regularity and succession, or to group; that is to say, they never can be seen in such a way as to give the idea of a whole. Where there are three windows, never more than one can be seen at a time; and this one, being complete in itself, forms a unity or whole. The best mode, however, is by having a number of windows, by which the piers between them are rendered so small that from every point of view several of them are seen; and this, with the obvious continuation of the series round the tower, produces an effect at once rich and grand, approaching even, as Burke observes, to the sublime.

Sutherland. — A monument to the memory of the late Duke of Sutherland is about to be erected on the summit of Benvrogie, a mountain in the parish of Golspie, in the county of Sutherland. The monument is to be erected by the tenantry on the estate, and will be 75 ft. high. (*Inverness Courier*, Oct. 1834.) [We should be much obliged to Mr. Barry (the duke's architect at Trentham), or to whatever other architect may be the designer of this pillar, for further particulars.]

ART. IV. *Restrospective Criticism.*

HOYLAKE *Church.* (fig. 134. p. 293.) — Your engraver has made rather an unfortunate mistake in the perspective view of Hoylake church. The arches at the west end are not pointed, as shown in the engraving, fig. 134.; but they constitute an arcade of intersecting semicircular arches, as shown in *fig.* 203. I should be glad if you would notice these errors, as at present it apears rather absurd to illustrate an article on Norman architecture by a building in which pointed arches occupy the most prominent place. — *J. A. Picton. Liverpool, October* 7. 1834.

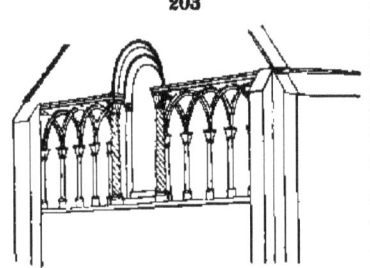

Huskisson's Monument at Liverpool. (p. 227.) — The author of the critique on this monument is in error, in stating that "the interior diameter of the columns is considerably less than the exterior." They are not fluted internally, as they are on the outside: the capitals are fully enriched outside, but inside they are merely blocked out with plain square stones. (See Stuart's *Athens*.) Nevertheless, in the general justness of the criticism I fully coincide. — *J. A. P. Liverpool, Oct. 7. 1834.*

Smirke's Suggestions for the Architectural Improvement of London. (p. 177.) — This work has been reviewed in the *Westminster Review* for July, 1834, in a manner which demands the attentive perusal of architects, and of all who are likely to have any thing to do with the improvement of towns. As we consider it a part of our duty to recommend to young architects every work that contains any useful article in the way of their profession, we would advise them to add this number of the *Westminster Review* to their library. Many, we trust, read this Review regularly; not only on account of its general merits, but because it and the *Foreign Quarterly* contain more articles on architecture and the fine arts than either the *Edinburgh* or the *Quarterly*. In the article to which we allude, the reviewer shows in detail what we have hinted at years ago in the *Gardener's Magazine*, viz., that no efficient and general system of improvement can be expected for the metropolis, till it is governed by a municipal body elected by a regular representative system; in short, a local parliament, in the election of the members of which every householder should have a vote. This would render altogether unnecessary the well-meant suggestions of Mr. Smirke for providing villages, partly at the expense of government or the public, in open spaces in the suburbs of the metropolis, for working mechanics. These, and every working class, must be put into a condition to take care of themselves.

Improved Shop Front. — I approve of the general principle set forth in the article in p. 113., on improving shop fronts, but consider that the blocks terminating the cornice ought not to be supported by brackets resting upon the pilasters; as the architrave is thus cut off, and prevented from having a bearing upon the end pilasters sufficient for the main beam which is to support the superstructure. The architrave, whatever it may really be, affects to be

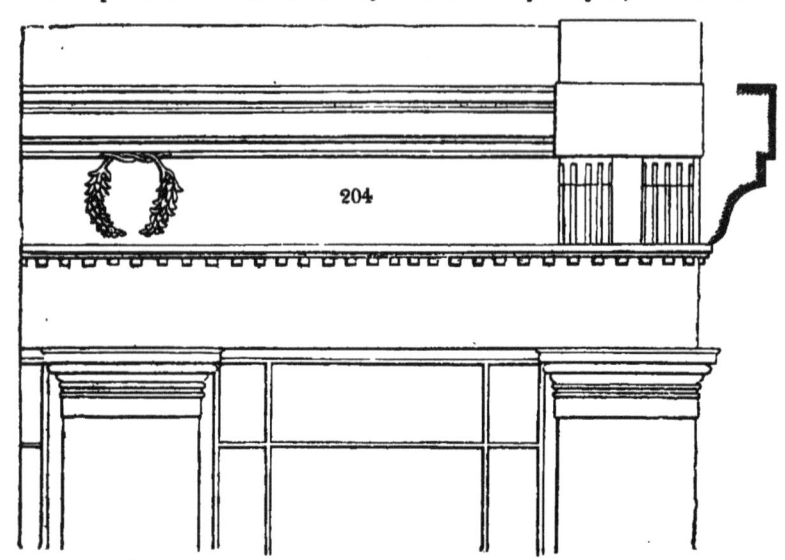

204

this main beam, and consequently ought to have a firm and long bearing at each end: now, with respect to the arrangement adopted, it may, perhaps, be said that the architrave has a firm bearing, the brackets being only attached to its face, and not taking its situation; but this does not appear to be the case; and, even if it could appear so, the arrangement, I apprehend, would be incorrect and faulty. The architrave is a beam of such importance that it ought to be of the same character and general appearance throughout its length, and its position seems to determine that it should be used for supporting upon its upper side only. The brackets ought to be laid upon it in the same manner as the frieze is, and in the way the smaller beams which support the floor, and which are frequently terminated in a triglyph, may be supposed to be: indeed, where only one bracket is used to support a terminating block, it may be considered as merely an elongation of one of these smaller beams.

I have used this arrangement both in a shop front, and in a public building under peculiar circumstances; adopting either the bracket which occupied the place of a triglyph, or two which extend to nearly the width of the pilaster, as appeared best suited to the case. I have sent a copy of the drawing (*fig.* 204.) which accompanied the original article, with only the necessary alteration, in order to facilitate comparison. — *Geo. Dymond. Bristol, June* 17. 1834.

The above we consider to be just, useful, and practical criticism; and we only wish this correspondent, and others who think like him, would be industrious in pointing out similar errors in public buildings. We also hope that Mr. Dymond has not forgotten the design for a villa, which he kindly promised to send us. — *Cond.*

A Curbed Roof. (p. 39.) — Lest the definition of a curbed roof, in p. 39., should not be clearly understood, allow me to illustrate it by a sketch (*fig.* 205.), in which *a* is the common rafter of the roof, and *b* the curbed rafter; *c* is the flooring joists, *d* the gutter, *e* the parapet wall, *f* a dormar window in the curb part of the roof, and *g* the ceiling and tie-joists; and *h* the wall plate of the flooring joists. — *J. I. K. Manor Place, Paddington,* 10*th March,* 1834.

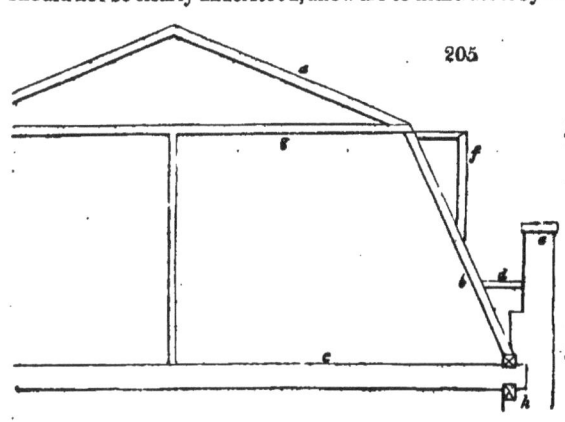

Curbed Roofs (p. 39.), in any situation, are unpleasing objects; both from the inelegance of their forms, and from the idea of insecurity that they present. Not only are these roofs to be found covering fourth-rate houses in the streets of London, where the price of ground is high; but they may also be seen in front of third and second rate houses in the vicinity of town.

It is much to be regretted, that, in and near London, we frequently find a curbed roof presenting its unshapely appearance high above a delicate balustrade attic, over an enriched entablature of the Corinthian or other order; while, in other countries, even the chimney stacks on one side of a street (that can be seen from the drawingroom windows on the other side) are composed of hewn stone, or covered with cement (as the case of the front may be), so as to present a pleasing appearance. The very intention of an attic at the wall head of a building is, that the roof, which is not very susceptible of being ornamented, may be hid: hence the inconsistency of the circumstance just mentioned relative to the houses in the vicinity of London. — *J. R. Bayswater, April,* 1834.

Emigration of Architects to North America. — At p. 90. you inform your readers of the emigration of two or three architects who have been contributors to your *Encyclopædia of Architecture*. I most heartily wish them success, and would not on any account try to keep a man at home who is fully bent upon leaving his native land; because nothing that can be said to such a person (considering the many conflicting statements respecting an emigrant's prospects) will ever satisfy him that he may as well stay at home; and, if he is restrained at first, he will in all probability still continue to cherish the desire, and, becoming indifferent to every thing about him, will eventually go (perhaps be in a manner compelled) under less favourable circumstances than if he had started at first. I feel convinced that nothing short of experience will satisfy such persons; friendly warnings go for nothing: those writers who give an unfavourable account of the country and its inhabitants are, if read at all, set down as aristocrats, or very illiberal persons; while those who speak in their praise are read with avidity, and every sentence taken in a more general sense, if possible, than even its author intended it to convey. Such is the effect of prejudice.

I am sorry to say I have purchased this experience; and dearly bought it was, I assure you. After struggling unsuccessfully through the six previous years, I began to think it was time to go further in search of employment; and having informed myself of the prospects offered in the United States, as well as I was able from the then recently published works on that subject, I came to the determination of visiting New York; having taken it for granted that I should certainly find employment there either as a clerk to a surveyor or builder, or, at all events, as a book-keeper in some other business, till I could turn myself about. The result, however, proved that I was wofully mistaken in coming to this conclusion. It was my wish to go alone; but I had a wife, and she had two orphan sisters who had been no less unsuccessful in life than myself. Their desire to accompany me was a natural one, and I could not resist it, although I was aware that considerable expense would attend it, as well as other inconveniences. We went. I traversed New York almost daily for two months, without being able to obtain a single day's employment; and being assured that there was not the least chance of meeting with any till the following spring, I at last determined upon returning.

I have never assumed the title of architect, but having had fifteen years' experience in the building line, with the superintendence of a brickfield and limekiln, I do think myself competent to act as a surveyor. Accordingly, to the several gentlemen in America to whom I took out letters of recommendation, I described myself as a building-surveyor; but they did not comprehend what that meant. They seemed to have some notion of what an architect was; and on my describing to one of them who had lately had a first-rate house built for himself, and was then building some others to let, what the office of a surveyor was, he said that he thought the services of such persons were very requisite in New York. I soon, however, ascertained there was not a shadow of chance for me in that branch; for the aforesaid gentleman assured me there had been no drawings made for his house, and that the almost invariable practice is, to fix upon a house already built, as a model, either to be copied exactly, or with such variations as the proprietor may think fit: an agreement is then drawn up, in few words, and, as you may suppose, in very vague and general terms, and the employer is left at the mercy of the builder for the completion of the contract. In consequence of this system prevailing to a great extent, I do not believe there is full employment throughout the year for half a dozen working architects or surveyors. This method of building from patterns, in America, is in some measure to be accounted for by the manner in which the building-ground is there disposed of: it is chiefly in the hands of the corporation, and as one portion gets filled up, another is brought into the market. The ground is sold in lots of 25 ft. frontage by 100 ft. deep; and, as the price of these has risen to a great height, there is, in almost every instance, a house built on each lot, the price being too high to allow of two lots being used for one house. The Americans are averse from paying for any things which appear to them superfluities; and it is the interest of the builders to persuade them that the services of the architect and surveyor are such. There is as little to be done in the way of keeping accounts, as in drawing; and they are, in general, both done by a journeyman who works the greater part of his time at the bench. The master builders are practical men, and, with very few exceptions, men who have gone over from this country as journeymen carpenters: being used to work so much by contract, they are not very particular in keeping accounts; and they are assisted in the little that is done, by the operations of a public officer, whose duty it is to inspect every cargo as it comes into port, when he measures every board, and scores the quantity upon it, reduced to 1 in. thick. In New York, timber is always brought in boards and scantling; and I do not recollect seeing any in the log during my stay there, except mahogany from the south. A part of a board or scantling, I was informed, is never taken to a job from a carpenter's yard. One the nearest the size required that can be found is picked out, and, if only half of it is used, the workmen carry home the remainder. I cannot answer for this practice being general; but I have seen large pieces of good fir timber hacked up for the fire, which could only have been obtained in this way. During my unhappy sojourn in New York, I could see by the advertisements in the different papers, which I daily searched (in doing which there is great facility afforded, an accommodation which I never could meet with in London), that there were several others in the same line as myself most anxious for employment; one of whom described himself as having served his articles under Mr. Nash in London.

With respect to the prospects of the gentleman you mention as going out with a cargo of chimney-pots and other ornaments, I would observe, that in New York they build their houses very lofty, many of them six stories high; consequently, if chimney-pots are required at all, they are seldom seen from the closely filled streets. The Americans are very fond of ornament, but at the same time they like to get it at a very cheap rate. There are many French in New York, and communications with their country are almost as frequent as with ours; consequently, I apprehend, they would put any Englishman out of the market in the way of *papier maché*. There are also several persons carrying on business as carvers; and very expert they are, I assure you, in carving mouldings, capitals, and other architectural ornaments in their soft pine; giving them a finish quite equal to the composition ornaments made in London. These are chiefly used in the frontispieces of their best houses and shops; comprising (in private houses) a richly moulded entrance door, columns, and pilasters (in some instances these are of marble), with mouldings over side lights between, and fan light above. This arrangement for the admission of light to the hall would no doubt be more generally followed in this country, but for a very obvious reason. I also saw some plaster ornaments used in inside finishing, equal to any thing of the kind, in point of design and finish, that I had ever seen in England.

I trust that in offering these remarks, I shall not be thought obtruding my private affairs; my object being, to prevent others from falling into the same errors, by coming to wrong conclusions, as I did. The only way to do this, is to teach people to discriminate, and to make proper allowance for the prejudices and predilections of the authors they read. Thus, Mr. Stuart's work will be found an unerring guide to any gentleman of small fortune making a pleasure excursion through the States; Mrs. Trollope's and Captain Hall's can only serve any lady or gentleman who has preconceived a very unfavourable opinion of the Americans, and is determined to confirm it by a transatlantic tour; while the small fry, and scraps in the periodical publications, are at best but blind guides. The safest way for a young man to act, especially if he has a wife and family, is to go over first alone, with a view of seeing and hearing what his prospects are likely to be; and then, if they appear favourable, returning for his family, &c. This is frequently done, but even then it is not safe to allow too long a period to elapse between the first and second visit : for a young man, who went out with his wife and child in the same vessel with us, afterwards told me he found trade so much altered for the worse, since his visit there three years ago, that he should never have returned if he had been aware of it.

Although I met with such a serious disappointment, I should be sorry to be thought as joining in the idle clamour raised by many against the Americans; as I do not lay the blame of my want of success either on them or their country. I had well informed myself on the subject of their peculiarities in manners and customs (except, as it turned out, in that which was for me the right one), and found no difficulty in accommodating myself to them. My expectations were as moderate as it was possible for a person to lay them; but I did expect to find employment, and utterly failed. It is frequently observed, that, notwithstanding the emigration of so many thousands of persons from this country, they are not missed; but this may in some degree be accounted for by the greater part of them returning; and I am of opinion that three fourths of the mechanics and others, not labourers or farmers, who have arrived in New York within the last two or three years, have made a hasty retreat. Trade there, as far as I had an opportunity of judging, appeared to me, in general, as much overdone as in London; and that curse to the mechanic, a Trades' Union, had got into operation. For the farmer and agricultural labourer, particularly the latter, there is an inexhaustible field for employment; there is also a good chance for rough hardworking mechanics, who are never likely to become any thing else here: but to all above them on the scale, I would say, stop at home, and put up with your difficulties if you can, rather than fly to others which you know not of. The Americans generally are not fond of laborious employment; consequently, they seize on the lighter occupations, to the exclusion of foreigners. I am afraid you will think I have already trespassed at too great a length, and I will therefore conclude by requesting you will make what use you please of the above, and I shall be happy to answer any queries for further information on the subject, as far as I am able, and for that reason I enclose a card with my real name and address. — *Z. Hertford, April* 24. 1834.

The Arch-headed Openings in the Chimney Top, proposed at p. 163., are said to " create a draught:" but I cannot conceive in what manner they can do so. I have, until now, conceived that such openings would have an opposite effect. We are not to consider wind as having any property different from that of water in motion. On the contrary, we know that, by exposing a solid to the action of either fluid, the current does not impinge against the body; but, by reacting, pushes up the moving mass quite clear of the top of the obstacle. That this is true, any person may satisfy himself, by observing how driving snow gets over a wall. It rises far above the wall before it gets over. Again, let him observe how the snow gets over a gate. He will see that the snow does not rise above the upper surface of the horizontal bars, but sweeps exactly across their upper surfaces. In like manner, it is presumed that, instead of the wind being "broken" by the arched openings between the flues, it will pass over the openings of the vents in a comparatively solid state, and so prevent their action. In short, there does not appear to be any known property of wind that can warrant our breaking and scattering it about at the chimney head, but every thing to induce us to keep it in a solid state, provided that the upper side of the coping is inclined about 45° to the current; and the margin of the flue is dressed as straight as possible; and also that the coping is made to project but very little over the shaft. It is only from these properties, and the additional altitude which a can confers on a chimney, that we may rationally explain its utility. — *John Milne. Edinburgh, July,* 1834.

Hinging Doors to Rooms. — I cannot conceive why we must hinge the " doors on the side nearest to the fire, whether they are in the same wall, or at right angles with it; otherwise they will draw out the smoke every time they are used." (p. 201.) An architectural maxim, like a definition in geometry, should be a simple idea, incapable of contradiction; or else it should be in the form of a proposition fully demonstrated. In the mean time, I cannot conceive what could induce smoke to come down the chimney by opening the door either to the right, or to the left; providing that I open or shut it in both cases with an equal velocity. — *Id.*

Blank Windows. — I beg leave to offer you a few remarks on the following " Architectural Maxim" given in your *Architectural Magazine*, p. 236. : — " If blank windows are ever allowable in original compositions, it can only be where they form part of a system of windows. To introduce them where they form no part of such a system, that is, where there are no real windows at all in the elevation, as in the exterior elevation of the Bank of England, and in the front of the National Gallery at Charing Cross, is contrary to every sound principle of architectural composition."

I presume that you would justify this censure, by observing that they are useless, and, consequently, inadmissible. Now, it appears to me, that even on this ground, at least as regards the latter example, these windows are capable of defence. It might be urged, that these partial openings are the means of lessening the great weight of wall above the lower windows. This seems to me equally satisfactory with the reasonings which some writers have made use of, when telling us why certain forms and objects may be admitted in design, and how it is that they give us pleasure in viewing them: I mean, those writers who would reduce all beauty in architecture to the principles of utility, aptitude, and conveniency.

But it is upon other ground than this that I would now attempt to defend the admission of blank windows, attached columns, &c., in architectural designs.

It cannot, I think, with any reason be denied, that the principles by which we are affected with what is termed *Beauty* are the same in Nature and Art; that, from whatever hidden cause it be that a man derives pleasure when viewing a beautiful object, this cause is the same both in the works of Nature and of Art. When the advocate for the Theory of Fitness suffers himself to be drawn into the wide field of natural beauties, he is immediately surrounded with insurmountable difficulties. This, I think, Burke has most satisfactorily shown. " On that principle," he observes, " the wedge-like snout of a swine, with its tough cartilage at the end, the little sunk eyes, and the whole make of the head, so well adapted to its offices of digging and rooting, would be extremely beautiful." (*Sublime and Beautiful*, part iii. sect. 6.) How admirably does the shell of the tortoise serve as a castle to its rightful occupier! but I fancy that more admiration is bestowed upon it when, by being wrought into ornaments, this fitness is at an end, than it could obtain while shielding the animal. Many things are very beautiful, though no use has ever yet been discerned in them; and I would, with Burke, appeal to the first and most natural feelings of mankind, whether, on beholding a lovely eye or mouth, any ideas of their being well fitted for seeing or eating ever present themselves. To apply this more immediately to our subject: When wholly occupied in admiring a noble portico, what is it that thus captivates us? Are we engaged in thinking how admirably the portico is adapted to afford shelter from the sun's rays, and from the rain? or, how efficiently the columns support the entablature and roof? When the eye is dwelling with pleasure on an Italian range of windows, is it the fact, that a great quantity of light is admitted by these windows which affords this pleasure? I trow not. It is said by some, that attached columns may be employed, as they strengthen, or appear to strengthen, the wall against which they are placed: but can any body tell me, when admiring their effect in a building, that his satisfaction springs from a knowledge of the additional stability which they give to the main walls? If it be so in fact, it must be first satisfactorily made out to him that the walls stand in need of extraneous support, and then that these columns are calculated to afford it. Upon finding these to be facts, we may call the building beautiful, and admire it: in other words, the absence or presence of beauty in an object is the result of a course of reasoning in the mind. But is not this a strange confusion of terms? Were it indeed true that attached columns are only to be admitted in design, on the ground that they appear to afford additional strength to the walls, we might, on some occasions, apply them thus without any entablature, as a Gothic buttress; nay, they would give equal stability to the wall, though we should even decapitate them.

In other branches of the fine arts, the judgment does not lay claim to this absolute sway. The sole end to which music aspires is to delight the ear. The same may be said of landscape-painting, and of some species of ornamental furniture. We call architecture the queen of the fine arts, and, in very deed, she is far too noble a queen to be placed *wholly* under the despotic jurisdiction of the cold dictates of judgment.

If I am unable to persuade the lover of the Aptitude Theory to forsake his favourite principle, I may, at least, urge him to follow this principle whither it will lead him. The only author I have met with, who attempts to do this, is Durand, in his *Précis des Leçons d'Architecture*. Now, what is the result at which he at length arrives? Were not men so prejudiced in their favour, he would prohibit the use of the Composite, Corinthian, Ionic, and Doric Orders! He would consign to oblivion those objects which most think to be the very pride of architecture, the richest diadems in her crown: he tells us that cornices are inadmissible in the interior of buildings, unless they support, or appear to support, the ceiling. As to beauty of contour in mouldings, it is all prejudice: since, however, mankind are so universally foolish as to admire some profiles more than others, on this account, and on this account alone (he says), we should give our mouldings certain forms in preference to others. Flutings (he observes) are useless; and then signs their death-warrant. M. Durand, who is professor of architecture at the Polytechnic School, finds that his theory must, when carried out, bring him to these determinations. One might suppose that he has been much with those whose slashing propensities, from their possessing a more extended field of action, brought on such disastrous results to their king and country, at the end of the last century: and thus can he, with more confidence than others, pronounce condemnation on those things which have been the objects of admiration for ages. Yet, although it be passing strange and surprisingly bold in a man to give utterance to such sentiments as these, it seems to me that they are nothing more than what one is constrained to allow, who holds that, in architecture, whatsoever is useless is inadmissible; and I believe that much praise is due to some portions of his work. In Gothic architecture, this theory is wholly untenable. Of what *use* are pinnacles, battlements to a church, and (what, I think, is, in a degree, analogous to blank windows) that panelling which we may sometimes see spreading itself over an old church tower with such wonderfully rich effect?

But, surely, it will be said, Fitness and Utility must be taken into consideration, when judging of the merits of an architectural composition. Undoubtedly they must: and I admit that they justly claim a large share of our attention. But I conceive that this is solely the province of Reason, and not of that which is usually termed Taste. A stranger passes by the London University: his first glance at the edifice would, I think, afford him much pleasure. A portico of ten Corinthian columns, elevated on a lofty basement, and crowned by a good proportioned dome, must command attention; and I think that, with most unbiassed observers, it would be a pleasurable attention: but, upon farther inspection, our observer perceives that the sole use of this portico is to shelter one doorway in the centre. This will cast a shade over his former satisfaction. It seems as though the portico and the entrance were not made for one another; it seems an application of a noble object to a purpose unworthy of it: as though we should yoke an elephant to a pony-carriage. Here the judgment is shocked, and that in no small degree; and we cannot divest ourselves of its influence, when judging of the structure as a work of art. But nothing of this kind can be said in reference to blank windows, and other objects of a similar nature. In the former case, there is a large assemblage of objects, evidently intended to answer a certain end; and we cannot help perceiving that the means used are not commensurate with the end proposed: while the sole aim of blank windows is to please the eye. It is, I believe, owing to this latter distinction that we are not molested by the whisperings of the judgment, when admiring such objects as the spires of Salisbury and Strasburgh. They are utterly useless; but they do not pretend to be otherwise.

I might extend these observations to works on literature which come within the cognizance of Taste; but I fear that I have already too far prolonged my remarks, and will hastily bring them to a close.

I entirely coincide with the spirit of the observations made by your correspondent Candidus, in the last Number of the *Architectural Magazine*, although I cannot agree with him on the comparative merits of the London University and the National Gallery. He will find some remarks in the *Anthenæum* of the 31st of May, 1834, relative to the propylæa in the new building, which he appears rather inclined to censure. — *Y. Z. London, Oct. 9. 1834.*

We leave the above criticism to produce its own effect on the minds of our readers. It is temperate; and that appears to us its principal merit. There is not a line in it which can be considered as a defence or justification of the use of blank windows in an elevation having no real windows. In such an elevation, the blank windows must either be introduced as ornaments, or for some useful purpose; but our critic offers no defence of them on either of these grounds. He supposes that we condemn blank windows simply because they are useless; and then he combats the idea which he has conjured up. If blank windows can be shown to be beautiful in themselves, that circumstance alone might justify their introduction, even in an elevation where there were no real windows. But he has not shown them to be beautiful at all; and we contend that, so far from being beautiful in themselves, they always convey the idea of imperfection or defect; and that they are only passable where they form part of a system of real windows. Even when they do form part of such a system, we think that, in many cases, it would be better to avoid them. The guide to their introduction or omission should be the necessity or non-necessity of maintaining the appearance of regularity and uniformity; because, in some elevations (for example, those of common street-houses), regularity and uniformity (as we have shown in p. 323.) are almost the only kinds of architectural beauty which are produced. In buildings of a higher character, such as the Bank of England and the National Gallery, the kind of beauty aimed at should be of a very superior description; and, so far from requiring blank windows to maintain the appearance of regularity and uniformity, these qualities are maintained by nobler parts of the edifice: and blank windows detract from the effect of the elevation, considered as a whole, by the vulgar or commonplace associations connected with them. In short, we think our maxim on the subject of blank windows unshaken by the objections of our correspondent: but we shall be glad to hear all that can be said against it; because it is mainly by discussions of this kind that the *Architectural Magazine* can be of service, either to young architects or to general readers. It is a fact, that, we believe, most people will assent to from their own experience, that instruction is much more effectually communicated by the correction of errors, than by the most perfect precepts. — *Cond.*

Ventilation by Mr. Milne and Mr. Picton. (p. 64. and p. 230.) — Having no copy of my answer [p. 279.] to the objections made by Mr. Dymond [p. 213.] to my equalising ventilator, I am not sure whether the statements of Mr. Picton are already answered: nevertheless, I shall say a few words in reply. Mr. Picton remarks (p. 230.) that my invention depends for "its efficacy entirely on the excess of temperature of the air in the room over that without." By reading my paper with attention, it will be seen that the use of my apparatus is to prevent excessive draught, caused by the variable force and direction of the wind, &c.; and that its action does not depend upon temperature, farther than that the damper permits an equal flow of air under all possible circumstances. In summer, my ventilator opens of its own accord; and, in winter, shuts itself just so far as to admit the same flow of air in both seasons. Mr. Picton continues: — " Should the difference be very slight, or the excess be the other way, it would become wholly inoperative." Why would it? I cannot conceive the possibility of the " excess " of temperature being ever the " other way;" that is, greater without than within a human dwelling. Mr. Picton next observes, that " were the temperature, within and without the house, equal, there would be no ventilation whatever." That, however, is an evil which is neither caused nor prevented by my ventilator. From what has been stated, I hope it will be understood that, even admitting it were evident that " it is quite possible for the air in a room to become unfit for respiration, with little or no increase of temperature," the equalising ventilator would not hinder the application of the proper remedy, rarefaction. For hospitals, and other public rooms, I did not propose to expose the " delicate balance" and " pivots of the louvre boards " of the ventilator " to the action " either " of a damp atmosphere or of high winds:" on the contrary, they are placed within the house, at the entrance of chimneys, or tubes, in which the rarefying process is directed to be made. " The obvious tendency of the apparatus is," not " to equalise the circulation when the difference of temperature is greater, and to diminish it when the difference is small." On the contrary, as regards the statement of Mr. Picton, it prevents a greater flow of air when the difference of heat is great; and permits an escape to the utmost extent possible when the difference is small; and gives complete control over its exit, from whatever cause it may be accelerated. Hence, as already shown, it also prevents " an enormous waste of heat in winter," without requiring the " equilibrium " of the damper to be adjusted by hand; and maintains its self-equalising properties, notwithstanding all that has been urged against it.

I have twice constructed this ventilator, and found its performance equal to my expectation: and I hereby offer to furnish it, at a very moderate charge; and to combine it with a mode of warming, ventilating, and preventing smoke, in any room or suite of apartments, in a more effectual and economical way than is, at this time, in general use; and to forfeit my remuneration if I fail.

I consider Mr. Picton's ventilating flues very good; but such are only advisable when the roof is exposed to the sun, and can be rationally expected to perform only when he is visible. It is, however, when the weather is close and sultry, and the sky cloudy, that ventilation is most wanted, and most difficult to produce, and at such a time such flues could not be of much use. Indeed, they frequently permit the entrance of cold air, instead of drawing off that which has become unfit for respiration. A very good illustration of the above observation will be found in my description of the Assembly Rooms and Theatre Royal. [This will appear in the Number for January.] But much depends upon circumstances; and I am far from doubting the efficacy of Mr. Picton's air-flues in many situations. — *John Milne. Edinburgh, August*, 1834.

The Plan for Curing Smoky Chimneys (p. 233.) which your correspondent Mr. Saul describes, and states to be the invention of Mr. Hall of Lancaster, although very simple and valuable, is by no means novel or original; for in the *Builder's Companion*, London, 8vo, 1831, by Mr. D. Boyers, surveyor, a precisely similar method is given; and I think it will be but justice to Mr. Boyers if you mention it in your Magazine. — *Amicus. London, Sept.* 16. 1834.

New Cock for Boilers, to admit and emit equal Quantities of cold and hot Water in equal Times. (p. 240.) — In order to the perfect action of this cock, the areas of the cold and hot water passages must be inversely as the altitudes of their supplying heads; and the areas being constant, if the altitude of the supplying head varies, there will be either too great or too small an expense of water in proportion to the supply: so that, after a certain number of openings of the cock, the boiler will either be quite full of water or quite empty. If I understand it, this appears to be the right view of the matter; and, if so, the contrivance is one needing far too nice an adjustment ever to be generally useful. I think, also, that the pin of the cock, by being exposed in one place to hot water and in another to cold, would not remain long tight. It would be easy to have the supplying head of water equal in altitude to that in the boiler; in which case, the areas of both passages would be equal, provided the water in both was of the same temperature, and that the conducting pipes were both of equal length : but, as they could not be so, two correctors would be necessary, one for temperature and the other for friction. All this it would be next to impossible to have done practically; moreover, sediment would deposit in the hot tube, and not in the cold one: so that, even if right at first, they would soon become wrong. — *Robert Mallet. Dublin, Aug.*, 1834.

ART. V. *Queries and Answers.*

NEW Exchange, Glasgow. — A correspondent enquires whether we can give any account of the new Exchange at Glasgow, which is reported to be far superior to any other structure of the kind in this country. We should feel obliged by the communication of some particulars respecting so important a structure. — *L.*

Towel Stands. — In reply to your querist (p. 96.), I would suggest, as in my opinion preferable to what he proposes, two brackets similar to *fig.* 206., 206 which may be of cast iron or of wood, carved or plain, and screwed to the side of the wash-hand stand, with a bar either turned or plain fixed between them. This would be ornamental rather than otherwise to the stand, and it would not be inconvenient to place the towel upon: if two sets could be fixed, they would have the appearance of handles, where an angular stand was used : if it should be more convenient, these brackets might be affixed to the side of a chest of drawers, or against any part of the wall. — *Z.*

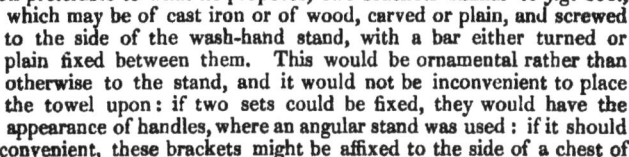

The River Wall at Woolwich Dock. (p. 42.) — I was led, by your query respecting this wall, to make a call at Woolwich Dockyard to inspect it, and I was much gratified with what I saw. Being so fortunate as to meet, on the wharf, with Mr. Ranger's superintendent (whose name I forget), I am enabled by his intelligent description to offer the following particulars of this truly national invention; or rather revival of an ancient mode of building, as many of our beautiful ecclesiastical as well as domestic and castellated remains bear a very close resemblance to Mr. Ranger's patent stone. The river wall at Woolwich, my informant says, is about 250 ft. long, and 28 ft. high, and breasting back 4 ft. from the plane of its base: it was erected in the early part of the year, and carried on at low water, the men working until the tide flowed and obliged them to leave off until the tide fell again, which, however my informant asserted, consolidated and hardened the work. The wall is now finished (June 24.), and makes a most excellent wharf wall, resembling granite, with bold horizontal joints, and perfectly sound, though no expense was incurred by piling for foundation, or by any other expensive measures usual on these works. The customary work of the wharf was not retarded during its erection, except at the point where the work was then carrying on. Upon the whole, I think it worth a journey to the amateur as well as the civil engineer, in whose department it must become a most important invention. I was also obliged by a description of a new dock in progress, which is building of the same material, but which I had not time to inspect. As soon as it is finished, which will be shortly, I shall take a scientific friend with me, and, if it appear worth a place in your valuable work, I shall endeavour to send you a more scientific description of it. I am informed that Mr. Ranger has erected a beautiful building, as a specimen of his material, at Sir H. Taylor's in the Regent's Park, in the early English style; also a guard-house in the Birdcage Walk, in the Grecian style, and another structure, showing a great alteration in street architecture, opposite the National Gallery, Pall-Mall.

These specimens I have not seen, but perhaps some of your numerous readers may oblige us with a description of them. — *Charles Manners, Woolwich Common, July* 14. 1834.

Which is the best Method of keeping a Dairy cool, or could not a draught be created in some way through it? That which I particularly have in view stands above ground, detached from any other building, and is about 10 ft. square; but, although it has a flat roof forming a cistern to contain water, it acquires such a degree of warmth, as to render it unfit for the purposes for which it was intended: perhaps some of my fellow-readers can assist me on the subject. — *Sam. Ap-Evan. Neath, Glamorganshire, Sept.* 22. 1834.

An Apparatus for cleaning the Outsides of lofty Windows is thus described by our correspondent G. B. W.: — I have supposed the window to be 8 ft. high, and 3 ft. 6 in. from the floor. *Fig.* 207. is a section, and *fig.* 208. the internal elevation of the window, &c.; *a a*, two stout standards, about 6 ft. 6 in. high, with two cross pieces *b b* securely screwed to them, and going across the window opening, to keep them firm, and two pieces *c c* notched into them: *d d* are two bearers, supported at the one end by the struts *e e*, which abut against the wood and stone sills, and at the other by the pieces *c c*; and screwed to the standards: *f f* are light standards of iron let into the ends of the bearers and the cross piece *g*, and screwed to them by nuts. A rope might go across the tops of these standards, and another crosswise, as shown by the dotted lines in *fig*. 208. For fear of their giving way outwards, a rope might be passed from their tops, through a ring on the top of the bearers, to the cross piece *b*, as shown in *fig.* 207. I have made this platform to project 2 ft. from the line of the sash frame; and the space afforded between the iron standard and the sash would be about 1 ft. 8 in., which I should think enough for a person to stand upon; but that, of course, is optional. A piece of 1 in. deal plank (11 in. wide) laid across the bearers, and, perhaps, screwed down to them, would complete the apparatus. The struts should be either tied or screwed to the bearers, and a cross piece put between them at the lower end to keep them in their places. I should think this would answer the purpose required. It might be easily taken to pieces or put up; and the expense of the materials would be very trifling. — *G. B. W. London, Sept.* 19. 1834.

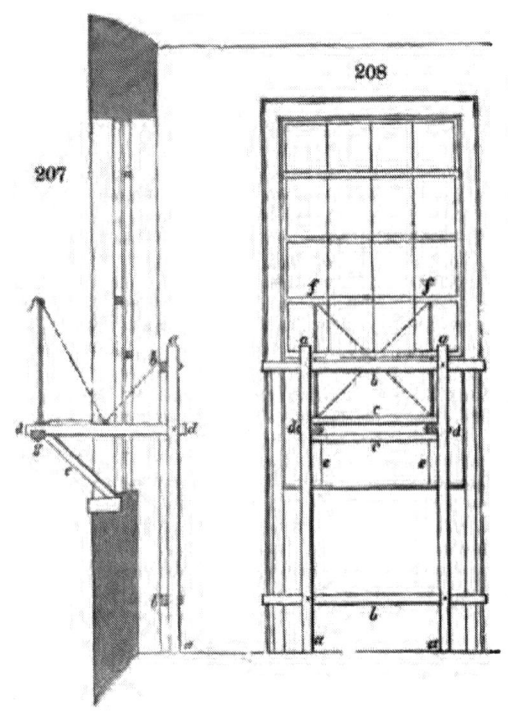

GLOSSARIAL INDEX.

ABACUS, 109 ; the upper member of the capital of a column.
Acroter, 193 ; a pedestal on the summit of a column for supporting a statue.
Acroteria, 150 ; small pedestals placed on the apex and other extremities of a pediment originally intended to support statues.
Antæ, 319 ; pilasters attached to a wall.
Antefixæ, 24 ; see *g*, in fig. 10.
Artesian wells, 210 ; wells formed by boring, and called Artesian because the practice originated at Artois.
Ashlar work, 6 ; rough stone laid in irregular courses.
Astragal, 109 ; a fillet moulding with a rounded edge.
Batten floors, 168 ; floors laid with narrow boards 1¼ in. thick.
Battened walls, see p. 171.
Beveled, 125 ; sloped off.
Blasting rocks, 93 ; splitting them into fragments by means of gunpowder.
Bond stones, 194 ; stones running through a wall at right angles with its face, in order to bind it together.
Borrshone, 372 ; a basket made of palm leaves, used by the Egyptians in brickmaking.
Boxed in, 74 ; filled up compactly.
Brick nogging, 37 ; a framework of timber filled in with brick.
Butt hinges, 83 ; hinges, which, when expanded, form a square.
Calorifère, 176 ; apparatus for heating by hot water, described at length, p. 359.
Cap of a chimney, 64 ; the upper and projecting part of the shaft.
Capotum, 269 ; a kind of Hindú torus moulding, with an ornament resembling a pigeon's head at its termination.
Castrametation, 148 ; camp-making, or the science of forming camps.
Cavetto, 111 ; a species of moulding, see fig. 45. p. 110.
Cella, 265 ; the part enclosed by walls, of a Grecian temple.
Check-plate, 196 ; the piece of wood in the lintel of a doorway, against which the door shuts.
Chevron mouldings, 292 ; indented mouldings in the Anglo-Norman style.
Chimney shafts, 118 ; the part of a chimney which rises above the roof.
Chunam, 315 ; an Indian cement or plaster.
Cincture, 32 ; a ring or fillet serving to divide the shaft of a column from its capital and base.
Clamps, 178 ; a quantity of bricks piled up for burning, but not enclosed in a kiln.
Clere-story, 290 ; the centre in a church, when it rises above the two ailes.
Clere-story windows, 331 ; windows in the clerestory of a church.
Clinker bricks, 238 ; small bricks burnt very hard.
Coins, 219 ; corners.
Concrete, 35 ; a mixture of clean gravel and quick-lime.
Congee, 112 ; a species of moulding, see fig. 51.
Corbel heads, 345 ; the extremities of corbel stones, often carved.
Corbeled, 89 ; one stone projecting over another to support a superincumbent stone.
Corona, 109 ; the crowning member of the entablature, see *e*, in fig. 10.
Corrugated, 72 ; wavy or fluted.
Crabs, 198 ; machines for being attached to and raising heavy weights.
Crowsteps, 6 ; the coping stones of a gable rising one above another, like steps.
Crypt, 96 ; a vault.
Cusmuda, 268 ; a kind of Hindú circular moulding.

Curbed, 39 ; contracted towards the ceiling by being carried up into the roof.
Cusps, 345 ; points formed in the upper corners of the window by uniting the two curves.
Cyclopian walls, 81 ; walls built with landstones heaped on each other without mortar.
Cyma recta, a species of moulding, see fig. 46. p. 110.
Cyma reversa, 111 ; a species of moulding, see fig. 50
Cyma talon, 111 ; a species of moulding, see fig. 47.
Dado, 156 ; the flat side of a pedestal between the plinth and the cornice ; applied also to the space between the skirting and the chairs' back moulding in rooms.
Deals, 83 ; deal boards sawn to a proper thickness for use.
Dormer windows, 184 ; windows in a roof.
Dovetailed groove and tenons, 80 ; two pieces of wood joined by one piece being cut into a particular shape, and the other cut out or hollowed out to receive it.
Doweled floors, 168 ; explained at length in p. 319.
Dressings to windows, 297 ; mouldings, or rather architectural lines and forms surrounding windows, so as to prevent them from being " mere holes in a wall."
Echinus, 111 ; a species of moulding, see fig. 49.
Engaged columns, 117 ; columns attached to a wall, and projecting from it half or three quarters of their diameters.
Entablature, 115 ; the horizontal mass placed on Grecian columns : it consists of three parts ; the architrave, the frieze, and the cornice.
Epistylium, 24 ; architrave.
Façade, the principal face, front, or elevation of any building.
Fascia, 112 ; the face or principal member of the architrave.
Feuars, 113 ; persons renting land for building on in Scotland, on very long leases, generally of 999 years.
Fillet, 109 ; a small square or flat moulding.
Finial, 238 ; a pointed ornament terminating a gable.
Fire bricks, 74 ; bricks made of a particular kind of clay not easily fused by fire.
Flanches, 41 ; projecting edges in iron work, generally curved, for the purpose of uniting and strengthening the parts to which they are applied.
Flashings, or *Flushings, of lead*, 36 ; strips of lead covering joints.
Fly wire, 306 ; wirecloth, or *toile métallique*, for putting in windows to admit the air, while it excludes the flies.
Folding floors, see an explanation at length, 319.
Footings, 209 ; the lower courses of a foundation.
Frets and *guillochés*, 256 ; frets are ornaments composed of a series of small straight fillets, and guillochés of a series of curved fillets.
Frieze, 109 ; see *b*, in fig. 10. p. 25.
Frustum of a pyramid, 192 ; the lower part, the upper having been cut off horizontally.
Geometrical drawing, 215 ; a drawing to a scale, as opposed to one in perspective.
Girders, 177 ; the principal beams for supporting the binding joists.
Greek cross, 133 ; a rectangular cross, the limbs of which are all equal.
Groined roof, 342 ; groins are lines formed at the intersection of two arches which cross each other.
Haunches of an arch, 140 ; the part behind the springing of the arch.
Headers, 125 ; bricks placed so as to have their heads to the surface of the wall.
Intercolumniation, 138 ; the distance between the columns of any building.

VOL. I. — No. 10.

Jamb, 343; the side pieces of any opening in a wall, which bear the piece that supports a superincumbent weight.
Jumper holes, 93; holes made to contain the gunpowder required to blast, or rend asunder, rocks.
Label moulding, 343; an outer moulding, crowning a door or window head, always returned at the ends.
Lancet windows, 293; windows formed with lancet heads, see fig. 155.
Landstone dikes, 81; dikes or walls built of landstones without mortar.
Lean-to, 93; shed or small room with a slanting roof projecting from the wall of the house to which it is attached.
Lintels, 125; the side pieces of a window frame or doorway.
Lotus ornaments, 22; see fig. 7.
Louvre-boards, 230; or luffer-boards; inclined narrow boards placed one above another in an aperture, so as to admit the air, but exclude the light.
Minutes, 154; subdivisions of Perrault's scale for drawing the orders of Classical architecture.
Modillions, 109; a species of ornament, in Classic architecture, resembling a bracket.
Modules, 153; equal parts into which a diameter is divided, for the purpose of facilitating its measurement or delineation.
Mullions, 125; upright pieces, dividing a window into three or more parts.
Mutules, 109; the modillions in the Doric order are called mutules.
Neck of a chimney, 64; part immediately under the cap.
Newel, 194; the turning-post of a staircase.
Nulling, see p. 570.
Octostyle, 140; a building with eight columns in front.
Ordonnance, 154; an order in Classic architecture.
Ovolo, 111; quarter-round moulding, see fig. 44. p. 110.
Pace, 168; a square landing-place dividing the stairs into flights, and used to form a turn without winders.
Padma, 269; one of the Hindú mouldings.
Pagoda caps, 232; caps for ventilation, made conical like the apex of a pagoda.
Palm-leaf ornaments, 22; see figs. 4, 5, and 6.
Panopticon, 208; all-seeing; a prison or workhouse so contrived as that the governor or inspector might, from a given situation, see into every part of it.
Parquetted floors, 319; floors laid in small pieces, so as to form patterns.
Patera, 68; an ornament something like a rose, used to conceal small openings.
Pilaster, 115; a rectangular pillar engaged in (attached to) a wall.
Pinnacle, 159; a pointed ornament terminating a pediment.
Pinned, 169; let into a wall, by a hole being cut into the wall for the purpose.
Pisé, 360; walls formed of mud or clay rammed into moulds.
Place bricks, 35; soft half burnt bricks.
Plate glass, 82; glass cast in a mould, instead of being blown.
Pugged, 37; filled in, between the ceiling and the floor above, with some substance to deaden sound, as hair, mortar, &c.
Quartering, 306; quarters are formed of upright pieces of timber, to which laths are nailed. Formerly, a tree, after being felled, was first sawn up into four equal parts: and hence the origin of this term.
Riser, 58; the upright part which supports the flat part, or tread, of every step in a flight of stairs.
Road metal, 91; broken stones and other material used for making or mending roads.
Roofs of a low pitch, 100; roofs not much elevated in the centre.
Row of blockings, 63; a row of projecting blocks of stone, or of projecting bricks, sometimes called a blocking course.
Rubblestone, 278; stone rough from the quarry.
Rusticwork, 120; stones made rough, on the outer surface, by tools. There are several kinds of rusticwork; the most common of which are the lined, in which the hollow marks are in straight; and the vermiculated, or wormed, in which they are in curved or tortuous lines.
Sailing over, 82; projecting.
Saw draughts, 198; longitudinal slits made by the saw in a thick board, but leaving the thin boards thus formed attached to both ends.
Scotia, 111; a species of moulding, see fig. 48.
Scroll hinges, 344; T-hinges with their projecting points terminating in scrolls, see fig. 169.
Sill, 125; the lower piece of a window-frame or doorway.
Sink stone, 305; a stone perforated with holes.
Sleepers, 37; joists to support a boarded floor, laid on the tops of dwarf walls.
Smithy, 144; a blacksmith's forge.
Snatch blocks, 198; blocks of pulleys with hooks attached.
Soffits, 168; the ceiling or under side of any member.
Spandrils, 131; the space between the springing of an arch and the flat surface it is intended to support.
Spiral stairs, 200; stairs winding round a newel or a well hole.
Splayed, 343; beveled off.
Spongy bricks, 34; porous bricks, from not being made of proper earth.
Spruce deals, 167; deals of the spruce fir, *Àbies communis*.
Stack of chimneys, 124; several smoke flues united in one column, and generally carried up to some height above the roof of the building to which they belong.
Standards, 392; straight upright pieces of wood.
Stays, 172; supports, generally of timber.
Stink trap, 305; or *Bell trap*, a metal vessel for permitting the escape of water into a drain or sewer, without admitting the fetid air from the drain. See *Encyclopædia of Cottage Architecture*, figs. 222. to 224. § 237.
Straight-jointed floors, see 319.
Stretchers, 195; bricks placed so as to have their length appear on the surface or outside of a wall.
Stocks, 36; sound, hard, well-burnt bricks.
Struts, 392; pieces of timber which resist crushing or thrusting; as ties are such as resist drawing or tension.
String-courses, 184; marked and projecting lines of separation on the face of a building.
Stylobates, 27; pedestals, see fig. 11. *ff*.
Swing door, 136; a door hinged so as to open either way.
Tazza, 302; cup.
Tie joists, 353; joists acting as strings or ties to keep two masses together which have a tendency to separate.
Torus, 111; a round moulding, larger and stronger than the astragal.
Transepts, 293. When a church is built in the form of a cross, the two shorter limbs are called transepts.
Transom, 238; a cross beam forming the horisontal bar of a window in the Gothic or Elizabethan styles.
Triglyphs, 109; certain distinctive marks in the frieze of the Doric order, shown at *d*, in fig. 10. p. 25., and formed by three glyphs, or grooves.
Truss, 177; to truss, in carpentry, is to form a system of ties and struts for the support of a roof or weight.
Vestibule, 119; an ante-hall, or inner porch.
Volutes, 263; scrolls.
Wall plate, 383; the plates on which the joists rest.
Water table, 293; a species of ledge left upon stone or brick walls, about 18 in. or 20 in., or more from the ground, from which place the thickness of the wall is diminished.
Weathered, 245; beveled off, to prevent the snow, &c., from lodging.
White deals, 167; deals formed of pine wood, generally of *Pìnus Stròbus*, in which there is little resin.
Winders, 168; angular steps, used where the stair makes a turn without a landing-place.
Yellow deals, 167; deals of fir wood; properly the wild pine, *Pìnus sylvèstris*, which abound in resin, and are, consequently, more durable than white deals.

GENERAL INDEX.

ABATTOIRS at Islington, 90; in France, 242.
Aberdeenshire, cottages of, 94.
Amiens, a public library established in, 88.
Architect and Surveyor, strictures on the professions of, 12.
Architects, emigration of, to North America, remarks on, 90. 384—386.
Architectural Drawings and Lectures, by Mr. Britton, notice of, 181; at Bristol, by Mr. Ross, notice of, 210.
Architectural Exhibitions, 89.
Architectural Fountains, designs for, in artificial stone, 295.
Architectural Improvement of London, remarks on, 382.
Architectural Magazine, objects of, 1; critical remarks on, 41. 212. 246.
Architectural Maxims, 80. 128. 201. 236. 266. 308. 351.
Architectural Societies, 89.
Architectural Students, 138.
Architecture, advantages of a taste for, 212; considered as an art of imagination, 145; Anglo-Norman style of, 238; as a study for ladies, 246; classic elementary forms of, 16; character in, 324; claim of, as a fine art, 223; common, or imitative, genius, and inventive, or original, genius in, compared, 185; the comparative value of simplicity in, 103; garden, 120; Gothic, elementary principles of, 328; Grecian, anticipated universality of, 275; on the means of forming a correct taste in, 49. 52; a just taste in, 49; modern, the alleged degeneracy in, 148; of China, 315; of Egypt, 17; on character in, 324; on heraldic ornaments in, 188; on those principles of composition in, which are common to all the fine arts, 217. 249. 281. 321. 353; science and subjects of, 1; taste for, 3; as a fine art, 5; Soane's lectures on, 89; the best general work on, enquired for, 320; the causes of the different degrees of taste in, 97; a delicate taste in, 97; the intensity of taste in, 98; a refined taste in, 98; a perfect taste in, 99; the circumstances which prevent individuals attaining a taste in, 99; on the harmony of enrichment in, 255; on uniformity in, 285.
Armagh Cathedral, 278.
Artificial stone, Austin's, 216; Bagshaw's, 87; Ranger's, 47. 302.
Ash pans and hearths, 96.
Athens, proposed new metropolis at, 243. 375.
Austin's artificial stone, durability of, 159. 216.
Bath, an oval hip, 92.
Bellingham bridge, 352.
Berlin, general introduction of cast iron in the edifices of, 88; improvements in, 88.
Biography of architects, suggested, 95.
Birmingham grammar school, 92; new market, 92; town hall, 92; critiques on, 379.
Blank windows, maxim respecting, 236; critique on, 387.
Blower, Clarke's improved, 87.
Boiler for steaming food for cattle, 48.
Bonnemain's apparatus for heating by hot water, 359.
Boring for water at Diss, 210.
Bricks, ancient, at Sutton Place, 210; British, proposed analysis of, 317; remarks on, 125.
Bricklayer, influence of, on rural architecture, 8.
Brickmaking, machines for, 18; among the Chinese, 125; in Egypt, 372.
Bridge at Chester, objections to, 140; of a novel description, 278; over the Dee, 67.
Bruges stove, improvements in, 77.
Buchanan's gate, 95.
Building, jobbing in, 211.
Cagnola, obituary of, 96.
Calorifère of Bonnemain, 359.

Camilla Cottage, query respecting, 48.
Cast-iron angles for outside doors, 233.
Cements, 290; in India, 315; new metallic, 46.
Cenotaph to the memory of Sir Walter Scott, 380.
Character in architecture, 394.
Chimney-pots, arch-headed openings in, critically examined, 386; ornamental, 159. 216.
Chimney-shafts, 144; ornamental, error in building of, 63.
Chimneys, smoky, plan for curing, 390.
Church at Hove, jobbing in building of, 211; spire of one in Cheshire set straight, 209.
Churches, new, hints respecting, 378.
Civil engineering, proposed course of lectures on, 208.
Classic architecture, the elementary principles of, 108. 112. 153. 259.
Clerkenwell, a Gothic church at, 90.
Closets in sitting-rooms, remarks on forming, 548.
Cock for boilers, a new kind, 46; query respecting, 240; criticism on, 390.
Concrete, composition of, 248; foundations of, 216. 248; forming walls of, 320.
Constantinople, a large building erected at, 208.
Cooking by gas, 93, 94.
Corinthian capital, a remarkable one in the Vatican, 357.
Cottages, premium offered by the Highland Society for designs of, 93.
County hall, Inverness-shire, 352.
Curved roof, description of, 383.
Dairy, query on the best method of keeping cool, 398; dairy and poultry house, 143.
Damp foundations and damp walls, remedies for, 125. 253.
Danish academy, exhibition at, 243.
Dining-room, position of, 95.
Doors to rooms, mode of hanging, criticised, 386.
Dover, improvements at, 209.
Dovetailed caps for wooden fences, 235.
Doweled floors, 319.
Drumlanrig, palace of, 94.
Dwelling-house, observations on the choice of, 34. 166.
Edinburgh, improvements in, 93. 317.
Edinburgh Society of Arts, 212.
Encyclopædia of Cottage Architecture, effects, produced by, 94.
Exeter new market, 352; Athenæum, 252.
Factories, a new mode of warming of, 88.
Fireproof floors, constructed of Caithness flagstones and cast iron, 71.
Fires in London, on the frequent cause of, 244.
Fishmongers' Hall, notice of, 90.
Fitzwilliam Museum, Cambridge, 378.
Freemasonry, 47.
Furniture, cleaning of, 86; French, inlaid, 244; use of slate and cast iron in, 41.
Garden architecture, 120.
Garden engine with iron frame, 92.
Germany, architects of, 276; buildings in, 276.
Gin temples of the metropolis, remarks on, 164.
Grecian tiles, 144.
Greek cross, explanation of, 95.
Gridiron, a covered one, 47.
Gothic arch of great antiquity, 96.
Gothic architecture, elements and principles of, 328.
Government house, a model for, 276.
Harmony in architecture, 354.
Heating by hot water, origin and progress of, 172. 358.
Holkham, improvements at, 245.
House, domestic offices of, 302.
Houses of Parliament, destruction of, and suggestion of new designs for, 378.
Hoylake church, description of, 292; correction of an error in the perspective view of, 381.

Huddersfield parish church, 211.
Hungerford new market, 55.
Huskisson's monument at Liverpool, critique on, 381.
Intricacy in architecture, 354.
Ironing stove, an improved one, 92.
Isometrical drawing, Mr. Sopwith's description of, 369.
Kitchen furniture, 92.
Labarre, M., a French architect, obituary of, 48.
Lamp-post, improved form of, in use in Edinburgh, 367.
Leeds court-house, improvements in, 211.
Leith harbour, proposed improvement of, 316.
Madeleine, church of, in Paris, 46.
Maple or satin wood, dyeing of, 240.
Market at Knightsbridge, 90.
Mason, influence of, on rural architecture, 6.
Masonic hall at Tiverton, 378.
Milepost, description of an improved one, 78.
Monument on Benvrogie, notice of, 381; at Liverpool, critique on, 277; on Bromsgrove Lickey, description of, 379.
Mortar, women carriers of, 243.
Naples, roads and bridges in the kingdom of, 207.
National Gallery, critique on, 90. 139; model of, 138.
New Exchange, Glasgow, query respecting, 391.
Newcastle, improvements in, 352.
Nicholson, Mr. Peter, proposed annuity for, 140. 245.
Northumberland, cottages of, 91.
Nuneham Courtenay, architectural improvements at, 92.
Obelisk on Bromsgrove Lickey, 379; of Luxor, where to be placed in Paris, 46. 245. 374.
Ornaments for cabinet work, 370; heraldic, in architecture, 188.
Oven with revolving shelves, 47.
Painted transparent blinds, remarks on, 127.
Pantheon in Oxford Street, 91. 184.
Pargetting, 184.
Partitions of lath and plaster, mode of rendering fireproof, 40.
Patent lever flooring-cramp, 96.
Penrhyn Castle, 93.
Perkins's mode of heating by hot water, 212.
Piles, wooden, 352.
Plan, studies of, 226.
Plaster casts, query respecting the colouring of, 248.
Plate warmer, improvements in, 216.
Preston, architecture, &c., at, 91.
Protestant church in the Rue d'Aguesseau, 242.
Public buildings, communication of sound in, 142.
Pyramids of Egypt, 91. 208.
Quay at Blackwall, 140; at Woolwich, 392.
Railroad between Dublin and Kingston, 317.
Railway, an experimental one, at Camden Town, 90.
Ranger's artificial stone, 47; used at Woolwich, 392.
Roads, underdraining of, 91.
Roaster, a portable one, 92.
Roasting oven, description of, 72.
Rocks, boring and blasting of, 93.
Roller blinds, 95.
Rosenburg Palace, 243.
Russel stove, description of, and strictures on, 75.
Sarcophagus in Hamilton Palace, 278.
Sea water, separation of from its salt, 214.

Shop fronts, improved design for, 113. 116; critique on, 382.
Shutters for shop fronts, an improved method of securing, 357.
Sideboards for small rooms, 247; with shelves of marble or slate, 95.
Slamming of a passage door, a preventive for, 126.
Slate, applicable to dairy shelves, &c., 143; slabs of, proposed as sleepers for iron rails, 241; as pavement and flooring, 241.
Smallwood, W. F., architect, obituary of, 184.
Smithy, portable, 144.
Smoky chimneys, a method of curing of, 233.
Somerset House, critique on the architectural designs exhibited at, 181.
St. James's Park, proposed entrance to, 316.
Stands for the extra-leaves of dining-tables, 143.
Statue, colossal, to be erected on the Pantheon in Paris, 88.
Street architecture, 96; of London, 90.
Street houses and shop fronts, remarks on, 113. 116.
Suspension bridge on the road between Naples and Rome, 207.
Suspension pier at Greenhithe, 47.
Swansea, architectural improvements at, 93.
Sydney, the pure sand of, used for the manufacture of glass, 89.
Table, marble, with a cast-iron pillar, 308; query respecting one, 143.
Telford, Thomas, F. R. S., obituary of, 320.
Theatre, a new method of diffusing light in, 276.
Tothill Fields prison, notice of, 90. 208.
Towel stands, query respecting, 96; answer to, 391.
Tower at Muthill in Aberdeenshire, critique on, 381; of the Southwark pin manufactury, query respecting the method of righting, 390.
Tredgold, Thomas, a subscription proposed for the children of, 208.
Trentham Hall, improvements at, 141.
University, London, and National Gallery, remarks on the porticoes of, 317.
Variety in architecture, 354.
Verandas and windows, remarks on, 314.
Versailles, fitting up the palace of, 88.
Ventilation, critical remarks on, 389; of bedrooms, 87; of hospitals and sick wards, 229; of living-rooms, 64. 213. 279.
Vibrating surfaces, Wheatstone's figures produced by, 138.
Villa at Ingress Park, 47; design of one for a sloping site, required, 48; in the Norman style, 333; one now building at Sydney, 376; deceptive practices in the designing of, 117. 214.
Wakefield, school-house and savings'-bank there, 142.
Washing and wringing machines, 247.
Water conducted in pipes by the ancients, 373.
Wilberforce memorial, 211.
Windows, blank, critical remarks on their introduction in buildings, 387—389; lofty, inconvenience of, 247; apparatus for cleaning the outsides of, described, 392; situation of the sites of, 280.
Witty's furnace, improvements in, 91.
Woburn Abbey, improvement of, 140.
Wooden fence, notice of, 79.
Working over-hours, 45.
Workmen, unions of, bad, 45. 86.
Worthing clock-tower, 245.
York monument, a descriptive account of, 192.

END OF THE FIRST VOLUME.

London:
Printed by A. Spottiswoode,
New-Street-Square.

Lightning Source UK Ltd.
Milton Keynes UK
UKHW020639270421
382707UK00004B/137